GUN TRADER'S GUIDE

On the cover, from top: The highly coveted Winchester Model 94 John Wayne Commemorative with its distinctive oversized bow on the lever; an equisitely engraved Ambassador-Side by-Side Shotgun by Renato Gamba of Italy; an extremely rare Colt Aircrewman 38 Special Revolver, courtesy of Frank Ercolino, of Centaur Firearms, Inc., of Lodi, New Jersey.

GUN TRADER'S GUIDE

TENTH EDITION

PAUL WAHL

Stoeger Publishing Company

Published by Stoeger Publishing Company
55 Ruta Court, South Hackensack, New Jersey 07606

ISBN: 0-88317-113-9

Manufactured in the United States of America

Distributed to the book trade and to the sporting goods trade
by Stoeger Industries, 55 Ruta Court, South Hackensack, New
Jersey 07606

In Canada, distributed to the book trade and to the sporting
goods trade by Stoeger Canada, Ltd., 165 Idema Road,
Markham, Ontario L3R 1A9

CONTENTS

INTRODUCTION

Nearly thirty years have passed since the first edition of GUN TRADER'S GUIDE appeared. In 1953, Paul Wahl wrote in the introduction to the first edition, "This is a book which the compiler—to whom guns are both business and pleasure—often wished someone would produce. Almost daily, my searches through shelves of arms books and files of manufacturers' literature gave me frequent pangs of regret for having discarded some now invaluable old gun catalog. Such an experience suggested the need for a one-volume source of specification and price data on modern small arms: a gun trader's vade mecum. It is earnestly hoped that this book will fill that need." GUN TRADER'S GUIDE has indeed filled that need.

The first edition of GUN TRADER'S GUIDE contained 225 pages and some 1,360 listings—accompanied by about 100 illustrations. Now, after nine revisions, the book has evolved into a complete catalog of rifles, shotguns and handguns of the twentieth century. It has more than 400 pages, over 4,000 listings and more than 2,000 illustrations, representing an enlargement of nearly 100 percent over the first edition. No wonder hundreds of thousands of gun buffs have made it their standard reference—and a perennial best seller. As a guide to the identification and evaluation of twentieth-century guns, this book is widely used by firearms dealers, gunsmiths, collectors, shooters, military and law enforcement personnel, shooting editors and writers, as well as pawnbrokers, auctioneers, appraisers and insurance adjusters.

In the previous nine editions of GUN TRADER'S GUIDE, no firearm manufactured prior to 1900 was listed. The same is true for this edition. Any firearm manufactured prior to 1900 is definitely an antique, and has no place in a book on "modern" firearms. We have, however, extended the range of some firearms that were not included in previous editions. For example, we have included L.C. Smith shotguns manufactured between 1900 and 1912. In previous editions, only those manufactured after 1913 were included. We have included all recently manufactured firearms, as well as filling in many gaps—for a total of nearly 150 additional listings not in the ninth edition.

Prices continue to rise on nearly all firearms, but perhaps not as rapidly as they did in the late '70s. Prices of some makes of guns are beginning to level off. Some firearms, however, are an exception. At a recent New York auction, a Parker A-1 Special Grade shotgun in 28 gauge brought the astonishing price of $95,000. A Winchester Model 73 One of One Thousand Rifle brought $45,000. These and other price changes are reflected in this new, tenth edition.

While collecting data for this new edition of GUN TRADER'S GUIDE, we found that geographic location influenced the value of a particular firearm. The Winchester Model 37 single-shot shotgun, for example, brought prices from $125 to $800. Yet, in some areas, Winchester Model 37 shotguns were bringing only $150 in excellent condition. In other areas, where shooting matches were prevalent, a good tightly-choked 12-gauge Model 37 would bring $600 or more. If a particular Model 37 had won in a couple of matches, the owner could practically name his own price.

Pre-1964 guns are still bringing top prices and continue to rise in value. Another point of interest is that the U.S. Repeating Arms Company has purchased the Winchester Repeating Arms Company and is under contract to manufacture all Winchester Model 94s and some other models. All Winchester rifles manufactured after January 1983 will also have

"U.S. Repeating Arms" stamped on the barrel. This means the end of the true Winchester Model 94s; most certainly, all pre-1983 Model 94s will be much sought after.

The prices shown in this book are based on exhaustive market research expertly interpreted and are close to the current national average *retail* prices of guns in excellent condition. Where possible, four price sources were obtained for each firearm. These prices were then averaged to obtain the prices in this book. For the values of extremely rare models in which little trading has been done, experienced collectors were consulted to obtain current values.

Before using this book, please read carefully "How to Use This Book" beginning on the following page. This will give you a better idea of how to evaluate a firearm's condition, and also how to convert the values shown in this book (for guns in excellent condition) to those for guns in other than excellent condition.

ACKNOWLEDGMENT

No book of this kind can be produced without the help of others. The editor expresses his appreciation to the many collectors, dealers, experts and others whose suggestions and advice have made this a better book. Thanks are also due the manufacturers who furnished specifications and photos of their products. Special thanks are due Triple K Manufactuing Co. for permission to use pistol illustrations (indicated by *) from their catalog.

HOW TO USE THIS BOOK

This GUN TRADER'S GUIDE catalogs most American and many foreign firearms produced from 1900 to date. Collectible military small arms are included. Omitted are products of some minor manufacturers, foreign guns rarely encountered in the United States, mail-order house brands, machine guns and other Class III weapons, black powder firearms, air and CO_2 guns.

The book is divided into three sections: Handguns, Rifles and Shotguns. Listings within each section are arranged alphabetically by maker or brand, whichever is more commonly used. For quick reference, turn to the Table of Contents, pages 5 and 6, where these guns are indexed.

Descriptions are limited to major specifications and years of production, together with such additional information as may assist in identification and evaluation. Almost every model listed is illustrated. If you don't find the illustration on the same page as the corresponding listing or on the opposite page, turn to the pages immediately preceding and following. In some instances, layout restrictions made such placement necessary.

Condition is a prime factor in determining the value of a secondhand gun. The following National Rifle Association Standards of Condition for Modern Firearms are used almost universally in grading such items offered for sale:

NEW—not previously sold at retail, in same condition as current factory production.
NEW, DISCONTINUED—same as NEW, but discontinued model.
The following definitions will apply to all second-hand articles:
PERFECT—in new condition in every respect.
EXCELLENT—new condition, used but little, no noticeable marring of wood or metal, bluing perfect (except at muzzle or sharp edges).
VERY GOOD—in perfect working condition, no appreciable wear on working surfaces, no corrosion or pitting, only minor surface dents or scratches.
GOOD—in safe working condition, minor wear on working surfaces, no broken parts, no corrosion or pitting that will interfere with proper functioning.
FAIR—in safe working condition, but well worn, perhaps requiring replacement of minor parts or adjustments which should be indicated in advertisement, no rust but may have corrosion pits which do not render the article unsafe or inoperable.
POOR—badly worn, rusty and battered, perhaps requiring major adjustments or repairs to place in operating condition."

There also are NRA Standards of Condition for Antique Firearms, sometimes used (improperly, in my opinion) to describe 20th-century collector firearms. Aside from the substitution of "factory new" for "perfect" and the addition of "fine," the terms are the same as used for grading modern guns but the definitions are very much different. To avoid misunderstanding as to condition, the seller should indicate which set of standards has been used.

For the purpose of assigning comparative values as a basis for trading, firearms listed in this book are assumed to be in *excellent* condition as defined in the NRA Standards of Condition for Modern Firearms. Exceptions are commemorative guns. Generally, these items are considered collectible only if in new condition, preferably with original box and papers. Values shown are for such specimens. Used commemoratives may bring as little as 10 percent more than comparable standard models.

To estimate prices for guns in other grades of condition, multiply the indicated "excellent" value by the appropriate factor: 1.1 for *new* or *perfect,* .8 for *very good,* .6 for *good,* .3 for *fair,* .15 for *poor.* Where a model is in big demand, a new or perfect specimen can command much more than 10 percent above the "excellent" figure and the price spread among other degrees of condition may be greater too.

If a modern firearm isn't listed in this book, values for comparable models, particularly those of like vintage and country of origin, generally will provide clues as to its worth.

For information on guns discontinued prior to 1900, refer to *The Gun Collector's Handbook of Values* by Charles Edward Chapel (Coward, McCann & Geoghegan), or *Flayderman's Guide to Antique American Firearms and Their Values* by Norm Flayderman (DBI Books).

Although close to current national average retail prices, GUN TRADER'S GUIDE values are approximate. Geographical location—involving regional economic conditions, state and municipal gun control laws, local preferences for certain models, etc.—has considerable influence on values. For the most part, prices of secondhand firearms are tied closely to those of similar new guns. Thus, where discount sales of the latter are prevalent, values of the former are depressed accordingly. Prices of many collector firearms fluctuate constantly. Some popular items have more than doubled in value in recent years.

When using this book, please remember that the values shown represent approximate retail prices for secondhand guns in excellent condition, unless otherwise indicated.

Section I
HANDGUNS

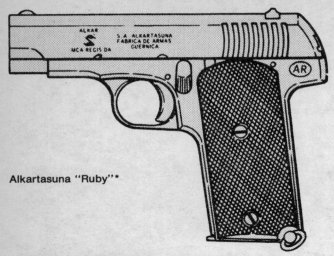

Alkartasuna "Ruby"*

S. A. Alkartasuna Fabrica de Armas, Guernica, Spain

Alkartasuna "Ruby" Automatic Pistol............$150
Caliber, 32 Automatic (7.65mm). 9-shot magazine. 3⅝-inch
barrel. 6⅜ inches overall. Weight, about 34 ounces. Fixed sights.
Blued finish. Checkered wood or hard rubber stocks. Made from
1917 to 1922. *Note:* Manufactured by a number of Spanish firms,
the Ruby was a secondary standard service pistol of the French
Army in World Wars I and II. Specimens made by Alkartasuna
bear the "Alkar" trademark.

American Firearms Manufacturing Co., Inc., San Antonio, Texas

American 25 Automatic Pistol
Caliber, 25 Automatic. 8-shot magazine. 2.1-inch barrel. 4.4
inches overall. Weight, 14½ ounces. Fixed sights. Stainless steel
or blued ordnance steel. Smooth walnut stocks. Made from 1966
to 1974.
Stainless Steel Model................................$160
Blued Steel Model................................... 140

American 380 Automatic

American 380 Automatic Pistol..................$210
Stainless steel. Caliber, 380 Automatic. 8-shot magazine. 3½-
inch barrel. 5½ inches overall. Weight, 20 ounces. Smooth
walnut stocks. Made from 1972 to 1974.

Astra Model 200 Firecat

Astra Pistols manufactured by Unceta y Compania, Guernica, Spain

**Astra Model 200 Firecat Vest Pocket Automatic
Pistol... $120**
Caliber, 25 Automatic (6.35mm). 6-shot magazine. 2¼-inch
barrel. 4⅜ inches overall. Weight, 11¾ ounces. Fixed sights.
Blued finish. Plastic stocks. Made from 1920 to date; U.S.
importation discontinued in 1968.

Astra Model 400

Astra Model 400 Automatic Pistol............... $210
Caliber, 9mm Bayard Long (38ACP, 9mm Browning Long, 9mm
Glisenti, 9mm Luger and 9mm Steyr cartridges may be used
interchangeably in this pistol because of its chamber design). 9-
shot magazine. 6-inch barrel. 10 inches overall. Weight, 35
ounces. Fixed sights. Blued finish. Plastic stocks. *Note:* This
pistol, as well as Astra Models 600 and 3000, is a modification of
the Browning Model 1912. Made from 1922 to 1945.

Astra Model 600

**Astra Model 600 Military & Police Type Automatic
Pistol... $350**
Calibers: 32 Automatic (7.65mm), 9mm Luger, 10-shot magazine
(32 cal.), 8-shot (9mm). 5¼-inch barrel. 8 inches overall. Weight,
about 33 ounces. Fixed sights. Blued finish. Plastic stocks. Made
from 1944 to 1945.

**Astra Model 800 Condor Military Automatic
Pistol... $175**
Similar to Models 400 and 600, except has an external hammer.
Caliber, 9mm Luger. 8-shot magazine. 5¼-inch barrel. 8¼ in-
ches overall. Weight, 32½ ounces. Fixed sights. Blued finish.
Plastic stocks. Made from 1958 to 1965.

Astra Model 800 Condor

Astra Model 3000

Astra Model 3000 Pocket Automatic Pistol...... $175
Calibers: 22 Long Rifle, 32 Automatic (7.65mm), 380 Automatic (9mm Short). 10-shot magazine (22 cal.), 7-shot (32 cal.), 6-shot (380 cal.). 4-inch barrel. 6⅜ inches overall. Weight, about 22 ounces. Fixed sights. Blued finish. Plastic stocks. Made from 1947 to 1956.

Astra Model 4000 Falcon

Astra Model 4000 Falcon Automatic Pistol...... $160
Similar to Model 3000, except has an external hammer. Calibers: 22 Long Rifle, 32 Automatic (7.65mm), 380 Automatic (9mm Short). 10-shot magazine in 22 caliber, 8-shot in 32 caliber, 7-shot in 380 caliber. 3⅔-inch barrel. 6½ inches overall. Weight: 20 ounces in 22 caliber, 24¾ ounces in 32 and 380 caliber. Fixed sights. Blued finish. Plastic stocks. Made from 1956 to 1971.

Astra Model 2000 Cub Pocket Automatic Pistol. $165
Calibers: 22 Short, 25 Auto. 6-shot magazine, 2¼-inch barrel. 4½ inches overall. Weight, about 11 ounces. Fixed sights. Blued or chromed finish. Plastic stocks. Made from 1954 to date; U.S. importation discontinued in 1968.

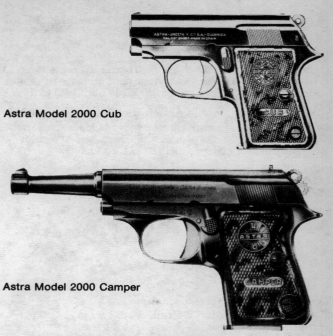

Astra Model 2000 Cub

Astra Model 2000 Camper

Astra Model 2000 Camper Automatic Pistol..... $165
Same as Model 2000 Cub, except chambered for 22 Short only, has 4-inch barrel; overall length, 6¼ inches; weight, 11½ ounces. Made from 1955 to 1960.

Astra Cadix

Astra Cadix Double Action Revolver............$160
Calibers: 22 Long Rifle, 38 Special. 9-shot cylinder in 22 caliber, 5-shot in 38 caliber. Barrels: 4-, 6-inch. Weight, about 27 ounces with 6-inch barrel. Ramp front sight, adjustable rear sight. Blued finish. Plastic stocks. Made from 1960 to 1968.

Astra Constable

Astra Constable Double Action Automatic Pistol
.... **$200**
Calibers: 22 Long Rifle, 32 Automatic (7.65mm), 380 Automatic
(9mm Short). 10-shot magazine in 22 caliber, 8-shot in 32
caliber, 7-shot in 380 caliber. 3½-inch barrel. 6½ inches overall.
Weight, about 24 ounces. Blade front sight, windage adjustable
rear sight. Blued or chromed finish. Made from 1965 to date.

Astra Model 44 Double Action Revolver........ **$315**
Similar to Astra 357, except chambered for 44 Magnum. Barrels:
6-, 8½-inch. 11½ inches overall with 6-inch barrel. Weight, 44
ounces with 6-inch barrel. Made from 1980 to date.

Astra Model 44

Astra Model 45 Double Action Revolver........ **$320**
Similar to Astra 357, except chambered for 45 Colt or 45 ACP.
Barrels: 6-, or 8½-inch. 11½ inches overall with 6-inch barrel.
Weight, 44 ounces with 6-inch barrel. Made from 1980 to date.

Astra Model A80

Astra Model A80 Auto Pistol..................... **$360**
Calibers, 9mm Parabellum, 38 Super, 45 ACP. 15-shot magazine
(9 shot for 45 ACP). Barrel: 3¾ inches, 7 inches overall. Weight,
36 ounces. Made from 1982 to date.

Astra 357, 3-inch barrel

Astra 357, 4-inch barrel

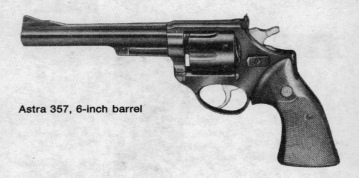

Astra 357, 6-inch barrel

Astra 357 Double Action Revolver.............. **$200**
Caliber, 357 Magnum. 6-shot cylinder. Barrels: 3-, 4-, 6-, 8½-
inch. 11¼ inches overall with 6-inch barrel. Weight, 42 ounces
with 6-inch barrel. Ramp front sight, adjustable rear sight.
Blued finish. Checkered wood stocks. Made from 1972 to date.

Bauer 25 Automatic

Bauer Firearms Corporation, Fraser, Michigan

Bauer 25 Automatic Pistol..................... **$ 85**
Stainless steel. Caliber, 25 Automatic. 6-shot magazine. 2⅛-inch
barrel. 4 inches overall. Weight, 10 ounces. Fixed sights. Checkered walnut or simulated pearl stocks. Made from 1972 to date.

Bauer 22 Automatic Pistol..................... **$ 90**
Same as 25 Automatic, except chambered for 22 Long Rifle, has
5-shot magazine, 2¼-inch barrel, is 4⅛ inches overall. Introduced in 1977.

Bayard Model 1908*

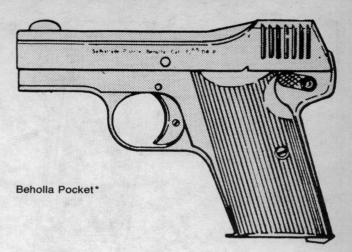

Beholla Pocket*

Bayard Pistols manufactured by Anciens Etablissements Pieper, Herstal, Belgium

Bayard Model 1908 Pocket Automatic Pistol.... $160
Calibers: 25 Automatic (6.35mm), 32 Automatic (7.65mm), 380 Automatic (9mm Short). 6-shot magazine. 2¼-inch barrel. 4⅞ inches overall. Weight, about 16 ounces. Fixed sights. Blued finish. Hard rubber stocks.

Bayard Model 1923 Pocket Automatic Pistol.... $140
Caliber, 25 Automatic (6.35mm). 2⅛-inch barrel. 4-5/16 inches overall. Weight, 12 ounces. Fixed sights. Blued finish. Checkered hard rubber stocks.

Bayard Model 1923 Pocket Automatic Pistol.... $150
Calibers: 32 Automatic (7.65mm), 380 Automatic (9mm Short). 6-shot magazine. 3-5/16-inch barrel. 5½ inches overall. Weight, about 19 ounces. Fixed sights. Blued finish. Checkered hard rubber stocks.

Beretta Model 1915*

Bayard Model 1930

Bayard Model 1930 Pocket 25 Automatic Pistol. $150
A modification of the Model 1923, which it closely resembles.

Beholla Pistol manufactured by Becker and Holländer, Stenda-Werke GmbH, both of Suhl, Germany

Beholla Pocket Automatic Pistol................. $135
Caliber, 32 Automatic (7.65mm). 7-shot magazine. 2.9-inch barrel. 5½ inches overall. Weight, 22 ounces. Fixed sights. Blued finish. Serrated wood or hard rubber stocks. Made from 1915 to 1920 by Becker and Holländer, circa 1920-1925 by Stenda-Werke. *Note:* Essentially the same pistol was manufactured concurrently with the Stenda version as the "Leonhardt" by H. M. Gering and as the "Menta" by August Menz.

Fabbrica d'Armi Pietro Beretta S.p.A., Gardone Valtrompia (Brescia), Italy

Beretta Model 1915 Automatic Pistol............ $260
Caliber, 32 Automatic (7.65mm). 8-shot magazine. 3.3-inch barrel. 5.9 inches overall. Weight, 20 ounces. Fixed sights. Blued finish. Wood stocks. Made from 1915 to 1930. *Note:* Specifications and illustration are of the 1919 modification; the earlier type is seven-shot. From 1915 to 1919, Beretta also made an enlarged version of Model 1915 chambered for the 9mm Luger cartridge.

Beretta Model 1923 Automatic Pistol............ $325
Caliber, 9mm Luger. 8-shot magazine. 4-inch barrel. 6½ inches overall. Weight, 30 ounces. Fixed sights. Blued finish. Plastic stocks. Made from 1923 to c. 1936.

Beretta Model 1934 Automatic Pistol
Caliber, 380 Automatic (9mm Short). 7-shot magazine. 3⅜-inch barrel. 5⅞ inches overall. Weight, 24 ounces. Fixed sights. Blued finish. Plastic stocks. Official pistol of the Italian Armed Forces. Wartime production is not as well made and finished as commercial models. Made from 1934 to 1959.
Commercial Model.................................... $230
War Model... 175

Beretta Model 1923*

Beretta Model 1934

Beretta Model 318 (1934)*

Beretta Model 318 (1934) Automatic Pistol......$210
Caliber, 25 Automatic (6.35mm). 8-shot magazine. 2½-inch barrel. 4½ inches overall. Weight, 14 ounces. Fixed sights. Blued finish. Plastic stocks. Made from 1934 to c. 1939.

Beretta Model 949 Olimpionico Automatic Pistol.. $450
Calibers: 22 Short, 22 Long Rifle. 5-shot magazine. 8¾-inch barrel. 12½ inches overall. Weight, 38 ounces. Target sights. Adjustable barrel weight. Muzzle brake. Checkered walnut stocks with thumb-rest. Made from 1959 to 1964.

Beretta Olimpionico

Beretta Model 950CC

Beretta Model 950CC Automatic Pistol.........$115
Caliber, 22 Short. 6-shot magazine. Hinged, 2⅜-inch barrel. 4¾ inches overall. Weight, 11 ounces. Fixed sights. Blued finish. Plastic stocks. Made from 1959 to date. *Note:* Formerly marketed in the U.S. as "Minx M2."

Beretta Model 950CC Special

Beretta Model 950B

Beretta Model 950CC Special Automatic Pistol. $130
Same general specifications as M2, except has 4-inch barrel. Made from 1959 to date. *Note:* Formerly marketed in U.S. as "Minx M4."

Beretta Model 950B Automatic Pistol...........$110
Same general specifications as Minx M2, except caliber, 25 Auto, has 7-shot magazine. Made from 1959 to date. *Note:* Formerly marketed in U.S. as "Jetfire."

Beretta Model 1935*

Beretta Model 70

Beretta Model 72

Beretta Model 1935 Automatic Pistol

Caliber, 32 Automatic (7.65mm). 8-shot magazine. 3½-inch barrel. 5¾ inches overall. Weight, 24 ounces. Fixed sights. Blued finish. Plastic stocks. A roughly finished version of this pistol was produced during World War II. Made from 1935 to 1959.
Commercial Model...................................$240
War Model.. 210

Beretta Model 72.................................$170
Same as Model 71, except has 6-inch barrel, weighs 18 ounces. Made from 1959 to date. *Note:* Formerly marketed in U.S. as "Jaguar Plinker."

Beretta Model 951 (1951)

Beretta Model 70T

Beretta Model 951 (1951) Military Automatic
Pistol..$285
Caliber, 9mm Luger. 8-shot magazine. 4½-inch barrel. 8 inches overall. Weight, 31 ounces. Fixed sights. Blued finish. Plastic stocks. Made from 1952 to date. *Note:* This is the standard pistol of the Italian Armed Forces, is also used by Egyptian and Israeli armies and by the police in Nigeria. Formerly marketed in the U.S. as the "Brigadier."

Beretta Model 70 Automatic Pistol..............$185
Improved version of Model 1935. Steel or lightweight alloy. Calibers: 32 Automatic (7.65mm), 380 Automatic (9mm Short). 8-shot magazine in 32, 7-shot in 380 caliber. 3½-inch barrel. 6½ inches overall. Weights: steel, 22¼ ounces; alloy, 16 ounces. Fixed sights. Blued finish. Checkered plastic stocks. Made from 1959 to date. *Note:* Formerly marketed in U.S. as "Pluma" for alloy model in 32 and "Cougar" for steel model in 380.

Beretta Model 71.................................$175
Same as lightweight alloy Model 70, except caliber 22 Long Rifle. Made from 1959 to date. *Note:* Formerly marketed in U.S. as "Jaguar Plinker."

Beretta Model 70T Automatic Pistol............$210
Similar to Model 70. Caliber, 32 Automatic (7.65mm). 9-shot magazine. 6-inch barrel. 9½ inches overall. Weight, 19 ounces. Adjustable rear sight, blade front sight. Blued finish. Checkered plastic stocks. Introduced in 1959. Discontinued.

Beretta Model 70S...............................$195
Similar to Model 70T, except chambered for 22 Auto and 380 Auto. Longer barrel guide, safety lever blocking hammer; sight and rear sight blade fixed on breech block. Weight, 1 pound 7 ounces. Made from 1977 to date.

Beretta Model 101...............................$210
Same as Model 70T, except caliber 22 Long Rifle, has 10-shot magazine. Introduced in 1959. Discontinued.

Beretta Model 76

Beretta Model 76 Automatic Target Pistol...... **$225**
Caliber, 22 Long Rifle. 10-shot magazine. 6-inch barrel. 8.8 inches overall. Weight, 33 ounces. Adjustable rear sight, front sight with interchangeable blades. Blued finish. Checkered plastic stocks. Made from 1966 to date. *Note:* Formerly marketed in the U.S. as the "Sable."

Beretta Model 90

Beretta Model 90 Double Action Automatic Pistol..................................... **$235**
Caliber, 32 Automatic (7.65mm). 8-shot magazine. 3⅝-inch barrel. 6⅝ inches overall. Weight, 19½ ounces. Fixed sights. Blued finish. Checkered plastic stocks. Made from 1969 to 1975.

Beretta Model 81

Beretta Model 81 Double Action Automatic Pistol................................. **$245**
Caliber, 32 Automatic (7.65mm). 12-shot magazine. 3.8-inch barrel. 6.8 inches overall. Weight, 23.5 ounces. Fixed sights. Blued finish. Plastic stocks. Made from 1976 to date.

Beretta Model 84................................. **$300**
Same as Model 81, except caliber 380 Automatic, has 13-shot magazine. Made from 1976 to date.

Beretta Model 92

Beretta Model 92 Double Action Automatic Pistol................................. **$375**
Caliber, 9mm Luger. 15-shot magazine. 4.9-inch barrel. 8.5 inches overall. Weight, 33.5 ounces. Fixed sights. Blued finish. Plastic stocks. Made from 1976 to date.

Bernardelli Vest Pocket

Vincenzo Bernardelli, S.p.A., Gardone V. T. (Brescia), Italy

Bernardelli Vest Pocket Automatic Pistol....... **$160**
Caliber, 25 Automatic (6.35mm). 5-shot or 8-shot magazine. 2⅛-inch barrel. 4⅛ inches overall. Weight, 9 ounces. Fixed sights. Blued finish. Bakelite stocks. Made from 1945 to 1968.

Bernardelli "Baby" Automatic Pistol............. **$185**
Calibers: 22 Short, 22 Long. 5-shot magazine. 2⅛-inch barrel. 4⅛ inches overall. Weight, 9 ounces. Fixed sights. Blued finish. Bakelite stocks. Made from 1949 to 1968.

Bernardelli "Sporter" Automatic Pistol......... **$225**
Caliber, 22 Long Rifle. 8-shot magazine. Barrel lengths: 6-, 8-, and 10-inch. 13 inches overall with 10-inch barrel. Weight, about 30 ounces with 10-inch barrel. Target sights. Blued finish. Walnut stocks. Made from 1949 to 1968.

Bernardelli "Baby"

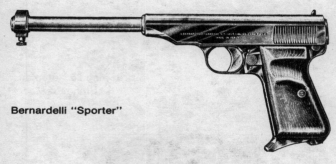

Bernardelli "Sporter"

Bernardelli Model 60

Bernardelli Model 60 Pocket Automatic Pistol.. $135
Calibers: 22 Long Rifle, 32 Auto (7.65mm), 380 Auto (9mm Short). 8-shot magazine in 22 and 32, 7-shot in 380. 3½-inch barrel. 6½ inches overall. Weight, about 25 ounces. Fixed sights. Blued finish. Bakelite stocks. Made from 1959 to date.

Bernardelli Model 80 Automatic Pistol......... $150
Calibers: 22 Long Rifle, 32 Automatic (7.65mm), 380 Automatic (9mm Short). Magazine capacity: 10-shot in 22, 8-shot in 32, 7-shot in 380 caliber. 3½-inch barrel. 6½ inches overall. Weight, 25.6 ounces. Adjustable rear sight, white dot front sight. Blued finish. Plastic thumb-rest stocks. Made from 1968 to date. *Note:* Model 80 is a modification of Model 60 designed to conform with U.S. import regulations.

Bernardelli Model 80

Bernardelli Model 90

Bernardelli Model 90 Sport Target.............. $175
Same as Model 80, except has 6-inch barrel, is 9 inches overall, weighs 26.8 ounces. Made from 1968 to date.

Bernardelli Model 100

Bernardelli Model 100 Target Automatic Pistol. $300
Caliber, 22 Long Rifle. 10-shot magazine. 5.9-inch barrel. 9 inches overall. Weight, 37¾ ounces. Adjustable rear sight, interchangeable front sight. Blued finish. Checkered walnut thumb-rest stocks. Made from 1969 to date: *Note:* Formerly designated Model 69.

Bersa Model 644

Bersa Pistol imported from Argentina by Interarms

Bersa Model 644 Auto Pistol................... **$ 95**
Caliber, 22 Long Rifle. 10-shot magazine. 3.5-inch barrel.
Weight, 26½ ounces. 6½ inches overall. Adjustable rear sight,
blade front sight. Contoured black nylon grips. Made from 1980
to date.

Bersa Model 622

Bersa Model 622 Auto Pistol.................... **$115**
Caliber, 22 Long Rifle. 7-shot magazine. 4- or 6-inch barrel. 7-,
9-inch overall length respectively. Weight, 2¼ pounds. Made
from 1982 to date.

Bersa Model 97

Bersa Model 97 Auto Pistol..................... **$140**
Caliber, 380 ACP. 7-shot magazine. 3½-inch barrel. 6½ inches
overall. Weight, 1¾ pounds. Made from 1982 to date.

Bronco Pistol manufactured by Echave y Arizmendi, Eibar, Spain

Bronco Model 1918 Pocket Automatic Pistol.... **$125**
Caliber, 32 Automatic (7.65mm). 6-shot magazine. 2½-inch

barrel. 5 inches overall. Weight, 20 ounces. Fixed sights. Blued
finish. Hard rubber stocks. Made circa 1918-1925.

Bronco Model 1918*

Browning 25 Automatic
Standard Model

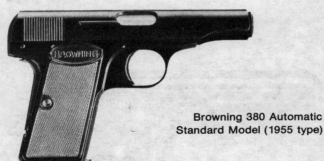

Browning 380 Automatic
Standard Model (1955 type)

Browning Pistols manufactured for Browning, Morgan, Utah, by Fabrique Nationale d'Armes de Guerre (now Fabrique Nationale Herstal), Herstal, Belgium, by Arms Technology Inc., Salt Lake City, Utah, and by J. P. Sauer & Sohn, Eckenforde, West Germany.

Browning 25 Automatic Pistol
Same general specifications as FN Browning Baby. Standard
Model, blued finish, hard rubber grips. Lightweight Model,
nickel-plated, Nacrolac pearl grips. Renaissance Engraved
Model, nickel-plated, Nacrolac pearl grips. Made by FN from
1955 to 1969.
Standard Model.................................$210
Lightweight Model................................ 300
Renaissance Model................................ 500

Browning 380 Automatic Pistol, 1955 Type
Same general specifications as FN Browning 380 Pocket Auto.
Standard Model, Renaissance Engraved Model, as furnished in
25 Automatic. Made by FN from 1955 to 1969.
Standard Model.................................$280
Renaissance Model................................ 780

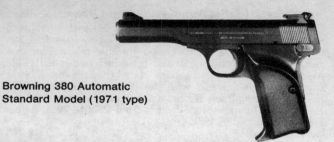

**Browning 380 Automatic
Standard Model (1971 type)**

Browning Nomad

Browning 380 Automatic Pistol, 1971 Type

Same as 380 Automatic, 1955 Type, except has longer slide, 4-7/16-inch barrel, is 7-1/16 inches overall, weighs 23 ounces. Rear sight adjustable for windage and elevation, plastic thumb-rest stocks. Made from 1971 to 1975.

Standard Model..$290
Renaissance Model.. 800

Browning Nomad Automatic Pistol.............. $225

Caliber, 22 Long Rifle. 10-shot magazine. Barrel lengths: 4½- and 6¾-inch. 8-15/16 inches overall with 4½-inch barrel. Weight, 34 ounces with 4½-inch barrel. Removable blade front sight, screw adjustable rear sight. Blued finish. Plastic stocks. Made by FN from 1962 to 1974.

**Browning Hi-Power
Standard Model**

**Browning Challenger
Standard Model**

**Browning Challenger
Gold Model**

Browning Hi-Power 9mm Automatic Pistol

Same general specifications as FN Browning Model 1935. 13-shot, fixed sights; also available with rear sight adjustable for windage and elevation and ramp front sight. Standard Model, blued finish, checkered walnut stocks. Renaissance Engraved Model, chrome-plated, Nacrolac pearl stocks. Made by FN from 1955 to date.

Standard Model, fixed sights.........................$ 310
Standard Model, adjustable sights..................... 380
Renaissance Model, fixed sights...................... 1100
Renaissance Model, adjustable sights............... 1150

**Browning Challenger
Renaissance Model**

Browning Renaissance Cased Set

Browning Renaissance Engraved Models,
Cased Set.. $3100

One pistol of each of the three models in a special walnut carrying case. Made by FN from 1955 to 1969.

Browning Challenger Automatic Pistol

Caliber, 22 Long Rifle. 10-shot magazine. Barrel lengths: 4½- and 6¾-inch. 11-7/16 inches overall with 6¾-inch barrel. Weight, 38 ounces with 6¾-inch barrel. Removable blade front sight, screw adjustable rear sight. Standard finish, blue; also furnished gold-inlaid (Gold Model) and engraved and chrome-plated (Renaissance Model). Checkered walnut stocks; finely figured and carved stocks on Gold and Renaissance Models. Standard made by FN from 1962 to 1975, higher grades introduced in 1971.

Standard Model.....................................$210
Gold Model... 510
Renaissance Model................................... 710

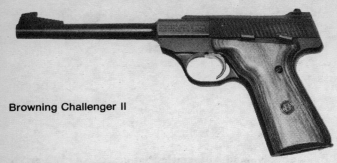

Browning Challenger II

Browning Challenger II Automatic Pistol....... $140
Same general specifications as Challenger Standard Model with
6¾-inch barrel. Aside from changed grip angle and impregnated
hardwood stocks, appearance is similar. Original Challenger
design was modified for lower production costs. Made by ATI
from 1976 to date.

Browning Challenger III

Browning Challenger III Automatic Pistol...... $180
Same general description as Challenger II, except has 5½-inch
bull barrel, alloy frame, and new sight system. Weight, 35
ounces. Made from 1982 to date.

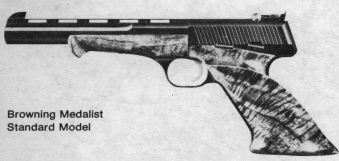

Browning Medalist
Standard Model

Browning Medalist
Renaissance Model

Browning Medalist Automatic Target Pistol
Caliber, 22 Long Rifle. 10-shot magazine. 6¾-inch barrel with
ventilated rib. 11-15/16 inches overall. Weight, 46 ounces. Re-
movable blade front sight, click-adjustable micrometer rear
sight. Standard finish, blue; also furnished gold-inlaid (Gold
Model) and engraved and chrome-plated (Renaissance Model).
Checkered walnut stocks with thumb-rest (for right- or left-
handed shooter); finely figured and carved stocks on Gold and
Renaissance Models. Made by FN from 1962 to 1975, higher
grades introduced in 1971.
Standard Model....................................**$475**
Gold Model.. 800
Renaissance Model................................. 925

Browning International Medalist

**Browning International Medalist Automatic
Target Pistol....................................... $480**
Modification of Medalist to conform with International Shooting Union rules; has 5.9-inch barrel, smaller grip, no forearm;
weight is 42 ounces. Made from 1970 to 1973.

Browning BDA

Browning BDA Double Action Automatic Pistol. $265
Same as SIG-Sauer P220. Calibers: 9mm Luger, 38 Super Auto,
45 Automatic. 9-shot magazine in 9mm and 38, 7-shot in 45. 4.4-
inch barrel. 7.8 inches overall. Weight, 29.3 ounces. Fixed sights.
Blued finish. Plastic stocks. Made from 1977 to 1979 by Sauer.

Browning BDA (1982) Double Action Automatic Pistol
Caliber, 380 Auto. 13-shot magazine. Barrel length, 3-13/16
inches. 6¾ inches overall. Weight, 23 ounces. Fixed blade front
sight, square notch drift adjustable rear sight. Made from 1982
to date.
Blue finish...**$300**
Nickel finish....................................... 340

Browning BDA-380

Browning BDA-380 Nickel

Budischowsky TP-70

Budischowsky Pistol manufactured by Norton Armament Corporation, Mt. Clemens, Michigan

Budischowsky TP-70 Double Action Automatic Pistol
Calibers: 22 Long Rifle, 25 Automatic. 6-shot magazine. 2.6-inch barrel. 4.65 inches overall. Weight, 12.3 ounces. Fixed sights. Stainless steel. Plastic stocks. Made from 1973 to 1977.

22 Long Rifle... $300
25 Automatic...   200

Charter Arms Corporation, Stratford, Connecticut

Charter Arms Undercover Double Action Revolver...$135
Caliber, 38 Special. 5-shot cylinder. Barrel lengths: 2-, 3-, 4-inch. 6¼ inches overall with 2-inch barrel and regular grips. Weight, 16 ounces, with 2-inch barrel. Fixed sights. Blued or nickel-plated finish. Plain walnut regular stocks, checkered Bulldog or square buttstocks. Made from 1965 to date.

Charter Arms Undercoverette Double Action Revolver...$130
Same as Undercover with 2-inch barrel, except caliber 32 S&W Long, 6-shot cylinder, blued finish only; weighs 16½ ounces. Made from 1972 to date.

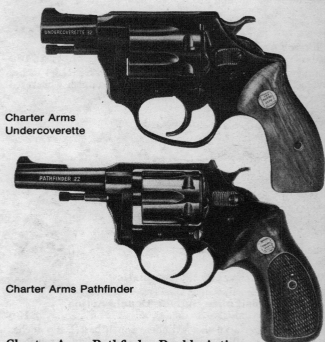

Charter Arms Undercoverette

Charter Arms Pathfinder

Charter Arms Pathfinder Double Action Revolver...$130
Calibers: 22 Long Rifle, 22 Win. Mag. R.F. 6-shot cylinder. Barrel lengths: 3-, 6-inch. 7⅛ inches overall with 3-inch barrel and regular stocks. Weight, with 3-inch barrel, 18½ ounces. Adjustable rear sight, ramp front sight. Blued finish. Plain walnut regular, checkered Bulldog or square buttstocks. Made from 1970 to date. *Note:* Originally designated "Pocket Target." Name changed to "Pathfinder" in 1971.

Charter Arms Bulldog 44

**Charter Arms Bulldog 44 Double Action
Revolver** **$150**
Caliber, 44 Special. 5-shot cylinder. 3-inch barrel. 7½ inches
overall. Weight, 19 ounces. Fixed sights. Blued or nickel-plated
finish. Checkered walnut Bulldog or square buttstocks. Made
from 1973 to date.

Charter Arms Bulldog 357

**Charter Arms Bulldog 357 Double Action
Revolver** **$160**
Caliber, 357 Magnum. 5-shot cylinder. 6-inch barrel. 11 inches
overall. Weight, 25 ounces. Fixed sights. Blued finish. Checkered
walnut square buttstocks. Introduced in 1977.

Charter Arms Police Bulldog

**Charter Arms Police Bulldog Double Action
Revolver** **$135**
Caliber, 38 Special. 6-shot cylinder. 4-inch barrel. 8½ inches
overall. Weight, 20½ ounces. Adjustable rear sight, ramp front
sight. Blued finish. Checkered walnut square buttstocks. Made
from 1976 to date.

Charter Arms Target Bulldog

**Charter Arms Target Bulldog Double Action
Revolver** **$145**
Calibers: 357 Magnum, 44 Special (latter introduced in 1977). 4-
inch barrel. 8½ inches overall. Weight, in 357, 20½ ounces.
Adjustable rear sight, ramp front sight. Blued finish. Checkered
walnut square buttstocks. Made from 1976 to date.

Colt's Firearms Division, Hartford, Connecticut
Colt Revolvers and Single Shot Pistols
Colt Single Action Army Revolver
Also called "Frontier Six Shooter" and "Peacemaker." Calibers:
22 Rimfire (Short, Long, Long Rifle), 22 W.R.F., 32 Rimfire, 32
Colt, 32 S&W, 32-20, 38 Colt, 38 S&W, 38 Special, 357 Magnum,
38-40, 41 Colt, 44 Rimfire, 44 Russian, 44 Special, 44-40, 45 Colt,
45 Auto, 450 Boxer, 450 Eley, 455 Eley, 476 Eley. 6-shot cylinder.
Barrel lengths: 4¾-, 5½- and 7½-inch with ejector; 3- and 4-
inches without ejector. 10¼ inches overall with 4¾-inch barrel.
Weight, 36 ounces in 45 caliber with 4¾-inch barrel. Fixed
sights. Also made in Target Model with flat top-strap and target
sights. Blued finish with casehardened frame or nickel-plated.
One-piece smooth walnut or checkered black rubber stocks. S.A.
Army Revolvers with serial numbers above 165,000 (circa 1896)
are adapted to smokeless powder; cylinder pin screw was
changed to spring catch at about the same time. Made from 1873
to 1942; production resumed in 1955 with serial number 1001SA.
Current calibers: 357 Magnum, 44 Special, 45 Long Colt.

Colt Single Action Army

U.S. Cavalry Model, 45 Colt, 7½-inch bbl. **$2000**
U.S. Artillery Model, 45 Colt, 5½-inch bbl. 2000
Frontier Six-Shooter, 44-40 2200
Storekeeper's Model, 3-inch/4-inch bbl., w/o ejector... 2500
Target Model, flat top-strap, target sights. 3500
*(Above values apply only to original models, not to
similar S.A.A. Revolvers of recent manufacture.)*
Standard Model, pre-1942 .... $950
Standard Model, current production 325

Colt Sheriff's Model 45
Limited edition of replica of "Storekeeper's Model" in caliber 45
Colt, made exclusively for Centennial Arms Corp., Chicago,
Illinois. Numbered from "1SM." Blued finish with casehardened
frame or nickel-plated. Walnut stocks. 478 were produced in
blue, 25 in nickel. Made in 1961.
Blued finish. **$1200**
Nickel finish. 3250

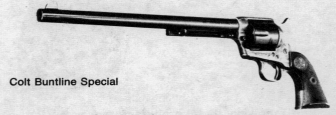

Colt Buntline Special

Colt Buntline Special 45 .... **$480**
Same as standard Single Action Army, except has 12-inch barrel,
caliber 45 Long Colt. Made from 1957 to 1975.

Colt New Frontier Single Action Army Revolver
.... **$375**
Same as Single Action Army, except has flat-top frame, adjustable target rear sight, ramp front sight, smooth walnut grips.

5½- or 7½-inch barrel. Calibers, 357 Magnum, 44 Special, 45 Colt. Made from 1961 to date.

Colt New Frontier

Colt New Frontier Buntline Special

Colt New Frontier Buntline Special............$540
Same as New Frontier Single Action Army, except has 12-inch barrel. Made from 1962 to 1966.

Colt Single Action Army—125th Anniversary Model...$545
Limited production deluxe version of Single Action Army issued in commemoration of Colt's 125th Anniversary. Caliber, 45 Long Colt. 7½-inch barrel. Gold-plated frame, trigger, hammer, cylinder pin, ejector rod tip, and stock medallion. Presentation case with anniversary medallion. Serial numbers from "50AM" 7368 were produced. Made in 1961.

Colt Single Action Army Commemorative Models
Limited production versions of Single Action Army 45 issued, with appropriate inscription, to commemorate historical events. Cased.

1963 issues:

West Virginia Statehood Centennial (600 produced)..	$ 600
Arizona Territorial Centennial (1280 produced).......	600

1964 issues:

Nevada Statehood Centennial (1877 produced).......	600
Nevada "Battle Born" (100 produced)...............	1330
Montana Territorial Centennial (851 produced).......	600
New Jersey Tercentenary (250 produced)............	740
St. Louis Bicentennial (450 produced)...............	600
Pony Express Presentation (1004 produced)..........	880
Chamizal Treaty (50 produced).....................	1410
Colonel Sam Colt Sesquicentennial	
Presentation (4750 produced)....................	740
Deluxe Presentation (200 produced)..............	1550
Special Deluxe Presentation (50 produced)........	2960
Wyatt Earp Buntline (150 produced)................	1550

1965 issues:

Old Fort Des Moines Reconstruction (200 produced)..	700
Appomattox Centennial (500 produced)..............	600

1966 issues:

General Meade (200 produced).....................	740
Abercrombie & Fitch Trailblazer—New York	
(200 produced)..................................	2000
California Gold Rush (130 produced)...............	840

Abercrombie & Fitch Trailblazer—Chicago	
(100 produced)..................................	$2040
Abercrombie & Fitch Trailblazer—San Francisco	
(100 produced)..................................	2000
Pony Express Four Square (4 guns).................	3250

1967 issues:

Lawman Series—Bat Masterson (500 produced)......	670
Alamo (1000 produced)............................	635

1968 issues:

Lawman Series—Pat Garrett (500 produced)........	645

1969 issues:

Lawman Series—Wild Bill Hickok (500 produced)....	640

1970 issues:

Texas Ranger (1000 produced).....................	1340
Missouri Sesquicentennial (501 produced)...........	555
Lawman Series—Wyatt Earp (501 produced)........	1340

1971 issues:

NRA Centennial, 357 or 45 (5001 produced)...........	550

Colt Single Action Army Commemorative Peacemaker Centennial 45

Colt Single Action Army Commemorative Peacemaker Centennial 44-40

Note: Values indicated are for commemorative revolvers in new condition.

1975 issues:

Peacemaker Centennial 45 (1501 produced)..........	$635
Peacemaker Centennial 44-40 (1501 produced).......	635
Peacemaker Centennial Cased Pair (501 produced)...	1700

1979 issues:

Ned Buntline 45 (3000 produced)...................	900

Colt Bisley Model Single Action Revolver
Variation of the Single Action Army, developed for target shooting; grips, trigger and hammer changed. Calibers, general specifications same as Single Action Army. Also made in Target Model with flat-topped frame and target sights. Made from 1894 to 1915.

Standard Model...................................	$ 845
Target Model....................................	2250

Colt Frontier Scout

Colt Frontier Scout Single Action Revolver

Single Action Army replica, ⅛ scale. Calibers: 22 Short, Long, Long Rifle; 22 W.R.F. Magnum (interchangeable cylinder available.) 6-shot cylinder. 4¾-inch barrel. 9-15/16 inches overall. Weight, 24 ounces. Fixed sights. Plastic stocks. Originally made with bright alloy frame; since 1959 with steel frame, blue finish, also in all nickel finish with wood stocks. Made from 1958 to 1971.

Blue finish, plastic stocks............................$195
Nickel finish, wood stocks............................ 200
Extra interchangeable cylinder....................... 20

Colt Buntline Scout

Colt Buntline Scout...............................$160
Same as "Frontier Scout," except has 9½-inch barrel. Made from 1959 to 1971.

Colt Frontier Scout Commemorative Models

Limited production versions of "Frontier Scout" issued, with appropriate inscription, to commemorate historical events. Cased.

1961 issues:
Kansas Statehood Centennial (6201 produced)........$ 275
Pony Express Centennial (1007 produced)........... 490

1962 issues:
Columbus, Ohio, Sesquicentennial (200 produced).... 600
Fort Findlay, Ohio, Sesquicentennial (130 produced).. 600
Fort Findlay Cased Pair, 22 Long Rifle and 22 Magnum
 (20 produced).................................. 3170

**Colt Frontier Scout Commemorative
Idaho Territorial Centennial**

New Mexico Golden Anniversary (1000 produced).... **$315**
West Virginia Statehood Centennial (3452 produced). 250

1963 issues:
Arizona Territorial Centennial (5355 produced)....... 275
Carolina Charter Tercentenary (300 produced)....... 350
Fort Stephenson, Ohio, Sesquicentennial
 (200 produced)................................. 600
Battle of Gettysburg Centennial (1019 produced)..... 275
Idaho Territorial Centennial (902 produced).......... 350
General John Hunt Morgan Indiana Raid
 (100 produced) 810

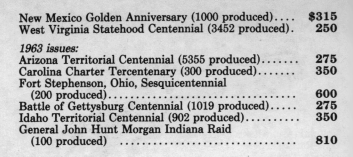

Montana Territory Centennial

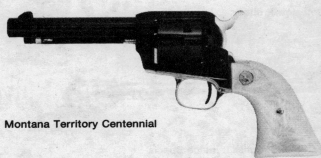

General Hood Centennial

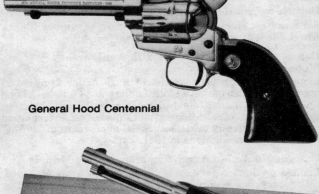

New Jersey Tercentenary

1964 issues:
Nevada Statehood Centennial (3984 produced)........ **$275**
Nevada "Battle Born" (981 produced)................ 275
Montana Territorial Centennial (2300 produced)....... 275
Wyoming Diamond Jubilee (2357 produced)........... 275
General Hood Centennial (1503 produced)............. 275
New Jersey Tercentenary (1001 produced)............. 275
St. Louis Bicentennial (802 produced)................ 275
California Gold Rush (500 produced)................. 320
Chamizal Treaty (450 produced)..................... 320

1965 issues:
Oregon Trail (1995 produced)......................... $275
Forty-Niner Miner (500 produced)................... 275
Old Fort Des Moines Reconstruction (700 produced)... 315
Appomattox Centennial (1001 produced).............. 275
General Meade Campaign (1197 produced)............. 275
St. Augustine Quadricentennial (500 produced)........ 315
Kansas Cowtown Series—Wichita (500 produced)...... 315

1966 issues:
Kansas Cowtown Series—Dodge City (500 produced)... $320
Colorado Gold Rush (1350 produced)................. 275
Oklahoma Territory (1343 produced)................. 275
Dakota Territory (1000 produced)................... 275

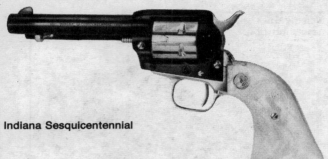

Indiana Sesquicentennial

Kansas Cowtown Series—Abilene (500 produced)...... 320
Indiana Sesquicentennial (1500 produced)............. 275

1967 issues:
Lawman Series—Bat Masterson (3000 produced)...... 320
Alamo (4500 produced)............................. 275
Kansas Cowtown Series—Coffeyville (500 produced).... 320
Kansas Trail Series—Chisholm Trail (500 produced)... 275

1968 issues:
Kansas Trail Series—Santa Fe Trail (501 produced)... 500
Nebraska Centennial (7001 produced)................ 275
Kansas Trail Series—Pawnee Trail (501 produced)..... 275
Lawman Series—Pat Garrett (3000 produced)......... 320

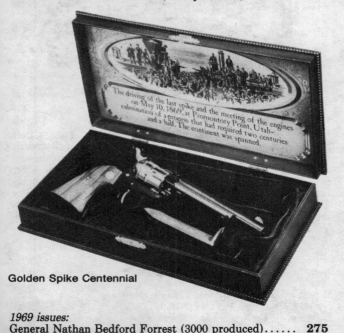

Golden Spike Centennial

1969 issues:
General Nathan Bedford Forrest (3000 produced)...... 275
Alabama Sesquicentennial (3001 produced)............ 275
Golden Spike (11,000 produced)..................... 275

Kansas Trail Series—Shawnee Trail (501 produced).... $275
Arkansas Territory Sesquicentennial (3500 produced).. 245
Lawman Series—Wild Bill Hickock (3000 produced)... 320
California Bicentennial (5000 produced).............. 275

1970 issues:
Kansas Fort Series—Fort Larned (500 produced)...... 275
Kansas Fort Series—Fort Hays (500 produced)........ 275
Maine Sesquicentennial (3000 produced).............. 275
Missouri Sesquicentennial (3000 produced)........... 275
Kansas Fort Series—Fort Riley (500 produced)........ 275
Lawman Series—Wyatt Earp (3000 produced)......... 350

1971 issue:
Kansas Fort Series—Fort Scott (500 produced)........ 275

1972 issues:
Florida Territory Sesquicentennial (2001 produced).... $275

1973 issues:
Arizona Ranger (3001 produced)...................... 275

Note: Values indicated are for commemorative revolvers in new condition.

Colt Peacemaker 22

Colt Peacemaker 22 Single Action Revolver.....$150
Calibers, 22 Long Rifle and 22 Win. Mag. R.F. Furnished with cylinder for each caliber. 6-shot. Barrels: 4⅜-, 6- or 7½-inch. 11¼ inches overall with 6-inch barrel. Weight, with 6-inch barrel, 30½ ounces. Fixed sights. Black composite stocks. Made from 1971 to 1976.

Colt Peacemaker 22
Second Amendment Commemorative

Colt Peacemaker 22 Second Amendment Commemorative....................................$275
Peacemaker 22 Single Action Revolver with 7½-inch barrel. Nickel-plated frame, barrel, ejector rod assembly, hammer and trigger; blued cylinder, backstrap and trigger guard. Black pearlite stocks. Barrel inscribed "The Right to Keep and Bear Arms." Presentation case. Limited edition of 3000 issued in 1977. Value is for revolver in new condition.

Colt New Frontier 22 Single Action Revolver... $175
Same as Peacemaker 22, except has flat-top frame, adjustable rear sight, ramp front sight. Made from 1971 to 1976.

Colt New Frontier 22

Colt
Deringer No. 4
(Cased Pair)

Colt Deringer No. 4

Replica of Deringer No. 3 (1872). Single shot with side-swing barrel. Caliber, 22 Short. 2½-inch barrel. 4-15/16 inches overall. Weight, 7¾ ounces. Fixed sights. Gold-finished frame, blued barrel, walnut grips; also available nickel-plated with simulated ivory grips. Cased. Made from 1959 to 1963.
Single pistol...................................... $100
Pair with consecutive serial numbers................. 200

Colt Deringer No. 4 Commemorative Models

Limited production version of 22 Deringer issued, with appropriate inscription, to commemorate historical events.
1961 issue:
Geneseo, Illinois, 125th Anniversary (104 produced).... $600
1962 issue:
Fort McPherson, Nebraska, Centennial (300 produced). 300

Note: Values indicated are for commemorative deringers in new condition.

Colt Lord and Lady Deringers

Same as Deringer No. 4. "Lord" model is blued with gold-plated frame and walnut stocks. "Lady" model is gold-plated with simulated pearl stocks. Furnished in cased pairs. Made from 1970 to 1972.
Lord Deringer, pair in case.......................... $180
Lady Deringer, pair in case.......................... 210
Lord and Lady Deringers, one each, in case........... 200

Colt
Civil War Centennial
(Cased Pair)

Colt Civil War Centennial Model Pistol

Single shot replica, ⅛ scale, of Colt Model 1860 Army Revolver. Caliber, 22 Short. 6-inch barrel. Weight, 22 ounces. Blued finish with gold-plated frame, grip frame, and trigger guard, walnut grips. Cased. 24,114 were produced. Made in 1961.
Single pistol... $ 95
Pair with consecutive serial numbers.................. 150

Colt Rock Island Arsenal Centennial Pistol...... $195

Limited production (550 pieces) version of Civil War Centennial Model single shot 22 pistol, made exclusively for Cherry's Sporting Goods, Geneseo, Illinois, to commemorate the centennial of the Rock Island Arsenal in Illinois. Cased. Made in 1962.

Note: Values indicated are for commemorative pistols in new condition.

Colt Bicentennial Commemorative Set

Colt U.S. Bicentennial Commemorative Set..... $3500

Replica Colt 3rd Model Dragoon Revolver with accessories, Colt Single Action Army Revolver, and Colt Python Revolver. Matching roll-engraved unfluted cylinders, blued finish, and rosewood stocks with Great Seal of the United States silver medallion. Dragoon revolver has silver grip frame. Serial numbers 0001 to 1776; all revolvers in set have same number. Deluxe drawer style presentation case of walnut, with book compartment containing a reproduction of "Armsmear." Issued in 1976. Value is for revolvers in new condition.

Colt Lightning Model

Colt New Double Action Central Fire Six Shot
Revolver..$450

Also called "Lightning Model." Calibers: 38 and 41 Centerfire. 6-shot cylinder. Barrel lengths: 2½-, 3½-, 4½- and 6-inch without ejector, 4½- and 6-inch with ejector. 8½ inches overall with 3½-inch barrel. Weight, 38 caliber with 3½-inch barrel, 23 ounces. Fixed sights. Blued or nickel finish. Hard rubber birdshead grips. Made from 1877 to 1909.

Colt Double Action Frontier

Colt Double Action Army Revolver.............. $950

Also called "Double Action Frontier." Similar in appearance to the smaller "Lightning Model," but has heavier frame of different shape, round disc on left side of frame, lanyard loop in butt. Calibers: 38-40, 44-40, 45 Colt. 6-shot cylinder. Barrel lengths: 3½- and 4-inch without ejector; 4¾-, 5½- and 7½-inch with ejector. 12½ inches overall with 7½-inch barrel. Weight, 45 caliber with 7½-inch barrel, 39 ounces. Fixed sights. Hard rubber birdshead grips. Blued or nickel finish. Made from 1878 to 1905.

Colt New Navy

Colt New Navy Double Action Revolver,
First Issue... $300

Also called "New Army." Calibers: 38 Short & Long Colt, 41 Short & Long Colt. 6-shot cylinder, left revolution. Barrel lengths: 3-, 4½- and 6-inch. 11¼ inches overall with 6-inch barrel. Weight 32 ounces, with 6-inch barrel. Fixed sights, knife-blade and V-notch. Blued or nickel-plated finish. Walnut or hard rubber grips. Made from 1889 to 1894. *Note:* This model, which was adopted by both the Army and Navy, was Colt's first revolver of the solid frame, swing-out cylinder type. It lacks the cylinder-locking notches found on later models made on this 41 frame; ratchet on the back of the cylinder is held in place by a double projection on the hand.

Colt New Navy Double Action Revolver,
Second Issue...................................... $270

Also called "New Army." General specifications same as First Issue, except this model has double cylinder notches and double locking bolt. Calibers: 38 Special added in 1904 and 32-30 in 1905. Made from 1892 to 1907. *Note:* The heavy 38 Special High Velocity loads should not be used in 38 Special arms of this model.

Colt Marine Corps Model Double Action
Revolver.. $750

General specifications same as "New Navy" Second Issue, except this model has round butt, was supplied only in 38 caliber (38 Short & Long Colt, 38 Special) and with 6-inch barrel. Made from 1905 to 1909.

Colt Army Special Double Action Revolver...... $260

41-caliber frame. Calibers: 32-20, 38 Special (41 Colt). 6-shot cylinder, right revolution. Barrel lengths: 4-, 4½-, 5- and 6-inch. 9¼ inches overall with 4-inch barrel. Weight, 32 ounces with 4-inch barrel. Fixed sights. Blued or nickel-plated finish. Hard rubber stocks. Made from 1908 to 1927. *Note:* This model has a somewhat heavier frame than the "New Navy" which it replaced. Serial numbers begin with 300,000. The heavy 38 Special High Velocity loads should not be used in 38 Special arms of this model.

Colt Official Police

Colt Official Police Double Action Revolver

Calibers: 22 Long Rifle (introduced 1930, embedded head-cylinder for high speed cartridges after 1932), 32-20 (discontinued 1942), 38 Special, 41 Long Colt (discontinued 1930). 6-shot cylinder. Barrel lengths: 4-, 5-, and 6-inch; 2-inch barrel and 6-inch heavy barrel in 38 Special only. 22 L.R. with 4- and 6-inch barrels only. 11¼ inches overall. Weight, 36 ounces, with standard 6-inch barrel in 38 Special. Fixed sights. Blued or nickel-plated finish. Checkered walnut stocks on all revolvers of this model, except some of postwar production had checkered plastic stocks. Made from 1927 to 1969. *Note:* This model is a refined version of the "Army Special," which it replaced in 1928 at about serial number 520,000. The "Commando" 38 Special was a wartime adaptation of the "Official Police" made to Government specifications. "Commando" can be identified by its sandblasted blued finish; serial numbers start with number 1 (1942).
Commercial Model.................................... $225
Commando Model................................... 200

Colt Official Police MK III Double Action
Revolver..$180

"J" frame, without shrouded ejector rod. Caliber, 38 Special. 6-shot cylinder. Barrel lengths: 4-, 5-, 6-inch. 9¼ inches overall with 4-inch barrel. Weight, with 4-inch barrel, 34 ounces. Fixed rear sight and ramp front sight. Service trigger and hammer or target trigger and wide-spur hammer. Blued or nickel-plated finish. Checkered walnut service stocks. Made from 1969 to 1975.

Colt Metropolitan MK III Double Action
Revolver..$180

Same as Official Police MK III, except has 4-inch barrel, option of service or target stocks; weighs 36 ounces. Made from 1969 to 1972.

Colt Officers' Model Target Double Action Revolver,
First Issue...$600

Caliber 38 Special. 6-inch barrel. Hand-finished action. Adjustable target sights. Checkered walnut stocks. General specifications same as "New Navy" Second Issue. Made from 1904 to 1908.

Colt Official Police MK III

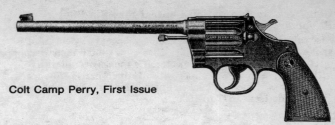

Colt Camp Perry, First Issue

**Colt Camp Perry Model Single Shot Pistol,
First Issue**..**$600**
Built on "Officers' Model" frame. Caliber, 22 Long Rifle
(embedded head chamber for high speed cartridges after 1930).
10-inch barrel. 13¾ inches overall. Weight, 34½ ounces. Adjustable target sights. Hand-finished action. Blued finish.
Checkered walnut stocks. Made from 1926 to 1934.

Colt Camp Perry, Second Issue

Colt Metropolitan MK III

Colt Camp Perry Model, Second Issue...........**$995**
General specifications same as First Issue, except this model has
shorter hammer fall and 8-inch barrel. 12 inches overall. Weight,
34 ounces. Made from 1934 to 1941 (about 440 produced).

Colt Officers' Model Special.....................**$275**
Target arm replacing "Officers' Model" Second Issue; basically
the same as that model, but with heavier, non-tapered barrel,
redesigned hammer, ramp front sight and "Coltmaster" rear
sight adjustable for windage and elevation. Calibers: 22 Long
Rifle, 38 Special. 6-inch barrel. 11¼ inches overall. Weights: 39
ounces (38 cal.), 43 ounces (22 cal.). Blued finish. Checkered
plastic stocks. Made from 1949 to 1953.

Colt Officers' Model Target
Second Issue

Colt Officers' Model Match

Colt Officers' Model Target, Second Issue.......**$650**
Calibers: 22 Long Rifle (introduced 1930, embedded head-
cylinder for high speed cartridges after 1932), 32 Police Positive
(introduced 1932, discontinued 1942), 38 Special. 6-shot
cylinder. Barrel lengths: 4-, 4½-, 5-, 6- and 7½-inch in 38
Special; 6-inch only in 22 L.R. and 32 P.P. 11¼ inches overall
with 6-inch barrel in 38 Special. Adjustable target sights. Blued
finish. Checkered walnut stocks. Hand-finished action. General
features same as "Army Special" and "Official Police" of same
date. Made from 1908 to 1949 (with exceptions noted).

Colt Officers' Model Match.......................**$300**
Same general design as previous Officers' Model revolvers, has
tapered heavy barrel, wide hammer spur, Accro rear sight, ramp
front sight, large target stocks of checkered walnut. Calibers: 22
Long Rifle, 38 Special. 6-inch barrel. 11¼ inches overall.
Weights: 43 ounces (22 cal.), 39 ounces (38 cal.). Blued finish.
Made from 1953 to 1970.

Colt Trooper

Colt Trooper Double Action Revolver

Same specifications as Officers' Model Match, except has 4-inch barrel with quick-draw ramp front sight, weighs 34 ounces in 38 caliber. Made from 1953 to 1969.
With standard hammer and service stocks............. **$235**
With wide-spur hammer and target stocks............. **255**

Colt Trooper MK III

Colt Trooper MK III Double Action Revolver... $225

"J" frame, shrouded ejector rod. Caliber, 357 Magnum. 6-shot cylinder. Barrel lengths: 4-, 6-inch. 9½ inches overall with 4-inch barrel. Weight, with 4-inch barrel, 39 ounces. Adjustable rear sight, ramp front sight. Target trigger and hammer. Blued or nickel-plated finish. Checkered walnut target stocks. Made from 1969 to date.

Colt Lawman MK III

Colt Lawman MK III Double Action Revolver... $175

"J" frame, shrouded ejector rod on 2-inch barrel only. Caliber, 357 Magnum. 6-shot cylinder. Barrel lengths: 2-, 4-inch. 9⅜ inches overall with 4-inch barrel. Weight, with 4-inch barrel, 35 ounces. Fixed rear sight and ramp front sight. Service trigger and hammer or target trigger and wide-spur hammer. Blued or nickel-plated finish. Checkered walnut service or target stocks. Made from 1969 to date.

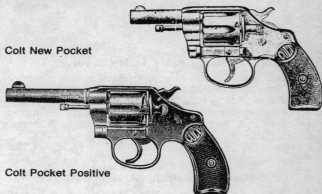

Colt New Pocket

Colt Pocket Positive

Colt New Pocket Double Action Revolver....... $260

Caliber, 32 Short & Long Colt. 6-shot cylinder. Barrel lengths: 2½-, 3½- and 6-inch. 7½ inches overall with 3½-inch barrel. Weight, 16 ounces with 3½-inch barrel. Fixed sights, knife-blade and V-notch. Blued or nickel finish. Rubber stocks. Made from 1895 to 1905.

Colt Pocket Positive Double Action Revolver....$230

General specifications same as "New Pocket," except this model has positive lock feature (see "Police Positive"). Calibers: 32 Short & Long Colt (discontinued 1914), 32 Colt New Police (32 S&W Short & Long). Fixed sights, flat top and square notch. Made from 1905 to 1940.

Colt New Police Double Action Revolver........ $255

Built on "New Pocket" frame, but with larger grip. Calibers: 32 Colt New Police, 32 Short & Long Colt. Barrel lengths: 2½-, 4- and 6-inch. 8½ inches overall with 4-inch barrel. Weight, 17 ounces with 4-inch barrel. Fixed sights, knife-blade and V-notch. Blued or nickel finish. Rubber stocks. Made from 1896 to 1905.

Colt Police Positive
First Issue

Colt Police Positive Double Action Revolver, First Issue... $325

Improved version of the "New Police" with the "Positive Lock," which prevents the firing pin from coming in contact with the cartridge except when the trigger is pulled. Calibers: 32 Short & Long Colt (discontinued 1915), 32 Colt New Police (32 S&W Short & Long), 38 New Police (38 S&W). 6-shot cylinder. Barrel lengths: 2½- (32 cal. only), 4-, 5- and 6-inch. 8½ inches overall with 4-inch barrel. Weight, 20 ounces with 4-inch barrel. Fixed sights. Blued or nickel finish. Rubber or checkered walnut stocks. Made from 1905 to 1947.

Colt Bankers' Special

Colt Bankers' Special Double Action Revolver

This is the "Police Positive" with a 2-inch barrel, otherwise specifications same as that model; rounded butt introduced in 1933. Calibers: 22 Long Rifle (embedded head-cylinder for high speed cartridges introduced 1933), 38 New Police. 6½ inches overall. Weight: 23 ounces in 22 caliber, 19 ounces in 38 caliber. Made from 1926 to 1940.

38 Caliber..	**$320**
22 Caliber..	640

Colt New Police Target Double Action
Revolver..**$285**

Target version of the "New Police" with same general specifications. Target sights. 6-inch barrel. Blued finish only. Made from 1896 to 1905.

Colt Police Positive Target

Colt Police Positive Target Double Action
Revolver..**$370**

Target version of the "Police Positive." Calibers: 22 Long Rifle (introduced 1910, embedded head-cylinder for high speed cartridges after 1932), 22 W.R.F. (introduced 1910, discontinued 1935), 32 Short & Long Colt (discontinued 1915), 32 New Police (32 S&W Short & Long). 6-inch barrel, blued finish only. 10½ inches overall. Weight, 26 ounces in 22 cal. Adjustable target sights. Checkered walnut stocks. Made from 1905 to 1940.

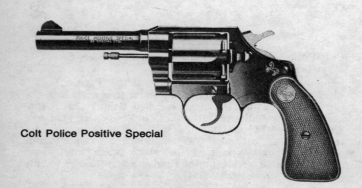

Colt Police Positive Special

Colt Police Positive Special Double Action
Revolver..**$215**

Based on the "Police Positive" with frame lengthened to permit longer cylinder. Calibers: 32-20 (discontinued 1942), 38 Special, 32 New Police and 38 New Police (introduced 1946). 6-shot cylinder. Barrel lengths: 4- (only length in current production), 5- and 6-inch. 8¾ inches overall with 4-inch barrel. Weight, 23 ounces in 38 Special with 4-inch barrel. Fixed sights. Checkered stocks of hard rubber, plastic or walnut. Made from 1907 to 1973.

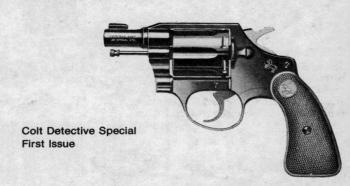

**Colt Detective Special
First Issue**

Colt Detective Special Double Action Revolver, First
Issue..**$280**

This is the "Police Positive Special" with a 2-inch barrel, otherwise specifications same as that model; rounded butt introduced in 1933. Originally supplied in 38 Special only, it was also made in calibers 32 New Police, 38 New Police. Weight, 17 ounces in 38 caliber in 1946. 6¾ inches overall. Weight, 21 ounces in 38 cal. Made from 1926 to 1972.

**Colt Cobra, Round Butt
First Issue**

Colt Cobra Double Action Revolver, Round Butt,
First Issue..**$300**

Lightweight "Detective Special" with same general specifications as that model, except with "Colt-alloy" frame. 2-inch barrel. Calibers: 38 Special, 38 New Police, 32 New Police. Weight, 15 ounces in 38 caliber. Blued finish. Checkered plastic or walnut stocks. Made from 1951 to 1973.

Colt Cobra Double Action Revolver,
Square Butt..**$315**

Lightweight "Police Positive Special" with same general specifications, except has "Colt-alloy" frame. 4-inch barrel. Calibers: 38 Special, 38 New Police, 32 New Police. Weight, 17 ounces in 38 caliber. Blued finish. Checkered plastic or walnut stocks. Made from 1951 to 1973.

Colt Agent, First Issue

Colt Agent Double Action Revolver, First Issue. $210
Same as Cobra—First Issue, except has short-grip frame, 38 Special only, weighs 14 ounces. Made from 1962 to 1973.

Colt Diamondback

Colt Diamondback Double Action Revolver......$275
"D" frame, shrouded ejector rod. Calibers: 22 Long Rifle, 38 Special. 6-shot cylinder. Barrels: 2½-, 4-inch; ventilated rib. 9 inches overall with 4-inch barrel. Weights (with 4-inch barrel): 22, 31¾ ounces; 38, 28½ ounces. Adjustable rear sight, ramp front sight. Blued or nickel finish. Checkered walnut stocks. Made from 1966 to date.

Colt Detective Special, Second Issue

Colt Detective Special Double Action Revolver, Second Issue... $225
"D" frame, shrouded ejector rod. Caliber, 38 Special. 6-shot cylinder. 2-inch barrel. 6⅞ inches overall. Weight, 21½ ounces. Fixed rear sight and ramp front sight. Blued or nickel-plated finish. Checkered walnut wrap-around stocks. Made from 1972 to date.

Colt Police Positive, Second Issue

Colt Police Positive Double Action Revolver, Second Issue...................................... $160
Same as Detective Special—Second Issue, except has 4-inch barrel, is 9 inches overall, weighs 26½ ounces. Introduced in 1977. *Note:* Original Police Positive (First Issue) has a shorter frame, is not chambered for 38 Special.

Colt Cobra, Second Issue

Colt Cobra Double Action Revolver, Second Issue...................................... $265
Lightweight version of Detective Special—Second Issue; has aluminum alloy frame, weighs 16½ ounces. Made from 1973 to 1981.

Colt Agent, Second Issue

Colt Agent Double Action Revolver, Second Issue...................................... $160
Same as Cobra—Second Issue, except has short service stocks, is 6⅝ inches overall, weighs 16 ounces. Made from 1973 to 1981.

Colt Viper

Colt Viper Double Action Revolver............ **$165**
Same as Cobra—Second Issue, except has 4-inch barrel, is 9
inches overall, weighs 20 ounces. Introduced in 1977.

Colt New Service

Colt New Service Target

Colt New Service Double Action Revolver
Calibers: 38 Special, 357 Magnum (introduced 1936), 38-40,
44-40, 44 Russian, 44 Special, 45 Auto, 45 Colt, 450 Eley, 455
Eley, 476 Eley. 6-shot cylinder. Barrel lengths: 4-, 5- and 6-inch
in 38 Special and 357 Magnum; 4½-, 5½- and 7½-inch in other
calibers. 9¾ inches overall with 4½-inch barrel. Weight, 39
ounces in 45 caliber with 4½-inch barrel. Fixed sights. Blued or
nickel finish. Checkered walnut stocks. Made from 1898 to 1942.
Note: More than 500,000 of this model in caliber 45 Auto
(designated "Model 1917 Revolver") were purchased by the U.S.
Government during World War I. These arms were later sold as
surplus to National Rifle Association members through the
Director of Civilian Marksmanship. Price was $16.15 plus pack-
ing charge. Supply exhausted during the early 1930's.
Commercial Model.................................. **$335**
Magnum.. **350**
1917 Army... **350**
Colt New Service Target...................... **$540**
Target version of the "New Service;" general specifications same
as that model. Calibers: originally chambered for 44 Russian, 450
Eley, 455 Eley and 476 Eley; later models in 44 Special, 45 Colt
and 45 Auto. Barrel lengths: 6- and 7½-inch. 12¾ inches overall
with 7½-inch barrel. Adjustable target sights. Hand-finished
action. Blued finish. Checkered walnut stocks. Made from 1900
to 1940.

Colt Shooting Master

Colt Shooting Master Double Action Revolver... **$640**
Deluxe target arm based on the "New Service" model. Calibers:
originally made only in 38 Special; 44 Special, 45 Auto and 45
Colt added in 1933 and 357 Magnum in 1936. 6-inch barrel. 11¼
inches overall. Weight, 44 ounces in 38 caliber. Adjustable target
sights. Hand-finished action. Blued finish. Checkered walnut
stocks. Rounded butt. Made from 1932 to 1941.

Colt Three-Fifty-Seven Double Action Revolver
Heavy frame. Caliber, 357 Magnum. 6-shot cylinder. 4- or 6-inch
barrel. Quick-draw ramp front sight, Accro rear sight. Blued
finish. Checkered walnut stocks. 9¼ or 11¼ inches overall.
Weights: 36 ounces (4-inch bbl.), 39 ounces (6-inch bbl.). Made
from 1953 to 1961.
With standard hammer and service stocks............. **$275**
With wide-spur hammer and target stocks............. **$300**

Colt Python

Colt Python Double Action Revolver............ **$375**
"I" frame, shrouded ejector rod. Caliber, 357 Magnum. 6-shot
cylinder. Barrels: 2½-, 4-, 6-inch; ventilated rib. 11¼ inches
overall with 6-inch barrel. Weight, 44 ounces with 6-inch barrel.
Adjustable rear sight, ramp front sight. Blued or nickel-plated.
Checkered walnut target stocks. Made from 1955 to date.

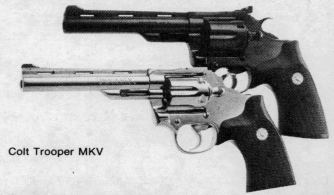

Colt Trooper MKV

Colt Trooper MK V Revolver.................... **$275**
Re-engineered Mark III for smoother, faster action. Caliber, 357
Magnum. 6-shot cylinder. Barrel lengths: 4-, 6-, 8-inch. Ad-
justable rear sight, ramp front sight, red insert and vent rib.
Checkered walnut stocks. Made from 1982 to date.

Colt Lawman MK V Revolver.................... **$225**
Similar to Trooper MK V, except available in 2- and 4-inch barrel lengths only. Fixed sight and solid rib. Made from 1982 to date.

Colt Automatic Pistols

Colt Model 1900 38 Automatic Pistol........... **$600**
Caliber, 38 ACP (modern high velocity cartridges should not be used in this pistol). 7-shot magazine. 6-inch barrel. 9 inches overall. Weight, 35 ounces. Fixed sights. Blued finish. Plain walnut stocks. Sharp-spur hammer. Combination rear sight and safety. Made from 1900 to 1903.

Colt Sporting 38 Automatic Pistol Model 1902.. **$600**
Caliber, 38 ACP (modern high velocity cartridges should not be used in this pistol). 7-shot magazine. 6-inch barrel. 9 inches overall. Weight, 35 ounces. Fixed sights, Knife-blade and V-notch. Blued finish. Checkered hard rubber stocks. Round back hammer. No safety. Made from 1902 to 1908.

Colt Model 1902 Military*

Colt Military 38 Automatic Pistol Model 1902...**$600**
Caliber, 38 ACP (modern high velocity cartridges should not be used in this pistol). 8-shot magazine. 6-inch barrel. 9 inches overall. Weight, 37 ounces. Fixed sights, knife-blade and V-notch. Blued finish. Checkered hard rubber stocks. Round back hammer, changed to spur type in 1908. No safety. Made from 1902 to 1929.

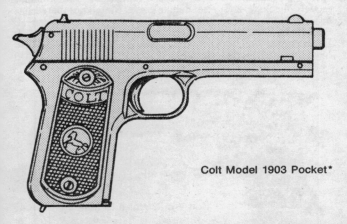

Colt Model 1903 Pocket*

Colt Pocket 38 Automatic Pistol Model 1903.... **$375**
Caliber, 38 ACP (modern high velocity cartridges should not be used in this pistol). Similar to Sporting 38 Model 1902, but with 4½-inch barrel. 7½ inches overall. Weight, 31 ounces. Fixed sights, knife-blade and V-notch. Blued finish. Checkered hard rubber stocks. Round back hammer, changed to spur type in 1908. No safety. Made from 1903 to 1929.

Colt Model 1905 Military*

Colt Military Model 45 Automatic Pistol Model 1905.. **$790**
Caliber, 45 Automatic. 7-shot magazine. 5-inch barrel. 8 inches overall. Weight, 32½ ounces. Fixed sights, knife-blade and V-notch. Blued finish. Checkered walnut stocks. Similar to Model 1902 38 Automatic Pistols. Made from 1905 to 1911.

Colt Pocket 32 Automatic

Colt Pocket Model 32 Automatic Pistol, First Issue.. **$300**
Caliber, 32 Auto. 8-shot magazine. 4-inch barrel. 7 inches overall. Weight, 23 ounces. Fixed sights. Blued finish. Checkered hard rubber stocks. Hammerless. Slide lock and grip safeties. Barrel-lock bushing similar to that on Government Model 45 Auto. Made from 1903 to 1911.

Colt Pocket Model 380 Automatic Pistol, First Issue.. **$340**
Same as Pocket 32 Auto—First Issue, except chambered for caliber 380 Auto, 7-shot magazine. Made from 1908 to 1911.

Colt Pocket Model 32 Automatic Pistol, Second Issue...................................... **$300**
Same as First Issue but without barrel-lock bushing. Made from 1911 to 1926.

Colt Pocket Model 380 Automatic Pistol, Second Issue...................................... **$280**
Same as Pocket 32 Auto—Second Issue, except chambered for 380 Auto, 7-shot magazine. Made from 1911 to 1926.

Colt Pocket Model 32 Automatic Pistol, Third Issue.. **$350**
Caliber, 32 Auto. Similar to First and Second Issues, but has safety disconnector on all pistols above No. 468097 which prevents firing of cartridge in chamber if magazine is removed. 3¾-inch barrel. 6¾ inches overall. Weight, 24 ounces. Fixed sights. Blued or nickel finish. Checkered walnut stocks. Made from 1926 to 1945.

Colt Pocket Model 380 Automatic Pistol, Third Issue....................................... $350
Same as Pocket 32 Auto—Third Issue, except chambered for 380 Auto, 7-shot magazine. Safety disconnector on all pistols above No. 92,894. Made from 1926 to 1945.

Colt Pocket 25 Automatic

Colt Pocket Model 25 Automatic Pistol......... $260
Caliber, 25 Automatic. 6-shot magazine. 2-inch barrel. 4½ inches overall. Weight, 13 ounces. Flat top front, square notch, rear sight in groove. Blued or nickel finish. Checkered hard rubber stocks on early models, checkered walnut on later type; special pearl stocks illustrated. Disconnector added in 1916 at pistol No. 141000. Made from 1908 to 1941.

Colt Government Model 45
Commercial, M1911A1 Type

Colt Government Model Automatic Pistol
U.S. Models 1911 and 1911A1. Caliber, 45 Automatic. 7-shot magazine. 5-inch barrel. 8½ inches overall. Weight, 39 ounces. Fixed sights. Blued finish on "Commercial Model," Parkerized or similar finish on most military pistols. Checkered walnut stocks formerly furnished, plastic grips on later production. Checkered, arched mainspring housing and longer grip safety spur adopted in 1923. (M1911A1 has these features.) Made from 1911 to 1970. Letter "C" precedes or follows serial number on "Commercial Model" 45's. *Note:* During both World Wars, Colt licensed other firms to make these pistols under government contract; they include: Ithaca Gun Co., North American Arms Co. Ltd. (Canada), Remington-Rand Co., Remington-UMC, Singer Sewing Machine Co., and Union Switch & Signal Co.; M1911 also produced at Springfield Armory.

U.S. Model 1911,	
Colt manufacture..................................	$ 365
North American manufacture......................	3300
Remington-UMC manufacture....................	490
Springfield manufacture..........................	580
Commercial Model, M1911 Type...................	430
U.S. Model 1911A1,	
Singer manufacture...............................	2440
Colt, Ithaca, Remington-Rand, Union Switch	
manufacture.....................................	375
Commercial Model, M1911A1 Type................	370

Colt World War I Commemorative 45
Standard Grade
Second Battle of the Marne

Colt World War I Commemorative 45
Deluxe Grade, Meuse Argonne

Colt World War I 50th Anniversary Commemorative Series 45 Auto
Limited production replica of Model 1911 45 Auto engraved with battle scenes, commemorating Battles at Chateau Thierry, Belleau Wood, Second Battle of the Marne, Meuse Argonne. In special presentation display cases. Production: 7400 standard model, 75 deluxe, 25 special deluxe grade. Match numbered sets offered. Made in 1967, 1968, 1969.

Standard grade.......................................	$ 410
Deluxe grade..	1050
Special deluxe grade.................................	2200

Colt World War II Commemorative 45
European Theater

Note: Values indicated are for commemorative 45 Autos in new condition.

Colt World War II Commemorative 45 Pacific Theater

Colt World War II Commemorative 45 Auto..... $475

Limited production replica of Model 1911A1 45 Auto engraved with respective names of locations where historic engagements occurred during World War II, as well as specific issue and theater identification. European model has oak leaf motif on slide; palm leaf design frames the Pacific issue. Cased. 11,500 of each model were produced. Made in 1970.

Colt National Match 45

Colt National Match Automatic Pistol

Identical with the Government Model 45 Auto, but with hand-honed action, match grade barrel, adjustable rear sight and ramp front sight or fixed sights. Made from 1932 to 1940.
With adjustable sights................................ $610
With fixed sights.................................... 485

Colt Gold Cup National Match 45

Colt Gold Cup National Match 45 Auto..........$450

Match version of Government Model 45 Automatic with same general specifications, except: match grade barrel with new design bushing, flat mainspring housing, long wide trigger with adjustable stop, hand-fitted slide with improved ejection port, adjustable rear sight, target front sight, checkered walnut grips with gold medallions. Weight, 37 ounces. Made from 1957 to 1970.

Colt NRA Centennial 45 Gold Cup National Match... $450

(2500 produced). Made in 1971.

Colt Gold Cup Mark III National Match 38 Special.. $525

Similar to Gold Cup National Match 45 Auto, except chambered for 38 Special mid-range. 5-shot magazine. Made from 1961 to 1974.

Colt Super 38

Colt Super 38 Automatic Pistol.................. $365

Identical with Government Model 45 Auto, except for caliber and magazine capacity. Caliber, 38 Automatic, 9-shot magazine. Made from 1928 to 1970.

Colt Super Match 38 Automatic Pistol

Identical with Super 38 Auto, but with hand-honed action, match grade barrel, adjustable rear sight and ramp front sight or fixed sights. Made from 1933 to 1940.
With adjustable sights.............................. $690
With fixed sights.................................... 475

Colt Ace

Colt Ace Automatic Pistol........................ $825

Caliber, 22 Long Rifle (regular or high speed). 10-shot magazine. Built on the same frame as the Government Model 45 Auto, with same safety features, etc. Hand-honed action, target barrel, adjustable rear sight. 4¾-inch barrel. 8¼ inches overall. Weight, 38 ounces. Made from 1930 to 1940.

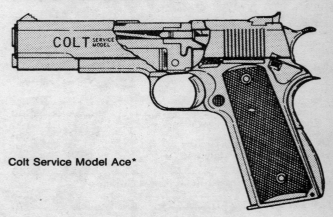

Colt Service Model Ace*

Colt Service Model Ace Automatic Pistol....... $1000
Identical with National Match Model 45 Auto, except for caliber, magazine capacity and weight; has "floating chamber" amplifying recoil to four times that normal in a 22. Caliber, 22 Long Rifle (regular or high speed). 10-shot magazine. Weight, 42 ounces. Made from 1938 to 1942.

Colt 22-45 Conversion Unit...................... $150
Converts Government Model 45 Auto to a 22 L.R. target pistol. Unit consists of slide assembly, barrel, floating chamber (as in Service Ace), bushing, ejector, recoil spring, recoil spring guide and plug, magazine and slide stop. Made from 1938 to date. *Note:* Now designated "22 Conversion Unit," postwar model of this unit is also adaptable to the Super 38 pistols.

Colt 45-22 Conversion Unit.................... $400
Converts Service Ace 22 to National Match 45 Auto. Unit consists of match grade slide assembly and barrel, bushing, recoil spring, recoil spring guide and plug, magazine and slide stop. Made from 1938 to 1942.

Colt's MK IV/Series '70
Government Model 45

Colt's MK IV/Series '70 Government Model Automatic Pistol.............................. $270
Calibers: 45 Automatic, 38 Super Auto, 9mm Luger. 7-shot magazine in 45, 9-shot in 38 and 9mm. 5-inch barrel. 8⅜ inches overall. Weight: 38 ounces in 45, 39 ounces in 38 and 9mm. Fixed rear sight and ramp front sight. Blued or nickel-plated finish. Checkered walnut stocks. Made from 1970 to date.

Colt's MK IV/Series '70
Gold Cup National Match 45

Colt's MK IV/Series '70 Gold Cup National Match 45 Auto............................... $350
Match version of MK IV/Series '70 Government Model. Caliber, 45 Automatic only. Flat mainspring housing. Accurizor barrel and bushing. Solid rib, Colt-Elliason adjustable rear sight, undercut front sight. Adjustable trigger, target hammer. 8¾ inches overall. Weight, 38½ ounces. Blued finish. Checkered walnut stocks. Made from 1970 to date.

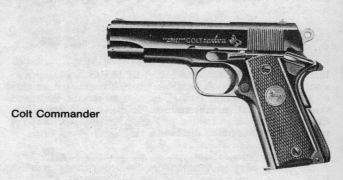

Colt Commander

Colt Commander Lightweight Automatic Pistol. $275
Same basic design as Government Model, but shorter and lighter in weight; receiver and mainspring housing are forged from a special lightweight metal, "Coltalloy." Calibers: 45 Automatic, 38 Super Auto, 9mm Luger. 7-shot magazine in 45 cal., 9-shot in 38 Auto and 9mm Luger. 4¼-inch barrel. 8 inches overall. Weight, 26½ ounces. Fixed sights. Round spur hammer. Improved safety lock. Blued finish. Checkered plastic or walnut stocks. Made from 1951 to date.

Colt Combat Commander

Colt Combat Commander Automatic Pistol....... $275
Same as lightweight Commander, except has steel frame, available in blued or nickel-plated finish, weighs 36 ounces. Made from 1970 to date.

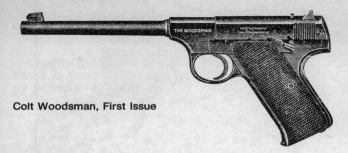

Colt Woodsman, First Issue

Colt Match Target Woodsman, First Issue

Colt Woodsman Target Model Automatic Pistol, First Issue $325

Caliber, 22 Long Rifle (regular velocity). 10-shot magazine. 6½-inch barrel. 10½ inches overall. Weight, 28 ounces. Adjustable sights. Blued finish. Checkered walnut stocks. Made from 1915 to 1932. *Note:* The mainspring housing of this model is not strong enough to permit safe use of high speed cartridges. Change to a new heat-treated mainspring housing was made at pistol No. 83,790. Many of the old models were converted by installation of new housings. The new housing may be distinguished from the earlier type by the checkering in the curve under the breech; new housing is grooved straight across, while the old type bears a diagonally checkered oval.

Colt Match Target Woodsman Automatic Pistol, First Issue $500

Same basic design as other Woodsman models. Caliber, 22 Long Rifle. 10-shot magazine. 6½-inch barrel, slightly tapered with flat sides. 11 inches overall. Weight, 36 ounces. Adjustable rear sight. Blued finish. Checkered walnut stock, one-piece design with extended sides. Made from 1938 to 1942.

Colt Woodsman Target, Second Issue

Colt Woodsman Target, Third Issue

Colt Woodsman Target Model Automatic Pistol, Second Issue $350

Caliber, 22 Long Rifle (regular or high speed). Same as original model, except has heavier barrel and high speed mainspring housing. See note under Woodsman—First Issue. Weight, 29 ounces. Made from 1932 to 1948.

Colt Woodsman Target Model Automatic Pistol, Third Issue $295

Same basic design as previous Woodsman pistols, but with these changes: longer grip, magazine catch on left side as on Government Model 45, larger thumb safety, slide stop, slide stays open on last shot, magazine disconnector, thumb-rest stocks. Caliber, 22 Long Rifle (regular or high speed). 10-shot magazine. 6-inch barrel. 10½ inches overall. Weight, 32 ounces. Click adjustable rear sight, ramp front sight. Blued finish. Checkered plastic or walnut stocks. Made from 1948 to 1976.

Colt Woodsman Sport Model First Issue

Colt Woodsman Sport Model, Second Issue

Colt Woodsman Sport Model Automatic Pistol, First Issue $325

Caliber, 22 Long Rifle (regular or high speed). Same as Target Woodsman—Second Issue, except has 4½-inch barrel. Adjustable rear sight, fixed or adjustable front sight. Weight, 27 ounces. 8½ inches overall. Made from 1933 to 1948.

Colt Woodsman Sport Model Automatic Pistol, Second Issue $295

Same as Target Woodsman—Third Issue, but with 4½-inch barrel. 9 inches overall. Weight, 30 ounces. Made from 1948 to 1976.

Colt Targetsman

Colt Targetsman...................................**$200**
Similar to "Woodsman Target" but has "economy" adjustable rear sight, lacks automatic slide stop. Made from 1959 to 1976.

Colt Match Target, Second Issue

**Colt Match Target Automatic Pistol,
Second Issue**......................................**$300**
Same basic design as Target Woodsman—Third Issue. Caliber, 22 Long Rifle (regular or high speed). 10-shot magazine. 6-inch flat-sided heavy barrel. 10½ inches overall. Weight, 40 ounces. Click adjustable rear sight, ramp front sight. Blued finish. Checkered plastic or walnut stocks. Made from 1948 to 1976.

Colt Match Target "4½" Automatic Pistol.......**$300**
Same as Match Target—Second Issue, except has a 4½-inch barrel. 9 inches overall. Weight, 36 ounces. Made from 1950 to 1976.

Colt Challenger Automatic Pistol................**$175**
Same basic design as Target Woodsman—Third Issue, but lacks some of the refinements. Fixed sights. Magazine catch on butt as in old Woodsman. Does not stay open on last shot. Lacks magazine safety. 4½-inch or 6-inch barrel. 9 inches or 10½ inches overall, depending upon barrel length. Weights: 30 ounces (4½-inch), 31½ ounces (6-inch). Blued finish. Checkered plastic stocks. Made from 1950 to 1955.

Colt Huntsman

Colt Huntsman.....................................**$190**
Same specifications as "Challenger." Made from 1955 to 1976.

Junior Colt

Junior Colt Pocket Model Automatic Pistol......**$140**
Made in Spain by Unceta y Cia. ("Astra"). Calibers: 22 Short, 25 Auto. 6-shot magazine. 2¼-inch barrel. 4¾ inches overall. Weight, 12 ounces. Fixed sights. Checkered walnut grips. Made from 1958 to 1968.

Note: Production of some Colt handguns spans the period from before World War II to the postwar years. Values shown for these models are for earlier production. Those manufactured c. 1946 and later generally are less desirable to collectors, and values are approximately 30 percent lower.

Data on commemorative Colts supplied by Mr. Robert E. P. Cherry, Cherry's Sporting Goods, Geneseo, Illinois.

CZ Duo

CZ Model 27

CZ Pistols manufactured by Ceska Zbrojovka-Nardoni Podnik, Strakonice, Czechoslovakia (formerly Böhmische Waffenfabrik A. G.)

CZ "Duo" Pocket Automatic Pistol...............**$125**
Caliber, 25 Automatic (6.35mm). 6-shot magazine. 2⅛-inch barrel. 4½ inches overall. Weight, 14½ ounces. Fixed sights. Blued or nickel finish. Plastic stocks. Made from 1926 to c. 1960.

CZ Model 27 Automatic Pistol....................**$170**
Caliber, 32 Automatic (7.65mm). 8-shot magazine. 4-inch barrel. 6 inches overall. Weight, 23½ ounces. Fixed sights. Blued finish. Plastic stocks. Made from 1927 to 1951.

CZ Model 38

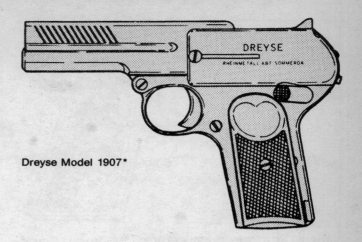

Dreyse Model 1907*

CZ Model 38 Double Action Automatic Pistol.... $180
Caliber, 380 Automatic (9mm). 9-shot magazine. 3¾-inch barrel. 7 inches overall. Weight, 26 ounces. Fixed sights. Blued finish. Plastic stocks. Made from 1939 to 1945.

Note: After the German occupation, March 1939, Models 27 and 38 were marked with manufacturer code "fnh." Designation of Model 38 was changed to "Pistole 39(t)."

CZ Model 1945

Dreyse Pistols manufactured by Rheinische Metallwaren und Maschinenfabrik ("Rheinmetall"), Sommerda, Germany

Dreyse Model 1907 Automatic Pistol............ $195
Caliber, 32 Automatic (7.65mm). 8-shot magazine. 3½-inch barrel. 6¼ inches overall. Weight, about 24 ounces. Fixed sights. Blued finish. Hard rubber stocks. Made from 1907- c. 1914.

**CZ Model 1945 Double Action Pocket Automatic
Pistol... $150**
Caliber, 25 Automatic (6.35mm). 8-shot magazine. 2½-inch barrel. 5 inches overall. Weight, 15 ounces. Fixed sights. Blued finish. Plastic stocks. Introduced 1945, production now discontinued.

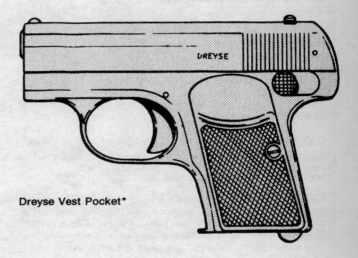

Dreyse Vest Pocket*

CZ New Model .006

Dreyse Vest Pocket Automatic Pistol............ $175
Conventional Browning type. Caliber, 25 Automatic (6.35mm). 6-shot magazine. 2-inch barrel. 4½ inches overall. Weight, about 14 ounces. Fixed sights. Blued finish. Hard rubber stocks. Made from c. 1909-1914.

Deutsche Waffen-und-Munitionsfabriken, Berlin, Germany

**CZ New Model .006 Double Action Automatic
Pistol... $185**
Caliber, 32 Automatic (7.65mm). 8-shot magazine. 3⅛-inch barrel. 6½ inches overall. Weight, 24 ounces. Fixed sights. Blued finish. Plastic stocks. Introduced 1951, production now discontinued. *Note:* Official designation of this pistol, used by the Czech National Police, is "VZ50." "New Model .006" is export designation.

DWM Pocket Automatic Pistol.................. $200
Similar to the FN Browning Model 1910. Caliber, 32 Automatic (7.65mm). 3½-inch barrel. 6 inches overall. Weight, about 21 ounces. Blued finish. Hard rubber stocks. Made from c. 1921-1931.

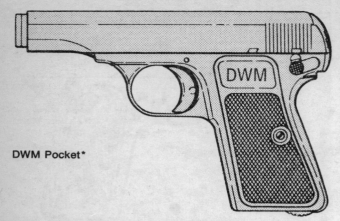

DWM Pocket*

Enfield Revolver manufactured by Royal Small Arms Factory, Enfield Lock, Middlesex, England

Enfield (British Service) No. 2 MK 1 Revolver.. $125
Webley pattern. Hinged frame. Double action. Caliber, 380 British Service (38 S&W with 200-grain bullet). 6-shot cylinder. 5-inch barrel. 10½ inches overall. Weight, about 27½ ounces. Fixed sights. Blued finish. Vulcanite stocks. First issued in 1932, this was the standard revolver of the British Army in World War II. Now obsolete. *Note:* This model was also produced with spurless hammer as No. 2 Mk 1* and Mk 1**.

Erma-Werke Model KGP68

Erma-Werke, Dachau, West Germany

Erma KGP68 Automatic Pistol.................. $160
Luger type. Calibers: 32 Automatic (7.65mm), 380 Automatic (9mm Short). 6-shot magazine in 32, 5-shot in 380. 4-inch barrel. 7⅜ inches overall. Weight, 22½ ounces. Fixed sights. Blued finish. Checkered walnut stocks. Made from 1968 to date.

Erma-Werke Model KGP69

Erma Model KGP69 Automatic Pistol........... $160
Luger type. Caliber, 22 Long Rifle. 8-shot magazine. 4-inch barrel. 7¾ inches overall. Weight, 29 ounces. Fixed sights. Blued finish. Checkered walnut stocks. Made from 1969 to date.

FN Browning 6.35mm

Fabrique Nationale D'Armes de Guerre, Liege, Belgium

**FN Browning 6.35mm Pocket Model Automatic
Pistol... $240**
Same specifications as Colt Pocket Model 25 Automatic Pistol.

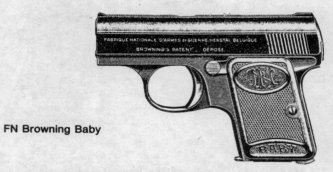

FN Browning Baby

FN Browning Baby Automatic Pistol............. $140
Caliber, 25 Automatic (6.35mm). 6-shot magazine. 2⅛-inch barrel. 4 inches overall. Weight, 10 ounces. Fixed sights. Blued finish. Hard rubber stocks. Made from 1940 to date.

FN Browning Model 1900*

**FN Browning Model 1900 Pocket Automatic
Pistol... $160**
Caliber, 32 Automatic (7.65mm). 7-shot magazine. 4-inch barrel. 6¾ inches overall. Weight, 22 ounces. Fixed sights. Blued finish. Hard rubber stocks. Made from 1899 to 1910.

FN Browning Model 1910

FN Browning Model 1910 Pocket Automatic Pistol... **$155**
Calibers: 32 Automatic (7.65mm), 380 Automatic (9mm). 7-shot magazine (32 cal.), 6-shot (380 cal.). 3½-inch barrel. 6 inches overall. Weight, 20½ ounces. Fixed sights. Blued finish. Hard rubber stocks. Made from 1910 to date.

FN Browning Military Model 1903 Automatic Pistol... **$180**
Caliber, 9mm Browning Long. 7-shot magazine. 5-inch barrel. 8 inches overall. Weight, 32 ounces. Fixed sights. Blued finish. Hard rubber stocks. *Note:* Aside from size, this pistol is of the same basic design as the Colt Pocket 32 and 380 Automatic Pistols. Made from 1903 to 1939.

FN Browning Model 1922

FN Browning Police & Military Model 1922 Automatic Pistol... **$135**
Calibers: 32 Automatic (7.65mm), 380 Automatic (9mm). 9-shot magazine (32 cal.), 8-shot (380 cal.). 4½-inch barrel. 7 inches overall. Weight, 25 ounces. Fixed sights. Blued finish. Hard rubber stocks. Made from 1922 to date.

FN Browning Model 1935 Hi-Power

FN Browning Military Model 1935 Hi-Power Automatic Pistol
Variation of the Browning-Colt 45 Auto design. Caliber, 9mm Luger. 13-shot magazine. 4⅝-inch barrel. 7¾ inches overall. Weight, about 35 ounces. Adjustable rear sight and fixed front sight or both fixed. Blued finish (Canadian manufacture Parkerized). Checkered walnut or plastic stocks. *Note:* Above specifications, in general, apply to both the original FN production and the pistols made by John Inglis Company of Canada for the Chinese Government. A smaller version, with shorter barrel and slide and 10-shot magazine, was made by FN for the Belgian and Rumanian Governments from about 1937 to 1940. Both types were made at the FN plant during the German Occupation of Belgian.
With adjustable rear sight............................ **$480**
FN manufacture, with fixed rear sight................ 320
Inglis manufacture, with fixed rear sight.............. 580

Fiala Outfitters, Inc., New York City

Fiala Repeating Pistol............................ **$375**
Despite its appearance, which closely resembles that of the early Colt Woodsman and High-Standard, this arm is not an automatic pistol. It is hand-operated by moving the slide to eject, cock and load. Caliber, 22 Long Rifle. 10-shot magazine. Barrel lengths: 3-, 7½- and 20-inch. 11¼ inches overall with 7½-inch barrel. Weight, 31 ounces with 7½-inch barrel. Target sights. Blued finish. Plain wood stocks. Shoulder stock was originally supplied for use with 20-inch barrel. Made from 1920 to 1923. Value shown is for pistol with one barrel and without shoulder stock.

Firearms International Regent

Firearms International Corporation, Washington, D.C.

Firearms International Regent Double Action Revolver... **$ 50**
Calibers: 22 Long Rifle, 32 S&W Long. 8-shot cylinder in 22 caliber, 7-shot in 32 caliber. Barrels: 3-, 4-, 6-inch in 22 caliber; 2½-, 4-inch in 32 caliber. Weight, with 4-inch barrel, 28 ounces. Fixed sights. Blue finish. Plastic stocks. Made from 1966 to 1972.

Firearms International Model D Automatic Pistol
.... **$145**
Caliber, 380 Automatic. 6-shot magazine. 3⅛-inch barrel. 6⅛ inches overall. Weight, 19½ ounces. Blade front sight, windage-adjustable rear sight. Blued, chromed, or military finish. Checkered walnut stocks. Made from 1974 to 1977.

Firearms International Model D

Forehand & Wadsworth, Worcester, Massachusetts

Forehand & Wadsworth Revolvers
See listings of similar Harrington & Richardson and Iver Johnson models for values.

French Model 1935A

French Military Pistol manufactured by Société Alsacienne de Constructions Mécaniques (S.A.C.M.), Cholet, France

French Model 1935A Automatic Pistol.......... $200
Caliber, 7.65mm Long. 8-shot magazine. 4.3-inch barrel. 7.6 inches overall. Weight, 26 ounces. Fixed sights. Blued finish. Checkered stocks. Made from 1935 to 1945. *Note:* This pistol was used by French troops during World War II and in Indo-China 1945-54.

Frommer Stop*

Frommer Pistols manufactured by Fémáru-Fegyver-és Gépgyár R.T., Budapest, Hungary

Frommer Stop Pocket Automatic Pistol......... $140
Locked-breech action, outside hammer. Calibers: 32 Automatic (7.65mm), 380 Automatic (9mm short). 7-shot magazine (32 cal.), 6-shot (380 cal.). 3⅞-inch barrel. 6½ inches overall. Weight, about 21 ounces. Fixed sights. Blued finish. Hard rubber stocks. Made from 1912 to 1920.

Frommer Baby*

Frommer Baby Pocket Automatic Pistol......... $175
Similar to "Stop" model except, has 2-inch barrel, is about 4¾ inches overall, weighs about 17½ ounces, magazine capacity is one round less. Introduced shortly after World War I.

Frommer Liliput*

Frommer Liliput Pocket Automatic Pistol....... $190
Caliber, 25 Automatic (6.35mm). 6-shot magazine. 2.14-inch barrel. 4.33 inches overall. Weight, 10½ ounces. Fixed sights. Blued finish. Hard rubber stocks. Made during early 1920s. *Note:* Although similar in appearance to the "Stop" and "Baby," this pistol is blowback operated.

Industria Armi Galesi, Collebeato (Brescia), Italy

Galesi Model 6 Pocket Automatic Pistol........ $105
Calibers: 22 Long, 25 Automatic (6.35mm). 6-shot magazine. 2¼-inch barrel. 4⅜ inches overall. Weight, about 11 ounces. Fixed sights. Blued finish. Plastic stocks. Made from 1930 to date.

Galesi Model 6*

Galesi Model 9*

Galesi Model 9 Pocket Automatic Pistol

Calibers: 22 Long Rifle, 32 Automatic (7.65mm), 380 Automatic (9mm Short). 8-shot magazine. 3¼-inch barrel. 5⅞ inches overall. Weight, about 21 ounces. Fixed sights. Blued finish. Plastic stocks. Made from 1930 to date. *Note:* Specifications vary; those shown are for 32 Automatic of common type.

22 Long Rifle or 380 Automatic	$115
32 Automatic	110

Glisenti Model 1910*

Societa Siderurgica Glisenti, Carcina (Brescia), Italy

Glisenti Model 1910 Italian Service Automatic Pistol **$220**
Caliber, 9mm, Glisenti. 7-shot magazine. 4-inch barrel. 8½ inches overall. Weight, about 32 ounces. Fixed sights. Blued finish. Checkered wood. Hard rubber or plastic stocks. Adopted 1910 and used through World War II.

Great Western Single Action

Great Western Arms Co., North Hollywood, California

Great Western Single Action Frontier Revolver. $175
Replica of the Colt Single Action Army Revolver. Calibers: 22 Long Rifle, 357 Magnum, 38 Special, 44 Special, 44 Magnum, 45 Colt. 6-shot cylinder. Barrel lengths: 4¾-, 5½- and 7½-inch. Weight, in 22 cal. with 5½-inch bbl., 40 ounces. Length overall, with 5½-inch bbl., 11⅛ inches. Fixed sights. Blued finish. Imitation stag grips. Made from 1951 to 1962. *Note:* Value shown is for improved late model revolvers; early Great Westerns are variable in quality and should be evaluated accordingly. It should also be noted that, beginning about July 1956, these revolvers were also offered in "do-it-yourself" kit form; values of guns assembled from these kits will, in general, be lower than for factory-completed weapons.

Great Western Double Barrel Derringer .... **$ 75**
Replica of Remington Double Derringer. Caliber, 38 S&W. Double barrels (superposed), 3-inch. Overall length, 5 inches. Fixed sights. Blued finish. Checkered black plastic grips. Made from 1953 to 1962.

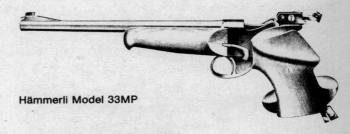

Hämmerli Model 33MP

Hämmerli AG Jagd- und Sportwaffenfabrik, Lenzburg, Switzerland

Hämmerli Model 33MP Free Pistol **$800**
System Martini single-shot action, set trigger. Caliber: 22 Long Rifle. 11½-inch octagon barrel. 16½ inches overall. Weight, 46 ounces. Micrometer rear sight, interchangeable front sights. Blued finish. Walnut stocks and forearm. Made from 1933 to 1949.

Hämmerli Model 100 Free Pistol

Same general specifications as Model 33MP. Improved action and sights, redesigned stock. Standard model has plain stocks and forearm; deluxe model has carved stocks and forearm. Made from 1950 to 1956.
Standard model......................................$805
Deluxe model... 960

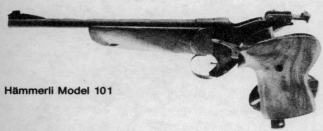

Hämmerli Model 101

Hämmerli Model 101..............................$655

Similar to Model 100, except has heavy round barrel with matte finish, improved action and sights, adjustable stocks. Weight, about 49 ounces. Made from 1956 to 1960.

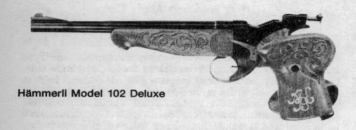

Hämmerli Model 102 Deluxe

Hämmerli Model 102

Same as Model 101, except barrel has highly polished blued finish. Deluxe model (illustrated) has carved stocks and forearm. Made from 1956 to 1960.
Standard model.................................... $ 650
Deluxe model...................................... 1000

Hämmerli Model 103.............................$880

Same as Model 101, except has lighter octagon barrel (as in Model 100) with highly polished blued finish, stocks and forearm of select French walnut. Weight, about 46 ounces. Made from 1956 to 1960.

Hämmerli Model 104..............................$675

Similar to Model 102, except has lighter round barrel, improved action, redesigned stocks and forearm. Weight, 46 ounces. Made from 1961 to 1965.

Hämmerli Model 105

Hämmerli Model 105..............................$875

Similar to Model 103, except has improved action, redesigned stocks and forearm. Made from 1961 to 1965.

Hämmerli Model 106

Hämmerli Model 106..............................$845

Similar to Model 104, except has improved trigger and stocks. Made from 1966 to 1971.

Hämmerli Model 107 Deluxe

Hämmerli Model 107

Similar to Model 105, except has improved trigger and stock. Deluxe model (illustrated) has engraved receiver and barrel, carved stocks and forearm. Made from 1966 to 1971.
Standard model.................................... $ 925
Deluxe model...................................... 1360

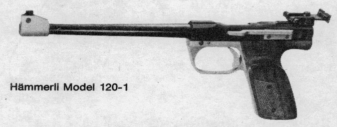

Hämmerli Model 120-1

Hämmerli Model 120-1 Single Shot Free Pistol. $520

Side lever-operated bolt action. Adjustable single-stage or two-stage trigger. Caliber, 22 Long Rifle. 9.999-inch barrel. 14¾ inches overall. Weight, 44 ounces. Micrometer rear sight, front sight on high ramp. Blued finish barrel and receiver, lever and grip frame anodized aluminum. Checkered walnut thumb-rest stocks. Made from 1972 to date.

Hämmerli Model 120-2..........................$540

Same as Model 120-1, except has hand-contoured stocks with adjustable palm-rest (available for right or left hand). Made from 1972 to date.

Hämmerli Model 120 Heavy Barrel adjustable stocks

Hämmerli Model 120 Heavy Barrel

Same as Models 120-1 and 120-2, except has 5.7-inch heavy barrel, weighs 41 ounces. Available with standard or adjustable stocks. Made from 1972 to date.
With standard stocks.................................$515
With adjustable stocks............................. 590

Hämmerli Model 150 Free Pistol

Hämmerli Model 150 Free Pistol.................$970

Improved Martini-type action with lateral-action cocking lever. Set trigger adjustable for weight, length and angle of pull. Caliber, 22 Long Rifle. 11.3-inch round barrel, free-floating. 15.4 inches overall. Weight, 43 ounces (with extra weights, 49½ ounces). Micrometer rear sight, front sight on high ramp. Blued finish. Select walnut forearm and stocks with adjustable palm-shelf. Made from 1972 to date.

Hämmerli-Walther Model 200, 1952 Type

Hämmerli-Walther Olympia Model 200 Automatic Pistol, 1952 Type..................................$640

Similar to 1936 Walther Olympia Funfkampf Model. Calibers: 22 Short, 22 Long Rifle. 6-shot magazine in 22 Short, 10-shot in 22 L.R. 7.5-inch barrel. 10.7 inches overall. Weights: 22 Short model (light alloy breechblock), 27.7 ounces; 22 L.R. model, 30.3 ounces; supplementary weights provided. Adjustable target sights. Blued finish. Checkered walnut thumb-rest stocks. Made from 1952 to 1958.

Hämmerli-Walther Model 200, 1958 Type
standard stocks

Hämmerli-Walther Olympia Model 200, 1958 Type......................................$725

Same as Model 200, 1952 Type, except has muzzle brake, 8-shot magazine in 22 Long Rifle model. 11.6 inches overall. Weights: 22 Short model, 30 ounces; 22 Long Rifle model, 33 ounces. Made from 1958 to 1963.

Hämmerli-Walther Olympia Model 201..........$645

Same as Model 200, 1952 Type, except has 9½-inch barrel. Made from 1955 to 1957.

Hämmerli-Walther Olympia Model 202..........$695

Same as Model 201, except has stocks with adjustable heel plate. Made from 1955 to 1957.

Hämmerli-Walther Olympia Model 203
1958 Type

Hämmerli-Walther Olympia Model 203

Same as corresponding Model 200 (1955 Type lacks muzzle brake), except has stocks with adjustable heel plate. Made from 1955 to 1963.
1955 Type...$725
1958 Type... 800

Hämmerli-Walther Olympia Model 204

American Model. Same as corresponding Model 200 (1956 Type lacks muzzle brake), except chambered for 22 Long Rifle only, has slide stop and micrometer rear sight. Made from 1956 to 1963.
1956 Type...$765
1958 Type... 845

Hämmerli-Walther Model 205

Hämmerli-Walther Olympia Model 205

American Model. Same as Model 204, except has stocks with adjustable heel plate. Made from 1956 to 1963.
1956 Type...$830
1958 Type... 800

Hämmerli Model 206

Hämmerli International Model 206 Automatic Pistol... $550

Calibers: 22 Short, 22 Long Rifle. 6-shot magazine in 22 Short, 8-shot in 22 L.R. 7-1/16-inch barrel with muzzle brake. 12½ inches overall. Weights: 22 Short model, 33 ounces; 22 L.R. model, 39 ounces (supplementary weights add 5 and 8 ounces). Micrometer rear sight, ramp front sight. Blued finish. Standard thumb-rest stocks. Made from 1962 to 1969.

Hämmerli Model 207

Hämmerli Model 207............................. $710

Same as Model 206, except has stocks with adjustable heel plate, weighs 2 ounces more. Made from 1962 to 1969.

Hämmerli Model 208

Hämmerli Model 208 Standard Automatic Pistol $840

Caliber, 22 Long Rifle. 3-shot magazine. 5.9-inch barrel. 10 inches overall. Weight, 35 ounces (barrel weight adds 3 ounces). Micrometer rear sight, ramp front sight. Blued finish. Checkered walnut stocks with adjustable heel plate. Made from 1966 to date.

Hämmerli Model 211............................. $780

Same as Model 208, except has standard thumb-rest stocks. Made from 1966 to date.

Hämmerli International Model 209 Automatic Pistol... $800

Caliber, 22 Short. 5-shot magazine. 4¾-inch barrel with muzzle brake and gas-escape holes. 11 inches overall. Weight, 39 ounces

Hämmerli Model 210

(interchangeable front weight adds 4 ounces). Micrometer rear sight, post front sight. Blued finish. Standard thumb-rest stocks of checkered walnut. Made from 1966 to 1970.

Hämmerli Model 210............................. $830

Same as Model 209, except has stocks with adjustable heel plate; is 0.8-inch longer and weighs one ounce more. Made from 1966 to 1970.

Hämmerli Model 230-1 Rapid Fire Automatic Pistol... $730

Caliber, 22 Short. 5-shot magazine. 6.3-inch barrel. 11.6 inches overall. Weight, 44 ounces. Micrometer rear sight, post front sight. Blued finish. Smooth walnut thumb-rest stocks. Made from 1970 to date.

Hämmerli Model 230-2

Hämmerli Model 230-2............................. $740

Same as Model 230-1, except has checkered walnut stocks with adjustable heel plate. Made from 1970 to date.

SIG-Hämmerli Model P240

SIG-Hämmerli Model P240 22 Conversion Unit

SIG-Hämmerli Model P240 Automatic Pistol

Caliber, 38 Special (wadcutter). 5-shot magazine. 6-inch barrel. 10 inches overall. Weight, 41 ounces. Micrometer rear sight, post front sight. Blued finish. Smooth walnut thumb-rest stocks. Accessory 22 Long Rifle conversion unit available. Made from 1975 to date.

Model P240.. **$735**
22 conversion unit................................... **370**

Hämmerli Virginian

Hämmerli Virginian Single Action Revolver..... **$240**

Similar to Colt Single Action Army, except has base pin safety system (SWISSAFE). Calibers: 357 Magnum, 45 Colt. 6-shot cylinder. Barrels: 4⅝-, 5½-, 7½-inch. 11 inches overall with 5½-inch barrel. Weight, with 5½-inch barrel, 40 ounces. Fixed sights. Blued barrel and cylinder, casehardened frame, chrome-plated grip frame and trigger guard. One-piece smooth walnut stock. Made from 1973 to 1976 for Interarms, Alexandria, Virginia.

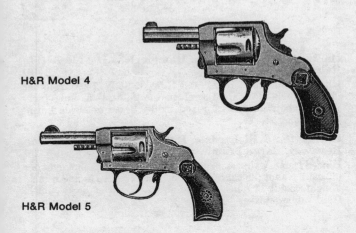

H&R Model 4

H&R Model 5

Harrington & Richardson, Inc., Gardner, Massachusetts (formerly Harrington & Richardson Arms Co., Worchester, Massachusetts)

Harrington & Richardson Model 4 (1904) Double Action Revolver... **$ 70**
Solid frame. Calibers: 32 S&W Long, 38 S&W. 6-shot cylinder (32 cal.), 5-shot (38 cal.). Barrel lengths: 2½-, 4½- and 6-inch. Weight, about 16 ounces in 32 caliber. Fixed sights. Blued or nickel finish. Hard rubber stocks.

Harrington & Richardson Model 5 (1905) Double Action Revolver... **$ 75**
Solid frame. Caliber, 32 S&W. 5-shot cylinder. Barrel lengths: 2½-, 4½- and 6-inch. Weight, about 11 ounces. Fixed sights. Blued or nickel finish. Hard rubber stocks.

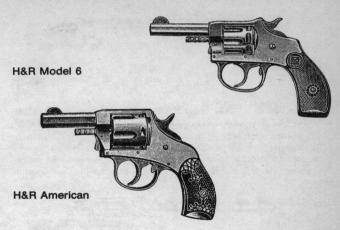

H&R Model 6

H&R American

Harrington & Richardson Model 6 (1906) Double Action Revolver..................................... **$ 70**
Solid frame. Caliber, 22 Long Rifle. 7-shot cylinder. Barrel lengths: 2½-, 4½- and 6-inch. Weight, about 10 ounces. Fixed sights. Blued or nickel finish. Hard rubber stocks.

Harrington & Richardson American Double Action Revolver.. **$ 70**
Solid frame. Calibers: 32 S&W Long, 38 S&W. 6-shot cylinder (32 cal.), 5-shot (38 cal.). Barrel lengths: 2½-, 4½- and 6-inch. Weight, about 16 ounces. Fixed sights. Blued or nickel finish. Hard rubber stocks.

H&R Young America

H&R Vest Pocket

Harrington & Richardson Young America Double Action Revolver..................................... **$ 70**
Solid frame. Calibers: 22 Long, 32 S&W. 7-shot cylinder (22 cal.), 5-shot (32 cal.). Barrel lengths: 2-, 4½- and 6-inch. Weight, about 9 ounces. Fixed sights. Blued or nickel finish. Hard rubber stocks.

Harrington & Richardson Vest Pocket Double Action Revolver... **$ 70**
Solid frame. Spurless hammer. Calibers: 22 Rimfire, 32 S&W. 7-shot cylinder, (22 cal.), 5-shot (32 cal.). 1⅛-inch barrel. Weight, about 9 ounces. Blued or nickel finish. Hard rubber stocks.

H&R Hunter

Harrington & Richardson Hunter Model Double Action Revolver..$100
Solid frame. Caliber, 22 Long Rifle. 9-shot cylinder. 10-inch octagon barrel. Weight, 26 ounces. Fixed sights. Blued finish. Checkered walnut stocks. Safety cylinder on later models. *Note:* An earlier "Hunter Model" was built on the smaller 7-shot frame.

H&R Trapper

Harrington & Richardson Trapper Model Double Action Revolver....................................$100
Solid frame. Caliber, 22 Long Rifle. 7-shot cylinder. 6-inch octagon barrel. Weight, 12¼ ounces. Fixed sights. Blued finish. Checkered walnut stocks. Safety cylinder on later models.

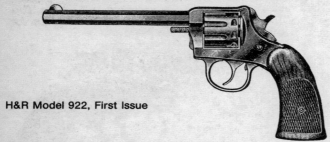

H&R Model 922, First Issue

Harrington & Richardson Model 922 Double Action Revolver, First Issue............................$100
Solid frame. Caliber, 22 Long Rifle. 9-shot cylinder. Barrel lengths: 6-inch on later production, formerly available with 10-inch barrel. Weight, with 6-inch bbl., 26 ounces. Fixed sights. Blued finish. Checkered walnut stocks. Safety cylinder and round barrel on later models, earlier production had octagon barrel.

H&R Automatic Ejecting

Harrington & Richardson Automatic Ejecting Double Action Revolver............................$125
Hinged frame. Calibers: 32 S&W Long, 38 S&W. 6-shot cylinder (32 cal.), 5-shot (38 cal.). Barrel lengths: 3¼ -, 4-, 5- and 6-inch. Weights: about 16 ounces (32 cal.), 15 ounces (38 cal.). Fixed sights. Blued or nickel finish. Black hard rubber stocks.

H&R Premier

Harrington & Richardson Premier Double Action Revolver...$ 80
Small hinged frame. Calibers: 22 Long Rifle, 32 S&W. 7-shot cylinder (22 cal.), 5-shot (32 cal.). Barrel lengths: 2-, 3-, 4-, 5- and 6-inch. Weights: 13 ounces (22 cal.), 12 ounces (32 cal.). Fixed sights. Blued or nickel finish. Black hard rubber stocks.

H&R Hammerless
Small Frame

Harrington & Richardson Hammerless Double Action Revolver, Small Frame...........................$ 90
Hinged frame. Calibers: 22 Long Rifle, 32 S&W. 7-shot cylinder (22 cal.), 5-shot (32 cal.). Barrel lengths: 2-, 3-, 4-, 5- and 6-inch. Weight, about 13 ounces. Fixed sights. Blued or nickel finish. Hard rubber stocks.

Harrington & Richardson Hammerless Double Action Revolver, Large Frame...........................$ 90
Hinged frame. Calibers: 32 S&W Long, 38 S&W. 6-shot cylinder (32 cal.), 5-shot (38 cal.). Barrel lengths: 3¼-, 4-, 5- and 6-inch. Weight, about 17 ounces. Fixed sights. Blued or nickel finish. Hard rubber stocks.

H&R Target Model

Harrington & Richardson Target Model Double Action Revolver.......................................$120
Small hinged frame. Calibers: 22 Long Rifle, 22 W.R.F. 7-shot cylinder. 6-inch barrel. Weight, 16 ounces. Fixed sights. Blued finish. Checkered walnut stocks.

H&R 22 Special

Harrington & Richardson 22 Special Double Action Revolver..**$125**
Heavy hinged frame. Calibers: 22 Long Rifle, 22 W.R.F. 9-shot cylinder. 6-inch barrel. Weight, 23 ounces. Fixed sights, front gold-plated. Blued finish. Checkered walnut stocks. Recessed safety cylinder on later models for high speed ammunition.

Harrington & Richardson Expert Model Double Action Revolver..**$125**
Same specifications as "22 Special," except has 10-inch barrel. Weight, 28 ounces.

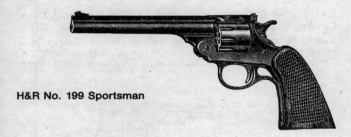

H&R No. 199 Sportsman

Harrington & Richardson No. 199 Sportsman Single Action Revolver................................. **$150**
Hinged frame. Caliber, 22 Long Rifle. 9-shot cylinder. 6-inch barrel. 11 inches overall. Weight, 30 ounces. Adjustable target sights. Blued finish. Checkered walnut stocks. Discontinued 1951.

H&R No. 999 Sportsman First Issue

Harrington & Richardson No. 999 Sportsman Double Action Revolver, First Issue.................... **$135**
Hinged frame. Calibers: 22 Long Rifle, 22 W.R.F. Same specifications as Sportsman Single Action.

H&R Bobby

Harrington & Richardson Bobby Double Action Revolver..**$115**
Hinged frame. Calibers: 32 S&W, 38 S&W. 6-shot cylinder (32 cal.), 5-shot (38 cal.). 4-inch barrel. 9 inches overall. Weight, 23 ounces. Fixed sights. Blued finish. Checkered walnut stocks. Discontinued 1946. *Note:* This revolver was originally designed and produced for use by London's Bobbies.

H&R Defender 38

Harrington & Richardson Defender 38 Double Action Revolver..**$120**
Hinged frame. Based on the "Sportsman" design. Caliber, 38 S&W. Barrel lengths: 4- and 6-inch. 9 inches overall with 4-inch barrel. Weight, 25 ounces with 4-inch barrel. Fixed sights. Blued finish. Black plastic stocks. Discontinued 1946. *Note:* This model was manufactured during World War II as an arm for plant guards, auxiliary police, etc.

H&R Ultra Sportsman

Harrington & Richardson Ultra Sportsman Revolver..**$180**
Single action. Hinged frame. Caliber, 22 Long Rifle. 9-shot cylinder. 6-inch barrel. Weight, 30 ounces. Adjustable target sights. Blued finish. Checkered walnut stocks. This model has short action, wide hammer spur; cylinder is length of a 22 Long Rifle cartridge.

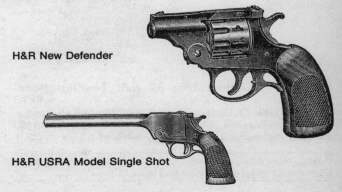

H&R New Defender

H&R USRA Model Single Shot

Harrington & Richardson New Defender Double Action Revolver **$180**
Hinged frame. Caliber, 22 Long Rifle. 9-shot cylinder. 2-inch barrel. 6¼ inches overall. Weight, 23 ounces. Adjustable sights. Blued finish. Checkered walnut stocks, round butt. *Note:* Basically, this is the Sportsman D.A. with a short barrel.

Harrington & Richardson USRA Model Single Shot Target Pistol **$390**
Hinged frame. Caliber, 22 Long Rifle. Barrel lengths: 7-, 8- and 10-inch. Weight, 31 ounces with 10-inch barrel. Adjustable target sights. Blued finish. Checkered walnut stocks. Made from 1928 to 1941.

H&R Self Loading 25*

Harrington & Richardson 25 Self Loading Pistol
. . . . **$270**
Modified Webley & Scott design. Caliber, 25 Auto. 6-shot magazine. 2-inch barrel. 4½ inches overall. Weight, 12 ounces. Fixed sights. Blued finish. Black hard rubber stocks.

H&R Self Loading 32*

Harrington & Richardson 32 Self Loading Pistol
. . . . **$270**
Modified Webley & Scott design. Caliber, 32 Auto. 8-shot magazine. 3½-inch barrel. 6½ inches overall. Weight, about 20 ounces. Fixed sights. Blued finish. Black hard rubber stocks.

Note: Unless otherwise indicated, all of the preceding models were discontinued prior to 1942.

H&R Model 922, Second Issue

Harrington & Richardson Model 922 Double Action Revolver, Second Issue . . . . **$ 65**
Solid frame. Caliber, 22 Long Rifle. 9-shot cylinder. Barrel lengths: 2½-, 4-, 6-inch. Weight, with 4-inch barrel, 24 ounces. Fixed sights. Blued finish. Plastic stocks. Made from 1950 to date. *Note:* Current Model 922 has a different frame from that of the First Issue. Model 923 is same as Model 922 Second Issue, except nickel finish.

Harrington & Richardson Model 999 Sportsman Double Action Revolver, Second Issue **$120**
Hinged frame. Caliber, 22 Long Rifle. 9-shot cylinder. 6-inch barrel with ventilated rib. Weight, 30 ounces. Adjustable sights. Blued finish. Checkered walnut stocks. Made from 1950 to date.

H&R Model 632

Harrington & Richardson Model 632 Guardsman Double Action Revolver . . . . **$ 70**
Solid frame. Caliber, 32 S&W Long. 6-shot cylinder. Barrel lengths: 2½- or 4-inch. Weight, with 2½-inch barrel, 19 ounces. Fixed sights. Blued or chrome finish. Checkered Tenite stocks (round butt on 2½-inch, square butt on 4-inch). Made from 1953 to date. *Note:* Model 633 is same, except chrome or nickel finish.

H&R Model 929

Harrington & Richardson Model 929 Sidekick Double Action Revolver..................................$ 75
Solid frame, swing-out cylinder. Caliber, 22 Long Rifle. 9-shot cylinder. Barrel lengths: 2½-, 4-, 6-inch. Weight, with 4-inch bbl., 24 ounces. Fixed sights. Blued finish. Checkered plastic stocks. Made from 1956 to date. *Note:* Model 930 is same, except nickel finish.

H&R Model 622

Harrington & Richardson Model 622 Double Action Revolver...$ 55
Solid frame. Caliber: 22 Short, Long, Long Rifle. 6-shot cylinder. Barrel lengths: 2½-, 4-, 6-inch. Weight, with 4-inch bbl., 26 ounces. Fixed sights. Blued finish. Plastic stocks. Made from 1957 to date. *Note:* Model 623 is same, except chrome or nickel finish.

Harrington & Richardson Model 732 Double Action Revolver...$ 75
Solid frame, swing-out cylinder. Calibers: 32 S&W, 32 S&W Long. 6-shot cylinder. Barrel lengths: 2½-, 4-inch. Weight, with 4-inch bbl., 26 ounces. Fixed sights (windage adjustable rear on 4-inch bbl. model). Blue finish. Plastic stocks. Made from 1958 to date. *Note:* Model 733 is same, except nickel finish.

H&R Model 733

H&R Model 939

Harrington & Richardson Model 939 Ultra Sidekick Double Action Revolver..........................$ 90
Solid frame, swing-out cylinder. Safety lock. Calibers: 22 Short, Long, Long Rifle. 9-shot cylinder. 6-inch barrel with flat sides, ventilated rib. Weight, 33 ounces. Adjustable rear sight, ramp front sight. Blued finish. Checkered walnut stocks. Made from 1958 to date. *Note:* Model 940 is same, except has round barrel.

H&R Model 949

Harrington & Richardson Model 949 Forty-Niner Double Action Revolver.............................$ 75
Solid frame. Side loading and ejection. Calibers: 22 Short, Long, Long Rifle. 9-shot cylinder. 5½-inch barrel. Weight, 31 ounces. Adjustable rear sight, blade front sight. Blue or nickel finish. One-piece, Western-style walnut grip. Made from 1960 to date. *Note:* Model 950 is same, except nickel finish.

H&R Model 950

Harrington & Richardson Model 976 Double Action Revolver...$ 80
Same as Model 949, except has color-casehardened frame, 7½-inch barrel, weighs 36 ounces. Introduced in 1977.

H&R Model 900

Harrington & Richardson Model 900 Double Action Revolver...$ 75
Solid frame, snap-out cylinder. Calibers: 22 Short, Long, Long Rifle. 9-shot cylinder. Barrel lengths: 2½-, 4-, 6-inch. Weight, with 6-inch bbl., 26 ounces. Fixed sights. Blued finish. Blade Cycolac stocks. Made from 1962 to 1973. *Note:* Model 901 (discontinued in 1963) is the same, except chrome finish, has white Tenite stocks.

Harrington & Richardson Model 925 Defender Double Action Revolver **$105**
Hinged frame. Caliber, 38 S&W. 5-shot cylinder. 2½-inch barrel. Weight, 22 ounces. Adjustable rear sight, fixed front sight. Blued finish. One-piece wrap-around grip. Made from 1964 to 1978. *Note:* Model 935 is same, except nickel finish.

H&R Model 925

H&R Model 926

Harrington & Richardson Model 926 Double Action Revolver **$105**
Hinged frame. Calibers: 22 Long Rifle, 38 S&W 9-shot cylinder in 22, 5-shot in 38. 4-inch barrel. Weight, 31 ounces. Adjustable rear sight, fixed front sight. Blued finish. Checkered walnut stocks. Made from 1968 to 1978.

H&R Model 666

Harrington & Richardson Model 666 Double Action Revolver . . . . **$ 75**
Solid frame. Convertible model with two cylinders. Calibers: 22 Long Rifle and 22 Win. Mag. R.F. 6-shot cylinders. 6-inch barrel. Weight, 28 ounces. Fixed sights. Blued finish. Plastic stocks. Made from 1976 to 1978.

H&R Model 649

Harrington & Richardson Model 649 Double Action Revolver **$100**
Solid frame. Side loading and ejection. Convertible model with two cylinders. Calibers: 22 Long Rifle and 22 Win. Mag. R.F. 6-shot cylinders. 5½-inch barrel. Weight, 32 ounces. Adjustable rear sight, blade front sight. Blued finish. One-piece, Western-style walnut stock. Made from 1976 to date. *Note:* Model 650 is same, except nickel finish.

H&R Model 650

H&R Model 676

Harrington & Richardson Model 676 Double Action Revolver **$110**
Solid frame. Side loading and ejection. Convertible model with two cylinders. Calibers: 22 Long Rifle and 22 Win. Mag. R.F. 6-shot cylinders. Barrel lengths: 4½-, 5½-, 7½-, 12-inch. Weight, with 5½-inch barrel, 32 ounces. Adjustable rear sight, blade front sight. Blued finish, color-casehardened frame. One-piece, Western-style walnut stock. Made from 1976 to 1980.

H&R Model 686

Harrington & Richardson Model 686 Double Action Revolver..**$105**
Caliber, 22 Long Rifle and 22 Win. Mag. R.F. Barrels: 4½-, 5½-, 7½-, 10- and 12-inches. 6-shot magazine. Adjustable rear sight, ramp and blade front sight. Blued with color casehardened frame. Weight, 31 ounces for 4½-inch barrel. Made from 1980 to date.

H&R Model 903

Harrington & Richardson Model 903 Target Revolver...**$105**
Caliber, 22 Long Rifle. 6-inch target weight flat side barrel. 9-shot capacity. Single and double action, swing-out cylinder. Blade front sight, adjustable rear sight. American walnut grips. Weight, 35 ounces. Made from 1980 to date.

Harrington & Richardson Model 603 Target Revolver...**$105**
Similar to Model 903, except in 22 Win. Mag. R.F. 6-shot capacity with unfluted cylinder. Made from 1980 to date.

Harrington & Richardson Model 604 Target Revolver...**$105**
Similar to Model 603, except with 6-inch bull barrel. Weight, 38 ounces. Made from 1980 to date.

H&R Model 904

Harrington & Richardson Model 904 Target Revolver...**$105**
Similar to Model 903, except 4- and 6-inch bull barrels. 4-inch barrel weighs 32 ounces. Made from 1980 to date.

H&R Model 905

Harrington & Richardson Model 905 Target Revolver...**$110**
Same as Model 904, except with 4-inch barrel only. Nickel finish. Made from 1981 to date.

Harrington & Richardson Model 826 Double Action Revolver...**$100**
Caliber, 22 Win. Mag. R.F. 6-shot magazine. 3-inch bull barrel. Ramp and blade front sight, adjustable rear sight. American walnut grips. Weight, 28 ounces. Made from 1981 to date.

Harrington & Richardson Model 829 Double Action Revolver...**$100**
Same as Model 826, except in 22 Long Rifle caliber. 9-shot capacity. Made from 1981 to date. Model 830 in nickel finish.

H&R Model 830

Harrington & Richardson Model 832 Double Action Revolver...**$100**
Same as Model 826, except in 32 S&W Long. Made from 1981 to date. Model 833 in nickel finish.

Hartford Automatic

Hartford Arms & Equipment Co., Hartford, Connecticut

Hartford Automatic Target Pistol...............**$325**
Caliber, 22 Long Rifle. 10-shot magazine. 6¾-inch barrel. 10¾ inches overall. Weight, 31 ounces. Target sights. Blued finish. Black rubber stocks. This arm closely resembles the early Colt Woodsman and High Standard pistols. Made from 1929 to 1930.

Hartford Repeating Pistol.......................**$290**
Same general design as the automatic pistol of this manufacture, but this model is a hand-operated repeating pistol on the order of the Fiala. Made from 1929 to 1930.

Hartford Single Shot Target Pistol.............**$290**
Similar in appearance to the Hartford Automatic. Caliber, 22 Long Rifle. 6¾-inch barrel. 10¾ inches overall. Weight, 38 ounces. Target sights. Mottled frame and slide, blued barrel. Black rubber or walnut stocks. Made from 1929 to 1930.

Note: The Hartford pistols were the forebears of the original High Standard line. High Standard Mfg. Corp. acquired Hartford Arms & Equipment Co. in 1932. The High Standard Model B is essentially the same as the Hartford Automatic.

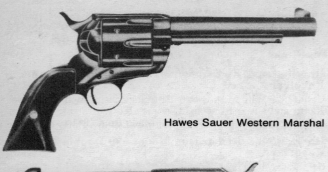

Hawes Sauer Western Marshal

Hawes Sauer Western Marshal 22

Hawes Firearms, Van Nuys, California

Hawes Sauer Western Marshal Single Action Revolver
Calibers: 22 Long Rifle (discontinued), 357 Magnum, 44 Magnum, 45 Auto; also, in two cylinder combinations, 22 Win. Mag. R.F. (discontinued), 9mm Luger, 44-40, 45 Auto. 6-shot cylinder. Barrel lengths: 5½-inch (discontinued), 6-inch. 11¾ inches overall with 6-inch barrel. Weight, 46 ounces. Fixed sights. Blued finish. Originally furnished with simulated stag plastic stocks; recent production has smooth rosewood stocks. Made from 1968 to date by J. P. Sauer & Sohn, Eckernforde, West Germany.
357 Magnum or 45 Colt.............................$135
44 Magnum... 140
Combination, 357 Magnum and 9mm Luger, 45 Colt and
  45 Auto.. 160
Combination, 44 Magnum and 44-40.................. 170
22 Long Rifle...................................... 110
Combination, 22 Long Rifle and 22 Win. Mag. R.F..... 140

Hawes Sauer Montana Marshal

Hawes Sauer Montana Marshal
Same as Western Marshal, except has brass grip frame. 22 caliber discontinued.
357 Magnum or 45 Colt.............................$150
44 Magnum... 155
Combination, 357 Magnum and 9mm Luger, 45 Colt and
  45 Auto.. 180
Combination, 44 Magnum and 44-40.................. 190
22 Long Rifle...................................... 135
Combination, 22 Long Rifle and 22 Win. Mag. R.F..... 160

Hawes Sauer Texas Marshal

Hawes Sauer Texas Marshal
Same as Western Marshal, except nickel-plated, has pearlite stocks. 22 caliber discontinued.
357 Magnum or 45 Colt.............................$155
44 Magnum... 165
Combination, 357 Magnum and 9mm Luger, 45 Colt and
  45 Auto.. 190
Combination, 44 Magnum and 44-40.................. 195
22 Long Rifle...................................... 140
Combination, 22 Long Rifle and 22 Win. Mag. R.F..... 170

Hawes Sauer Federal Marshal

Hawes Sauer Federal Marshal
Same as Western Marshal, except has color-casehardened frame, brass grip frame, one-piece walnut stock. Not made in 22 caliber.
357 Magnum or 45 Colt.............................$160
44 Magnum... 165
Combination, 357 Magnum and 9mm Luger, 45 Colt and
  45 Auto.. 195
Combination, 44 Magnum and 44-40.................. 200

Hawes Sauer Silver City Marshal

Hawes Sauer Silver City Marshal
Same as Western Marshal, except has nickel-plated frame, brass grip frame, blued cylinder and barrel, pearlite stocks.
44 Magnum...$170
Combination, 357 Magnum and 9mm Luger, 45 Colt and
  45 Auto.. 195
Combination, 44 Magnum and 44-40.................. 200

Hawes Sauer Chief Marshal

Hawes Deputy Montana Marshal

Hawes Deputy Montana Marshal

Same as Deputy Marshal, except has brass grip frame, walnut stocks only.
22 Long Rifle..$ 70
Combination, 22 Long Rifle and 22 Win. Mag. R.F.....   80

Hawes Sauer Chief Marshal Single Action Target Revolver

Same as Western Marshal, except has adjustable rear sight and front sight, oversized rosewood stocks. Not made in 22 caliber.
357 Magnum or 45 Colt..............................$160
44 Magnum..   170
Combination, 357 Magnum and 9mm Luger, 45 Colt and
    45 Auto..   195
Combination, 44 Magnum and 44-40.................   200

Hawes Deputy Texas Marshal

Hawes Deputy Texas Marshal

Same as Deputy Marshal, except has chrome finish.
22 Long Rifle, plastic stocks.........................$ 65
Combination, 22 Long Rifle and 22 Win. Mag. R.F., plastic
    stocks..   80
Extra for walnut stocks..............................   5

Hawes Deputy Marshal

Hawes Deputy Marshal Single Action Revolver

Caliber, 22 Long Rifle; also 22 Win. Mag. R.F. in two cylinder combination. 6-shot cylinder. 5½-inch barrel. 11 inches overall. Weight, 34 ounces. Adjustable rear sight, blade front sight. Blued finish. Plastic or walnut stocks. Made from 1973 to date.
22 Long Rifle, plastic stocks.........................$ 60
Combination, 22 Long Rifle and 22 Win. Mag. R.F., plastic
    stocks..   70
Extra for walnut stocks..............................   5

Hawes Deputy Silver City Marshal

Hawes Deputy Silver City Marshall

Same as Deputy Marshal, except has chrome-plated frame, brass grip frame, blued cylinder and barrel.
22 Long Rifle, plastic stocks.........................$65
Combination, 22 Long Rifle and 22 Win. Mag. R.F., plastic
    stocks..   75
Extra for walnut stocks..............................   5

Hawes Deputy Denver Marshal

Hawes Deputy Denver Marshal

Same as Deputy Marshal, except has brass frame.
22 Long Rifle, plastic stocks.........................$ 70
Combination, 22 Long Rifle and 22 Win. Mag. R.F., plastic
    stocks..   80
Extra for walnut stocks..............................   5

Hawes Favorite

Hawes Favorite Single Shot Target Pistol.......$ 75
Replica of Stevens No. 35. Tip-up action. Caliber, 22 Long Rifle. 8-inch barrel. 12 inches overall. Weight, 24 ounces. Target sights. Chrome-plated frame. Blued barrel. Plastic or rosewood stocks (add $5 for the latter). Made from 1968 to 1976.

Heckler & Koch
Model P9S 9mm Target

Heckler & Koch Model HK4

Heckler & Koch Model P9S 9mm Target........ $550
Same as standard Model P9S 9mm, except has adjustable trigger, trigger stop, adjustable rear sight.

Heckler & Koch GmbH, Oberndorf/Neckar, West Germany

Heckler & Koch Model HK4 Double Action Automatic Pistol
Calibers: 380 Automatic (9mm Short); also 22 Long Rifle, 25 Automatic (6.35mm), and 32 Automatic (7.65mm) with conversion kits. 7-shot magazine in 380; 8-shot in other calibers. 3-11/32-inch barrel. 6-3/16 inches overall. Weight, 18 ounces. Fixed sights. Blued finish. Plastic stock.
380 Automatic....................................... **$295**
380 Automatic with 22 conversion unit............... 320
380 Automatic with 22, 25 and 32 conversion units..... 405

Heckler & Koch Model P9S 9mm Competition Kit

Heckler & Koch Model P9S 9mm Competition Kit
Same as Model P9S 9mm Target, except comes with extra 5½-inch barrel and barrel weight. Also available with walnut competition stock.
With standard stock.................................**$560**
With competition stock............................. 640

Heckler & Koch Model P9S 45...................$490
Same as standard Model P9S 9mm, except caliber 45 Automatic; has 7-shot magazine.

Heckler & Koch Model VP'70Z Double Action Automatic Pistol.......................................$240
Caliber, 9mm Luger. 18-shot magazine. 4½-inch barrel. 8 inches overall. Weight, 32½ ounces. Fixed sights. Blued slide, plastic receiver and stock.

Heckler & Koch Model P9S 9mm

Heckler & Koch Model P9S 9mm Double Action Automatic Pistol.......................................$475
Caliber, 9mm Luger. 9-shot magazine. 4-inch barrel. 7⅝ inches overall. Weight, 32 ounces. Fixed sights. Blued finish. Plastic stock.

Note: All Heckler & Koch pistols listed are currently manufactured.

Heckler & Koch Model P9S 45

Heckler & Koch Model VP'70Z

High Standard Sporting Firearms, East Hartford, Connecticut (formerly High Standard Mfg. Co., Hamden, Connecticut)

High Standard Model B Automatic Pistol....... $220
Original Standard pistol. Hammerless. Caliber, 22 Long Rifle. 10-shot magazine. Barrel lengths: 4½- and 6¾-inch. 10¾ inches overall with 6¾-inch barrel. Weight, 33 ounces with 6¾-inch barrel. Fixed sights. Blued finish. Hard rubber stocks. Made from 1932 to 1942.

High Standard Model B

High Standard Model H-B Automatic Pistol..... $175
Same as Model B, but with visible hammer, no thumb safety. Made from 1940 to 1942.

High Standard Model C Automatic Pistol........ $190
Same as Model B except chambered for 22 Short. Made from 1935 to 1942.

High Standard Model H-B

High Standard Model A

High Standard Model A Automatic Pistol....... $175
Hammerless. Caliber, 22 Long Rifle. 10-shot magazine. Barrel lengths: 4½-, and 6¾-inch. 11½ inches overall with 6¾-inch barrel. Weight, 36 ounces with 6¾-inch barrel. Adjustable target sights. Blued finish. Checkered walnut stocks. Made from 1938 to 1942.

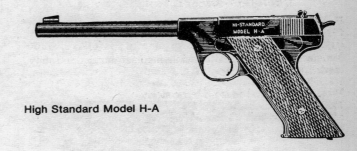

High Standard Model H-A

High Standard Model H-A Automatic Pistol..... $175
Same as Model A, but with visible hammer, no thumb safety. Made from 1939 to 1942.

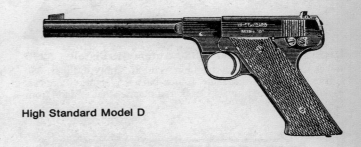

High Standard Model D

High Standard Model D Automatic Pistol........ $225
Same general specifications as Model A, but with heavier barrel. Weight, 40 ounces with 6¾-inch barrel. Made from 1937 to 1942.

High Standard Model H-D Automatic Pistol..... $225
Same as Model D, but with visible hammer, no thumb safety. Made from 1939 to 1942.

High Standard Model H-DM Automatic Pistol... $225

Also called H-D Military. Same as Model H-D, but with thumb safety. Made from 1941 to 1951.

High Standard Model E

High Standard Model E Automatic Pistol....... $270

Same general specifications as Model A, but with extra heavy barrel and thumb-rest stocks. Weight, 42 ounces with 6¾-inch barrel. Made from 1937 to 1942.

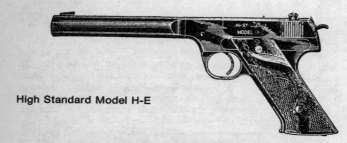

High Standard Model H-E

High Standard Model H-E Automatic Pistol..... $250

Same as Model E, but with visible hammer, no thumb safety. Made from 1939 to 1942.

High Standard Model G-380

High Standard Model G-380 Automatic Pistol... $255

Lever takedown. Visible hammer. Thumb safety. Caliber, 380 Automatic. 6-shot magazine. 5-inch barrel. Weight, 40 ounces. Fixed sights. Blued finish. Checkered plastic stocks. Made from 1943 to 1950.

High Standard Model G-B

High Standard Model G-B Automatic Pistol

Lever takedown. Hammerless. Interchangeable barrels. Caliber, 22 Long Rifle. 10-shot magazine. Barrel lengths: 4½- and 6¾-inch. 10¾ inches overall with 6¾-inch barrel. Weight, 36 ounces with 6¾-inch barrel. Fixed sights. Blued finish. Checkered plastic stocks. Made from 1948 to 1951.
With one barrel......................................$180
With both barrels.................................. 220

High Standard Model G-D Automatic Pistol

Lever takedown. Hammerless. Interchangeable barrels. Caliber, 22 Long Rifle. 10-shot magazine. Barrel lengths: 4½- and 6¾-inch. 11½ inches overall with 6¾-inch barrel. Weight, 41 ounces with 6¾-inch barrel. Target sights. Blued finish. Checkered walnut stocks. Made from 1948 to 1951.
With one barrel......................................$220
With both barrels.................................. 275

High Standard Model G-E

High Standard Model G-E Automatic Pistol

Same general specifications as Model G-D, but with extra heavy barrel and thumb-rest stocks. Weight, 44 ounces with 6¾-inch barrel. Made from 1949 to 1951.
With one barrel......................................$275
With both barrels.................................. 300

High Standard Olympic, First Model

High Standard Olympic Automatic Pistol—First Model

Same general specifications as Model G-E, but chambered for 22 Short, has light alloy slide. Made from 1950 to 1951.
With one barrel......................................$390
With both barrels.................................. 435

High Standard Sport-King Automatic Pistol—First Model

Takedown. Hammerless. Interchangeable barrels. Caliber, 22 Long Rifle. 10-shot magazine. Barrel lengths: 4½- and 6¾-inch. 11½ inches overall, with 6¾-inch barrel. Weight, 39 ounces with 6¾-inch barrel. Fixed sights. Blued finish. Checkered plastic thumb-rest stocks. Made from 1951 to 1958. *Note:* 1951-54 production has lever takedown as in "G" series; later version illustrated has push-button takedown.
With one barrel......................................$150
With both barrels.................................. 175

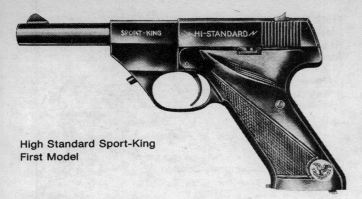

**High Standard Sport-King
First Model**

High Standard Flite-King Automatic Pistol—First Model

Same general specifications as Sport-King, except caliber 22 Short, has aluminum alloy frame and slide, weighs 26 ounces with 6½-inch bbl. Made from 1953 to 1958.
With one barrel.................................... **$160**
With both barrels.................................. 175

High Standard Lightweight Sport-King

Same as standard Sport-King, except has forged aluminum alloy frame, weighs 30 ounces with 6¾-inch barrel. Made from 1954 to 1965.
With one barrel.................................... **$160**
With both barrels.................................. 175

High Standard Dura-Matic

High Standard Dura-Matic Automatic Pistol.... $ 90

Takedown. Caliber, 22 Long Rifle. 10-shot magazine. Barrels: 4½- or 6½-inch, interchangeable. Overall length, with 6½-inch bbl., 10⅞ inches. Weight, with 6½-inch bbl., 35 ounces. Fixed sights. Blued finish. Checkered grips. Made from 1952 to 1970.

High Standard Plinker

High Standard Plinker........................... $110

Similar to Dura-Matic with same general specifications. Made from 1971 to 1973.

High Standard Field-King Automatic Pistol

Same general specifications as Sport-King, but with heavier barrel and target sights. Late model 6¾-inch barrels have recoil stabilizer feature. Weight, 43 ounces with 6¾-inch barrel. Made from 1951 to 1958.
With one barrel.................................... **$150**
With both barrels.................................. 190

High Standard Supermatic

High Standard Supermatic Automatic Pistol

Takedown. Hammerless. Interchangeable barrels. Caliber, 22 Long Rifle. 10-shot magazine. Barrel lengths: 4½- and 6¾-inch. Late model 6¾-inch barrels have recoil stabilizer feature. Weight, with 6¾-inch bbl., 43 ounces. 11½ inches overall with 6¾-inch bbl. Target sights. Elevated serrated rib between sights. Adjustable barrel weights add 2 or 3 ounces. Blued finish. Checkered plastic thumb-rest stocks. Made from 1951 to 1958.
With one barrel.................................... **$200**
With both barrels.................................. 215

High Standard Olympic Second Model

High Standard Olympic Automatic Pistol—Second Model

Same general specifications as Supermatic, but chambered for 22 Short, has light alloy slide. Weight, 39 ounces with 6¾-inch barrel. Made from 1951 to 1958.
With one barrel.................................... **$220**
With both barrels.................................. 240

**High Standard Sport-King
Second Model**

High Standard Sport-King Automatic Pistol—Second Model...................................$125

Caliber, 22 Long Rifle. 10-shot magazine. Barrels: 4½- or 6¾-inch, interchangeable. 11¼ inches overall with 6¾-inch bbl. Weight, with 6¾-inch bbl., 42 ounces. Fixed sights. Blued finish. Checkered grips. Made from 1958 to 1970.

High Standard Sport-King
Third Model

High Standard Sport-King Automatic Pistol—Third Model...................................... $120

Similar to Sport-King—Second Model, with same general specifications; available in blued or nickel finish. Introduced in 1974. Discontinued.

High Standard Flite-King Automatic Pistol—Second Model....................................$125

Same as Sport-King—Second Model, except caliber 22 Short and weighs 2 ounces lighter. Made from 1958 to 1966.

High Standard Supermatic Tournament
bull barrel

High Standard Supermatic Tournament Automatic Pistol.. $200

Takedown. Caliber, 22 Long Rifle. 10-shot magazine. Barrels (interchangeable): 5½-inch bull, 6¾-inch heavy tapered, notched and drilled for stabilizer and weights. 10 inches overall with 5½-inch bbl. Weight, with 5½-inch bbl., 44 ounces. Click adjustable rear sight, undercut ramp front sight. Blued finish. Checkered grips. Made from 1958 to 1966.

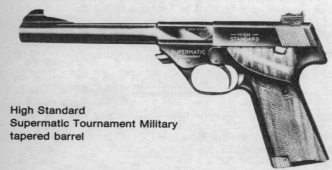

High Standard
Supermatic Tournament Military
tapered barrel

High Standard Supermatic Tournament Military...$225

Same as Supermatic Tournament, except has military grip. Made from 1965 to 1971.

High Standard Supermatic Citation
bull barrel

High Standard Supermatic Citation

Same as Supermatic Tournament, except: barrels—6¾-, 8-, 10-inch—tapered and with stabilizer and two removable weights; also furnished with Tournament's 5½-inch bull barrel; adjustable trigger pull; recoil-proof click adjustable rear sight; (barrel-mounted on 8-inch and 10-inch barrels) checkered walnut thumb-rest grips on bull barrel model. Currently manufactured only with bull barrel. Made from 1958 to date.
With bull barrel...................................... $215
With tapered barrel................................ 225

High Standard Supermatic Citation Military
fluted barrel

High Standard Supermatic Citation Military

Same as Supermatic Citation, except has military grip and bracket rear sight, barrels as in Supermatic Trophy. Made from 1965 to date.
With bull barrel...................................... $225
With fluted barrel.................................. 240

High Standard Supermatic Trophy
bull barrel

High Standard Supermatic Trophy

Same as Supermatic Citation, except: 5½-inch bull barrel or 7¼-inch fluted barrel with detachable stabilizer and weights: extra magazine; high-lustre blued finish; checkered walnut thumb-rest grips. Made from 1963 to 1966.
With bull barrel...................................... $225
With fluted barrel.................................. 310

High Standard Supermatic Trophy Military
fluted barrel

High Standard Olympic I.S.U. Military

High Standard Supermatic Trophy Military
Same as Supermatic Trophy, except has military grip and bracket rear sight. Made from 1965 to date.
With bull barrel..................................... $225
With fluted barrel.................................... 305

High Standard Olympic Commemorative Model. $845
Limited edition of Supermatic Trophy Military issued to commemorate the only American made rimfire target pistol ever to win an Olympic Gold Medal. Highly engraved with Olympic rings inlaid in gold. Deluxe presentation case. Made in 1972. *Note:* Value shown is for pistol in new, unfired condition.

High Standard Olympic—Third Model.......... $210
Same as Supermatic Trophy with bull barrel, except caliber 22 Short. Made from 1963 to 1966.

High Standard Olympic I.S.U. Military.......... $220
Same as Olympic I.S.U., except has military grip and bracket rear sight. Introduced in 1965. Discontinued.

High Standard Sharpshooter

High Standard Sharpshooter Automatic Pistol.. $135
Takedown. Hammerless. Caliber, 22 Long Rifle. 10-shot magazine. 5½-inch bull barrel. 9 inches overall. Weight, 42 ounces. Micrometer rear sight, blade front sight. Blued finish. Plastic stocks. Made from 1971 to date.

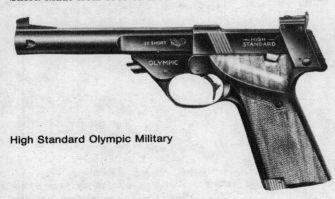

High Standard Olympic Military

High Standard Olympic Military................. $220
Same as Olympic—Third Model, except has military grip and bracket rear sight. Made in 1965.

High Standard Victor
solid rib barrel

High Standard Derringer

High Standard Olympic I.S.U.

High Standard Olympic I.S.U...................... $225
Same as Supermatic Citation, except: caliber, 22 Short; 6¾-inch and 8-inch tapered barrels with stabilizer, detachable weights. Made from 1958 to date; 8-inch barrel discontinued in 1964.

High Standard Victor Automatic Pistol......... $210
Takedown. Caliber, 22 Long Rifle. 10-shot magazine. Barrels: 4½-inch solid or ventilated rib, 5½-inch ventilated rib; interchangeable. 9¾ inches overall with 5½-inch barrel. Weight, with 5½-inch barrel, 52 ounces. Rib-mounted target sights. Blued finish. Checkered walnut thumb-rest stocks. Standard or military grip configuration. Made from 1972 to date (standard-grip model, 1974-75).

High Standard Derringer

Hammerless, double action, double barrel (over/under). Calibers: 22 Short, Long, Long Rifle; 22 Magnum Rimfire. 2-shot. 3½-inch barrels. 5 inches overall. Weight, 11 ounces. Standard model has blued or nickel finish, plastic grips; presentation model is gold-plated, comes in walnut case. Standard model made from 1963 (22 S-L-LR) and 1964 (22 MRF) to date; gold model made from 1965 to date.

Gold presentation, one derringer.....................$150
Gold presentation, matched pair, consecutive
   numbers.. 330
Standard model..................................... 90

High Standard Sentinel

High Standard Sentinel Double Action Revolver...$ 90

Solid frame, swing-out cylinder. Caliber, 22 Long Rifle. 9-shot cylinder. Barrels: 3-, 4- or 6-inch. Overall length, with 4-inch bbl., 9 inches. Weight, with 4-inch bbl., 19 ounces. Fixed sights. Aluminum frame. Blued or nickel finish. Checkered grips. Made from 1955 to 1956.

High Standard Sentinel Imperial.................$105

Same as Sentinel, except has onyx-black or nickel finish, two-piece checkered walnut grips, ramp front sight. Made from 1962 to 1965.

High Standard Sentinel Deluxe

High Standard Sentinel Deluxe..................$105

Same as Sentinel, except 4- and 6-inch barrels only; has wide trigger, movable rear sight, two-piece square-butt grips. Made from 1957 to 1974. *Note:* Designated "Sentinel" after 1971.

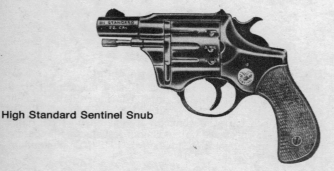

High Standard Sentinel Snub

High Standard Sentinel Snub....................$120

Same as Sentinel Deluxe, except 2⅜-inch barrel (7¼-inch overall; weight, 15 ounces), checkered birdshead-type grips. Made from 1957 to 1974.

High Standard Double-Nine Double Action Revolver—Aluminum Frame................................$110

Western-style version of Sentinel. Blued or nickel finish with simulated ivory, ebony or stag grips. 5½-inch barrel. 11 inches overall. Weight, 27¼ ounces. Made from 1959 to 1971.

High Standard Posse

High Standard Posse.............................$100

Similar to Double-Nine—Aluminum Frame, except 3½-inch barrel (9-inch overall; weight, 23¼ ounces), blued finish, brass-grip frame and trigger guard, walnut grips. Made from 1961 to 1966.

High Standard Natchez

High Standard Natchez..........................$125

Similar to Double-Nine—Aluminum Frame, except 4½-inch barrel (10-inch overall; weight, 25¼ ounces), blued finish, simulated ivory birdshead grips. Made from 1961 to 1966.

High Standard Longhorn-Aluminum Frame

High Standard Longhorn—Aluminum Frame

Similar to Double-Nine—Aluminum Frame. Longhorn hammer spur. Blued finish 4½-inch barrel with simulated pearl grips; 5½-inch, simulated stag grips; 9½-inch, walnut grips. Latter model made from 1960 to 1971, others made from 1961 to 1966.

With 4½- or 5½-inch barrel.........................$125
With 9½-inch barrel................................ 130

High Standard Kit Gun

High Standard Kit Gun Double Action Revolver. $125

Solid frame, swing-out cylinder. Caliber, 22 Long Rifle. 9-shot cylinder. 4-inch barrel. 9 inches overall. Weight, 19 ounces. Adjustable rear sight, ramp front sight. Blued finish. Checkered walnut stocks. Made from 1970 to 1973.

High Standard Double-Nine—Steel Frame

High Standard Double-Nine—Steel Frame....... $100

Similar to Double-Nine—Aluminum Frame, with same general specifications, except has extra cylinder for 22 Win. Mag. R.F., walnut stocks. Introduced in 1971. Discontinued.

High Standard Double-Nine Deluxe............. $125

Same as Double-Nine—Steel Frame, except has adjustable target rear sight. Introduced in 1971. Discontinued.

High Standard Hombre

High Standard Durango

High Standard Hombre........................... $100

Similar to Double-Nine—Steel Frame, except 22 Long Rifle only, lacks single-action type ejector rod and tube, has 4½-inch barrel. Made from 1971 to 1973.

High Standard Durango........................ $110

Similar to Double-Nine—Steel Frame, except 22 Long Rifle only, available with 4½-, as well as 5½-inch barrel. Made from 1971 to 1973.

High Standard Longhorn—Steel Frame

High Standard Longhorn—Steel Frame

Similar to Double-Nine—Steel Frame, except has 9½-inch barrel; available with either fixed or adjustable sights. Made from 1971 to date.
With fixed sights...................................... $125
With adjustable sights............................... 130

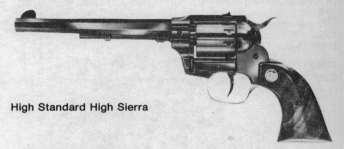

High Standard High Sierra

High Standard High Sierra Double Action Revolver

Similar to Double-Nine—Steel Frame, except has 7-inch octagon barrel, gold-plated grip frame; available with either fixed or adjustable sights. Made from 1973 to date.
With fixed sights...................................... $125
With adjustable sights............................... 130

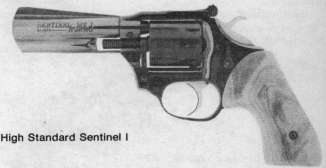

High Standard Sentinel I

High Standard Sentinel I Double Action Revolver

Steel frame. Caliber, 22 Long Rifle. 9-shot cylinder. Barrel lengths: 2-, 3-, 4-inch. 6⅞ inches overall with 2-inch barrel. Weight, with 2-inch barrel, 21½ ounces. Ramp front sight, fixed or adjustable rear sight. Blued or nickel finish. Smooth walnut stocks. Made from 1974 to date.
With fixed sights.................................... $ 95
With adjustable sights............................. 100

High Standard Sentinel Mark IV

Same as Sentinel Mark I, except chambered for 22 Winchester Magnum Rimfire. Made from 1974 to date.
With fixed sights....................................$100
With adjustable sights............................. 105

High Standard Sentinel Mark II

High Standard Sentinel Mark II Double Action Revolver...$125

Caliber, 357 Magnum. 6-shot cylinder. Barrel lengths: 2½-, 4-, 6-inch. 9 inches overall with 4-inch barrel. Weight, with 4-inch barrel, 38 ounces. Fixed sights. Blued finish. Walnut service or combat-style stocks. Made from 1974 to 1976.

High Standard Sentinel Mark III

High Standard Sentinel Mark III................ $135

Same as Sentinel Mark II, except has ramp front sight and adjustable rear sight. Made from 1974 to 1976.

High Standard Camp Gun

High Standard Camp Gun........................ $125

Same as Sentinel Mark I/Mark IV, except has 6-inch barrel, adjustable rear sight, target-style checkered walnut stocks; available in either 22 Long Rifle or 22 Win. Mag. R.F. Made from 1976 to date.

Hopkins & Allen Arms Co., Norwich, Connecticut

Hopkins & Allen Revolvers

See listings of comparable Harrington & Richardson and Iver Johnson models for values.

Interarms, Alexandria, Virginia

Interarms Virginian Single Action Revolver.....$175

See listings under Hämmerli (manufacturer).

Interarms Virginian Dragoon Single Action Revolver

Calibers: 357 Magnum, 44 Magnum, 45 Colt. 6-shot cylinder. Barrels: 5- (not available in 44 Magnum), 6-, 7½-, 8⅜-inch (latter only in 44 Magnum model with adjustable sights). 11⅞ inches overall with 6-inch barrel. Weight, with 6-inch barrel, 48 ounces. Fixed sights or micrometer rear sight and ramp front sight. Blued finish with color-casetreated frame. Smooth walnut stocks. SWISSAFE base pin safety system. Manufactured by Interarms Industries Inc., Midland, Virginia. Introduced in 1977.
With fixed sights....................................$135
With adjustable sights............................. 145

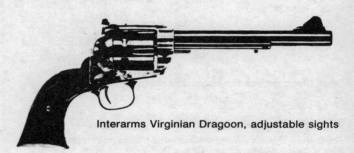

Interarms Virginian Dragoon, adjustable sights

Japanese Military Pistols manufactured by Government plant at Tokyo, Japan

Japanese Nambu Model 1914 Automatic Pistol.. $225

Original Japanese service pistol, resembles Luger in appearance and Glisenti in operation. Caliber, 8mm Nambu. 7-shot magazine, 4½-inch barrel. 9 inches overall. Weight, about 30 ounces. Fixed front sight, adjustable rear sight. Blued finish. Checkered wood stocks. Made from 1914 to 1925.

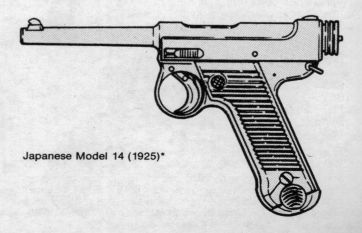

Japanese Model 14 (1925)*

Japanese Model 14 (1925) Automatic Pistol.... $190
Modification of the Nambu Model 1914, changes chiefly intended to simplify mass production. Either standard round trigger guard or oversize guard to permit firing while wearing glove. Caliber, 8mm Nambu. 8-shot magazine. 4¾-inch barrel. 9 inches overall. Weight, about 29 ounces. Fixed sights. Blued finish. Grooved wood stocks. Introduced 1925, manufactured through World War II.

Japanese Model 94*

Japanese Model 94 (1934) Automatic Pistol..... $190
This weapon is of extremely poor design and construction; the sear is exposed on the left side, and the pistol can be fired by pressure on this part. Caliber, 8mm Nambu. 6-shot magazine. 3⅛-inch barrel. 7⅛ inches overall. Weight, about 27 ounces. Fixed sights. Blued finish. Hard rubber or wood stocks. Introduced in 1934, principally for export to Latin American countries. Production was continued through World War II.

Iver Johnson Model 1900

Iver Johnson's Arms & Cycle Works, Fitchburg, Massachusetts

Iver Johnson Model 1900 Double Action Revolver.. $ 75
Solid frame. Calibers: 22 Long Rifle, 32 S&W, 32 S&W Long, 38 S&W. 7-shot cylinder (22 cal.), 6-shot (32 S&W), 5-shot (32 S&W Long, 38 S&W). Barrel lengths: 2½-, 4½- and 6-inch. Weight, 12 ounces (32 S&W with 2½-inch barrel). Fixed sights. Blued or nickel finish. Hard rubber stocks. Made from 1900 to 1947.

Iver Johnson Model 1900 Target Double Action Revolver.. $ 85
Solid frame. Caliber, 22 Long Rifle, 7-shot cylinder. Barrel lengths: 6- and 9½-inch. Fixed sights. Blued finish. Checkered walnut stocks. This earlier model does not have counterbored chambers as in the Target Sealed 8. Made from 1925 to 1942.

Iver Johnson Target Sealed 8

Iver Johnson Target Sealed 8 Double Action Revolver.. $ 95
Solid frame. Caliber, 22 Long Rifle. 8-shot cylinder. Barrel lengths: 6- and 10-inch. 10¾ inches overall with 6-inch barrel. Weight, 24 ounces with 6-inch barrel. Fixed sights. Blued finish. Checkered walnut stocks. Made from 1931 to 1957.

Iver Johnson Target 9 Shot Double Action Revolver.. $ 85
Same as Target Sealed 8, except this model has nine chambers, not counterbored. Made from 1929 to 1946.

Iver Johnson Safety Hammer

Iver Johnson Safety Hammer Double Action Revolver.. $ 75
Hinged frame. Calibers: 22 Long Rifle, 32 S&W, 32 S&W Long, 38 S&W. 7-shot cylinder (22 cal.), 6-shot (32 S&W Long), 5-shot (32 S&W, 38 S&W). Barrel lengths: 2-, 3-, 3¼-, 4-, 5- and 6-inch. Weights with 4-inch barrel: 15 ounces (22, 32 S&W), 19½ ounces (32 S&W Long), 19 ounces (38 S&W). Fixed sights. Blued or nickel finish. Hard rubber stocks, round butt; square butt, rubber and walnut stocks available. *Note:* 32 S&W Long and 38 S&W models built on heavy frame. Made from 1892 to 1950.

Iver Johnson Safety Hammerless

Iver Johnson Safety Hammerless Double Action Revolver.. $ 95
Hinged frame. Calibers: 22 Long Rifle, 32 S&W, 32 S&W Long, 38 S&W. 7-shot cylinder (22 cal.), 6-shot (32 S&W Long), 5-shot (32 S&W, 38 S&W). Barrel lengths: 2-, 3-, 3¼-, 4-, 5- and 6-inch. Weights with 4-inch barrel: 15 ounces (22, 32 S&W), 20½ ounces (32 S&W Long), 20 ounces (38 S&W). Fixed sights. Blued or nickel finish. Hard rubber stocks, round butt. Square butt, rubber and walnut stocks available. *Note:* 32 S&W Long & 38 S&W models built on heavy frame. Made from 1895 to 1950.

Iver Johnson 22 Supershot Double Action Revolver .... $ 75

Hinged frame. Caliber, 22 Long Rifle. 7-shot cylinder. 6-inch barrel. Fixed sights. Blued finish. Checkered walnut stocks. This earlier model does not have counterbored chambers as in the Supershot Sealed 8. Made from 1929 to 1949.

Iver Johnson Trigger-Cocking

Iver Johnson Trigger-Cocking Single Action Target Revolver $110

Hinged frame. First pull on trigger cocks hammer, second pull releases hammer. Caliber, 22 Long Rifle. 8-shot cylinder, counterbored chambers. 6-inch barrel. 10¾ inches overall. Weight, 24 ounces. Adjustable target sights. Blued finish. Checkered walnut stocks. Made from 1940 to 1947.

Iver Johnson Champion

Iver Johnson Champion 22 Target Single Action Revolver $110

Hinged frame. Caliber, 22 Long Rifle. 8-shot cylinder. Counterbored chambers as in Sealed 8 models. 6-inch barrel. 10¾ inches overall. Weight, 28 ounces. Adjustable target sights. Blued finish. Checkered walnut stocks, adjustable finger-rest. Made from 1938 to 1948.

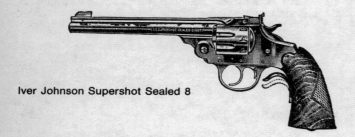

Iver Johnson Supershot Sealed 8

Iver Johnson Supershot Sealed Eight Double Action Revolver $125

Hinged frame. Caliber, 22 Long Rifle. 8-shot cylinder. 6-inch barrel. 10¾ inches overall. Weight, 24 ounces. Adjustable target sights. Blued finish. Checkered walnut stocks. Postwar model does not have adjustable finger-rest found on earlier version. Made from 1931 to 1957.

Iver Johnson Supershot 9-Shot Double Action Revolver .... $ 95

Same as Supershot Sealed Eight except this model has nine chambers, not counterbored. Made from 1929 to 1949.

Iver Johnson Protector Sealed 8

Iver Johnson Protector Sealed Eight Double Action Revolver $125

Hinged frame. Caliber, 22 Long Rifle. 8-shot cylinder. 2½-inch barrel. 7¼ inches overall. Weight, 20 ounces. Fixed sights. Blued finish. Checkered walnut stocks. Made from 1933 to 1949.

Iver Johnson Supershot Model 844 Double Action Revolver .... $ 95

Hinged frame. Caliber, 22 Long Rifle. 8-shot cylinder. Barrel lengths: 4½- or 6-inch. Overall length, with 4½-inch bbl., 9¼ inches. Weight, with 4½-inch bbl., 27 ounces. Adjustable sights. Blued finish. Checkered walnut one-piece grip. Made from 1955 to 1956.

Iver Johnson Armsworth Model 855 Single Action Revolver $125

Hinged frame. Caliber, 22 Long Rifle. 8-shot cylinder. Barrel length, 6-inches. Overall length, 10¾ inches. Weight, 30 ounces. Adjustable sights. Blued finish. Checkered walnut one-piece grip. Adjustable finger-rest. Made from 1955 to 1957.

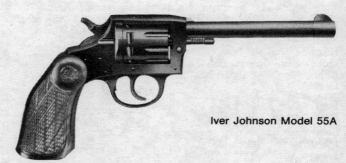

Iver Johnson Model 55A

Iver Johnson Model 55A Target Double Action Revolver .... $ 60

Solid frame. Caliber, 22 Long Rifle. 8-shot cylinder. Barrel lengths: 4½-, 6-inch. 10¾ inches overall (6-inch bbl.). Weight, 30½ ounces (6-inch bbl.). Fixed sights. Blued finish. Walnut stocks. Made from 1955 to date. *Note:* Original model designation was 55, changed to 55A when loading gate was added in 1961.

Iver Johnson Cadet Double Action Revolver

Solid frame. Calibers: 22 Long Rifle, 22 Win. Mag. R.F., 32 S&W Long, 38 S&W, 38 Special. 6- or 8-shot cylinder in 22, 5-shot in other calibers. 2½-inch barrel. 7 inches overall. Weight, 22 ounces. Fixed sights. Blued finish; nickel finish also available in 32 and 38 Special models. Plastic stocks. Made from 1955 to date. *Note:* Loading gate added in 1961; 22 cylinder capacity changed from 8 to 6 rounds in 1975.

38 Special .... $ 90
Other calibers 85

Iver Johnson Model 57A Target

Iver Johnson Model 57A Target Double Action Revolver...$ 75

Solid frame. Caliber, 22 Long Rifle. 8-shot cylinder. Barrel lengths: 4½-, 6-inch. 10¾ inches overall (6-inch bbl.). Weight, 30½ ounces (6-inch bbl.). Adjustable sights. Blued finish. Walnut stocks. Made from 1956 to 1975. *Note:* Original model designation was 57, changed to 57A when loading gate was added in 1961.

Iver Johnson Model 66 Trailsman

Iver Johnson Model 66 Trailsman Double Action Revolver...$ 85

Hinged frame. Rebounding hammer. Caliber, 22 Long Rifle. 8-shot cylinder. 6-inch barrel. 11 inches overall. Weight, 34 ounces. Adjustable sights. Blued finish. Walnut stocks. Made from 1958 to 1975.

Iver Johnson Sidewinder Double Action Revolver...$ 85

Solid frame. Caliber, 22 Long Rifle. 6- or 8-shot cylinder. Barrel lengths: 4¾-, 6-inch. 11¼ inches overall with 6-inch barrel. Weight, with 6-inch barrel, 31 ounces. Fixed sights. Blued or nickel finish; also available with color-casehardened frame. Plastic "staghorn" stocks; model with casehardened frame has walnut stocks. Made from 1961 to date. *Note:* Cylinder capacity changed from 8 to 6 rounds in 1975.

Iver Johnson Sidewinder "S"...................$ 95

Same as Sidewinder, except has interchangeable cylinders in 22 Long Rifle and 22 Win. Mag. R.F., adjustable sights. Made from 1974 to date.

Iver Johnson Model 67 Viking

Iver Johnson Model 67 Viking Double Action Revolver...$100

Hinged frame. Caliber, 22 Long Rifle. 8-shot cylinder. Barrel lengths: 4½- and 6-inch. 11 inches overall with 6-inch barrel. Weight, with 6-inch barrel, 34 ounces. Adjustable sights. Walnut stocks with thumb-rest. Made from 1964 to 1975.

Iver Johnson Model 67S Viking Snub

Iver Johnson Model 67S Viking Snub Double Action Revolver...$ 95

Hinged frame. Calibers: 22 Long Rifle; 32 S&W Short and Long; 38 S&W. 8-shot cylinder in 22; 5-shot in 32 and 38 calibers. 2¾-inch barrel. Weight, 25 ounces. Adjustable sights. Tenite grips. Made from 1964 to 1975.

Iver Johnson American Bulldog

Iver Johnson American Bulldog Double Action Revolver

Solid frame. Calibers: 22 Long Rifle, 22 Win. Mag. R.F., 38 Special. 6-shot cylinder in 22, 5-shot in 38. Barrel lengths: 2½-, 4-inch. 9 inches overall with 4-inch barrel. Weight, with 4-inch barrel, 30 ounces. Adjustable sights. Blued or nickel finish. Plastic stocks. Made from 1974 to 1976.
38 Special...$100
Other calibers................................... 95

Iver Johnson Rookie

Iver Johnson Rookie Double Action Revolver... $ 75
Solid frame. Caliber, 38 Special. 5-shot cylinder. 4-inch barrel.
9 inches overall. Weight, 30 ounces. Fixed sights. Blued or nickel
finish. Plastic stocks. Made from 1975 to date.

Iver Johnson Sportsman Double Action
Revolver... **$ 75**
Solid frame. Caliber, 22 Long Rifle. 6-shot cylinder. Barrel
lengths: 4¾-, 6-inch. 10¾ inches overall with 6-inch barrel.
Weight, with 6-inch barrel, 30½ ounces. Fixed sights. Blued
finish. Plastic stocks. Made from 1974 to 1976.

Iver Johnson Deluxe Target

Iver Johnson Deluxe Target...................... **$ 90**
Same as Sportsman, except has adjustable sights. Made from
1975 to 1976.

Iver Johnson Swing Out

Iver Johnson Swing Out Double Action Revolver
Calibers: 22 Long Rifle, 22 Win. Mag. R.F., 32 S&W Long, 38
Special. 6-shot cylinder in 22, 5-shot in 32 and 38. Barrels:
Plain—2-, 3-, 4-inch; ventilated rib—4-, 6-inch. 8¾ inches over-
all with 4-inch barrel. Fixed or adjustable sights. Blued or nickel
finish. Walnut stocks. Introduced in 1977.
With plain barrel, fixed sights........................ **$100**
With ventilated rib, adjustable sights................. **140**

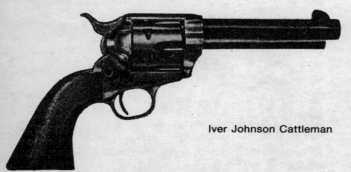

Iver Johnson Cattleman

Iver Johnson Cattleman Single Action Revolver
Calibers: 357 Magnum, 44 Magnum, 45 Colt. 6-shot cylinder.
Barrel lengths: 4¾-, 5½- (not available in 44), 6- (44 only), 7¼-
inch. Weight, about 41 ounces. Fixed sights. Blued barrel and
cylinder, color-casehardened frame, brass grip frame. One-piece
walnut stock. Made by Aldo Uberti, Brescia, Italy, from 1973 to
date.
44 Magnum.. **$170**
Other calibers.. **150**

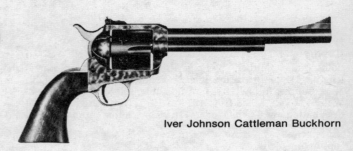

Iver Johnson Cattleman Buckhorn

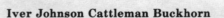

Iver Johnson Cattleman Buntline

Iver Johnson Cattleman Buckhorn
Same as standard Cattleman, except has adjustable rear sight
and ramp front sight; barrels: 4¾- (44 only), 5¾- (not available
in 44), 6- (44 only), 7½-, 12-inch. Weight, almost 44 ounces.
Made from 1973 to date.
357 Magnum or 45 Colt, 12-inch barrel............... **$195**
357 Magnum or 45 Colt, other barrels................. **150**
44 Magnum, 12-inch barrel........................... **225**
44 Magnum, other barrels............................ **200**

Iver Johnson Cattleman Buntline
Same as Cattleman Buckhorn, except has 18-inch barrel, walnut
shoulder stock with brass fittings. Weight, about 56 ounces.
Made from 1973 to date.
44 Magnum.. **$325**
Other calibers.. **300**

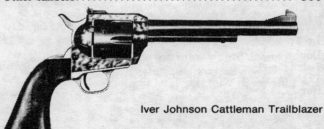

Iver Johnson Cattleman Trailblazer

Iver Johnson Cattleman Trailblazer............. **$130**
Similar to Cattleman Buckhorn, except 22 caliber; has interchangeable 22 Long Rifle and 22 Win. Mag. R.F. cylinders,
5½- or 6½-inch barrel; weight, about 40 ounces. Made from
1973 to date.

Note: For engraved Cattleman revolvers, add $450 to values
indicated.

Lahti, Swedish Model

Lahti Pistols manufactured by Husqvarna Vapen-fabriks A. B. Huskvarna, Sweden, Valtion Kivaar Tedhas ("VKT") Jyväskyla, Finland

Lahti Automatic Pistol

Caliber, 9mm Luger, 8-shot magazine. 4¾-inch barrel. Weight, about 46 ounces. Fixed sights. Blued finish. Plastic stocks. Specifications given are those of the Swedish Model 40 but also apply in general to the Finnish Model L-35 which differs only slightly. A considerable number of Swedish "Lahti" pistols were imported and sold in the U.S. a few years ago; the Finnish Model, which is somewhat better made, is a rather rare modern pistol. Finnish Model L-35 adopted in 1935. Swedish Model 40 adopted in 1940, manufactured through 1944.

Finnish model.......................................$520
Swedish model...................................... 230

Le Francais Policeman*

Le Francais Pistols produced by Manufacture Francaise d'Armes et Cycles de St. Etienne, France

Le Francais Policeman Model Automatic Pistol..$110
Double action. Hinged barrel. Caliber, 25 Automatic (6.35mm). 7-shot magazine. 3½-inch barrel. 6 inches overall. Weight, about 12 ounces. Fixed sights. Blued finish. Hard rubber stocks. Made from 1914 to date.

Le Francais Staff Officer Model Automatic Pistol...$105
Caliber, 25 Automatic. Similar to the "Policeman" Model, except does not have cocking-piece head, barrel is about an inch shorter and weight is an ounce less. Made from 1914 to date.

Le Francais Army Model Automatic Pistol.......$110
Similar in operation to the Le Francais 25 Automatics. Caliber, 9mm Browning Long. 8-shot magazine, 5-inch barrel. 7¾ inches overall. Weight, about 34 ounces. Fixed sights. Blued finish. Checkered walnut stocks. Made from 1928 to 1938.

Le Francais Staff Officer*

Lignose Einhand Model 2A*

Aktien-Gesellschaft "Lignose" Abteilung, Suhl, Germany

Lignose Einhand Model 2A Pocket Automatic Pistol..$180
As the name implies, this pistol is designed for one-hand operation; pressure on a "trigger" at the front of the guard retracts the slide. Caliber, 25 Automatic (6.35mm). 6-shot magazine. 2-inch barrel. 4¾ inches overall. Weight, about 14 ounces. Blued finish. Hard rubber stocks.

Lignose Einhand Model 3A

Lignose Einhand Model 3A Pocket Automatic Pistol..$180
Same as the Model 2A except has longer grip, 9-shot magazine, weighs about 16 ounces.

Lignose Model 2 Pocket Automatic Pistol......... $135
Conventional Browning type. Same general specifications as Model 2A "Einhand," but lacks the one-hand operation feature.

Note: These Lignose pistols were manufactured from 1920 to the mid-1930's. Also marketed under the Bergmann name.

Llama Model IIIA

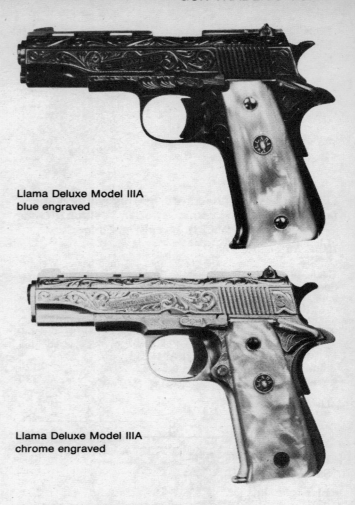

Llama Deluxe Model IIIA
blue engraved

Llama Deluxe Model IIIA
chrome engraved

Llama Pistols manufactured by Gabilondo y Cia., Vitoria, Spain

Llama Model IIIA Automatic Pistol............. $170
Caliber, 380 Automatic. 7-shot magazine. 3-11/16-inch barrel. 6½ inches overall. Weight, 23 ounces. Adjustable target sights. Blued finish. Plastic stocks. Made from 1951 to date.

Llama Model XA Automatic Pistol.............. $170
Same as Model IIIA, except caliber 32 Automatic, 8-shot magazine.

Llama Model XV Automatic Pistol.............. $210
Same as Model XA, except caliber 22 Long Rifle.

Llama Models C-IIIA, C-XA, C-XV.............. $210
Same as Models IIIA, XA and XV, except satin-chrome finish.

Llama Model CE-IIIA

Llama Models CE-IIIA, CE-XA, CE-XV......... $290
Same as Models IIIA, XA and XV, except chrome-engraved finish. Introduced in 1977.

Llama Models BE-IIIA, BE-XA, BE-XV......... $285
Same as Models IIIA, XA and XV, except blue-engraved finish. Introduced in 1977.

Llama Deluxe Models IIIA, XA, XV
Same as standard Model IIIA, XA and XV, except finish—chrome engraved or blue engraved—and simulated pearl stocks.
Chrome-engraved finish............................$235
Blue-engraved finish................................ 230

Llama Model G-IIIA Deluxe.................... $975
Same as Model IIIA, except gold damascened, has simulated pearl stocks.

Llama Model VIII

Llama Model VIII Automatic Pistol............. $210
Caliber, 38 Super. 9-shot magazine. 5-inch barrel. 8½ inches overall. Weight, 40 ounces. Fixed sights. Blued finish. Wood stocks. Made from 1952 to date.

Llama Model IXA Automatic Pistol $210
Same as Model VIII, except caliber 45 Automatic, 7-shot magazine.

Llama Model XI

Llama Model XI Automatic Pistol $210
Same as Model VIII, except caliber 9mm Luger.

Llama Model C-XI

Llama Models C-VIII, C-IXA, C-XI $270
Same as Models VIII, IXA and XI, except satin-chrome finish.

Llama Models CE-VIII, CE-IXA, CE-XI $280
Same as Models VIII, IXA and XI, except chrome-engraved finish. Introduced in 1977.

Llama Models BE-VIII, BE-IXA, BE-XI $260
Same as Models VIII, IXA and XI, except blue-engraved finish. Introduced in 1977.

Llama Deluxe Models VIII, IXA, XI
Same as standard Models VIII, IXA and XI, except finish—chrome engraved or blue engraved—and simulated pearl stocks.
Chrome-engraved finish $250
Blue-engraved finish 225

Llama Double Action Automatic Pistol $290
Calibers, 38 Super, 9mm, 45 Auto. 9-shot magazine (7-shot for 45 Auto). 5-inch barrel, 8½ inches overall. Weight: 2 pounds, 8 ounces. Introduced in 1981.

Llama Martial Double Action Revolver

Llama Martial Double Action Revolver $180
Calibers: 22 Long Rifle, 38 Special. 6-shot cylinder. Barrel lengths: 4-inch (38 Special only), 6-inch. 11¼ inches overall with 6-inch barrel. Weight, with 6-inch barrel, about 36 ounces. Target sights. Blued finish. Checkered walnut stocks. Made from 1969 to 1976.

Llama Deluxe Martial, gold damascened

Llama Deluxe Martial
Same as standard Martial, except finish–satin chrome, chrome engraved, blue engraved, gold damascened; has simulated pearl stocks.
Satin-chrome finish $210
Chrome-engraved finish 260
Blue-engraved finish 245
Gold-damascened finish 825

Llama Comanche

Llama Comanche I Double Action Revolver $175
Same general specifications as Martial 22. Introduced in 1977.

Llama Comanche II $175
Same general specifications as Martial 38. Introduced in 1977.

Llama Comanche III Double Action Revolver $200
Caliber, 357 Magnum. 6-shot cylinder. 4-inch barrel. 9¼ inches overall. Weight, 36 ounces. Adjustable rear sight, ramp front sight. Blued finish. Checkered walnut stocks. Made from 1975 to date. *Note:* Prior to 1977, this model was designated "Comanche."

Llama Chrome Comanche III $255
Same general specifications as Comanche III, except has satin chrome finish. 4- or 6-inch barrels. Made from 1979 to date.

Llama Super Comanche IV Double Action Revolver $310
Caliber, 44 Magnum. 6-shot cylinder. 6-inch barrel. 11¾ inches overall. Weight, 3 pounds, 2 ounces. Adjustable rear sight, ramp front sight. Polished deep blue finish. Checkered walnut grips. Made from 1980 to date.

Luger Pistol manufactured by Deutsche Waffen- und Munitionsfabriken (DWM), Berlin, Germany; also by Königlich Gewehrfabrik Erfurt, Heinrich Krieghoff Waffenfabrik, Mauser-Werke, Simson & Co., Vickers Ltd., Waffenfabrik, Bern.

Luger (Parabellum) Automatic Pistol

Calibers: 7.65mm Luger, 9mm Luger. 8-shot magazine. Barrel lengths: 3⅝-, 4½-, 6-inch (7.65mm); 4-, 6-, 8-inch (9mm). Overall length with 4-inch barrel, 8¾ inches. Weight, with 4-inch barrel, 30 ounces. Fixed sights, adjustable rear sight on long barrel models. Blued finish. Checkered walnut stocks. Lugers manufactured prior to 1908 have a flat mainspring, and a number of other parts differ from later models. Early pistols have grip safety (not found on later production, except for export to Switzerland), some pre-World War I models lack the shoulder stock lug found on most Lugers. German Service Lugers bear a year stamp on the receiver, not found on the commercial models, which are also better finished. Pistols made for export to the United States were generally stamped with an American Eagle on receiver or breechblock; those imprted by A. F. Stoeger, Inc. after World War I bear that firm's name. Made from 1900 to 1942; production resumed in 1970 by Mauser. Specialist collectors recognize a great many Luger variations with a wide range of values.

Luger Parabellum

1900 Commercial, 7.65mm	$ 2300
1900 Eagle, 7.65mm	2500
1900 Swiss Commercial, 7.65mm	3500
1900 Swiss Military 7.65mm	3000
1900 Swiss Military, 7.65mm, wide trigger	3000
1902 7.65mm and 9mm Luger, Carbine	7500
1902 9mm Luger, Cartridge Counter	10,000
1902 Commercial, 9mm Luger	5000
1902 Eagle, 9mm Luger	7000
1902 Prototype, 7.65mm and 9mm Luger	18,000
1902-3 Presentation, 7.65mm, Carbine	45,000
1904 Navy, 9mm Luger	9500
1906 Brazilian, 7.65mm	1200
1906 Bulgarian, 9mm Luger	4750
1906 Bulgarian, 7.65mm	5000
1906 Commercial, 9mm Luger	4000
1906 Dutch, 9mm Luger	1150
1906 Eagle, 9mm Luger	1850
1906 Eagle, 7.65mm	2200
1906 Navy Commercial, 9mm Luger	4000
1906 Navy Military, 9mm Luger	2650
1906 Portuguese Army, 7.65mm	1400
1906 Portuguese Navy Crown, 7.65mm and 9mm Luger	10,000
1906 Portuguese Navy, RP, 7.65mm	7000
1906 Russian, 9mm Luger	10,000
1906 Swiss Commercial, 7.65mm	3000
1906 Swiss Police, 7.65mm	2800

1908 Bolivian, 9mm Luger	8000
1908 DWM Commercial, 9mm Luger	1250
1908 Military, 9mm Luger	950
1908 Navy Commercial, 7.65mm	3400
1908 Navy Military, 9mm Luger	2200
1914 Artillery, 9mm Luger	1400
1914 Military, 9mm Luger	750
1914 Navy, 9mm Luger	2200
1918 Spandau, 9mm Luger	5500
1920 Abercrombie & Fitch, 7.65mm and 9mm Luger	6500
1920 Artillery, 9mm Luger	2500
1920 Commercial, 7.65mm and 9mm Luger	900
1920 Navy, 9mm Luger	3200
1920 Swiss Commercial, 7.65mm and 9mm Luger	3000
1920-22 7.65mm and 9mm Luger	1100
1921 Krieghoff, 7.65mm	2500
1923 Commercial, 7.65mm and 9mm Luger	2000
1923 Commercial Krieghoff 9mm Luger	2500
1923 Commercial "Safe-Loaded", 7.65mm and 9mm Luger	2000
1923 Simson Commercial, 9mm Luger	1700
1923 Simson Military, 9mm Luger	2000
1923 Stoeger, 7.65mm and 9mm Luger	7000
1929 Bern, 7.65mm and 9mm Luger	3000
1930-33 Death Head, 9mm Luger	3000
1933-35 Mauser Commercial, 9mm Luger	7000
1934 Sideframe, Krieghoff, 6" barrel, 9mm Luger	6500
1934 Sideframe, 9mm Luger, Krieghoff, 6" barrel	4500
1934 Simson, 9mm Luger	2200
1935 Portuguese, 7.65mm	2000
1936 Persian, 9mm Luger	8500
1936-40 Dutch Banner, 9mm Luger	2000
1936-9 S/42, 9mm Luger	750
1937-39 Banner Commercial, 7.65mm 4" barrel	2000
1938 9mm Luger, Krieghoff	3500
1939-40 42, 9mm Luger	750
1940 9mm Luger, Krieghoff	2700
1940 42/42 BYF, 9mm Luger	2200
1940 Mauser Banner, 7.65mm and 9mm Luger	1800
1940-1 S/42, 9mm Luger	900
1941-2 BYF, 9mm Luger	1500
1941-4, 9mm Luger, Krieghoff	2750
1945 9mm Luger, Krieghoff	5000
36, 9mm Luger, Krieghoff	5000
Banner Commercial, 7.65mm, 4" barrel	2250
G.L. Baby, 9mm Luger	100,000
K U 9mm Luger	2200
Mauser Banner Commercial, 9mm Luger	2000
Mauser Parabellum Bulgarian, 7.65mm, Commemorative	1800
Mauser Parabellum Russian, 7.65mm, Commemorative	1800
Mauser Parabellum Sport, 7.65mm or 9mm Luger	3500
Post War, 9mm Luger, Krieghoff	3000
Vickers Commercial, 9mm Luger	2500
Vickers Military, 9mm Luger	2100

Luna Model 300 Free Pistol

Luna Free Pistol originally manufactured by Ernst Friedr. Büchel and later by Udo Anschütz, both of Zella-Mehlis, Germany.

Luna Model 300 Free Pistol.....................$920
Single shot. System Aydt action. Set trigger. Caliber, 22 Long Rifle. 11-inch barrel. Weight, 40 ounces. Target sights. Blued finish. Checkered and carved walnut stock and forearm; improved design with adjustable hand base on later models of Udo Anschütz manufacture. Made prior to World War II.

Mauser Model 1898 Military

Waffenfabrik Mauser of Mauser-Werke A.G., Oberndorf, Germany

Mauser Model 1898 Military Automatic Pistol. $1200
Caliber, 7.63mm Mauser; also chambered for 9mm Mauser and 9mm Luger; the latter is identified by a large red "9" in the stocks. Box magazine, 10-shot. 5¼-inch barrel. 12 inches overall. Weight, 45 ounces. Adjustable rear sight. Blued finish. Walnut stocks. Made from 1898 to 1945. *Note:* Specialist collectors recognize a number of varieties of this pistol at higher values. Price shown is for the more common type.

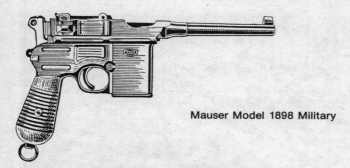

Mauser WTP Model I

Mauser WTP Model II

Mauser WTP Model I Automatic Pistol..........$225
"Westentaschen-Pistole" (Vest Pocket Pistol). Caliber, 25 Automatic (6.35mm). 6-shot magazine. 2½-inch barrel. 4½ inches overall. Weight, 11½ ounces. Blued finish. Hard rubber stocks. Made from c. 1922 to 1937.

Mauser WTP Model II Automatic Pistol.........$250
Similar to Model I, but smaller and lighter. Caliber, 25 Automatic (6.35mm). 6-shot magazine. 2 inch barrel. 4 inches overall. Weight, 9½ ounces. Blued finish. Hard rubber stocks. Made from 1938 to 1940.

Mauser Pocket Model 1910 Automatic Pistol....$200
Caliber, 25 Automatic (6.35mm). 9-shot magazine. 3.1-inch barrel. 5.4 inches overall. Weight, 15 ounces. Fixed sights. Blued finish. Checkered walnut or hard rubber stocks. Made from 1910 to 1934.

Mauser Pocket Model 1914.....................$200
Similar to Pocket Model 1910. Caliber, 32 Automatic (7.65mm). 8-shot magazine. 3.4-inch barrel. 6 inches overall. Weight, 21 ounces. Fixed sights. Blued finish. Checkered walnut or hard rubber stocks. Made from 1914 to 1934.

Mauser Pocket Model 1934.....................$275
Similar to Pocket Models 1910 and 1914 in the respective calibers. Chief difference is in the more streamlined one-piece stocks. Made from 1934 to c. 1939.

Mauser Model HSc

Mauser Model HSc Double Action Automatic Pistol..$325
Calibers: 32 Automatic (7.65mm), 380 Automatic (9mm Short). 8-shot magazine in 32, 7-shot in 380. 3.4-inch barrel. 6.4 inches overall. Weight, 23.6 ounces. Fixed sights. Blued or nickel finish. Checkered walnut stocks. Made from 1938 to 1945, from 1968 to date.

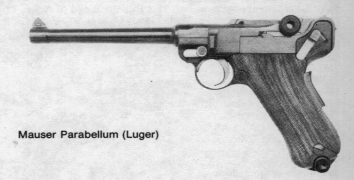

Mauser Parabellum (Luger)

Mauser Parabellum (Luger) Automatic Pistol...$900
Current commercial model. Swiss pattern with grip safety. Calibers: 7.65mm Luger, 9mm Luger. 8-shot magazine. Barrel lengths: 4-, 6-inch. 8¾ inches overall with 4-inch barrel. Weight, with 4-inch barrel, 30 ounces. Fixed sights. Blued finish. Checkered walnut stocks. Made from 1970 to date. *Note:* Pistols of this model sold in the United States have the American Eagle stamped on the receiver.

MKE Kirikkale*

MKE Pistol manufactured by Makina ve Kimya Endüstrisi Kurumu, Ankara, Turkey

MKE Kirikkale Double Action Automatic Pistol. $150
Similar to Walther PP. Calibers: 32 Automatic (7.65mm), 380 Automatic (9mm Short). 7-shot magazine. 3.9-inch barrel. 6.7 inches overall. Weight, 24 ounces. Fixed sights. Blued finish. Checkered plastic stocks. Made from 1948 to date. *Note:* This is a standard service pistol of the Turkish Army.

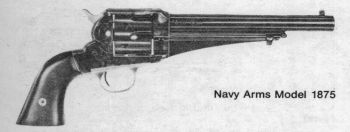

Navy Arms Model 1875

Navy Arms Company, Ridgefield, New Jersey

Navy Arms Model 1875 Single Action Revolver. $155
Replica of Remington Model 1875. Calibers: 357 Magnum, 44-40, 45 Colt. 6-shot cylinder. 7½-inch barrel. 13½ inches overall. Weight, about 48 ounces. Fixed sights. Blued or nickel finish. Smooth walnut stocks. Made in Italy from c. 1955 to date. *Note:* Originally marketed in the U.S. as Replica Arms Model 1875; that firm was acquired by Navy Arms Company.

Navy Arms Rolling Block

Navy Arms Rolling Block Single Shot Pistol.... $100
Calibers: 22 Long Rifle, 22 Hornet, 357 Magnum. 8-inch barrel. 12 inches overall. Weight, about 40 ounces. Adjustable sights. Blued barrel, color-casehardened frame, brass trigger guard. Smooth walnut stock and forearm. Introduced in 1965. Discontinued.

Navy Arms Standard Frontier

Navy Arms Standard Frontier Single Action Revolver... $140
Calibers: 22 Long Rifle, 22 Win. Mag. R.F., 357 Magnum, 45 Colt. 6-shot cylinder. Barrel lengths: 4½-, 5½-, 7½-inch. 10¼ inches overall with 4½-inch barrel. Weight, with 4½-inch barrel, about 36 ounces. Fixed sights. Blued barrel and cylinder, color-casehardened frame, brass grip frame. One-piece smooth walnut stock. Introduced in 1975. Discontinued.

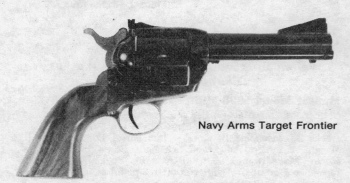

Navy Arms Target Frontier

Navy Arms Target Frontier...................... $155
Same as Standard Frontier, except has adjustable rear sight and ramp front sight. Introduced in 1975. Discontinued.

Navy Arms Buntline Frontier

Navy Arms Buntline Frontier.................... $250
Same as Target Frontier, except has detachable shoulder stock and 16½-inch barrel; calibers: 357 Magnum and 45 Colt only. Introduced in 1975. Discontinued.

North American Arms Model 22S

North American Arms, Freedom, Wyoming

North American Arms Model 22S Mini Revolver.. $ 85

Single action. Caliber, 22 Short. 5-shot cylinder. 1⅛-inch barrel. 3½ inches overall. Weight, 4 ounces. Fixed sights. Stainless steel. Plastic stocks. Made from 1975 to date.

North American Arms Model 22LR

North American Arms Model 22LR.............. $ 85

Same as Model 22S, except chambered for 22 Long Rifle, is 3⅞ inches overall, weighs 4½ ounces. Made from 1976 to date.

North American Arms Model 454C

North American Arms Model 454C Single Action Revolver.. $500

Caliber, 454 Casull. 5-shot cylinder. 7½-inch barrel. 14 inches overall. Weight, 50 ounces. Fixed sights. Stainless steel. Smooth hardwood stocks. Introduced in 1977.

Norwegian Model 1914

Norwegian Military Pistol manufactured by Kongsberg Vaapenfabrikk, the government arsenal at Kongsberg, Norway

Norwegian Model 1914 Automatic Pistol....... $240

Similar to Colt Model 1911 45 Automatic with same general specifications, except has lengthened slide stop. Made from 1919

to 1946. *Note:* Model 1912 is same except has conventional slide stop; only 500 were made and this is a very rare collector's item.

Ortgies Vest Pocket*

Ortgies Pistols manufactured by Deutsche Werke A. G., Erfurt, Germany

Ortgies Vest Pocket Automatic Pistol.......... $130

Caliber, 25 Automatic (6.35mm). 6-shot magazine. 2¾-inch barrel. 5-3/16 inches overall. Weight, 13½ ounces. Fixed sights. Blued finish. Plain walnut stocks. Made in 1920's.

Ortgies Pocket*

Ortgies Pocket Automatic Pistol................. $130

Calibers: 32 Automatic (7.65mm), 380 Automatic (9mm). 7-shot magazine (380 cal.), 8-shot (32 cal.). 3¼-inch barrel. 6½ inches overall. Weight, 22 ounces. Fixed sights. Blued finish. Plain walnut stocks. Made in 1920's.

Plainfield Machine Company, Plainfield, New Jersey

Plainfield Model 71 Automatic Pistol

Calibers: 22 Long Rifle, 25 Automatic; conversion kit available. 10-shot magazine in 22, 8-shot in 25. 2½-inch barrel. 5⅛ inches overall. Weight 25 ounces. Fixed sights. Stainless steel frame and slide. Checkered walnut stocks. Made from 1970 to date.

22 Long Rifle or 25 Auto only......................... $ 60
With conversion kit.................................... 75

Plainfield Model 72

Same as Model 71, except has aluminum slide, 3½-inch barrel, is 6 inches overall. Made from 1970 to date.

22 Long Rifle or 25 Auto only......................... $ 60
With conversion kit.................................... 75

Plainfield Model 71

Record-Match Model 210

Record-Match Model 200

Record-Match Pistols manufactured by Udo Anschütz, Zella-Mehlis, Germany

Record-Match Model 210 Free Pistol...........$1100
System Martini action, set trigger with button release. Caliber, 22 Long Rifle. Single shot. 11-inch barrel. Weight, 46 ounces. Target sights, micrometer rear. Blued finish. Carved and checkered walnut stock and forearm, adjustable hand base. Also made with dural action (Model 210A); weight of this model, 35 ounces. Made prior to World War II.

Record-Match Model 200 Free Pistol............$800
Basically the same as Model 210 except plainer, with different stock design and conventional set trigger, spur trigger guard. Made prior to World War II.

Plainfield Model 72

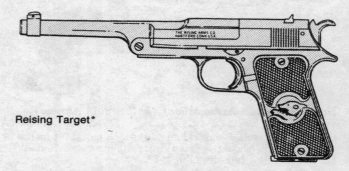

Reising Target*

Reising Arms Co., Hartford, Connecticut

Reising Target Automatic Pistol.................$345
Hinged frame. Outside hammer. Caliber, 22 Long Rifle. 12-shot magazine. 6½-inch barrel. Fixed sights. Blued finish. Hard rubber stocks. Made from 1921 to 1924.

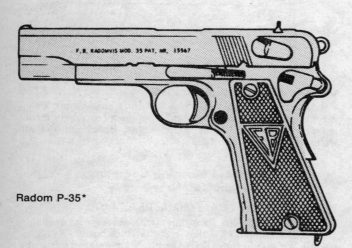

Radom P-35*

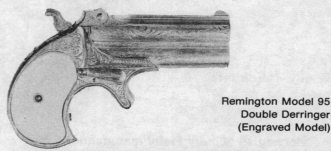

Remington Model 95
Double Derringer
(Engraved Model)

Radom Pistol manufactured by Polish Arsenal at Radom

Radom P-35 Automatic Pistol....................$270
Variation of the Colt Government Model 45 Auto. Caliber, 9mm Luger. 8-shot magazine. 4¾-inch barrel. 7¾ inches overall. Weight, 29 ounces. Fixed sights. Blued finish. Plastic stocks. Made from 1935 through World War II.

Remington Arms Company, Ilion, New York

Remington Model 95 Double Derringer
Single action. Caliber, 41 Short Rimfire. Double barrels (superposed), 3-inch. 4⅞ inches overall. Early models have long hammer spur and two-armed extractor; later production have short

hammer spur and sliding extractor (a few have no extractor). Fixed sights: front blade integral with barrels, rear groove. Finishes: all blued, blued with nickel-plated frame, fully nickel-plated; also furnished with factory engraving. Grips: walnut, checkered hard rubber, pearl, ivory. Weight, 11 ounces. Made from 1866 to 1935. Approximately 150,000 were manufactured. *Note:* During the seventy years of its production, serial numbering of this model was repeated two or three times. Therefore aside from hammer and extractor differences between the earlier model and the later type, the best clue to the age of a Double Derringer is the stamping of the company's name on the top of the barrel or side rib. Prior to 1888, derringers were stamped "E. Remington & Sons;" from 1888 to 1910, "Remington Arms Co.;" from 1910 to 1935, "Remington Arms-U.M.C. Co."
Plain model.. **$700**
Factory-engraved model with ivory or pearl grips...... 850

Remington New Model Single Shot Target Pistol
.... **$900**
Also called Model 1901 Target. Rolling-block action. Calibers: 22 Short, 22 Long Rifle, 44 S&W Russian. 10-inch barrel, half-octagon. 14 inches overall. Weight, 45 ounces (22 cal.). Target sights. Blued finish. Checkered walnut grips and forearm. Made from 1901 to 1909.

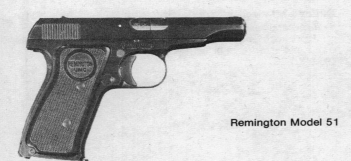

Remington Model 51

Remington Model 51 Automatic Pistol..........$350
Calibers: 32 Auto, 380 Auto. 7-shot magazine. 3½-inch barrel. 6⅝ inches overall. Weight, 21 ounces. Fixed sights. Blued finish. Hard rubber stocks. Made from 1918 to 1934.

Remington Model XP-100

Remington Model XP-100 Single Shot Pistol....$190
Bolt action. Caliber, 221 Remington "Fire Ball." 10½-inch barrel with ventilated rib. 16¾ inches overall. Weight, 3¾ pounds. Adjustable rear sight, blade front sight; receiver drilled and tapped for scope mounts. Blued finish. One-piece brown nylon stock. Made from 1963 to date.

Rossi

Amadeo Rossi S.A., Sáo Leopoldo, Brazil
Rossi Double Action Revolver...................$100
Calibers: 22 Long Rifle, 32 S&W Long, 38 Special. 5-shot cylinder in 38, 6-shot in other calibers. Barrel lengths: 3-, 6-inch. Weight, with 3-inch barrel, 22 ounces. Adjustable rear sight, ramp front sight. Blued or nickel finish. Wood or plastic stocks. Made from 1965 to date.

Ruby Pistol manufactured by Gabilondo y Urresti, Eibar, Spain, and others
Ruby 7.65mm Automatic Pistol.................$ 75
Secondary standard service pistol of the French Army in World War I and II. Essentially the same as the Alkartasuna; see listing of that pistol for specifications. Other manufacturers: Armenia Elgoibarresa y Cia., Eceolaza y Vicinai y Cia., Hijos de Angel Echeverria y Cia., Bruno Salaverria y Cia., Zulaika y Cia., all of Eibar, Spain; Gabilondo y Cia., Elgoibar, Spain; Ruby Arms Company, Guernica, Spain. Made from 1914 to 1922.

Ruby 7.65mm*

Ruger Handguns manufactured by Sturm, Ruger & Co., Southport, Connecticut
Ruger Standard Model Automatic Pistol
Caliber, 22 Long Rifle. 9-shot magazine. 4¾- or 6-inch barrel. 8¾ inches overall with 4¾-inch bbl. Weight, with 4¾-inch bbl., 36 ounces. Fixed sights. Blued finish. Hard rubber or checkered walnut stocks. Made from 1949 to date. *Note:* In 1951, after

death of Alexander Sturm, the color of the eagle on the stock medallion was changed from red to black as a memorial. Known as the "Red Eagle Automatic," this early type is now a collector's item.

With red eagle medallion............................. **$280**
With black eagle medallion........................... **90**
Extra for walnut stocks.............................. **10**

Ruger Standard Model

Ruger Mark I Target

Ruger Mark I Target Model Automatic Pistol... $120
Caliber, 22 Long Rifle. 9-shot magazine. Barrels: 5¼- or 6⅞-inch heavy tapered, 5½-inch untapered bull barrel. 10⅞ inches overall with 6⅞-inch barrel. Weight, with 5½- or 6⅞-inch barrel, 42 ounces. Adjustable rear sight, under-cut target front sight. Blued finish. Hard rubber stocks or checkered walnut thumb-rest stocks (add $10 to value for latter). Made from 1951 to date.

Ruger Mark II Automatic Pistol................. $105
Caliber, 22 Long Rifle. 4¾- or 6-inch barrel. 10-shot magazine. Blued finish. Similar in appearance to Standard Model. Introduced 1982.

Ruger Mark II Target Pistol..................... $125
Same as standard Mark II, except has 5½-inch target bull barrel.

Ruger Mark II Automatic Stainless.............. $435
Same as standard Mark II, except in stainless steel. Production limited to 5000.

Ruger Single-Six

Ruger Single-Six Revolver....................... $110
Single Action. Calibers: 22 Long Rifle, 22 Win. Magnum Rimfire. 6-shot cylinder. Barrel lengths: 4⅝-, 5½-, 6½-, 9½-inch. Overall length with 5½-inch bbl., 10⅞ inches. Weight, about 35 ounces. Fixed sights. Blued finish. Checkered hard rubber or smooth walnut grips. made from 1953 to 1972. *Note:* Pre-1956 model has flat loading gate, is worth about twice as much as later version.

Ruger Single-Six Convertible.................... $155
Same as Single-Six, except has two cylinders for 22 Long Rifle and 22 Win. Mag. R.F.

Ruger Lightweight Single-Six

Ruger Lightweight Single-Six................... $240
Same general specifications as Single-Six, except: 4⅝-inch barrel, 10 inches overall length, weighs 23 ounces; cylinder, cylinder frame and grip frame of lightweight alloy. Made from 1955 to 1958.

Ruger Convertible Super Single-Six

Ruger Super-Single Six Convertible Revolver...$170
Same general specifications as Single-Six, except: ramp front sight, click-adjustable rear sight with protective ribs integral with frame; 5½- or 6½-inch barrel only; two interchangeable cylinders, 22 LR and 22WMR. Made from 1964 to 1972.

Ruger Blackhawk

Ruger Blackhawk Single Action Revolver....... $150
Calibers: 30 Carbine, 357 Magnum, 41 Magnum, 45 Colt. 6-shot cylinder. Barrel lengths: 4⅝-inch (357, 41, 45 caliber), 6½-inch (357, 41 caliber), 7½-inch (30, 45 caliber). 10⅛ inches overall in 357 model with 4⅝-inch barrel. Weight, 357 model with 4⅝-

inch barrel, 38 ounces. Adjustable rear sight, ramp front sight. Blued finish. Checkered hard rubber or smooth walnut stocks. Made from 1955 to 1972.

Ruger Blackhawk Convertible.................... $200
Same as Blackhawk, except has extra cylinder. Caliber combinations: 357 Magnum and 9mm Luger, 45 Colt and 45 Automatic.

Ruger Super Bearcat

Ruger Blackhawk 44

Ruger Hawkeye

Ruger Super Blackhawk

Ruger Blackhawk 44 Magnum Revolver....... $275
Single action with heavy frame and cylinder. Caliber, 44 Magnum. 6-shot cylinder. 6½-inch barrel. Overall length, 12⅛ inches. Weight, 40 ounces. Adjustable rear sight, ramp front sight. Blued finish. Smooth walnut stocks. Made from 1956 to 1963.

Ruger Super Blackhawk Single Action Revolver... $275
Caliber, 44 Magnum. 6-shot cylinder. 7½-inch barrel. 13⅜ inches overall. Weight, 48 ounces. Click adjustable rear sight, ramp front sight. Blued finish. Steel or brass grip frame. Smooth walnut stocks. Made from 1959 to 1972.

Ruger Hawkeye Single Shot Pistol............. $800
Single action; cylinder replaced by rotating breechblock; chamber is in barrel. Caliber, 256 Magnum. 8½-inch barrel. 14½ inches overall. Weight, 45 ounces. Blued finish. Click adjustable rear sight, ramp front sight. Smooth walnut stocks. Made from 1963 to 1964.

Ruger New Model Super Single-Six Convertible Revolver
Single action with interlocked mechanism. Calibers: 22 Long Rifle and 22 Win. Mag. R.F. Interchangeable 6-shot cylinders. Barrel lengths: 4⅝-, 5½-, 6½-, 9½-inch. 10-13/16 inches overall with 4⅝-inch barrel. Weight, with 4⅝-inch barrel, 33 ounces. Adjustable rear sight, ramp front sight. Blued finish or stainless steel; latter only with 5½- or 6½-inch barrel. Smooth walnut stocks. Made from 1972 to date.
Blued finish.. $105
Stainless steel....................................... 125

Ruger Bearcat

Ruger New Model Blackhawk

Ruger Bearcat Single Action Revolver......... $185
Aluminum frame. Caliber, 22 Long Rifle. 6-shot cylinder. 4-inch barrel. 8⅞ inches overall. Weight, 17 ounces. Fixed sights. Blued finish. Smooth walnut stocks. Made from 1958 to 1971.

Ruger Super Bearcat............................. $165
Same general specifications as Bearcat, except has steel frame; weight, 25 ounces. Made from 1971 to 1973.

Ruger New Model Blackhawk Single Action Revolver
Interlocked mechanism. Calibers: 30 Carbine, 357 Magnum, 41 Magnum, 45 Colt. 6-shot cylinder. Barrel lengths: 4⅝-inch (357, 41, 45 caliber), 6½-inch (357, 41 caliber), 7½-inch (30, 45 caliber). 10⅜ inches overall in 357 model with 4⅝-inch barrel. Weight, 357 model with 4⅝-inch barrel, 40 ounces. Adjustable rear sight, ramp front sight. Blued finish or stainless steel; latter only in 357 model. Smooth walnut stocks. Made from 1973 to date.
Blued finish.. $150
Stainless steel....................................... 170

Ruger New Model Blackhawk Convertible......$170
Same as New Model Blackhawk, except has extra cylinder; blued finish only. Caliber combinations: 357 Magnum and 9mm Luger, 45 Colt and 45 Automatic.

Ruger New Model Super Blackhawk

Ruger New Model Super Blackhawk Single Action Revolver..$170
Interlocked mechanism. Caliber, 44 Magnum. 6-shot cylinder. 7½-inch barrel. 13⅜ inches overall. Weight, 48 ounces. Adjustable rear sight, ramp front sight. Blued finish. Smooth walnut stocks. Made from 1973 to date.

Ruger Security-Six

Ruger Security-Six Double Action Revolver
Caliber, 357 Magnum. 6-shot cylinder. Barrel lengths: 2¾-, 4-, 6-inch. 9¼ inches overall with 4-inch barrel. Weight, with 4-inch barrel, 33½ ounces. Adjustable rear sight, ramp front sight. Blued finish or stainless steel. Square butt. Checkered walnut stocks. Made from 1970 to date.
Blued finish...**$160**
Stainless steel....................................... 180

Ruger Speed-Six

Ruger Speed-Six Double Action Revolver
Calibers: 38 Special, 357 Magnum, 9mm Luger. 6-shot cylinder. Barrel lengths: 2¾-, 4-inch; 9mm available only with 2¾-inch barrel. 7¾ inches overall with 2¾-inch barrel. Weight, with 2¾-inch barrel, 31 ounces. Fixed sights. Blued finish or stainless steel; latter available in 38 Special with 2¾-inch barrel, 357 Magnum with either barrel. Round butt. Checkered walnut stocks. Made from 1973 to date.
38 Special, blued finish............................**$125**
38 Special, stainless steel........................... 140
357 Magnum or 9mm Luger, blued finish............. 140
357 Magnum, stainless steel......................... 190

Ruger Police Service-Six, stainless steel

Ruger Police Service-Six
Same general specifications as Speed-Six, except has square butt: stainless steel models and 9mm Luger caliber available only with 4-inch barrel. Made from 1973 to date.
38 Special, blued finish............................**$115**
38 Special, stainless steel........................... 140
357 Magnum or 9mm Luger, blued finish............. 140
357 Magnum, stainless steel......................... 190

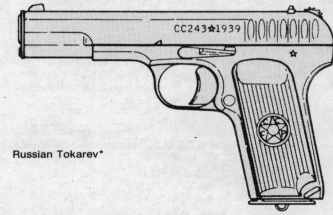

Russian Tokarev*

Russian Service Pistol manufactured by Government plants at Tula and elsewhere

Russian Model 30 Tokarev Service Automatic Pistol...$225
Modified Colt-Browning type. Caliber, 7.62mm Russian Automatic (also uses 7.63mm Mauser Automatic cartridge). 8-shot magazine. 4½-inch barrel. 7¾ inches overall. Weight, about 29 ounces. Fixed sights. Made from 1930 to mid-1950's. *Note:* A slightly modified version with improved locking system and different disconnector was adopted in 1933. Tokarev-type pistols also have been made in Hungary, Poland, Yugoslavia, People's Republic of China and North Korea.

Sauer Model 1913*

Sauer Pistols manufactured prior to and during World War II by J. P. Sauer & Sohn, Suhl, Germany

Sauer Model 1913 Pocket Automatic Pistol.... $160
Caliber, 32 Automatic (7.65mm). 7-shot magazine. 3-inch barrel. 5⅞ inches overall. Weight, 22 ounces. Fixed sights. Blued finish. Black hard rubber stocks. Made from 1913 to 1930.

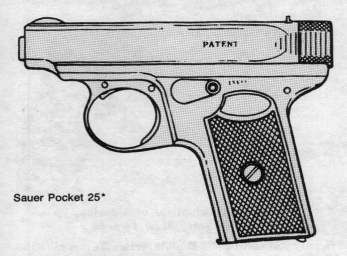

Sauer Pocket 25*

Sauer Pocket 25 Automatic Pistol............... $160
Smaller version of Model 1913, issued about same time as 32 caliber model. Caliber, 25 Automatic (6.35mm). 7-shot magazine. 2½-inch barrel. 4¼ inches overall. Weight, 14½ ounces. Fixed sights. Blued finish. Black hard rubber stocks. Made from 1913 to 1930.

Sauer Model 1930

Sauer Model 1930 Pocket Automatic Pistol..... $220
Authority Model (Behorden Modell). Successor to Model 1913, has improved grip and safety. Caliber, 32 Automatic (7.65mm). 7-shot magazine. 3-inch barrel. 5¾ inches overall. Weight, 22 ounces. Fixed sights. Blued finish. Black hard rubber stocks. Made from 1930 to 1938. *Note:* Some pistols of this model have indicator pin showing when cocked. Also manufactured with dural slide and receiver; this type weighs about ⅓ less than the standard model.

Sauer Model H

Sauer Model H Double Action Automatic Pistol. $225
Calibers: 25 Auto (6.35mm), 32 Auto (7.65mm), 380 Auto (9mm). Specifications shown are for 32 Auto model. 7-shot magazine. 3¼-inch barrel. 6¼ inches overall. Weight, 20 ounces. Fixed sights. Blued finish. Black plastic stocks. Also made in dural model weighing about ⅓ less. Made from 1938 to 1945. *Note:* This pistol, designated Model 38, was manufactured during World War II for military use. These wartime models are inferior to the earlier production, some lack safety lever.

Sauer Handguns currently manufactured by J. P. Sauer & Sohn GmbH, Eckernförde, West Germany

Sauer Single Action Revolvers
See listing under Hawes.

SIG-Sauer Model P220

SIG-Sauer Model P220 Double Action Automatic Pistol... $340
Calibers: 22 Long Rifle, 7.65mm Luger, 9mm Luger, 38 Super, 45 Automatic. 10-shot magazine in 22, 7-shot in 45, 9-shot in other calibers. 4.4-inch barrel. 7.8 inches overall. Weight, in 9mm, 26.5 ounces. Fixed sights. Blued finish. Checkered plastic stocks. Made from 1976 to date. *Note:* Also sold in Untied States as Browning BDA.

SIG-Sauer Model P230

SIG-Sauer Model P230 Double Action Automatic Pistol $290

Calibers: 22 Long Rifle, 32 Automatic (7.65mm), 380 Automatic (9mm Short), 9mm Police. 10-shot magazine in 22, 8-shot in 32, 7-shot in 9mm. 3.6-inch barrel. 6.6 inches overall. Weight, in 32 Automatic, 18.2 ounces. Fixed sights. Blued finish. Plastic stocks. Made from 1976 to date.

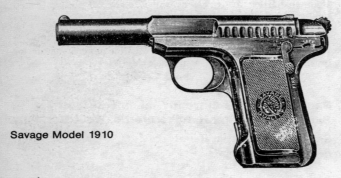

Savage Model 1910

Savage Arms Co., Utica, New York

Savage Model 1910 Automatic Pistol $145

Calibers: 32 Auto, 380 Auto. 10-shot magazine (32 cal.), 9-shot (380 cal.), 3¾-inch barrel (32 cal.), 4½-inch (380 cal.), 6½ inches overall (32 cal.), 7 inch (380 cal.). Weight, about 23 ounces. Fixed sight. Blued finish. Hard rubber stocks. *Note:* This model was made in hammerless type with grip safety as well as with exposed hammer spur. Made from 1910 to 1917.

Savage Model 1917*

Savage Model 1917 Automatic Pistol $175

Same specifications as 1910 Model, except has spur-type hammer and redesigned heavier grip. Made from 1917 to 1928.

Savage Model 101

Savage Model 101 Single Action Single Shot Pistol $100

Barrel integral with swing-out cylinder. Caliber, 22 Short, Long, Long Rifle. 5½-inch barrel. Weight, 20 ounces. Blade front sight, slotted rear sight adjustable for windage. Blued finish. Grips of compressed, impregnated wood. Made from 1960 to 1968.

Security Model PSS38

Security Industries of America, Little Ferry, New Jersey

Security Model PSS38 Double Action Revolver. $155

Caliber, 38 Special. 5-shot cylinder. 2-inch barrel. 6½ inches overall. Weight, 18 ounces. Fixed sights. Stainless steel. Walnut stocks. Introduced in 1973. Discontinued.

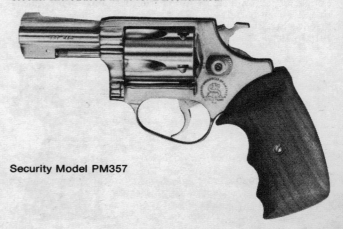

Security Model PM357

Security Model PM357 Double Action Revolver. $180

Caliber, 357 Magnum. 5-shot cylinder. 2½-inch barrel. 7½ inches overall. Weight, 21 ounces. Fixed sights. Stainless steel. Walnut stocks. Introduced in 1975. Discontinued.

Security Model PPM357

Security Model PPM357 Double Action Revolver...$180

Caliber, 357 Magnum, 5-shot cylinder. 2-inch barrel. 6⅛ inches overall. Weight, 18 ounces. Fixed sights. Stainless steel. Walnut stocks. Made from 1976 to date. *Note:* Spurless hammer (illustrated) was discontinued in 1977; this model now has the same conventional hammer as in other Security revolvers.

R. F. Sedgley, Inc., Philadelphia, Pennsylvania

Sedgley Baby Hammerless Ejector Double Action Revolver...$130

Solid frame. Folding trigger. Caliber, 22 Long. 6-shot cylinder. 4 inches overall. Weight, 6 ounces. Fixed sights. Blued or nickel finish. Rubber stocks. Made c. 1930 to 1939.

Sheridan Knocabout

Sheridan Products, Inc., Racine, Wisconsin

Sheridan Knocabout Single Shot Pistol.........$ 70

Tip-up type. Caliber, 22 Long Rifle, Long, Short. 5-inch barrel. 6¾ inches overall. Weight, 24 ounces. Fixed sights. Checkered plastic stocks. Blued finish. Made from 1953 to 1960.

SIG Schweizerische Industrie-Gesellschaft, Neuhausen am Rheinfall, Switzerland

SIG Model P210-1 Automatic Pistol............$700

Calibers: 22 Long Rifle, 7.65mm Luger, 9mm Luger. 8-shot magazine. 4¾-inch barrel. 8½ inches overall. Weights: 33 ounces in 22 caliber, 35 ounces in 7.65mm and 9mm. Fixed sights. Polished blued finish. Checkered wood stocks. Made from 1949 to date.

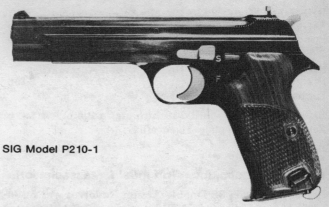

SIG Model P210-1

SIG Model P210-2...............................$700

Same as Model P210-1, except has sandblasted finish, plastic stocks; not available in 22 Long Rifle.

SIG Model P210-5 Target Pistol.................$975

Same as Model P210-2, except has 6-inch barrel, micrometer adjustable rear sight, target front sight, adjustable trigger stop. 9.7 inches overall. Weight, about 38.3 ounces. Discontinued.

SIG Model P210-6

SIG Model P210-6 Target Pistol.................$975

Same as Model P210-2, except has micrometer adjustable rear sight, target front sight, adjustable trigger stop. Weight, about 37 ounces.

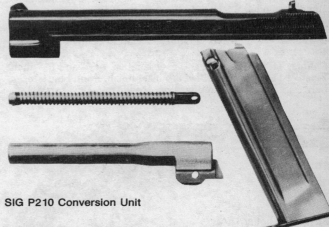

SIG P210 Conversion Unit

SIG P210 22 Conversion Unit....................$300

Converts P210 pistol to 22 Long Rifle. Consists of barrel with recoil spring, slide and magazine.

SIG-Sauer Model P220 Double Action Automatic Pistol... $450
For data see listing under Sauer. *Note:* Also sold in United States as Browning BDA.

SIG-Sauer Model P230 Double Action Automatic Pistol... $400
For data see listing under Sauer.

SIG-Hämmerli Model P240 Automatic Pistol.... $975
For data see listing under Hämmerli.

Smith & Wesson, Inc., Springfield, Massachusetts

Smith & Wesson 38 Double Action Revolver..... $650
Hinged frame. Caliber, 38 S&W. 5-shot cylinder. Barrel lengths: 4¼-, 4-, 5-, 6-, 8- and 10-inch. Fixed sights. Blued or nickel finish. Hard rubber stocks. Made from 1880 to 1911. *Note:* Value shown applies generally to the several varieties. Exceptions are the first issue of 1880 (identified by squared side plate and serial number 1 to 4000) and the 8- and 10-inch barrel models of the third issue (1884-1895), which bring about $300.

Smith & Wesson Perfected Model 38 Double Action Revolver.. $475
Hinged frame. Similar to earlier 38 Double Action Model, but heavier frame, side latch as in solid frame models, improved lockwork. Caliber, 38 S&W. 5-shot cylinder. Barrel lengths: 3¼-, 4-, 5- and 6-inch. Fixed sights. Blued or nickel finish. Hard rubber stocks. Made from 1909 to 1920.

Smith & Wesson 32 Double Action Revolver..... $205
Hinged frame. Caliber, 32 S&W. 5-shot cylinder. Barrel lengths: 3-, 3½- and 6-inch. Fixed sights. Blued or nickel finish. Hard rubber stocks. Made from 1880 to 1919. *Note:* Value shown applies generally to the several varieties. Exception is the very rare first issue of 1880 (identified by squared side plate and serial number 1 to 30); value, $2000.

Smith & Wesson No. 3 Single Action (New Model) Revolver.. $1000
Hinged frame. 6-shot cylinder. Caliber, 44 S&W Russian. Barrel lengths: 4-, 5-, 6-, 6½-, 7½- and 8-inch. Fixed or target sights. Blued or nickel finish. Round buttstocks, hard rubber or checkered walnut. Made from 1878 to 1908. *Note:* Value shown is for standard model. Specialist collectors recognize numerous variations with a wide range of higher values.

Smith & Wesson No. 3 Single Action (Frontier) Revolver.. $950
Caliber, 44-40 Winchester. Barrel lengths: 4-, 5- and 6½-inch. Fixed or target sights. Blued or nickel finish. Round buttstocks, hard rubber or checkered walnut. Made from 1885 to 1908.

S&W 44 Frontier D.A.

Smith & Wesson No 3 Single Action Target Revolver.. $1200
Hinged frame. 6-shot cylinder. Calibers: 32/44 S&W, 38/44 S&W Gallery & Target. 6½-inch barrel only. Fixed or target sights. Blued or nickel finish. Round buttstocks, hard rubber or checkered walnut. Made from 1887 to 1910.

Smith & Wesson 44 Double Action Revolver
Also called Wesson Favorite (lightweight model), Frontier (caliber 44-40). Hinged frame. 6-shot cylinder. Calibers: 44 S&W Russian, 38-40, 44-40. Barrel lengths: 4-, 5-, 6- and 6½-inch. Weight, with 6½-inch barrel, 37½ ounces. Fixed sights. Blued or nickel finish. Hard rubber stocks. Made from 1881 to 1913, except "Frontier" which was discontinued in 1910.
Standard Model, 44 Russian........................ $ 700
Standard Model, 38-40............................. 1200
Frontier Model.................................... 550
Favorite Model.................................... 2000

S&W Safety Hammerless

Smith & Wesson Safety Hammerless Revolver.. $340
Also called New Departure Double Action. Hinged frame. Calibers: 32 S&W, 38 S&W. 5-shot cylinder. Barrel lengths: 32 cal.—2-, 3- and 3½-inch; 38 cal.—2-, 3¼-, 4-, 5- and 6-inch. Length overall: 32 cal. with 3-inch barrel—6¾ inches; 38 cal. with 3¼-inch barrel—7½ inches. Weights: 32 cal. with 3-inch barrel—14¼ ounces; 38 cal. with 3¼-inch barrel—18¼ ounces. Fixed sights. Blued or nickel finish. Hard rubber stocks. 32 cal. made from 1888 to 1937, 38 cal. from 1887 to 1941. Various minor changes.

Smith & Wesson Model 1891 Single Action Revolver
Hinged frame. Caliber, 38 S&W. 5-shot cylinder. Barrel lengths: 3¼-, 4-, 5- and 6-inch. Fixed sights. Blued or nickel finish. Hard rubber stocks. Made 1891 to 1911. *Note:* Until 1906, an accessory single-shot target barrel (see Model 1891 Single Shot Target Pistol) was available for this revolver.
Revolver only..................................... $ 505
Set with 22 single-shot barrel.................... 1015

S&W Model 1891 Single Shot

Smith & Wesson Model 1891 Single Shot Target Pistol, First Model
Hinged frame. Calibers: 22 Long Rifle, 32 S&W, 38 S&W. Barrel lengths: 6-, 8- and 10-inch. Approximately 13½ inches overall with 10-inch barrel. Weight, about 25 ounces. Target sights, barrel catch rear sight adjustable for windage and elevation.

Blued finish. Square butt, hard rubber stocks. Made from 1893 to 1905. *Note:* This model was available also as a combination arm with accessory 38 revolver barrel and cylinder to convert the single-shot target pistol to a pocket revolver. It has the frame of the 38 Single Action Revolver Model 1891 with side flanges, hand and cylinder stop slots.

Single-shot pistol, 22 Long Rifle	$ 340
Single-shot pistol, 32 S&W or 38 S&W	1000
Combination set, revolver and single-shot barrel	945

Smith & Wesson Model 1891 Single Shot Target Pistol, Second Model..................................$340
Basically the same as the First Model, except side flanges, hand and stop slots eliminated, cannot be converted to revolver, redesigned rear sight. Caliber, 22 Long Rifle only. 10-inch barrel only. Made from 1905 to 1909.

Smith & Wesson Perfected Single Shot Target Pistol
Also called Olympic Model (see note below). Similar to 1891 Single Shot Second Model except has double-action lockwork. Caliber, 22 Long Rifle only. 10-inch barrel. Checkered walnut stocks, extended square butt target type. Made from 1909 to 1923. *Note:* In 1920 and thereafter, pistols of this model were made with barrels having bore diameter of .223 instead of .226 and tight, short chambering. The first of these pistols were produced for the U.S. Olympic Team of 1920 and, therefore, the designation Olympic Model was adopted.

Pre-1920 Type	$400
Olympic Model	550

Smith & Wesson Model I

Smith & Wesson Model I Hand Ejector Double Action Revolver..$465
First Model. Forerunner of the current 32 Hand Ejector and Regulation Police models, this was the first S&W revolver of the solid-frame, swing-out cylinder type. Top strap of this model is longer than later models and it lacks the usual S&W cylinder latch. Caliber, 32 S&W Long. Barrel lengths: 3¼-, 4¼-, and 6-inch. Fixed sights. Blued or nickel finish. Round butt, hard rubber stocks. Made from 1896 to 1903.

S&W Model 30

Smith & Wesson Model 30 32 Hand Ejector Double Action Revolver...................................$200
Caliber, 32 S&W Long. 6-shot cylinder. Barrel lengths: 2- (introduced 1949), 3-, 4- and 6-inch. 8 inches overall with 4-inch

barrel. Weight, 18 ounces with 4-inch barrel. Fixed sights. Blued or nickel finish. Checkered walnut or hard rubber stocks, round butt. Made from 1903 to 1976. Numerous changes, mostly minor, as in M & P model.

S&W Model 31

Smith & Wesson Models 31 & 33 Regulation Police Double Action Revolver.........................$200
Same basic type as 32 Hand Ejector, except has square butt stocks. Calibers: 32 S&W Long (Model 31), 38 S&W (Model 33). 6-shot cylinder in 32 caliber, 5-shot in 38 caliber. Barrel lengths: 2- (introduced 1949), 3-, 4- and 6-inch in 32 cal.; 4-inch only in 38 cal. 8½ inches overall with 4-inch barrel. Weights: 18 ounces in 38 cal. with 4-inch barrel, 32 cal. ¾-ounce heavier. Fixed sights. Blued or nickel finish. Checkered walnut stocks. Made from 1917 to date; Model 33 discontinued in 1974.

S&W Regulation Police Target

Smith & Wesson Regulation Police Target Double Action Revolver....................................$215
Target version of the Regulation Police with standard features of that model. Caliber, 32 S&W Long. 6-inch barrel. 10¼ inches overall. Weight, 20 ounces. Adjustable target sights. Blued finish. Checkered walnut stocks. Made from about 1917 to 1940.

S&W Model 32

S&W Model 36

Smith & Wesson Model 32 Terrier Double Action Revolver...$225
Caliber, 38 S&W. 5-shot cylinder. 2-inch barrel. 6¼ inches overall. Weight, 17 ounces. Fixed sights. Blued or nickel finish. Checkered walnut or hard rubber stocks. Built on 32 Hand Ejector frame. Made from 1936 to 1974.

Smith & Wesson Model 36 Chiefs Special Double Action Revolver.......................................$175

Based on 32 Hand Ejector with frame lengthened to permit longer cylinder necessary for 38 Special cartridge. Caliber, 38 Special. 5-shot cylinder. Barrel lengths: 2- or 3-inch. Overall length, with 2-inch bbl., 6½ inches. Weight, 19 ounces. Fixed sights. Blued or nickel finish. Checkered walnut stocks, round or square butt. Made from 1952 to date.

Smith & Wesson Model 37 Airweight Chiefs Special..$195

Same general specifications as standard Chiefs Special, except has light alloy frame, weighs 12½ ounces with 2-inch bbl., blued finish only. Made from 1954 to date.

S&W Model 60

Smith & Wesson Model 60 38 Chiefs Special Stainless...$300

Same as standard Chiefs special, except satin-finished stainless steel: 2-inch barrel only. Made from 1965 to date.

S&W Model 38

S&W Model 40

Smith & Wesson Model 40 Centennial Double Action Hammerless Revolver...........................$325

Similar to Chiefs Special, but has Safety Hammerless type mechanism with grip safety. 2-inch barrel. Weight, 19 ounces. Made from 1953 to 1974.

Smith & Wesson Model 42 Centennial Airweight..$350

Same as standard Centennial model except has light alloy frame, weighs 13 ounces. Made from 1954 to 1974.

Smith & Wesson Model 38 Bodyguard Airweight Double Action Revolver.............................. $225

"Shrouded" hammer. Light alloy frame. Caliber, 38 Special. 5-shot cylinder. 2-inch barrel. 6⅜ inches overall. Weight, 14½ ounces. Fixed sights. Blued or nickel finish. Checkered walnut stocks. Made from 1955 to date.

Smith & Wesson Model 49 Bodyguard.......... $190

Same as Model 38 Bodyguard Airweight, except has steel frame, weighs 20½ ounces. Made from 1959 to date.

S&W 22/32 Target

Smith & Wesson 22/32 Target Double Action Revolver...$450

Also known as the Bekeart Model. Design based upon "32 Hand Ejector." Caliber, 22 Long Rifle (recessed head cylinder for high speed cartridges introduced 1935). 6-shot cylinder. 6-inch barrel. 10½ inches overall. Weight, 23 ounces. Adjustable target sights. Blued finish. Checkered walnut stocks. Made from 1911 to 1953. *Note:* In 1911, San Francisco gun dealer Phil Bekeart, who suggested this model, received 292 pieces. These are the true "Bekeart Model" revolvers worth about double the value shown for the standard 22/32 Target.

S&W Model 35

Smith & Wesson Model 35 1953 22/32 Target... $300

Same general specifications as previous model 22/32 Target, except has new micrometer click rear sight, Magna-type target stocks, weighs 25 ounces. Made from 1953 to 1974.

S&W 22/32 Kit Gun

Smith & Wesson 22/32 Kit Gun................. $215

Same as 22/32 Target, except has 4-inch barrel and round buttstocks. 8 inches overall. Weight, 21 ounces. Made from 1935 to 1953.

S&W Model 34

Smith & Wesson Model 34 1953 22/32 Kit Gun.. $190

Same general specifications as previous model Kit Gun, except furnished in choice of 2-inch or 4-inch barrel and round or square buttstocks, blue or nickel finish. Made from 1953 to date.

S&W Model 43

Smith & Wesson Model 43 1955 22/32 Kit Gun Airweight...$300

Same as Model 34 Kit Gun, except has light alloy frame, furnished with 3½-inch barrel only, weighs 14¼ ounces, square buttstock. Made from 1954 to 1974.

S&W Model 51

Smith & Wesson Model 51 1960 22/32 Kit Gun M.R.F...$325

Same as Model 34 Kit Gun, except chambered for 22 Winchester Magnum Rim Fire; has 3½-inch barrel, weighs 24 ounces. Made from 1960 to 1974.

Smith & Wesson Ladysmith (Model M Hand Ejector) Double Action Revolver

Caliber, 22 Long Rifle. 7-shot cylinder. Barrel lengths: 2¼-, 3-, 3½- and 6-inch (Third Model only). Approximately 7 inches overall with 3½-inch barrel. Weight, about 9½ ounces. Fixed sights, adjustable target sights were available on Third Model. Blued or nickel finish. Round butt, hard rubber stocks on First and Second Model; Checkered walnut or hard rubber square buttstocks on Third Model. First Model—1902 to 1906: cylinder locking bolt operated by button on left side of frame, no barrel lug and front locking bolt. Second Model—1906 to 1911: rear

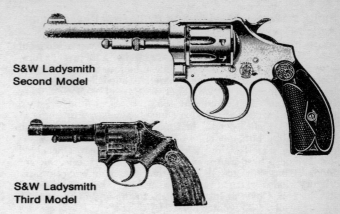

S&W Ladysmith
Second Model

S&W Ladysmith
Third Model

cylinder latch eliminated, has barrel lug, forward cylinder lock with draw-bolt fastening. Third Model—1911 to 1921: same as Second Model except has square buttstocks, target sights and 6-inch barrel available. *Note:* Legend has it that a straight-laced D. B. Wesson ordered discontinuance of the Ladysmith when he learned of the little revolver's reputed popularity with ladies of the evening. The story, which undoubtedly has enhanced the appeal of this model to collectors, is not true: Wesson Ladysmith was discontinued because of difficulty of manufacture and high frequency of repairs.

First Model...	$ 715
Second Model...	610
Third Model, fixed sights, 3- or 3½-inch barrel.......	535
Third Model, fixed sights, 2¼- or 6-inch barrel.......	1000
Third Model, adjustable sights, 6-inch barrel.........	1000

Smith & Wesson Model 38 Hand Ejector Double Action Revolver...$600

Military & Police—First Model. Resembles Colt New Navy in general appearance, lacks barrel lug and locking bolt common to all later S&W hand ejector models. Caliber 38 Long Colt. 6-shot cylinder. Barrel lengths: 4-, 5-, 6- and 6½-inch. 11½ inches overall with 6½-inch barrel. Fixed sights. Blued or nickel finish. Checkered walnut or hard rubber stocks, round butt. Made from 1899 to 1902.

S&W Military & Police
Model of 1905

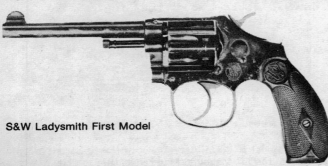

S&W Ladysmith First Model

S&W Model 10 Round Butt

Smith & Wesson Model 10 38 Military & Police Double Action Revolver

Also called Hand Ejector Model of 1902, Hand Ejector Model of 1905, Model K. Manufactured substantially in its present form since 1902, this model has undergone numerous changes, most of them minor. Both round and square butt models available, the latter introduced in 1904. Caliber, 38 Special. 6-shot cylinder. Barrel lengths: 2- (introduced 1933), 4-, 5-, 6- and 6½-inch (latter discontinued 1915), also 4-inch heavy barrel (introduced 1957). 11⅛ inches overall in square butt model with 6-inch barrel. Round butt model is ¼-inch shorter, weighs about ½-ounce less. Fixed sights. Blued or nickel finish. Checkered walnut stocks, hard rubber available in round butt style. Current Model 10 has short action. Made from 1902 to date. *Note:* S&W Victory Model, wartime version of the M & P 38, was produced for the U.S. Government from 1940 to the end of the war. A similar revolver, designated 38/200 British Service Revolver, was produced for the British Government during the same period. These arms have either brush-polish or sand-blast blue finish, and most of them have plain, smooth walnut stocks and lanyard swivels.

Model of 1902 (1902-1905)............................. $360
Model of 1905 (1905-1940)............................. 290
38/200 British Service (1940-1945).................... 220
Victory Model (1942-1945)............................. 220
Model of 1944 (1945-1948)............................. 195
Model 10 (1948-date)................................. 180

Smith & Wesson Military & Police 32-20 Double Action Revolver

Same as M & P 38, except chambered for 32-20 Winchester cartridge. First introduced in the 1899 model, M & P Revolvers were produced in this caliber until about 1940. Values same as for corresponding M & P 38 models.

S&W Model 12

Smith & Wesson Model 12 38 Military & Police Airweight...................................$170

Same as standard Military & Police, except has light alloy frame, furnished with 2- or 4-inch barrel only, weighs 18 ounces (with 2-inch barrel). Made from 1952 to date.

S&W Model 58

Smith & Wesson Model 58 41 Military & Police Double Action Revolver...................................$270

Caliber, 41 Magnum. 6-shot cylinder. 4-inch barrel. Overall length, 9¼ inches. Weight, 41 ounces. Fixed sights. Checkered walnut stocks. Made from 1964 to date.

S&W Model 64

Smith & Wesson Model 64 38 Military & Police Stainless...$215

Same as standard Model 10, except satin-finished stainless steel; available in square butt type with 4-inch heavy barrel, round butt type with 2-inch barrel. Made from 1970 to date.

S&W Model 10 Heavy Barrel

Smith & Wesson Model 10 38 Military & Police Heavy Barrel...$155

Same as standard Model 10, except has heavy 4-inch barrel, weighs 34 ounces. Made from 1957 to date.

S&W Model 13

Smith & Wesson Model 13 357 Military & Police...$180

Same as Model 10 38 Military & Police Heavy Barrel, except chambered for 357 Magnum. Made from 1974 to date.

S&W Model 65

Smith & Wesson Model 65 357 Military & Police Stainless..$190

Same as Model 13, except satin-finished stainless steel. Made from 1974 to date.

S&W 38 M&P Target

Smith & Wesson 38 Military & Police Target Double Action Revolver

Target version of the Military & Police with standard features of that model. Caliber, 38 Special. 6-inch barrel. Weight, 32¼ ounces. Adjustable target sights. Blued finish. Checkered walnut stocks. Made from 1899 to 1940. For values, add $50 to those shown for corresponding M&P 38 models.

Smith & Wesson K-32 Target Double Action Revolver...$700

Same as 38 Military & Police Target, except chambered for 32 S&W Long cartridge, slightly heavier barrel. Weight, 34 ounces. Only 98 produced. Made from 1938 to 1940.

S&W K-22 Outdoorsman

Smith & Wesson K-22 Outdoorsman Double Action Revolver.......................................$390

Design based upon the 38 Military & Police Target. Caliber, 22 Long Rifle. 6-shot cylinder barrel. 11⅛ inches overall. Weight, 35 ounces. Adjustable target sights. Blued finish. Checkered walnut stock. Made from 1931 to 1940.

Smith & Wesson K-22 Masterpiece Double Action Revolver...$595

Improved version of K-22 Outdoorsman with same specifications but with micrometer click rear sight, short action and anti-backlash trigger. Manufactured 1940.

S&W Model 17

Smith & Wesson Models 17 (K22), 48 (K22-MRF), 16 (K32) and 14 (K38) Masterpiece Double Action Revolvers

Calibers: 22 Long Rifle, 22 Magnum Rim Fire, 32 S&W Long, 38 Special. 6-shot cylinder. Barrel lengths: 4- (22 MRF only), 6-, 8⅜-inch (latter not available in K32). 11⅛ inches overall (6-inch bbl.). Weight, 38½ ounces (K22 with 6-inch bbl.). Click adjustable rear sights, Partridge front sight. Blued finish. Checkered walnut stocks. Made from 1947 to date. (Model 16 discontinued 1974; only 3630 were produced.)

Model 17 or 14.......................................$175
Model 48.. 200
Above with 8⅜-inch barrel, add...................... 5
Model 16.. 250

Smith & Wesson K32 and K38 Heavy Masterpiece Double Action Revolvers

Same as K32 and K38 Masterpiece, but with heavy weight barrel. Weight, 38½ ounces. Made from 1950 to 1953. *Note:* All K32 and K38 revolvers made after September 1953 have heavy barrels and the "Heavy Masterpiece" designation was discontinued. Values for Heavy Masterpiece models are the same as shown for Models 14 and 16.

S&W Model 15

Smith & Wesson Models 18(22) and 15(38) Combat Masterpiece Double Action Revolvers

Same as K22 and K38 Masterpiece but with 2- (38) or 4-inch barrel and Baughman quick-draw front sight. 9⅛ inches overall (with 4-inch barrel). Weight, 34 ounces in 38 cal. Made from 1950 to date.

Model 18..$180
Model 15.. 195

S&W Model 14 Single Action

Smith & Wesson Model 14 K38 Masterpiece Single Action

Same as standard Model 14, except single action only, with target hammer and trigger.

With 6-inch barrel................................... **$175**
With 8⅜-inch barrel................................. **180**

S&W Model 67

Smith & Wesson Model 67 38 Combat Masterpiece Stainless..$190

Same as Model 15, except satin-finished stainless steel; available only with 4-inch barrel. Made from 1972 to date.

S&W Model 53

Smith & Wesson Model 53 22 Magnum Double Action Revolver...$475

Caliber, 22 Remington Jet C.F. Magnum. 6-shot cylinder (inserts permit use of 22 Short, Long, or L.R. cartridges). Barrel lengths: 4-, 6-, 8⅜-inches. Overall length (with 6-inch barrel), 11¼ inches. Weight (with 6-inch barrel), 40 ounces. Micrometer click rear sight, ramp front sight. Checkered walnut stocks. Made from 1960 to 1974.

Smith & Wesson New Century Model Hand Ejector Double Action Revolver..........................$570

Also called "Triple Lock" because of its third cylinder lock at the crane. 6-shot cylinder. Calibers: 44 S&W Special, 450 Eley, 455

Mark II. Barrel lengths: 4-, 5-, 6½- and 7½-inch. Weight, with 6½-inch barrel, 39 ounces. Fixed sights. Blued or nickel finish. Checkered walnut stocks. Made from 1907 to 1915.

S&W 44 Hand Ejector Second Model

Smith & Wesson 44 Hand Ejector Second Model Double Action Revolver..................................$750

Basically the same as "New Century," except crane lock ("Triple Lock" feature) and extractor rod casing eliminated. Calibers: 44 S&W Special, 44-40 Winchester, 45 Colt. Barrel lengths: 4-, 5-, 6½- and 7½-inch. 11¾ inches overall with 6½-inch barrel. Weight, 38 ounces with 6½-inch barrel. Fixed sights. Blued or nickel finish. Checkered walnut stocks. Made from 1915 to 1937.

Smith & Wesson 1917 Army Double Action Revolver

Caliber, 45 Automatic, using 3-cartridge half-moon clip; 45 Auto Rim, without clip. 6-shot cylinder. 5½-inch barrel. 10¾ inches overall. Weight, 36¼ ounces. Fixed sights. Blued finish (blue-black finish on commercial model, brush polish on military). Checkered walnut stocks (commercial model, smooth on military). Made under U.S. Government contract from 1917 to 1919; produced commercially from 1919 to 1941. *Note:* About 175,000 of these revolvers were produced during World War I. The DCM sold these to NRA members during the 1930's at $16.15 each.

Commercial model................................... **$400**
Military model... **325**

S&W Model 22

Smith & Wesson Model 22 1950 Army Double Action Revolver..$440

Postwar version of the 1917 Army. Same specifications as that model. Redesigned hammer. Made from 1950 to 1967.

Smith & Wesson 1926 Model 44 Military Double Action Revolver..$600

Basically the same as the early "New Century" model, having the extractor rod casing but lacking the "Triple Lock" feature. Caliber, 44 S&W Special. 6-shot cylinder. Barrel lengths: 4-, 5- and 6½-inch. 11¾ inches overall with 6½-inch barrel. Weight, 39½ ounces with 6½-inch barrel. Fixed sights. Blued or nickel finish. Checkered walnut stocks. Made from 1926 to 1941.

S&W Model 21

S&W Model 23

Smith & Wesson Model 21 1950 44 Military Double Action Revolver $360

Postwar version of the 1926 Model 44 Military. Same specifications as that model. Redesigned hammer. Made from 1950 to 1967.

Smith & Wesson 1926 Model 44 Target Double Action Revolver $500

Target version of the 1926 Model 44 Military. 6½-inch barrel only. Target sights. Blued finish only. Made from 1926 to 1941.

Smith & Wesson Model 23 38/44 Outdoorsman Double Action Revolver $450

Target version of the 38/44 Heavy Duty. 6½-inch barrel only. Weight, 41¾ ounces. Target sights, micrometer click rear on postwar models. Blued finish only. 1950 model has ribbed barrel, redesigned hammer. Made from 1930 to 1967.

Pre-War:	$525
Post-War:	450

S&W Model 24

S&W Model 27

S&W Model 28

Smith & Wesson Model 24 1950 44 Target Double Action Revolver $490

Postwar version of the 1926 Model 44 Target with same general specifications, except has redesigned hammer, ribbed barrel, micrometer click rear sight. Made from 1950 to 1967.

Smith & Wesson Model 25 1950 45 Target Double Action Revolver $450

Same as 1950 Model 44 Target but chambered for 45 Automatic cartridge. Made from 1950 to date.

S&W Model 20

Smith & Wesson Model 20 38/44 Heavy Duty Double Action Revolver

Caliber, 38 Special (especially designed for high speed ammunition). 6-shot cylinder. Barrel lengths: 4-, 5- and 6½-inch. 10⅜ inches overall with 5-inch barrel. Weight, 40 ounces with 5-inch barrel. Fixed sights. Blued or nickel finish. Checkered walnut stocks. Short action after 1948. Made from 1930 to 1967.

Pre-World War II	$400
Post-War	300

Smith & Wesson Model 27 357 Magnum Double Action Revolver

Caliber, 357 S&W Magnum. 6-shot cylinder. Barrel lengths: 3½-, 5-, 6-, 6½- and 8⅜-inch. 11⅜ inches overall with 6-inch barrel. Weight, 44 ounces with 6-inch barrel. Adjustable target sights, Baughman quick-draw ramp front sight on 3½-inch barrel. Blued or nickel finish. Checkered walnut stocks. Made from 1935 to date. *Note:* Until 1938, the 357 Magnum was custom made in any barrel length from 3½-inch to 8¾-inch; each of these revolvers was accompanied by a registration certificate and has its registration number stamped on the inside of the yoke. Postwar Magnums have a redesigned hammer with shortened fall and the new S&W micrometer click rear sight.

Prewar registered model	$895
Prewar model without registration number	550
Current model with 8⅜-inch barrel	325
Current model, other barrel lengths	300

Smith & Wesson Model 28 Highway Patrolman Double Action Revolver $230

Caliber, 357 Magnum. 6-shot cylinder. Barrel lengths: 4- or 6-inch. Overall length, with 6-inch bbl., 11¼ inches. Weight with 6-inch bbl., 44 ounces. Adjustable rear sight, ramp front sight. Blued finish. Checkered walnut stocks, Magna or target type. Made from 1954 to date.

S&W Model 19

S&W Model 19
Round Butt

S&W Model 66

Blued or nickel finish. Target stocks of checkered Goncalo Alves.
Made from 1956 to date.
With 8⅜-inch barrel.................................... $345
Other barrel lengths.................................. 325

S&W Texas Ranger Commemorative

S&W Model 29

S&W Model 57

**Smith & Wesson Model 19 357 Combat Magnum Double
Action Revolver**.................................. **$230**
Caliber, 357 Magnum. 6-shot cylinder. Barrel lengths: 2½-, 4-,
6-inch. 9½ inches overall (4-inch bbl.). Weight, 35 ounces (4-
inch bbl.). Click adjustable rear sight, ramp front sight. Blued or
nickel finish. Target stocks of checkered Goncalo Alves. Model
with 2½-inch barrel has round butt. Made from 1956 to date.

**Smith & Wesson Model 66 357 Combat Magnum
Stainless**... **$340**
Same as Model 19, except satin-finished stainless steel. Made
from 1971 to date.

Smith & Wesson Texas Ranger Commemorative
.... **$575**
Issued to honor the 150th anniversary of the Texas Rangers.
Model 19 357 Combat Magnum with 4-inch barrel, sideplate
stamped with Texas Ranger Commemorative Seal, smooth Goncalo Alves stocks. Special Bowie knife. In presentation case. 8000
sets were made in 1973. Value is for set in new condition.

**Smith & Wesson Model 29 44 Magnum Double Action
Revolver**
Caliber, 44 Magnum. 6-shot cylinder. Barrel lengths: 4-, 6½-,
8⅜-inch. 11⅛ inches overall (6½-inch bbl.). Weight, 47 ounces
(6½-inch bbl.). Click adjustable rear sight, ramp front sight.

**Smith & Wesson Model 57 41 Magnum Double Action
Revolver**
Caliber, 41 Magnum. 6-shot cylinder. Barrel lengths: 4-, 6-, 8⅜-
inches. Weight (with 6-inch barrel), 40 ounces. Micrometer click
rear sight, ramp front sight. Target stocks of checkered Goncalo
Alves. made from 1964 to date.
With 8⅜-inch barrel.................................. $300
Other barrel lengths................................. 290

S&W 125th Anniversary
Commemorative, Standard Edition

S&W 125th Anniversary
Commemorative, Deluxe Edition

Smith & Wesson 125th Anniversary Commemorative
Issued to celebrate the 125th anniversary of the 1852 partnership of Horace Smith and Daniel Baird Wesson. Standard Edition is Model 25 revolver, caliber 45 Colt, with 6½-inch barrel, bright blued finish, gold-filled barrel roll mark "Smith & Wesson 125th Anniversary," sideplate marked with gold-filled Anniversary seal, smooth Goncalo Alves stocks, in presentation case with nickel silver Anniversary medallion and book, "125 Years with Smith & Wesson" by Roy Jinks. Deluxe Edition is same, except revolver is Class A engraved with gold-filled seal on sideplate, ivory stocks; Anniversary medallion is sterling silver and book is leather bound; limited to 50 units. Total issue is 10,000 units, of which 50 are Deluxe Edition and two are a Custom Deluxe Edition not for sale. Made in 1977. Values are for revolvers in new condition.

Standard Edition.................................. $ 495
Deluxe Edition.................................... 1500

Smith & Wesson 35 Automatic Pistol............ $800
Caliber, 35 S&W Automatic. 7-shot magazine. 3½-inch barrel (hinged to frame). 6½ inches overall. Weight, 25 ounces. Fixed sights. Blued or nickel finish. Plain walnut stocks. Made from 1913 to 1921.

S&W 35 Automatic

S&W 32 Automatic

Smith & Wesson 32 Automatic Pistol.......... $1200
Caliber, 32 Automatic. Same general specifications as 35 caliber model, but barrel is fastened to the receiver instead of hinged. Made from 1924 to 1937.

S&W Straight Line

Smith & Wesson Straight Line Single Shot Target Pistol.. $600
Frame shaped like that of an automatic pistol, barrel swings to the left on pivot for extracting and loading, straight line trigger and hammer movement. Caliber, 22 Long Rifle. 10-inch barrel. Approximately 11¼ inches overall. Weight, 34 ounces. Target sights. Blued finish. Smooth walnut stocks. Supplied in metal case with screwdriver and cleaning rod. Made from 1925 to 1936.

S&W Model 39

Smith & Wesson Model 39 9mm Double Action Automatic Pistol

Caliber, 9mm Luger. 8-shot magazine. 4-inch barrel. Overall length, 7-7/16 inches. Weight, 26½ ounces. Click adjustable rear sight, ramp front sight. Blued or nickel finish. Checkered walnut stocks. Made from 1954 to date. *Note:* Between 1954 and 1966, 927 pistols of this model were made with steel, instead of alloy, frames.

With steel frame.....................................**$750**
With alloy frame..................................**190**

S&W Model 59

Smith & Wesson Model 59 9mm Double Action Automatic Pistol......................................**$230**

Similar to Model 39 with same general specifications, except has 14-shot magazine, checkered nylon stocks. Made from 1971 to date.

S&W Model 52

Smith & Wesson Model 52 38 Master Automatic Pistol..**$420**

Caliber, 38 Special (mid-range wadcutter only). 5-shot magazine. 5-inch barrel. Overall length, 8⅝ inches. Weight, 41 ounces. Micrometer click rear sight, Patridge front sight on ramp base. Blued finish. Checkered walnut stocks. Made from 1961 to date.

Smith & Wesson Model 41 22 Automatic Pistol.. **$300**

Caliber: 22 Long Rifle, 22 Short (not interchangeably). 10-shot magazine. Barrel lengths: 5-, 5½-, 7⅜-inch; latter has detachable muzzle brake. 12 inches overall (7⅜-inch bbl.). Weight, 43½ ounces (7⅜-inch bbl.). Click adjustable rear sight, undercut Patridge front sight. Blued finish. Checkered walnut stocks with thumb-rest. Made from 1957 to date.

Smith & Wesson Model 46 22 Automatic Pistol.. **$400**

Caliber, 22 Long Rifle. 10-shot magazine. Barrel lengths: 5-, 5½-, 7-inch. 10-9/16 inches overall (7-inch bbl.). Weight, 42 ounces (7-inch bbl.). Click adjustable rear sight, under cut Patridge front sight. Blue finish. Molded nylon stocks with thumb-rest. Only 4000 produced. Made from 1957 to 1966.

S&W Model 41

S&W Model 46

S&W Model 61

Smith & Wesson Model 61 Escort Pocket Automatic Pistol...**$150**

Caliber, 22 Long Rifle. 5-shot magazine. 2⅛-inch barrel. 4-13/16 inches overall. Weight, 14 ounces. Fixed sights. Blued or nickel finish. Checkered plastic stocks. Made from 1970 to 1974.

Star Model H*

Star, Bonifacio Echeverria, S.A., Eibar, Spain

Star Model HN Automatic Pistol $135
Caliber, 380 Automatic (9mm Short). 6-shot magazine. 2¾-inch barrel. 5-9/16 inches overall. Weight, 20 ounces. Fixed sights. Blued finish. Plastic stocks. Made from 1934 to 1941.

Star Model H $135
Same as Model HN except caliber 32 Automatic (7.65mm). 7-shot magazine. Weight, 20 ounces. Made from 1934 to 1941.

Star Model I*

Star Model I Automatic Pistol $135
Caliber, 32 Automatic (7.65mm). 9-shot magazine. 4-13/16-inch barrel. 7½ inches overall. Weight, 24 ounces. Fixed sights. Blued finish. Plastic stocks. Made from 1934 to 1936.

Star Model IN $135
Same as Model I, except caliber 380 Automatic (9mm Short), 8-shot magazine, weighs 24½ ounces. Made from 1934 to 1936.

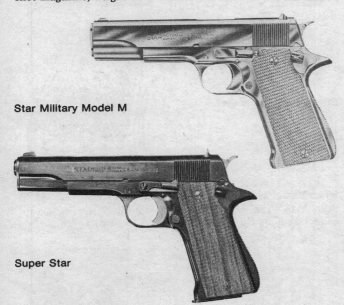

Star Military Model M

Super Star

Star Military Model M Automatic Pistol $185
Modification of the Colt Government Model 45 Auto, which it closely resembles; lacks grip safety. Calibers: 9mm Bergmann, 38 Super, 9mm Luger. 8-shot magazine, except 7-shot in 45 caliber. 5-inch barrel. 8½ inches overall. Weight, 36 ounces. Fixed sights. Blued finish. Checkered stocks. Made from 1934 to 1939.

Super Star Automatic Pistol $230
Improved version of the Model M with same general specifications; has disarming bolt permitting easier takedown, indicator of cartridge in chamber, magazine safety, takedown magazine, improved sights with luminous spots for aiming in darkness. Calibers: 38 Super, 9mm Luger. This is the standard service pistol of the Spanish Armed Forces, adopted 1946.

Super Star Target Model $260
Same as regular Super Star, except with adjustable target rear sight. Discontinued.

Star Model A Automatic Pistol $195
Modification of the Colt Government Model 45 Auto which it closely resembles; lacks grip safety. Caliber, 38 Super. 8-shot magazine. 5-inch barrel. 8-inches overall. Weight, 35 ounces. Fixed sights. Blued finish. Checkered stocks. Made from 1934 to date.

Star Model B $200
Same as Model A, except caliber 9mm Luger. Made from 1934 to 1975.

Star Model P $210
Same as Model A, except caliber 45 Automatic; has 7-shot magazine. Made from 1934 to 1975.

Star Models Super A, Super B, Super P $225
Same as Models A, B and P, except with improvements described under Super Star. Made from c. 1946 to date.

Star Model AS

Star Models AS, BS, PS $200
Same as Models A, B and P, except have magazine safety. Made from 1975 to date.

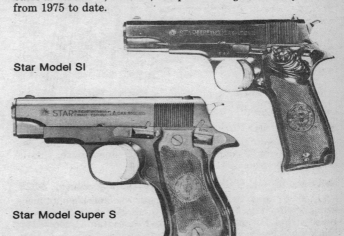

Star Model SI

Star Model Super S

Star Model SI Automatic Pistol.................. **$175**
Reduced-size modification of the Colt Government Model 45
Auto; lacks grip safety. Caliber, 32 Automatic (7.65mm). 8-shot
magazine. 4-inch barrel. 6½ inches overall. Weight, 20 ounces.
Fixed sights. Blued finish. Plastic stocks. Made from 1941 to
1965.

Star Model S....................................... **$190**
Same as Model SI except caliber 380 Automatic (9mm), 7-shot
magazine, weighs 19 ounces. Made from 1941 to 1965.

Star Models Super SI, Super S................... **$200**
Same general specifications as the regular Model SI and S,
except with improvements described under Super Star. Made
from c. 1946 to 1972.

Star Model Super SM

Star Model Super SM........................... **$200**
Similar to Model Super S, except has adjustable rear sight, wood
stocks. Made from 1973 to date.

Star Model CO*

Star Model CO Pocket Automatic Pistol........ **$135**
Caliber, 25 Automatic (6.35mm). 2¾-inch barrel. 4½ inches
overall. Weight, 13 ounces. Fixed sights. Blued finish. Plastic
stocks. Made from 1941 to 1957.

Star Model CU Starlet Pocket Automatic Pistol. $150
Light alloy frame. Caliber, 25 Automatic (6.35mm). 8-shot magazine. 2⅜-inch barrel. 4¾ inches overall. Weight, 10½ ounces.
Fixed sights. Blued or chrome-plated slide; frame anodized in
black, blue, green, gray or gold. Plastic stocks. Made from 1957
to date. U.S. importation discontinued in 1968.

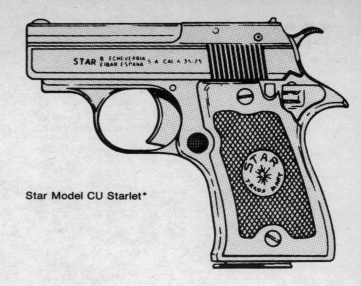

Star Model CU Starlet*

Star Starfire Automatic Pistol.................. **$175**
Light alloy frame. Caliber, 380 Automatic (9mm Short). 7-shot
magazine. 3⅛-inch barrel. 5½ inches overall. Weight, 14½
ounces. Fixed sights. Blued or chrome-plated slide; frame
anodized in black, blue, green, gray or gold. Plastic stocks. Made
from 1957 to date. U.S. importation discontinued in 1968.

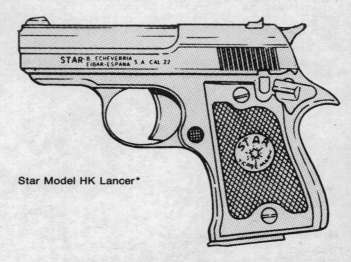

Star Model HK Lancer*

Star Model HK Lancer Automatic Pistol........ **$170**
Similar to Starfire with same general specifications, except
caliber 22 Long Rifle. Made from 1955 to 1968.

Star Model F

Star Model F Automatic Pistol.................. **$135**
Caliber, 22 Long Rifle. 10-shot magazine. 4½-inch barrel. 7¼ inches overall. Weight, 25 ounces. Fixed sights. Blued finish. Plastic stocks. Made from 1942 to 1967.

Star Model FS

Star Model FS..................................... **$140**
Same as regular Model F, but with 6-inch barrel and adjustable sights. Weighs 27 ounces. Made from 1942 to 1967.

Star Model F Olympic Rapid-Fire............... **$200**
Caliber, 22 Short. 9-shot magazine. 7-inch barrel. 11-1/16 inches overall. Weight, 52 ounces with weights. Adjustable target sight. Adjustable 3-piece barrel weight. Aluminum alloy slide. Muzzle brake. Plastic stocks. Made from 1942 to 1967.

Star Model FR..................................... **$145**
Similar to Model F with same general specifications, but restyled, has slide stop and adjustable rear sight. Made from 1967 to 1972.

Star Model FRS

Star Model FRS................................... **$145**
Same as Model FR, except has 6-inch barrel, weighs 28 ounces; also available in chrome finish. Made from 1967 to date.

Star Model FM

Star Model FM..................................... **$145**
Similar to Model FR, except has heavier frame with web in front of trigger guard, 4¼-inch heavy barrel; weighs 32 ounces. Made from 1972 to date.

Star Model BKS

Star Model BKS Starlight Automatic Pistol..... **$200**
Light alloy frame. Caliber, 9mm Luger. 8-shot magazine. 4¼-inch barrel. 7 inches overall. Weight, 25 ounces. Fixed sights. Blued or chrome finish. Plastic stocks. Made from 1970 to date.

Star Model BKM.................................. **$220**
Similar to Model BKS, except has 4-inch barrel, checkered backstrap, checkered walnut stocks. Made from 1976 to date.

Star Model PD

Star Model PD Automatic Pistol................. **$245**
Caliber, 45 Automatic. 6-shot magazine. 3¾-inch barrel. 7 inches overall. Weight, 25 ounces. Adjustable rear sight, ramp front sight. Blued finish. Checkered walnut stocks. Made from 1975 to date.

Stenda Pistol manufactured by Stenda-Werke, Suhl, Germany

Stenda Pocket Automatic Pistol.................. **$110**
Essentially the same as the Beholla; see listing of that pistol for specifications. Made circa 1920 to 1925. *Note:* This pistol may be marked "Beholla" along with the Stenda name and address.

Sterling Model 283

Sterling Model 284

Sterling Model 285

Sterling Model 286

Sterling Model PPL-22

Sterling Arms Corporation, Gasport, New York

Sterling Model 283 Target 300 Automatic Pistol **$145**
Caliber, 22 Long Rifle. 10-shot magazine. Barrel lengths: 4½-, 6-, 8-inch. 9 inches overall with 4½-inch barrel. Weight, with 4½-inch barrel, 36 ounces. Adjustable sights. Blued finish. Plastic stocks. Made from 1970 to 1971.

Sterling Model 284 Target 300L **$145**
Same as Model 283, except has 4½- or 6-inch "Luger"-type barrel. Made from 1970 to 1971.

Sterling Model 285 Husky **$130**
Same as Model 283, except has fixed sights, 4½-inch barrel only. Made from 1970 to 1971.

Sterling Model 286 Trapper **$130**
Same as Model 284, except has fixed sights. Made from 1970 to 1971.

Note: Total production of Models 283, 284, 285 and 286 was 2700 pieces.

Sterling Model PPL-22 Automatic Pistol **$130**
Caliber, 22 Long Rifle. 10-shot magazine. 1-inch barrel. 5½-inches overall. Weight, about 24 ounces. Fixed sights. Blued finish. Wood stocks. Made from 1970 to 1971. *Note:* Only 382 were produced.

Sterling Model 287 PPL-380 Automatic Pistol . . **$ 70**
Caliber, 380 Automatic. 6-shot magazine. 1-inch barrel. 5⅜ inches overall. Weight, 22½ ounces. Fixed sights. Blued finish. Plastic stocks. Made from 1971 to 1972.

Sterling Model 300

Sterling Model 300 Pocket Automatic Pistol.... $ 75
Caliber, 25 Automatic. 6-shot magazine. 2⅓-inch barrel. 4½ inches overall. Weight, 13 ounces. Fixed sights. Blued or nickel finish. Plastic stocks. Made from 1972 to date.

Sterling Model 300S............................. $ 90
Same as Model 300, except stainless steel. Made from 1976 to date.

Sterling Model 302.............................. $ 80
Same as Model 300, except caliber 22 Long Rifle. Made from 1973 to date.

Sterling Model 302S............................ $ 90
Same as Model 302, except stainless steel. Made from 1976 to date.

Sterling Model 400

Sterling Model 400 Double Action Automatic Pistol.. $150
Caliber, 380 Automatic. 7-shot magazine. 3½-inch barrel. 6½ inches overall. Weight, 24 ounces. Adjustable rear sight. Blued or nickel finish. Checkered walnut stocks. Made from 1975 to date.

Sterling Model 400S............................ $195
Same as Model 400, except stainless steel. Introduced in 1977.

Sterling Model 450

Sterling Model 450 Double Action Automatic Pistol.. $300
Caliber, 45 Automatic. 8-shot magazine. 4-inch barrel. 7½ inches overall. Weight, 36 ounces. Adjustable rear sight. Blued finish. Smooth walnut stocks. Introduced in 1977.

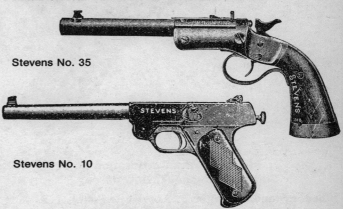

Stevens No. 35

Stevens No. 10

J. Stevens Arms Co., Chicopee Falls, Massachusetts

Stevens No. 35 Offhand Model Single Shot Target Pistol... $170
Tip-up action. Caliber, 22 Long Rifle. Barrel lengths: 6-, 8-, 10- and 12¼-inch. Weight, 24 ounces with 6-inch barrel. Target sights. Blued finish. Walnut stocks. *Note:* This pistol is similar to the earlier "Gould" model. No. 35 was also supplied chambered for 410 shotshell. Made from 1907 to 1939.

Stevens No. 10 Single Shot Target Pistol....... $180
Caliber, 22 Long Rifle. 8-inch barrel. 11½ inches overall. Weight, 37 ounces. Target sights. Blued finish. Hard rubber stocks. In external appearance this arm resembles an automatic pistol; it has a tip-up action. Made from 1919 to 1939.

Steyr-Hahn M12

Steyr-Hahn Pistol manufactured by Osterreichische Waffenfabrik-Gesellschaft, Steyr, Austria

Steyr-Hahn M12 Automatic Pistol............... $255
Caliber, 9mm Steyr. 8-shot fixed magazine, charger loaded. 5.1-inch barrel. 8.5 inches overall. Weight, 35 ounces. Fixed sights. Blued finish. Checkered wood stocks. Made from 1911 to 1919. Adopted by the Austro-Hungarian Army in 1912. *Note:* Confiscated by the Germans in 1938, an estimated 250,000 of these pistols were converted to 9mm Luger and stamped with an identifying "08" on the left side of the slide.

Stoeger Standard Luger

Taurus Model 80

Taurus Model 82

Stoeger Arms Corporation
South Hackensack, New Jersey

Stoeger Standard Luger 22 Automatic Pistol.... $145
Caliber, 22 Long Rifle. 10-shot magazine. Barrels: 4½-, 5½-inch.
8⅞ inches overall with 4½-inch barrel. Weight, with 4½-inch
barrel. Weight, with 4½-inch barrel, 29½ ounces. Fixed sights.
Black finish. Smooth wood stocks. Made from 1969 to date.

Stoeger Target Luger 22 Automatic Pistol...... $150
Same as Standard Luger 22, except has target sights: 9⅜ inches
overall with 4½-inch barrel. Checkered wood stocks. Made from
1975 to date.

Stoeger Steel Frame Luger 22 Automatic Pistol. $145
Caliber, 22 LR. 10-shot magazine. Barrel, 4½ inches; 8⅞ inches
overall. Blued finish. Checkered wood stocks. Features one-piece
solidly forged and machined steel frame. Made from 1980 to
date.

Taurus Model 80 Double Action Revolver....... $ 85
Caliber, 38 Special. 6-shot cylinder. Barrel lengths: 3-, 4-inch.
9¼ inches overall with 4-inch barrel. Weight, with 4-inch barrel,
30 ounces. Fixed sights. Blued or nickel finish. Checkered walnut
stocks. Made from 1971 to date.

Taurus Model 82 Heavy Barrel.................. $ 90
Same as Model 80, except has heavy barrel; weight, with 4-inch
barrel, 33 ounces. Made from 1971 to date.

Taurus Model 74

Taurus Model 84

Taurus Model 83

Taurus Revolvers manufactured by Forjas Taurus
S. A., Porto Alegre, Brazil

Taurus Model 74 Target Grade Double Action
Revolver.. $ 80
Caliber, 32 S&W Long. 6-shot cylinder. 3-inch barrel. 8¼ inches
overall. Weight, 20 ounces. Adjustable rear sight, ramp front
sight. Blued or nickel finish. Checkered walnut stocks. Made
from 1971 to date.

Taurus Model 94 Target Grade.................. $ 80
Same as Model 74, except caliber 22 Long Rifle, 4-inch barrel,
9¼ inches overall, weighs 23 ounces. Made from 1971 to date.

Taurus Model 84 Target Grade Revolver....... $100
Caliber, 38 Special. 6-shot cylinder. 4-inch barrel. 9¼ inches
overall. Weight, 31 ounces. Adjustable rear sight, ramp front
sight. Blued or nickel finish. Checkered walnut stocks. Made
from 1971 to date.

Taurus Model 83 Heavy Barrel Target Grade... $110
Same as Model 84, except has heavy barrel, weighs 34½ ounces. Introduced in 1977.

Taurus Model 86

Taurus Model 86 Target Master Double Action Revolver...................................**$125**
Caliber, 38 Special. 6-shot cylinder. 6-inch barrel. 11¼ inches overall. Weight, 34 ounces. Adjustable rear sight, Patridge-type front sight. Blued finish. Checkered walnut stocks. Made from 1971 to date.

Taurus Model 96 Target Master.................**$125**
Same as Model 86, except caliber 22 Long Rifle. Made from 1971 to date.

Thompson Model 27A-5
with drum magazine

Thompson Pistol manufactured by Auto-Ordnance Corporation, West Hurley, New York

Thompson Model 27A-5 Semiautomatic Pistol
Similar to Thompson Model 1928A submachine gun, except has no provision for automatic firing, does not have detachable buttstock. Caliber, 45 Automatic. 20-shot detachable box magazine (5-, 15- and 30-shot box magazines, 39-shot drum also available). 13-inch finned barrel. Overall length, 26 inches. Weight, about 6¾ pounds. Adjustable rear sight, blade front sight. Blued finish. Walnut grips. Introduced in 1977.
With box magazine.....................................$360
With drum magazine (as illustrated)..................400

Thompson/Center Contender
Standard Model, 1967 Type

Thompson/Center Contender
Standard Model 1972 Type

Thompson/Center Contender
Ventilated Rib Model

Thompson/Center Contender
Bull Barrel Model, with scope

Thompson/Center Arms, Rochester, New Hampshire

Thompson/Center Contender Single Shot Pistol
Break frame, underlever action. Calibers: (rimfire) 22 LR, 22 WMR, 5mm RRM; (standard centerfire), 218 Bee, 22 Hornet, 22 Rem. Jet, 221 Fireball, 222 Rem., 25-35, 256 Win. Mag., 30 M1 Carbine, 30-30, 38 Auto, 38 Special, 357 Mag./Hot Shot, 9mm Luger, 45 Auto, 45 Colt, 44 Magnum/Hot Shot; (wildcat centerfire) 17 Ackley Bee, 17 Bumblebee, 17 Hornet, 17 K Hornet, 17 Mach IV, 17-222, 17-223, 22 K Hornet, 30 Herrett, 357 Herrett, 357-4 B&D. Interchangable barrels: 8¾- or 10-inch standard octagon (357 Mag., 44 Mag. and 45 Colt available with detachable choke for use with Hot Shot cartridges); 10-inch with ventilated rib and detachable internal choke tube for Hot Shots, 357 and 44 Magnum only; 10-inch bull barrel, 30 or 357 Herret only. 13½ inches overall with 10-inch barrel. Weight, with standard 10-inch barrel, about 43 ounces. Adjustable rear sight, ramp front sight; ventilated-rib model has folding rear sight, adjustable front sight; bull barrel available with or without sights; Lobo 1½X scope and mount (add $40 to value). Blued finish. Receiver photoengraved. Checkered walnut thumb-rest stock and forearm (pre-1972 model has different stock with silver grip cap). Made from 1967 to date.
Standard Model.......................................$175
Ventilated-Rib Model................................. 180
Bull Barrel Model, with sights...................... 185
Bull Barrel Model, without sights................... 180
Extra standard barrel...............................   65
Extra ventilated rib or bull barrel.................   70

Unique Kriegsmodell

Unique Pistol made by Manufacture d'Armes des Pyrénées Francaises, Hendaye, France

Unique Kriegsmodell Automatic Pistol.......... $130
Caliber, 32 Automatic (7.65mm). 9-shot magazine. 3.2-inch barrel. 5.8 inches overall. Weight, 26.5 ounces. Fixed sights. Blued finish. Plastic stocks. Manufactured during German occupation of France 1940-1945. *Note:* Bears German military acceptance marks, may have stocks marked "7.65m/m 9 SCHUSS."

Unique Model Rr Automatic Pistol.............. $170
Postwar commercial version of WWII Kriegsmodell with same general specifications. Made from 1951 to date.

Unique Model B/cf Automatic Pistol............. $175
Calibers: 32 Automatic (7.65mm), 380 Automatic (9mm Short). 9-shot magazine in 32, 8-shot in 380. 4-inch barrel. 6.6 inches overall. Weight, 24.3 ounces. Blued finish. Plain or thumb-rest plastic stocks. Made from 1954 to date.

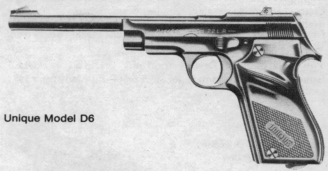

Unique Model D6

Unique Model Rr

Unique Model D6 Automatic Pistol.............. $225
Caliber, 22 Long Rifle. 10-shot magazine. 6-inch barrel. 9¼ inches overall. Weight, about 26 ounces. Adjustable sights. Blued finish. Plain or thumb-rest plastic stocks. Made from 1954 to date.

Unique Model D2................................. $225
Same as Model D6, except has 4¼-inch barrel; 7½ inches overall, weighs 24½ ounces. Made from 1954 to date.

Unique Model L

Unique Model B/cf

Unique Model L Automatic Pistol............... $175
Calibers: 22 Long Rifle, 32 Automatic (7.65mm), 380 Automatic (9mm Short). 10-shot magazine in 22, 7-shot in 32, 6-shot in 380. 3.3-inch barrel. 5.8 inches overall. Weights: about 16½ ounces in 380 with light alloy frame, about 23 ounces with steel frame. Fixed sights. Blued finish. Plastic stocks. Made from 1955 to date.

Unique Model Mikros

Unique Model Mikros Pocket Automatic Pistol..$150
Calibers: 22 Short, 25 Automatic (6.35mm). 6-shot magazine. 2¼-inch barrel. 4-7/16 inches overall. Weights: 9½ ounces with light alloy frame, 12½ ounces with steel frame. Fixed sights. Blued finish. Plastic stocks. Made from 1957 to date.

Unique Model DES/69

Unique Model DES/69 Standard Match Automatic Pistol.. $400
Caliber, 22 Long Rifle. 5-shot magazine. 5.9-inch barrel. 10.6 inches overall. Weight, 35 ounces (barrel weight adds about 9 ounces). Click adjustable rear sight, ramp front sight. Blued finish. Checkered walnut thumb-rest stocks with adjustable hand-rest. Made from 1969 to date.

Unique Model DES/VO

Unique Model DES/VO Rapid Fire Match Automatic Pistol... $425
Caliber, 22 Short. 5-shot magazine. 5.9-inch barrel. 10.4 inches overall. Weight, 43 ounces. Click adjustable rear sight, blade front sight. Checkered walnut thumb-rest stocks with adjustable hand-rest. Trigger adjustable for length of pull. Made from 1974 to date.

U.S. Revolvers manufactured by Iver Johnson's Arms & Cycle Works, Fitchburg, Massachusetts
See listings of comparable Iver Johnson models for values.

U.S. Arms Abilene

United States Arms Corporation, Riverhead, New York

U.S. Arms Abilene Single Action Revolver
Safety Bar action. Calibers: 357 Magnum, 41 Magnum, 44 Magnum, 45 Colt; also 9mm Luger and 357 convertible model with two cylinders. 6-shot cylinder. Barrel lengths: 4⅝-, 5½-, 6½-inch. 7½- and 8½-inch available in 44 Magnum only. Weight, about 48 ounces. Adjustable rear sight, ramp front sight. Blued finish or stainless steel. Smooth walnut stocks. made from 1976 to date.

44 Magnum, blued finish.............................$150
44 Magnum, stainless steel...........................   190
Other calibers, blued finish..........................   130
357 Magnum, stainless steel..........................   165
Convertible, 357 Magnum/9mm Luger, blued finish....   140

Universal Enforcer

Universal Firearms Corporation, Hialeah, Florida

Universal Enforcer Semi-Automatic Pistol...... $190
M-1 Carbine type action. Caliber, 30 Carbine. 5-, 15- or 30-shot clip magazine. 10¼-inch barrel. 17¾ inches overall. Weight, with 30-shot magazine, 4½ pounds. Adjustable rear sight, blade front sight. Blued finish. Walnut stock with pistol grip and handguard. Made from 1964 to date.

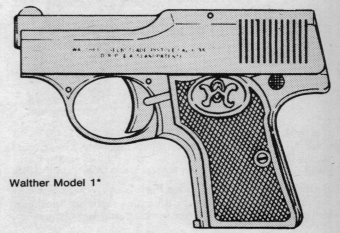

Walther Model 1*

Walther Pistols made prior to and during World War II by Waffenfabrik Walther, Zella-Mehlis (Thür.), Germany

Walther Model 1 Automatic Pistol **$260**
Caliber, 25 Automatic (6.35mm). 6-shot magazine. 2.1-inch barrel. 4.4 inches overall. Weight, 12.8 ounces. Fixed sights. Blued finish. Checkered hard rubber stocks. Introduced in 1908.

Walther Model 2*

Walther Model 2 Automatic Pistol **$260**
Caliber, 25 Automatic (6.35mm). 6-shot magazine. 2.1-inch barrel. 4.2 inches overall. Weight, 9.8 ounces. Fixed sights. Blued finish. Checkered hard rubber stocks. Introduced in 1909.

Walther Model 3 Automatic Pistol **$260**
Caliber, 32 Automatic (7.65mm). 6-shot magazine. 2.6-inch barrel. 5 inches overall. Weight, 16.6 ounces. Fixed sights. Blued finish. Checkered hard rubber stocks. Introduced in 1910.

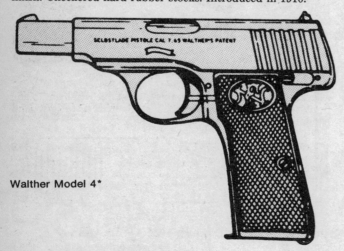

Walther Model 4*

Walther Model 4 Automatic Pistol **$290**
Caliber, 32 Automatic (7.65mm). 8-shot magazine. 3.5-inch barrel. 5.9 inches overall. Weight, 18.6 ounces. Fixed sights. Blued finish. Checkered hard rubber stocks. Made from 1910 to 1918.

Walther Model 5 Automatic Pistol **$295**
Improved version of Model 2 with same general specifications. Distinguished chiefly by better workmanship and appearance. Introduced in 1913.

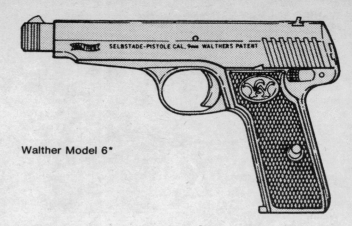

Walther Model 6*

Walther Model 6 Automatic Pistol **$375**
Caliber, 9mm Luger. 8-shot magazine. 4¾-inch barrel. 8¼ inches overall. Weight, 34 ounces. Fixed sights. Blued finish. Checkered hard rubber stocks. Made from 1915 to 1917. *Note:* Powerful 9mm Luger cartridge really is too much for the simple blowback system of this pistol and firing is not recommended.

Walther Model 7*

Walther Model 7 Automatic Pistol **$260**
Caliber, 25 Automatic (6.35mm). 8-shot magazine. 3-inch barrel. 5.3 inches overall. Weight, 11.8 ounces. Fixed sights. Blued finish. Checkered hard rubber stocks. Made from 1917 to 1918.

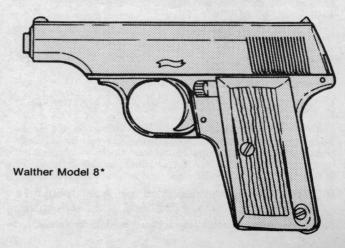

Walther Model 8*

Walther Model 8 Automatic Pistol.............. **$260**
Caliber, 25 Automatic (6.35mm). 8-shot magazine. 2⅞-inch barrel. 5⅛ inches overall. Weight, 12⅜ ounces. Fixed sights. Blued finish. Checkered plastic stocks. Made from 1920 to 1945.

Walther Model 8 Lightweight Automatic Pistol. **$295**
Same as standard Model 8 except about 25 percent lighter due to use of aluminum alloys.

Walther Model 9

Walther Model 9 Vest Pocket Automatic Pistol.. **$350**
Caliber, 25 Automatic (6.35mm). 6-shot magazine. 2-inch barrel. 3-15/16 inches overall. Weight, 9 ounces. Fixed sights. Blued finish. Checkered plastic stocks. Made from 1921 to 1945.

Walther Model PP (Prewar)

Walther Model PP Double Action Automatic Pistol
Polizeipistole (Police Pistol). Calibers: 22 Long Rifle (5.6mm), 25 Automatic (6.35mm), 32 Automatic (7.65mm), 380 Automatic (9mm). 8-shot magazine, 7-shot in 380. 3⅞-inch barrel. 6-5/16 inches overall. Weight, 23 ounces. Fixed sights. Blued finish. Checkered plastic stocks. *Note:* Wartime models are inferior in workmanship to prewar commercial pistols. Made from 1929 to 1945.

22 caliber, commercial model..........................	$445
25 caliber, commercial model..........................	480
32 and 380 caliber, commercial model.................	550
Wartime model.......................................	295

Walther Model PP Lightweight
Same as standard Model PP, except about 25 percent lighter due to use of aluminum alloys. Values 50 percent higher.

Walther Presentation Model PP 7.65mm....... **$1350**
Made of soft aluminum alloy in green-gold color, these pistols were not intended to be fired.

Walther Model PPK Double Action Automatic Pistol
Polizeipistole Kriminal (Detective Pistol). Calibers: 22 Long Rifle (5.6mm), 25 Automatic (6.35mm), 32 Automatic (7.65mm), 380 Automatic (9mm). 7-shot magazine, 6-shot in 380. 3¼-inch barrel. 5⅞ inches overall. Weight, 19 ounces. Fixed sights. Blued

finish. Checkered plastic stocks. *Note:* Wartime models are inferior in workmanship to prewar commercial pistols. Made from 1931 to 1945.

22 and 25 caliber, commercial model..................	$700
32 and 380 caliber, commercial model.................	650
Wartime model.......................................	450

Walther Model PPK (WWII)

Walther Model PPK Lightweight
Same as standard Model PPK, except about 25 percent lighter due to use of aluminum alloys. Values 50 percent higher.

Walther Presentation Model PPK 7.65mm..... **$1150**
Made of soft aluminum alloy in green-gold color, these pistols were not intended to be fired.

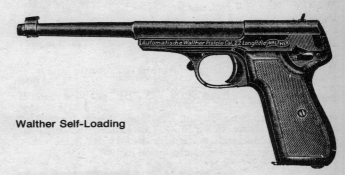

Walther Self-Loading

Walther Self-Loading Sport Pistol.............. **$600**
Caliber, 22 Long Rifle. 10-shot magazine. Barrel lengths: 6-, and 9-inch. 9⅞ inches overall with 6-inch barrel. Target sights. Blued finish. One-piece, wood or plastic stocks, checkered. Introduced in 1932.

Walther Olympia Sport Model Automatic Pistol. **$650**
Caliber, 22 Long Rifle. 10-shot magazine. 7.4-inch barrel. 10.7 inches overall. Weight, 30½ ounces, less weight. Adjustable target sights. Blued finish. Checkered stocks. Set of four detachable weights was supplied at extra cost. Introduced about 1936.

Walther Olympia Hunting Model Automatic Pistol... **$675**
Same general specifications as Olympia Sport Model, but with 4-inch barrel. Weight, 28½ ounces.

Walther Olympia Rapid Fire Model Automatic Pistol... **$1000**
Caliber, 22 Short. 6-shot magazine. 7.4-inch barrel. 10.7 inches overall. Weight (without 12⅜-ounce detachable muzzle weight), 27½ ounces. Adjustable target sights. Blued finish. Checkered stocks. Introduced 1936.

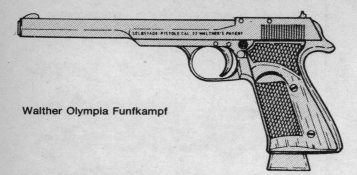

Walther Olympia Funfkampf

Walther Olympia Funfkampf Model Automatic Pistol. **$1250**
Caliber, 22 Long Rifle. 10-shot magazine. 9.6-inch barrel. 13 inches overall. Weight, 33 ounces. less weight. Set of 4 detachable weights. Adjustable target sights. Blued finish. Checkered stocks.

Walther Model HP pf*

Walther Model HP Double Action Automatic Pistol. **$1000**
Prewar commercial version of the P38. "HP" is abbreviation of "Heeres Pistole" (Army Pistol). Caliber, 9mm Luger. 8-shot magazine. 5-inch barrel. 8⅜ inches overall. Weight, about 34½ ounces. Fixed sights. Blued finish. Checkered wood or plastic stocks. The Model HP is distinguished by its notably fine material and workmanship. Introduced in 1937.

Walther Model P38 (WWII)

Walther P38 Military Double Action Automatic Pistol. **$450**
Modification of the Model HP adopted as an official German Service arm in 1938 and produced throughout World War II by Walther (code "ac"), Mauser (code "byf") and a number of other manufacturers. General specifications are the same as Model HP, but there is a vast difference in quality, the P38 being a mass-produced military pistol; some of the late wartime models were very roughly finished and tolerances were quite loose.

Walther Olympia Model Pistols manufactured 1952-1963 by Hämmerli AG Jagd-und Sportwaffenfabrik, Lenzburg, Switzerland. Marketed as "Hämmerli-Walther."

Hämmerli-Walther Olympia Model 200 Automatic Pistol, 1952 Type **$620**
Similar to 1936 Walther Olympia Funfkampf Model. See Hämmerli listing for data.

Hämmerli-Walther Olympia Model 200, 1958 Type **$700**
See Hämmerli listing for data.

Hämmerli-Walther Olympia Model 201 . . . . **$620**
See Hämmerli listing for data.

Hämmerli-Walther Olympia Model 202 . . . . **$700**
See Hämmerli listing for data.

Hämmerli-Walther Olympia Model 203
See Hämmerli listing for data.
1955 Type. **$700**
1958 Type. 775

Hämmerli-Walther Olympia American Model 204
See Hämmerli listing for data.
1956 Type. **$735**
1958 Type. 810

Hämmerli-Walther Olympia American Model 205
See Hämmerli listing for data.
1956 Type. **$810**
1958 Type. 890

Walther Pistols made in France, since 1950, by Manufacture de Machines du Haut-Rhin (MANURHIN) at Mulhouse-Bourtzwiller

Walther Mark II Model PP Automatic Pistol. **$360**
Same general specifications as prewar Model PP.

Walther Mark II Model PPK Automatic Pistol. . . **$495**
Same general specifications as prewar Model PPK

Walther Mark II Model PPK Lightweight. **$490**
Same as standard PPK except has dural receiver. Calibers: 22 Long Rifle and 32 Auto.

Note: The designation "Mark II" is used here to distinguish between these and the prewar models. Early (1950-1954) production bears MANURHIN trademark on slide and grips. Later models are marked "Walther Mark II." U.S. importation discontinued.

Walther Model PP (Current)

Walther Pistols currently manufactured in West Germany by Carl Walther Waffenfabrik, Ulm/Donau

Walther Model PP Double Action Automatic Pistol

Calibers: 22 Long Rifle, 32 Automatic (7.65mm), 380 Automatic (9mm Short). 8-shot magazine in 22 and 32, 7-shot in 380. 3.9-inch barrel. 6.7 inches overall. Weight, in 32 caliber, 23.3 ounces. Fixed sights. Blued finish. Checkered plastic stocks. Made from 1963 to date.

22 Long Rifle $430
Other calibers 400

Walther Model PPK (Current)

Walther Model PPK Double Action Automatic Pistol

Steel or dural frame. Calibers: 22 Long Rifle, 32 Automatic (7.65mm), 380 Automatic (9mm Short); latter caliber not available in model with dural frame. 3.3-inch barrel. 6.1 inches overall. Weight (32 caliber): with steel frame, 20.8 ounces; with dural frame, 16.6 ounces. Fixed sights. Blued finish. Checkered plastic stocks. Made from 1963 to date. U.S. importation discontinued in 1968.

22 Long Rifle $500
Other calibers 400

Walther Model PPK/S

Walther Model PPK/S Double Action Automatic Pistol

Designed to meet the requirements of the U.S. Gun Control Act of 1968, this model has the frame of the PP and the shorter slide and barrel of the PPK. Overall length is 6.1 inches; weight is 23 ounces. Other specifications are the same as those of standard PPK, except steel frame only. Made from 1971 to date.

22 Long Rifle $450
Other calibers 420

Walther Deluxe Engraved Pistols, Models PP, PPK, PPK/S

These elaborately engraved models are available in blued finish, chrome-, silver- or gold-plated.

Blued finish . . . . $ 995
Chrome-plated 1130
Silver-plated 1175
Gold-plated 1270
Add for 22 Long Rifle 25

Walther Model PP Super

Walther Model PP Super Double Action Automatic Pistol $630

Caliber, 9x18mm. 7-shot magazine. 3.6-inch barrel. 6.9 inches overall. Weight, 30 ounces. Fixed sights. Blued finish. Checkered plastic stocks. Made from 1974 to date.

Walther Model TPH

Walther Model TPH Double Action Pocket Automatic Pistol $540

Light alloy frame. Calibers: 22 Long Rifle, 25 Automatic (6.35mm). 6-shot magazine. 2.8-inch barrel. 5.3 inches overall. Weight, 11.5 ounces. Fixed sights. Blued finish. Checkered plastic stocks. Made from 1969 to date. *Note:* Few of these pistols have reached the United States, due to import restrictions.

Walther Model P38 (P1) Double Action Automatic Pistol

Postwar commercial version of the P38, has light alloy frame. Calibers: 22 Long Rifle, 7.65mm Luger, 9mm Luger. 8-shot magazine. Barrel lengths: 5.1-inch in 22 caliber, 4.9-inch in 7.65mm and 9mm. 8.5 inches overall. Weight, 28.2 ounces. Fixed sights. Non reflective black finish. Checkered plastic stocks.

Made from 1957 to date. *Note:* As "P1," this is the official pistol of the West German Armed Forces.

22 Long Rifle... **$635**
Other calibers.. **560**

Walther Model P38 (Current)

Walther Model P38K

Walther Deluxe Engraved Model P38
Elaborately engraved. Available in blued finish, chrome-, silver- or gold-plated.

Blued finish................................. **$1175**
Chrome-plated................................ **1300**
Silver-plated................................. **1400**
Gold-plated................................... **1500**

Walther Model P38K........................... **$590**
Short-barreled version of current P38—"K" is for *kurz* (short). Same general specifications as standard model, except 2.8-inch barrel, 6.3 inches overall, weighs 27.2 ounces, front sight is slide mounted; caliber, 9mm Luger only. Made from 1974 to date.

Walther Model P4

Walther Model P4 (P38-IV) Double Action Automatic Pistol... **$585**
Similar to P38, except has an uncocking device instead of a manual safety; caliber, 9mm Luger only, 4.3-inch barrel, 7.9 inches overall. Other general specifications same as for current model P38. Made from 1974 to date.

Walther Model GSP, 22 Long Rifle

**Walther Model GSP
32 S&W Long Wadcutter**

Walther Model GSP Target Automatic Pistol
Calibers: 22 Long Rifle, 32 S&W Long Wadcutter. 5-shot magazine. 4.5-inch barrel. 11.8 inches overall. Weights: 44.8 ounces in 22 caliber, 49.4 ounces in 32 caliber. Adjustable target sights. Black finish. Walnut thumb-rest stocks with adjustable hand-rest. Made from 1969 to date.

22 Long Rifle....................................... **$675**
32 S&W Long Wadcutter........................... **820**
Conversion unit, 22 Short or 22 Long Rifle, extra...... **495**

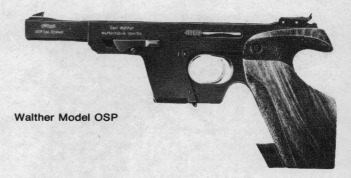

Walther Model OSP

Walther Model OSP Rapid Fire Target Automatic Pistol... **$675**
Caliber, 22 Short. 5-shot magazine. 4.5-inch barrel. 11.8 inches overall. Weight, 42.3 ounces. Adjustable target sights. Black finish. Walnut thumb-rest stocks with adjustable hand-rest. 22 Long Rifle conversion unit available (add $275). Made from 1968 to date.

Warner Arms Corp. (or Davis-Warner Arms Co.), Norwich, Connecticut

Warner Infallible Pocket Automatic Pistol...... **$195**
Caliber, 32 Automatic. 7-shot magazine. 3-inch barrel. 6½ inches overall. Weight, about 24 ounces. Fixed sights. Blued finish. Hard rubber stocks. Made from 1917 to 1919.

Warner Infallible*

Webley 25 Hammer Model

Webley 25 Hammerless

Webley Metropolitan Police

Webley 9mm Military & Police

Webley Mark I 455 Automatic*

Webley Single Shot Target

Webley & Scott Ltd., London and Birmingham, England

Webley 25 Hammer Model Automatic Pistol.....$140
Caliber, 25 Automatic. 6-shot magazine. Length overall, 4¾ inches. Weight, 11¾ ounces. No sights. Blued finish. Checkered vulcanite stocks. Made from 1906 to 1940.

Webley 25 Hammerless Model Automatic Pistol. $145
Caliber, 25 Automatic. 6-shot magazine. Length overall, 4¼ inches. Weight, 9¾ ounces. Fixed sights. Blued finish. Checkered vulcanite stocks. Made from 1909 to 1940.

Webley Metropolitan Police Automatic Pistol... $145
Calibers: 32 Automatic, 380 Automatic. 8-shot magazine (32 cal.), 7-shot (380 cal.). 3½-inch barrel. 6¼ inches overall. Weight, 20 ounces. Fixed sights. Blued finish. Checkered vulcanite stocks. Made from 1906 to 1940 (32), 1908 to 1920 (380).

Webley "Semiautomatic" Single Shot Pistol..... $200
Similar in appearance to the Webley Metropolitan Police Model Automatic, this pistol is "semiautomatic" in the sense that the fired case is extracted and ejected and the hammer cocked as in a blowback automatic pistol; it is loaded singly and the slide manually operated in loading. Caliber, 22 Long. Barrel lengths: 4½- and 9-inch. Overall length with 9-inch barrel, 10¾ inches. Weight, with 9-inch barrel, 24 ounces. Adjustable sights. Blued finish. Checkered vulcanite stocks. Made from 1911 to 1927.

Webley 9mm Military & Police Automatic Pistol.. $225
Caliber, 9mm Browning Long. 8-shot magazine. 8 inches overall. Weight, 32 ounces. Fixed sights. Blued finish. Checkered vulcanite stocks. Made from 1909 to 1930.

Webley Mark I 455 Automatic Pistol........... $325
Caliber, 455 Webley Automatic. 7-shot magazine. 5-inch barrel. 8½ inches overall. Weight, about 39 ounces. Fixed sights. Blued finish. Checkered vulcanite stocks. Made from 1912 to 1945. *Note:* Mark I No. 2 is same pistol with adjustable rear sight and modified manual safety.

Webley Single Shot Target Pistol................ $225
Hinged frame. Caliber, 22 Long Rifle. 10-inch barrel. 15 inches overall. Weight, 37 ounces. Fixed sights on earlier models, current production has adjustable rear sight. Blued finish. Checkered walnut or vulcanite stocks. Made from 1909 to date.

Webley Mark III

Webley Mark III 38 Military & Police Model Revolver...$150

Hinged frame. Double action. Caliber, 38 S&W, 6-shot cylinder. Barrel lengths: 3- and 4-inch. Overall length, with 4-inch barrel, 9½ inches. Weight, with 4-inch barrel, 21 ounces. Fixed sights. Blued finish. Checkered walnut or vulcanite stocks. Made from 1897 to 1945.

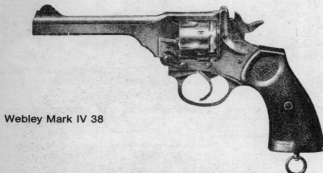

Webley Mark IV 38

Webley Mark IV 38 Military & Police Model Revolver...$150

Hinged frame. Double Action. Caliber, 38 S&W. 6-shot cylinder. Barrel lengths: 3-, 4- and 5-inch. 9⅛ inches overall with 5-inch barrel. Weight, with 5-inch barrel, 27 ounces. Fixed sights. Blued finish. Checkered stocks. Made from 1929 to c. 1957.

Webley Mark IV 22

Webley Mark IV 22 Caliber Target Revolver... $170

Same frame and general appearance as Mark IV 38. Caliber, 22 Long Rifle. 6-shot cylinder. 6-inch barrel. 10⅛ inches overall. Weight, 34 ounces. Target sights. Blued finish. Checkered stocks. Discontinued 1945.

Webley No. 1 Mark VI 455 British Service Revolver...$135

Double action. Hinged frame. Caliber, 455 Webley. 6-shot cylinder. Barrel lengths: 4-, 6- and 7½-inch. Overall length, with 6-inch barrel, 11¼ inches. Weight, with 6-inch barrel, 38 ounces. Fixed sights. Blued finish. Checkered walnut or vulcanite stocks. Made from 1915 to 1947.

Webley Mark VI 22 Target Revolver............$170

Same frame and general appearance as the Mark VI 455. Caliber, 22 Long Rifle. 6-shot cylinder. 6-inch barrel. 11¼ inches overall. Weight, 40 ounces. Target sights. Blued finish. Checkered walnut or vulcanite stocks. Discontinued 1945.

Webley No. 1 Mark VI 455

Webley Mark VI 22

Webley RIC Model

Webley "RIC" Model Revolver....................$140

Royal Irish Constabulary or "Bulldog" Model. Double action. Solid frame. Caliber, 455 Webley. 5-shot cylinder. 2¼-inch barrel. Weight, 21 ounces. Fixed sights. Blued finish. Checkered walnut or vulcanite stocks. Discontinued.

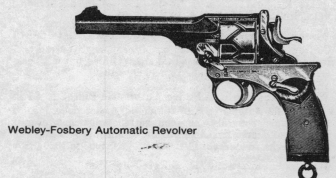

Webley-Fosbery Automatic Revolver

Webley-Fosbery Automatic Revolver............$375

Hinged frame. Recoil action revolves cylinder and cocks hammer. Caliber, 455 Webley. 6-shot cylinder. 6-inch barrel. 12 inches overall. Weight, 42 ounces. Fixed sights. Blued finish. Checkered walnut stocks. Made from 1901 to 1939. *Note:* A few were produced in caliber 38 Colt Auto with an 8-shot cylinder; this is a very rare collector's item.

Dan Wesson Model 11

Dan Wesson Model 12

Dan Wesson Arms, Inc., Monson, Massachusetts

Dan Wesson Model 11 Service Double Action Revolver
Caliber, 357 Magnum. 6-shot cylinder. Barrel lengths: 2½-, 4-, 6-inch; interchangeable barrel assemblies. 9 inches overall with 4-inch barrel. Weight, with 4-inch barrel, 38 ounces. Fixed sights. Blued finish. Interchangeable stocks. Made from 1970 to 1971. *Note:* Model 11 has external barrel nut.

With one barrel assembly and stock..................	$120
Extra barrel assembly...............................	35
Extra stock...	12

Dan Wesson Model 12 Target
Same general specifications as Model 11, except has adjustable sights. Made from 1970 to 1971.

With one barrel assembly and stock..................	$160
Extra barrel assembly...............................	35
Extra stock...	12

Dan Wesson Model 14 Service Double Action Revolver
Caliber, 357 Magnum. 6-shot cylinder. Barrel lengths: 2¼-, 3¾-, 5¾-inch; interchangeable barrel assemblies. 9 inches overall with 3¾-inch barrel. Weight, with 3¾-inch barrel, 36 ounces. Fixed sights. Blued or nickel finish. Interchangeable stocks. Made from 1971 to 1975. *Note:* Model 14 has recessed barrel nut.

With one barrel assembly and stock..................	$130
Extra barrel assembly...............................	40
Extra stock...	12

Dan Wesson Model 8 Service
Same general specifications as Model 14, except caliber 38 Special. Made from 1971 to 1975. Values same as for Model 14.

Dan Wesson Model 15 Target
Same general specifications as Model 14, except has adjustable sights. Made from 1971 to 1975.

With one barrel assembly and stock..................	$170
Extra barrel assembly...............................	40
Extra stock...	12

Dan Wesson Model 9 Target
Same as Model 15, except caliber 38 Special. Made from 1971 to 1975. Values same as for Model 15.

Dan Wesson Model 14-2 Service Double Action Revolver
Caliber, 357 Magnum. 6-shot cylinder. Barrel lengths: 2½-, 4-, 6-, 8-inch; interchangeable barrel assemblies. 9¼ inches overall with 4-inch barrel. Weight, with 4-inch barrel, 34 ounces. Fixed sights. Blued finish. Interchangeable stocks. Made from 1975 to date. *Note:* Model 14-2 has recessed barrel nut.

With one barrel assembly—8-inch—and stock........	$145
With one barrel assembly—other lengths—and stock...	135
Extra barrel assembly, 8-inch.......................	50
Extra barrel assembly, other lengths................	40
Extra stock...	15

Dan Wesson Model 14

Dan Wesson Model 15

Dan Wesson Model 14-2

Dan Wesson Model 8-2 Service
Same general specifications as Model 14-2, except caliber 38 Special. Made from 1975 to date. Values same as for Model 14-2.

Dan Wesson Model 15-2 Target
Same general specifications as Model 14-2, except has adjustable rear sight and interchangeable blade front sight; also available with 10-, 12- and 15-inch barrels. Made from 1975 to date.

With one barrel assembly—8-inch—and stock........	$180
With one barrel assembly—10-inch—and stock........	190
With one barrel assembly—12-inch—and stock........	200
With one barrel assembly—15-inch—and stock........	255
With one barrel assembly—other lengths—and stock...	165
Extra barrel assembly, 8-inch.......................	60
Extra barrel assembly, 10-inch......................	75
Extra barrel assembly, 12-inch......................	95
Extra barrel assembly, 15-inch......................	120
Extra barrel assembly, other lengths................	45
Extra stock...	13

Dan Wesson Model 9-2 Target
Same as Model 15-2, except caliber 38 Special. Made from 1975 to date. Values same as for Model 15-2.

Dan Wesson Model 15-2

Dan Wesson Model 15-2H
interchangeable heavy barrel assemblies

Dan Wesson Model 15-2H Heavy Barrel

Same as Model 15-2, except has heavy barrel assembly; weight, with 4-inch barrel, 38 ounces. Made from 1975 to date.

With one barrel assembly—8-inch—and stock	$200
With one barrel assembly—10-inch—and stock	210
With one barrel assembly—12-inch—and stock	240
With one barrel assembly—15-inch—and stock	275
With one barrel assembly—other lengths—and stock	180
Extra barrel assembly, 8-inch	80
Extra barrel assembly, 10-inch	100
Extra barrel assembly, 12-inch	120
Extra barrel assembly, 15-inch	160
Extra barrel assembly, other lengths	60
Extra stock	13

Dan Wesson Model 9-2H Heavy Barrel

Same as Model 15-2H, except caliber 38 Special. Made from 1975 to date. Values same as for Model 15-2H.

Dan Wesson Model 15-2V
Interchangeable ventilated-rib barrel assemblies

Dan Wesson Model 15-2V Ventilated Rib

Same as Model 15-2, except has ventilated-rib barrel assembly;

weight, with 4-inch barrel, 35 ounces. Made from 1975 to date. Values same as for 15-2H.

Dan Wesson Model 9-2V Ventilated Rib

Same as Model 15-2V, except caliber 38 Special. Made from 1975 to date. Values same as for Model 15-2H.

Dan Wesson Model 15-2HV
Interchangeable ventilated-rib heavy barrel assemblies

Dan Wesson Model 15-2HV Ventilated-Rib Heavy Barrel

Same as Model 15-2, except has ventilated-rib heavy barrel assembly; weight, with 4-inch barrel, 37 ounces. Made from 1975 to date.

With one barrel assembly—8-inch—and stock	$195
With one barrel assembly—10-inch—and stock	220
With one barrel assembly—12-inch—and stock	245
With one barrel assembly—15-inch—and stock	290
With one barrel assembly—other lengths—and stock	180
Extra barrel assembly, 8-inch	90
Extra barrel assembly, 10-inch	110
Extra barrel assembly, 12-inch	140
Extra barrel assembly, 15-inch	180
Extra barrel assembly, other lengths	70
Extra stock	12

Dan Wesson Model 9-2HV Ventilated-Rib Heavy Barrel

Same as Model 15-2H, except caliber 38 Special. Made from 1975 to date. Values same as for Model 15-2HV.

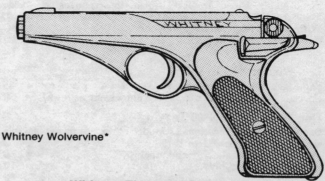

Whitney Wolvervine*

Whitney Firearms Company, Hartford, Connecticut

Whitney Wolverine Automatic Pistol............$150
Dural frame/shell contains all operating components. Caliber, 22 Long Rifle. 10-shot magazine. 4⅝-inch barrel. 9 inches overall. Weight, 23 ounces. Patridge-type sights. Blue or nickel finish. Plastic stocks. Made from 1955 to 1962.

Section II
RIFLES

Anschutz Model 1411

Anschutz Model 1413

Anschutz Model 1407

Anschutz Model 1408-ED

Anschutz Model 1418

Anschutz Model 1432

Anschutz Model 1433

Anschutz Model 1422D Classic

J. G. Anschutz G. m. b. H. Jagd-und Sportwaffenfabrik, Ulm, West Germany

Anschutz Model 1411 Match 54 Rifle

Bolt action single shot. Caliber, 22 Long Rifle. 27½-inch extra heavy barrel. Scope bases. Receiver grooved for Anschutz sights. Single-stage adjustable trigger. Select walnut target stock with cheekpiece (adjustable in 1973 and later production), full pistol grip, beavertail forearm, adjustable butt plate, hand stop and swivel. Model 1411-L has left-hand stock. Weight, about 11 pounds. Discontinued.

With nonadjustable cheekpiece.......................	$495
With adjustable cheekpiece...........................	600
Extra for Anschutz International sight set.............	100

Anschutz Model 1413 Super Match 54 Rifle

Freestyle international target rifle with specifications similar to those of Model 1411, except has special stock with thumb hole, adjustable pistol grip, adjustable cheekpiece in 1973 and later production, adjustable hook butt plate, adjustable palmrest. Model 1413-L has left-hand stock. Weight, about 15½ pounds. Discontinued.

With nonadjustable cheekpiece.......................	$775
With adjustable cheekpiece...........................	830
Extra for Anschutz International sight set.............	100

Anschutz Model 1407 ISU Match 54 Rifle....... $650

Bolt action single shot. Caliber, 22 Long Rifle. 26⅞-inch barrel. Scope bases. Receiver grooved for Anschutz sights. Single-stage adjustable trigger. Select walnut target stock with deep forearm for position shooting, adjustable butt plate, hand stop and swivel. Model 1407-L has left-hand stock. Weight, about 10 pounds. Made from 1970. Discontinued. Value is for rifle less sights; add $65 for Anschutz International sight set.

Anschutz Model 1408-ED Super Running Boar Rifle.. $600

Bolt action single shot. Caliber, 22 Long Rifle. 23½-inch barrel with sliding weights. No metallic sights. Receiver drilled and tapped for scope bases. Single-stage adjustable trigger. Oversize bolt knob. Select walnut stock with thumb hole, adjustable comb and butt plate. Weight, about 9½ pounds. Made from 1976. Discontinued.

Anschutz Model 1418 Bolt Action Sporter...... $300

Caliber, 22 Long Rifle. 5- or 10-shot magazine. 19¾-inch barrel. Folding leaf rear sight, hooded ramp front sight. Receiver grooved for scope mounting. Select walnut stock, Mannlicher type, with cheekpiece, pistol grip and forearm skip checkered. Weight, 5½ pounds. Made from 1976. Discontinued.

Anschutz Model 1518............................. $325

Same as Model 1418 except chambered for 22 Magnum RF, 4-shot box magazine. Made from 1976. Discontinued.

Anschutz Model 1432 Bolt Action Sporter...... $535

Caliber, 22 Hornet. 5-shot box magazine. 24-inch barrel. Folding leaf rear sight, hooded ramp front sight. Receiver grooved for scope mounting. Select walnut stock with Monte Carlo comb and cheekpiece, pistol grip and forearm skip checkered. Weight, 6¾ pounds. Made from 1974. Discontinued.

Anschutz Model 1433 Bolt Action Sporter...... $610

Caliber, 22 Hornet, 5-shot box magazine. 19¾-inch barrel. Folding leaf rear sight, hooded ramp front sight. Receiver grooved for scope mounting. Single-stage or double-set trigger. Select walnut stock, Mannlicher type, with cheekpiece, pistol grip and forearm skip checkered. Weight, 6½ pounds. Made from 1976. Discontinued.

Anschutz Model 1533............................. $600

Same as Model 1433 except chambered for 222 Rem., 3-shot box magazine. Made from 1976. Discontinued.

Note: All of the above Anschutz rifles were marketed in the United States by Savage Arms. In addition, Anschutz Models 1403, 1416, 1516, 1422D, 1522D and 1441 were sold as "Savage/Anschutz" with Savage model designations. See listings under Savage Arms. In January 1982, Talo Distributors, Inc. became the exclusive United States distributor for all Anschutz rifles. The new models are listed below.

Anschutz Model 1422D Classic................... $406

Bolt action sporter. Caliber, 22 Long Rifle. 5-shot removable straight feed clip magazine. 24-inch barrel. Folding leaf rear sight, hooded ramp front sight. Select European walnut stock, classic type. Weight: 7¼ pounds. Made from 1982 to date.

Anschutz Model 1522D Classic................... $425

Same as Model 1422D except chambered for 22 Magnum RF, 4-shot magazine. Made from 1982 to date.

Anschutz Model 1432D Classic................... $450

Bolt action sporter similar to Model 1422D except chambered for 22 Hornet. 4-shot magazine. 23½-inch barrel. Weight, 7¾ pounds. Made from 1982 to date.

Anschutz Model 1532D............................ $450

Same as Model 1432D except chambered for 222 Rem. 3-shot magazine. Made from 1982 to date.

Anschutz Model 1813

Anschutz Model 1427B

Anschutz Model 1403B

Anschutz Mark 2000

Anschutz Model 1416D

Anschutz Sporter Model 1432D

Anschutz Model 54.18 MS

Anschutz Model 1808 ED Super

Anschutz Model 1422D Custom................. **$430**
Same as Model 1422D Classic except has fancy grade Monte Carlo stock of European walnut with hand-carved rollover cheekpiece. Weight, 6½ pounds. Made from 1982 to date.

Anschutz Model 1522D Custom................. **$470**
Same as Model 1522D Classic except has fancy grade Monte Carlo stock of European walnut with hand-carved rollover cheekpiece. Weight, 6½ pounds. Made from 1982 to date.

Anschutz Model 1432D Custom................. **$490**
Same as Model 1432D Classic except has fancy grade Monte Carlo stock of European walnut with hand-carved rollover cheekpiece. Weight, 6½ pounds. Made from 1982 to date.

Anschutz Model 1532D Custom................. **$490**
Same as Model 1532D Classic except has fancy grade Monte Carlo stock of European walnut with hand-carved rollover cheekpiece. Weight, 6½ pounds. Made from 1982 to date.

Anschutz Model 1416D.......................**$240**
Bolt action sporter. Caliber, 22 Long Rifle. 22½-inch barrel. Folding leaf rear sight, hooded ramp front sight. Receiver grooved for scope mounting. Select European stock, with cheekpiece, pistol grip and forearm skip checkered. Weight, 6 pounds. Made from 1982 to date.

Anschutz Model 1516D Bolt Action Sporter..... **$250**
Same as Model 1416D except chambered for 22 Magnum RF. Made from 1982 to date.

Anschutz Model 1418D Bolt Action Sporter **$360**
Caliber, 22 Long Rifle. 5- or 10-shot magazine. 19¾-inch barrel. European walnut Monte Carlo stock, Mannlicher type, with cheekpiece, pistol grip and fore-end skip line checkering, buffalo horn schnabel tip. Weight, 5½ pounds. Made from 1982 to date.

Anschutz Model 1518D.......................**$370**
Same as Model 1418D except chambered for 22 Magnum RF, 4-shot magazine. Made from 1982 to date.

Anschutz Model 520/61 Semiautomatic......... **$170**
Caliber, 22 Long Rifle. 10-shot magazine. 24-inch barrel. Folding leaf rear sight, hooded ramp front sight. Receiver grooved for scope mounting. Rotary style safety. Monte Carlo stock and beavertail fore-end checkered. Weight, 6½ pounds. Made from 1982 to date.

Anschutz Mark 2000 Match..................... **$135**
Takedown. Bolt action single shot. Caliber, 22 Long Rifle. 26-inch heavy barrel. Walnut stock with deep fluted thumb groove, Wundhammer swell pistol grip, beavertail-style fore-end. Adjustable butt plate, single-stage adjustable trigger. Weight, 8½ pounds. Made from 1982 to date.

Anschutz Model 1430D Match.................. **$260**
Improved version of Model 64S. Bolt action single shot. Caliber, 22 Long Rifle. 26-inch medium heavy barrel. Walnut Monte Carlo stock with cheekpiece, adjustable butt plate, deep mid stock tapered to fore-end. Pistol grip and contoured thumb groove with stipple checkering. Single-stage adjustable trigger. Weight, 8⅜ pounds. Made from 1982 to date.

Anschutz Super Match Model 1813............. **$785**
Bolt action single shot. Caliber, 22 Long Rifle. 27¼-inch barrel. Improved Super Match 54 action with light firing pin, one-point adjustable trigger. European walnut thumb hole stock, adjustable palm rest, fore-end and pistol grip stipple checkered. Adjustable cheekpiece and hook butt-plate. Weight, 15¼ pounds. Made from 1982 to date.

Anschutz Model 1810 Super Match II.......... **$700**
A less detailed version of the Super Match 1813 Model. Tapered fore-end with deep receiver area. Select European hardwood stock. Weight, about 13½ pounds. Made from 1982 to date.

Anschutz Model 1811 Prone Match............. **$540**
Bolt action single shot. Caliber, 22 Long Rifle. 27¼-inch barrel. Improved Super Match 54 action. Select European hardwood stock with beaver-tail fore-end, adjustable cheekpiece, and deep thumb flute. Thumb groove and pistol grip with stipple checkering. Adjustable butt plate. Weight, about 11½ pounds. Made from 1982 to date.

Anschutz Model 1807 ISU Standard Match...... **$490**
Bolt action single shot. Caliber, 22 Long Rifle. 26-inch barrel. Improved Super Match 54 action. Two stage match trigger. Removable cheekpiece, adjustable butt plate, thumb piece and fore stock with stippled checkering. Weight, 10 pounds. Made from 1982 to date.

Anschutz Model 1808ED Super-Running Target... **$550**
Bolt action single shot. Caliber, 22 Long Rifle. 23½-inch barrel with sliding weights. Improved Super Match 54 action. Heavy beavertail fore-end, adjustable cheekpiece and butt plate. Adjustable single-stage trigger. Weight, 9¼ pounds. Made from 1982 to date.

Anschutz Model 64MS

Anschutz Model 1403D

Argentine Model 1891 Carbine

Armalite AR-7

Anschutz Model 54.18MS........................ **$475**
Bolt action single shot. Caliber, 22 Long Rifle, 20-inch barrel. European hardwood stock with cheekpiece. Fore-end and Wundhammer swell pistol grip stipple checkered. Receiver grooved, drilled and tapped for scope blocks. Weight, 8⅜ pounds. Made from 1982 to date.

Anschutz Model 64 MS........................ **$255**
Bolt action single shot. Caliber, 22 Long Rifle. 21¼-inch barrel. European hardwood stock with cheekpiece. Fore-end base and Wundhammer swell pistol grip stipple-checkered. Adjustable two-stage trigger. Receiver grooved, drilled and tapped for scope blocks. Weight, 8 pounds. Made from 1982 to date.

Anschutz Model 1403B........................ **$465**
A lighter weight model designed for Biathlon competition. Caliber, 22 Long Rifle. 21½-inch barrel. Adjustable two-stage trigger. Adjustable grooved wood butt plate, stipple-checkered deep thumb rest flute and straight pistol grip. Weight, about 9 pounds with sights. Made from 1982 to date.

Anschutz Model 1427B Biathlon Rifle........... **$675**
Bolt action clip repeater. Caliber, 22 Long Rifle. 21½-inch barrel. Two stage trigger with wing type safety. Hardwood stock with deep fluting, pistol grip and deep forestock with adjustable hand stop rail. Weight, about 9 pounds with sights. Made from 1982 to date.

Argentine Military Rifles manufactured in Germany by D. W. M. and Ludwig Loewe & Co., Berlin

Argentine Model 1891 Mauser Military Rifle....**$ 95**
Bolt action. Caliber, 7.65mm Mauser, 5-shot semi-fixed box magazine, clip loaded. 29-inch barrel. Weight, about 8¾ pounds. Open rear sight, inverted "V" front sight. Military-type full stock. (Adopted 1891 by Argentina, also Boliva, Colombia, Ecuador, Paraguay, Peru and Uruguay).

Argentine Model 1891 Carbine.................. **$115**
Same as Model 1891 Rifle, except has 17.6-inch barrel, is stocked to muzzle, has no bayonet stud.

ArmaLite Inc., Costa Mesa, California

Armalite AR-7 "Explorer" Survival Rifle........ **$ 85**
Takedown. Semiautomatic. Caliber, 22 Long Rifle. 8-shot box magazine. 16-inch cast aluminum barrel with steel liner. Peep rear sight, blade front sight. Brown plastic stock, recessed to stow barrel, action, and magazine. Weight, 2¾ pounds. Will float, either stowed or assembled. Made from 1959 to 1973. *Note:* Now manufactured by Charter Arms Corp., Stratford, Conn.

Armalite Custom AR-7 Rifle.................... **$125**
Same as AR-7 Survival Rifle, except has deluxe walnut stock with cheekpiece and pistol grip. Weight, 3½ pounds. Made from 1964 to 1970.

Armalite Custom AR-7

Armalite AR-180

Armi Jager, Turin, Italy

Armi Jager AP-74 Semiautomatic Rifle

Styled after U.S. M16 military rifle. Calibers: 22 Long Rifle, 32 Auto (pistol cartridge). Detachable clip magazine; capacity: 14 rounds 22 LR, 9 rounds 32 ACP. 20-inch barrel with flash suppressor. Weight, about 6½ pounds. M16 type sights. Stock, pistol grip and forearm of black plastic, swivels and sling. Made from 1974 to date.

22 Long Rifle...................................... **$125**
32 Automatic......................................   **130**

Armi Jager AP-74 with Wood Stock

Same as standard AP-74, except has wood stock, pistol grip and forearm, weighs about 7 pounds.

22 Long Rifle...................................... **$125**
32 Automatic......................................   **135**

Armalite AR-180 Semiautomatic Rifle.......... **$285**

Commercial version of full-automatic AR-18 Combat Rifle. Gas-operated semiautomatic. Caliber, 223 Rem. (5.56mm). 5-, 20-, 30-round magazines. 18¼-inch barrel with flash hider/muzzle brake. Flip-up "L" type rear sight, adjustable for windage; post front sight, adjustable for elevation. Accessory 3x scope and mount (add $60 to value). Folding buttstock of black nylon, rubber butt plate, pistol grip, heat-dissipating fiberglass fore-end (hand guard), swivels, sling. 38 inches overall, 28¾ inches folded. Weight, 6½ pounds. Made by Armalite Inc. 1969 to 1972; manufactured for Armalite by Howa Machinery Ltd., Nagoya, Japan, 1972 to 1973, by Sterling Armament Co. Ltd., Dagenham, Essex, England, 1976 to date.

Armi Jager AP-74 Commando

Armi Jager Model AP-74

Armi Jager AP-74 Commando................$150

Similar to standard AP-74, but styled to resemble original version of Uzi 9mm submachine gun with wood buttstock; lacks carrying handle and flash suppressor, has different type front sight mount and guards, wood stock, pistol grip and forearm. Made from 1976 to date.

Austrian Model 95 Rifle

Austrian Military Rifles manufactured at Steyr Armory, Steyr, Austria

Austrian Model 95 Steyr-Mannlicher Service Rifle.............................$100

Straight-pull bolt action. Caliber, 8x50R Mannlicher (many of these rifles were altered during World War II to use the 7.9mm German service ammunition). 5-shot Mannlicher-type box magazine, 30-inch barrel. Weight, about 8½ pounds. Blade front sight, rear sight adjustable for elevation. Military-type full stock.

Austrian Model 90 Steyr-Mannlicher Carbine... $100

Same general specifications as Model 95 Rifle, except has 19½-inch barrel, weighs about 7 pounds.

Belgian Military Rifles manufactured by Fabrique Nationale D'Armes de Guerre, Herstal, Belgium; Fabrique D'Armes de L'Etat, Luttich, Belgium, Hopkins & Allen Arms Co. of Norwich, Connecticut, as well as contractors in Birmingham, England, also produced these arms during World War I

Belgian Model 1889 Mauser Military Rifle...... $125

Caliber, 7.65mm Belgian Service (7.65mm Mauser). 5-shot projecting box magazine. 30¾-inch barrel with jacket. Weight, about 8½ pounds. Adjustable rear sight, blade front sight. Straight-grip military stock. Made from 1889 to about 1935; this and the carbine model of the same type were the principal weapons of the Belgian Army at the start of World War II.

Belgian Model 1889 Mauser Carbine............ $125

Same as Model 1889 Rifle except has 20¾-inch barrel, weighs about 8 pounds. The Model 1916 Carbine is virtually the same except for minor difference in the rear sight graduations, the lower band which is closer to the muzzle and the swivel plate located on the side of the buttstock.

Belgian Military Rifles manufactured by Fabrique Nationale D'Armes de Guerre, Herstal, Belgium

Belgian Model 1935 Mauser Military Rifle...... $155

Same general specifications as F.N. Model 1924; differences are minor. Caliber, 7.65mm Belgian Service.

Belgian Model 1936 Mauser Military Rifle...... $150

An adaptation of the Model 1889 with German M/98-type bolt, Belgian M/89 protruding box magazine. Caliber 7.65mm Belgian Service.

Pietro Beretta, Brescia, Italy

Beretta Small Bore Sporting Carbine............ $175

Semiautomatic with bolt handle raised, conventional bolt action repeater with handle in lowered position. Caliber, 22 Long Rifle. 4-, 8-, or 20-shot magazines. 20½-inch barrel. 3-leaf folding rear sight, patridge front sight. Stock with checkered pistol grip, sling swivels. Weight, 5½ pounds.

British Military Rifles manufactured at Royal Small Arms Factory, Enfield Lock, Middlesex, England, as well as private contractors

British Army Rifle No. 1 Mark III*.............. $150

Short Magazine Lee-Enfield (S.M.L.E.). Bolt Action. Caliber, 303 British Service. 10-shot box magazine. 25¼-inch barrel. Weight, about 8¾ pounds. Adjustable rear sight, blade front sight with guards. Two-piece, full length military stock. *Note:* The earlier Mark III (approved 1907) is virtually the same as the Mark III* (adopted 1918) except for sights and different magazine cut-off which was eliminated on the latter.

British Army Rifle No. 3 Mark I* (Pattern '14).. $150

Modified Mauser-type bolt action. Except for caliber, 303 British Service, and long range sights, this rifle is the same as U.S. Model 1917 Enfield. See listing of the latter for general specifications.

British Army Rifle No. 4 Mark I*................ $125

Post World War I modification of the S.M.L.E. intended to simplify mass production. General specifications same as Rifle No. 1 Mark III* except weighs 9¼ pounds, has aperture rear sight, minor differences in construction.

British Army Light Rifle No. 4 Mark I*......... $125

Modification of the S.M.L.E. Caliber, 303 British Service, 10-shot box magazine. 23-inch barrel. Weight, about 6¾ pounds. Micrometer click rear peep sight, blade front sight. One-piece military-type stock with recoil pad. Made during World War II.

British S.M.L.E. No. 1 Mark III*

British No. 3 Mark I*

Brno Hornet

Brno Model 21H

Brno Model 22F

Brno Model II

Brown Precision "High Country"

British Army Rifle No. 5 Mark I* $140
Jungle Carbine. Modification of the S.M.L.E. similar to Light
Rifle No. 4 Mark I* except has 20½-inch barrel with flash hider,
carbine-type stock. Made during World War II, originally designed for use in the Pacific Theater.

Brno Sporting Rifles manufactured by
Ceska Zbrojovka, Brno, Czechoslovakia

Brno Hornet Bolt Action Sporting Rifle $635
Miniature Mauser action. Caliber, 22 Hornet. 5-shot detachable
box magazine. 23-inch barrel. Double set trigger. Weight, about
6¼ pounds. Three-leaf open rear sight, hooded ramp front sight.
Sporting stock with checkered pistol grip and forearm, swivels.
Discontinued. *Note:* This rifle was also marketed in the U.S. as
the "Z-B Mauser."

Brno Model 21H Bolt Action Sporting Rifle $635
Mauser-type action. Calibers: 6.5x57, 7x57, 8x57mm. 5-shot box
magazine. 20½-inch barrel. Double set trigger. Weight, about
6¾ pounds. Two-leaf open rear sight, hooded ramp front sight.
Half-length sporting stock with cheekpiece, checkered pistol
grip and forearm, swivels. Discontinued.

Brno Model 22F $650
Same as Model 21H except has full-length Mannlicher-type
stock, weighs about 6 pounds 14 ounces. Discontinued.

Brno Model I Bolt Action Sporting Rifle $395
Caliber, 22 Long Rifle, 5-shot detachable magazine. 22¾-inch
barrel. Weight, about 6 pounds. Three-leaf open rear sight,
hooded ramp front sight. Sporting stock with checkered pistol
grip, swivels. Discontinued.

Brno Model II $410
Same as Model I except with deluxe grade stock. Discontinued.

Brown Precision Company, San Jose, California

Brown Precision "High Country" Bolt Action Sporter... $300
Calibers: 243 Win., 25-06, 270 Win., 7mm Rem. Mag., 308 Win., 30-06. 5-shot magazine (except 4-shot in 7mm Magnum). Remington Model 700 action. 22- or 24-inch barrel. No sights. Fiberglass stock with recoil pad and sling swivels. Weight, about 6½ pounds. Made from 1975 to date.

Browning Rifles manufactured for Browning, Morgan, Utah, by Fabrique Nationale d'Armes de Guerre (now Fabrique Nationale Herstal), Herstal, Belgium; Miroku Firearms Mfg. Co., Tokyo, Japan; Oy Sako Ab, Riihimaki, Finland

Browning 22 Automatic Rifle, Grade I
Similar to discontinued Remington Model 241A. Autoloading. Takedown. Calibers: 22 Long Rifle, 22 Short (not interchangeably). Tubular magazine in buttstock holds 11 Long Rifle, 16 Short. Barrel lengths: 19¼-inch in 22 L.R., 22¼-inch in 22 Short. Weight, about 4¾ pounds in L.R., 5 pounds in Short. Receiver scroll engraved. Open rear sight, bead front sight. Pistol-grip buttstock, semi-beavertail forearm, both checkered. Made from 1965 to 1972 by FN, from 1972 to date by Miroku. *Note:* Illustrations are of rifles manufactured by FN.
FN manufacture..................................... $260
Miroku manufacture.............................. 160

Browning 22 Automatic Rifle, Grade II
Same as Grade I, except satin chrome-plated receiver engraved with small game animal scenes, gold-plated trigger, select walnut stock and forearm. 22 Long Rifle only
FN manufacture..................................... $360
Miroku manufacture.............................. 250

Browning 22 Automatic Rifle, Grade III
Same as Grade I, except satin chrome-plated receiver elaborately hand-carved and engraved with dog and gamebird scenes, scrolls and leaf clusters; gold-plated trigger, extra fancy walnut stock and forearm, skip-checkered. 22 Long Rifle only.
FN manufacture..................................... $825
Miroku manufacture.............................. 600

F.N. Browning Semiautomatic Rifle............. $2000
Same as F.N. FAL Semiautomatic Rifle. See listing of that rifle for specifications. Sold by Browning for a brief period c.1960.

Browning High-Power Bolt Action Rifle, Safari Grade, Standard Action................................. $700
Mauser-type action. Calibers: 270 Win., 30-06, 7mm Rem. Mag., 300 H&H Mag., 300 Win. Mag., 308 Norma Mag., 338 Win. Mag., 375 H&H Mag., 458 Win. Mag. Cartridge capacity: 6 rounds in 270, 30-06; 4 in magnum calibers. Barrel length: 22" in 270, 30-06; 24" in magnum calibers. Weight: 7lbs. 2 oz. in 270, 30-06; 8¼ lbs. in magnum calibers. Folding leaf rear sight, hooded ramp front sight. Checkered stock with pistol grip, Monte Carlo cheekpiece, QD swivels; recoil pad on magnum models. Made from 1959 to 1974 by FN.

Browning High-Power Bolt Action Rifle, Safari Grade, Short Action................................... $650
Same as Standard, except short action. Calibers: 222 Rem., 222 Rem. Mag. 22-inch lightweight barrel or 24" heavy barrel. No sights. Weight: 6 lbs. 2 oz. with lightweight barrel, 7½ lbs. with heavy barrel. Made from 1963 to 1974 by Sako.

Browning High-Power Bolt Action Rifle, Safari Grade, Medium Action................................. $675
Same as Standard, except medium action. Calibers: 22/250, 243 Win., 264 Win. Mag., 284 Win. Mag., 308 Win. Barrel: 22-inch lightweight barrel; 22/250 and 243 also available with 24" heavy barrel. Weight: 6 lbs. 12 oz. with lightweight barrel; 7lbs. 13 oz. with heavy barrel. Made from 1963 to 1974 by Sako.

Browning High-Power Bolt Action Rifle, Medallion Grade.. $1125
Same as Safari Grade, except: receiver and barrel scroll engraved, ram's head engraved on floorplate; select walnut stock with rosewood forearm tip and grip cap. Made from 1961 to 1974.

Browning High-Power Bolt Action Rifle, Olympian Grade.. $1700
Same as Safari Grade, except: barrel engraved; receiver, trigger guard and floor plate satin-chrome-plated and engraved with game scenes appropriate to caliber; finest figured walnut stock with rosewood forearm tip and grip cap, latter with 18K gold medallion. Made from 1961 to 1974.

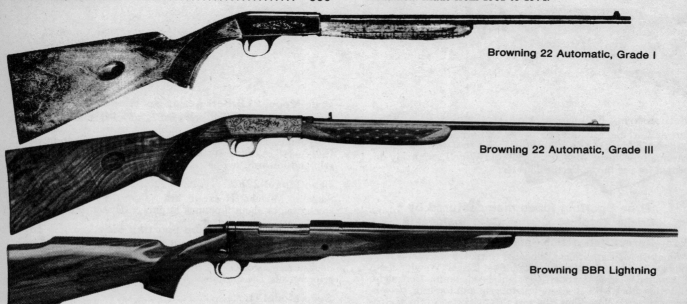

Browning 22 Automatic, Grade I

Browning 22 Automatic, Grade III

Browning BBR Lightning

Browning High-Power, Safari Grade Standard Action

Browning High-Power, Safari Grade, Short Action

Browning High-Power, Safari Grade, Medium Action, Heavy Barrel

Browning High-Power, Safari Grade, Medium Action, Lightweight Barrel

Browning High-Power, Medallion Grade

Browning High-Power, Olympian Grade

Browning "T-Bolt", T-1

Browning "T-Bolt", T-2

Browning BAR, Grade I

Browning BAR, Grade II

Browning BAR, Grade III

Browning BAR, Grade IV

Browning BAR, Grade V

Browning BL-22, Grade I

Browning BL-22, Grade II

Browning BLR

Browning BBR Lightning Bolt Action Rifle......$300
Bolt action rifle with short throw bolt of 60-degrees. Calibers, 25-06 Rem., 270 Win., 30-06, 7mm Rem. Mag., 300 Win. Mag. 24-inch barrel. Weight, 8 pounds. Made from 1979 to date.

Browning "T-Bolt" 22 Repeating Rifle, T-1......$150
Straight-pull bolt action. Caliber, 22 Long Rifle. 5-shot clip magazine. 24-inch barrel. Peep rear sight, blade/ramp front sight. Plain walnut stock with pistol grip. Weight, 6 lbs. Also available in left-hand model. Made from 1965 to 1974 by FN.

Browning "T-Bolt" T-2.....................$250
Same as T-1, except fancy figured walnut stock, checkered. Discontinued 1974.

Browning BAR Automatic Rifle, Grade I, Standard Calibers.............................$400
Gas-operated semiautomatic. Calibers: 243 Win., 270 Win., 308 Win., 30-06. 4-round box magazine. 22-inch barrel. Weight, about 7½ pounds. Folding leaf rear sight, hooded ramp front sight. French walnut stock and forearm, checkered, QD swivels. Made from 1967 to date by FN.

Browning BAR, Grade I, Magnum Calibers......$425
Same as BAR in standard calibers, except chambered for 7mm Rem. Mag., 300 Win. Mag.; has 3-round box magazine, 24-inch barrel, recoil pad; weighs about 8½ pounds. Made from 1969 to date by FN.

Browning BAR, Grade II
Same as Grade I, except receiver engraved with big game heads (deer and antelope on standard-caliber rifles, ram and grizzly on magnum-caliber) and scrollwork, higher grade wood. Made from 1967 to 1974 by FN.
Standard calibers...................................$500
Magnum calibers....................................550

Browning BAR, Grade III......................$800
Same as Grade I, except receiver of grayed steel engraved with big game heads (deer and antelope on standard-caliber rifles, moose and elk on magnum-caliber) framed in fine-line scrollwork, gold-plated trigger, stock and forearm of highly figured French walnut, hand-checkered and carved. Made from 1971 to 1974 by FN.

Browning BAR, Grade IV.....................$1200
Same as Grade I, except: receiver of grayed steel engraved with full detailed rendition of running deer and antelope on standard-caliber rifles, moose and elk on magnum-caliber, gold-plated trigger, stock and forearm of highly figured French walnut, hand checkered and carved. Made from 1971 to date by FN.

Browning BAR, Grade V......................$1600
Same as Grade I, except: receiver with complete big game scenes executed by a master engraver and inlaid with 18K gold (deer and antelope on standard-caliber rifles, moose and elk on magnum-caliber), gold-plated trigger, stock and forearm of finest French walnut, intricately hand checkered and carved. Made from 1971 to 1974 by FN.

Browning BL-22 Lever Action Repeating Rifle, Grade I............................$150
Short-throw lever action. Caliber, 22 Long Rifle, Long, Short. Tubular magazine holds 15 Long Rifle, 17 Long, 22 Short. 20-inch barrel. Weight, 5 pounds. Folding leaf rear sight, bead front sight. Receiver grooved for scope mounting. Walnut straight-grip stock and forearm, barrel band. Made from 1970 to date by Miroku.

Browning BL-22, Grade II......................$160
Same as Grade I, except scroll engraving on receiver, hand checkered grip and forearm. Made from 1970 to date by Miroku.

Browning BLR Lever Action Repeating Rifle....$275
Calibers: 243 Win., 308 Win., 358 Win. 4-round detachable box magazine. 20-inch barrel. Weight, about 7 pounds. Windage and elevation adjustable open rear sight, hooded ramp front sight. Walnut straight-grip stock and forearm, checkered, barrel band, recoil pad. Made 1971 by FN, 1972 to date by Miroku.

Browning Model '81 BLR......................$275
Redesigned version of the Browning BLR. Calibers, 22-250 Rem., 243 Win., 308 Win., 358 Win. 4-round detachable box magazine. 20-inch barrel. Weight, about 7 pounds. Walnut straight-grip stock and forearm, cut checkering, recoil pad. Introduced in 1982.

Browning BLR (81 Model)

Browning 78, 45-70

Browning 78

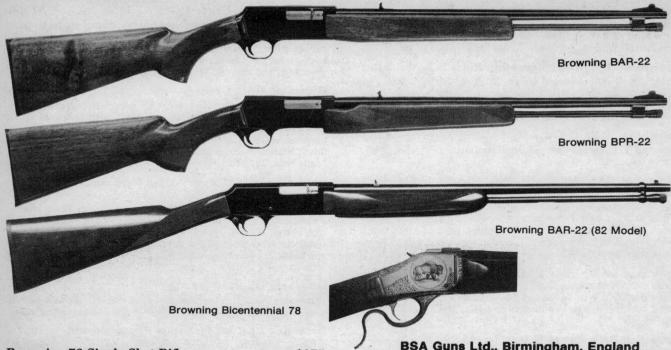

Browning BAR-22

Browning BPR-22

Browning BAR-22 (82 Model)

Browning Bicentennial 78

BSA Guns Ltd., Birmingham, England

Browning 78 Single Shot Rifle................... **$375**

Falling-block lever action similar to Winchester 1885 High Wall S.S. Calibers: 22-250, 6mm Rem., 243 Win., 25-06, 7mm Rem. Mag., 30-06, 45-70 Govt. 26-inch octagon or heavy round barrel; 24-inch octagon bull barrel on 45-70 model. Weights: with octagon barrel, about 7¾ pounds; with round barrel, about 8½ pounds; 45-70, about 8¾ pounds. Furnished without sights, except 45-70 model has open rear sight, blade front sight. Fancy walnut stock and forearm, both checkered. 45-70 model has straight-grip stock with curved butt plate; others have stock with Monte Carlo comb and cheekpiece, pistol grip with cap, recoil pad. Made from 1973 to date by Miroku.

Browning Bicentennial 78 Set................... **$2300**

Special Model 78 45-70 with same specifications as standard type, except sides of receiver engraved with bison and eagle, scroll engraving on top of receiver, lever, both ends of barrel, and butt plate; high grade walnut stock and forearm. Accompanied by an engraved hunting knife and stainless steel commemorative medallion, all in an alder wood presentation case. Each item in set has matching serial number beginning with "1776" and ending with numbers 1 to 1000. Edition limited to 1000 sets. Made in 1976. Value is for set in new condition.

Browning BAR-22 Automatic Rifle.............**$155**

Semiautomatic. Caliber, 22 Long Rifle. Tubular magazine holds 15 rounds. 20¼-inch barrel. Weight, 6¼ pounds. Folding leaf rear sight, gold bead front sight on ramp. Receiver grooved for scope mounting. French walnut pistol-grip stock and forearm, checkered. Introduced 1977; made by Miroku.

Browning BAR-22, 1982 Version............... **$175**

Similar to BAR-22 Automatic Rifle except redesigned with new look and weight-forward balance. Weight, 6 pounds. Introduced in 1982.

Browning BPR-22 Pump Rifle................... **$160**

Hammerless slide-action repeater. Specifications same as for BAR-22, except also available chambered for 22 Magnum RF; magazine capacity, 11 rounds. Introduced 1977; made by Miroku. Discontinued, 1982.

BSA No. 12 Martini Single Shot Target Rifle.... **$230**

Caliber, 22 Long Rifle. 29-inch barrel. Weight, about 8¾ pounds. Parker-Hale Model 7 rear sight and Model 2 front sight. Straight-grip stock, checkered forearm. *Note:* This model was also available with open sights or with BSA No. 30 and 20 sights. Made prior to World War II.

BSA Model 15 Martini Single Shot Target Rifle. **$375**

Caliber, 22 Long Rifle. 29-inch barrel. Weight, about 9½ pounds. BSA No. 30 rear sight and No. 20 front sight. Target stock with cheekpiece and pistol grip, long semi-beavertail forearm. Made prior to World War II.

BSA Centurian Model Match Rifle.............. **$310**

Same general specifications as Model 15 except has "Centurion" match barrel, 1½" groups at 100 yards guaranteed. Made prior to World War II.

BSA Model 12/15 Martini Single Shot Target Rifle.. **$305**

Caliber, 22 Long Rifle. 29-inch barrel. Weight, about 9 pounds. Parker-Hale No. PH-7A rear sight and No. FS-22 front sight. Target stock with high comb and cheekpiece, beavertail forearm. *Note:* This is a post World War II model; however, a similar rifle, the BSA-Parker Model 12/15 was produced about 1938.

BSA Heavy Model 12/15......................... **$340**

Same as Standard Model 12/15 except has extra heavy barrel, weighs about 11 pounds.

BSA No. 13 Martini Single Shot Target Rifle.... **$235**

Caliber, 22 Long Rifle. Lighter version of the No. 12 with same general specifications, except has 25-inch barrel, weighs 6½ pounds. Made prior to World War II.

BSA No. 13 Sporting Rifle

Same as No. 13 Target except fitted with Parker-Hale "Sportarget" rear sight and bead front sight. Also available in caliber 22 Hornet. Made prior to World War II.

22 Long Rifle.. **$230**
22 Hornet.. **325**

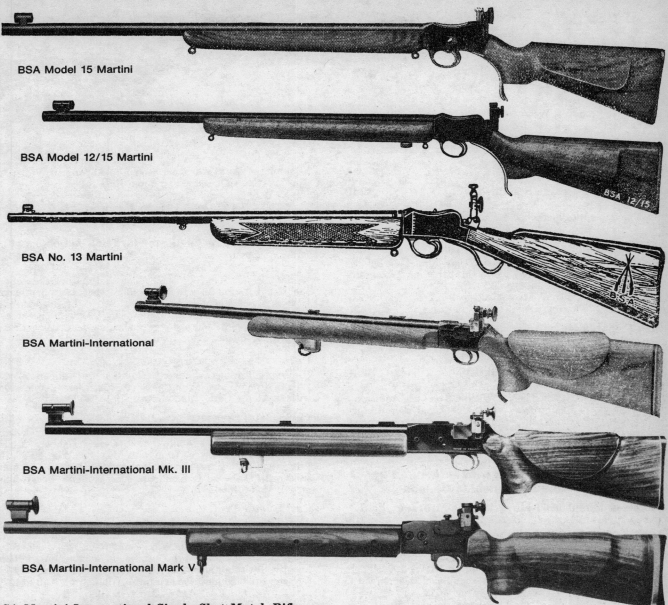

BSA Model 15 Martini

BSA Model 12/15 Martini

BSA No. 13 Martini

BSA Martini-International

BSA Martini-International Mk. III

BSA Martini-International Mark V

**BSA Martini-International Single Shot Match Rifle—
Heavy Pattern.....................................$350**
Caliber, 22 Long Rifle. 29-inch heavy barrel. Weight, about 14
pounds. Parker-Hale "International" front and rear sights. Target stock with full cheekpiece and pistol grip, broad beavertail
forearm, handstop, swivels. Available in right-hand and left-
hand models. Manufactured from 1950 to 1953.

BSA Martini-International—Light Pattern...... $375
Same general specifications as Heavy Pattern, except has 26-
inch lighter weight barrel. Weight, about 11 pounds.

BSA Martini-International MK II Match Rifle... $350
Same general specifications as original model. Heavy and Light
Pattern. Improved trigger mechanism and ejection system. Re-
designed stock and forearm. Made from 1953 to 1959.

BSA Martini-International MK III Match Rifle.. $410
Same general specifications as MK II Heavy Pattern. Longer
action frame with I-section alloy strut to which forearm is

attached; barrel is fully floating. Redesigned stock and forearm.
Made from 1959 to 1967.

BSA Martini-International ISU Match Rifle..... $425
Similar to MK III, but modified to meet International Shooting
Union "Standard Rifle" specifications. 28-inch standard weight
barrel. Weight, 10¾ pounds. Redesigned stock and forearm;
latter attached to barrel with "V" section alloy strut. Made from
1968 to date.

BSA Martini-International Mark V Match Rifle. $420
Same is ISU model, except has heavier barrel. Weight, 12¼
pounds. Made from 1976 to date.

**BSA Majestic Deluxe Featherweight Bolt Action Hunt-
ing Rifle**
Mauser-type action. Calibers: 243 Win., 270 Win., 308 Win.,
30-06, 458 Win. Mag. 4-shot magazine. 22-inch barrel with

BSA Monarch Deluxe Varmint

BESA recoil reducer. Weight, 6¼ lbs., except 8¾ lbs. in 458. Folding leaf rear sight, hooded ramp front sight. European-style walnut stock, checkered, with cheekpiece, pistol grip, schnabel fore-end, swivels, recoil pad. Made from 1959 to 1965.

458 Win. Mag. caliber	$280
Other calibers	235

BSA Majestic Deluxe Standard Weight **$240**
Same as Featherweight Model, except heavier barrel without recoil reducer. Calibers: 22 Hornet, 222 Rem., 243 Win., 7x57mm, 308 Win., 30-06. Weight, 7¼ to 7¾ pounds.

BSA Monarch Deluxe Bolt Action Hunting Rifle. $250
Same as Majestic Deluxe Standard Weight Model, except has redesigned stock of U.S. style with contrasting hardwood fore-end tip and grip cap. Calibers: 222 Rem., 243 Win., 270 Win., 7mm Rem. Mag., 308 Win., 30-06. 22-inch barrel. Weight, 7 to 7¼ pounds. Made from 1965 to 1974.

BSA Monarch Deluxe Varmint Rifle **$270**
Same as Monarch Deluxe, except has 24-inch heavy barrel and weighs 9 pounds. Calibers: 222 Rem., 243 Win.

BSA CF-2 Bolt Action Hunting Rifle **$290**
Mauser-type action. Calibers: 7mm Rem. Mag., 300 Win. Mag. 3-shot magazine. 23.6-inch barrel. Weight, 8 pounds. Adjustable rear sight, hooded ramp front sight. Checkered walnut stock with Monte Carlo comb, roll-over cheekpiece, rosewood fore-end tip, recoil pad, sling swivels. Made from 1975 to date. *Note:* Also marketed in U.S.A. as Ithaca-BSA CF-2. See that listing for illustration.

Canadian Military Rifles manufactured by Ross Rifle Co., Quebec, Canada

Canadian Model 1907 Mark II Ross Military Rifle **$150**
Straight pull bolt action. Caliber, 303 British. 5-shot box magazine. 28-inch barrel. Weight, about 8½ pounds. Adjustable rear sight, blade front sight. Military-type full stock. *Note:* The Ross was originally issued as a Canadian service rifle in 1907. There were a number of variations; it was the official weapon at the beginning of World War I, has been obsolete for many years. For Ross sporting rifle, see listing under Ross Rifle Co.

Carl Gustafs Stads Gevärsfaktori, Eskilstuna, Sweden

Carl Gustaf Monte Carlo Standard Bolt Action Sporting Rifle **$410**
Carl Gustaf 1900 action. Calibers: 6.5x55, 7x64, 270 Win., 7mm Rem. Mag., 308 Win., 30-06, 9.3x62. 5-shot magazine, except 4-shot in 9.3x62 and 3-shot in 7mm Rem. Mag. 23½-inch barrel. Weight, about 7 pounds. Folding leaf rear sight, hooded ramp front sight. French walnut Monte Carlo stock with cheekpiece, checkered forearm and pistol grip, sling swivels. Also available in left-hand model. Made from 1970 to 1977.

Carl Gustaf Standard **$380**
Same specifications as Monte Carlo Standard. Calibers: 6.5x55, 7x64, 270 Win., 308 Win., 30-06, 9.3x62. Classic style stock without Monte Carlo. Made from 1970 to 1977.

Carl Gustaf Special **$505**
Also designated "Grade II" in U.S. and "Model 9000" in Canada. Same specifications as Monte Carlo Standard. Calibers: 22-250, 243 Win., 25-06, 270 Win., 7mm Rem. Mag., 308 Win., 30-06, 300 Win. Mag. 3-shot magazine in magnum calibers. Select wood stock with rosewood fore-end tip. Also available in left-hand model. Made from 1970 to 1977.

Carl Gustaf Trofé **$635**
Also designated "Grade III" in U.S. and "Model 8000" in Canada. Same specifications as Monte Carlo Standard. Calibers: 22-250, 25-06, 6.5x55, 270 Win., 7mm Rem. Mag., 308 Win., 30-06, 300 Win. Mag. 3-shot magazine in magnum calibers. Furnished without sights. Stock of fancy wood with rosewood fore-end tip, high-gloss lacquer finish. Made from 1970 to 1977.

Carl Gustaf Monte Carlo Standard

Carl Gustaf Special

Carl Gustaf Trofé

Carl Gustaf Deluxe

Carl Gustaf Sporter

Carl Gustaf Grand Prix

Charter AR-7

(disassembled and stowed in stock)

Carl Gustaf Deluxe.............................. $730
Same specifications as Monte Carlo Standard. Calibers: 6.5x55, 308 Win., 30-06, 9.3x62. 4-shot magazine in 9.3x62. Jewelled bolt. Engraved floorplate and trigger guard. Stock of deluxe French walnut with rosewood fore-end tip. Made from 1970 to 1977.

Carl Gustaf Sporter............................ $475
Also designated "Varmint-Target" in U.S. Fast bolt action with large bakelite bolt knob. Trigger pull adjusts down to 18 ounces. Calibers: 222 Rem., 22-250, 243 Win., 6.5x55. 5-shot magazine, except 6-shot in 222 Rem. 26¾-inch heavy barrel. Weight, about 9½ pounds. Furnished without sights. Target-type Monte Carlo stock of French walnut. Made from 1970 to date.

Carl Gustaf Grand Prix Single Shot
Target Rifle...................................... $500
Special bolt action with "world's shortest lock time." Single-stage trigger adjusts down to 18 ounces. Caliber, 22 Long Rifle. 26¾-inch heavy barrel with adjustable trim weight. Weight, about 9¾ pounds. Furnished without sights. Target-type Monte Carlo stock of French walnut, adjustable cork butt plate. Made from 1970 to date.

Charter Arms Corporation
Stratford, Connecticut

Charter AR-7 "Explorer" Survival Rifle........ $ 75
Same as Armalite AR-7, except has black, instead of brown "wood grain" plastic stock. See listing of that rifle for specifications. Made from 1973 to date.

Churchill, Gunmakers, Ltd., London, England

Churchill "One of One Thousand" Rifle........ $1300
Made for Interarms to commemorate that firm's 20th anniversary. Mauser-type action. Calibers: 270, 7mm Rem. Mag., 308, 30-06, 300 Win. Mag., 375 H&H Mag., 458 Win. Mag. 5-shot magazine (3-shot in magnum calibers). 24-inch barrel. Weight, about 8 pounds. Classic style French walnut stock with cheekpiece, black fore-end tip, checkered pistol grip and fore-arm, swivel-mounted recoil pad with cartridge trap, pistol-grip cap with trap for extra front sight, barrel-mounted sling swivel. Issue limited to 1000 rifles. Made in 1973.

Clerke Recreation Products,
Santa Monica, California

Clerke Hi-Wall Single Shot Rifle................. $240
Falling-block lever action similar to Winchester 1885 High Wall S.S. Color casehardened investment-cast receiver. Calibers: 222 Rem., 22-250, 243 Rem., 6mm Rem., 25-06, 270 Win., 7mm Rem. Mag., 30-06, 45-70 Govt. 26-inch medium-weight barrel. Weight,

Churchill "One of One Thousand"

Clerke Hi-Wall

about 8 pounds. Furnished without sights. Checkered walnut pistol-grip stock and schnabel forearm. Made from 1972 to 1974.

Clerke Deluxe Hi-Wall **$300**
Same as standard model, except has adjustable trigger, half-octagon barrel, select wood, stock with cheekpiece and recoil pad. Made from 1972 to 1974.

Colt Industries, Firearms Division, Hartford, Connecticut

Colt Lightning Magazine Rifle **$875**
Slide action. Calibers: 32-20, 38-40, 44-40. 15-shot tubular magazine. 26-inch barrel, round or octagon. Weight, 6¾ pounds (round barrel model). Open rear sight, bead or blade front sight. Walnut stock and forearm. Made from 1885 to 1900.

Colt Lightning Carbine **$1375**
Same as Lightning Magazine Rifle, except has 12-shot magazine, 20-inch barrel, weighs 6¼ pounds.

Colt Lightning Baby Carbine **$2800**
Same as Lightning Carbine, except lighter weight (5½ pounds).

Colt 22 Lightning Magazine Rifle **$695**
Slide action. Caliber, 22 Rim Fire (Short or Long). Tubular magazine holding 15 long or 16 short. 24-inch barrel, round or octagon. Weight, 5¾ pounds (round barrel model). Open rear sight, bead front sight. Walnut stock and forearm. Made from 1885 to 1903.

Coltsman "Custom" Bolt Action Sporting Rifle ... **$400**
FN Mauser action, side safety, engraved floorplate. Calibers: 30-06, 300 H&H Mag. 5-shot box magazine. 24-inch barrel, ramp

front sight. Fancy walnut stock, Monte Carlo comb, cheekpiece, pistol grip, checkered, Q.D. swivels. Weight, about 7¼ pounds. Made from 1957 to 1961. Value shown is for rifle, as furnished by manufacturer, without rear sight.

Coltsman "Deluxe" Rifle **$375**
FN Mauser action. Same as "Custom" model except plain floorplate, plainer wood and checkering. Made from 1957 to 1961. Value shown is for rifle, as furnished by manufacturer, without rear sight.

Coltsman "Standard" Rifle **$320**
FN Mauser action. Same as "Deluxe" model except stock has no cheekpiece, barrel length is 22 inches. Made from 1957 to 1961. Value shown is for rifle, as furnished by manufacturer, without rear sight.

Coltsman Rifles, Models of 1957
Sako Medium action. Calibers: 243, 308. Weight, about 6¾ pounds. Other specifications similar to those of models with FN actions. Made from 1957 to 1961.
"Custom" **$400**
"Deluxe" 375
"Standard" 325

Colteer 1-22 Single Shot Bolt Action Rifle .... **$ 50**
Caliber, 22 Long Rifle, Long, Short. 20 or 22-inch barrel. Open rear sight, ramp front sight. Pistol-grip stock with Monte Carlo comb. Weight, about 5 pounds. Made from 1957 to 1967.

Coltsman "Custom" Rifle, Model of 1961 .... **$440**
Sako action. Calibers: 222, 222 Mag., 223, 243, 264, 270, 308, 30-06, 300 H&H. 23-, 24-inch barrel. Folding leaf rear sight, hooded ramp front sight. Fancy French walnut stock with Monte Carlo comb, rosewood fore-end tip and grip cap, skip checkering, recoil pad, sling swivels. Weight, 6½ to 7½ pounds depending upon caliber. Made from 1963 to 1965.

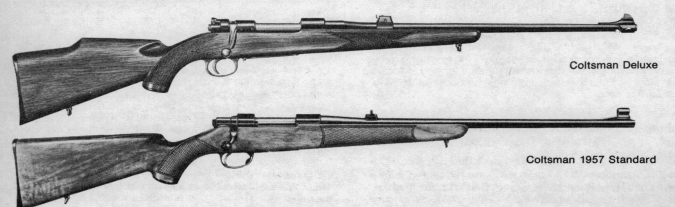

Coltsman Deluxe

Coltsman 1957 Standard

Colteer 1-22

Coltsman 1961 Custom

Coltsman 1961 Standard

Colt AR-15 Sporter

Colteer Autoloader

Colt Stagecoach

Colt AR-15 Adjustable Stock

Coltsman "Standard" Rifle, Model of 1961....... **$375**
Same as "Custom" model, except plainer, American walnut
stock. Made from 1963 to 1965.

Colt AR-15 Sporter................................**$375**
Commercial semiautomatic version of U.S. M16 rifle. Gas-operated. Takedown. Caliber, 223 Rem. (5.56mm). 20-round maga-

zine with spacer to reduce capacity to 5 rounds. 20-inch barrel
with flash suppressor. Rear peep sight with windage adjustment
in carrying handle. Front sight adjustable for windage, 3x scope
and mount available as accessory equipment (adds $70 to value).
Black molded buttstock of high-impact synthetic material, rubber butt plate. Barrel surrounded by handguards of black
fiberglass with heat-reflecting inner shield. Swivels, black web
sling strap. Weight, without accessories, 6.3 pounds. Made from
1964 to date.

Colt AR-15 Adjustable Stock....................**$400**
Same as AR-15, except has collapsible buttstock and redesigned
forearm.

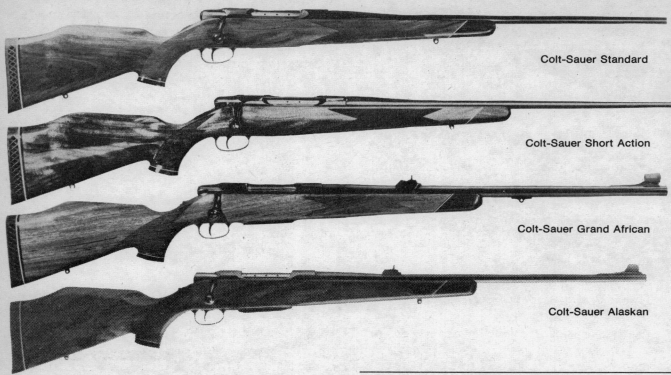

Colt-Sauer Standard

Colt-Sauer Short Action

Colt-Sauer Grand African

Colt-Sauer Alaskan

Colteer 22 Autoloader............................$135
Caliber, 22 Long Rifle. 15-round tubular magazine. 19⅜-inch
barrel. Open rear sight, hooded ramp front sight. Straight-grip
stock, Western carbine style forearm with barrel band. Weight,
about 4¾ pounds. Made from 1964 to 1975.

Colt Stagecoach 22 Autoloader...................$145
Same as Colteer 22 Autoloader, except has engraved receiver,
saddle ring, 16½-inch barrel. Weight, 4 lbs. 10 oz. Made from
1965 to 1975.

Colt-Sauer Sporting Rifle, Standard Model......$725
Sauer 80 nonrotating bolt action. Calibers: 25-06, 270 Win.,
30-06. 3-round detachable box magazine. 24-inch barrel. Weight,
7¾ pounds; 8½ pounds in 25-06. Furnished without sights.
American walnut stock with Monte Carlo cheekpiece, checkered
pistol grip and forearm, rosewood fore-end tip and pistol-grip
cap, recoil pad. Made from 1973 to date.

Colt-Sauer Magnum............................$800
Same specifications as standard model, except calibers: 7mm
Rem. Mag., 300 Win. Mag., 300 Weatherby; weight, 8½ pounds.
Made from 1973 to date.

Colt-Sauer Short Action.........................$750
Same specifications as standard model, except calibers; 22-250,
243 Win., 308 Win.; weighs 7½ pounds, 8¼ pounds in 22-250.
Made from 1973 to date.

Colt-Sauer Grand Alaskan......................$825
Same specifications as standard model, except caliber 375 H&H,
weighs 8½ pounds, adjustable leaf rear sight, hooded ramp front
sight, magnum-style stock of walnut.

Colt-Sauer Grand African......................$875
Same specifications as standard model, except caliber 458 Win.
Mag., weighs 9½ pounds, adjustable leaf rear sight, hooded
ramp front sight, magnum-style stock of Bubinga. Made from
1973 to date.

Note: Colt-Sauer rifles are manufactured for Colt by J. P.
Sauer & Sohn, Eckernforde, West Germany.

Commando Carbines manufactured by Volunteer Enterprises, Inc., Knoxville, Tennessee

Commando Mark III Semiautomatic Carbine
Blow-back action, fires from closed bolt. Caliber, 45 ACP. 15- or
30-shot magazine. 16½-inch barrel with cooling sleeve and
muzzle brake. Weight, 8 pounds. Peep rear sight, blade front
sight. "Tommy Gun" style stock and forearm or grip. Made from
1969 to 1976.
With horizontal forearm.............................**$135**
With vertical foregrip............................... 145

Commando Mark 45
Same specifications as Mark III. Has redesigned trigger housing
and magazine. 5-, 15-, 30- and 90-shot magazines available.
Made from 1976 to date.
With horizontal forearm.............................**$140**
With vertical foregrip............................... 150

Commando Mark 9
Same specifications as Mark III and Mark 45, except caliber
9mm Luger. Made from 1976 to 1981.
With horizontal forearm.............................**$140**
With vertical foregrip............................... 150

Continental Rifles manufactured in Belgium for Continental Arms Corp., New York, N.Y.

Continental Double Rifle......................**$3800**
Calibers: 270, 303 Sav., 30-40, 348 Win., 30-06, 375 H&H, 400
Jeffrey, 465, 470, 475 No. 2, 500, 600. Side-by-side. Anson-Deeley
reinforced box lock action with triple bolting lever-work. Two
triggers. Nonautomatic safety. 24- or 26-inch barrels. Express
rear sight, bead front sight. Checkered cheekpiece stock and
fore-end. Weight, from 7 pounds, depending upon caliber.

Commando Mark III

Commando Mark 45

Commando Mark 9

Daisy V/L Standard

Czechoslovakian Military Rifles manufactured by Ceska Zbrojovka, Brno, Czechoslovakia

Czech Model 1924 (VZ24) Mauser Military Rifle **$150**
Basically the same as the German Kar., 98k and F.N. (Belgian Model 1924.) Caliber, 7.9mm Mauser. 5-shot box magazine. 23¼-inch barrel. Weight, about 8½ pounds. Adjustable rear sight, blade front sight with guards. Military stock of Belgian-type, full handguard. Manufactured from 1924 through World War II. Many of these rifles were made for export. As produced during the German occupation, this model was known as Gewehr 24t.

Czech Model 1933 (VZ33) Mauser Military Carbine **$150**
Modification of the German M/98 action with smaller receiver ring. Caliber, 7.9mm Mauser. 19¼-inch barrel. Weight, about 7½ pounds. Adjustable rear sight, blade front sight with guards. Military-type full stock. Manufactured from 1933 through World War II; a similar model produced during the German occupation was designated Gew., 33/40.

Daisy Division, Victor Comptometer Corporation, Rogers, Arkansas

Daisy V/L Standard Rifle **$140**
Single shot, under-lever action. Caliber, 22 V/L (caseless cartridge; propellant ignited by jet of hot air). 18-inch barrel. Weight, 5 pounds. Adjustable open rear sight, ramp with blade front sight. Wood-grained Lustran stock (foam-filled). Approximately 19,000 manufactured 1968-1969.

Daisy V/L Collector's Kit

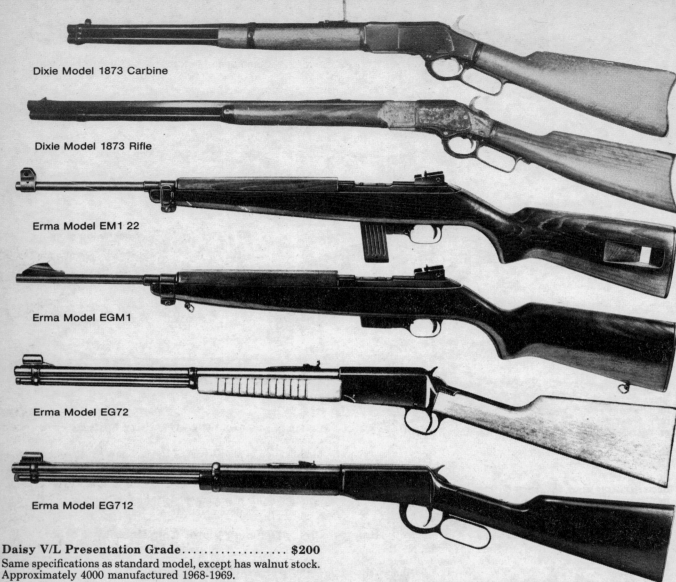

Dixie Model 1873 Carbine

Dixie Model 1873 Rifle

Erma Model EM1 22

Erma Model EGM1

Erma Model EG72

Erma Model EG712

Daisy V/L Presentation Grade.................. **$200**
Same specifications as standard model, except has walnut stock.
Approximately 4000 manufactured 1968-1969.

Daisy V/L Collector's Kit........................ **$300**
Presentation grade rifle with a gold plate inscribed with the
owner's name and gun serial number mounted on the stock. Kit
also includes a special gun case, pair of brass gun cradles for wall-
hanging, 300 rounds of 22 V/L ammunition, and a certificate
signed by Daisy president Cass S. Hough. Approximately 1000
manufactured 1968-1969.

Note: Daisy V/L is the first and only commercial caseless
cartridge system. It is expected that these rifles will ap-
preciate considerably in future years. The cartridge, no
longer made, also is a collector's item.

Charles Daly Rifle made by Franz Jaeger & Co., Suhl, Germany, and distributed in the U.S. by Charles Daly, Inc. of New York City

Charles Daly Hornet Rifle...................... **$890**
Same as Herold Rifle. See listing of that rifle for specifications.
Imported during the 1930's.

Dixie Rifles manufactured in Italy for Dixie Gun Works, Inc., Union City, Tennessee

**Dixie Model 1873 Lever Action Repeating
Carbine**... **$270**
Replica Winchester '73. Caliber, 44-40. 11-shot tubular magazine. 20-inch barrel. Weight, 7¼ pounds. Leaf rear sight, blade
front sight. Walnut stock and forearm, barrel band.

Dixie Model 1873 Rifle........................... **$295**
Same general specifications as carbine, except receiver engraved
with fancy scrollwork, elk and buffalo, casehardened in colors;
23½-inch octagon barrel; weight, 9 pounds.

Erma Werke, Dachau, West Germany

Erma Model EM1 22 Semiautomatic Carbine.... **$130**
Styled after U.S. Carbine Cal. 30 M1. Caliber, 22 Long Rifle. 10-
or 15-round magazine. 18-inch barrel. Weight, about 5½
pounds. Carbine-type sights. Receiver grooved for scope mounting. Military stock and handguard. Introduced, 1966. Discontinued.

FN Model 1950 Mauser

FN Model 1949 Semiautomatic Rifle

F.N. FAL Semiautomatic Rifle

Erma Model EGM1............................. **$130**
Same as Model EM1, except has unslotted buttstock, ramp front sight, 5-shot magazine standard. Introduced, 1970. Discontinued.

Erma EG72 Pump Action Repeater............. **$110**
Visible hammer. Caliber, 22 Long Rifle. 15-shot magazine. 18½-inch barrel. Weight, about 5¼ pounds. Open rear sight, hooded ramp front sight. Receiver grooved for scope mounting. Straight-grip stock, grooved slide handle. Made from 1970 to 1976.

**Erma Model EG712 Lever Action Repeating
Carbine**.. **$150**
Styled after Winchester Model 94. Caliber, 22 Long Rifle, Long, Short. Tubular magazine holds 15 LR, 17 Long, 21 Short. 18½-inch barrel. Weight, about 5½ pounds. Open rear sight, hooded ramp front sight. Receiver grooved for scope mounting. Western carbine-style stock and forearm with barrel band. Made from 1976 to date. *Note:* A similar carbine of Erma manufacture is marketed in the U.S. as Ithaca Model 72 Saddlegun.

Erma Model EG73............................. **$160**
Same as Model EG712, except chambered for 22 Winchester Magnum Rimfire, has 12-shot tubular magazine, 19.3-inch barrel. Made from 1973 to date.

Fabrique Nationale D'Armes de Guerre, Herstal, Belgium

**F. N. Models 1924, 1934/30 and 1930 Mauser Military
Rifles**.. **$150**
Basically the same as the German Kar. 98k. Straight bolt handle. Calibers: 7mm, 7.65mm and 7.9mm Mauser. 5-shot box magazine. 23½-inch barrel. Weight, about 8½ pounds. Adjustable rear sight, blade front sight. Military stock of M/98 pattern with slight modification. Model differences are minor. Also produced in a short carbine model with 17¼-inch barrel. *Note:* These rifles were manufactured under contract for Abyssinia, Argentina, Belgium, Bolivia, Brazil, Chile, China, Colombia, Ecuador, Iran, Luxembourg, Mexico, Peru, Turkey, Uruguay and Yugoslavia. Such arms usually bear the coat of arms of the country for which they were made, together with the contractor's name and the date of manufacture. Also sold commercially and exported to all parts of the world.

F. N. Model 1950 Mauser Military Rifle........ **$175**
Same as previous F.N. models of Kar. 98k type, except chambered for 30-06.

F. N. Model 1949 Semiautomatic Military Rifle.. **$375**
Gas-operated. Calibers: 7mm, 7.65mm, 7.92mm, 30M² (30-06). 10-round box magazine, clip fed or loaded singly. 23.2-inch barrel. Weight, 9½ pounds. Tangent rear sight, shielded post front sight. Pistol-grip stock, handguard. *Note:* Adopted in cal. 30 by Belgium in 1949 and also by Belgian Congo, Brazil, Colombia, Luxemburg, and Netherlands East Indies; Venezuela bought this rifle in 7mm, Egypt in 7.92mm. Approximately 160,000 were made.

F. N. FAL Semiautomatic Rifle.................. **$490**
Same as the standard FAL military rifle except without provision for automatic firing. Gas-operated. Caliber, 7.62mm NATO (.308 Win.). 10- or 20-round box magazine. 25½-inch barrel (including flash hider). Weight, about 9 pounds. Post front sight, aperture rear sight. Wood buttstock, pistol grip, forearm/handguard; carrying handle, sling swivels. Made from 1950 to date.

F. N. Deluxe Mauser Bolt Action Sporting Rifle. **$585**
American calibers: 220 Swift, 243 Win., 244 Rem., 250/3000, 257 Roberts, 270 Win., 7mm, 300 Sav., 308 Win., 30-06; European calibers: 7x57, 8x57JS, 8x60S, 9.3x62, 9.5x57, 10.75x68mm. 5-shot box magazine. 24-inch barrel. Weight, about 7½ pounds; in 270, 8¼ pounds. American model is standard with hooded ramp front sight and Tri-Range rear sight; Continental model has two-leaf rear sight. Checkered stock with cheekpiece, pistol grip, swivels. Made from 1947 to 1963.

F. N. Deluxe Mauser — Presentation Grade..... **$980**
Same as regular model, except has select grade stock; engraving on receiver, trigger guard, floorplate and barrel breech. Discontinued 1963.

FN Deluxe Mauser

FN Supreme Mauser

Finnish Lion Match

Finnish Lion Champion

Finnish Lion Standard

F. N. Supreme Mauser Bolt Action Sporting Rifle... **$590**
Calibers: 243, 270, 7mm, 308, 30-06. 4-shot magazine in 243 and 308; 5-shot in other calibers. 22-inch barrel in 308; 24-inch in other calibers. Hooded ramp front sight, Tri-range peep rear sight. Checkered stock with Monte Carlo cheekpiece, pistol grip, swivels. Weight, about 7¾ pounds. Made from 1957 to 1975.

F. N. Supreme Magnum Mauser.................. **$595**
Calibers: 264 Mag., 7mm Mag., 300 Win. Mag. Specifications same as for standard-caliber model except 3-shot magazine capacity.

Finnish Lion Rifles manufactured by Valmet Oy, Tourula Works, Jyväskylä, Finland

Finnish Lion Match Rifle......................... **$450**
Bolt action single shot. Caliber, 22 Long Rifle. 28¾-inch heavy barrel. Weight, about 14½ pounds. Extension rear peep sight, aperture front sight. Walnut free-rifle stock with full pistol grip, thumb-hole, beavertail forearm, hook buttplate, palm-rest, hand stop, swivel. Made from 1937 to 1972.

Finnish Lion Champion Free Rifle............... **$525**
Bolt action single shot. Double-set trigger. Caliber, 22 Long Rifle. 28¾-inch heavy barrel. Weight, about 16 pounds. Ex-

tension rear peep sight, aperture front sight. Walnut free-rifle stock with full pistol grip, thumb-hole, beavertail forearm, hook butt plate, palm-rest, hand stop, swivel. Made from 1965 to 1972.

Finnish Lion Standard ISU Target Rifle......... **$375**
Bolt action single shot. Caliber, 22 Long Rifle. 27½-inch barrel. Weight, about 10½ pounds. Extension rear peep sight, aperture front sight. Walnut target stock with full pistol grip, checkered beavertail forearm, adjustable butt plate, sling swivel. Made from 1966 to 1977.

Luigi Franchi, S.p.A. Brescia, Italy

Franchi Centennial Automatic Rifle
Commemorates Franchi's 100th anniversary (1868-1968). Centennial seal engraved on receiver. Semiautomatic. Take-down. Caliber, 22 Long Rifle. 11-shot magazine in buttstock. 21-inch barrel. Weight, 5⅛ pounds. Open rear sight, goldbead front sight on ramp. Checkered walnut stock and fore-end. Deluxe model has fully engraved receiver, premium grade wood. Made in 1968.
Standard Model.....................................**$230**
Deluxe Model....................................... 320

French Government Plants, Chatellerault, St. Etienne

French Model 1886 Lebel Military Rifle......... **$100**
Bolt action. Caliber, 8mm Lebel. 8-shot tubular magazine. 31½-inch barrel. Weight, about 9¼ pounds. Adjustable rear sight, blade front sight. Two-piece military stock. Made from 1886 through World War II with various modifications.

French Military Rifle manufactured by Manufacture Francaise d'Armes et de Cycles de St. Etienne (MAS), St. Etienne, Loire, France

French Model 1936 MAS Military Rifle.........$100
Bolt action. Caliber, 7.5mm MAS. 5-shot box magazine. 22½-inch barrel. Weight, about 8¼ pounds. Adjustable rear sight, blade front sight. Two-piece military-type stock. Bayonet carried in fore-end tube. Made from 1936 to 1940.

Garcia Corporation, Teaneck, New Jersey

Garcia Bronco 22 Single Shot Rifle..............$ 45
Swing-out action. Takedown. Caliber, 22 Long Rifle, Long, Short. 16½-inch barrel. Weight, 3 pounds. Open rear sight, blade front sight. One-piece stock and receiver, crackle finish. Introduced, 1967. Discontinued.

German Military Rifles manufactured by Ludwig Loewe & Co., Berlin; also by all German arsenals as well as other contractors such as Haenel and Schilling

German Model 1888 (Gew. 88) Mauser-Mannlicher Service Rifle.....................................$100
Bolt action, straight handle. Caliber, 7.9mm Mauser (8x57mm). 5-shot Mannlicher box magazine. 29-inch barrel with jacket. Weight, about 8½ pounds. Fixed front sight, adjustable rear. Military-type full stock.

German Model 1888 (Kar. 88) Mauser-Mannlicher Carbine...$100
Same general specifications as Gew. 88, except has 18-inch

barrel, without jacket, flat turned-down bolt handle, weighs about 6¾ pounds.

German Military Rifles manufactured by various plants under German Government control

German Model 1898 (Gew. 98) Mauser Military Rifle... $150
Bolt action, straight handle. Caliber, 7.9mm Mauser (8x57mm). 5-shot box magazine. 29-inch barrel. Weight, 9 pounds. Blade front sight, adjustable rear sight. Military-type full stock with rounded bottom pistol grip. Adopted in 1898.

German Model 1898A (Kar. 98A) Mauser Carbine... $150
Same general specifications as Model 1898 (Gew. 98) Rifle, except has turned-down bolt handle, smaller receiver ring, light 23½-inch straight taper barrel, front sight guards, sling is attached to left side of stock, weighs 8 pounds. *Note:* Some of these carbines are marked "Kar. 98;" the true Kar. 98 is the earlier original M/98 carbine with 17-inch barrel and is rarely encountered.

German Model 1898B (Kar. 98B) Mauser Carbine... $125
Same general specifications as Model 1898 (Gew. 98) Rifle, except has turned-down bolt handle and sling attached to left side of stock. This is the post World War I model.

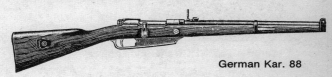

German Kar. 88

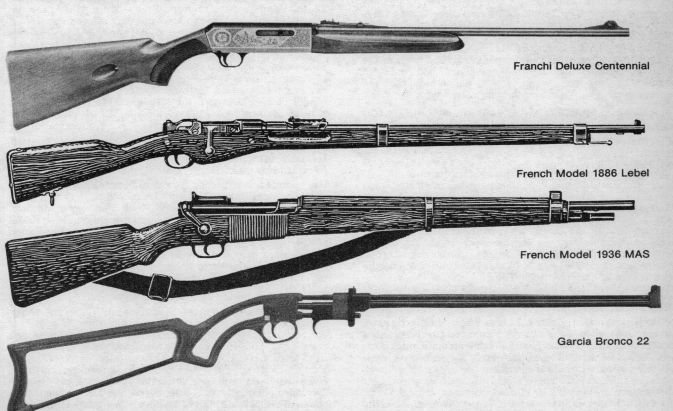

Franchi Deluxe Centennial

French Model 1886 Lebel

French Model 1936 MAS

Garcia Bronco 22

German Gew. 98

German Kar. 98K

German Gew. 33/40

German Gew. 43

German Model 1898K (Kar. 98K) Mauser Carbine **$150**
Same general specifications as Model 1898 (Gew. 98) Rifle except has turned-down bolt handle, 23½-inch barrel, may have hooded front sight, sling is attached to left side of stock, weighs about 8½ pounds. Adopted in 1935, this was the standard German Service rifle during World War II. *Note:* Late war models had stamped sheet steel trigger guards and many of the Model 98k carbines made during World War II had laminated wood stocks; these weigh about ½ to ¾ pound more than the previous model 98k. Value shown is for earlier type.

German Model 29/40 (Gew. 29/40) Mauser Rifle. $120
Same general specifications as Kar. 98k, differences are minor. Made in Poland during German occupation. Adopted in 1940.

German Model 33/40 (Gew. 33/40) Mauser Rifle. $120
Same general specifications as the Czech Model 33 (VZ33) Mauser Carbine with minor modifications, has laminated wood stock as found in war-time Model 98k carbines. Made in Czechoslovakia during German occupation. Adopted in 1940.

German Model 24T (Gew. 24T) Mauser Rifle **$120**
Same general specifications as the Czech Model 24 (VZ24) Mauser Rifle with minor modifications, has laminated wood stock, weighs about 9¼ pounds. Made in Czechoslovakia during German occupation. Adopted in 1940.

German Model VK 98 People's Rifle ("Volksgewehr") . . . . **$ 85**
Kar. 98K-type action. Caliber, 7.9mm. Single shot or repeater (latter with rough hole-in-the-stock 5-shot "magazine" or fitted with 10-shot clip of German Model 43 semiautomatic rifle). 20.9-inch barrel. Weight, 7 pounds. Fixed V-notch rear sight dovetailed into front receiver ring; front blade welded to barrel. Crude, unfinished, half-length stock without butt plate. Last ditch weapon made in 1945 for issue to German civilians. *Note:* Of value only as a military arms collector's item, this hastily made rifle should be regarded as *unsafe* to shoot.

Note: German Mauser Military Rifles (Gew. 98, Kar. 98) were made prior to and during World War I at the government arsenals at Amberg, Brunn, Danzig, Erfurt and Spandau; they were also manufactured by contractors such as Haenel, Loewe, Mauser, Schilling and Steyr. These rifles bear the Imperial Crown, maker's name and date of manufacture on the receiver ring. Post World War I Kar. 98b bears maker's name and date. During World War II as well as the years immediately preceding (probably from c. 1935), a letter or number code was used to indicate maker. This code and date of manufacture will be found stamped on the receiver ring of rifles of this period. German Service Mausers also bear the model number (Gew. 98, Kar. 98k, G. 33/40, etc.) on the left side of the receiver. An exception is Model VK98, which usually bears no identifying marks. Gew. is abbreviation for *gewehr* (rifle), Kar. for *karabiner* (carbine).

German Models 41 and 41-W (Gew. 41, Gew. 41-W) Semiautomatic Military Rifles **$200**
Gas-operated, muzzle cone system. Caliber, 7.9mm Mauser. 10-shot box magazine, 22½-inch barrel. Weight, about 10¾ pounds. Adjustable leaf rear sight, blade front sight. Military-type stock with semi-pistol grip, plastic handguard. *Note:* Model 41 lacks bolt release found on Model 41-W, otherwise the two models are the same. This is a Walther design and the early models were manufactured in that firm's Zella-Mehlis plant. Made from about 1941 to 1943.

German Model 43 (Gew. 43, Kar. 43) Semiautomatic Military Rifles **$225**
Gas-operated, barrel vented as in Russian Tokarev. Caliber, 7.9mm Mauser. 10-shot detachable box magazine. 22- or 24-inch barrel. Weight, about 9 pounds. Adjustable rear sight, hooded front sight. Military-type stock with semi-pistol grip, wooden handguard. *Note:* These rifles are alike except for minor details, have characteristic late World War II manufacturing short cuts: cast receiver and bolt cover, stamped steel parts, etc. Gew. 43 may have either 22- or 24-inch barrel; the former length was standardized in late 1944 when weapon designation was changed to "Kar. 43." Made from 1943 to 1945.

Gévarm Rifle manufactured by Gévelot, Saint Etienne, France

Gévarm E-1 Autoloading Rifle.................. **$135**
Caliber, 22 Long Rifle, 8-shot clip magazine, 19½-inch barrel. Open rear sight, post front sight. Pistol-grip stock and forearm of French walnut.

Golden Eagle Rifles manufactured for Golden Eagle Firearms Inc., Houston, Texas, by Nikko Firearms Ltd., Tochigi, Japan

Golden Eagle Model 7000 Grade I Big Game Rifle.................................. **$450**
Bolt action. Calibers: 22-250, 243 Win., 25-06, 270 Win., 270 Weatherby Mag., 7mm Rem. Mag., 30-06, 300 Weath. Mag., 300 Win. Mag., 338 Win. Mag. Magazine capacity: 4 rounds in 22-250, 3 rounds in other calibers. 24- or 26-inch barrel (26-inch only in 338). Weights: 7 pounds in 22-250, 8¾ pounds in other calibers. Furnished without sights. Fancy American walnut stock, skip-checkered, contrasting wood fore-end tip and grip cap with gold eagle head, recoil pad. Introduced, 1976. Discontinued.

Golden Eagle Model 7000 Grade I African....... **$500**
Same as standard model, except calibers 375 H&H Mag. and 458 Win. Mag., 2-shot magazine in 458, weighs 8¾ pounds in 375 and 10½ pounds in 458, furnished with sights. Introduced, 1976. Discontinued.

Greifelt & Co., Suhl Germany

Greifelt Sport Model 22 Hornet Bolt Action Rifle.................................. **$825**
Caliber, 22 Hornet. 5-shot box magazine. 22-inch Krupp steel barrel. Weight, 6 pounds. Two-leaf rear sight, ramp front sight. Walnut stock, checkered pistol grip and forearm. Made prior to World War II.

Hämmerli AG Jagd-und Sportwaffenfabrik, Lenzburg, Switzerland

Hämmerli Model Olympia 300 Meter Bolt Action Single Shot Free Rifle............................... **$750**
Calibers: 30-06, 300 H&H Magnum for U.S.A.; ordinarily produced in 7.5mm, other calibers available on special order. 29½-inch heavy barrel. Double-pull trigger or double-set trigger. Micrometer peep rear sight, globe front sight. Free rifle stock with cheekpiece, full pistol grip, thumb-hole, beavertail forearm, palm-rest, Swiss-type butt plate, swivels. Made from 1945 to 1959.

Hämmerli Model 45 Smallbore Bolt Action Single Shot Match Rifle.. **$550**
Calibers: 22 Long Rifle, 22 Extra Long. 27½-inch heavy barrel. Weight, about 15½ pounds. Micrometer peep rear sight, globe front sight. Free rifle stock with cheekpiece, full pistol grip, thumb-hole, beavertail forearm, palm-rest, Swiss-type butt plate, swivels. Made from 1945 to 1957.

Gévarm E-1

Golden Eagle Model 7000

Hämmerli Olympia

Hämmerli Model 45

Hämmerli-Tanner 300 Meter Free Rifle........ $820
Bolt action single shot. Caliber, 7.5mm standard, available in most popular centerfire calibers. 29½-inch heavy barrel. Weight, about 16¾ pounds. Micrometer peep rear sight, globe front sight. Free rifle stock with cheekpiece, thumb-hole, adjustable hook butt plate, palm-rest, swivel. Made from 1962 to date.

Hämmerli Model 54 Smallbore Match Rifle...... $545
Bolt action single shot. Caliber, 22 Long Rifle. 27½-inch heavy barrel. Weight, about 15 pounds. Micrometer peep rear sight, globe front sight. Free rifle stock with cheekpiece, thumb-hole, adjustable hook butt plate, palm-rest, swivel. Made from 1954 to 1957.

Hämmerli Model 503 Free Rifle................. $550
Bolt action single shot. Caliber, 22 Long Rifle, 27½-inch heavy barrel. Weight, about 15½ pounds. Micrometer peep rear sight, globe front sight. Free rifle stock with cheekpiece, thumb-hole, adjustable hook butt plate, palm-rest, swivel. Made from 1957 to 1962.

Hämmerli Model 506 Smallbore Match Rifle.... $580
Bolt action single shot. Caliber, 22 Long Rifle. 26¾-inch heavy barrel. Weight, about 16½ pounds. Micrometer peep rear sight, globe front sight. Free rifle stock with cheekpiece, thumb-hole, adjustable hook butt plate, palm-rest, swivel. Made from 1963 to 1966.

C. G. Haenel, Suhl, Germany

Haenel Mauser-Mannlicher Bolt Action Sporting Rifle
... $300
Mauser M/88 type action. Calibers: 7x57, 8x57, 9x57mm, Mannlicher clip-loading box magazine, 5-shot. 22- or 24-inch half- or full-octagon barrel with raised matted rib. Double-set trigger. Weight, about 7½ pounds. Leaf type open rear sight, ramp front sight. Sporting stock with cheekpiece, checkered pistol grip, raised side-panels, schnabel tip, swivels.

Haenel '88 Mauser Sporter...................... $275
Same general specifications as Haenel Mauser-Mannlicher, except has Mauser 5-shot box magazine.

Harrington & Richardson Inc., Gardner, Massachusetts

Harrington & Richardson Reising Model 60 Semi-automatic Rifle................................... $375
Caliber, 45 Automatic. 12-shot and 20-shot detachable box magazines. 18¼-inch barrel. Weight, about 7½ pounds. Open rear sight, blade front sight. Plain pistol-grip stock. Made from 1944 to 1946.

Harrington & Richardson Model 65 Military Autoloading Rifle... $200
Also called "General." Caliber, 22 Long Rifle, 10-shot detachable box magazine. 23-inch heavy barrel. Weight, about 9 pounds. Redfield 70 rear peep sight, blade front sight with protecting "ears." Plain pistol-grip stock, "Garand" dimensions. Made from 1944 to 1946. *Note:* This model was used as a training rifle by the U.S. Marine Corps.

Harrington & Richardson Model 165 "Leatherneck" Autoloading Rifle................................... $100
Caliber, 22 Long Rifle. 10-shot detachable box magazine. 23-inch barrel. Weight, about 7½ pounds. Redfield 70 rear peep sight, blade front sight on ramp. Plain pistol-grip stock, swivels, web sling. Made from 1945 to 1961.

Harrington & Richardson Model 265 "Reg'lar" Bolt Action Repeating Rifle........................... $ 50
Caliber, 22 Long Rifle. 10-shot detachable box magazine. 22-inch barrel. Weight, about 6½ pounds. Lyman 55 rear peep sight, blade front sight on ramp. Plain pistol-grip stock. Made from 1946 to 1949.

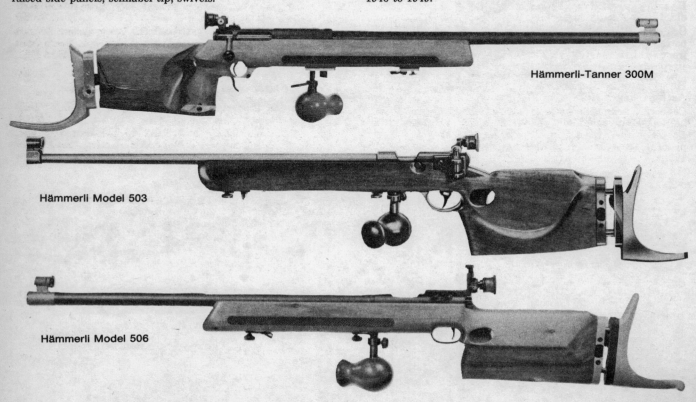

Hämmerli-Tanner 300M

Hämmerli Model 503

Hämmerli Model 506

H&R Reising Model 60

H&R Model 65

H&R Model 165

Harrington & Richardson Model 450............**$125**
Same as Model 451, except without front and rear sights.

Harrington & Richardson "Targeteer Jr." Bolt Action Rifle..**$ 85**
Caliber, 22 Long Rifle. 5-shot detachable box magazine. 20-inch barrel. Weight, about 7 pounds. Redfield 70 rear peep sight. Lyman 17A front sight. Target stock, junior size with pistol grip, swivels and sling. Made from 1948 to 1951.

Harrington & Richardson Model 365 "Ace" Bolt Action Single Shot Rifle............................**$ 40**
Caliber, 22 Long Rifle. 22-inch barrel. Weight, about 6½ pounds. Lyman 55 rear peep sight, blade front sight on ramp. Plain pistol-grip stock. Made from 1946-1947.

Harrington & Richardson Model 465 "Targeteer Special" Bolt Action Repeating Rifle............**$ 90**
Caliber, 22 Long Rifle. 10-shot detachable box magazine. 25-inch barrel. Weight, about 9 pounds. Lyman 57 rear peep sight, blade front sight on ramp. Plain pistol-grip stock, swivels, web sling strap. Made from 1946 to 1947.

Harrington & Richardson Model 451 "Medalist" Bolt Action Target Rifle............................**$150**
Caliber, 22 Long Rifle. 5-shot detachable box magazine. 26-inch barrel. Weight, about 10½ pounds. Lyman 524F extension rear sight, Lyman 77 front sight, scope bases. Target stock with full pistol grip and forearm, swivels and sling. Made from 1948 to 1961.

Harrington & Richardson Model 250 "Sportster" Bolt Action Repeating Rifle............................**$ 50**
Caliber, 22 Long Rifle. 5-shot detachable box magazine. 23-inch barrel. Weight, about 6½ pounds. Open rear sight, blade front sight on ramp. Plain pistol-grip stock. Made from 1948 to 1961.

Harrington & Richardson Model 251............**$ 55**
Same as Model 250 except has Lyman 55H rear sight.

Harrington & Richardson Model 765 "Pioneer" Bolt Action Single Shot Rifle........................**$ 30**
Caliber, 22 Long Rifle, Long, Short. 24-inch barrel. Weight, about 5 pounds. Open rear sight, hooded bead front sight. Plain pistol-grip stock. Made from 1948 to 1954.

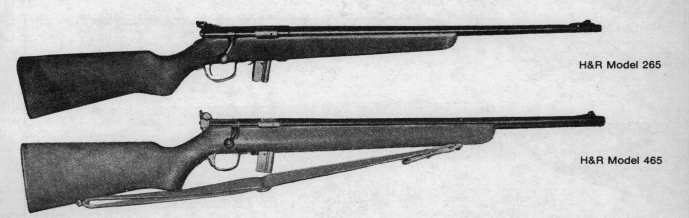

H&R Model 265

H&R Model 465

Harrington & Richardson Model 865 "Plainsman" Bolt Action Repeating Rifle . . . . $ 60
Caliber, 22 Long Rifle, Long, Short. 5-shot detachable box magazine. 22- or 24-inch barrel. Weight, about 5¼ pounds. Open rear sight and bead front sight. Plain pistol-grip stock. Made from 1949 to date.

Harrington & Richardson Model 866 Bolt Action Repeating Rifle . . . . $ 65
Same as Model 865, except has Mannlicher-style stock. Made in 1971.

Harrington & Richardson Model 150 "Leatherneck" Autoloading Rifle $100
Caliber, 22 Long Rifle only. 5-shot detachable box magazine, 22-inch barrel. Weight, about 7¼ pounds. Open rear sight, blade front sight on ramp. Plain pistol-grip stock. Made from 1949 to 1953.

Harrington & Richardson Model 151 . . . . $125
Same as Model 150 except with Redfield 70 rear peep sight.

Harrington & Richardson Model 852 "Fieldsman" Bolt Action Repeating Rifle . . . . $ 65
Caliber, 22 Long Rifle, Long, Short. Tubular magazine holds 21 Short, 17 Long, 15 Long Rifle. 24-inch barrel. Weight, about 5½ pounds. Open rear sight, bead front sight. Plain pistol-grip stock. Made from 1952 to 1953.

Harrington & Richardson Model 750 "Pioneer" Bolt Action Single Shot Rifle . . . . $ 40
Caliber, 22 Long Rifle, Long, Short. 22- or 24-inch barrel. Weight, about 5 pounds. Open rear sight, bead front sight. Plain pistol-grip stock. Made from 1954 to 1981. Redesigned in 1982.

Harrington & Richardson Model 751 Single Shot Rifle . . . . $ 50
Same as Model 750, except has Mannlicher-style stock. Made in 1971.

Harrington & Richardson Model 422 Slide Action Repeater . . . . $ 85
Caliber, 22 Long Rifle, Long, Short. Tubular magazine holds 21 Short, 17 Long, 15 Long Rifle. 24-inch barrel. Weight, about 6 pounds. Open rear sight, ramp front sight. Plain pistol-grip stock, grooved slide handle. Made from 1956 to 1958.

Harrington & Richardson Model 755 "Sahara" Single Shot Rifle . . . . $ 40
Blow-back action, automatic ejection. Caliber, 22 Long Rifle, Long, Short. 18-inch barrel. Weight, 4 pounds. Open rear sight, military type front sight. Mannlicher-style stock. Made from 1963 to 1971.

Harrington & Richardson Model 760 Single Shot Rifle . . . . $ 40
Same as Model 755, except has conventional sporter stock. Made from 1965 to 1970.

Harrington & Richardson Model 800 "Lynx" Autoloading Rifle . . . . $ 65
Caliber, 22 Long Rifle. 5 or 10-shot clip magazine. 22-inch barrel. Open sights. Weight, 6 pounds. Plain pistol-grip stock. Made from 1958 to 1960.

Harrington & Richardson Model 158 "Topper Jet" Single Shot Combination Rifle
Shotgun-type action with visible hammer, side lever, automatic ejector. Caliber, 22 Rem. Jet. 22-inch barrel (interchanges with 30-30, 410 ga., 20 ga. barrels). Weight, 5 pounds. Lyman folding adjustable open rear sight, ramp front sight. Plain pistol-grip stock and forearm, recoil pad. Made from 1963 to 1967.
Rifle only. . . . . $ 85
Interchangeable barrel — 30-30, shotgun. . . . . $ 25

Harrington & Richardson Model 158C . . . . $ 85
Same as Model 158 "Topper Jet," except calibers 22 Hornet and 30-30. Straight-grip stock. Made from 1963 to date.

Harrington & Richardson Model 163 "Mustang" Single Shot Rifle . . . . $ 85
Same as Model 158 "Topper" except has gold-plated hammer and trigger, straight-grip stock and contoured forearm. Made from 1964 to 1967.

H&R Model 866

H&R Model 750

H&R Model 755 "Sahara"

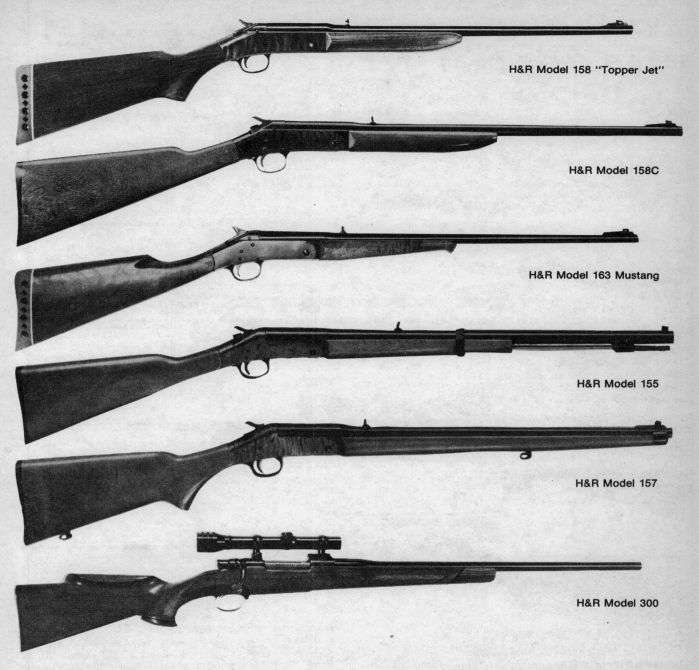

H&R Model 158 "Topper Jet"

H&R Model 158C

H&R Model 163 Mustang

H&R Model 155

H&R Model 157

H&R Model 300

Harrington & Richardson Model 155 Single Shot Rifle.................................$ 90

Model 158 action. Calibers: 44 Rem. Mag., 45-70 Govt. 24-or 28-inch barrel (latter in 44 only). Weight, 7 or 7½ pounds. Folding leaf rear sight, blade front sight. Straight-grip stock, forearm with barrel band, brass cleaning rod. Made from 1972 to date.

Harrington & Richardson Model 157 Single Shot Rifle.................................$ 90

Model 158 action. Calibers: 22 Win. Mag. RF, 22 Hornet, 30-30. 22-inch barrel. Weight, 6¼ pounds. Folding leaf rear sight, blade front sight. Pistol-grip stock, full-length forearm, swivels. Made from 1976 to date.

Harrington & Richardson Model 300 Ultra Bolt Action Rifle...$350

Mauser-type action. Calibers: 22-250, 243 Win., 270 Win., 30-06, 308 Win., 7mm Rem. Mag., 300 Win. Mag. 3-round magazine in 7mm and 300 Mag. calibers, 5-round in others. 22- or 24-inch barrel. Open rear sight, ramp front sight. Checkered stock with roll-over cheekpiece and full pistol grip, contrasting wood forearm tip and pistol grip, rubber butt plate, swivels. Weight, 7¼ pounds. Made from 1965 to date.

Harrington & Richardson Model 301 Carbine....$380

Same as Model 300, except has 18-inch barrel, Mannlicher-style stock, weighs 7¼ pounds; not available in caliber 22-250. Made from 1967 to 1976.

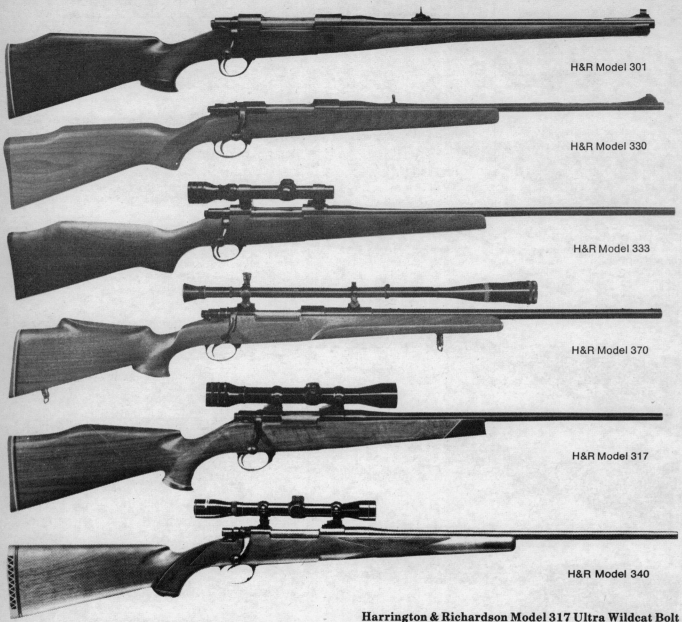

H&R Model 301

H&R Model 330

H&R Model 333

H&R Model 370

H&R Model 317

H&R Model 340

**Harrington & Richardson Model 330
Hunter's Rifle**....................................**$275**
Similar to Model 300, but with plainer stock. Calibers: 243 Win.,
270 Win., 30-06, 308 Win., 7mm Rem. Mag., 300 Win. Mag.
Weight, about 7⅛ pounds. Made from 1967 to 1972.

Harrington & Richardson Model 333............**$225**
Plainer version of Model 300 with uncheckered walnut-finished
hardwood stock. Calibers: 7mm Rem. Mag., 30-06. 22-inch barrel. Weight, 7¼ pounds. No sights. Made in 1974.

**Harrington & Richardson Model 370
Ultra Medalist**....................................**$350**
Varmint and target rifle based on Model 300. Calibers: 22-250,
243 Win., 6mm Rem. 5-round magazine. 24-inch varmint weight
barrel. No sights. Target-style stock with semi-beavertail forearm. Weight, 9½ pounds. Made from 1968 to 1973

**Harrington & Richardson Model 317 Ultra Wildcat Bolt
Action Rifle**......................................**$325**
Sako short action. Calibers: 17 Rem., 17/223 (handload), 222
Rem., 223 Rem. 6-round magazine. 20-inch barrel. No sights,
receiver dovetailed for scope mounts. Checkered stock with
cheekpiece and full pistol grip, contrasting wood forearm tip and
pistol-grip cap, rubber butt plate. Weight, 5¼ pounds. Made
from 1968 to 1976.

**Harrington & Richardson Model 317P Presentation
Grade**...**$565**
Same as Model 317, except has select grade fancy walnut stock
with basketweave carving on forearm and pistol grip. Made from
1968 to 1976.

Harrington & Richardson Model 340............**$245**
Mauser-type action. Calibers: 243 Win., 308 Win., 270 Win.,
30-06, 7x57mm. 22-inch barrel. Weight, 7¼ pounds. Hand-
checkered stock of American walnut. Made from 1982 to date.

Harrington & Richardson Model 360 Ultra Automatic Rifle **$310**
Gas-operated semiautomatic. Calibers: 243 Win., 308 Win. 3-round detachable box magazine. 22-inch barrel. Open rear sight, ramp front sight. Checkered stock with roll-over cheekpiece, full pistol grip, contrasting wood forearm tip and pistol-grip cap, rubber butt plate, sling swivels. Weight, 7½ pounds. Introduced, 1965. Discontinued. (*Note:* Originally designated Model 308, number changed to 360 in 1967).

Harrington & Richardson Model 361 . . . . **$325**
Same as Model 360, except has full roll-over cheekpiece for right- or left-hand shooters. Made 1970 to 1973.

Harrington & Richardson 100th Anniversary (1871-1971) Commemorative Officer's Model Springfield Replica, Model 1873 . . . . **$400**
Model 1873 "trap door" single-shot action. Engraved breech block, receiver, hammer, lock, band and butt plate. Caliber, 45-70. 26-inch barrel. Peep rear sight, blade front sight. Checkered walnut stock with anniversary plaque. Ramrod. Weight, about 8 pounds. 10,000 made in 1971. Value is for rifle in new, unfired condition.

Harrington & Richardson Model 171 . . . . **$200**
Model 1873 Springfield Cavalry Carbine replica. Caliber, 45-70. 22-inch barrel. Weight, 7 pounds. Leaf rear sight, blade front sight. Plain walnut stock. Made from 1972 to 1981.

Harrington & Richardson Model 171 Deluxe **$250**
Same as Model 171, except engraved action. Made from 1972 to date.

Harrington & Richardson Model 172 . . . . **$1150**
Same as Model 171 Deluxe, except silver-plated, has fancy walnut stock, checkered, with grip adapter; tang-mounted aperture sight. Made from 1972 to date.

Harrington & Richardson Model 173 . . . . **$285**
Model 1873 Springfield Officer's Model replica, same as 100th Anniversary Commemorative, except without plaque on stock. Made from 1972 to date.

Harrington & Richardson Model 174 . . . . **$275**
Little Big Horn Commemorative Carbine. Same as Model 171 Deluxe, except has tang-mounted aperture sight, grip adapter. Made in 1972. Value is for carbine in new, unfired condition.

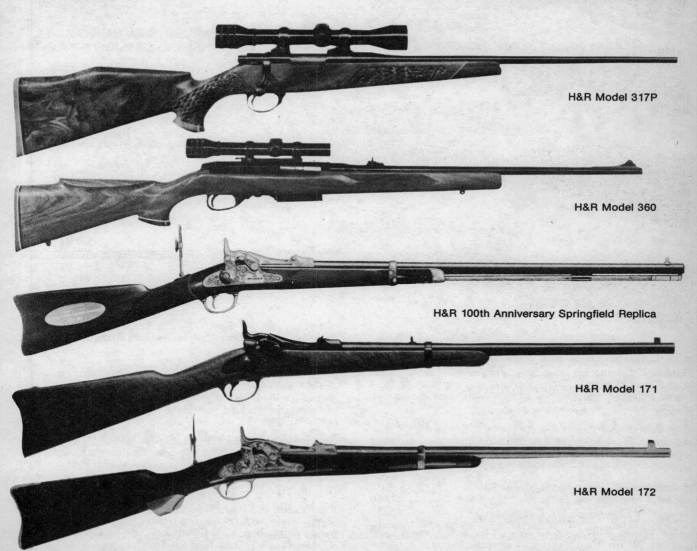

H&R Model 317P

H&R Model 360

H&R 100th Anniversary Springfield Replica

H&R Model 171

H&R Model 172

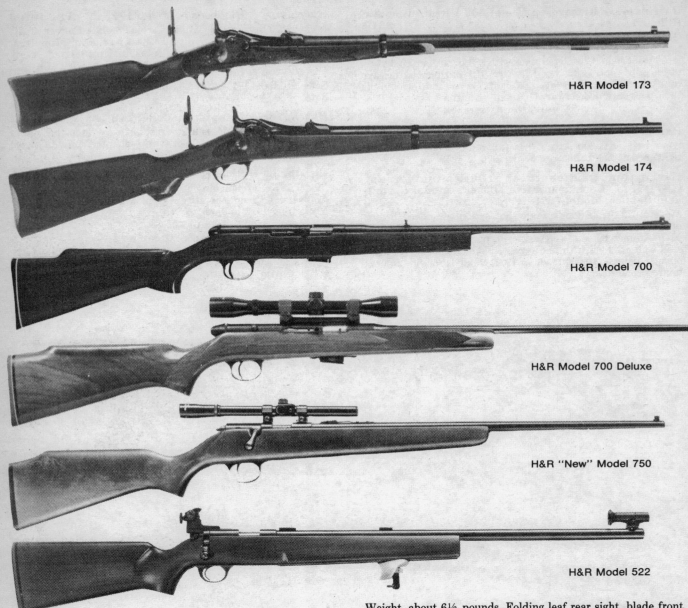

H&R Model 173

H&R Model 174

H&R Model 700

H&R Model 700 Deluxe

H&R "New" Model 750

H&R Model 522

Harrington & Richardson Model 178............$225
Model 1873 Springfield Infantry Rifle replica. Caliber, 45-70. 32-inch barrel. Weight, 8 lbs. 10 oz. Leaf rear sight, blade front sight. Full-length stock with barrel bands, swivels, ramrod. Made from 1973 to date.

Harrington & Richardson Custer Memorial Issue
Limited Edition Model 1873 Springfield Carbine replica, richly engraved and inlaid with gold, fancy walnut stock, in mahogany display case. Made in 1973. Value is for carbine in new, unfired condition.
Officers' Model, limited to 25 pieces................ **$3500**
Enlisted Men's Model, limited to 243 pieces.......... **2250**

**Harrington & Richardson Model 700
Autoloading Rifle...............................$155**
Caliber, 22 Win. Mag. Rimfire, 5-shot magazine. 22-inch barrel.

Weight, about 6½ pounds. Folding leaf rear sight, blade front sight on ramp. Monte Carlo-style stock of American walnut. Introduced in 1977.

Harrington & Richardson Model 700 Deluxe.... $200
Same as Model 700 Standard except has select custom polished and blued finish, select walnut stock, hand checkering, and no iron sights. Fitted with H&R Model 432 4x scope. Made from 1980 to date.

Harrington & Richardson Model 5200 Sporter.. $260
Turn-bolt repeater. Caliber, 22 Long Rifle. 24-inch barrel. Classic style American walnut stock. Adjustable trigger. Peep receiver sight, hooded ramp front sight. Weight, 6½ pounds.

**Harrington & Richardson Model 5200
Match Rifle...$225**
Same action as 5200 Sporter. Caliber, 22 Long Rifle. 28-inch target weight barrel. Target stock of American walnut. Weight, 11 pounds. Made from 1982 to date.

Heckler & Koch Model HK300

Heckler & Koch Model HK91 A-2

Heckler & Koch Model HK91 A-3

Heckler & Koch Model HK93 A-2

Heckler & Koch, GMBH,
Oberndorf/Neckar, West Germany

**Heckler & Koch Model HK300 Semiautomatic
Rifle** **$275**
Caliber, 22 Win. Mag. Rimfire. 5- or 15-round box magazine.
19.7-inch barrel. Weight, about 5¾ pounds. V-notch rear sight,
ramp front sight. European walnut stock with cheekpiece,
checkered forearm and pistol grip. Currently manufactured.

**Heckler & Koch Model HK91 A-2 Semiautomatic
Rifle** **$525**
Delayed roller-locked blow-back action. Caliber, 7.62mm x 51
NATO (308) Win.). 5- or 20-round box magazine. 19-inch barrel.
Weight, without magazine, 9.37 pounds. "V" and aperture rear

sight, post front sight. Plastic buttstock and forearm. Currently
manufactured.

Heckler & Koch Model HK91 A-3 . . . . **$650**
Same as Model HK91 A-2, except has retractable metal buttstock, weighs 10.56 pounds. Currently manufactured.

**Heckler & Koch Model HK93 A-2 Semiautomatic
Rifle** **$500**
Delayed roller-locked blow-back action. Caliber, 5.56mm x 45
(223 Rem.). 5- or 20-round magazine. 16.13-inch barrel. Weight,
without magazine, 7.6 pounds. "V" and aperture sight, post front
sight. Plastic buttstock and forearm. Currently manufactured.

Heckler & Koch Model HK93 A-3

Heckler & Koch Model HK93 A-3 .... **$630**
Same as Model HK93 A-2, except has retractable metal buttstock, weighs 8.42 pounds. Currently manufactured.

Herold Rifle made by Franz Jaeger & Co., Suhl, Germany

Herold Bolt Action Repeating Sporting Rifle **$860**
"Herold-Repetierbüchse." Miniature Mauser-type action with unique 5-shot box magazine on hinged floorplate. Double-set triggers. Caliber, 22 Hornet. 24-inch barrel. Leaf rear sight, ramp front sight. Weight, about 7¾ pounds. Fancy checkered stock. Made prior to World War II. *Note:* These rifles were imported by Charles Daly and A. F. Stoeger Inc. of New York City and sold under their own names.

The High Standard Mfg. Corp., Hamden, Connecticut

High Standard Sport-King "Field" Autoloading Rifle .... **$ 75**
Caliber, 22 Long Rifle, 22 Long, 22 Short (high speed). Tubular magazine holds 15 L.R., 17 Long, or 21 Short. 22¼-inch barrel. Weight, 5½ pounds. Open rear sight, beaded post front sight. Plain pistol-grip stock. Made from 1960 to 1966.

High Standard Sport-King "Special" Autoloading Rifle .... **$ 85**
Same as Sport-King "Field", except stock has Monte Carlo comb and semi-beavertail forearm. Made from 1960 to 1966.

High Standard Sport-King Autoloading Carbine. **$100**
Same as Sport-King "Field" Autoloader, except has 18¼-inch barrel, Western style straight-grip stock with barrel band, sling and swivels. Made from 1964 to 1973.

High Standard Sport-King Deluxe Autoloader ... **$ 95**
Same as Sport-King "Special" Autoloader, except has checkered stock. Made from 1966 to 1975.

High Standard Hi-Power Deluxe Bolt Action Rifle **$250**
Mauser-type action, sliding safety. Calibers: 270, 30-06. 4-shot magazine. 22-inch barrel. Weight, 7 pounds. Folding open rear sight, ramp front sight. Walnut stock with checkered pistol grip and forearm, Monte Carlo comb, Q.D. swivels. Made from 1962 to 1966.

High Standard Hi-Power "Field" Bolt Action Rifle **$225**
Same as Hi-Power Deluxe, except has plain field style stock. Made from 1962 to 1966.

High Standard Flite-King Pump Rifle .... **$ 95**
Hammerless slide action. Caliber, 22 Long Rifle, 22 Long, 22 Short. Tubular magazine holds 17 Long Rifle, 19 Long, or 24 Short. 24-inch barrel. Weight, 5½ pounds. Patridge rear sight, bead front sight. Monte Carlo stock with pistol grip, serrated semi-beavertail forearm. Made from 1962 to 1975.

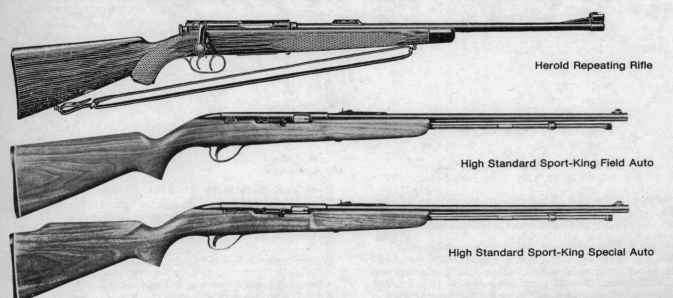

Herold Repeating Rifle

High Standard Sport-King Field Auto

High Standard Sport-King Special Auto

High Standard Sport-King Auto Carbine

High Standard Sport-King Deluxe Auto

High Standard Hi-Power Deluxe

High Standard Hi-Power Field

High Standard Flite-King Pump

H & H Royal Double Rifle

Holland & Holland, Ltd., London, England

Holland & Holland Royal Hammerless Ejector Double Rifle **$18,000**
Side lock. Calibers: 240 Apex, 7mm H&H Mag., 300 H&H Mag., 300 Win. Mag., 30-06, 375 H&H Mag., 458 Win. Mag., 465 H&H Mag. 24- to 28-inch barrels. Weights, from 7½ pounds up, depending upon caliber and barrel length. Folding leaf rear sight, ramp front sight. Cheekpiece stock of select French walnut, checkered pistol grip and forearm. Currently manufactured. Same general specifications apply to prewar model.

Holland & Holland Royal Deluxe Double Rifle **$15,000**
Formerly designated "Modele Deluxe." Same specifications as Royal Model, except has exhibition grade stock and special engraving. Currently manufactured.

Holland & Holland No. 2 Model Hammerless Ejector Double Rifle **$9000**
Same general specifications as Royal Model, except plainer finish. Discontinued 1960.

H & H Best Quality Magazine Rifle

Holland & Holland Best Quality Magazine Rifle... $2500

Mauser or Enfield action. Calibers: 240 Apex, 300 H&H Magnum, 375 H&H Magnum. 4-shot box magazine. 24-inch barrel. Weight, about 7¼ pounds in 300 Magnum caliber; about 8¼ pounds in 300 Magnum caliber; about 8¼ pounds in 375 Magnum caliber. Folding leaf rear sight, hooded ramp front sight. Detachable French walnut stock with cheekpiece, checkered pistol grip and forearm, swivels. Currently manufactured. Specifications given are those of the present model; however, in general they apply also to prewar models.

Holland & Holland Deluxe Magazine Rifle...... $3000

Same specifications as Best Quality, except has exhibition grade stock and special engraving. Currently manufactured.

Hungarian Military Rifles manufactured at Government Arsenal, Budapest, Hungary

Hungarian Model 1935M Mannlicher Military Rifle.. $175

Caliber, 8x52mm Hungarian. Bolt action, straight handle. 5-shot projecting box magazine. 24-inch barrel. Weight, about 9 pounds. Adjustable leaf rear sight, hooded front blade. Two-piece military-type stock. Made from 1935 to c.1940.

Hungarian Model 1943M (German Gew. 98/40) Mannlicher Military Rifle............................. $200

Modification, during German occupation, of the Model 1935M. Caliber, 7.9mm Mauser. Turned down bolt handle and Mauser M/98-type box magazine; other differences are minor. Made from 1940 to end of war in Europe.

Husqvarna Vapenfabrik A.B., Huskvarna, Sweden

Husqvarna Hi-Power Bolt Action Sporting Rifle. $245

Mauser-type action. Calibers: 220 Swift, 270 Win., 30-06 (see note below), 5-shot box magazine. 23¾-inch barrel. Weight, about 7¾ pounds. Open rear sight, hooded ramp front sight. Sporting stock of Arctic beech, checkered pistol grip and forearm, swivels. *Note:* Husqvarna sporters were first introduced in the United States about 1948; earlier models were also available in calibers 6.5x55, 8x57 and 9.3x57. Specifications given above are those of the 1950 model. Made from 1946 to 1951.

Husqvarna 1951 Model............................ $250

Same as 1950 Model, except has high comb stock, low safety.

Husqvarna Deluxe Model Hi-Power Bolt Action Sporting Rifles, Series 1100........................... $325

Same as 1951 Model, except has "jewelled" bolt, European walnut stock. Made from 1952 to 1956.

Husqvarna Super Grade, Series 1000............ $325

Same as 1951 Model, except has European walnut sporter stock with Monte Carlo comb and cheekpiece. Made from 1952 to 1956.

Husqvarna Crown Grade, Series 3100........... $350

HVA improved Mauser action. Calibers: 243, 270, 7mm, 30-06, 308 Win. 5-shot box magazine, 23¾-inch barrel. Weight, 7¼ pounds. Open rear sight, hooded ramp front sight. European walnut stock, checkered, cheekpiece, pistol-grip cap, black foretip, swivels. Made from 1954 to 1972.

Husqvarna Crown Grade, Series 3000........... $350

Same as Series 3100, except has Monte Carlo comb stock.

Husqvarna Lightweight Rifle, Series 4100...... $325

HVA improved Mauser action. Calibers: 243, 270, 7mm, 30-06, 308 Win. 5-shot box magazine. 20½-inch barrel. Weight, about 6¼ pounds. Open rear sight, hooded ramp front sight. Lightweight walnut stock with cheekpiece, pistol grip, schnabel foretip, checkered, swivels. Made from 1954 to 1972.

Husqvarna Lightweight Rifle, Series 4000...... $350

Same as Series 4100, except has no rear sight and has Monte Carlo comb stock.

Husqvarna Model 456 Lightweight Full-Stock Sporter.. $375

Same as Series 4000/4100 except has sporting-style full stock with slope-away cheek rest. Weight, 6½ pounds. Made from 1959 to 1970.

Husqvarna Imperial Custom Grade, Series 6000.. $425

Same as Series 3100, except fancy grade stock, 3-leaf folding rear sight, adjustable trigger. Calibers: 243, 270, 7mm Rem. Mag., 308, 30-06. Made from 1968 to 1970.

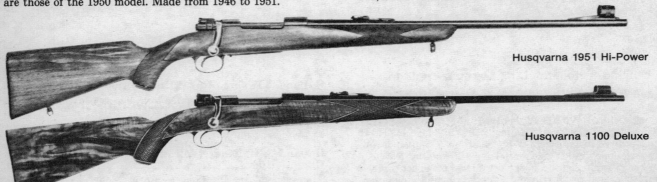

Husqvarna 1951 Hi-Power

Husqvarna 1100 Deluxe

Husqvarna 3000 Crown Grade

Husqvarna 4100 Lightweight

Husqvarna Model 456

Husqvarna 6000 Imperial Custom

Husqvarna 7000 Imperial Lightweight

Husqvarna P-3000 Presentation Grade

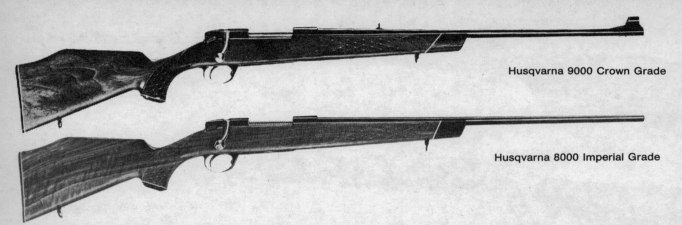

Husqvarna 9000 Crown Grade

Husqvarna 8000 Imperial Grade

Husqvarna Imperial Monte Carlo Lightweight, Series 7000 . . . . **$450**
Same as Series 4000 Lightweight, except fancy grade stock, 3-leaf folding rear sight, adjustable trigger. Calibers: 243, 270, 308, 30-06. Made from 1968 to 1970.

Husqvarna Presentation Rifle, Series P-3000 . . . **$600**
Same as Crown Grade Series 3000, except specially selected stock, engraved action, adjustable trigger. Calibers: 243, 270, 7mm Rem. Mag., 30-06. Made from 1968 to 1970.

Husqvarna Model 9000 Crown Grade Rifle **$325**
New design Husqvarna bolt action. Adjustable trigger. Calibers: 270, 7mm Rem. Mag., 30-06, 300 Win. Mag. 5-shot box magazine, hinged floorplate. 23¾-inch barrel. Folding leaf rear sight, hooded ramp front sight. Checkered walnut stock with Monte Carlo cheekpiece, rosewood forearm tip and pistol-grip cap. Weight, 7 lbs. 3 oz. Made from 1971 to 1972.

Husqvarna Model 8000 Imperial Grade Rifle **$450**
Same as Model 9000, except has jeweled bolt, engraved floorplate, deluxe French walnut stock, no sights. Made from 1971 to 1972.

Interarms Mark X Rifles manufactured for Interarms, Alexandria, Virginia, by Zavodi Crvena Zastava, Belgrade, Yugoslavia

Interarms Mark X Bolt Action Sporting Rifle **$210**
Mauser-type action. Calibers: 22-250, 243, 25-06, 270, 7x57, 7mm Rem. Mag., 308, 30-06, 300 Win. Mag. 5-shot magazine (3-shot in magnum calibers). 24-inch barrel. Weight, 7½ pounds. Adjustable leaf rear sight, ramp front sight with hood. Classic style stock of European walnut with Monte Carlo comb and cheekpiece, checkered pistol grip and forearm, black fore-end tip, QD swivels. Made from 1972 to date.

Interarms Mark X Cavalier **$275**
Same specifications as Mark X, except has contemporary style stock with roll-over cheekpiece, rosewood fore-end tip and grip cap, recoil pad. Made from 1974 to date.

Interarms Mark X Viscount **$200**
Same specifications as Mark X, except has plainer field grade stock. Made from 1974 to date.

Interarms Mark X

Interarms Mark X Cavalier

Interarms Mark X Viscount

Interarms Mark X Whitworth

Italian Model 38

Ithaca Model X5-T

Interarms Mark X Marquis Mannlicher Style Carbine.. **$275**
Same specifications as Mark X, except has 20-inch barrel, full-length Mannlicher-type stock with metal fore-end/muzzle cap. Calibers: 270, 7x57, 308, 30-06. Made from 1976 to date.

Interarms Mark X Continental Mannlicher Style Carbine.. **$280**
Same specifications as Mark X, except straight European-style comb stock with sculptured cheek-piece. Precise double-set triggers and classic "butter-knife" bolt handle. French checkering. Weight, about 7¼ pounds.

Interarms Mark X Alaskan...................... **$300**
Same specifications as Mark X, except calibers 375 H&H Mag. and 458 Win. Mag., 3-round magazine, weighs 8¼ pounds, has stock with recoil-absorbing cross bolt and heavy duty recoil pad. Made from 1976 to date.

Interarms Whitworth Express Rifle............. **$435**
Mauser-type action. Calibers: 7mm Rem. Mag., 375 H & H, 458 Win. 24-inch barrel. Traditional hand-checkered, oil finished, English style European walnut stock fitted with solid steel recoil bearing cross block. Three leaf express sights, rubber recoil pad.

Italian Military Rifles manufactured by Government plants at Brescia, Gardone, Terni and Turin, Italy

Italian Model 1891 Mannlicher-Carcano Military Rifle...................................... **$ 85**
Bolt action, straight handle. Caliber, 6.5mm. Italian Service. 6-shot modified Mannlicher-type box magazine. 30¾-inch barrel. Weight, about 9 pounds. Adjustable rear sight, blade front sight. Military-type straight-grip stock. Adopted 1891.

Italian Model 38 Military Rifle.................. **$ 85**
Modification of Model 1891, has turned-down bolt handle, detachable folding bayonet. Caliber, 7.35mm Italian Service (many arms of this model were later converted to the old 6.5mm caliber). 6-shot box magazine. 21¼-inch barrel. Weight, about 7½ pounds. Adjustable rear sight, blade front sight. Military-type straight-grip stock. Adopted 1938.

Ithaca Gun Company, Inc., Ithaca, New York

Ithaca Model X5-C Lightning Autoloader Clip Repeater... **$ 65**
Takedown. Caliber, 22 Long Rifle. 7-shot clip magazine. 22-inch barrel. Weight, 6 pounds. Open rear sight. Raybar front sight. Pistol-grip stock, grooved forearm. Made from 1958 to 1964.

Ithaca Model X5-T Lightning Autoloader Tubular Repeater... **$ 65**
Same as Model X5-C except has 16-shot tubular magazine, stock with plain forearm. Made from 1959 to 1963.

Ithaca Model X-15 Lightning Autoloader........ **$ 65**
Same general specifications as Model X5-C, except forearm is not grooved. Made from 1964 to 1967.

Ithaca Model 49 Saddlegun Lever Action Single Shot Rifle... **$ 40**
Martini-type action. Hand-operated rebounding hammer. Caliber, 22 Long Rifle, Long, Short. 18-inch barrel. Open sights. Western carbine-style stock. Weight, 5½ pounds. Made from 1961 to 1978.

Ithaca Model 49 Youth Saddlegun.............. **$ 40**
Same as standard Model 49, except shorter stock for young shooters. Made from 1961 to 1978.

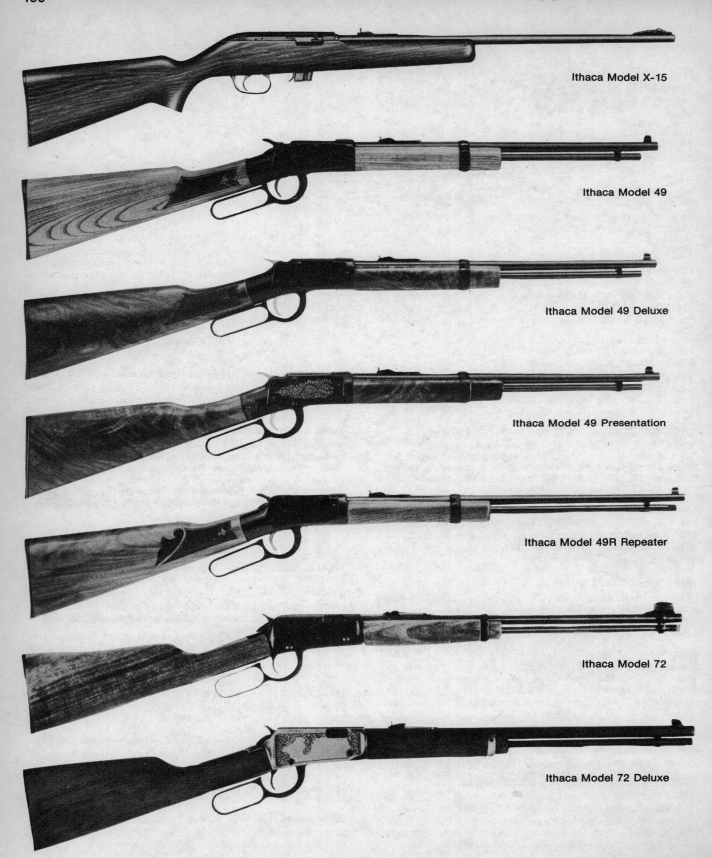

Ithaca Model X-15

Ithaca Model 49

Ithaca Model 49 Deluxe

Ithaca Model 49 Presentation

Ithaca Model 49R Repeater

Ithaca Model 72

Ithaca Model 72 Deluxe

Ithaca Model 49 Magnum Saddlegun............ **$ 45**
Same as standard Model 49, except chambered for 22 Win. Mag.
R.F. cartridge. Made from 1962 to 1978.

Ithaca Model 49 Deluxe Saddlegun............. **$ 55**
Same as standard Model 49, except has gold-plated hammer and
trigger, figured walnut stock, sling swivels. Made from 1962 to
1975.

**Ithaca St. Louis Bicentennial Model 49
Saddlegun**.. **$150**
Same as Model 49 Deluxe, except has commemorative inscription. 200 made in 1964. Value is for rifle in new, unfired condition.

Ithaca Model 49 Presentation Saddlegun....... **$175**
Same as standard Model 49 Saddlegun, except has gold-plated
hammer and trigger, engraved receiver, full fancy figured walnut
stock with gold nameplate. Available in 22 Long Rifle or 22
WMR. Made from 1962 to 1974.

Ithaca Model 49R Saddlegun Repeater......... **$110**
Similar in appearance to Model 49 Single Shot. Caliber, 22 Long
Rifle, Long, Short. Tubular magazine holds 15 LR, 17 Long, 21
Short. 20-inch barrel. Weight, 5½ pounds. Open rear sight, bead
front sight. Western-style stock, checkered grip. Made from
1968 to 1971.

**Ithaca Model 72 Saddlegun Lever Action Repeating
Carbine**.. **$130**
Caliber, 22 Long Rifle, Long, Short. Tubular magazine holds 15
LR, 17 Long, 21 Short. 18½-inch barrel. Weight, about 5½
pounds. Open rear sight, hooded ramp front sight. Receiver
grooved for scope mounting. Western carbine stock and forearm
of American walnut. Made from 1973 to 1978. *Note:* Barrel and
action are manufactured by Erma Werke, Dachau, West Germany; wood is installed by Ithaca.

Ithaca Model 72 Deluxe........................ **$180**
Same as standard Model 72, except has silver-finished and
engraved receiver, octagon barrel, higher grade walnut stock and
forearm. Made from 1974 to 1976.

Ithaca Model 72 Magnum....................... **$150**
Same as standard Model 72, except chambered for 22
Winchester Magnum Rimfire, has 11-shot tubular magazine,
18½-inch barrel. Made from 1975 to 1978.

**Ithaca Model LSA-55 Standard Grade Bolt Action Re-
peating Rifle**..................................... **$300**
Mauser-type action. Calibers: 222 Rem., 22-250, 6mm Rem., 243
Win., 308 Win. 3-shot detachable clip magazine. 22-inch barrel.
Weight, 6½ pounds. Folding leaf rear sight, hooded ramp front
sight. Checkered walnut stock with Monte Carlo cheekpiece,
detachable swivels. Made from 1969 to 1977. Manufactured by
Oy Tikkakoski AB, Tikkakoski, Finland.

Ithaca Model LSA-55 Deluxe................... **$350**
Same as Model LSA-55 Standard Grade, except has roll-over
cheekpiece, rosewood grip-cap and fore-end tip, skip checkering,
high-lustre blue, no iron sights, scope mount standard equipment. Made from 1969 to 1977.

Ithaca Model LSA-55 Heavy Barrel............. **$375**
Same as Model LSA-55, except calibers 222 Rem. and 22-250
only; has 23-inch heavy barrel, no sights, special stock with
beavertail forearm, weighs about 8½ pounds. Made from 1974
to 1977.

Ithaca Model LSA-65 Standard Grade........... **$300**
Same as Model LSA-55 Standard Grade, except calibers 25-06,
270, 30-06; 4-shot magazine, 23-inch barrel, weighs 7 pounds.
Made from 1969 to 1977.

Ithaca Model LSA-65 Deluxe................... **$330**
Same as Model LSA-65 Standard Grade, except has special
features of Model LSA-55 Deluxe. Made from 1969 to date.

Ithaca Model LSA-55 Standard

Ithaca Model LSA-55 Deluxe

Ithaca Model LSA-65 Standard

Ithaca-BSA CF-2

Ithaca-BSA CF-2 Bolt Action Repeating Rifle....$300
Mauser-type action. Calibers: 7mm Rem. Mag., 300 Win. Mag. 3-shot magazine. 23.6-inch barrel. Weight, 8 pounds. Adjustable rear sight, hooded ramp front sight. Checkered walnut stock with Monte Carlo comb, roll-over cheekpiece, rosewood fore-end tip, recoil pad, sling swivels. Made from 1976 to 1977. Manufactured by BSA Guns Ltd., Birmingham, England.

Iver Johnson's Arms & Cycle Works, Fitchburg, Massachusetts

Iver Johnson Model X Bolt Action Single Shot Rifle.. $100
Takedown. Caliber, 22 Long Rifle, Long, Short. 22-inch barrel. Weight, about 4 pounds. Open rear sight, blade front sight. Pistol-grip stock with knob fore-end tip. Made from 1928 to 1932.

Iver Johnson Model 2X...........................$125
Improved version of the Model X, has heavier 24-inch barrel, larger stock (without knob tip), weighs about 4½ pounds. Made from 1932 to 1955.

Iver Johnson's Arms, Inc. Middlesex, New Jersey

Iver Johnson Model M1 Semiautomatic Carbine. $170
Similar to U.S. Carbine, Cal. 20, M1. 18-inch barrel. Weight, about 5½ pounds. 15- or 30-round detachable magazine.

Iver Johnson Model PM30P Paratrooper........ $200
Same as the standard M1 except telescoping walnut stock.

Japanese Military Rifles manufactured by Government plant at Tokyo, Japan

Japanese Model 38 Arisaka Service Rifle....... $130
Mauser-type bolt action. Caliber, 6.5mm Japanese. 5-shot box magazine. Barrel lengths: 25⅜ inches, 31¼ inches. Weight,

about 9¼ pounds with long barrel. Fixed front sight, adjustable rear sight. Military-type full stock. Adopted in 1905, the 38th year of the Meiji reign, hence designation "Model 38."

Japanese Model 38 Arisaka Carbine............ $125
Same general specifications as Model 38 Rifle except has 19-inch barrel, heavy folding bayonet, weighs about 7¼ pounds.

Japanese Model 44 Cavalry Carbine............ $125
Same general specifications as Model 38 Rifle except has 19-inch barrel, heavy folding bayonet, weighs about 8½ pounds. Adopted in 1911, the 44th year of the Meiji reign, hence the designation "Model 44."

Japanese Model 99 Service Rifle................ $125
Modified Model 38. Caliber, 7.7mm Japanese. 5-shot box magazine. 25¾-inch barrel. Weight, about 8¾ pounds. Fixed sight, adjustable aperture rear sight, anti-aircraft sighting bars on some early models; fixed rear sight on some late World War II rifles. Military-type full stock, may have bipod. Takedown paratroop model was also made during World War II. Adopted in 1939, Japanese year 2599 from which the designation "Model 99" is taken. *Note:* The last Model 99 rifles made were of very poor quality, some have cast steel receivers. Value shown is for earlier type.

Johnson Automatics, Inc., Providence, R.I.

Johnson Model 1941 Semiautomatic Military Rifle... $675
Short-recoil-operated. Removable, air-cooled, 22-inch barrel. Calibers: 30-06, 7mm Mauser. 10-shot rotary magazine. Two-piece, wood stock, pistol grip; perforated metal radiator sleeve over rear half of barrel. Receiver peep sight, protected post front sight. Weight, 9½ pounds. *Note:* The Johnson M/1941 was adopted by the Netherlands Government in 1940-41 and the major portion of the production of this rifle, 1941 to 1943, was on Dutch orders. A quantity was also purchased by the U.S. Government for use by Marine Corps parachute troops (1943) and for Lend Lease. All of these rifles were caliber 30-06; the 7mm Johnson rifles were made for a South American government.

Japanese Model 38

Japanese Model 99

Johnson Model 1941

Iver Johnson Model 2X

Iver Johnson M-1 Carbine

Iver Johnson PM30 P Paratrooper

Krico Rifle

Krico Special Varmint Rifle

Krico Rifles manufactured by Sportwaffenfabrik Kriegeskorte G.m.b.H., Stuttgart-Hedelfingen, West Germany

Krico Bolt Action Sporting Rifle................ **$520**
Miniature Mauser action. Single- or double-set trigger. Calibers: 22 Hornet, 222 Rem. 4-shot clip magazine. 22-, 24- or 26-inch barrel. Weight, about 6¼ pounds. Open rear sight, hooded ramp front sight. Checkered stock with cheekpiece, pistol grip, black fore-end tip, sling swivels. Made from 1956 to 1962.

Krico Carbine...................................... **$525**
Same as Krico Rifle, except has 20- or 22-inch barrel, full-length Mannlicher-type stock.

Krico Special Varmint Rifle...................... **$520**
Same as Krico Rifle, except has heavy barrel, no sights, weighs about 7¼ pounds; caliber 222 Rem. only.

Krico Model 311

Krico Model 311 Small Bore Rifle
Bolt action. Caliber, 22 Long Rifle. 5- or 10-shot clip magazine. 22-inch barrel. Weight, about 6 pounds. Single- or double-set trigger. Open rear sight, hooded ramp front sight; available with factory-fitted Kaps 2½ x scope. Checkered stock with cheekpiece and pistol grip, swivels.
With scope sight.................................... $345
With iron sights only................................ 260

H. Krieghoff Jagd-und Sportwaffenfabrik, Ulm (Donau), West Germany

Krieghoff "Teck" Over-and-Under Rifle
Kersten action, double crossbolt, double underlugs. Box lock. Calibers: 7x57R, 7x64, 7x65R, 30-30, 308 Win., 30-06, 300 Win. Mag., 9.3x74R, 375 H&H Mag., 458 Win. Mag. 25-inch barrels. Weight, 8 to 9½ pounds, depending upon caliber. Express rear sight, ramp front sight. Checkered walnut stock and forearm. Made from 1967 to date.
Standard Calibers.............................$2100
375 H&H Mag., 458 Win. Mag...................... 2400

Krieghoff "Ulm" Over-and-Under Rifle......... $3000
Same general specifications as "Teck" model, except has side locks with leaf arabesque engraving. Made from 1963 to date.

Krieghoff "Ulm-Primus" Over-and-Under Rifle.$3500
Deluxe version of "Ulm" model, has detachable side locks, higher grade engraving and stock wood. Made from 1963 to date.

Luna Rifle manufactured by Ernst Friedr. Büchel, Mehlis, Germany

Luna Single Shot Target Rifle....................$750
Falling block action. Calibers: 22 Long Rifle, 22 Hornet. 29-inch barrel. Weight, about 8¼ pounds. Micrometer peep rear tang sight, open rear sight, ramp front sight. Cheekpiece stock with full pistol grip, semi-beavertail forearm, checkered, swivels. Made prior to World War II.

Mannlicher Sporting Rifles manufactured by Steyr-Daimler-Puch, A.-G., Steyr, Austria

Mannlicher-Schoenauer Model 1903 Bolt Action Sporting Carbine.................................... $750
Caliber, 6.5x53mm (referred to in some European gun catalogues as 6.7x53mm, following the Austrian practice of designating calibers by bullet diameter). 5-shot rotary magazine. 450mm

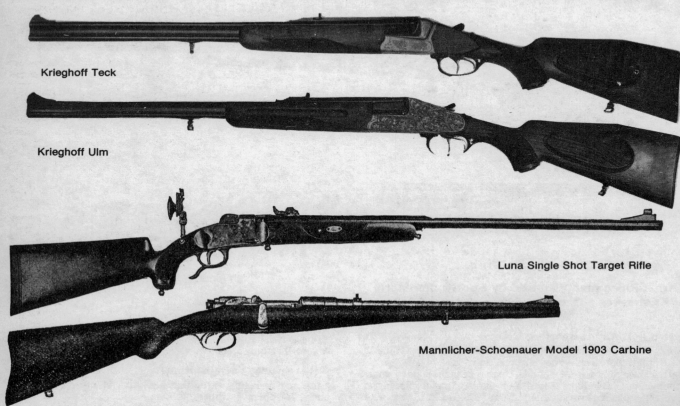

Krieghoff Teck

Krieghoff Ulm

Luna Single Shot Target Rifle

Mannlicher-Schoenauer Model 1903 Carbine

Mannlicher-Schoenauer Model 1905 Carbine

Mannlicher-Schoenauer High Velocity

Mannlicher-Schoenauer Model 1950 Rifle

Mannlicher-Schoenauer Model 1950 Carbine

Mannlicher-Schoenauer Model 1952 Rifle

(17.7-inch) barrel. Weight, about 6½ pounds. Double-set trigger. Two-leaf rear sight, ramp front sight. Full-length sporting stock with cheekpiece, pistol grip, trap butt plate, swivels.

Mannlicher-Schoenauer Model 1905 Carbine.... $700
Same as Model 1903, except caliber 9x56mm and has 19.7-inch barrel, weighs about 6¾ pounds.

Mannlicher-Schoenauer Model 1908 Carbine.... $700
Same as Model 1905, except calibers 7x57mm and 8x56mm.

Mannlicher-Schoenauer Model 1910 Carbine.... $700
Same as Model 1905, except caliber 9.5x57mm.

Mannlicher-Schoenauer Model 1924 Carbine.... $900
Same as Model 1905, except caliber 30-06 (7.62x63mm).

Mannlicher-Schoenauer High Velocity Bolt Action Sporting Rifle.......................................$750
Calibers: 7x64 Brenneke, 30-06 (7.62x63), 8x60 Magnum, 9.3x62, 10.75x68mm. 23.6-inch barrel. Weight, about 7½ pounds. British-style 3-leaf open rear sight, ramp front sight. Half-length sporting stock with cheekpiece, pistol grip, checkered, trap butt plate, swivels. Also produced in takedown model.

Note: The preceding Mannlicher-Schoenauer models were produced prior to World War II. Manufacture of sporting

rifles and carbines was resumed at the Steyr-Daimler-Puch plant in Austria during 1950 and the Model 1950 Rifles and Carbines were introduced at that time.

Mannlicher-Schoenauer Model 1950 Bolt Action Sporting Rifle.. $700
Calibers: 257 Roberts, 270 Win., 30-06. 5-shot rotary magazine. 24-inch barrel. Weight, about 7¼ pounds. Single trigger or double-set trigger. Redesigned low bolt handle, shot-gun-type safety. Folding leaf open rear sight, hooded ramp front sight. Improved half-length stock with cheekpiece, pistol grip, checkered, ebony fore-end tip, swivels. Made from 1950 to 1952.

Mannlicher-Schoenauer Model 1950 Carbine.... $700
Same general specifications as Model 1950 Rifle except has 20-inch barrel, full-length stock, weighs about 7 pounds. Made from 1950 to 1952.

Mannlicher-Schoenauer Model 1950 6.5 Carbine... $625
Same as other Model 1950 Carbines except caliber 6.5x53mm, has 18¼-inch barrel, weighs 6¾ pounds. Made from 1950 to 1952.

Mannlicher-Schoenauer Improved Model 1952 Sporting Rifle.. $625
Same as Model 1950 except has swept-back bolt handle, redesigned stock. Calibers: 257, 270, 30-06, 9.3x62mm. Made from 1952 to 1956.

Mannlicher-Schoenauer Improved Model 1952 Carbine $625

Same as Model 1950 Carbine except has swept-back bolt handle, redesigned stock. Calibers: 257, 270, 7mm, 30-06. Made from 1952 to 1956.

Mannlicher-Schoenauer Improved Model 1952 6.5 Carbine $650

Same as Model 1952 Carbine except caliber 6.5x53mm, has 18¼-inch barrel. Made from 1952 to 1956.

Mannlicher-Schoenauer Custom Model 1956 Sporting Rifle $625

Same general specifications as Models 1950 and 1952, except 22-inch barrel, redesigned stock with high comb. Calibers: 243 and 30-06. Made from 1956 to 1960.

Mannlicher-Schoenauer Custom Model 1956 Carbine $625

Same general specifications as Model 1950 and 1952 Carbines except has redesigned stock with high comb. Calibers: 243, 6.5mm, 257, 270, 7mm, 30-06, 308. Made from 1956 to 1960.

Mannlicher-Schoenauer Carbine, Model 1961-MCA $630

Same as Model 1956 Carbine, except has universal Monte Carlo design stock. Calibers: 243 Win., 6.5mm, 270, 308, 30-06. Made from 1961 to 1971.

Mannlicher-Schoenauer Rifle, Model 1961-MCA $600

Same as Model 1956 Rifle, except has universal Monte Carlo design stock. Calibers: 243, 270, 30-06. Made from 1961 to 1971.

Note: In 1967, Steyr-Daimler-Puch introduced a new series of sporting rifles with a bolt action that is a departure from the familiar Mannlicher-Schoenauer system of earlier models. In the latter, the action is locked by lugs symmetrically arranged behind the bolt head as well as by placing the bolt handle ahead of the right flank of the receiver, the rear section of which is open on top for backward movement of the bolt handle. The current action, made in four lengths to accommodate different ranges of cartridges, has a closed-top receiver; the bolt locking lugs are located toward the rear of the bolt (behind the magazine), and the Mannlicher-Schoenauer rotary magazine has been redesigned as a detachable box type of Makrolon.

Mannlicher Model SL Rifle $625

Steyr-Mannlicher SL bolt action. Calibers: 222 Rem., 222 Rem. Mag., 223 Rem. 5-shot rotary magazine, detachable. 23⅝-inch barrel. Weight, about 6.05 pounds. Single- or double-set trigger (mechanisms interchangeable). Open rear sight, hooded ramp front sight. Half stock of European walnut with Monte Carlo comb and cheekpiece, skip-checkered forearm and pistol grip, rubber butt pad, QD swivels. Made from 1967 to date.

Mannlicher-Schoenauer Model 1952 Carbine

Mannlicher-Schoenauer Model 1956 Rifle

Mannlicher-Schoenauer Model 1956 Carbine

Mannlicher-Schoenauer Model 1961-MCA Carbine

Mannlicher-Schoenauer Model 1961-MCA Rifle

Mannlicher Model SL Rifle
double-set trigger

Mannlicher Model SL Rifle
single-stage trigger

Mannlicher Model SL Carbine

Mannlicher Model L Rifle

Mannlicher Model SL Carbine................... **$645**
Same general specifications as Model SL Rifle, except has 20-inch barrel and full-length stock, weighs about 5.95 pounds. Made from 1968 to date.

Mannlicher Model SL Varmint Rifle............. **$500**
Same general specifications as Model SL Rifle, except caliber 222 Rem. only, has 25⅝-inch heavy barrel, no sights, weighs about 7.92 pounds. Made from 1969 to date.

Mannlicher Model L Rifle........................ **$515**
Same general specifications as Model SL Rifle, except has type "L" action, weighs about 6.3 pounds. Calibers: 22-250, 5.6x57, 243 Win., 6mm Rem., 308 Win. Made from 1968 to date.

Mannlicher Model L Carbine..................... **$735**
Same general specifications as Model SL Carbine, except has type "L" action, weighs about 6.2 pounds. Calibers same as for Model L Rifle. Made from 1968 to date.

Mannlicher Model L Varmint Rifle............... **$550**
Same general specifications as Model SL Varmint Rifle, except has type "L" action. Calibers: 22-250, 243 Win., 308 Win. Made from 1969 to date.

Mannlicher Model SSG Match Target Rifle
Type "L" action. Caliber, 308 Win. (7.62x51 NATO). 5- or 10-round magazine, single-shot plug. 25½-inch heavy barrel. Weight, 10¼ pounds. Single trigger. Micrometer peep rear sight, globe front sight. Target stock, European walnut or synthetic,

with full pistol grip, wide forearm with swivel rail, adjustable rubber butt plate. Made 1969 to date.
With walnut stock.................................... **$725**
With synthetic stock................................ **700**

Mannlicher Model M Rifle........................ **$550**
Same general specifications as Model SL Rifle, except has type "M" action, stock with fore-end tip and recoil pad, weighs about 6.9 pounds. Calibers: 6.5x57, 270 Win., 7x57, 7x64, 30-06, 8x57JS, 9.3x62. Made from 1969 to date.

Mannlicher Model M Carbine.................... **$565**
Same general specifications as Model SL Carbine, except has type "M" action, stock with recoil pad, weighs about 6.8 pounds. Made from 1969 to date.

Mannlicher Left-handed Model M Rifle......... **$635**
Same as right-handed Model M Rifle, except has bolt handle on left, cheekpiece on right. Additional calibers, 6.5x55 and 7.5 Swiss. Introduced 1977.

Mannlicher Left-handed Model M Carbine...... **$655**
Same as right-handed Model M Carbine, except has bolt handle on left, cheekpiece on right. Additional calibers, 6.5x55 and 7.5 Swiss. Introduced 1977.

Mannlicher Model M Professional Rifle......... **$500**
Same as standard Model M Rifle, except has synthetic (Cycolac) stock, weighs about 7½ pounds. Calibers: 6.5x55, 6.5x57, 270 Win., 7x57, 7x64, 7.5 Swiss, 30-06, 8x57JS, 9.3x62. Introduced 1977.

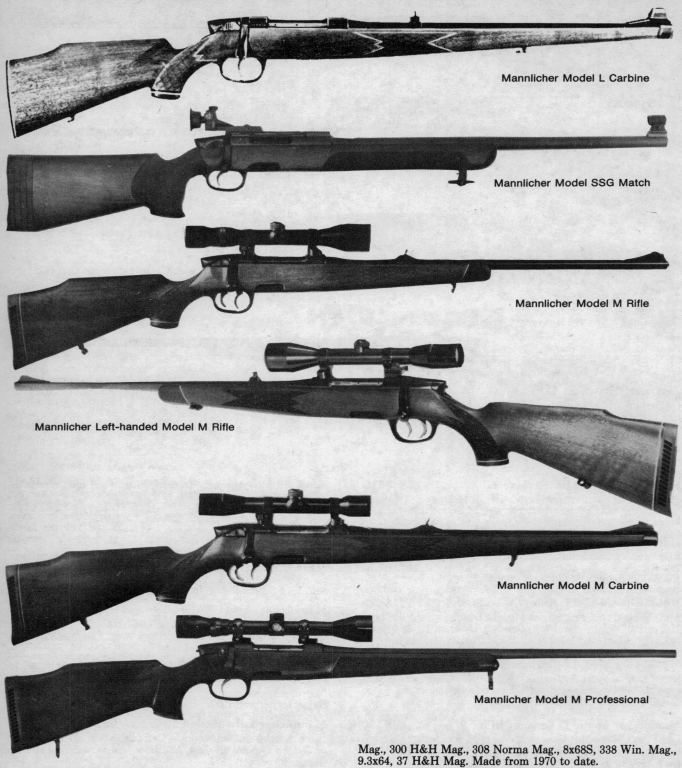

Mannlicher Model L Carbine

Mannlicher Model SSG Match

Mannlicher Model M Rifle

Mannlicher Left-handed Model M Rifle

Mannlicher Model M Carbine

Mannlicher Model M Professional

Mag., 300 H&H Mag., 308 Norma Mag., 8x68S, 338 Win. Mag., 9.3x64, 37 H&H Mag. Made from 1970 to date.

Mannlicher Model S Rifle **$650**
Same general specifications as Model SL Rifle, except has type "S" action, 4-round magazine, 25⅝-inch barrel, stock with fore-end tip and recoil pad, weighs about 8.4 pounds. Calibers: 6.5x68, 257 Weatherby Mag., 264 Win. Mag., 7mm Rem. Mag., 300 Win.

Mannlicher Model S/T Rifle **$645**
Same as Model S Rifle, except has heavy 25⅝-inch barrel, weighs about 9.02 pounds. Calibers: 9.3x64, 375 H&H Mag., 458 Win. Mag. Option of 23⅝-inch barrel in latter caliber. Made from 1975 to date.

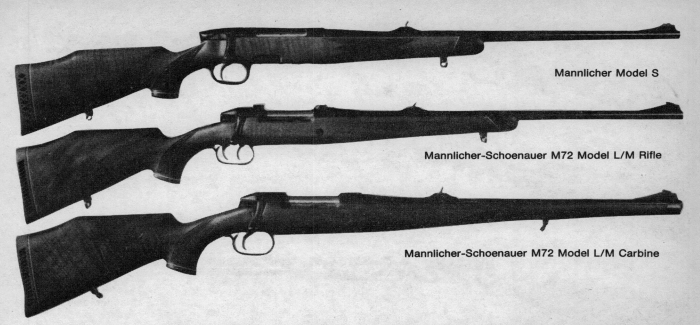

Mannlicher Model S

Mannlicher-Schoenauer M72 Model L/M Rifle

Mannlicher-Schoenauer M72 Model L/M Carbine

Mannlicher-Schoenauer M72 Model L/M Rifle...$650
M72 bolt action, type L/M receiver, front-locking bolt, internal rotary magazine (5-round). Calibers: 22-250, 5.6x57, 6mm Rem., 243 Win., 6.5x57, 270 Win., 7x57, 7x64, 308 Win., 30-06. 23⅝-inch barrel. Weight, about 7.3 pounds. Single- or double-set trigger (mechanisms interchangeable). Open rear sight, hooded ramp front sight. Half stock of European walnut, checkered forearm and pistol grip, Monte Carlo cheekpiece, rosewood fore-end tip, recoil pad, QD swivels. Made from 1972 to date.

Mannlicher-Schoenauer M72 Model L/M Carbine...$650
Same general specifications as M72 Model L/M Rifle, except has 20-inch barrel and full-length stock, weighs about 7.2 pounds. Made from 1972 to date.

Mannlicher-Schoenauer M72 Model S Rifle......$700
Same general specifications as M72 Model L/M Rifle, except has magnum action, 4-round magazine, 25⅝-inch barrel, weighs about 8.6 pounds. Calibers: 6.5x68, 7mm Rem. Mag., 8x68S, 9.3x64, 375 H&H Mag. Made from 1972 to date.

Mannlicher-Schoenauer M72 Model S/T Rifle... $750
Same as M72 Model S Rifle, except has heavy 25⅝-inch barrel, weighs about 9.3 pounds. Calibers: 300 Win. Mag., 9.3x64, 375 H&H Mag., 458 Win. Mag. Option of 23⅝-inch barrel in latter caliber. Made from 1975 to date.

Marlin Firearms Co., North Haven, Connecticut

Marlin Model 92 Lever Action Repeating Rifle.. $430
Calibers: 22 Short, Long, Long Rifle; 32 Short, Long (rimfire or centerfire by changing firing pin). Tubular magazines: holding 25 Short, 20 Long, 18 Long Rifle (22); 17 Short, 14 Long (32); 16-inch barrel model has shorter magazine holding 15 Short, 12 Long, 10 Long Rifle. Barrel lengths: 16-(22 cal. only), 24-, 26-, 28-inches. Weight, with 24-inch barrel, about 5½ pounds. Open rear sight, blade front sight. Plain straightgrip stock and forearm. Made from 1892 to 1916 *Note:* Originally designated "Model 1892."

Marlin Model 93 Lever Action Repeating Rifle.. $375
Solid frame or takedown. Calibers: 25-36 Marlin, 30-30, 32 Special, 32-40, 38-55. Tubular magazine holds 10 cartridges. 26-inch round or octagon barrel standard; also made with 28-,-30- and 32-inch barrels. Weight, about 7¼ pounds. Open rear sight, bead front sight. Plain straight-grip stock and forearm. Made from 1893 to 1936. *Note:* Prior to 1915, was designated "Model 1893."

Marlin Model 93 Carbine..........................$550
Same as Standard Model 93, except calibers 30-30 and 32 Special only. 7-shot magazine, 20-inch round barrel, weighs about 6¾ pounds, carbine sights.

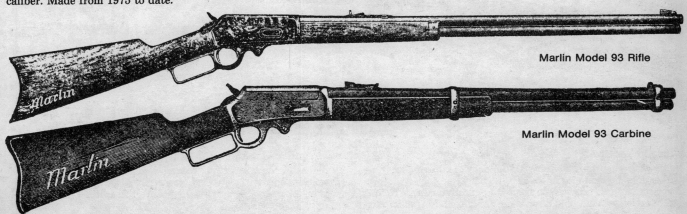

Marlin Model 93 Rifle

Marlin Model 93 Carbine

Marlin Model 1895

Marlin Model 20

Marlin Model 27

Marlin Model 29

Marlin Model 38

Marlin Model 39

Marlin 90th Anniversary Model 39A Rifle

Marlin Model 93SC Sporting Carbine........... **$575**
Same as Model 93 Carbine, except has ⅔ magazine holding 5 shots, weighs 6½ pounds.

Marlin Model 93 Musket........................ **$680**
Same as Standard Model 93, except has 30-inch barrel, angular bayonet, ramrod under barrel, musket stock, full-length military-style forearm. Weight, 8 pounds. Made from 1893 to 1915.

Marlin Model 94 Lever Action Repeating Rifle.. **$425**
Solid frame or takedown. Calibers: 25-20, 32-20, 38-40, 44-40. 10-shot tubular magazine. 24-inch round or octagon barrel. Weight, about 7 pounds. Open rear sight, bead front sight. Plain straight-grip stock and forearm (also available with pistol-grip stock). Made from 1894 to 1934. _Note:_ Prior to 1906, was designated "Model 1894."

Marlin Model 1895 Lever Action Repeating Rifle.. **$530**
Solid frame or takedown. Calibers: 33 WCF, 38-56, 40-65, 40-70, 40-82, 45-70. 9-shot tubular magazine. 24-inch round or octagon barrel standard (other lengths available). Weight, about 8 pounds. Open rear sight, bead front sight. Plain stock and forearm (also available with pistol-grip stock). Made from 1895 to 1915.

Marlin Model 97 Lever Action Repeating Rifle.. **$300**
Takedown. Caliber, 22 Long Rifle, Long, Short. Tubular magazine; full length holds 25 Short, 20 Long, 18 Long Rifle; half length holds 16 Short, 12 Long and 10 Long Rifle. Barrel lengths: 16,-24,-26,-28-inches. Weight, about 6 pounds. Open rear sight and bead front sight. Plain straight-grip stock and forearm (also available with pistol-grip stock). Made from 1897 to 1922. _Note:_ Prior to 1905 was designated "Model 1897."

Marlin Model 18 Baby Slide Action Repeater... **$190**
Exposed hammer. Solid frame. Caliber, 22 Long Rifle, Long, Short. Tubular magazine holds 14 Short. 20-inch barrel, round or octagon. Weight, 3¾ pounds. Open rear sight, bead front sight. Plain straight-grip stock and slide handle. Made from 1906 to 1909.

Marlin Model 20 Slide Action Repeating Rifle... **$180**
Exposed hammer. Takedown. Caliber, 22 Long Rifle, Long, Short. Tubular magazine: half-length holds 15 Short, 12 Long, 10 Long Rifle; full-length holds 25 Short, 20 Long, 18 Long Rifle. 24-inch octagon barrel. Weight, about 5 pounds. Open rear sight, bead front sight. Plain straight-grip stock, grooved slide handle. Made from 1907 to 1922. _Note:_ After 1920 was designated "Model 20-S."

Marlin Model 25 Slide Action Repeating Rifle... **$225**
Exposed hammer. Takedown. Caliber, 22 Short (also handles 22 CB Caps). Tubular magazine holds 15 Short. 23-inch barrel. Weight, about 4 pounds. Open rear sight, beaded front sight. Plain straight-grip stock and slide handle. Made from 1909 to 1910.

Marlin Model 27 Slide Action Repeating Rifle... **$210**
Exposed hammer. Takedown. Calibers: 25-20, 32-20. ⅔ magazine (tubular) holds 7 shots. 24-inch octagon barrel. Weight, about 5¾ pounds. Open rear sight, bead front sight. Plain straight-grip stock, grooved slide handle. Made from 1910 to 1916.

Marlin Model 27S.............................. **$190**
Same as Model 27, except has round barrel, also chambered for 25 Stevens R.F. Made from 1920 to 1932.

Marlin Model 29 Slide Action Repeating Rifle... **$200**
Similar to Model 20, has 23-inch round barrel, half magazine only, weighs about 5¾ pounds. Model 37 is same type except has 24-inch barrel and full magazine. Made from 1913 to 1916.

Marlin Model 32 Slide Action Repeating Rifle... **$200**
Hammerless. Takedown. Caliber, 22 Long Rifle, Long, Short. ⅔ tubular magazine holds 15 Short, 12 Long, 10 L.R.; full magazine, 25 Short, 20 Long, 18 L.R. 24-inch octagon barrel. Weight, about 5½ pounds. Open rear sight, bead front sight. Plain pistol-grip stock, grooved slide handle. Made from 1914 to 1915.

Marlin Model 38 Slide Action Repeating Rifle... **$200**
Hammerless. Takedown. Caliber, 22 Long Rifle, Long, Short. ⅔ magazine (tubular) holds 15 Short, 12 Long, 10 Long Rifle. 24-inch octagon barrel. Weight, about 5½ pounds. Open rear sight, bead front sight. Plain pistol-grip stock, grooved slide handle. Made from 1920 to 1930.

Marlin Model 39 Lever Action Repeating Rifle.. **$275**
Takedown. Casehardened receiver. Caliber, 22 Long Rifle, Long, Short. Tubular magazine holds 25 Short, 20 Long, 18 Long Rifle. 24-inch octagon barrel. Weight, about 5¾ pounds. Open rear sight, bead front sight. Plain pistol-grip stock and forearm, weighs about 6½ pounds. Made from 1922 to 1947.

Marlin Model 39A............................... **$135**
General specifications same as Model 39, except has blued receiver, round barrel, heavier stock with semi-beavertail forearm, weighs about 6½ pounds. Made from 1938 to 1960.

Marlin Golden 39A Rifle......................... **$135**
Same as Model 39A, except has gold-plated trigger, hooded ramp front sight, sling swivels. Made from 1960 to date.

Marlin Model 39A "Mountie" Lever Action Repeating Rifle.. **$175**
Same as Model 39A, except has lighter, straight-grip stock, slimmer forearm. Weight, 6¼ pounds. Made from 1953 to 1960.

Marlin 90th Anniversary Model 39A Rifle....... **$510**
Commemorates Marlin's 90th anniversary. Same general specifications as Golden 39A, except has chrome-plated barrel and action, stock and forearm of select walnut, finely checkered, carved figure of a squirrel on right side of buttstock. 500 made in 1960. Value is for rifle in new, unfired condition.

Marlin Golden 39A Rifle

Marlin 90th Anniversary Model 39 Carbine

Marlin Model 39A-DL

Marlin Model 39A Octagon

Marlin Golden 39M Carbine

Marlin Model 39 Carbine

Marlin Model 39D

Marlin 90th Anniversary Model 39 Carbine..... $500
Carbine version of 90th Anniversary Model 39A. 500 made in 1960. Value is for carbine in new, unfired condition.

Marlin Model 39A-DL...........................$195
Same as 90th Anniversary Model 39A, except blued barrel and action. Made from 1960 to 1963.

Marlin Model 39A Octagon.......................$160
Same as Golden 39A, except has octagon barrel, plain bead front sight, slimmer stock and forearm, no pistol-grip cap or swivels. Made in 1973.

Marlin Model 65E................................ $ 40
Same as Model 65, except has rear peep sight and hooded front sight.

Marlin Model 39M "Mountie" Carbine........... $140
Same as Model 39A "Mountie" Rifle, except has 20-inch barrel and reduced magazine capacity: 21 Short, 16 Long, 15 Long Rifle. Weight, 6 pounds. Made from 1954 to 1960.

Marlin Golden 39M Carbine..................... $135
Same as Model 39M, except has gold-plated trigger, hooded ramp front sight, sling swivels. Made from 1960 to date. *Note:* This model originally was designated "Golden 39 Mountie."

Marlin Model 39 Carbine....................... $135
Same as Model 39M, except has lightweight barrel, ¾ magazine (capacity: 18 Short, 14 Long, 12 Long Rifle), slimmer forearm. Weight, 5¼ pounds. Made from 1963 to 1967.

Marlin Model 39D.............................. $130
Same as Model 39M, except has pistol-grip stock, forearm with barrel band. Made from 1970 to 1974.

Marlin Model 39M Octagon..................... $175
Same as Golden 39M, except has octagon barrel, plain bead front sight, no swivels. Made in 1973.

Marlin 39 Century Ltd.......................... $225
Commemorative version of Model 39A. Receiver inlaid with brass medallion, Marlin Centennial 1870-1970. Square lever. 20-inch octagon barrel. Fancy walnut straight-grip stock and forearm; brass fore-end cap, butt plate, nameplate in buttstock. 35,388 made in 1970.

Marlin 39A Article II Rifle..................... $200
Commemorates National Rifle Association Centennial 1871-1971. "The Right to Bear Arms" medallion inlaid in receiver. Similar to Model 39A. Magazine capacity — 26 Shorts, 21 Longs, 19 Long Rifles. 24-inch octagon barrel. Fancy walnut pistol-grip stock and forearm; brass fore-end cap, butt plate. 6,244 made in 1971.

Marlin 39M Article II Carbine.................. $200
Same as 39A Article II Rifle, except has straight-grip buttstock, square lever, 20-inch octagon barrel, reduced magazine capacity. 3,824 made in 1971.

Marlin Model 65 Bolt Action Single Shot Rifle.. $ 35
Takedown. Caliber, 22 Long Rifle, Long, Short. 24-inch barrel. Weight, about 5 pounds. Open rear sight, bead front sight. Plain pistol-grip stock with grooved forearm. Made from 1932 to 1938.

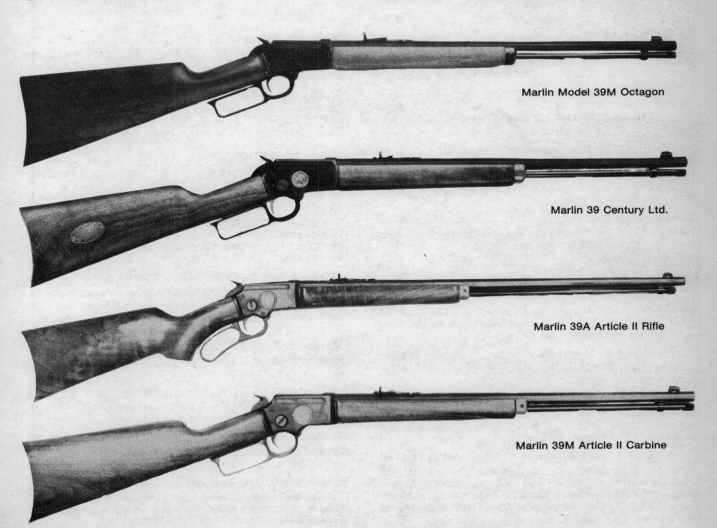

Marlin Model 39M Octagon

Marlin 39 Century Ltd.

Marlin 39A Article II Rifle

Marlin 39M Article II Carbine

Marlin Model 50

Marlin Model 80 C

Marlin Model 80 DL

Marlin Model 50 Autoloading Rifle.............$ 55
Takedown. Caliber, 22 Long Rifle. 6-shot detachable box magazine. 22-inch barrel. Weight, about 6 pounds. Open rear sight, bead front sight. Plain pistol-grip stock, forearm with finger grooves. Made from 1931 to 1934.

Marlin Model 50E................................$ 60
Same as Model 50, except has peep rear sight, hooded front sight.

Marlin Model 80 Bolt Action Repeating Rifle....$ 45
Takedown. Caliber, 22 Long Rifle, Long, Short. 8-shot detachable box magazine. 24-inch barrel. Weight, about 6 pounds. Open rear sight, bead front sight. Plain pistol-grip stock. Made from 1934 to 1939.

Marlin Model 80E................................$ 55
Same as Model 80, except has peep rear sight, hooded front sight. Made from 1934 to 1940.

Marlin Model 80C................................$ 55
Improved version of Model 80 with same general specifications, has stock with semi-beavertail forearm. Made from 1940 to 1970.

Marlin Model 80DL..............................$ 65
Same as Model 80C except has peep rear sight, hooded front sight, swivels. Made from 1940 to 1965.

Marlin-Glenfield Model 80G.....................$ 45
Same as Model 80C, except has plainer stock, bead front sight. Made from 1960 to 1965.

Marlin-Glenfield Model 20......................$ 45
Same as Model 80/780, except has bead front sight, walnut-finished hardwood stock. Made from 1966 to date. *Note:* Recent production has checkered pistol grip.

Marlin Model 780 Bolt Action Repeating Rifle...$ 65
Caliber, 22 Long Rifle, Long, Short. 7-shot clip magazine. 22-inch barrel. Weight, about 5½ pounds. Open rear sight, hooded ramp front sight. Receiver grooved for scope mounting. Monte Carlo stock with checkered pistol grip and forearm. Made from 1971 to date.

Marlin Model 781................................$ 70
Same general specifications as Model 780, except has tubular magazine (capacity: 17 LR, 19 Long, 25 Short), weighs about 6 pounds. Made from 1971 to date.

Marlin Model 782................................$ 75
Same general specifications as Model 780, except chambered for 22 Win. Magnum R.F., weighs about 6 pounds, has swivels and sling. Made from 1971 to date.

Marlin Model 783................................$ 75
Same as Model 782, except has 12-shot tubular magazine. Made from 1971 to date.

Marlin Model 980 22 Magnum....................$ 85
Bolt action. Caliber, 22 Win. Magnum R.F. 8-shot clip magazine. 24-inch barrel. Weight, about 6 pounds. Open rear sight, hooded ramp front sight. Monte Carlo stock, swivels, sling. Made from 1962 to 1970.

Marlin Model A-1 Autoloading Rifle............$ 85
Takedown. Caliber, 22 Long Rifle. 6-shot detachable box magazine. 24-inch barrel. Weight, about 6 pounds. Open rear sight. Plain pistol-grip stock. Made from 1935 to 1946.

Marlin Model A-1E..............................$ 60
Same as Model A-1, except has peep rear sight, hooded front sight.

Marlin Model A-1C Autoloading Rifle...........$ 60
Improved version of Model A-1 with same general specifications, has stock with semi-beavertail forearm. Made from 1940 to 1946.

Marlin Model A-1DL.............................$ 70
Same as Model A-1C, except has peep rear sight, hooded front sight, swivels.

Marlin Model 100 Bolt Action Single Shot Rifle.$ 35
Takedown. Caliber, 22 Long Rifle, Long, Short. 24-inch barrel. Weight, about 4½ pounds. Open rear sight, bead front sight. Plain pistol-grip stock. Made from 1936 to 1960.

Marlin-Glenfield Model 80G

Marlin-Glenfield Model 20

Marlin Model 780

Marlin Model 781

Marlin Model 782

Marlin Model 783

Marlin Model 980

Marlin Model A-1

Marlin Model 100

Marlin-Glenfield Model 10

Marlin Model 81 DL

Marlin-Glenfield Model 81 G

Marlin-Glenfield Model 30A

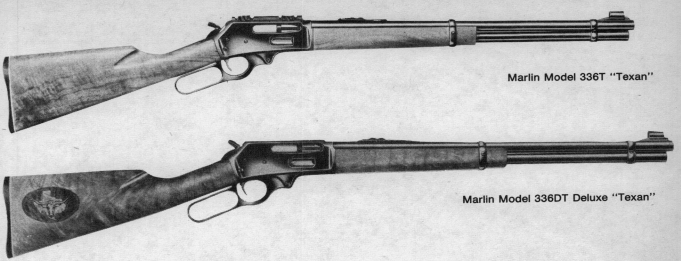

Marlin Model 336T "Texan"

Marlin Model 336DT Deluxe "Texan"

Marlin Model 100S "Tom Mix Special" .... **$ 70**
Same as Model 100 except has peep rear sight and hooded front sight, sling. Made from 1936 to 1946.

Marlin Model 100SB .... **$ 35**
Same as Model 100 except smoothbore for use with 22 shot cartridges, shotgun sight. Made from 1936 to 1941.

Marlin Model 101 .... **$ 40**
Improved version of Model 100 with same general specifications except has stock with beavertail forearm, weighs about 5 pounds. Introduced, 1951. Discontinued.

Marlin Model 101DL .... **$ 50**
Same as Model 101 except has peep rear sight, hooded front sight, swivels. Discontinued.

Marlin-Glenfield Model 101G .... **$ 35**
Same as Model 101, except has plainer stock. Made from 1960 to 1965.

Marlin-Glenfield Model 10 .... **$ 35**
Same as Model 101, except has walnut-finished hardwood stock. Made from 1966 to 1979. *Note:* Later production has checkered pistol grip.

Marlin Model 81 Bolt Action Repeating Rifle .... **$ 50**
Takedown. Caliber, 22 Long Rifle, Long, Short. Tubular magazine holds 24 Short, 20 Long, 18 Long Rifle. 24-inch barrel. Weight, about 6¼ pounds. Open rear sight, bead front sight. Plain pistol-grip stock. Made from 1937 to 1940.

Marlin Model 81E .... **$ 55**
Same as Model 81, except has peep rear sight, hooded front sight.

Marlin Model 81C .... **$ 60**
Improved version of Model 81 with same general specifications, has stock with semi-beavertail forearm. Made from 1940 to 1970.

Marlin Model 81DL .... **$ 70**
Same as Model 81C, except has peep rear sight, hooded front sight, swivels. Discontinued 1965.

Marlin-Glenfield Model 81G .... **$ 55**
Same as Model 81C, except has plainer stock, bead front sight. Made from 1960 to 1965.

Marlin Model 36 Lever Action Repeating Carbine **$295**
Calibers: 30-30, 32 Special. 6-shot tubular magazine. 20-inch barrel. Weight, about 6½ pounds. Open rear sight, bead front sight. Pistol-grip stock, semi-beavertail forearm with carbine barrel band. Made from 1936 to 1948. *Note:* In 1936, this was designated "Model 1936."

Marlin Model 36A Lever Action Repeating Rifle **$205**
Same as Model 36 Carbine, except has ⅔ magazine holding 5 cartridges, 24-inch barrel, weighs 6¾ pounds, has hooded front sight, semi-beavertail forearm.

Marlin Model 36A-DL **$240**
Same as Model 36A, except has deluxe checkered stock and forearm, swivels and sling.

Marlin Model 36 Sporting Carbine **$205**
Same as Model 36A rifle except has 20-inch barrel, weighs 6¼ pounds.

Marlin Model 336C Lever Action Carbine **$140**
Improved version of Model 36 Carbine with same general specifications, has improved action with round breech bolt. Made from 1948 to date. *Note:* Cal. 35 Rem. introduced 1953. Cal. 32 Win. Spl. discontinued in 1963. Recent production has squared finger lever.

Marlin-Glenfield Model 36G **$125**
Same as Model 336C, except chambered for 30-30 only, has 5-shot magazine, plainer stock. Made from 1960 to 1965.

Marlin-Glenfield Model 30 .... **$ 90**
Same as Model 336C, except chambered for 30-30 only, has 4-shot magazine, plainer stock and forearm of walnut-finished hardwood. Made from 1966 to 1968.

Marlin-Glenfield Model 30A .... **$ 95**
Same as Model 336C, except chambered for 30-30 only, has checkered stock of walnut-finished hardwood. Made from 1969 to date.

Marlin Model 336T "Texan" Lever Action Carbine **$140**
Same as Model 336 Carbine, except has straight-grip stock and is not available in caliber 32 Special. Made from 1953 to date. Caliber 44 Magnum made from 1963 to 1967.

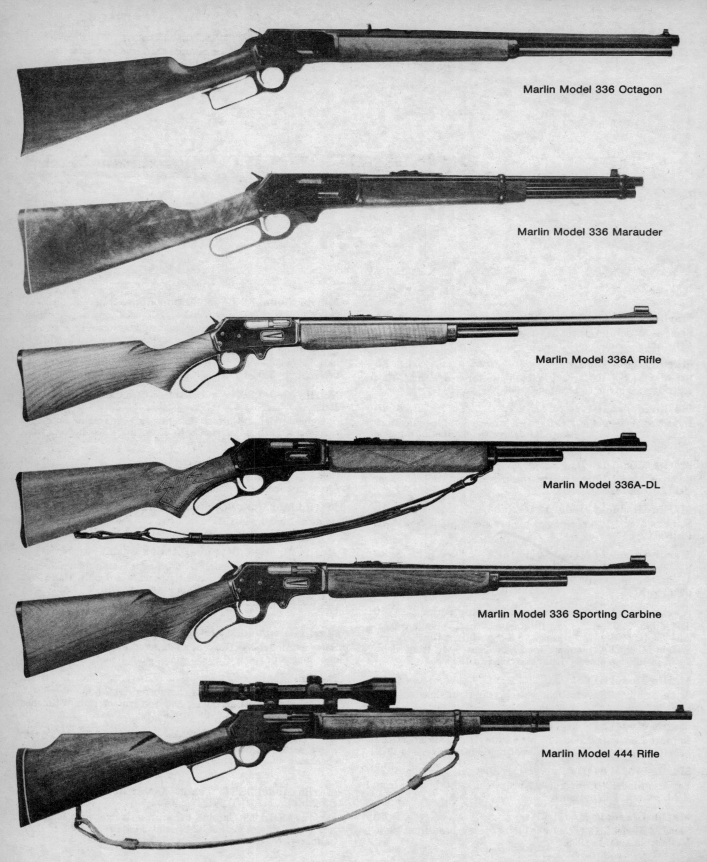

Marlin Model 336 Octagon

Marlin Model 336 Marauder

Marlin Model 336A Rifle

Marlin Model 336A-DL

Marlin Model 336 Sporting Carbine

Marlin Model 444 Rifle

Marlin 444 Sporter

Marlin Model 336DT Deluxe "Texan".......... **$205**
Same as Model 336T, except has select walnut stock and forearm, hand-carved longhorn steer and map of Texas on buttstock. Made from 1962 to 1964.

Marlin Model 336 Octagon...................... **$165**
Same as Model 336T, except chambered for 30-30 only, has 22-inch octagon barrel. Made in 1973.

Marlin Model 336 "Marauder".................. **$275**
Same as Model 336 "Texan" Carbine except has 16¼-inch barrel, weighs about 6¼ pounds. Made from 1963 to 1964.

Marlin Model 336A Lever Action Repeating Rifle... **$145**
Improved version of Model 36A Rifle with same general specifications, has improved action with round breech bolt. Calibers: 30-30, 32 Special (discontinued 1963), 35 Rem. (introduced 1952). Made from 1948 to 1963; reintroduced 1973, still in production. *Note:* Recent production has sling swivels and carrying strap.

Marlin Model 336A-DL........................ **$170**
Same as Model 336A Rifle except has deluxe checkered stock and forearm, swivels and sling. Made from 1948 to 1963.

Marlin Model 336 Sporting Carbine............. **$135**
Same as Model 336A rifle, except has 20-inch barrel, weighs 6¼ pounds. Made from 1948 to 1963.

Marlin Model 336 "Micro Goove Zipper"........ **$275**
General specifications same as Model 336 Sporting Carbine, except caliber 219 Zipper. Made from 1955 to 1961.

Marlin Model 444 Lever Action Repeating Rifle. **$205**
Action similar to Model 336. Caliber, 444 Marlin. 4-shot tubular magazine. 24-inch barrel. Weight, 7½ pounds. Open rear sight, hooded ramp front sight. Monte Carlo stock with straight grip, recoil pad. Carbine-style forearm with barrel band. Swivels, sling. Made from 1965 to 1971.

Marlin 444 Sporter............................... **$155**
Same as Model 444 Rifle, except has 22-inch barrel, pistol-grip stock and forearm as on Model 336A, recoil pad, QD swivels and sling. Made from 1972 to date.

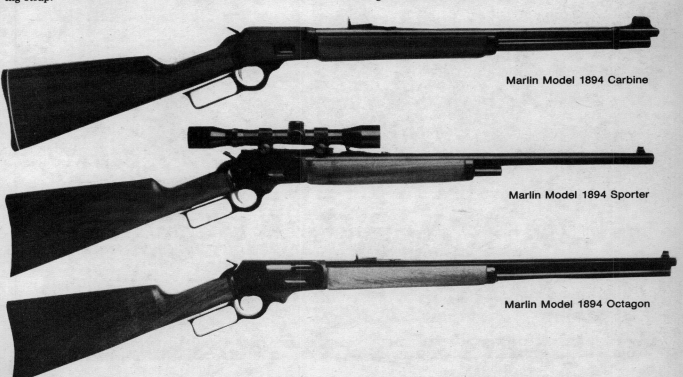

Marlin Model 1894 Carbine

Marlin Model 1894 Sporter

Marlin Model 1894 Octagon

Marlin Model 1894 Carbine......................$140
Replica of original Model 94. Caliber, 44 Rem. 10-shot magazine. 20-inch round barrel. Weight, 6 pounds. Open rear sight, ramp front sight. Straight-grip stock, forearm with barrel band. Made from 1969 to date.

Marlin Model 1894 Sporter.....................$135
Same general specifications as Model 1894 Carbine, except has 22-inch barrel, 6-shot magazine. Made in 1973.

Marlin Model 1894 Octagon.....................$165
Same general specifications as Model 1894 Carbine, except has octagon barrel, bead front sight. Made in 1973.

Marlin Centennial 1870-1970 Matched Pair, Models 336 and 39.......................................$1460
Presentation grade rifles in luggage-style case. Matching serial numbers. Fancy walnut straight-grip buttstock and forearm, brass butt plate and fore-end cap. Engraved receiver with inlaid medallion; square lever. 20-inch octagon barrel. Model 336: 30-30, 7-shot, 7 pounds. Model 39: 22 Short, Long, Long Rifle; tubular magazine holds 21 Short, 16 Long, 15 Long Rifle. 1,000 sets produced. Made in 1970. Value is for rifles in new, unfired condition.

Marlin Model 336 Zane Grey Century...........$225
Similar to Model 336A, except has 22-inch octagonal barrel, caliber 30-30; Zane Grey Centennial 1872-1972 medallion inlaid in receiver; selected walnut stock with classic pistol grip and forearm; brass butt plate, fore-end cap. Weight, 7 pounds. 10,000 produced (numbered ZG1 through ZG10,000). Made in 1972.

Marlin 1895 45/70 Repeater....................$175
Model 336 type action. Caliber, 45/70 Government. 4-shot magazine. 22-inch barrel. Weight, about 7 pounds. Open rear sight, bead front sight. Straight-grip stock, forearm with metal end cap, QD swivels, leather sling. Made fron 1972 to date.

Marlin Model 88-C Autoloading Rifle............$ 60
Takedown. Caliber, 22 Long Rifle. Tubular magazine in buttstock holds 14 cartridges. 24-inch barrel. Weight, about 6¾ pounds. Open rear sight, hooded front sight. Plain pistol-grip stock. Made from 1947 to 1956.

Marlin Model 88-DL............................$ 70
Same as Model 88-C except has receiver peep sight, checkered stock and sling swivels. Made from 1953 to 1956.

Marlin Zane Grey Century

Marlin Centennial Matched Pair

Marlin Model 1895

Marlin Model 88-C

Marlin Model 89-C

Marlin Model 98

Marlin-Glenfield Model 99G

Marlin-Glenfield Model 60

Marlin Model 99 DL

Marlin Model 49DL

Marlin Model 89-C Autoloading Rifle .... $ 60
Clip magazine version of Model 88-C. 7-shot clip (12-shot in later models). Other specifications same. Made from 1950 to 1961.

Marlin Model 89-DL .... $ 70
Same as Model 89-C except has receiver peep sight and sling swivels.

Marlin Model 98 Autoloading Rifle .... $ 60
Solid frame. Caliber, 22 Long Rifle. Tubular magazine holds 15 cartridges. 22-inch barrel. Weight, about 6¾ pounds. Open rear sight, hooded ramp front sight. Monte Carlo stock with cheekpiece. Made from 1950 to 1961.

Marlin Model 99 Autoloading Rifle .... $ 60
Caliber, 22 Long Rifle. Tubular magazine holds 18 cartridges. 22-inch barrel. Weight, about 5½ pounds. Open rear sight, hooded ramp front sight. Plain pistol-grip stock. Made from 1959 to 1961.

Marlin Model 99C .... $ 60
Same as Model 99 except has gold-plated trigger, receiver grooved for tip-off scope mounts, Monte Carlo stock (checkered in current production.) Made from 1962 to date.

Marlin-Glenfield Model 99G .... $ 55
Same as Model 99C, except has plainer stock, bead front sight. Made from 1960 to 1965.

Marlin-Glenfield Model 60 .... $ 45
Same as Model 99C, except has walnut-finished hardwood stock. Made from 1966 to date. *Note:* Recent production has checkered pistol grip and forearm.

Marlin Model 99DL .... $ 55
Same as Model 99 except has gold-plated trigger, jeweled breechbolt, Monte Carlo stock with pistol grip, swivels and sling. Made from 1960 to 1965.

Marlin Model 49 .... $ 70
Same as Model 99C, except has two-piece stock, checkered after 1970. Made from 1968 to 1971.

Marlin Model 49DL .... $ 75
Same as Model 49, except has scrollwork on sides of receiver, checkered stock and forearm. Made from 1971 to date.

Marlin Model 99M1 Carbine .... $ 70
Same as Model 99C except styled after U.S. 30M1 Carbine; 9-shot tubular magazine, 18-inch barrel, open rear sight, military-style ramp front sight, carbine stock with handguard and barrel band, sling swivels. Weight, 4½ pounds. Made from 1966 to 1979.

Marlin Model 989M2

Marlin-Glenfield Model 70

Marlin Model 989

Marlin-Glenfield Model 989 G

Marlin Model 122

Marlin Model 455

Marlin Model 57

Marlin Model 56

Marlin Model 62

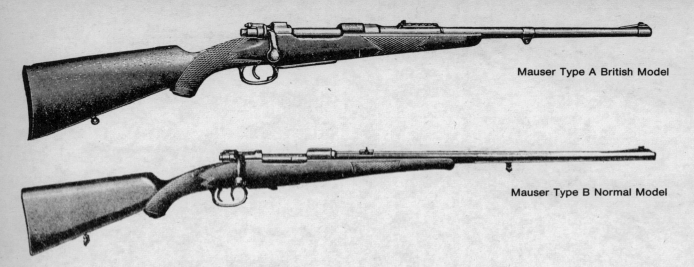

Mauser Type A British Model

Mauser Type B Normal Model

Marlin Model 989M2 Carbine . . . . $ 75
Same as Model 99M1, except clip-loading—7-shot magazine.
Made from 1966 to 1979.

Marlin-Glenfield Model 70 . . . . $ 55
Same as Model 989M2, except has walnut-finished hardwood
stock, no handguard. Made from 1966 to 1969.

Marlin Model 989 Autoloading Rifle . . . . $ 65
Caliber, 22 Long Rifle, 7-shot clip magazine. 22-inch barrel.
Weight, about 5½ pounds. Open rear sight, hooded ramp front
sight. Monte Carlo walnut stock with pistol grip. Made from
1962 to 1966.

Marlin-Glenfield Model 989G Autoloading Rifle . $ 60
Same as Model 989, except plain stock, bead front sight. Made
from 1962 to 1964.

**Marlin Model 122 Single Shot Junior
Target Rifle** . . . . $ 55
Bolt action. Caliber, 22 Long Rifle, 22 Long, 22 Short. 22-inch
barrel. Weight, about 5 pounds. Open rear sight, hooded ramp
front sight. Monte Carlo stock with pistol grip, swivels, sling.
Made from 1961 to 1965.

Marlin Model 322 Bolt Action Varmint Rifle $350
Sako short Mauser action. Caliber, 222 Rem. 3-shot clip magazine. 24-inch medium weight barrel. Checkered stock. Two-
position peep sight, hooded ramp front sight. Weight, about 7½
pounds. Made from 1954 to 1957.

Marlin Model 455 Bolt Action Sporter $370
FN Mauser action with Sako trigger. Calibers: 270, 30-06, 308. 5-
shot box magazine. 24-inch medium weight stainless steel barrel.
Monte Carlo stock with cheekpiece, checkered pistol grip and
forearm. Lyman 48 receiver sight, hooded ramp front sight.
Weight, about 8½ pounds. Made from 1957 to 1959.

Marlin Model 57 Levermatic Rifle $105
Lever action. Caliber, 22 Long Rifle, 22 Long, 22 Short. Tubular
magazine holds 19 Long Rifle, 21 Long, 27 Short. 22-inch barrel.
Weight, about 6¼ pounds. Open rear sight, hooded ramp front
sight. Monte Carlo-style stock with pistol grip. Made from 1959
to 1965.

Marlin Model 57M Levermatic $120
Same as Model 57, except chambered for 22 Winchester
Magnum Rim Fire cartridge, has 24-inch barrel, 15-shot maga-
zine. Made from 1960 to 1969.

Marlin Model 56 Levermatic Rifle $105
Same as Model 57 except clip-loading. Magazine holds eight
rounds. Weight, about 5¾ pounds. Made from 1955 to 1964.

Marlin Model 62 Levermatic Rifle $135
Lever action. Calibers: 256 Magnum, 30 Carbine. 4-shot clip
magazine. 23-inch barrel. Weight, 7 pounds. Open rear sight,
hooded ramp front sight. Monte Carlo-style stock with pistol
grip, swivels and sling. Made in 256 Magnum from 1963 to 1966;
in 30 Carbine from 1966 to 1969.

Mauser Sporting Rifles manufactured by
Mauser-Werke, Oberndorf am Neckar, Germany

Mauser Bolt Action Sporting Rifle $475
Calibers: 6.5x55, 6.5x58, 7x57, 8x57, 9x57, 9.3x62, 10.75x68. 5-
shot box magazine. 23½-inch barrel. Weight, about 7 to 7½
pounds. Double-set trigger. Tangent curve rear sight, ramp front
sight. Pistol-grip stock, forearm with schnabel tip, swivels.

Mauser Bolt Action Sporting Rifle, Short Model . $475
Calibers: 6.5x54, 8x51mm. 19¾-inch barrel. Weight, about 6¼
pounds. Other specifications same as for Standard Rifle.

Mauser Bolt Action Sporting Carbine $480
Calibers: 6.5x54, 6.5x58, 7x57, 8x57, 957mm. 19¾-inch barrel.
Weight, about 7 pounds. Full-stocked to muzzle. Other specifica-
tions same as for standard rifle.

**Mauser Bolt Action Sporting Rifle,
Military Type** $400
So-called because of "stepped" M/98-type barrel, military front
sight and double-pull trigger. Calibers 7x57, 8x57, 9x57mm.
Other specifications same as standard rifle.

Note: The foregoing Mauser Sporting Rifles were manufactured prior to World War I. Those that follow were produced
during the period between World Wars I and II. The early
Mauser models can generally be identified by the pistol grip
which is rounded instead of capped and the M/98 military-
type magazine floorplate and catch; the later models have
hinged magazine floorplate with lever or button release.
Prior to the end of World War I, the name of the firm was
"Waffenfabrik Mauser A.-G." Shortly after World War I, it
was changed to "Mauser-Werke A.-G." This may be used as
a general clue to the age of genuine Original-Mauser sporting rifles made prior to World War II since all bear either of
these firm names as well as the "Mauser" banner trademark.

Mauser Type M

Mauser Standard Model

Mauser Model MS350B

Mauser Bolt Action Sporting Rifle Type "A"..... $525
Special British Model. Calibers: 7x57, 30-06 (7.62x63), 8x60, 9x57, 9.3x62mm. 5-shot box magazine. 23½-inch round barrel. Weight, about 7¼ pounds. Military-type single trigger. Express rear sight, hooded ramp front sight. Circassian walnut sporting stock with checkered pistol grip and forearm, with or without cheekpiece, buffalo horn fore-end tip and grip cap, detachable swivels. Variations: octagon barrel, double-set trigger, shotgun-type safety, folding peep rear sight, tangent curve rear sight, three-leaf rear sight.

Mauser Bolt Action Sporting Rifle Type "A"..... $525
Short Model. Same as standard Type "A" except has short action, 21½-inch round barrel, weighs about 6 pounds, calibers: 250-3000, 6.5x54, 8x51mm.

Mauser Bolt Action Sporting Rifle, Type "A".... $600
Magnum Model. Same general specifications as standard Type "A" except has Magnum action, weighs 7½ to 8½ pounds, calibers 280 Ross, 318 Westley Richards Express, 10.75x68mm. 404 Nitro Express.

Mauser Bolt Action Sporting Rifle, Type "B".... $475
Normal Model. Calibers: 7x57, 30-06 (7.62x63), 8x57, 8x60, 9x57, 9.3x62, 10.75x68mm. 5-shot box magazine. 23½-inch round barrel. Weight, about 7¼ pounds. Double-set trigger. Three-leaf rear sight, ramp front sight. Fine walnut stock with checkered pistol grip, schnabel fore-end tip, cheekpiece, grip cap, swivels. Variations: octagon or half-octagon barrel, military-type single trigger, shotgun-type trigger, shotgun-type safety, folding peep rear sight, tangent curve rear sight, telescopic sight.

Mauser Bolt Action Sporting Rifle, Type "K".... $475
Light Short Model. Same general specifications as Normal Type "B" model except has short action, 21½-inch round barrel, weighs about 6 pounds; calibers: 250-3000, 6.5x54, 8x51mm.

Mauser Bolt Action Sporting Carbine, Type "M"... $525
Calibers: 6.5x54, 7x57, 30-06 (7.62x63), 8x51, 8x60, 9x57mm. 5-shot box magazine. 19¾-inch round barrel. Weight, about 6 to 6¾ pounds. Double-set trigger, flat bolt handle. Three-leaf rear sight, ramp front sight. Stocked to muzzle, cheekpiece, checkered pistol grip and forearm, grip cap, steel fore-end cap, swivels. Variations: military-type single trigger, shotgun-type trigger, shotgun-type safety, tangent curve rear sight, telescopic sight.

Mauser Bolt Action Sporting Carbine, Type "S". $500
Calibers: 6.5x54, 7x57, 8x51, 8x60, 9x57mm. 5-shot box magazine. 19¾-inch round barrel. Weight, about 6 to 6¾ pounds. Double-set trigger. Three-leaf rear sight, ramp front sight. Stocked to muzzle, schnabel fore-end tip, cheekpiece, checkered pistol grip with cap, swivels. Variations: same as listed for Normal Model Type "B."

Mauser Standard Model Rifle.................... $450
Refined version of the German Service Kar.98k. Straight bolt handle. Calibers: 7mm Mauser (7x57mm), 7.9mm Mauser (8x57mm). 5-shot box magazine. 23½-inch barrel. Weight, about 8½ pounds. Blade front sight, adjustable rear sight. Walnut stock of M/98 military-type. *Note:* These rifles were made for commercial sale and are of the high quality found in the Oberndorf Mauser sporters. They bear the Mauser trademark on the receiver ring.

Mauser Model ES340 Bolt Action Single Shot Target Rifle.. **$225**
Caliber, 22 Long Rifle. 25½-inch barrel. Weight, about 6½ pounds. Tangent curve rear sight, ramp front sight. Sporting stock with checkered pistol grip and grooved forearm, swivels.

Mauser Model ES350 Bolt Action Single Shot Target Rifle.. **$375**
"Meistershaftsbüchse" (Championship Rifle). Caliber, 22 Long Rifle, 27½-inch barrel. Weight, about 7¾ pounds. Open micrometer rear sight, ramp front sight. Target stock with checkered pistol grip and forearm, grip cap, swivels.

Mauser Model M410 Bolt Action Repeating Sporting Rifle.. **$300**
Caliber, 22 Long Rifle. 5-shot detachable box magazine. 23½-inch barrel. Weight, about 5 pounds. Tangent curve open rear sight, ramp front sight. Sporting stock with checkered pistol grip, swivels.

Mauser Model MS420 Bolt Action Repeating Sporting Rifle.. **$300**
Caliber, 22 Long Rifle. 5-shot detachable box magazine. 25½-inch barrel. Weight, about 6½ pounds. Tangent curve open rear sight, ramp front sight. Sporting stock with checkered pistol grip, grooved forearm swivels.

Mauser Model EN310 Bolt Action Single Shot Sporting Rifle.. **$195**
Caliber, 22 Long Rifle. ("22 Lang für Büchsen.") 19¾-inch barrel. Weight, about 4 pounds. Fixed open rear sight, blade front sight. Plain pistol-grip stock.

Mauser Model EL320 Bolt Action Single Shot Sporting Rifle.. **$225**
Caliber, 22 Long Rifle. 23½-inch barrel. Weight, about 4¼ pounds. Adjustable open rear sight, bead front sight. Sporting stock with checkered pistol grip, swivels.

Note: The foregoing series of Mauser 22 Rifles was superseded about 1935 by the "B" series (Model MS-350B, ES-350B, etc.) of improved models, as well as the Sportmodel DSM34. The Military Model KKW was introduced just prior to World War II.

Mauser Model MS350B, Bolt Action Repeating Target Rifle.. **$400**
Caliber, 22 Long Rifle. 5-shot detachable box magazine. Receiver and barrel grooved for detachable rear sight or scope. 26¾-inch barrel. Weight, about 8½ pounds. Micrometer open rear sight, ramp front sight. Target stock with checkered pistol grip and forearm, grip cap, sling swivels.

Mauser Model ES350B Bolt Action Single Shot Target Rifle.. **$350**
Same general specifications as Model MS350B except single shot, weighs about 8¼ pounds.

Mauser Model ES340B Bolt Action Single Shot Target Rifle.. **$300**
Caliber, 22 Long Rifle. 26¾-inch barrel. Weight, about 8 pounds. Tangent curve open rear sight, ramp front sight. Plain pistol-grip stock, swivels.

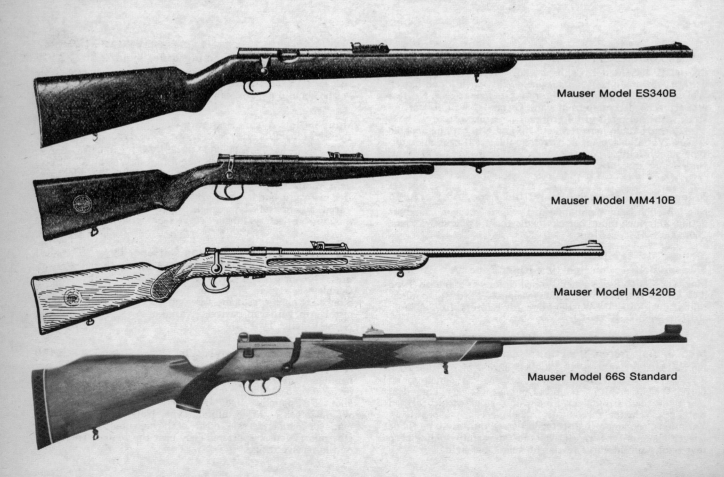

Mauser Model ES340B

Mauser Model MM410B

Mauser Model MS420B

Mauser Model 66S Standard

Mauser Model 66S Ultra

Mauser Model 66ST

Mauser Model 66SG

Mauser Model 66S Deluxe

Mauser Model MM410B Bolt Action Repeating Sporting Rifle...................................... **$360**
Caliber, 22 Long Rifle. 5-shot detachable box magazine. 23½-inch barrel. Weight, about 6¼ pounds. Tangent curve open rear sight, ramp front sight. Lightweight sporting stock with checkered pistol grip, swivels.

Mauser Model MS420B Bolt Action Repeating Target Rifle.. **$350**
Caliber, 22 Long Rifle. 5-shot detachable box magazine. 26¾-inch barrel. Weight, about 8 pounds. Tangent curve open rear sight, ramp front sight. Target stock with checkered pistol grip, grooved forearm, swivels.

Mauser Model DSM34 Bolt Action Single Shot Sporting Rifle...................................... **$330**
Also called "Sport-model." Caliber, 22 Long Rifle. 26-inch barrel. Weight, about 7¾ pounds. Tangent curve open rear sight, barleycorn front sight. M/98 military-type stock, swivels.

Mauser Model KKW Bolt Action Single Shot Target Rifle.. **$350**
Caliber, 22 Long Rifle. 26-inch barrel. Weight, about 8¾ pounds. Tangent curve open rear sight, barleycorn front sight.

M/98 military-type stock, swivels. *Note:* This rifle has an improved design Mauser 22 action with separate non-rotating bolt head. In addition to being produced for commercial sale, this model was used as a training rifle by the German armed forces; it was also made by Walther and Gustloff.

Note: Production of Original-Mauser sporting rifles was resumed at the Oberndorf plant in 1965 by Mauser-Jagdwaffen GmbH, now Mauser-Werke Oberndorf GmbH. The Series 2000-3000-4000 rifles, however, were made for Mauser by Friedrich Wilhelm Heym Gewehrfabrik, Muennerstadt, West Germany.

Mauser Model 66S Standard Bolt Action Sporting Rifle
Telescopic short action. Barrels interchangeable within caliber group. Single- or double-set trigger (interchangeable). Calibers: 243 Win., 6.5x57, 270 Win., 7x64, 308 Win., 30-06. 3-round magazine. 23.6-inch barrel (25.6-inch in 7x64). Weight, about 7.3 pounds (7.5 pounds in 7x64). Adjustable open rear sight, hooded ramp front sight. Select European walnut stock, Monte Carlo with cheekpiece, rosewood fore-end tip and pistol-grip cap, skip checkering, recoil pad, sling swivels. Made from 1965 to date; export to U.S. discontinued 1974. *Note:* U.S. designation, 1971-73, was "Model 660".
With one barrel.. **$730**
Extra barrel assembly................................. **200**

Mauser Model 66SP

Mauser Model 3000

Mauser Model 4000

Mauser Model 66S Ultra

Same general specifications as Model 66S Standard, except has 20.9-inch barrel, weighs about 6.8 pounds.

With one barrel.....................................**$750**
Extra barrel assembly.............................. 200

Mauser Model 66ST Carbine

Same general specifications as Model 66S Standard, except has 20.9-inch barrel, full-length stock, weighs about 7.1 pounds.

With one barrel.....................................**$775**
Extra barrel assembly.............................. 200

Mauser Model 66SH High Performance

Same general specifications as Model 66S Standard, except has 25.6-inch barrel, weighs about 7.5 pounds (9.3 pounds in 9.3x64). Calibers: 6.5x68, 7mm Rem. Mag., 7mm S.E.v.Hofe, 300 Win. Mag., 8x68S, 9.3x64.

With one barrel.....................................**$700**
Extra barrel assembly.............................. 200

Mauser Model 66SG Big Game

Same general specifications as Model 66S Standard, except has 25.6-inch barrel, weighs about 9.3 pounds. Calibers: 375 H&H Mag., 458 Win. Mag. *Note:* U.S. designation, 1971-73, was "Model 660 Safari."

With one barrel.....................................**$800**
Extra barrel assembly.............................. 200

Mauser Model 66S Deluxe

On special order, Model 66S rifles and carbines are available with elaborate engraving, gold and silver inlays, and carved stocks of the finest select walnut. Added value is upwards of $1000.

Mauser Model 66SP Super Match Bolt Action Target Rifle..**$800**

Telescopic short action. Adjustable single-stage trigger. Caliber, 308 Win. (chambering for other cartridges available on special order). 3-shot magazine. 27.6-inch heavy barrel with muzzle brake, dovetail rib for special scope mount. Weight, about 12 pounds. Target stock with wide and deep forearm, full pistol grip, thumb-hole, adjustable cheekpiece, adjustable rubber butt plate.

Mauser Model 2000 Bolt Action Sporting Rifle.. **$275**

Modified Mauser type action. Calibers: 270 Win., 308 Win., 30-06. 5-shot magazine. 24-inch barrel. Weight, about 7½ pounds. Folding leaf rear sight, hooded ramp front sight. Checkered walnut stock with Monte Carlo comb and cheekpiece, fore-end tip, sling swivels. Made from 1969 to 1971. *Note:* Model 2000 is similar in appearance to Model 3000.

Mauser Model 3000 Bolt Action Sporting Rifle.. **$390**

Modified Mauser type action. Calibers: 243 Win., 270 Win., 308 Win., 30-06. 5-shot magazine. 22-inch barrel. Weight, about 7 pounds. No sights. Select European walnut stock, Monte Carlo style with cheekpiece, rosewood fore-end tip and pistol-grip cap, skip checkering, recoil pad, sling swivels. Made from 1971 to 1974.

Mauser Model 3000 Magnum.....................**$425**

Same general specifications as standard Model 3000, except has 3-shot magazine, 26-inch barrel, weighs about 8 pounds. Calibers: 7mm Rem. Mag., 300 Win. Mag., 375 H&H Mag.

Mauser Model 4000 Varmint Rifle..............**$340**

Same general specifications as standard Model 3000, except has smaller action, folding leaf rear sight and hooded ramp front sight, rubber butt plate instead of recoil pad, weighs about 6¾ pounds. Calibers: 222 Rem., 223 Rem.

Mossberg Model K

Mossberg Model L

Mossberg Model 35

Mossberg Model 45

Mossberg Model 46

Mossberg Model L42A

Gebrüder Merkel, Suhl, Germany

Merkel Over-And-Under Rifles ("Bockdoppelbüchsen")
See listing under Merkel Shotguns.

Mexican Military Rifle manufactured by Government Arsenal, Mexico, D.F.

Mexican Model 1936 Mauser Military Rifle..... $175
Same as the German Kar.98k with minor variations, has U.S. M/1903 Springfield-type knurled cocking piece.

O. F. Mossberg & Sons, Inc. North Haven, Connecticut

Mossberg Model K Slide Action Repeater....... $100
Hammerless. Takedown. Caliber, 22 Long Rifle, Long, Short. Tubular magazine holds 20 Short, 16 Long, 14 Long Rifle. 22-inch barrel. Weight, about 5 pounds. Open rear sight, bead front sight. Plain straight-grip stock, grooved slide handle. Made from 1922 to 1931.

Mossberg Model M Slide Action Repeater...... $115
Specifications same as for Model K except has 24-inch octagon barrel, pistol-grip stock, weighs about 5½ pounds. Made from 1928 to 1931.

Mossberg Model L Single Shot Rifle............ $225
Martini-type falling-block lever action. Takedown. Caliber, 22 Long Rifle, Long, Short. 24-inch barrel. Weight, about 5 pounds.

Open rear sight and bead front sight. Plain pistol-grip stock and forearm. Made from 1929 to 1932.

Mossberg Model B Single Shot Bolt Action Rifle.. $ 40
Takedown. Caliber, 22 Long Rifle, Long, Short. 22-inch barrel. Open rear sight, bead front sight. Plain pistol-grip stock. Made from 1930 to 1932.

Mossberg Model R Bolt Action Repeating Rifle.. $ 45
Takedown. Caliber, 22 Long Rifle, Long, Short. Tubular magazine. 24-inch barrel. Open rear sight, bead front sight. Plain pistol-grip stock. Made from 1930 to 1932.

Mossberg Model 10 Bolt Action Single Shot Rifle.. $ 40
Takedown. Caliber, 22 Long Rifle, Long, Short. 22-inch barrel. Weight, about 4 pounds. Open rear sight, bead front sight. Plain pistol-grip stock with swivels and sling. Made from 1933 to 1935.

Mossberg Model 20 Bolt Action Single Shot Rifle.. $ 40
Takedown. Caliber, 22 Long Rifle, Long, Short. 24-inch barrel. Weight, about 4½ pounds. Open rear sight, bead front sight. Plain pistol-grip stock and forearm with finger grooves, sling and swivels. Made from 1933 to 1935.

Mossberg Model L43

Mossberg Model 30 Bolt Action Single Shot Rifle.. $ 40
Takedown. Caliber, 22 Long Rifle, Long, Short. 24-inch barrel. Weight, about 4½ pounds. Peep rear sight, bead front sight on hooded ramp. Plain pistol-grip stock, forearm with finger grooves. Made from 1933 to 1935.

Mossberg Model 40 Bolt Action Repeating Rifle. $ 45
Same specifications as Model 30, except has a tubular magazine (holds 16 Long Rifle) and weighs about 5 pounds. Made from 1933 to 1935.

Mossberg Model 14 Bolt Action Single Shot Rifle.. $ 40
Takedown. Caliber, 22 Long Rifle, Long, Short. 24-inch barrel. Weight, about 5¼ pounds. Peep rear sight, hooded ramp front sight. Plain pistol-grip stock with semi-beavertail forearm, 1¼-inch swivels. Made from 1934 to 1935.

Mossberg Model 34 Bolt Action Single Shot Rifle.. $ 40
Takedown. Caliber, 22 Long Rifle, Long, Short. 24-inch barrel. Weight, 5½ pounds. Peep rear sight, hooded ramp front sight. Plain pistol-grip stock with semi-beavertail forearm, 1¼-inch swivels. Made from 1934 to 1935.

Mossberg Model 44 Bolt Action Repeating Rifle. $ 55
Takedown. Caliber, 22 Long Rifle, Long, Short. Tubular magazine holds 16 Long Rifle. 24-inch barrel. Weight, 6 pounds. Peep rear sight, hooded ramp front sight. Plain pistol-grip stock with semi-beavertail forearm, 1¼-inch swivels. Made from 1934 to 1935. *Note:* Do not confuse this rifle with the later Models 44B and 44US which are clip repeaters.

Mossberg Model 25 Bolt Action Single Shot Rifle .... $ 40
Takedown. Caliber, 22 Long Rifle, Long, Short. 24-inch barrel. Weight, about 5 pounds. Peep rear sight, hooded ramp front sight. Plain pistol-grip stock with semi-beavertail forearm. 1¼-inch swivels. Made from 1935 to 1936.

Mossberg Model 25A.............................. $ 40
Same as Model 25 with minor improvements. Made from 1936 to 1938.

Mossberg Model 35 Target Grade Bolt Action Single Shot Rifle.. $ 90
Caliber, 22 Long Rifle. 26-inch heavy barrel. Weight, about 8¼ pounds. Micrometer click rear peep sight, hooded ramp front sight. Large target stock with full pistol grip, cheekpiece, full beavertail forearm, 1¼-inch swivels. Made from 1935 to 1937.

Mossberg Model 42 Bolt Action Repeating Rifle. $ 55
Takedown. Caliber, 22 Long Rifle, Long, Short. 7-shot detachable box magazine. 24-inch barrel. Weight, about 5 pounds. Receiver peep sight, open rear sight, hooded ramp front sight. Pistol-grip stock. 1¼-inch swivels. Made from 1935 to 1937.

Mossberg Model 45 Bolt Action Repeating Rifle. $ 55
Takedown. Caliber, 22 Long Rifle, Long, Short. Tubular magazine holds 15 Long Rifle, 18 Long, 22 Short. 24-inch barrel. Weight, about 6¾ pounds. Rear peep sight, hooded ramp front sight. Plain pistol-grip stock, 1¼-inch swivels. Made from 1935 to 1937.

Mossberg Model 45C.............................. $ 45
Same as Model 45 but without rear peep sight and ramp front sight; intended for use with telescopic sight only. Made from 1935 to 1937.

Mossberg Model 46 Bolt Action Repeating Rifle. $ 55
Takedown. Caliber, 22 Long Rifle, Long, Short. Tubular magazine holds 15 Long Rifle, 18 Long, 22 Short. 26-inch barrel. Weight, 7½ pounds. Micrometer click rear peep sight, hooded ramp front sight. Pistol-grip stock with cheekpiece, full beavertail forearm, 1¼-inch swivels. Made from 1935 to 1937.

Mossberg Model 46C.............................. $ 60
Same as Model 46 except has a heavier barrel and stock than that model, weighs 8½ pounds. Made from 1936 to 1937.

Mossberg Model 35A Bolt Action Single Shot Rifle.. $ 60
Caliber, 22 Long Rifle. 26-inch heavy barrel. Weight, about 8¼ pounds. Micrometer click peep rear sight and hooded front sight. Target stock with cheekpiece, full pistol grip and forearm, 1¼-inch sling swivels. Made from 1937 to 1938.

Mossberg Model 35A-LS.......................... $ 75
Same as Model 35A but with Lyman 57 rear sight and 17A front sight.

Mossberg Model 42A Bolt Action Repeating Rifle.. $ 55
Takedown. Caliber, 22 Long Rifle, Long, Short. 7-shot detachable box magazine. 24-inch barrel. Weight, about 5 pounds. Receiver peep sight, open rear sight, ramp front sight. Plain pistol-grip stock. Made from 1937 to 1938.

Mossberg Model L42A........................... $ 55
Same as Model 42A but with left-hand action. Made from 1937 to 1941.

Mossberg Model 43 Bolt Action Repeating Rifle. $ 75
Speedlock, adjustable trigger pull. Caliber, 22 Long Rifle. 7-shot detachable box magazine. 26-inch heavy barrel. Weight, about 8¼ pounds. Lyman 57 rear sight, selective aperture front sight. Target stock with cheekpiece, full pistol grip, beavertail forearm, adjustable front swivel. Made from 1937 to 1938.

Mossberg Model L43.............................. $ 75
Same as Model 43 except has left-hand action. Made from 1937 to 1938.

Mossberg Model 45A Bolt Action Repeating Rifle.. $ 55
Takedown. Caliber, 22 Long Rifle, Long, Short. Tubular magazine holds 15 Long Rifle, 18 Long, 22 Short. 24-inch barrel. Weight, about 6¾ pounds. Receiver peep sight, open rear sight, hooded ramp front sight. Plain pistol-grip stock, 1¼-inch swivels. Made from 1937 to 1938.

Mossberg Model 45AC............................ $ 45
Same as Model 45A, except without receiver peep sight.

Mossberg Model L45A............................ $ 60
Same as Model 45A, except has left-hand action. Made from 1937 to 1938.

Mossberg Model L45A

Mossberg Model L46A-LS

Mossberg Model 26B

Mossberg Model 42B

Mossberg Model 42C

Mossberg Model 46A Bolt Action Repeating Rifle .... $ 60

Takedown. Caliber, 22 Long Rifle, Long, Short. Tubular magazine holds 15 Long Rifle, 18 Long, 22 Short. 26-inch barrel. Weight, about 7¼ pounds. Micrometer click receiver peep sight, open rear sight, hooded ramp front sight. Pistol-grip stock with cheekpiece and beavertail forearm, quick-detachable swivels. Made from 1937 to 1938.

Mossberg Model 46AC .... $ 60

Same as Model 46A, except without open rear sight.

Mossberg Model 46A-LS .... $ 75

Same as Model 46A, except with Lyman 57 receiver sight.

Mossberg Model L-46A-LS .... $ 75

Same as Model 46A-LS, except has left-hand action. Made from 1937 to 1938.

Mossberg Model 26B Bolt Action Single Shot Rifle .... $ 45

Takedown. Caliber, 22 Long Rifle, Long, Short. 26-inch barrel. Weight, about 5½ pounds. Micrometer click rear peep sight, open rear sight, hooded ramp front sight. Plain pistol-grip stock, swivels. Made from 1938 to 1941.

Mossberg Model 26C .... $ 40

Same as Model 26B except without rear peep sight and swivels.

Mossberg Model 42B Bolt Action Repeating Rifle .... $ 55

Takedown. Caliber, 22 Long Rifle, Long, Short. 5-shot detachable box magazine. 24-inch barrel. Weight, about 6 pounds. Micrometer click receiver peep sight, open rear sight, hooded ramp front sight. Plain pistol-grip stock, swivels. Made from 1938 to 1941.

Mossberg Model 42C .... $ 55

Same as Model 42B except without rear peep sight.

Mossberg Model 44B Bolt Action Target Rifle .. $ 90

Caliber, 22 Long Rifle. 7-shot detachable box magazine. 26-inch heavy barrel. Weight, about 8 pounds. Micrometer click receiver peep sight, hooded front sight. Target stock with full pistol grip, cheekpiece, beavertail forearm, adjustable swivel. Made from 1938 to 1941.

Mossberg Model 35B .... $ 75

Same specifications as Model 44B, except single shot. Made from 1938 to 1940.

Mossberg Model 43B $105

Same as Model 44B, except with Lyman 57 receiver sight and 17A front sight. Made from 1938 to 1939.

Mossberg Model 45B Bolt Action Repeating Rifle .... $ 60

Takedown. Caliber, 22 Long Rifle, Long, Short. Tubular magazine holds 15 Long Rifle, 18 Long, 22 Short. 24-inch barrel. Weight, about 6¼ pounds. Open rear sight, hooded front sight. Plain pistol-grip stock, swivels. Made from 1938 to 1940.

Mossberg Model 44B

Mossberg Model 43B

Mossberg Model 45B

Mossberg Model 46B

Mossberg Model 51

Mossberg Model 50

Mossberg Model 46B Bolt Action Repeating Rifle .... **$ 60**
Takedown. Caliber, 22 Long Rifle, Long, Short. Tubular magazine holds 15 Long Rifle, 18 Long, 22 Short. 26-inch barrel. Weight, about 7 pounds. Micrometer click receiver peep sight, open rear sight, hooded front sight. Plain pistol-grip stock with cheekpiece, swivels. *Note:* Postwar version of this model has full magazine holding 20 Long Rifle, 23 Long, 30 Short. Made from 1938 to 1950.

Mossberg Model 46BT .... **$ 75**
Same as Model 46B, except has heavier barrel and stock, weighs 7¾ pounds. Made from 1938 to 1939.

Mossberg Model 51 Autoloading Rifle .... **$ 75**
Takedown. Caliber, 22 Long Rifle. 15-shot tubular magazine in buttstock. 24-inch barrel. Weight, about 7¼ pounds. Micrometer click receiver peep sight, open rear sight, hooded ramp front sight. Cheekpiece stock with full pistol grip and beavertail forearm, swivels. Made in 1939 only.

Mossberg Model 50 Autoloading Rifle .... **$ 70**
Same as Model 51, except has plain stock without beavertail, cheekpiece, swivels or receiver peep sight. Made from 1939 to 1942.

Mossberg Model 51M Autoloading Rifle .... **$ 75**
Caliber, 22 Long Rifle. 15-shot tubular magazine. 20-inch barrel. Weight, about 7 pounds. Microclick receiver peep sight, open rear sight, hooded ramp front sight. Two-piece Mannlicher-type stock with pistol grip and cheekpiece, swivels. Made from 1939 to 1946.

Mossberg Model 151M Autoloading Rifle .... **$ 75**
Improved version of Model 51M with same general specifications, complete action is instantly removable without use of tools. Made from 1946 to 1958.

Mossberg Model 151K .... **$ 70**
Same as Model 151M except has 24-inch barrel, weighs about 6 pounds, has no peep sight, plain stock with Monte Carlo comb and cheekpiece, pistol-grip knob, fore-end tip, without swivels. Made from 1950 to 1951.

Mossberg Model 51M

Mossberg Model 151M

Mossberg Model 151K

Mossberg Model 46M

Mossberg Model 44US

Mossberg Model 152

Mossberg Model 42M Bolt Action Repeating Rifle... **$ 85**
Caliber, 22 Long Rifle, Long, Short. 7-shot detachable box magazine. 23-inch barrel. Weight, about 6¾ pounds. Microclick receiver peep sight, open rear sight, hooded ramp front sight. Two-piece Mannlicher-type stock with cheekpiece and pistol grip, swivels. Made from 1940 to 1950.

Mossberg Model 46M Bolt Action Repeating Rifle... **$ 70**
Caliber, 22 Long Rifle, Long, Short. Tubular magazine holds 22 Short, 18 Long, 15 Long Rifle. 23-inch barrel. Weight, about 7 pounds. Microclick receiver peep sight, open rear sight, hooded

ramp front sight. Two-piece Mannlicher-type stock with cheekpiece and pistol grip, swivels. Made from 1940 to 1952.

Mossberg Model 44US Bolt Action Repeating Rifle... **$100**
Caliber, 22 Long Rifle. 7-shot detachable box magazine. 26-inch heavy barrel. Weight, about 8½ pounds. Micrometer click receiver peep sight, hooded front sight. Target stock, swivels. Made from 1943 to 1948. *Note:* This model was used as a training rifle by the U.S. Armed Forces during World War II.

Mossberg Model 152 Autoloading Carbine......**$ 90**
Caliber, 22 Long Rifle. 7-shot detachable box magazine. 18-inch barrel. Weight, about 5 pounds. Peep rear sight, military-type front sight. Monte Carlo stock with pistol grip, hinged forearm pulls down to form hand grip, sling mounted on swivels on left side of stock. Made from 1948 to 1957.

Mossberg Model 152K........................ **$ 90**
Same as Model 152, except with open instead of peep rear sight. Made from 1950 to 1957.

Mossberg Model 142-A Bolt Action Repeating Carbine............................ **$ 60**
Caliber, 22 Short, Long, Long Rifle. 7-shot detachable box magazine. 18-inch barrel. Weight, about 6 pounds. Peep rear sight, military-type front sight. Monte Carlo stock with pistol grip, hinged forearm pulls down to form hand grip, sling swivels mounted on left side of stock. Made from 1949 to 1957.

Mossberg Model 142K........................ **$ 60**
Same as Model 142, except has open rear sight. Made from 1953 to 1957.

Mossberg Model 144 Bolt Action Target Rifle... **$ 95**
Caliber, 22 Long Rifle. 7-shot detachable box magazine. 26-inch heavy barrel. Weight, about 8 pounds. Microclick receiver peep sight, hooded front sight. Pistol-grip target stock with beavertail forearm, adjustable hand stop, swivels. Made from 1949 to 1954. *Note:* This model designation was resumed c. 1973 for previous Model 144LS. See that listing.

Mossberg Model 144LS........................ **$105**
Same as Model 144 except has Lyman 57MS or Mossberg S331

receiver sight and Lyman 17A front sight. Made from 1954 to date. *Note:* This model since c.1973 has been marketed as Model 144.

Mossberg Model 146B Bolt Action Repeating Rifle............................... **$ 70**
Takedown. Caliber, 22 Long Rifle, Long, Short. Tubular magazine holds 30 Short, 23 Long, 20 Long Rifle. 26-inch barrel. Weight, about 7 pounds. Micrometer click rear peep sight, open rear sight, hooded front sight. Plain stock with pistol grip, Monte Carlo comb and cheekpiece, knob fore-end tip, swivels. Made from 1949 to 1954.

Mossberg Model 140K Bolt Action Repeating Rifle............................... **$ 60**
Caliber, 22 Long Rifle, 22 Long, 22 Short. 7-shot clip magazine. 24½-inch barrel. Weight, 5¾ pounds. Open rear sight, bead front sight. Monte Carlo stock with cheekpiece and pistol grip, sling swivels. Made from 1955 to 1958.

Mossberg Model 140B Sporter-Target Rifle..... **$ 70**
Same as Model 140K, except has peep rear sight, hooded ramp front sight. Made from 1957 to 1958.

Mossberg Model 144LS

Mossberg Model 146B

Mossberg Model 140K

Mossberg Model 140B

Mossberg Model 346K

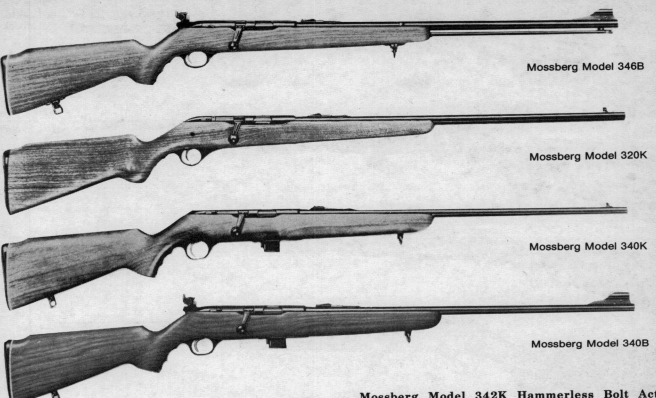

Mossberg Model 346B

Mossberg Model 320K

Mossberg Model 340K

Mossberg Model 340B

Mossberg Model 346K Hammerless Bolt Action Repeating Rifle................................... **$ 70**
Caliber, 22 Short, Long, Long Rifle. Tubular magazine holds 25 Short, 20 Long, 18 Long Rifle. 24-inch barrel. Weight, about 6½ pounds. Open rear sight, bead front sight. Walnut stock with Monte Carlo comb, cheekpiece, pistol grip, sling swivels. Made from 1958 to 1971.

Mossberg Model 346B........................... **$ 75**
Same as Model 346K, except has peep rear sight, hooded ramp front sight. Made from 1958 to 1967.

Mossberg Model 320K Hammerless Bolt Action Single Shot... **$ 55**
Same as Model 346K except single shot, has drop-in loading platform, automatic safety. Weight, about 5¾ pounds. Made from 1958 to 1960.

Mossberg Model 340K Hammerless Bolt Action Repeating Rifle...................................... **$ 60**
Same as Model 346K, except clip type, 7-shot magazine. Made from 1958 to 1971.

Mossberg Model 340B Target Sporter........... **$ 65**
Same as Model 340K, except has peep rear sight, hooded ramp front sight. Made from 1958 to date.

Mossberg Model 320B Boy Scout Target Rifle.. **$ 70**
Same as Model 340K, except single shot with automatic safety. Made from 1960 to 1971.

Mossberg Model 340M........................... **$ 75**
Same as Model 340K, except has 18½-inch barrel, Mannlicher-style stock with swivels and sling. Weight, 5¼ pounds. Made from 1970 to 1971.

Mossberg Model 342K Hammerless Bolt Action Carbine.. **$ 60**
Same as Model 340K, except has 18-inch barrel, stock has no cheekpiece, extension fore-end is hinged, pulls down to form hand grip; sling swivels and web strap on left side of stock; weight, about 5 pounds. Made from 1958 to 1974.

Mossberg Model 350K Autoloading Rifle—Clip Type.. **$ 70**
Caliber, 22 Short (high speed), Long, Long Rifle. 7-shot clip magazine. 23½-inch barrel. Weight, about 6 pounds. Open rear sight, bead front sight. Monte Carlo stock with pistol grip. Made from 1958 to 1971.

Mossberg Model 352K Autoloading Carbine..... **$ 70**
Caliber, 22 Short, Long, Long Rifle. 7-shot clip magazine. 18-inch barrel. Weight, about 5 pounds. Open rear sight, bead front sight. Monte Carlo stock with pistol grip; extension fore-end of Tenite is hinged, pulls down to form hand grip; sling swivels, web strap. Made from 1958 to 1971.

Mossberg Model 351K Automatic Sporter....... **$ 60**
Caliber, 22 Long Rifle. 15-shot tubular magazine in buttstock. 24-inch barrel. Weight, about 6 pounds. Open rear sight, bead front sight. Monte Carlo stock with pistol grip. Made from 1960 to 1971.

Mossberg Model 351C Automatic Carbine....... **$ 70**
Same as Model 351K, except has 18½-inch barrel, Western carbine-style stock with barrel band and sling swivels. Weight, 5½ pounds. Made from 1965 to 1971.

Mossberg Model 640K "Chuckster" Hammerless Bolt Action Rifle.................................... **$ 70**
Caliber, 22 R.F. Magnum. 5-shot detachable clip magazine. 24-inch barrel. Weight, about 6 pounds. Open rear sight, bead front sight. Monte Carlo stock with cheekpiece, pistol grip, sling swivels. Made from 1959 to date.

Mossberg Model 320B

Mossberg Model 342K

Mossberg Model 350K

Mossberg Model 352K

Mossberg Model 351K

Mossberg Model 640K

Mossberg Model 640KS

Mossberg Model 640M

Mossberg Model 640KS.......................... $ 90
Deluxe version of Model 640K, has select walnut stock, hand checkering; gold-plated front sight, rear sight elevator, and trigger. Made from 1960 to 1964.

Mossberg Model 640M.......................... $100
Similar to Model 640K, except chambered for 22 Win. Mag. R.F.; has 20-inch barrel, Mannlicher-style stock with Monte Carlo comb and cheekpiece, swivels. Made from 1967 to 1973.

Mossberg Model 642K.......................... $ 75
Same as Model 640K, except has 18½-inch barrel, forearm with black Tenite extension that pulls down to form hand grip. Made from 1961 to 1964.

Mossberg Model 620K.......................... $ 55
Same as Model 640K, except single shot. Made from 1960 to 1964.

Mossberg Model 400 "Palomino" Lever Action Rifle.. $ 90
Hammerless. Caliber, 22 Short, Long, Long Rifle. Tubular magazine holds 20 Short, 17 Long, 15 Long Rifle. 24-inch barrel. Weight, about 5½ pounds. Open rear sight, bead front sight. Monte Carlo stock with checkered pistol grip; and beavertail forearm. Made from 1959 to 1964.

Mossberg Model 402 "Palomino" Carbine........ $ 90
Same as Model 400, except has 18½-inch (1961-64) or 20-inch barrel (1964-71), forearm with barrel band, swivels; magazine holds two less rounds; weight, about 4¾ pounds. Made from 1961 to 1971.

Mossberg Model 430 Automatic Rifle............ $ 75
Caliber, 22 Long Rifle, 18-shot tubular magazine. 24-inch barrel. Weight, about 6¼ pounds. Open rear sight, bead front sight. Monte Carlo stock with checkered pistol grip; checkered forearm. Made from 1970 to 1971.

Mossberg Model 432 Western Style Auto Carbine... $ 70
Same as Model 430 except has plain straight-grip carbine-type stock and forearm, barrel band, sling swivels. Magazine capacity, 15 cartridges. Weight, about 6 pounds. Made from 1970 to 1971.

Mossberg Model 341 Bolt Action Repeater...... $ 60
Caliber, 22 Short, Long, Long Rifle. 7-shot clip magazine. 24-inch barrel. Weight, 6½ pounds. Open rear sight, ramp front sight. Monte Carlo stock with checkered pistol grip and forearm, sling swivels. Made from 1972 to date.

Mossberg Model 321K Bolt Action Single Shot.. $ 60
Same as Model 341, except single shot. Made from 1972 to 1980.

Mossberg Model 321B.......................... $ 60
Same as Model 321K, except has receiver peep sight. Made from 1972 to 1975.

Mossberg Model 333 Autoloading Carbine.......$ 90
Caliber, 22 Long Rifle. 15-shot tubular magazine. 20-inch barrel. Weight, about 6¼ pounds. Open rear sight, ramp front sight. Monte Carlo stock with checkered pistol grip and forearm, barrel band, swivels. Made from 1972 to 1973.

Mossberg Model 642K

Mossberg Model 400

Mossberg Model 402

Mossberg Model 341

Mossberg Model 333

Mossberg Model 353

Mossberg Model 800

Mossberg Model 800VT

Mossberg Model 800M

Mossberg Model 800D

Mossberg Model 353 Autoloading Carbine......$ 75
Caliber, 22 Long Rifle. 7-shot clip magazine. 18-inch barrel. Weight, about 5 pounds. Open rear sight, ramp front sight. Monte Carlo stock with checkered pistol grip and forearm; black Tenite extension fore-end pulls down to form hand grip. Made from 1972 to date.

Mossberg Model 800 Bolt Action Center Fire Rifle.. **$190**
Calibers: 222 Rem., 22-250, 243 Win., 308 Win. 4-shot magazine, 3-shot in 222, 22-inch barrel. Weight, about 7½ pounds. Folding leaf rear sight, ramp front sight. Monte Carlo stock with cheekpiece, checkered pistol grip and forearm, sling swivels. Made from 1967 to 1979.

Mossberg Model 800VT Varmint/Target........ **$205**
Similar to Model 800, except has 24-inch heavy barrel, no sights; weight, about 9½ pounds. Calibers: 222 Rem., 22-250, 243 Win. Made from 1968 to 1979.

Mossberg Model 800M........................... **$250**
Same as Model 800, except has flat bolt handle, 20-inch barrel, Mannlicher-style stock; weight, 6½ pounds. Calibers: 22-250, 243 Win., 308 Win. Made from 1969 to 1972.

Mossberg Model 800D Super Grade............. **$240**
Deluxe version of Model 800, has stock with roll-over comb and cheekpiece, rosewood fore-end tip and pistol-grip cap; weight, about 6¾ pounds. Not chambered for 222 Rem. Made from 1970 to 1973.

Mossberg Model 810

Mossberg Model 472 Carbine (pistol-grip)

Mossberg Model 472 Carbine (straight-grip)

Mossberg Model 472 Rifle

Mossberg Model 472 Brush Gun

Mossberg Model 472 "One in Five Thousand"
(right side)

Mossberg Model 472 "One in Five Thousand"
(left side)

Mossberg Model 377

Mossberg Model 380

Mossberg Model 810 Bolt Action Center Fire Rifle
Calibers: 270 Win., 30-06, 7mm Rem. Mag., 338 Win. Mag. Detachable box magazine (1970-75) or internal magazine with hinged floorplate (1972 to date); capacity: 4-shot in 270 and 30-06, 3-shot in magnums. 22-inch barrel in 270 and 30-06, 24-inch in magnums. Weight, 7½ to 8 pounds. Leaf rear sight, ramp front sight. Stock with Monte Carlo comb and cheekpiece, checkered pistol grip and forearm, grip cap, sling swivels. Made from 1970 to 1979.
Standard calibers..................................... $195
Magnum calibers.................................... 210

Mossberg Model 472 Lever Action Center Fire
Carbine... $150
Calibers: 30-30, 35 Rem. 6-shot tubular magazine. 20-inch barrel. Weight, 6¾ to 7 pounds. Open rear sight, ramp front sight. Pistol-grip or straight-grip stock, forearm with barrel band; sling swivels on pistol-grip model, saddle ring on straight-grip model. Made from 1972 to 1979.

Mossberg Model 472 Rifle........................ $150
Same as Model 472 Carbine with pistol-grip stock, except has 24-inch barrel, 5-shot magazine; weight, about 7 pounds. Made from 1974 to 1976.

Mossberg Model 472 Brush Gun................. $160
Same as Model 472 Carbine with straight-grip stock, except has 18-inch barrel; weight, about 6½ pounds. Caliber, 30-30. Magazine capacity, 5 rounds. Made from 1974 to 1976.

Mossberg Model 472 "One in Five Thousand"... $265
Same as Model 472 Brush Gun, except has Indian scenes etched on receiver; brass butt plate, saddle ring and barrel bands, gold-plated trigger; bright blued finish; select walnut stock and forearm. Limited edition of 5000, serial numbered 1 to 5000. Made in 1974.

Mossberg Model 377 "Plinkster" Autoloading
Rifle... $ 60
Caliber, 22 Long Rifle. 15-shot tubular magazine. 20-inch barrel. Weight, about 6¼ pounds. 4X scope sight. Thumbhole stock with roll-over cheekpiece, Monte Carlo comb, checkered forearm; molded of modified polystyrene foam in walnut finish; sling swivel studs. Introduced 1977.

Mossberg Model 380 Semiautomatic Rifle....... $ 80
Caliber, 22 Long Rifle. 15-shot butt stock magazine. 20-inch barrel. Weight, 5½ pounds. Open rear sight, bead front sight. Made from 1980 to date.

Musgrave Manufacturers & Distributors (Pty) Ltd., Bloemfontein, South Africa

Musgrave Premier NR5 Bolt Action Hunting
Rifle.. $285
Calibers: 243 Win., 270 Win., 30-06, 308 Win., 7mm Rem. Mag. 5-shot magazine. 25½-inch barrel. Weight, 8¼ pounds. Furnished without sights. Select walnut Monte Carlo stock with cheekpiece, checkered pistol grip and forearm, contrasting pistol-grip cap and fore-end tip, recoil pad, swivel studs. Made from 1971 to 1976.

Musgrave Valiant NR6 Bolt Action Hunting
Rifle.. $225
Similar to Premier, except has 24-inch barrel; stock with straight comb, skip checkering, no grip cap or fore-end tip; leaf rear sight, hooded ramp front sight; weight, 7¾ pounds. Made from 1971 to 1976.

Musgrave Premier

Musgrave Valiant

Musgrave RSA

Musketeer Mauser

Musgrave RSA NR1 Bolt Action Single Shot Target Rifle... $270
Caliber, 308 Win. (7.62mm NATO). 26.4-inch heavy barrel. Weight, about 10 pounds. Aperture receiver sight, tunnel front sight. Walnut target stock with beavertail forearm, handguard, barrel band, rubber butt plate, sling swivels. Made from 1971 to 1976.

Musketeer Rifles manufactured by Firearms International Corp., Washington, D.C.

Musketeer Mauser Sporter......................$230
FN Mauser bolt action. Calibers: 243, 25-06, 270, 264 Mag., 308, 30-06, 7mm Mag., 300 Win. Mag. Magazine holds 5 standard, 3 magnum cartridges. 24-inch barrel. Weight, about 7¼ pounds. No sights. Monte Carlo stock with checkered pistol grip and forearm, swivels. Made from 1963 to 1972.

Navy Arms Co., Ridgefield, New Jersey

Navy Arms "Yellowboy" Lever Action Repeating Rifle.. $250
Replica of Winchester Model 1866. Calibers: 38 Special, 44-40. 15-shot magazine. 24-inch octagon barrel. Weight, about 8 pounds. Folding leaf rear sight, blade front sight. Straight-grip stock, forearm with end cap. Introduced, 1966. Discontinued.

Navy Arms "Yellowboy" Carbine................ $175
Similar to "Yellowboy" Rifle, except has 19-inch barrel, 10-shot magazine (14-shot in 22 Long Rifle), carbine-style forearm with barrel band, weighs about 6¾ pounds.

Navy Arms "Yellowboy" Trapper's Model....... $175
Same as "Yellowboy" Carbine, except has 16½-inch barrel, magazine holds two fewer rounds, weighs about 6¼ pounds. Discontinued.

Navy Arms Model 1873 Lever Action Repeating Rifle.. $250
Replica of Winchester Model 1873. Casehardened receiver. Calibers: 22 Long Rifle, 357 Magnum, 44-40. 15-shot magazine. 24-inch octagon barrel. Weight, about 8 pounds. Open rear sight, blade front sight. Straight-grip stock, forearm with end cap. Made in Italy from 1972 to date.

Navy Arms Model 1873 Carbine................ $200
Similar to Model 1873 Rifle, except has blued receiver, 10-shot magazine, 19-inch round barrel, carbine-style forearm with barrel band, weighs about 6¾ pounds. Discontinued.

Navy Arms 1873 Trapper's Model.............. $205
Same as Model 1873 Carbine, except has 16½-inch barrel, 8-shot magazine, weighs about 6¼ pounds. Discontinued.

Navy Arms Engraved Models
"Yellowboy" and Model 1873 rifles and carbines are available in deluxe models with select walnut stocks and forearms and engraving in three grades. Grade "A" is delicate scrollwork in limited areas. Grade "B" is more elaborate with about 40 percent coverage. Grade "C" is highest grade engraving. Add to value:
Grade "A"..$100
Grade "B".. 135
Grade "C".. 350

Navy Arms Revolving Carbine................... $160
Action resembles that of Remington Model 1875 Revolver. Casehardened frame. Calibers: 357 Magnum, 44-40, 45 Colt. 6-shot cylinder. 20-inch barrel. Weight, about 5 pounds. Open rear sight, blade front sight. Straight-grip stock, brass trigger guard and butt plate. Introduced, 1968. Discontinued.

Navy Arms Rolling Block Baby Carbine........ $145
Replica of small Remington Rolling Block single-shot action. Casehardened frame, brass trigger guard. Calibers: 22 Long Rifle, 22 Hornet, 357 Magnum, 44-40. 20-inch octagon or 22-inch round barrel. Weight, about 5 pounds. Open rear sight, blade front sight. Straight-grip stock, plain forearm, brass butt plate. Made from 1968 to date.

Navy Arms Rolling Block Buffalo Rifle.......... $150
Replica Remington Rolling Block single-shot action. Casehardened frame, brass trigger guard. Calibers: 444 Marlin, 45-70, 50-70. 26- or 30-inch heavy half-octagon or full-octagon barrel. Weight, about 11 to 12 pounds. Open rear sight, blade front sight. Straight-grip stock with brass butt plate, forearm with brass barrel band. Made from 1971 to date.

Navy Arms Rolling Block Buffalo Carbine....... $150
Same as Buffalo Rifle, except has 18-inch barrel, weighs about 10 pounds.

Navy Arms Rolling Block Creedmoor Rifle...... $195
Same as Buffalo Rifle, except calibers 45-70 and 50-70 only, 28- or 30-inch heavy half-octagon or full-octagon barrel, Creedmoor tang peep sight.

Navy Arms Martini Target Rifle................. $210
Martini single-shot action. Calibers: 444 Marlin, 45-70. 26- or 30-inch half-octagon or full-octagon barrel. Weight, about 9 pounds with 26-inch barrel. Creedmore tang peep sight, open middle sight, blade front sight. Stock with cheekpiece and pistol grip, forearm with schnabel tip, both checkered. Introduced, 1972. Discontinued.

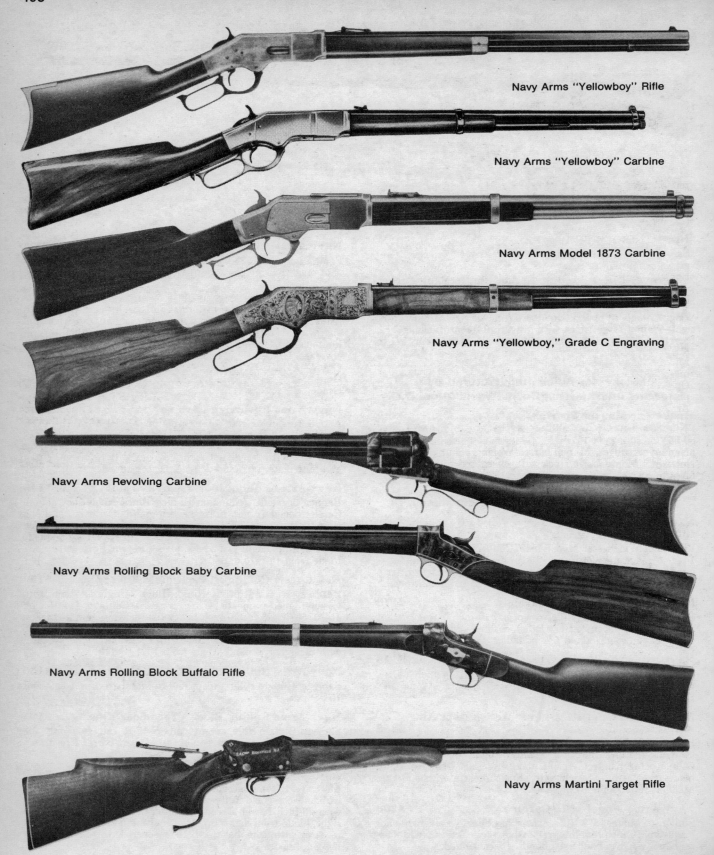

Navy Arms "Yellowboy" Rifle

Navy Arms "Yellowboy" Carbine

Navy Arms Model 1873 Carbine

Navy Arms "Yellowboy," Grade C Engraving

Navy Arms Revolving Carbine

Navy Arms Rolling Block Baby Carbine

Navy Arms Rolling Block Buffalo Rifle

Navy Arms Martini Target Rifle

Navy Arms 45-70 Mauser Rifle

Navy Arms 45-70 Mauser Rifle.................. **$150**
Siamese Mauser bolt action. Caliber, 45-70 Government. 3-round magazine. 24- or 26-inch barrel. Weight, about 8½ pounds with 26-inch barrel. Open rear sight, ramp front sight. Checkered stock with Monte Carlo comb. Introduced, 1973. Discontinued.

Navy Arms 45-70 Mauser Carbine............... **$155**
Same as 45-70 Mauser Rifle, except has 18-inch barrel, straight-grip stock with low comb, weighs about 7½ pounds. Discontinued.

Newton Sporting Rifles manufactured by Newton Arms Co., Charles Newton Rifle Corp., and Buffalo Newton Rifle Co., all of Buffalo, N.Y.

Newton-Mauser Sporting Rifle................... **$500**
Mauser (Oberndorf) action. Caliber, 256 Newton. 5-shot box magazine, hinged floorplate. Double-set triggers. 24-inch barrel. Open rear sight, ramp front sight. Sporting stock with checkered pistol grip. Weight, about 7 pounds. Made c. 1914 by Newton Arms Co.

Newton Standard Model Sporting Rifle—First Type... **$550**
Newton bolt action, interrupted screw-type breech-locking mechanism, double-set triggers. Calibers: 22, 256, 280, 30, 33, 35 Newton; 30-06. 24-inch barrel. Open rear sight or cocking-piece peep sight, ramp front sight. Checkered pistol-grip stock. Weight, 7 to 8 pounds, depending upon caliber. Made c. 1916-18 by Newton Arms Co.

Newton Standard Model Sporting Rifle—Second Type... **$575**
Newton bolt action, improved design; distinguished by reversed-set trigger and 1917-Enfield-type bolt handle. Calibers: 256, 30, 35 Newton; 30-06. 5-shot box magazine. 24-inch barrel. Open rear sight, ramp front sight. Checkered pistol-grip stock. Weight, 7¾ to 8¼ pounds, depending on caliber. Made c. 1921 by Charles Newton Rifle Corp.

Buffalo Newton Sporting Rifle................... **$550**
Same general specifications as Standard Model—2nd Type. Made c. 1922-32 by Buffalo Newton Rifle Co.

Nikko Firearms Ltd., Tochiga, Japan
See listings under Golden Eagle Rifles.

Noble Mfg. Co., Haydenville, Massachusetts

Noble Model 33 Slide Action Repeater.......... **$ 50**
Hammerless. Caliber, 22 Long Rifle, Long, Short. Tubular magazine holds 21 Short, 17 Long, 15 Long Rifle. 24-inch barrel. Weight, 6 pounds. Open rear sight, bead front sight. Tenite stock and slide handle. Made from 1949 to 1953.

Nobel Model 33A................................. **$ 45**
Same general specifications as Model 33 except has wood stock and slide handle. Made from 1953 to 1955.

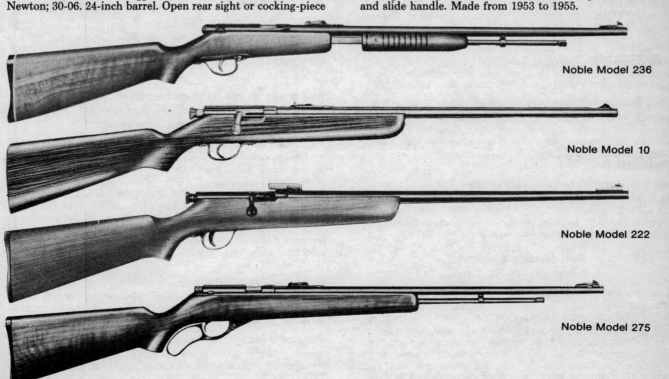

Noble Model 236

Noble Model 10

Noble Model 222

Noble Model 275

Parker-Hale 1200 Super

Parker-Hale 1200V Varmint

Pedersen Model 3000 Grade I

Noble Model 236 Slide Action Repeating Rifle...$ 45
Hammerless. Caliber, 22 Short, Long, Long Rifle. Tubular magazine holds 21 Short, 17 Long, 15 Long Rifle. 24-inch barrel. Weight, about 5½ pounds. Open rear sight, ramp front sight. Pistol-grip stock, grooved slide handle. Made from 1951 to date.

Noble Model 10 Bolt Action Single Shot Rifle... $ 30
Caliber, 22 Long Rifle, Long, Short. 24-inch barrel. Plain pistol-grip stock. Open rear sight, bead front sight. Weight, about 4 pounds. Made from 1955 to 1958.

Noble Model 20 Bolt Action Single Shot Rifle... $ 30
Manually cocked. Caliber, 22 Long Rifle, Long, Short. 22-inch barrel. Weight, about 5 pounds. Open rear sight, bead front sight. Walnut stock with pistol grip. Made from 1958 to 1963.

Noble Model 222 Bolt Action Single Shot Rifle.. $ 35
Manually cocked. Caliber, 22 Long Rifle, Long, Short Barrel integral with receiver. Overall length, 38 inches. Weight, about 5 pounds. Interchangeable V-notch and peep rear sight, ramp front sight. Scope mounting base. Pistol-grip stock. Made from 1958 to 1971.

Nobel Model 275 Lever Action Rifle............. $ 80
Hammerless. Caliber, 22 Short, Long, Long Rifle. Tubular magazine holds 21 Short, 17 Long, 15 Long Rifle. 24-inch barrel. Weight, about 5½ pounds. Open rear sight, ramp front sight. Stock with semi-pistol grip. Made from 1958 to 1971.

Parker-Hale Limited, Birmingham, England

Parker-Hale 1200 Super Bolt Action Sporting Rifle.. $260
Mauser type bolt action. Calibers: 22-250, 243 Win., 6mm Rem., 25-06, 270 Win., 30-06, 308 Win. 4-shot magazine. 24-inch barrel. Weight, 7¼ pounds. Folding open rear sight, hooded ramp front sight. European walnut stock with rollover Monte Carlo cheekpiece, rosewood fore-end tip and pistol-grip cap, skip checkering, recoil pad, sling swivels. Made from 1968 to date.

Parker-Hale 1200 Super Magnum............... $275
Same general specifications as 1200 Super, except calibers 7mm Rem. Mag. and 300 Win. Mag., 3-shot magazine.

Parker-Hale 1200P Presentation............... $330
Same general specifications as 1200 Super, except has scroll-engraved action, trigger guard and floorplate, no sights, QD swivels. Calibers, 243 Win. and 30-06. Made from 1969 to 1975.

Parker-Hale 1200V Varmint..................... $280
Same general specifications as 1200 Super, except has 24-inch heavy barrel, no sights, weighs 9½ pounds. Calibers: 22-250, 6mm Rem., 25-06, 243 Win. Made from 1969 to date.

Pedersen Rifles manufactured by Pedersen Custom Guns, division of O. F. Mossberg & Sons, Inc., North Haven, Connecticut

Pedersen Model 3000 Grade I Bolt Action Rifle. $700
Richly engraved with silver inlays, full-fancy American black walnut stock. Mossberg Model 810 action. Calibers: 270 Win., 30-06, 7mm Rem. Mag., 338 Win. Mag. 3-shot magazine, hinged floorplate. 22-inch barrel in 270 and 30-06, 24-inch in magnums. Weight, 7 to 8 pounds, depending upon caliber. Open rear sight, hooded ramp front sight. Monte Carlo stock with roll-over cheekpiece, wrap-around hand checkering on pistol grip and forearm, rosewood pistol-grip cap and fore-end tip, recoil pad or steel butt plate with trap, detachable swivels. Made from 1973 to 1975.

Pedersen Model 3000 Grade II.................. $550
Same as Model 3000 Grade I, except less elaborate engraving, no inlays, fancy grade walnut stock with recoil pad. Made from 1973 to 1975.

Pedersen Model 3000 Grade III................. $470
Same as Model 3000 Grade I, except no engraving or inlays, select grade walnut stock with recoil pad. Made from 1973 to 1974.

Pedersen Model 3000 Grade III

Plainfield M-1 Carbine

Plainfield Military Sporter

Plainfield Commando

Plainfielder Deluxe Sporter

Pedersen Model 4700 Custom Deluxe Lever Action Rifle **$175**
Mossberg Model 472 action. Calibers: 30-30, 35 Rem. 5-shot tubular magazine. 24-inch barrel. Weight, 7½ pounds. Open rear sight, hooded ramp front sight. Hand-finished black walnut stock and beavertail forearm, barrel band swivels. Made in 1975.

Plainfield Machine Company, Dunellen, New Jersey

Plainfield M-1 Carbine **$145**
Same as U.S. Carbine, Cal. 30, M-1, except also available in caliber 5.7mm (22 with necked-down 30 Carbine cartridge case). Current production has ventilated metal handguard and barrel band without bayonet lug; earlier models have standard military-type fittings. Made from 1960 to 1977.

Plainfield M-1 Carbine, Military Sporter **$145**
Same as M-1 Carbine, except has unslotted buttstock and wood handguard. Made from 1960 to 1977.

Plainfield M-1 Carbine, Commando Model **$150**
Same as M-1 Carbine, except has paratrooper-type stock with telescoping wire shoulderpiece. Made from 1960 to 1977.

Plainfielder Deluxe Sporter **$175**
Same as M-1 Carbine, except has Monte Carlo sporting stock. Made from 1960 to 1973.

Polish Military Rifles manufactured by Government Arsenals at Radom and Warsaw

Polish Model 1898 (Karabin 98, WZ98A) Mauser Military Rifle **$125**
Same, except for minor details, as the German Gew. 98 used in World War I. Manufacture begun c. 1921.

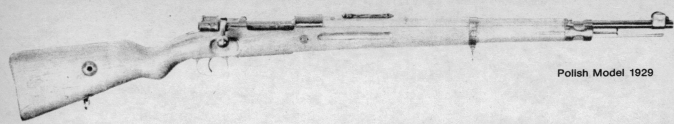

Polish Model 1929

Polish Model 1898 (Karabin 98, K98) Mauser Military Carbine **$125**

Same, except for minor details, as the German Kar. 98a. First manufactured during early 1920's.

Polish Model 1929 (Karabin 29, WZ29) Mauser Military Rifle **$125**

Same, except for minor details, as the Czech Model 24. Manufactured from 1929 through World War II; a similar model produced during the German occupation was designated Gew. 29/40.

James Purdey & Sons Ltd., London, England

Purdey Double Rifle **$17,000**

Side lock action, hammerless, ejectors. Calibers: 375 Flanged Magnum Nitro Express, 500/465 Nitro Express, 470 Nitro Express, 577 Nitro Express. 25½-inch barrels (25-inch in 375). Weight, 9½ to 12¾ pounds, depending upon caliber. Folding leaf rear sight, ramp front sight. Cheekpiece stock, checkered forearm and pistol grip, recoil pad, swivels. Currently manufactured; same general specifications apply to pre-WWII model.

Purdey Single Rifle **$3500**

Mauser-type bolt action. Calibers: 7x57, 300 H&H Magnum, 375 H&H Magnum, 10.75x73. 3-shot magazine. 24-inch barrel. Weight, 7½ to 8¾ pounds, depending upon caliber. Folding leaf rear sight, hooded ramp front sight. Cheekpiece stock, checkered forearm and pistol grip, swivels. Currently manufactured; same general specifications apply to pre-WWII model.

Remington Arms Company, Ilion, New York

Remington No. 2 Sporting Rifle

Single-shot, rolling-block action. Calibers: 22, 25, 32, 38, 44 rimfire or centerfire. Barrel lengths: 24-, 26-, 28- or 30-inches. Weight, 5 to 6 pounds. Open rear sight, bead front sight. Straight-grip sporting stock and knobtip forearm of walnut. Made from 1873 to 1910.
Calibers 22 through 32 .... **$245**
Calibers 38 through 44 425

Remington No. 3 Sporting Rifle **$675**

Single-shot. Hepburn falling-block action with side lever. Calibers: 22 WCF, 22 Extra Long, 25/20 Stevens, 25/21 Stevens, 25/25 Stevens, 32 WCF, 32/40 Ballard & Marlin, 32/40 Remington, 38 WCF, 38/40 Remington, 38/50 Remington, 38/55 Ballard & Marlin, 40/60 Ballard & Marlin, 40/60 WCF, 40/65 Remington Straight, 40/82 WCF, 45/70 Government, 45/90 WCF; also was supplied on special order in bottle-necked 40/50, 40/70, 40/90, 44/77, 44/90, 44/105, 50/70 Government, 50/90 Sharps Straight. Barrel lengths: 26-inch (22, 25, 32 cal. only), 28-inch, 30-inch; half-octagon or full-octagon. Weight, from 8 to 10 pounds depending upon barrel length and caliber. Open rear sight, blade front sight. Checkered pistol-grip stock and forearm. Made from 1880 to about 1911.

Remington No. 3 Creedmoor and Schuetzen Rifles .... **$5000+**

Produced in a variety of styles and calibers, these are collector's items and bring far higher prices than the sporting types. The Schuetzen Special, which has an under-lever action, is especially rare—perhaps less than 100 having been made.

Purdey Double Rifle

Purdey Single Rifle

Remington No. 2

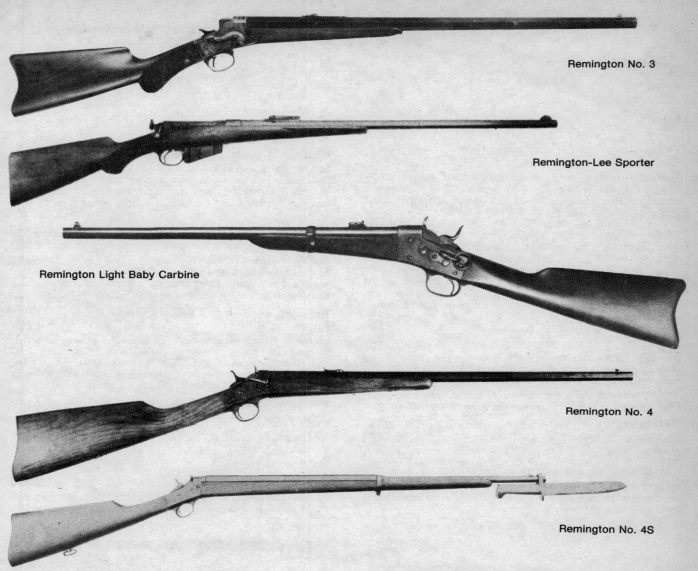

Remington No. 3

Remington-Lee Sporter

Remington Light Baby Carbine

Remington No. 4

Remington No. 4S

Remington No. 3 High Power Rifle

Single-shot. Hepburn falling-block action with side lever. Calibers: 30/30, 30/40, 32 Special, 32/40, 38/55, 38/72 (high-power cartridges). Barrel lengths: 26-inch, 28-inch, 30-inch. Weight, about 8 pounds. Open sporting sights. Checkered pistol-grip stock and forearm. Made from 1893 to 1907.

Calibers 30/30, 30/40, 32 Special, 32/40 . . . . $425
Calibers 38/55, 38/72 750

Remington-Lee Bolt Action Sporting Rifle

Calibers: 6mm U.S.N., 30-30, 30-40, 7mm Mauser, 7.65 Mauser, 32 Rem., 32-40, 35 Rem., 38-55, 38-72, 405 Win., 43 Spanish, 44/77 Sharps, 45/70, 45/90. Detachable box magazine holding 5 cartridges. 24- or 26-inch barrel. Weight, 7 pounds. Open rear sight, bead or blade front sight. Walnut stock with checkered pistol grip. Made from 1886 to 1906. *Note:* A limited number of this model were produced in "Special" Grade with deluxe walnut stock, half-octagon barrel, Lyman sights; these sold for approximately twice the price of the Standard Grade.

Standard Model $500
Deluxe Model 750

Remington Light Baby Carbine $300

Single-shot. Rolling-block action. Caliber, 44 Winchester. 20-inch barrel. Weight, 5¾ pounds. Open rear sight, blade front sight. Plain straight-grip carbine-stock and forearm, barrel band. Made from 1883 to 1910.

Remington No. 4 Single Shot Rifle $175

Rolling-block action. Solid frame or takedown. Calibers: 22 Short and Long, 22 Long Rifle, 25 Stevens R.F., 32 Short and Long R.F. 22½-inch octagon barrel, 24-inch available in 32 caliber only. Weight, about 4½ pounds. Open rear sight, blade front sight. Plain walnut stock and forearm. Made from 1890 to 1933.

Remington No. 4S Military Model 22 Single Shot Rifle $270

Rolling-block action. Calibers: 22 Short only, 22 Long Rifle only. 28-inch barrel. Weight, about 5 pounds. Military-type rear sight, blade front sight. Military-type stock with handguard, stacking swivel, sling. Has a bayonet stud on the barrel; bayonet and scabbard were regularly supplied. *Note:* At one time the "Military Model" was the official rifle of the Boy Scouts of America and was called the "Boy Scout Rifle." Made from 1913 to 1933.

Remington No. 5

Remington No. 5 Special Rifle
Single-shot. Rolling-block action. Calibers: 7mm Mauser, 30-30, 30-40 Krag, 303 British, 32-40, 32 Special, 38-55 (high power cartridges). Barrel lengths: 24-, 26- and 28-inches. Weight, about 7 pounds. Open sporting sights. Plain straight-grip stock and forearm. Made from 1902 to 1918. *Note:* Models 1897 and 1902 Military Rifles, intended for the export market, are almost identical with the No. 5 except for 30-inch barrel, full military stock and weight (about 8½ pounds); a carbine was also supplied. The military rifles were produced in caliber 8mm Lebel for France, 7.62mm Russian for Russia and 7mm Mauser for the Central and South American government trade. At one time, Remington also offered these military models to retail purchasers.
Sporting Model....................................... $350
Military Model....................................... 225

Remington No. 6 Takedown Rifle............... $150
Single-shot. Rolling-block action. Calibers: 22 Short, 22 Long, 22 Long Rifle, 32 Short and Long R.F. 20-inch barrel. Weight, about 4 pounds. Open front and rear sights, tang peep sight. Plain straight-grip stock and forearm. Made from 1901 to 1933.

Remington No. 7 Target and Sporting Rifle...... $525
Single-shot. Rolling-block Army Pistol frame. Calibers: 22 Short, 22 Long Rifle, 25 Stevens R.F. (other calibers as available in No. 2 Rifle were supplied on special order). Half-octagon barrels: 24-, 26-, 28-inch. Weight, about 6 pounds. Lyman combination rear sight, Beach combination front sight. Fancy walnut stock and forearm; Swiss butt plate available as an extra. Made from 1903 to 1911.

Remington Model 8A Autoloading Rifle......... $235
Standard Grade. Takedown. Calibers: 25, 30, 32 and 35 Rem. Detachable box magazine holds five cartridges. 22-inch barrel. Weight, 7¾ pounds. Open rear sight, bead front sight. Plain straight-grip stock and forearm of walnut. Made from 1906 to 1936.

Remington Model 81A "Woodsmaster" Autoloading Rifle... $250
Standard Grade. Takedown. Calibers: 30, 32 and 35 Rem., 300 Sav. 5-shot box magazine (not detachable). 22-inch barrel. Weight, 8¼ pounds. Open rear sight, bead front sight. Plain, pistol-grip stock and forearm of walnut. Made from 1936 to 1950.

Remington Model 12A Slide Action Repeating Rifle...................................... $160
Standard Grade. Hammerless. Takedown. Caliber, 22 Short, Long or Long Rifle. Tubular magazine holds 15 Short, 12 Long or 10 Long Rifle cartridges. 22-inch round barrel. Weight, 4½ pounds. Open rear sight, bead front sight. Plain, straight-grip stock, grooved slide handle. Made from 1909 to 1936.

Remington Model 12B............................$150
Same as Model 12A, except chambered for 22 Short only.

Remington Model 2C............................ $275
Target Grade. Same as Model 12A, except has 24-inch octagon barrel, pistol-grip stock.

Remington Model 12CS..........................$200
Same as Model 12C, except chambered for 22 Remington Special (22 W.R.F.). Magazine holds 12 rounds.

Remington No. 6

Remington No. 7

Remington Model 8A

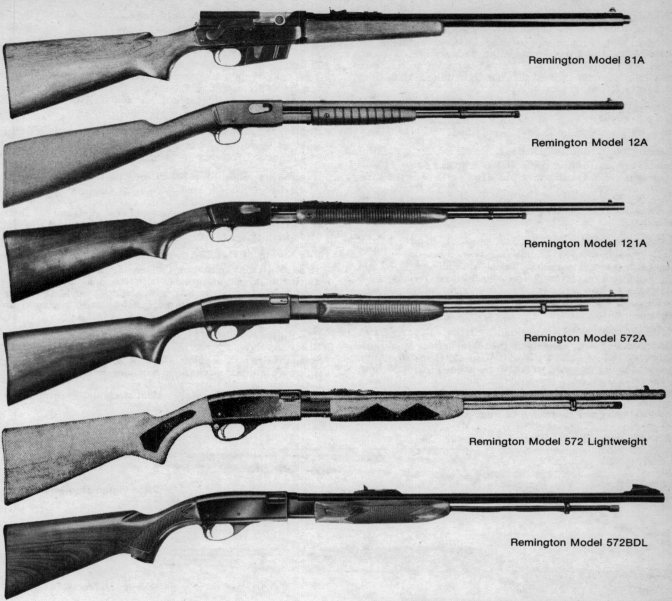

Remington Model 81A

Remington Model 12A

Remington Model 121A

Remington Model 572A

Remington Model 572 Lightweight

Remington Model 572BDL

Remington Model 121A "Fieldmaster" Slide Action Repeating Rifle.. **$210**
Standard Grade. Hammerless. Takedown. Caliber, 22 Short, Long, Long Rifle. Tubular magazine holds 20 Short, 15 Long or 14 Long Rifle cartridges. 24-inch round barrel. Weight, 6 pounds. Plain, pistol-grip stock and grooved semi-beavertail slide handle. Made from 1936 to 1954.

Remington Model 121S........................... **$175**
Same as Model 121A, except chambered for 22 Remington Special (22 W.R.F.). Magazine holds 12 rounds. Discontinued.

Remington Model 121SB.......................... **$175**
Same as Model 121A, except smoothbore. Discontinued.

Remington Model 572A "Fieldmaster" Slide Action Repeater.. **$100**
Hammerless. Caliber, 22 Short, Long, Long Rifle. Tubular maga-

zine holds 20 Short, 17 Long, 15 Long Rifle. 23-inch barrel. Weight, about 5½ pounds. Open rear sight, ramp front sight. Pistol-grip stock, grooved forearm. Made from 1955 to date.

Remington Model 572 Lightweight.............. **$125**
Same as Model 572A, except has aluminum alloy receiver and outer barrel casing anodized in colors, chrome-plated magazine tube, trigger and trigger guard, checkered stock and forearm of light tan walnut; weight, about 4 pounds. Colors: Buckskin Tan (Model 572BT), Teal Wing Blue (Model 572TWB), Crown Wing Black (Model 572CWB). Made from 1958 to 1962.

Remington Model 572SB Smooth Bore.......... **$150**
Same as Model 572A, except smooth bore for 22 Long Rifle shot cartridges. Made from 1961 to date.

Remington Model 572BDL Deluxe............... **$175**
Same as Model 572A, except has blade ramp front sight, sliding ramp rear sight, checkered stock and forearm. Made from 1966 to date.

Remington Model 14A High Power Slide Action Repeating Rifle **$225**
Standard Grade. Hammerless. Takedown. Calibers: 25, 30, 32 and 35 Rem. 5-shot tubular magazine. 22-inch barrel. Weight, about 6¾ pounds. Open rear sight, head front sight. Plain, pistol-grip stock and grooved slide handle of walnut. Made from 1912 to 1935.

Remington Model 14R Carbine **$275**
Same as Model 14A except has 18½-inch barrel, straight-grip stock, weighs about 6 pounds.

Remington Model 14½ Rifle **$550**
Similar to Model 14A, except calibers 38/40 and 44/40, 11-shot full magazine, 22½-inch barrel. Made from 1912 to early 1920's.

Remington Model 14½ Carbine **$650**
Same as Model 14½ Rifle, except has 9-shot magazine, 18½-inch barrel.

Remington Model 141A "Gamemaster" Slide Action Repeating Rifle **$275**
Standard Grade. Hammerless. Takedown. Calibers: 30, 32 and 35 Rem. 5-shot tubular magazine. 24-inch barrel. Weight, about 7¾ pounds. Open rear sight, bead front sight on ramp. Plain, pistol-grip stock, semi-beavertail fore-end (slide-handle). Made from 1936 to 1950.

Remington Model 16 Autoloading Rifle **$195**
Takedown. Closely resembles the Winchester Model 03. Calibers: 22 Short, 22 Long Rifle, 22 W.R.F., 22 Remington Auto. 15-shot tubular magazine in buttstock. 22-inch barrel. Weight, 5¾ pounds. Open rear sight, bead front sight. Plain straight-grip stock and forearm. Made from 1914 to 1928. *Note:* This model was discontinued in all calibers except 22 Rem. Auto in 1918 and specifications given are for the 22 Rem. Auto model.

Remington Model 30A Bolt Action Express Rifle **$495**
Standard Grade. Modified M/1917 Enfield Action. Calibers: 25, 30, 32 and 35 Rem., 7mm Mauser, 30-06. 5-shot box magazine. 22-inch barrel. Weight, about 7¼ pounds. Open rear sight, bead front sight. Walnut stock with checkered pistol grip and forearm. Made from 1921 to 1940. *Note:* Early Model 30's had a slender fore-end with schnabel tip, military-type double-pull trigger, 24-inch barrel.

Remington Model 30R Carbine **$290**
Same as Model 30A, except has 20-inch barrel, plain stock, weighs about 7 pounds.

Remington Model 30S Sporting Rifle **$325**
Special Grade. Same action as Model 30A. Calibers: 257 Roberts, 7mm Mauser, 30-06. 5-shot box magazine. 24-inch barrel. Weight, about 8 pounds. Lyman #48 Receiver sight, bead front sight. Special high comb stock with long, full forearm, checkered. Made from 1930 to 1940.

Remington Model 24A Autoloading Rifle **$225**
Standard Grade. Takedown. Calibers: 22 Short only, 22 Long Rifle only, or 10 Long Rifle. 21-inch barrel. Weight, about 5 pounds. Open rear sight, bead front sight. Plain walnut stock and forearm. Made from 1922 to 1935.

Remington Model 241A "Speedmaster" Autoloading Rifle **$250**
Standard Grade. Takedown. Calibers: 22 Short only, 22 Long Rifle only. Tubular magazine in buttstock, holds 15 Short or 10 Long Rifle. 24-inch barrel. Weight, about 6 pounds. Open rear sight, bead front sight. Plain walnut stock and forearm. Made from 1935 to 1951.

Remington Model 14A

Remington Model 141A

Remington Model 16

Remington Model 30A

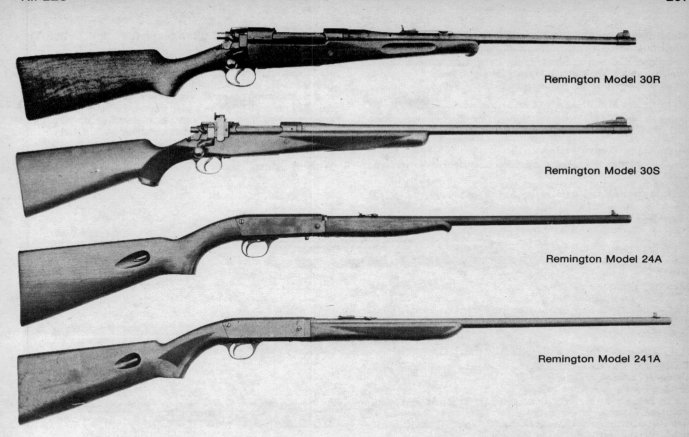

Remington Model 30R

Remington Model 30S

Remington Model 24A

Remington Model 241A

Remington Model 552A "Speedmaster" Autoloading Rifle . . . . **$ 95**
Caliber, 22 Short, Long, Long Rifle. Tubular magazine holds 20 Short, 17 Long, 15 Long Rifle. 25-inch barrel. Weight, about 5½ pounds. Open rear sight, bead front sight. Pistol-grip stock, semi-beavertail forearm. Made from 1957 to date.

Remington Model 552BDL Deluxe **$105**
Same as Model 552A, except has checkered walnut stock and forearm. Made from 1966 to date.

Remington Model 552GS Gallery Special . . . . **$ 95**
Same as Model 552A, except chambered for 22 Short only. Made from 1957 to 1977.

Remington Model 552C Carbine **$100**
Same as Model 552A, except has 21-inch barrel. Made from 1961 to 1977.

Remington Model 25A Slide Action Repeating Rifle **$250**
Standard Grade. Hammerless. Takedown. Calibers: 25/20, 32/20. 10-shot tubular magazine. 24-inch barrel. Weight, about 5½ pounds. Open rear sight, bead front sight. Plain, pistol-grip stock, grooved slide handle. Made from 1923 to 1936.

Remington Model 25R Carbine **$275**
Same as Model 25A, except has 18-inch barrel. 6-shot magazine, straight-grip stock, weighs about 4½ pounds.

Remington Model 33 Bolt Action Single Shot Rifle . . . . **$ 55**
Takedown. Caliber, 22 Short, Long, Long Rifle. 24-inch barrel. Weight, about 4½ pounds. Open rear sight, bead front sight.

Plain, pistol-grip stock, forearm with grasping grooves. Made from 1931 to 1936.

Remington Model 33 NRA Junior Target Rifle . . **$ 75**
Same as Model 33 Standard, except has Lyman peep rear sight, Patridge-type front sight, ⅞-inch sling and swivels, weighs about 5 pounds.

Remington Model 34 Bolt Action Repeating Rifle . . . . **$ 95**
Takedown. Caliber, 22 Short, Long, Long Rifle. Tubular magazine holds 22 Short, 17 Long or 15 Long Rifle. 24-inch barrel. Weight, about 5¼ pounds. Open rear sight, bead front sight. Plain, pistol-grip stock, forearm with grasping grooves. Made from 1932 to 1936.

Remington Model 34 NRA Target Rifle . . . . **$ 80**
Same as Model 34 Standard, except has Lyman peep rear sight, Patridge-type front sight, ⅞-inch sling and swivels, weighs about 5¾ pounds.

Remington Model 341A "Sportsmaster" Bolt Action Repeating Rifle . . . . **$ 60**
Takedown. Caliber, 22 Short, Long, Long Rifle. Tubular magazine holds 22 Short, 17 Long, 15 Long Rifle. 27-inch barrel. Weight, about 6 pounds. Open rear sight, bead front sight. Plain pistol-grip stock. Made from 1936 to 1940.

Remington Model 341P . . . . **$ 95**
Same as Model 341A, except has peep rear sight, hooded front sight.

Remington Model 341SB . . . . **$ 55**
Same as Model 341A, except smoothbore for use with shot cartridges.

Remington Model 41A "Targetmaster" Bolt Action Single Shot Rifle .... **$ 55**
Takedown. Caliber, 22 Short, Long, Long Rifle. 27-inch barrel. Weight, about 5½ pounds. Open rear sight, bead front sight. Plain pistol-grip stock. Made from 1936 to 1940.

Remington Model 41AS .... **$ 45**
Same as Model 41A, except chambered for 22 Remington Special (22 W.R.F.).

Remington Model 41P .... **$ 60**
Same as Model 41A, except has peep rear sight, hooded front sight.

Remington Model 41SB .... **$ 50**
Same as Model 41A, except smoothbore for use with shot cartridges.

Remington Model 37 "Rangemaster" Bolt Action Target Rifle
Model of 1937. Caliber, 22 Long Rifle. 5-shot box magazine, single shot adapter also supplied as standard equipment. 28-inch heavy barrel. Weight, about 12 pounds. Remington front and rear sights, scope bases. Target stock, swivels, sling. *Note:* original 1937 model had a stock with outside barrel band similar in appearance to that of the old style Winchester Model 52; forearm design was modified and barrel band eliminated in 1938. Made from 1937 to 1940.
With factory sights **$425**
Without sights 375

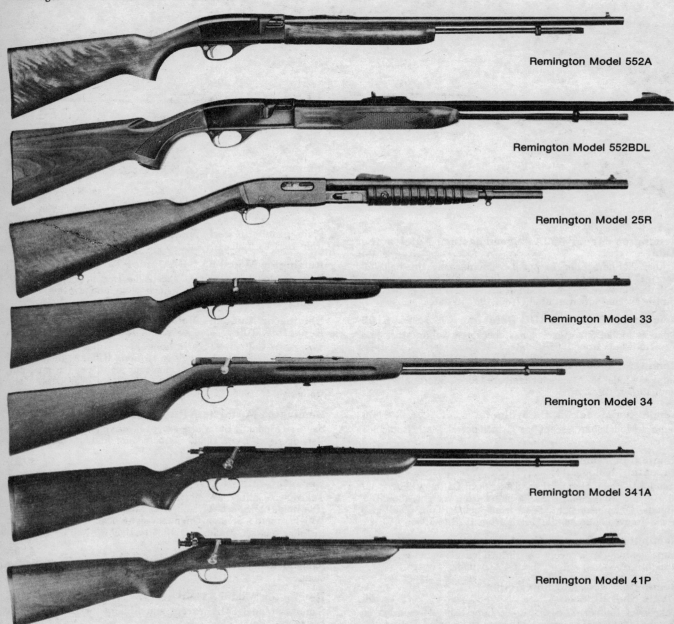

Remington Model 552A

Remington Model 552BDL

Remington Model 25R

Remington Model 33

Remington Model 34

Remington Model 341A

Remington Model 41P

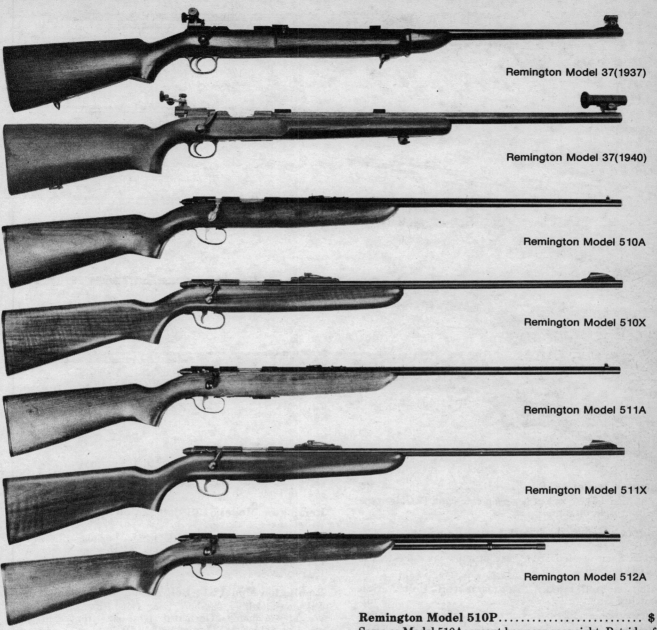

Remington Model 37(1937)

Remington Model 37(1940)

Remington Model 510A

Remington Model 510X

Remington Model 511A

Remington Model 511X

Remington Model 512A

Remington Model 510P........................... **$ 55**
Same as Model 510A, except has peep rear sight, Patridge front
sight on ramp.

Remington Model 510SB........................... **$ 50**
Same as Model 510A, except smoothbore for use with shot
cartridges, shotgun bead front sight, no rear sight.

**Remington Model 510X Bolt Action Single Shot
Rifle**.. **$ 55**
Same as Model 510A, except improved sights. Made from 1964
to 1966.

**Remington Model 511A "Scoremaster" Bolt Action Box
Magazine Repeating Rifle**........................ **$ 65**
Takedown. Caliber, 22 Short, Long, Long Rifle. 6-shot detachable box magazine. 25-inch barrel. Weight, about 5½
pounds. Open rear sight, bead front sight. Plain pistol-grip
stock. Made from 1939 to 1962.

**Remington Model 37 "Rangemaster" Bolt Action Tar-
get Rifle**
Model of 1940. Same as Model of 1937, except has "Miracle"
trigger mechanism and Randle design stock with high comb, full
pistol grip and wide beavertail fore-end. Made from 1940 to
1954.
With factory sights.................................$350
Without sights...................................... 295

**Remington Model 510A "Targetmaster" Bolt Action
Single Shot Rifle**................................. **$ 75**
Takedown. Caliber, 22 Short, Long, Long Rifle. 25-inch barrel.
Weight, about 5½ pounds. Open rear sight, bead front sight.
Plain pistol-grip stock. Made from 1939 to 1962.

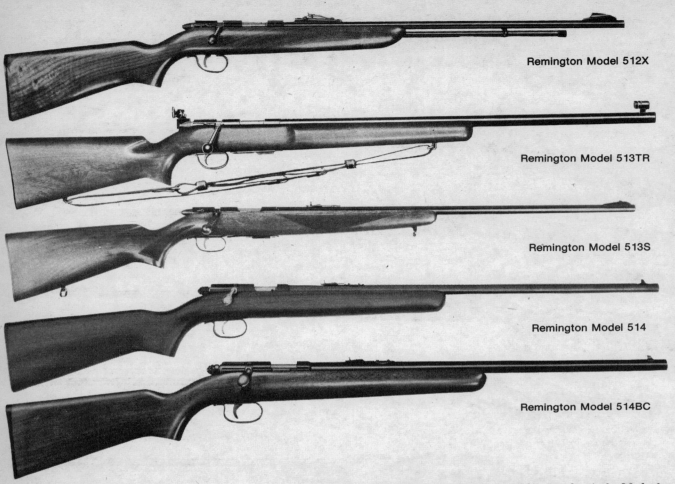

Remington Model 512X

Remington Model 513TR

Remington Model 513S

Remington Model 514

Remington Model 514BC

Remington Model 511P . . . . **$ 65**
Same as Model 511A, except has peep rear sight, Patridge type
blade front sight on ramp.

**Remington Model 511X Bolt Action Repeating
Rifle** . . . . **$ 65**
Clip type. Same as Model 511A, except improved sights. Made
from 1964 to 1966.

**Remington Model 512A "Sportsmaster" Bolt Action
Repeating Rifle** . . . . **$ 65**
Takedown. Caliber, 22 Short, Long, Long Rifle. Tubular maga-
zine holds 22 Short, 17 Long, 15 Long Rifle. 25-inch barrel.
Weight, about 5¾ pounds. Open rear sight, bead front sight.
Plain pistol-grip stock with semi-beavertail fore-end. Made from
1940 to 1962.

Remington Model 512P . . . . **$ 70**
Same as Model 512A, except has peep rear sight, blade front
sight on ramp.

**Remington Model 512X Bolt Action Repeating
Rifle** . . . . **$ 75**
Tubular magazine type. Same as Model 512A, except has im-
proved sights. Made from 1964 to 1966.

**Remington Model 513TR "Matchmaster" Bolt Action
Target Rifle** **$160**
Caliber, 22 Long Rifle. 6-shot detachable box magazine. 27-inch
barrel. Weight, about 9 pounds. Redfield No. 75 rear sight and

globe front sight. Target stock. Sling and swivels. Made from
1941 to 1969.

**Remington Model 513S Bolt Action Sporting
Rifle** **$150**
Caliber, 22 Long Rifle. 6-shot detachable box magazine. 27-inch
barrel. Weight, about 6¾ pounds. Marble open rear sight,
Patridge type front sight. Checkered sporter stock. Made from
1941 to 1956.

Remington Model 514 Bolt Action Single Shot . . **$ 90**
Takedown. Caliber, 22 Short, Long, Long Rifle. 24-inch barrel.
Weight, 4¾ pounds. Open rear sight, bead front sight. Plain
pistol-grip stock. Made from 1948 to 1971.

Remington Model 514P . . . . **$ 65**
Same as Model 514, except has receiver peep sight.

Remington Model 514BC Boy's Carbine . . . . **$ 60**
Same as Model 514, except has 21-inch barrel, 1-inch shorter
stock. Made from 1961 to 1971.

**Remington Model 720A Bolt Action High Power
Rifle** **$245**
Modified M/1917 Enfield action. Calibers: 257 Roberts, 270
Winchester, 30-06. 5-shot box magazine. 22-inch barrel. Weight,
about 8 pounds. Open rear sight, bead front sight on ramp.
Pistol-grip stock, checkered. Made in 1941.

Remington Model 720R **$245**
Same as Model 720A, except has 20-inch barrel.

Remington Model 550A

Remington Model 521TL

Remington Model 720A

Remington Model 720S..........................$245
Same as Model 720, except has 24-inch barrel.

Remington Model 550A Autoloading Rifle....... $100
Has "Power Piston" or floating chamber which permits interchangeable use of 22 Short, Long or Long Rifle cartridges. Tubular magazine holds 22 Short, 17 Long, 15 Long Rifle. 24-inch barrel. Weight, about 6¼ pounds. Open rear sight, bead front sight. Plain, one-piece pistol-grip stock. Made from 1941 to 1971.

Remington Model 550P..........................$110
Same as Model 550A, except has peep rear sight, blade front sight on ramp.

Remington Model 550-2G.........................$100
"Gallery Special." Same as Model 550A, except has 22-inch barrel, screweye for counter chain and fired shell deflector.

Remington Model 521TL Junior Target Bolt Action Repeating Rifle...................................$100
Takedown. Caliber, 22 Long Rifle. 6-shot detachable box magazine. 25-inch barrel. Weight, about 7 pounds. Lyman No. 57RS rear sight, blade front sight. Target stock. Sling and swivels. Made from 1947 to 1969.

Remington Model 721A Standard Grade Bolt Action High Power Rifle...................................$190
Calibers: 264 Win., 270 Win., 30-06. 4-shot box magazine. 24-inch barrel. Weight, about 7¼ pounds. Open rear sight, bead front sight on ramp. Plain sporting stock. Made from 1948 to 1962.

Remington Model 721ADL Deluxe Grade....... $200
Same as Model 721A, except has deluxe checkered stock.

Remington Model 721BDL Deluxe Special Grade...................................$225
Same as Model 721ADL, except selected wood.

Remington Model 721A 300 Magnum Standard Grade...................................$200
Caliber, 300 H&H Magnum. Same as standard model, except has 26-inch heavy barrel, 3-shot magazine, recoil pads, weighs 8¼ pounds.

Remington Model 721ADL 300 Magnum Deluxe Grade...................................$250
Same as Model 721A 300 Magnum, except has deluxe checkered stock.

Remington Model 721BDL 300 Magnum Deluxe Special Grade...................................$335
Same as Model 721ADL 300 Magnum, except selected wood.

Remington Model 722A Standard Grade Bolt Action Sporting Rifle...................................$275
Same as Model 721A, except shorter action, calibers 257 Roberts, 308 Win., 300 Savage, weighs 7 pounds. Made from 1948 to 1962.

Remington Model 722ADL Deluxe Grade....... $295
Same as Model 722A, except has deluxe checkered stock.

Remington Model 722BDL Deluxe Special Grade...................................$395
Same as Model 722ADL, except selected wood.

Remington Model 722A 222 Standard Grade.... $295
Caliber, 222 Rem. Same as standard model, except has 26-inch barrel, 5-shot magazine, weighs about 8 pounds. Made from 1950 to 1962.

Remington Model 722ADL 222 Deluxe Grade... $300
Same as Model 722A 222, except has deluxe checkered stock.

Remington Model 722BDL 222 Deluxe Special Grade...................................$325
Same as Model 722ADL 222, except selected wood.

Remington Model 722A 244 Standard Grade.... $200
Caliber, 244 Rem. Specifications same as Model 722A 222, except magazine capacity is four rounds. Made from 1955 to 1962.

Remington Model 722ADL 244 Deluxe Grade... $335
Same as Model 722A 244, except has deluxe checkered stock.

**Remington Model 722BDL 244 Deluxe
Special Grade**.................................$400
Same as Model 722ADL, except selected wood.

**Remington Model 725ADL Bolt Action
Repeating Rifle**...................................$325
Calibers: 222, 243, 244, 270, 280, 30-06. 4-shot box magazine (5-shot in 222). 22-inch barrel (24-inch in 222). Weight, about 7 pounds. Open rear sight, hooded ramp front sight. Monte Carlo comb stock with pistol grip, checkered, swivels. Made from 1958 to 1961.

Remington Model 725 "Kodiak" Magnum Rifle.. $550
Similar to Model 725ADL. Calibers: 375 H&H Mag., 458 Win. Mag. 3-shot magazine. 26-inch barrel with recoil reducer built into muzzle. Weight, about 9 pounds. Deluxe, reinforced Monte Carlo stock with recoil pad, black fore-end tip, swivels, sling. Made in 1961.

**Remington Model 760 "Gamemaster" Standard Grade
Slide Action Repeating Rifle**...................... $230
Hammerless. Calibers: 223 Rem., 6mm Rem., 243 Win., 257 Roberts, 270 Win., 280 Rem., 30-06, 300 Sav., 308 Win., 35 Rem. 22-inch barrel. Weight, about 7½ pounds. Open rear sight, bead front sight on ramp. Plain pistol-grip stock, grooved slide handle on early models; current production has checkered stock and slide handle. Made from 1952 to 1980.

Remington Model 760ADL Deluxe Grade....... $240
Same as Model 760, except has deluxe checkered stock, standard or high comb, grip cap, sling swivels. Made from 1953 to 1963.

Remington Model 760BDL Custom Deluxe...... $260
Same as Model 760 Rifle, except made in calibers 270, 30-06 and 308 only, has Monte Carlo cheekpiece stock, forearm with black tip, basket-weave checkering. Available in right- or left-hand models. Made from 1953 to 1980.

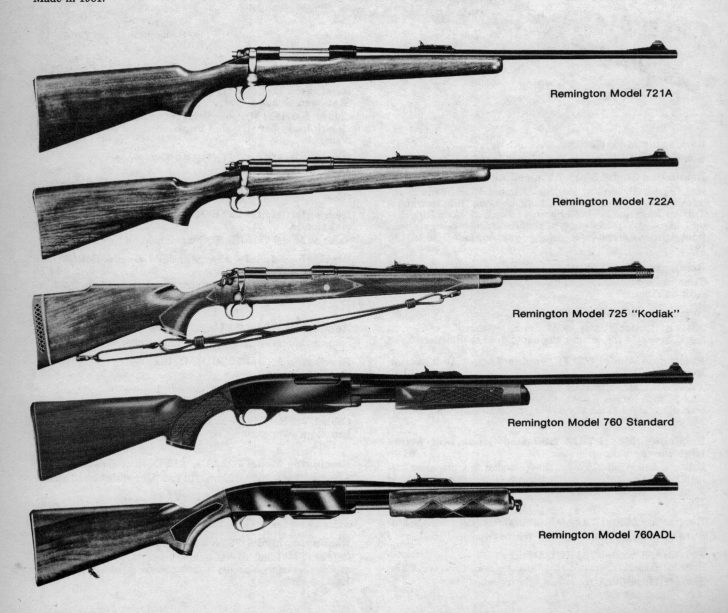

Remington Model 721A

Remington Model 722A

Remington Model 725 "Kodiak"

Remington Model 760 Standard

Remington Model 760ADL

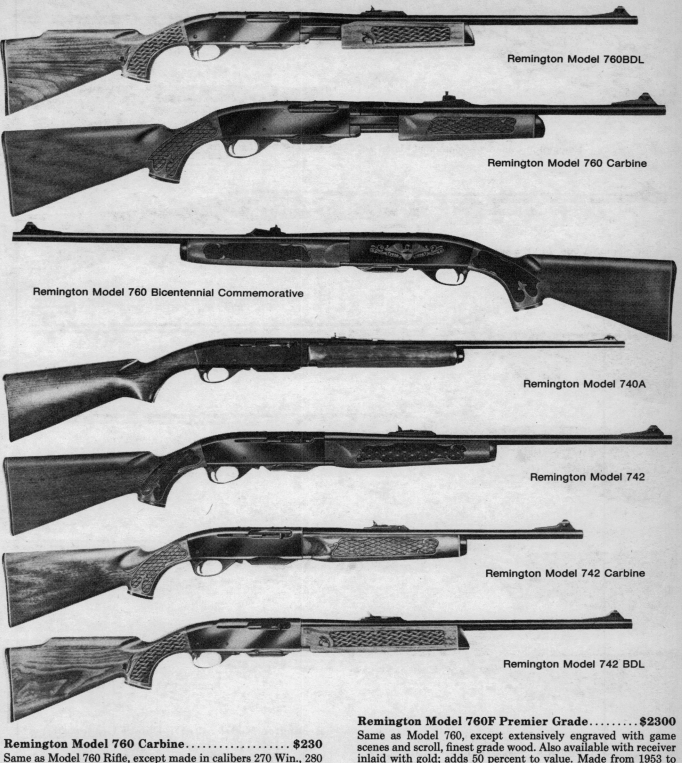

Remington Model 760BDL

Remington Model 760 Carbine

Remington Model 760 Bicentennial Commemorative

Remington Model 740A

Remington Model 742

Remington Model 742 Carbine

Remington Model 742 BDL

Remington Model 760 Carbine.................. **$230**
Same as Model 760 Rifle, except made in calibers 270 Win., 280 Rem., 30-06 and 308 Win. only, has 18½-inch barrel, weighs 7¼ pounds. Made from 1960 to date.

Remington Model 760D Peerless Grade....... **$1190**
Same as Model 760, except scroll engraved, fancy wood. Made from 1953 to 1980.

Remington Model 760F Premier Grade........ **$2300**
Same as Model 760, except extensively engraved with game scenes and scroll, finest grade wood. Also available with receiver inlaid with gold; adds 50 percent to value. Made from 1953 to 1980.

Remington Model 760 Bicentennial Commemorative................................... **$400**
Same as Model 760, except has commemorative inscription on receiver. Made in 1976.

Remington Model 742F

Remington Canadian Centennial Model 742

Remington Model 742 Bicentennial Commemorative

Remington Model 40X Standard Rim Fire

Remington International Match

Remington Model 40XB Rim Fire

Remington Model 40XB Center Fire

Remington Model 740A "Woodsmaster" Autoloading Rifle... **$180**
Standard Grade. Gas-operated. Calibers, 30-06 or 308. 4-shot detachable box magazine. 22-inch barrel. Weight, about 7½ pounds. Plain pistol-grip stock, semi-beavertail fore-end with finger grooves. Open rear sight, ramp front sight. Made from 1955 to 1960.

Remington Model 740ADL Deluxe Grade....... **$195**
Same as Model 740A, except has deluxe checkered stock, standard or high comb, grip cap, sling swivels. Made from 1955 to 1960.

Remington Model 740BDL Deluxe Special Grade...................................**$200**
Same as Model 740ADL, except selected wood. Made from 1955 to 1960.

Remington Model 742 "Woodsmaster" Automatic Big Game Rifle.................................... **$280**
Gas-operated semiautomatic. Calibers: 6mm Rem., 243 Win., 280 Rem., 30-06, 308 Win. 4-shot clip magazine. 22-inch barrel. Weight, 7½ pounds. Open rear sight, bead front sight on ramp. Checkered pistol-grip stock and forearm. Made from 1960 to 1980.

Remington Model 742 Carbine................... **$280**
Same as Model 742 Rifle, except made in calibers 30-06 and 308 only, has 18½-inch barrel, weighs 6¾ pounds. Made from 1961 to 1980.

Remington Model 742BDL Custom Deluxe...... **$300**
Same as Model 742 Rifle, except made in calibers 30-06 and 308 only, has Monte Carlo cheekpiece stock, forearm with black tip, basket-weave checkering. Available in right- and left-hand models. Made from 1966 to 1980.

Remington Model 742D Peerless Grade........ **$1050**
Same as Model 742 except scroll engraved, fancy wood. Made from 1961 to 1980.

Remington Model 742F Premier Grade......... **$2100**
Same as Model 742 except extensively engraved with game scenes and scroll, finest grade wood. Also available with receiver inlaid with gold; adds 50 percent to value. Made from 1961 to 1980.

Remington Canadian Centennial Model 742 Rifle... **$400**
Same as Model 742, except has commemorative inscription on receiver. Made in 1967. Value is for rifle in new, unfired condition.

Remington Model 742 Bicentennial Commemorative.................................. **$400**
Same as Model 742, except has commemorative inscription on receiver. Made in 1976.

Remington Model 40X Heavyweight Bolt Action Target Rifle
Caliber, 22 Long Rifle. Single shot. Action similar to Model 722. Click adjustable trigger. 28-inch heavy barrel. Redfield Olympic sights. Scope bases. High comb target stock, bedding device,

adjustable swivel, rubber butt plate. Weight, 12¾ pounds. Made from 1955 to 1964.
With sights.. **$300**
Without sights... 275

Remington Model 40X Standard Barrel
Same as Model 40X Heavyweight except has lighter barrel. Weight, 10¾ pounds.
With sights.. **$285**
Without sights... 250

Remington Model 40X Center Fire.............. **$350**
Specifications same as for Model 40X Rim Fire. Calibers: 222 Rem., 222 Rem. Mag., 7.62mm NATO, 30-06 (others were available on special order). Made from 1961 to 1964. Value shown is for rifle without sights.

Remington International Match Free Rifle...... **$600**
Calibers: 22 Long Rifle, 222 Rem., 222 Rem. Mag., 7.62mm NATO, 30-06 (others were available on special order). Model 40X type bolt action, single shot. 2-oz. adjustable trigger. 28-inch heavy barrel. Weight, about 15½ pounds. "Free rifle"-style stock with thumb-hole (furnished semi-finished by manufacturer); interchangeable and adjustable rubber butt plate and hook butt plate, adjustable palm-rest, adjustable sling swivel. Made from 1961 to 1964. Value shown is for rifle with professionally-finished stock, no sights.

Remington Model 40-XB "Rangemaster" Rim Fire Match Rifle....................................... **$400**
Bolt action single shot. Caliber, 22 Long Rifle. 28-inch standard or heavy barrel. Target stock with adjustable front swivel block on guide rail, rubber butt plate. Weight, without sights: standard barrel, 10 pounds; heavy barrel, 11¼ pounds. Value shown is for rifle without sights. Made from 1964 to 1974.

Remington Model 40-XB Center Fire Match Rifle....................................... **$525**
Bolt action single shot. Calibers: 222 Rem., 222 Rem. Mag., 223 Rem., 22-250, 6x47mm, 6mm Rem., 243 Win., 25-06, 7mm Rem. Mag., 30-06, 308 Win. (7.62mm NATO), 30-338, 300 Win. Mag. 27¼-inch standard or heavy barrel. Target stock with adjustable front swivel block on guide rail, rubber butt plate. Weight, without sights: standard barrel, 9¼ pounds; heavy barrel, 11¼ pounds. Value shown is for rifle without sights. Made from 1964 to date.

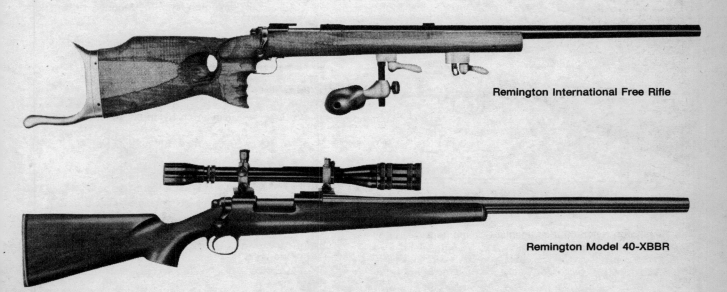

Remington International Free Rifle

Remington Model 40-XBBR

Remington Model 40-XC

Remington Model 40-XR

Remington Model 540-X

Remington Model 540-XR

Remington Nylon 66 Mohawk Brown

Remington Nylon 66 Apache Black

Remington Nylon 66 Bicentennial Commemorative

Remington Nylon 77

Remington Nylon 76

Remington Model 40-XB Center Fire Repeater..$500
Same as Model 40-XB Center Fire except 5-shot repeater. Calibers: 222 Rem., 222 Rem. Mag., 223 Rem., 22-250, 6x47mm, 6mm Rem., 243 Win., 308 Win. (7.62mm NATO). Heavy barrel only.

Remington International Free Rifle............. $550
Same as Model 40-XB rim fire and center fire, except has "free rifle"-type stock with adjustable butt plate and hook, adjustable palm-rest, movable front sling swivel, 2-ounce trigger; weight, about 15 pounds. Made from 1964 to 1974. Value shown is for rifle with professionally finished stock, no sights.

Remington Model 40-XBBR Bench Rest Rifle... $425
Bolt action single shot. Calibers: 222 Rem., 222 Rem. Mag., 223 Rem., 6x47mm, 308 Win. (7.62mm NATO). 20- or 26-inch un-blued stainless steel barrel. Supplied without sights. Weights: with 20-inch barrel, 9¼ pounds; with 26-inch barrel, 12 pounds. Varmint style stock. Made from 1969 to date.

Remington Model 40-XC National Match Course Rifle.. $520
Bolt action repeater. Caliber, 308 Win. (7.62mm NATO). 5-shot magazine; clip slot in receiver. 24-inch barrel. Supplied without sights. Weight, 11 pounds. Thumb groove stock with adjustable hand stop and sling swivel, adjustable butt plate. Made from 1974 to date.

Remington Model 40-XR Rim Fire Position Rifle.. $375
Bolt action single shot. Caliber, 22 Long Rifle. 24-inch heavy barrel. Supplied without sights. Weight, about 10 pounds. Position style with thumb groove, adjustable hand stop and sling swivel on guide rail, adjustable butt plate. Made from 1974 to date.

Remington Model 40-X Sporter................. $775
Same general specifications as Model 700C Custom (see that listing), except chambered for 22 Long Rifle. Made from 1972 to date.

Remington Model 540-X Rim Fire Target Rifle.. $185
Bolt action single shot. Caliber, 22 Long Rifle. 26-inch heavy barrel. Supplied without sights. Weight, about 8 pounds. Target stock with Monte Carlo cheekpiece and thumb groove, guide rail for hand stop and swivel, adjustable butt plate. Made from 1969 to 1974.

Remington Model 540-XR Rim Fire Position Rifle.. $200
Bolt action single shot. Caliber, 22 Long Rifle. 26-inch medium-weight barrel. Supplied without sights. Weight, 8 lbs. 13 oz. Position style stock with thumb groove, guide rail for hand stop and swivel, adjustable butt plate. Made from 1974 to date.

Remington Model 540-XRJR..................... $200
Same as Model 540-XR, except 1¾-inch shorter stock. Made from 1974 to date.

Remington Nylon 66 "Mohawk Brown" Autoloading Rifle... $ 75
Caliber, 22 Long Rifle. Tubular magazine in buttstock holds 14 rounds. 19½-inch barrel. Weight, about 4 pounds. Open rear sight, blade front sight. Brown nylon stock and forearm. Made from 1959 to date.

Remington Nylon 66 "Apache Black"............ $ 75
Same as Nylon 66 "Mohawk Brown," except barrel and receiver cover chrome-plated, black stock.

Remington Nylon 66 GS Gallery Special........ $ 75
Same as Nylon 66 "Mohawk Brown" except chambered for 22 Short only. Made from 1959 to 1980.

Remington Nylon 66 Bicentennial Commemorative.................................. $100
Same as Nylon 66, except has commemorative inscription on receiver. Made in 1976.

Remington Nylon 77 Clip Repeater.............. $ 75
Same as Nylon 66, except has 5-shot clip magazine. Made from 1970 to 1971.

Remington Nylon 76 Lever Action Repeating Rifle................................... $ 75
Short-throw lever action. Other specifications same as for Nylon 66. Made from 1962 to 1964.

Remington Nylon 10 Bolt Action Single Shot Rifle.. $ 35
Same as Nylon 11 except single shot. Made from 1962 to 1966.

Remington Nylon 11 Bolt Action Repeating Rifle.. $ 70
Clip type. Caliber, 22 Short, Long, Long Rifle, 6 or 10-shot clip magazine. 19⅝-inch barrel. Weight, about 4½ pounds. Open rear sight, blade front sight. Nylon stock. Made from 1962 to 1966.

Remington Nylon 12 Bolt Action Repeating Rifle................................... $ 65
Same as Nylon 11 except has tubular magazine holding 22 Short, 17 Long, 15 Long Rifle. Made from 1962 to 1966.

Remington Model 600 Bolt Action Carbine...... $220
Calibers: 222 Rem., 6mm Rem., 243 Win., 308 Win., 35 Rem. 5-shot box magazine (6-shot in 222 Rem.). 18½-inch barrel with ventilated rib. Weight, 6 pounds. Open rear sight, blade ramp front sight. Monte Carlo stock with pistol grip. Made from 1964 to 1967.

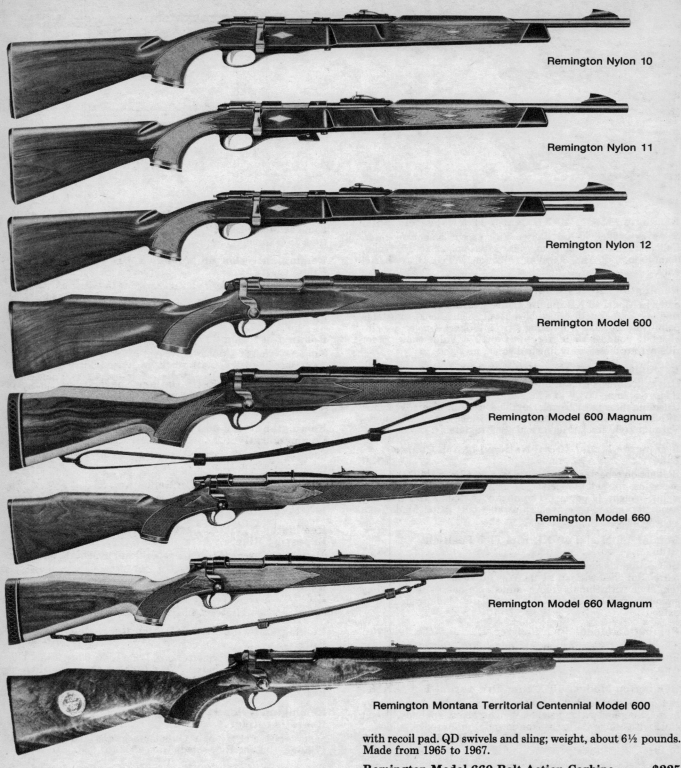

Remington Nylon 10

Remington Nylon 11

Remington Nylon 12

Remington Model 600

Remington Model 600 Magnum

Remington Model 660

Remington Model 660 Magnum

Remington Montana Territorial Centennial Model 600

with recoil pad. QD swivels and sling; weight, about 6½ pounds. Made from 1965 to 1967.

Remington Model 660 Bolt Action Carbine...... $225
Calibers: 222 Rem., 6mm Rem., 243 Win., 308 Win. 5-shot box magazine (6-shot in 222). 20-inch barrel. Weight, 6½ pounds. Open rear sight, bead front sight on ramp. Monte Carlo stock, checkered, black pistol-grip cap and fore-end tip. Made from 1968 to 1971.

Remington Model 600 Magnum.................. $250
Same as Model 600, except calibers 6.5mm Rem. Mag. and 350 Rem. Mag., 4-shot magazine, special magnum type barrel with racket for scope back-up, laminated walnut-and-beech stock

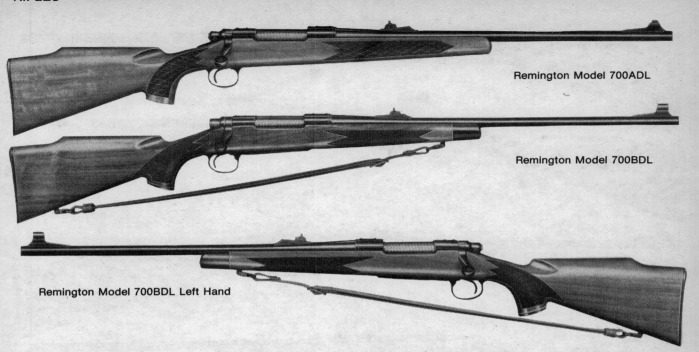

Remington Model 700ADL

Remington Model 700BDL

Remington Model 700BDL Left Hand

Remington Model 660 Magnum.................. **$275**
Same as Model 660, except calibers 6.5mm Rem. Mag. and 350 Rem. Mag., 4-shot magazine, laminated walnut-and-beech stock with recoil pad, QD swivels and sling. Made from 1968 to 1971.

Remington Montana Territorial Centennial Model 600... **$400**
Same as Model 600, except has commemorative medallion embedded in buttstock. Made in 1964. Value is for rifle in new, unfired condition.

Remington Model 700ADL Center Fire Bolt Action Rifle
Calibers: 22-250, 222 Rem., 25-06, 6mm Rem., 243 Win., 270 Win., 30-06, 308 Win., 7mm Rem. Mag. Magazine capacity: 6-shot in 222 Rem., 4-shot in 7mm Rem. Mag., 5-shot in other calibers. Barrel lengths: 24-inch in 22-250, 222 Rem., 25-06, 7mm Rem. Mag.; 22-inch in other calibers. Weight, 7 pounds standard, 7½ pounds in 7mm Rem. Mag. Ramp front sight, sliding ramp open rear sight. Monte Carlo stock with cheekpiece, skip checkering, recoil pad on magnum. Made from 1962 to date.
Standard calibers.................................... **$210**
7mm Rem. Mag...................................... **225**

Remington Model 700BDL Custom Deluxe
Same as Model 700 ADL, except has hinged floorplate, hooded ramp front sight, stock with black fore-end tip and pistol-grip cap, cut checkering, QD swivels and sling. Additional calibers: 17 Rem., 264 Win. Mag., 300 Win. Mag., 8mm Rem. Mag.; all with 24-inch barrels; magnums have 4-shot magazine, recoil pad, weighs 7½ pounds; 17 Rem. has 6-shot magazine, weighs 7 pounds. Made from 1962 to date.
Standard calibers except 17 Rem.....................**$245**
Magnum calibers and 17 Rem....................... **325**

Remington Model 700BDL Left Hand
Same as Model 700BDL, except has left-hand bolt action, stock with cheekpiece on right side. Calibers: 270 Win., 30-06, 7mm Rem. Mag. Made from 1973 to date.
270 and 30-06.......................................**$250**
7mm Rem. Mag....................................... **275**

Remington Model 700BDL Varmint Special..... **$300**
Same as Model 700BDL, except has 24-inch heavy barrel, no sights. weighs 9 pounds (8¾ pounds in 308 Win.). Calibers: 22-250, 222 Rem., 223 Rem., 25-06, 6mm Rem., 243 Win., 308 Win. Made from 1967 to date.

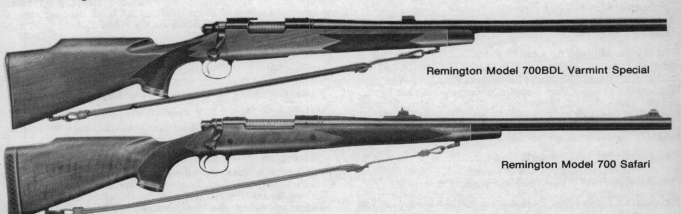

Remington Model 700BDL Varmint Special

Remington Model 700 Safari

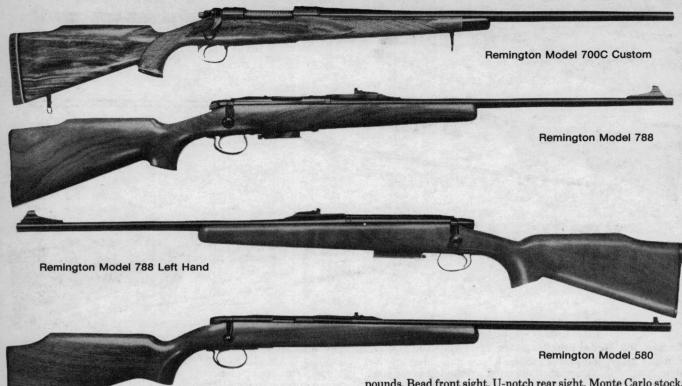

Remington Model 700C Custom

Remington Model 788

Remington Model 788 Left Hand

Remington Model 580

Remington Model 700 Safari Grade.............$430
Similar to magnum Model 700BDL, except calibers 375 H&H Mag. and 458 Win. Mag., has heavier barrel and stock, weighs 9 pounds. Made from 1962 to date.

Remington Model 700C Custom..................$450
Same general specifications as Model 700BDL, except special made-to-order grade with higher quality wood and high-gloss blued finish. Available in all Model 700BDL calibers except 17 Rem., 223 Rem., 8mm Rem. Mag., 264 Win. Mag., 375 H&H Mag., 458 Win. Mag. Made from 1965 to date.

Remington Model 700D Peerless Grade........ $900
Same as Model 700C Custom, except scroll engraved, fancy wood. Made from 1965 to date.

Remington Model 700F Premier Grade........$2000
Same as Model 700D Peerless Grade, except more elaborately engraved, finest grade wood. Made from 1965 to date.

Remington Model 788 Center Fire Bolt Action Rifle... $190
Calibers: 222 Rem., 22-250, 223 Rem., 6mm Rem., 243 Win., 308 Win., 30-30, 44 Rem. Mag. 3-shot clip magazine (4-shot in 222 and 223 Rem.). 24-inch barrel in 22's, 22-inch in other calibers. Weights: 7½ pounds with 24-inch barrel, 7¼ pounds with 22-inch barrel. Blade front sight on ramp, U-notch rear sight. Monte Carlo stock, no checkering. Made from 1967 to date.

Remington Model 788 Left Hand................ $200
Same as Model 788, except has left-hand bolt action, calibers 6mm Rem. and 308 Win. only. Made from 1972 to 1979.

Remington Model 580 Bolt Action Single Shot.. $ 70
Caliber, 22 Short, Long, Long Rifle. 24-inch barrel. Weight, 4¾

pounds. Bead front sight, U-notch rear sight. Monte Carlo stock. Made from 1967 to 1978.

Remington Model 580SB Smooth Bore.......... $ 80
Same as Model 580, except smooth bore for 22 Long Rifle shot cartridges. Made from 1967 to 1978.

Remington Model 580BR Boy's Rifle............. $ 70
Same as Model 580, except has 1-inch shorter stock. Made from 1971 to 1978.

Remington Model 581 Clip Repeater............. $ 85
Same general specifications as Model 580, except has 5-shot clip magazine. Made from 1967 to date.

Remington Model 581 Left Hand................. $ 90
Same as Model 581, except has left-hand bolt action. Made from 1969 to date.

Remington Model 582 Tubular Repeater........ $100
Same general specifications as Model 580, except has tubular magazine holding 20 Short, 15 Long, 14 Long Rifle cartridges; weight, about 5 pounds. Made from 1967 to date.

Remington Model 591 Bolt Action Clip Repeater...................................... $125
Caliber, 5mm Rim Fire Magnum. 4-shot clip magazine. 24-inch barrel. Weight, 5 pounds. Bead front sight, U-notch rear sight. Monte Carlo stock. Made from 1970 to 1973.

Remington Model 592 Tubular Repeater........ $125
Same as Model 591, except has tubular magazine holding 10 rounds, weighs 5½ pounds. Made from 1970 to 1973.

Remington Model 541-S Custom Sporter........ $175
Bolt action repeater. Scroll engraving on receiver and trigger guard. Caliber, 22 Short, Long, Long Rifle. 5-shot clip magazine. 24-inch barrel. Weight, 5½ pounds. Supplied without sights. Checkered walnut stock with rosewood-finished fore-end tip, pistol-grip cap and butt plate. Made from 1972 to date.

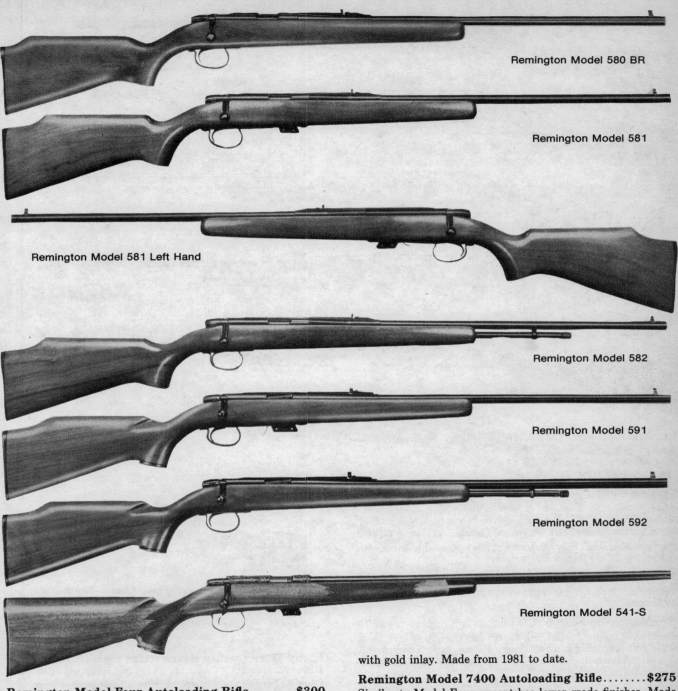

Remington Model 580 BR

Remington Model 581

Remington Model 581 Left Hand

Remington Model 582

Remington Model 591

Remington Model 592

Remington Model 541-S

Remington Model Four Autoloading Rifle........ **$300**
Hammerless. Calibers: 6mm Rem., 243 Win., 270 Win., 7mm
Express Rem., 30-06, 308 Win. 22-inch barrel. Weight, 7½
pounds. Open rear sight, bead front sight on ramp. Monte Carlo
checkered stock and checkered forearm. Made from 1981 to
date.

Remington Model Four Peerless Grade........ **$1200**
Same as Model Four Standard, except has engraved receiver.
Made from 1981 to date.

Remington Model Four Premier Grade........ **$3400**
Same as Model Four Standard, except has engraved receiver

with gold inlay. Made from 1981 to date.

Remington Model 7400 Autoloading Rifle........ **$275**
Similar to Model Four, except has lower grade finishes. Made
from 1981 to date.

**Remington Model Six Slide Action
Repeating Rifle**.................................... **$275**
Hammerless. Caliber: 6mm Rem., 243 Win., 270 Win., 7mm
Express Rem., 30-06, 308 Win. 22-inch barrel. Weight, 7½
pounds. Checkered Monte Carlo stock and forearm. Made from
1981 to date.

Remington Model Six Peerless Grade........... **$1200**
Same as Model Six Standard, except has engraved receiver.
Made from 1981 to date.

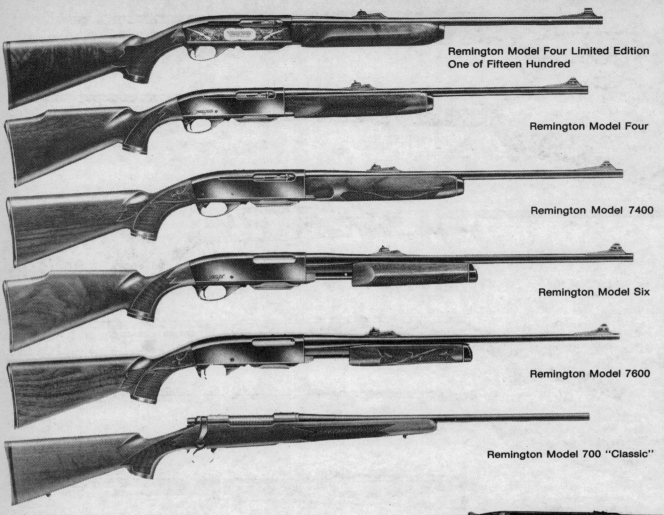

Remington Model Four Limited Edition
One of Fifteen Hundred

Remington Model Four

Remington Model 7400

Remington Model Six

Remington Model 7600

Remington Model 700 "Classic"

Remington Model Six Premier Grade **$3400**
Same as Model Six Standard, except has engraved receiver with
gold inlay. Made from 1981 to date.

Remington Model 7600 .... **$265**
Similar to Model Six, except has lower grade finishes. Made from
1981 to date.

Remington Model 700 "Classic" **$375**
Same as standard Model 700, except has quality walnut stock
with full-pattern cut checkering; special satin-wood finish.
Brown rubber butt pad. Hinged floor plate. No sights. Weight,
7 pounds. Introduced in 1981.

John Rigby & Co., London, England

**Rigby Best Quality Hammerless Ejector Double
Rifle** **$16,000**
Side locks. Calibers: 275 Magnum, 350 Magnum, 470 Nitro
Express. 24- to 28-inch barrels. Weights, from 7½ to 10½
pounds depending upon caliber. Folding leaf rear sight, bead
front sight. Checkered pistol-grip stock and forearm.

**Rigby Second Quality Hammerless Ejector Double
Rifle** **$12,000**
Same general specifications as Best Quality double rifle, except
box lock.

Rigby Best Quality Double Rifle

**Rigby Third Quality Hammerless Ejector Double
Rifle** **$9,000**
Same as Second Quality double rifle, except plainer finish and
not of as high quality.

Rigby 350 Magnum Magazine Sporting Rifle .. **$2,500**
Mauser action. Caliber, 350 Magnum. 5-shot box magazine. 24-
inch barrel. Weight, about 7¾ pounds. Folding leaf rear sight,
bead front sight. Sporting stock with full pistol grip, checkered.
Currently manufactured.

Rigby 416 Big Game Magazine Sporting Rifle . **$2,500**
Mauser action. Caliber, 416 Big Game. 4-shot box magazine. 24-
inch barrel. Weight, about 9 to 9¼ pounds. Folding leaf rear
sight, bead front sight. Sporting stock with full pistol grip,
checkered. Currently manufactured.

Rigby Second Quality Double Rifle

Rigby 275 Magazine Sporting Rifle **$2,500**
Mauser action. Caliber, 275 High Velocity or 7x57mm. 5-shot box magazine. 25-inch barrel. Weight, about 7½ pounds. Folding leaf rear sight, bead front sight. Sporting stock with half-pistol grip, checkered. Specifications given are those of current model; however, in general, they apply also to pre-war model.

Rigby 275 Light-Weight Model Magazine Rifle **$2,500**
Same as standard 275 rifle, except has 21-inch barrel and weighs only 6¾ pounds.

Ross Rifle Co., Quebec, Canada

Ross Model 1910 Bolt Action Sporting Rifle **$250**
Straight pull bolt action with interrupted-screw-type lugs. Calibers: 280 Ross, 303 British. 4-shot or 5-shot magazine. Barrel lengths: 22-, 24-, 26-inch. Two-leaf open rear sight, bead front sight. Checkered sporting stock. Weight, about 7 pounds. Made from c. 1910 to end of World War I. *Note:* Most firearm authorities are of the opinion that this and other Ross models with interrupted-screw-type lugs are unsafe to fire.

Amadeo Rossi, S.A., Sao Leopoldo, Brazil

Rossi Gallery Model Slide Action Repeater **$110**
Similar to Winchester Model 62. Caliber, 22 Long Rifle, Long, Short. Tubular magazine holds 13 LR, 16 Long, 20 Short. 23-inch barrel. Weight, 5¾ pounds. Open rear sight, bead front sight. Straight-grip stock, grooved slide handle. Made from 1970 to date.

Rossi Gallery Model Carbine **$110**
Same as standard Gallery Model, except has 16¼-inch barrel, weighs 5½ pounds. Made from 1975 to date.

Rigby 350 Magnum

Rigby 275 Magazine

Rossi Gallery Model Magnum **$125**
Same as standard Gallery Model, except chambered for 22 Win. Mag. R.F., 10-shot magazine. Made in 1975.

Rossi Lever Action Carbine **$160**
Similar to Winchester Model 92. Caliber, 357 Mag. Tubular magazine. 20-inch barrel. Weight, 5¾ pounds. Open rear sight, bead front sight. Straight-grip walnut stock. Made from 1978 to date.

Rossi Lever Action Carbine Engraved Model **$200**
Same as standard model, except has engraved action. Made from 1981 to date.

Ruger Rifles manufactured by Sturm, Ruger & Co., Southport, Connecticut

Ruger Model 44 Standard Autoloading Carbine . **$180**
Gas-operated. Caliber, 44 Magnum. 4-shot tubular magazine (with magazine release button since 1967). 18½-inch barrel. Weight, 5¾ pounds. Folding leaf rear sight, gold bead front sight. Carbine-style stock with barrel band and curved butt plate. Made from 1961 to date.

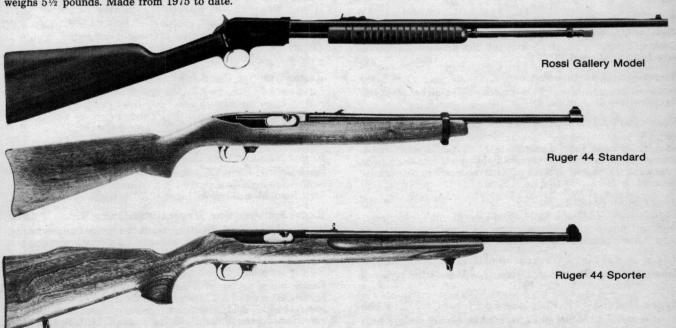

Rossi Gallery Model

Ruger 44 Standard

Ruger 44 Sporter

Ruger 10/22 Standard

Ruger 10/22 Sporter

Ruger 10/22 International

Ruger Model 10/22SP Deluxe Sporter

Ruger Model 44RS Carbine...................... $190
Same as Standard Model 44, except has built-in peep sight, sling swivels.

Ruger Model 44 Sporter........................ $225
Same as Standard Model 44, except has Monte Carlo sporter stock with finger-grooved forearm, grip cap, flat butt plate, sling swivels. Discontinued 1971.

Ruger Model 44 International.................... $400
Same as Standard Model 44, except has Mannlicher-style full stock, swivels. Discontinued 1971.

Ruger Model 10/22 Standard Autoloading Carbine.. $ 70
Caliber, 22 Long Rifle. Detachable 10-shot rotary magazine. 18½-inch barrel. Weight, 5 pounds. Folding leaf rear sight, bead front sight. Carbine-style stock with barrel band and curved butt plate. Made from 1964 to date.

Ruger Model 10/22 Sporter...................... $ 80
Same as Standard Model 10/22, except has Monte Carlo sporter stock with finger-grooved forearm, grip cap, flat butt plate, sling swivels. Discontinued 1971.

Ruger Model 10/22 International................ $300
Same as Standard Model 10/22, except has Mannlicher-style full stock, swivels. Discontinued 1971.

Ruger Model 10/22SP Deluxe Sporter........... $ 95
Same as Standard Model 10/22, except has checkered stock with flat butt plate and sling swivels. Made from 1971 to date.

Ruger Number One Standard Rifle.............. $275
Falling-block single-shot action with Farquharson type lever. Calibers: 22-250, 243 Win., 6mm Rem., 25-06, 270 Win., 30-06, 7mm Rem. Mag., 300 Win. Mag. 26-inch barrel. Weight, 8 pounds. No sights, has quarter-rib for scope mounting. Checkered pistol-grip buttstock and semi-beavertail forearm, QD swivels, rubber butt plate. Made from 1966 to date.

Ruger Number One Special Varminter.......... $275
Same as No. 1 Standard, except has heavy 24-inch barrel with target scope bases, no quarter-rib; weight is 9 pounds. Calibers: 22-250, 25-06, 7mm Rem. Mag., 300 Win. Mag. Made from 1966 to date.

Ruger Number One Light Sporter.............. $275
Same as No. 1 Standard, except has 22-inch barrel, folding leaf rear sight on quarter-rib and ramp front sight, Henry pattern forearm, front swivel on barrel band; weight is 7¼ pounds. Calibers: 243 Win., 270 Win., 7x57mm, 30-06. Made from 1966 to date.

Ruger Number One Medium Sporter........... $275
Same as No. 1 Light Sporter, except has 26-inch barrel (22-inch in 45-70); weight is 8 pounds (7¼ pounds in 45-70). Calibers: 7mm Rem. Mag., 300 Win. Mag., 45-70. Made from 1966 to date.

Ruger Number One Tropical Rifle.............. $300
Same as No. 1 Light Sporter, except has heavy 24-inch barrel, calibers are 375 H&H Mag. and 458 Win. Mag.; weights, 8¼ pounds for 375, 9 pounds for 458. Made from 1966 to date.

Ruger Number Three Single Shot Carbine...... $235
Falling-block action with American-style lever. Calibers: 22 Hornet, 30-40, 45-70. 22-inch barrel. Weight, 6 pounds. Folding leaf rear sight, gold bead front sight. Carbine-style stock with curved butt plate, forearm with barrel band. Made from 1972 to date.

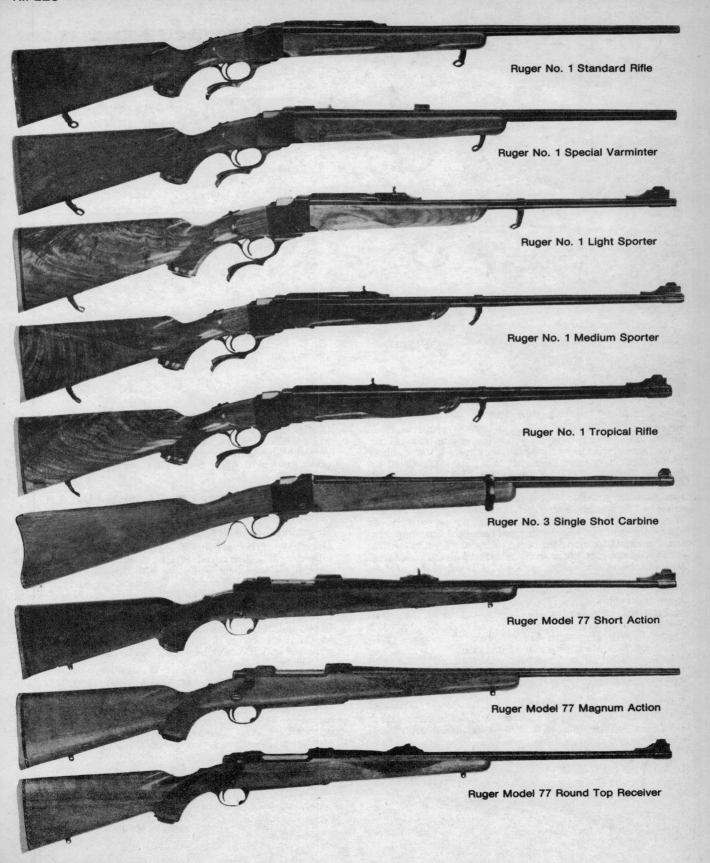

Ruger No. 1 Standard Rifle

Ruger No. 1 Special Varminter

Ruger No. 1 Light Sporter

Ruger No. 1 Medium Sporter

Ruger No. 1 Tropical Rifle

Ruger No. 3 Single Shot Carbine

Ruger Model 77 Short Action

Ruger Model 77 Magnum Action

Ruger Model 77 Round Top Receiver

Ruger Model 77V Varmint

Ruger Mini-14

Ruger Model 77 - MANNLICHER

Ruger Mini - 14/5

Ruger Model 77 Bolt Action Rifle

Receiver with integral scope mount base or with round top. Short stroke or magnum length action (depending upon caliber) in the former type receiver, magnum only in the latter. Calibers: 22-250, 220 Swift, 6mm Rem., 243 Win., 250-3000, 25-06, 257 Roberts, 270 Win., 7x57mm, 7mm Rem. Mag., 280 Rem., 308 Win., 30-06, 300 Win. Mag., 338 Win. Mag., 458 Win. Mag. 5-shot magazine standard, 4-shot in 220 Swift, 3-shot in magnum calibers. 22-, 24-, or 26-inch barrel (depending upon caliber). Weight, about 7 pounds (458 Mag. model, 8¾ pounds). Round top model furnished with folding leaf rear sight and ramp front sight; integral base model furnished with scope rings and with or without open sights. Stock with checkered pistol grip and forearm, pistol-grip cap, rubber recoil pad, QD swivel studs. Made from 1968 to date.

Model 77R, integral base, no sights	$200
Same, 338 Win. Mag.	225
Model 77RS, integral base, open sights	340
Same, 338 Win. Mag.	375
Same, 458 Win. Mag., with standard stock	375
Same, 458 Win. Mag., with fancy Circassian walnut stock	400
Model 77ST, round top, open sights	375
Same, 338 Win. Mag.	375

Ruger Model 77V Varmint Rifle $250

Same as standard Model 77 with integral base receiver, except has heavy 24-inch (26-inch in 220 Swift) barrel drilled and tapped for target scope bases; weight is 9 pounds. Calibers: 22-250, 220 Swift, 243 Win., 6mm Rem., 25-06, 308. Made from 1968 to date.

Ruger Mini-14 Semiautomatic Rifle $275

Gas-operated. Caliber, 223 Rem. (5.56mm). 5-, 10-, or 20-shot box magazine. 18½-inch barrel. Weight, about 6½ pounds. Peep rear sight, blade front sight. Pistol-grip stock with curved butt plate, handguard. Made from 1976 to date.

Russian Military Rifles. Principal U.S.S.R. Arms Plant is located at Tula

Russian Model 1891 Mosin Military Rifle $125

Nagant system bolt action. Caliber, 7.62mm Russian. 5-shot box magazine. 31½-inch barrel. Weight, about 9 pounds. Open rear sight, blade front sight. Full stock with straight grip. Specifications given are for World War II version, earlier types differ slightly. *Note:* In 1916, Remington Arms Co. and New England Westinghouse Co. produced 250,000 of these rifles on a contract from the Imperial Russian Government. Few were delivered to Russia and the balance were purchased by the U.S. Government for training purposes in 1918. Eventually, many of these rifles were sold to N.R.A. members for about $3 each by the Director of Civilian Marksmanship.

Russian Tokarev Model 40 Semiautomatic Military Rifle $300

Gas-operated. Caliber, 7.62mm Russian. 10-shot detachable box magazine. 24½-inch barrel. Muzzle brake. Weight, about 9 pounds. Leaf rear sight, hooded post front sight. Full stock with pistol grip. Differences between Models 1938, 1940 and 1941 are minor.

Russian Model 1891 Moisin

Sako Rifles manufactured by Oy Sako Ab, Riihimaki, Finland

Sako "Vixen" Sporter........................... **$370**
Short Mauser-type bolt action. Calibers: 218 Bee, 22 Hornet, 222 Rem., 222 Rem. Mag., 223 Rem. 5-shot magazine. 23½-inch barrel. Weight, 6½ pounds. Hooded ramp front sight. Sporter stock with Monte Carlo cheekpiece, checkered pistol grip and forearm, swivels. Made from 1946 to 1971.

Sako "Vixen" Carbine........................... **$500**
Same as Vixen Sporter, except has 20-inch barrel, Mannlicher-type full stock. Made from 1947 to 1971.

Sako "Vixen" Heavy Barrel...................... **$390**
Same as Vixen Sporter, except calibers (222 Rem., 222 Rem. Mag., 223 Rem.), heavy barrel, target-style stock with beavertail forearm; weight, 7½ pounds. Made from 1947-1971.

Sako High-Power Mauser Sporting Rifle....... **$350**
FN Mauser action. Calibers: 270, 30-06, 5-shot magazine. 24-inch barrel. Open rear leaf sight, Patridge front sight, hooded ramp. Checkered stock with Monte Carlo comb and cheekpiece. Weight, about 7½ pounds. Made from 1950 to 1957.

Sako Magnum Mauser........................... **$425**
Same general specifications as standard model, except has recoil pad. Calibers: 300 H&H Magnum, 375 H&H Magnum.

Sako "Forester" Sporter........................ **$425**
Medium-length Mauser-type bolt action. Calibers: 22-250, 243 Win., 308 Win. 5-shot magazine. 23-inch barrel. Weight, 6½ pounds. Hooded ramp front sight. Sporter stock with Monte Carlo cheekpiece, checkered pistol grip and forearm, swivels. Made from 1957 to 1971.

Sako "Forester" Carbine........................ **$600**
Same as Forester Sporter, except has 20-inch barrel, Mannlicher-type full stock. Made from 1958 to 1971.

Sako "Forester" Heavy Barrel................... **$450**
Same as Forester Sporter, except has 24-inch heavy barrel, weighs 7½ pounds. Made from 1958 to 1971.

Sako "Finnbear" Sporter........................ **$400**
Long Mauser-type bolt action. Calibers: 25-06, 264 Mag., 270, 30-06, 300 Win. Mag., 338 Mag., 7mm Mag., 375 H&H Mag. Magazine holds 5 standard or 4 magnum cartridges. 24-inch barrel. Weight, about 7 pounds. Hooded ramp front sight. Sporter stock with Monte Carlo cheekpiece, checkered pistol grip and forearm, recoil pad, swivels. Made from 1961 to 1971.

Sako "Finnbear" Carbine........................ **$535**
Same as Finnbear Sporter, except has 20-inch barrel, Mannlicher-type full stock. Made in 1971.

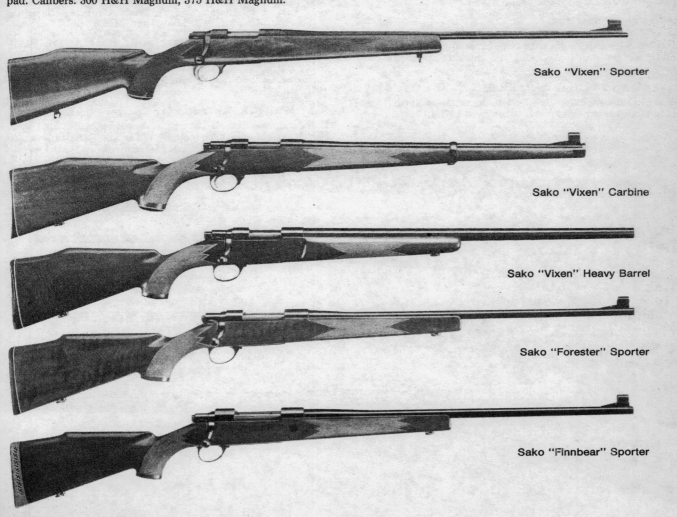

Sako "Vixen" Sporter

Sako "Vixen" Carbine

Sako "Vixen" Heavy Barrel

Sako "Forester" Sporter

Sako "Finnbear" Sporter

Sako "Finnwolf" Lever Action Rifle **$400**
Hammerless. Calibers: 243 Win., 308 Win. 4-shot clip magazine. 23-inch barrel. Weight, 6¾ pounds. Hooded ramp front sight. Sporter stock with Monte Carlo cheekpiece, checkered pistol grip and forearm, swivels (available with right- or left-hand stock). Made from 1963 to 1972.

Sako Model 72 .... **$365**
Single model designation replacing Vixen Sporter, Vixen Carbine, Vixen Heavy Barrel, Forester Sporter, Forester Carbine, Forester Heavy Barrel, Finnbear Sporter, and Finnbear Carbine, with same specifications except all but heavy barrel models fitted with open rear sight. Values same as for corresponding earlier models. Made from 1972 to 1974.

Sako Golden Anniversary Model **$1300**
Special presentation grade rifle issued in 1973 to commemorate Sako's 50th anniversary. 1000 (numbered 1 to 1000) made. Same specifications as Deluxe Sporter, long action, 7mm Rem. Mag. Receiver, trigger guard and floorplate decorated with gold oak leaf and acorn motif. Stock of select European walnut, checkering bordered with hand-carved oak leaf pattern.

Sako Model 74 Super Sporter, Short Action **$410**
Mauser-type bolt action. Calibers: 222 Rem., 223 Rem. 5-shot magazine. 23½-inch barrel. Weight, about 6½ pounds. No sights. Checkered European walnut stock with Monte Carlo cheekpiece, QD swivel studs. Made from 1974 to date.

Sako Deluxe Sporter **$475**
Same as Vixen, Forester, Finnbear, and Model 74, except has fancy French walnut stock with skip checkering, rosewood fore-end tip and pistol-grip cap, recoil pad, inlaid trigger guard and floorplate.

Sako Model 73 Lever Action Rifle **$360**
Same as Finnwolf, except has 3-shot clip magazine, flush floorplate; stock has no cheekpiece. Made from 1973 to 1975.

Sako Model 74 Super Sporter, Medium Action .. **$400**
Same specifications as with short action, except weight is 7¼ pounds. Calibers: 220 Swift, 22-250, 243 Win. Made from 1974 to 1978.

Sako Model 74 Super Sporter, Long Action **$350**
Same specifications as with short action, except has 24-inch barrel, weighs about 8 pounds; magnums have 4-shot magazine, recoil pad. Calibers: 25-06, 270 Win., 7mm Rem. Mag., 30-06, 300 Win. Mag., 338 Win. Mag., 375 H&H Mag. Made from 1974 to 1978.

Sako Model 74 Carbine **$405**
Long Mauser-type bolt action. Caliber, 30-06. 5-shot magazine. 20-inch barrel. Weight, about 7½ pounds. No sights. Mannlicher-type full stock of European walnut, checkered, Monte Carlo. Made from 1974 to 1978.

Sako Model 74 Heavy Barrel Rifle, Short Action **$400**
Mauser-type bolt action. Calibers: 222 Rem., 223 Rem. 5-shot magazine. 23½-inch heavy barrel. Weight, about 8¼ pounds. No sights. Checkered European walnut stock, target style with beavertail forearm. Made from 1974 to 1978.

Sako Model 74 Heavy Barrel Rifle, Medium Action **$400**
Same specifications as with short action, except has 23-inch heavy barrel, weighs about 8½ pounds. Calibers: 220 Swift, 22-250, 243 Win., 308 Win. Made from 1974 to 1978.

Sako Model 74 Heavy Barrel Rifle, Long Action . **$400**
Same specifications as with short action, except has 24-inch heavy barrel, weighs about 8¾ pounds; magnum has 4-shot magazine. Calibers: 25-06, 7mm Rem. Mag. Made from 1974 to 1978.

Sako Model 78 Super Rimfire Sporter **$220**
Bolt action. Caliber, 22 Long Rifle. 5-shot magazine. 22½-inch barrel. Weight, about 6¾ pounds. No sights. European walnut stock, checkered, Monte Carlo. Introduced in 1977. Discontinued.

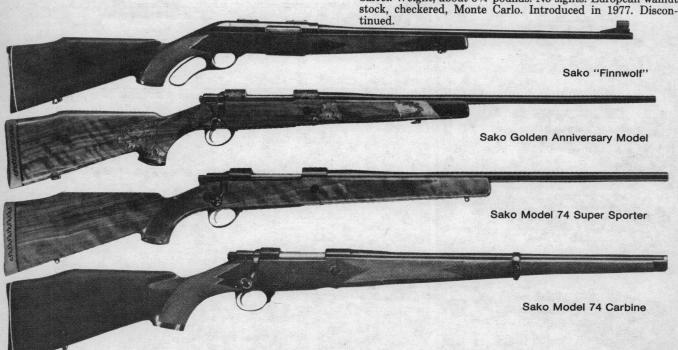

Sako "Finnwolf"

Sako Golden Anniversary Model

Sako Model 74 Super Sporter

Sako Model 74 Carbine

Sako Deluxe Sporter

Sako Model 73

Sako Model 78 Rimfire

Sako Model 78 Super Hornet Sporter............**$260**
Same specifications as Model 78 Rimfire, except caliber 22
Hornet, 4-shot magazine. Introduced in 1977. Discontinued.

Sako Model A1 Standard........................**$460**
Short bolt action. Calibers: 17 Rem., 222 Rem., 223 Rem. 5-shot
magazine. 23½-inch barrel. Weight, about 6½ pounds. No
sights. Checkered European walnut stock with Monte Carlo
cheekpiece, OD swivel studs. Made from 1978 to date.

Sako Model A1 Deluxe Grade...................**$610**
Same specifications as standard grade, except with 22 lines to
the inch French checkering, rosewood grip cap and fore-end tip,
semi-beavertail fore-end.

Sako Model A11 Standard.......................**$460**
Medium bolt action. Calibers: 22-250 Rem., 243 Win., 308 Win.
23½-inch barrel in 22-250; 23-inch barrel in 243 Win., and 308
Win. 5-shot magazine. Weight, about 7¼ pounds. Checkered
European walnut stock with Monte Carlo cheekpiece, OD swivel
studs. Made from 1978 to date.

Sako Model A11 Deluxe Grade..................**$610**
Same specifications as standard grade, except with 22 lines per
inch French checkering, rosewood grip cap and fore-end tip,
semi-beavertail fore-end.

Sako Model A111 Standard....................**$500**
Long bolt action. Calibers 25-06 Rem., 270 Win., 30-06, 7mm
Rem Mag., 300 Win. Mag., 338 Win. Mag., 375 H&H. 24-inch
barrel. 4-shot magazine. Weight, 8 pounds. Made from 1978 to
date.

Sako Model A111 Deluxe.......................**$640**
Same specifications as with standard, except with French checkering, rosewood grip cap and fore-end tip, semi-beavertail fore-
end.

Sako Safari Grade.............................**$1100**
Classic bolt action. Calibers: 300 Win. Mag., 338 Win. Mag., 375
H&H. Oil finished European walnut stock with hand checkering.
Barrel band swivel, express-type sight rib; satin blue finish.

Sako Classic Bolt Action Rifle...................**$560**
Type A11 action. Calibers 243 Win., 270 Win., 30-06, 7mm Rem.
Mag. American walnut stock.

Sako Super Deluxe Rifle........................**$1100**
Available in A1, A11, A111 calibers. Select European walnut
stock, hand checkered, deep oak leaf hand engraved design.

J. P. Sauer & Sohn, Suhl, Germany

Sauer Mauser Bolt Action Sporting Rifle........**$475**
Calibers: 7x57 and 8x57mm are the most common, but these
rifles were produced in a variety of calibers including most of the
popular Continental numbers as well as our 30-06. 5-shot box
magazine. 22- or 24-inch Krupp steel barrel, half-octagon with
raised matted rib. Double set trigger. Weight, about 7½ pounds.
Three-leaf open rear sight, ramp front sight. Sporting stock with
cheekpiece, checkered pistol grip, raised side-panels, schnabel
tip, swivels. Also made with 20-inch barrel and full-length stock.
Manufactured prior to World War II.

Savage Arms, formerly of Utica, N.Y. now located at Westfield, Massachusetts

Savage Model 99 Lever Action Repeating Rifle
Introduced in 1899, this model has been produced in a variety of
styles and calibers. Original designation, "Model 1899," was
changed to "Model 99" circa 1920. Earlier rifles and carbines—
similar to Models 99A, 99B and 99H—were supplied in calibers
25-35, 30-30, 303 Sav., 32-40 and 38-55. Post-World War II
Models 9A, 99C, 99CD, 99DL, 99F, 99PE and 99DE have top
tang safety; other 99s have slide safety on right side of trigger
guard. Current Models 99C and 99CD have detachable box
magazine instead of traditional Model 99 rotary magazine.

Savage Model 99A..............................**$425**
Hammerless. Solid frame. Calibers: 30/30, 300 Sav., 303 Sav.
Five-shot rotary magazine. 24-inch barrel. Weight, about 7¼
pounds. Open rear sight, bead front sight on ramp. Plain
straight-grip stock, tapered forearm. Made from 1920 to 1936.

Savage Model 99A..............................**$225**
Current model. Similar to original Model 99A, except has top
tang safety, 22-inch barrel, folding leaf rear sight, does not have
crescent butt plate; weight, 7 pounds. Calibers: 243 Win., 250
Sav., 300 Sav., 308 Win. Made from 1971 to date.

Savage Model 99B..............................**$600**
Takedown. Otherwise same as Model 99A, except weight about
7½ pounds. Made from 1920 to 1936.

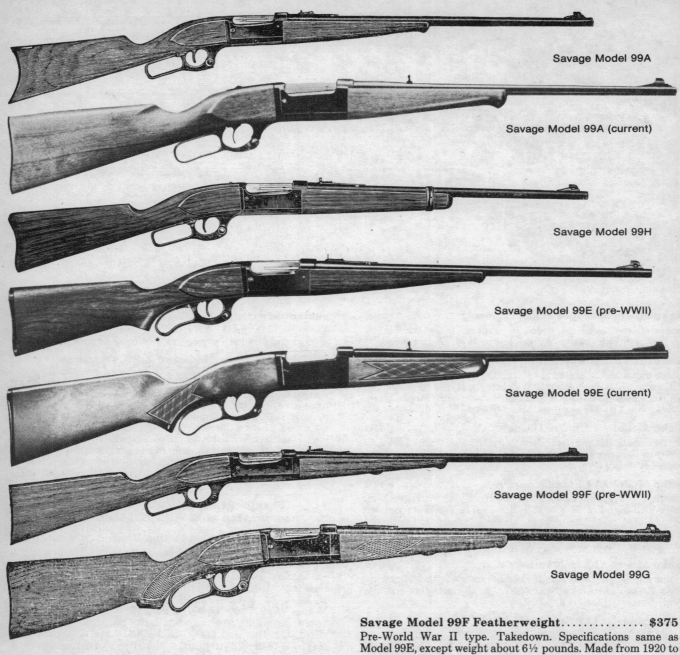

Savage Model 99A

Savage Model 99A (current)

Savage Model 99H

Savage Model 99E (pre-WWII)

Savage Model 99E (current)

Savage Model 99F (pre-WWII)

Savage Model 99G

Savage Model 99H Carbine **$425**
Solid frame. Calibers: 250/3000, 30/30, 303 Sav. Carbine stock and forearm. Weight, about 6½ pounds. Other specifications same as Model 99A. Made from 1931 to 1942.

Savage Model 99E **$600**
Pre-World War II type. Solid frame. Calibers: 22 Hi-Power, 250/3000, 30/30, 300 Sav., 303 Sav. with 22-inch barrel; 300 Sav. 24-inch. Weight, about 7 pounds. Other specifications same as Model 99A. Made from 1920 to 1936.

Savage Model 99E Carbine **$185**
Current model. Solid frame. Calibers: 243 Win., 300 Sav., 308 Win. 20- or 22-inch barrel. Checkered pistol-grip stock and forearm. Weight, about 7 pounds. Made from 1960 to date.

Savage Model 99F Featherweight **$375**
Pre-World War II type. Takedown. Specifications same as Model 99E, except weight about 6½ pounds. Made from 1920 to 1942.

Savage Model 99F Featherweight **$225**
Postwar model. Solid frame. Calibers: 243 Win., 300 Sav., 308 Win. 22-inch barrel. Checkered pistol-grip stock and forearm. Weight, about 6½ pounds. Made from 1955 to 1973.

Savage Model 99G **$425**
Takedown. Checkered pistol-grip stock and forearm. Weight, about 7¼ pounds. Other specifications same as Model 99E. Made from 1920 to 1942.

Savage Model 99RS **$425**
Pre-World War II type. Same as prewar Model 99R, except equipped with Lyman rear peep sight and folding middle sight, quick detachable swivels and sling. Made from 1936 to 1942.

Savage Model 99K

Savage Model 99EG (post-WWII)

Savage Model 99K.............................. $1100
Deluxe version of Model G with same specifications, except has fancy stock and engraving on receiver and barrel, Lyman peep rear sight and folding middle sight. Made from 1931 to 1942.

Savage Model 99EG............................... $300
Pre-World War II type. Solid frame. Plain pistol-grip stock and forearm. Otherwise same as Model G. Made from 1936 to 1941.

Savage Model 99EG............................... $375
Post-World War II type. Same as prewar model, except has checkered stock and forearm. Calibers: 250 Sav., 300 Sav., 308 Win. (introduced 1955), 243 Win. and 358 Win. Made from 1946 to 1960.

Savage Model 99T.................................$340
Feather-weight. Solid frame. Calibers: 22 Hi-Power, 30/30, 303 Sav. with 20-inch barrel. 300 Sav. with 22-inch barrel. Checkered pistol-grip stock and beavertail forearm. Weight, about 7 pounds. General specifications same as other Model 99 rifles. Made from 1936 to 1942.

Savage Model 99R............................... $420
Pre-World War II type. Solid frame. Calibers: 250/3000 with 22-inch barrel; 300 Sav. with 24-inch barrel. Weight, about 7½ pounds. Special large pistol-grip stock and forearm, checkered. General specifications same as other Model 99 rifles. Made from 1936 to 1942.

Savage Model 99R............................... $255
Post-World War II type. Same as prewar model, except made with 24-inch barrel only, has screw eyes for sling swivels. Calibers: 250 Sav., 300 Sav., 308 Win., 243 Win. and 358 Win. Made from 1946 to 1960.

Savage Model 99RS............................... $305
Post-World War II type. Same as postwar Model 99R, except equipped with Redfield 70LH receiver sight, blank in middle sight slot. Made from 1946 to 1958.

Savage Model 99DL Deluxe..................... $220
Postwar model. Calibers: 243 Win., 308 Win. Same as Model 99F, except has high comb Monte Carlo stock, sling swivels; weight, about 6¾ pounds. Made from 1960 to 1973.

Savage Model 99C.................................$215
Current model. Same as Model 99F, except has clip magazine instead of rotary. Calibers: 243 Win., 284 Win., 308 Win. (4-shot detachable magazine holds one round less in 284). Weight, about 6¾ pounds. Made from 1965 to date.

Savage Model 99CD............................... $250
Deluxe version of Model 99C. Calibers: 243 Win., 250 Sav., 308 Win. Hooded ramp front sight. Weight, 8¼ pounds. Stock with Monte Carlo comb and cheekpiece, checkered pistol grip, grooved forearm, swivels and sling. Made from 1975 to 1981.

Savage Model 99PE Presentation Grade........$700
Same as Model 99DL, except has engraved receiver (game scenes on sides), tang and lever; fancy walnut Monte Carlo stock and forearm with hand checkering, QD swivels. Calibers: 243, 284, 308. Made from 1968 to 1970.

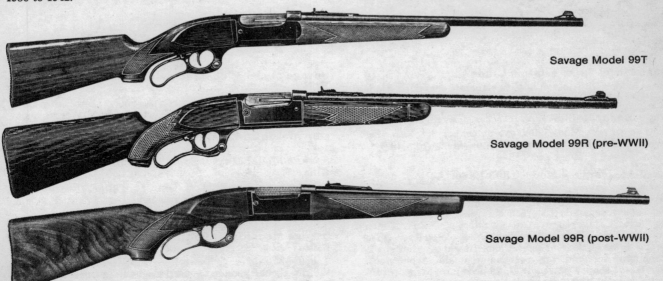

Savage Model 99T

Savage Model 99R (pre-WWII)

Savage Model 99R (post-WWII)

Savage Model 99RS (pre-WWII)

Savage Model 99C

Savage Model 99CD

Savage Model 99PE

Savage Model 99DE

Savage Model 99-358

Savage Model 99DE Citation Grade............. **$510**
Same as Model 99PE, except has less elaborate engraving. Made
from 1968 to 1970.

Savage Model 99-358............................ **$240**
Similar to current Model 99A, except caliber 358 Win., has
grooved forearm, recoil pad, swivel studs. Made from 1977 to
1980.

**Savage Anniversary Model 1895 Lever Action
Rifle**... **$275**
Replica of Savage Model 1895 Hammerless Lever Action Rifle
issued to commemorate the 75th anniversary (1895-1970) of
Savage Arms. Caliber, 308 Win. 5-shot rotary magazine. 24-inch
full-octagon barrel. Engraved receiver. Brass-plated lever. Open
rear sight, brass blade front sight. Plain straight-grip buttstock,
schnabel-type fore-end; brass medallion inlaid in buttstock,
brass crescent-shaped butt plate. 9,999 produced. Made in 1970
only. Value is for new, unfired specimen.

**Savage Model 1903 Slide Action Repeating
Rifle**.. **$145**
Hammerless. Takedown. Caliber, 22 Short, Long, Long Rifle.
Detachable box magazine. 24-inch octagon barrel. Weight, about
5 pounds. Open rear sight, bead front sight. Pistol-grip stock,
grooved slide handle. Made from 1903 to 1921.

**Savage Model 1904 Bolt Action Single Shot
Rifle**... **$ 55**
Takedown. Caliber, 22 Short, Long, Long Rifle. 18-inch barrel.
Weight, about 3 pounds. Open rear sight, bead front sight. Plain,
straight-grip, one-piece stock. Made from 1904 to 1917.

**Savage Model 1905 Bolt Action Single Shot
Rifle**... **$ 55**
Takedown. Caliber, 22 Short, Long, Long Rifle. 22-inch barrel.
Weight, about 5 pounds. Open rear sight, bead front sight. Plain,
straight-grip one-piece stock. Made from 1905 to 1919.

Savage Anniversary Model 1895

Savage Model 19 NRA (1933)

Savage Model 20 (1926)

Savage Model 23A

Savage Model 1909 Slide Action Repeater...... $175
Hammerless. Takedown. Similar to Model 1903, except has 20-inch round barrel, plain stock and forearm, weighs about 4¾ pounds. Made from 1909 to 1915.

Savage Model 1912 Autoloading Rifle........... $325
Takedown. Caliber, 22 Long Rifle only. 7-shot detachable box magazine. 20-inch barrel. Weight, about 4½ pounds. Open rear sight, bead front sight. Plain straight-grip stock and forearm. Made from 1912 to 1916.

Savage Model 1914 Slide Action Repeating
Rifle.. $200
Hammerless. Takedown. Caliber, 22 Short, Long, Long Rifle. Tubular magazine holds 20 Short, 17 Long, 15 Long Rifle. 24-inch octagon barrel. Weight, about 5¾ pounds. Open rear sight, bead front sight. Plain pistol-grip stock, grooved slide handle. Made from 1914 to 1924.

Savage Model 19 NRA Bolt Action Match Rifle..$175
Model of 1919. Caliber, 22 Long Rifle. 5-shot detachable box magazine. 25-inch barrel. Weight, about 7 pounds. Adjustable rear peep sight, plade front sight. Full military stock with pistol grip. Made from 1919 to 1933.

Savage Model 19 Bolt Action Target Rifle....... $180
Model of 1933. Speed lock. Caliber, 22 Long Rifle. 5-shot detachable box magazine. 25-inch barrel. Weight, about 8 pounds. Adjustable rear peep sight and blade front sight on early models, later production equipped with extension rear sight and hooded front sight. Target stock with full pistol grip and beavertail forearm. Made from 1933 to 1946.

Savage Model 19L...................................$200
Same as standard Model 19 (1933), except equipped with Lyman 48Y receiver sight and 17A front sight. Made from 1933 to 1942.

Savage Model 19M...................................$210
Same as standard Model 19 (1933), except has heavy 28-inch

barrel with scope bases, weighs about 9¼ pounds. Made from 1933 to 1942.

Savage Model 19H.............................. $290
Same as standard Model 19 (1933), except chambered for 22 Hornet, has Model 23D-type bolt mechanism, loading port and magazine. Made from 1933 to 1942.

Savage Model 1920 Hi-Power Bolt Action Rifle. $350
Short Mauser-type action. Calibers: 250/3000, 300 Sav. 5-shot box magazine. 22-inch barrel in 250 cal.; 24-inch in 300 cal. Weight, about 6 pounds. Open rear sight, bead front sight. Checkered pistol-grip stock with slender forearm and schnabel tip. Made from 1920 to 1926.

Savage Model 20-1926 Hi-Power Bolt Action
Rifle... $300
Same as Model 1920, except has 24-inch medium weight barrel, improved stock, Lyman 54 rear peep sight, weighs about 7 pounds. Made from 1926 to 1929.

Savage Model 23A Bolt Action Sporting Rifle... $150
Caliber, 22 Long Rifle. 5-shot detachable box magazine. 23-inch barrel. Weight, about 6 pounds. Open rear sight, blade or bead front sight. Plain pistol-grip stock with slender forearm and schnabel tip. Made from 1923 to 1933.

Savage Model 23AA................................ $175
Model of 1933. Improved version of the Model 23A with same general specifications, except has speed lock, improved stock, weighs about 6½ pounds. Made from 1933 to 1942.

Savage Model 23B.............................. $130
Same as Model 23A, except caliber 25/20, has 25-inch barrel. Model of 1933 has improved stock with full forearm instead of the slender forearm with schnabel found on earlier production, weighs about 6½ pounds. Made from 1923 to 1942.

Savage Model 23C.................................$175
Same as Model 23B, except caliber 32/20. Made from 1923 to 1942.

Savage Model 23D.............................. $250
Same as Model 23B, except caliber 22 Hornet. Made from 1933 to 1947.

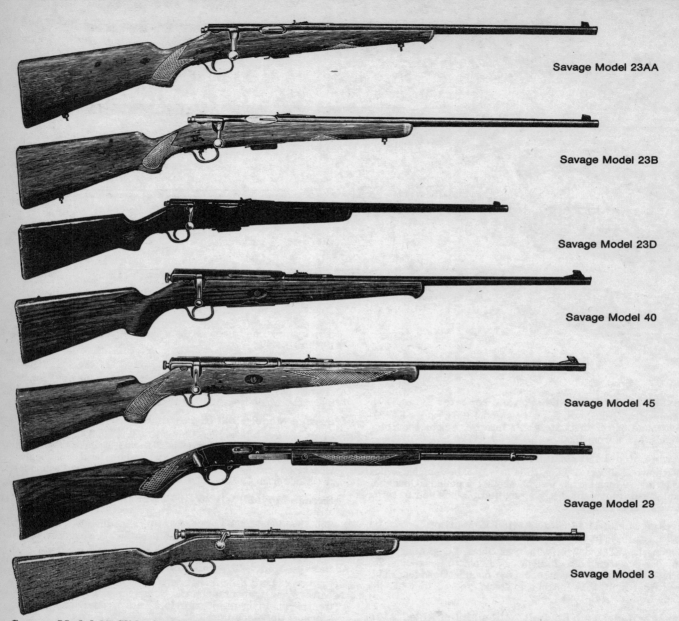

Savage Model 23AA

Savage Model 23B

Savage Model 23D

Savage Model 40

Savage Model 45

Savage Model 29

Savage Model 3

Savage Model 25 Slide Action Repeating Rifle.. $200
Takedown. Hammerless. Caliber, 22 Short, Long, Long Rifle. Tubular magazine holds 20 Short, 17 Long, 15 Long Rifle. 24-inch octagon barrel. Weight, about 5¾ pounds. Open rear sight, blade front sight. Plain pistol-grip stock, grooved slide handle. Made from 1925 to 1929.

Savage Model 40 Bolt Action Sporting Rifle..... $250
Standard Grade. Calibers: 250/3000, 300 Sav., 30/30, 30/06. 4-shot detachable box magazine. 22-inch barrel in calibers 250/3000 and 30/30; 24-inch in 300 Sav. and 30/06. Weight, about 7½ pounds. Open rear sight, bead front sight on ramp. Plain pistol-grip stock with tapered forearm and schnabel tip. Made from 1928 to 1940.

Savage Model 45 Super Sporter.................. $295
Special Grade. Same as Model 40, except has checkered pistol grip and forearm, Lyman No. 40 receiver sight. Made from 1928 to 1940.

Savage Model 29 Slide Action Repeating Rifle.. $175
Takedown. Hammerless. Caliber, 22 Short, Long, Long Rifle. Tubular magazine holds 20 Short, 17 Long, 15 Long Rifle. 24-inch barrel, octagon on prewar, round on postwar production. Weight, about 5½ pounds. Open rear sight, bead front sight. Stock with checkered pistol grip and slide handle on prewar, plain stock and grooved forearm on postwar production. Made from 1929 to 1967.

Savage Model 3 Bolt Action Single Shot Rifle... $ 55
Takedown. Caliber, 22 Short, Long, Long Rifle. 26-inch barrel on prewar rifles, postwar production has 24-inch barrel. Weight, about 5 pounds. Open rear sight, bead front sight. Plain pistol-grip stock. Made from 1933 to 1952.

Savage Model 3S............................... $ 70
Same as Model 3, except has peep rear sight and hooded front sight. Made from 1933 to 1942.

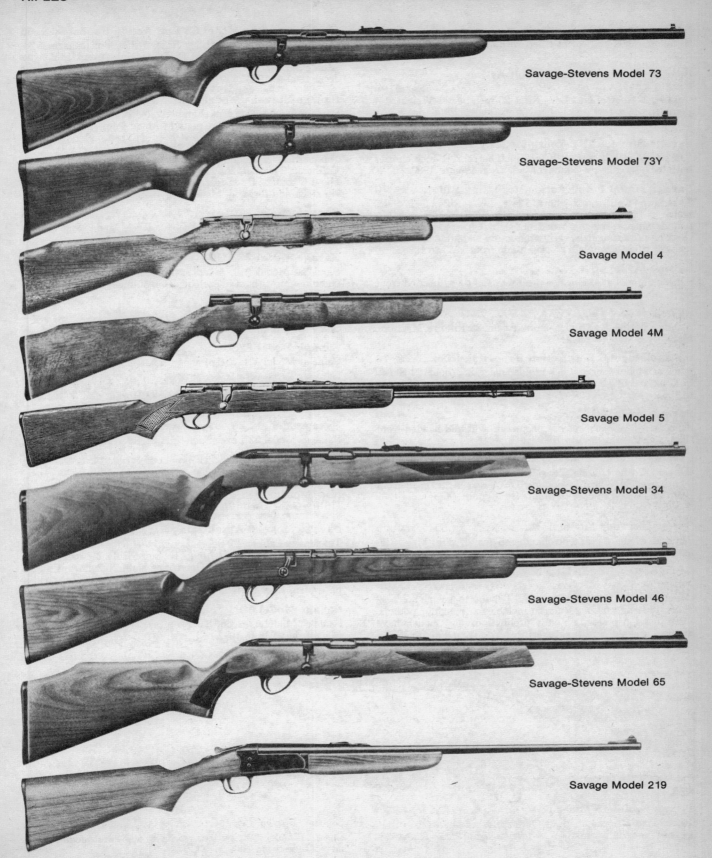

Savage-Stevens Model 73

Savage-Stevens Model 73Y

Savage Model 4

Savage Model 4M

Savage Model 5

Savage-Stevens Model 34

Savage-Stevens Model 46

Savage-Stevens Model 65

Savage Model 219

Savage Model 3ST..............................$ 80
Same as Model 3S, except fitted with swivels and sling. Made from 1933 to 1942.

**Savage-Stevens Model 73 Bolt Action
Single Shot**..$ 55
Caliber, 22 Short, Long, Long Rifle. 20-inch barrel. Weight, 4¾ pounds. Open rear sight, bead front sight. Plain pistol-grip stock. Made from 1965 to 1980.

Savage-Stevens 73Y Youth Model...............$ 55
Same as Model 73, except has 18-inch barrel, 1½-inch shorter buttstock, weighs 4½ pounds. Made from 1965 to 1980.

Savage Model 4 Bolt Action Repeating Rifle.....$ 70
Takedown. Caliber, 22 Short, Long, Long Rifle. 5-shot detachable box magazine. 24-inch barrel. Weight, about 5½ pounds. Open rear sight, bead front sight. Checkered pistol-grip stock on prewar models, early production had grooved forearm; postwar rifles have plain stocks. Made from 1933 to 1965.

Savage Model 4S..................................$ 75
Same as Model 4, except has peep rear sight and hooded front sight. Made from 1933 to 1942.

Savage Model 4M.................................$ 70
Same as Model 4, except chambered for 22 Rimfire Magnum. Made from 1961 to 1965.

Savage Model 5 Bolt Action Repeating Rifle.....$ 70
Same as Model 4, except has tubular magazine (holds 21 Short, 17 Long, 15 Long Rifle), weighs about 6 pounds. Made from 1936 to 1961.

Savage Model 5S..................................$ 80
Same as Model 5, except has peep rear sight and hooded front sight. Made from 1936 to 1942.

Savage-Stevens Model 34 Bolt Action Repeater.$ 60
Caliber, 22 Short, Long, Long Rifle. 5-shot clip magazine. 20-inch barrel. Weight, 5½ pounds. Open rear sight, bead front sight. Checkered stock with Monte Carlo comb. Made from 1969 to 1981.

Savage-Stevens Model 34M.....................$ 65
Same as Model 34, except chambered for 22 Win. Mag. R.F. Made from 1969 to 1973.

Savage-Stevens Model 46 Bolt Action Tubular Repeater..$ 60
Caliber, 22 Short, Long, Long Rifle. Tubular magazine holds 22 Short, 17 Long, 15 Long Rifle. 20-inch barrel. Weight, 5 pounds. Plain pistol-grip stock on early production; later models have Monte Carlo stock with checkering. Made from 1969 to 1973.

Savage-Stevens Model 65 Bolt Action Repeater.$ 65
Caliber, 22 Short, Long, Long Rifle. 5-shot clip magazine. 20-inch barrel. Weight, 5 pounds. Open rear sight, ramp front sight. Monte Carlo stock with checkered pistol grip and forearm. Made from 1969 to 1973.

Savage-Stevens Model 65M.....................$ 70
Same as Model 65, except chambered for 22 Win. Mag. R.F., has 22-inch barrel, weighs 5¾ pounds. Made from 1969 to 1981.

Savage Model 219 Single Shot Rifle.............$ 75
Hammerless. Takedown. Shotgun-type action with top lever. Calibers: 22 Hornet, 25/20, 32/20, 30/30. 26-inch barrel. Weight, about 6 pounds. Open rear sight, bead front sight. Plain pistol-rip stock and forearm. Made from 1938 to 1965.

Savage Model 219L...............................$ 75
Same as Model 219, except has side lever. Made from 1965 to 1967.

Savage Model 221 Utility Gun....................$ 85
Same as Model 219, except caliber 30/30 only, supplied in combination with an interchangeable 30-inch 12 gauge shotgun barrel.

Savage Model 222................................$ 85
Same as Model 221, except shotgun barrel is 28-inch, 16 gauge.

Savage Model 223................................$ 85
Same as Model 221, except shotgun barrel is 28-inch, 20 gauge.

Savage Model 227................................$ 85
Same as Model 221, except caliber 22 Hornet and 30-inch, 12 gauge barrel.

Savage Model 228................................$ 85
Same as Model 227, except shotgun barrel is 28-inch, 16 gauge.

Savage Model 229................................$ 85
Same as Model 227, except shotgun barrel is 28-inch, 20 gauge.

Note: Model 219 in 25/20 and 32/20, as well as all models of Utility Gun, discontinued.

Savage Model 6 Autoloading Rifle...............$ 90
Takedown. Caliber, 22 Short, Long, Long Rifle. Tubular magazine holds 21 Short, 17 Long, 15 Long Rifle. 24-inch barrel. Weight, about 6 pounds. Open rear sight, bead front sight. Checkered pistol-grip stock on prewar models, postwar rifles have plain stocks. Made from 1938 to 1968.

Savage Model 6S.................................$ 95
Same as Model 6, except has peep rear sight, bead front sight. Made from 1938 to 1942.

Savage Model 219L

Savage Model 6

Savage Model 60

Savage Model 90

Savage Model 7 Autoloading Rifle.............. $ 90
Same general specifications as Model 6, except has 5-shot detachable box magazine. Made from 1939 to 1951.

Savage Model 7S................................. $ 90
Same as Model 7, except has peep rear sight and hooded front sight. Made from 1938 to 1942.

Savage Model 60 Autoloading Rifle............. $ 70
Caliber, 22 Long Rifle. 15-shot tubular magazine. 20-inch barrel. Weight, 6 pounds. Open rear sight, ramp front sight. Monte Carlo stock of walnut with checkered pistol grip and forearm. Made from 1969 to 1972.

Savage Model 90 Autoloading Carbine.......... $ 75
Similar to Model 60, except has 16½-inch barrel, 10-shot tubular magazine, folding leaf rear sight, bead front sight, carbine-style stock of uncheckered walnut with barrel band and sling swivels; weight, 5¾ pounds. Made from 1969 to 1972.

Savage-Stevens Model 88 Autoloading Rifle..... $ 55
Similar to Model 60, except has walnut-finished hardwood stock, plain bead front sight; weight, 5¾ pounds. Made from 1969 to 1972.

Savage-Stevens Model 80 Autoloading Rifle..... $ 60
Caliber, 22 Long Rifle, 15-shot tubular magazine. 20-inch barrel. Weight, 6 pounds. Open rear sight, bead front sight. Monte Carlo stock of walnut with checkered pistol grip and forearm. Made from 1976 to date. (*Note:* This rifle is essentially the same as Model 60 of 1969-72, except that it has a different style of checkering, side instead of top safety, and plain bead instead of ramp front sight.)

Savage Model 63K Key Lock Bolt Action Single Shot.. $ 55
Trigger locked with key. Caliber, 22 Short, Long, Long Rifle. 18-inch barrel. Weight, 4 pounds. Open rear sight, hooded ramp front sight. Full-length stock with pistol grip, swivels. Made from 1970 to 1972.

Savage Model 63KM............................ $ 60
Same as Model 63K, except chambered for 22 Win. Mag. R.F. Made from 1970 to 1972.

Savage Model 340 Bolt Action Repeating Rifle
Calibers: 22 Hornet, 222 Rem., 223 Rem., 225 Win., 30-30. Clip magazine; 4-shot capacity (3-shot in 30-30). Barrel lenghts: originally 20-inch in 30-30, 22-inch in 22 Hornet; later 22-inch in 30-30, 24-inch in other calibers. Weight, 6½ to 7½ pounds depending upon caliber and vintage. Open rear sight (folding leaf on recent production), ramp front sight. Early models had plain pistol-grip stock; checkered since 1965. Made from 1950 to date. (*Note:* From 1947 to 1950, this was Stevens Model 322 22 Hornet and Model 325 30-30.)
Pre-1965 with plain stock........................... $130
Current model...................................... 155

Savage Model 340C Carbine.................... $130
Same as Model 340, except caliber 30-30, 18½-inch barrel; weight about 6 pounds. Made from 1962 to 1964.

Savage Model 340S Deluxe...................... $150
Same as Model 340, except has checkered stock, screw eyes for sling, peep rear sight and hooded front sight. Made from 1955 to 1960.

Savage Model 342.............................. $130
Designation, 1950 to 1955, of Model 340 22 Hornet.

Savage Model 342S Deluxe...................... $150
Designation, 1950 to 1955, of Model 340S 22 Hornet.

Savage Model 110 Sporter Bolt Action Repeating Rifle.................................... $160
Calibers: 243, 270, 308, 30-06. 4-shot box magazine. 22-inch barrel. Weight, about 6¾ pounds. Open rear sight, ramp front sight. Standard sporter stock with pistol grip, checkered. Made from 1958 to 1963.

Savage-Stevens Model 80

Savage Model 63K

Savage Model 340 Rifle

Savage Model 340C Carbine

Savage Model 110

Savage Model 110MCL

Savage Model 110MC...........................**$175**
Same as Model 110, except has Monte Carlo-style stock. Calibers: 22-250, 243, 270, 308, 30-06. 24-inch barrel in 22-250. Made from 1959 to 1969.

Savage Model 110MCL.........................**$200**
Same as Model 110MC, except has left-hand action. Made from 1959 to 1969.

Savage Model 110M Magnum....................**$210**
Same as Model 110MC, except calibers: 7mm Rem. Mag., 264, 300 and 338 Win. 24-inch barrel. Stock with recoil pad. Weight, 7¾ to 8 pounds. Made from 1963 to 1969.

Savage Model 110ML Magnum..................**$215**
Same as Model 110M Magnum, except has left-hand action.

Savage Model 110E
Calibers: 243 Win., 7.308, 30-06, 4-shot box magazine (3-shot in Magnum). 20- or 22-inch barrel (24-inch stainless steel in Magnum). Weight, 6¾ pounds (Magnum 7¾ pounds). Open rear sight, ramp front sight. Plain Monte Carlo stock on early production; current models have checkered stocks of walnut-finished hardwood (Magnum has recoil pad). Made from 1963 to date.
Caliber 243 Win. or 30-06...........................**$200**
Caliber 7mm Rem. Mag............................. 215

Savage Model 110EL
Same as Model 110E, excpet has left-hand action, made in calibers 30-06 and 7mm Rem. Mag. only. Made from 1969 to 1973.
Caliber 30-06.......................................**$200**
Caliber 7mm Rem. Mag............................. 215

Savage Model 110B.............................**$240**
Similar to Model 110E, except has a select walnut stock with Monte Carlo comb and cheekpiece, checkered, pistol-grip cap. Calibers: 243 Win., 270 Win., 30-06. Made from 1976 to 1979.

Savage Model 110BL............................**$240**
Same as Model 110B, except has left-hand action.

Savage Model 110P Premier Grade
Calibers: 243 Win., 7mm Rem. Mag., 30-06. 4-shot magazine (3-shot in Magnum). 22-inch barrel (24-inch stainless steel in Magnum). Weight, 7 pounds (Magnum 7¾ pounds). Open rear folding leaf sight, ramp front sight. French walnut stock with Monte Carlo comb and cheekpiece, rosewood fore-end tip and pistol-grip cap, skip checkering, sling swivels (Magnum has recoil pad). Made from 1964 to 1970.
Calibers 243 Win. and 30-06........................**$400**
Caliber 7mm Rem. Mag............................. 420

Savage Model 110M

Savage Model 110E

Savage Model 110PL Premier Grade
Same as Model 110P, except has left-hand action.
Calibers 243 Win. and 30-06......................... $400
Caliber 7mm Rem. Mag.............................. 425

Savage Model 110PE Presentation Grade
Same as Model 110P, except has engraved receiver, floorplate and trigger guard, stock of choice grade French walnut. Made from 1968 to 1970.
Calibers 243 and 30-06............................. $670
Caliber 7mm Rem. Mag.............................. 700

Savage Model 110PEL Presentation Grade
Same as Model 110PE, except has left-hand action.
Calibers 243 and 30-06............................. $670
Caliber 7mm Rem. Mag.............................. 695

Savage Model 110C
Calibers: 22-250, 243, 25-06, 270, 308, 30-06, 7mm Rem. Mag. 4-shot detachable clip magazine (3-shot in Magnum calibers). 22-inch barrel (24-inch in 22-250 Magnum calibers). Weight, 6¾ pounds (Magnum 7¾ to 8 pounds). Open rear sight, ramp front sight. Checkered Monte Carlo-style walnut stock (Magnum has recoil pad). Made from 1966 to date.
Standard calibers.................................. $200
Magnum calibers................................... 220

Savage Model 110CL
Same as Model 110C, except has left-hand action. (Only available in 243 Win., 30-06, 270 and 7mm mag.)
Standard calibers.................................. $200
Magnum calibers................................... 220

Savage Model 110D
Similar to Model 110C, except has internal magazine with hinged floorplate. Calibers: 243 Win., 270 Win., 30-06, 7mm Rem. Mag., 300 Win. Mag. Made from 1972 to 1975.
Standard calibers.................................. $200
Magnum calibers................................... 220

Savage Model 110DL
Same as Model 110D, except has left-hand action.
Standard calibers.................................. $200
Magnum calibers................................... 220

Savage Model 111 Chieftain Bolt Action Rifle
Calibers: 243 Win., 270 Win., 7x57mm, 7mm Rem. Mag., 30-06. 4-shot clip magazine (3-shot in magnum). 22-inch barrel (24-inch in magnum). Weight, 7½ pounds (8¼ pounds in magnum). Leaf rear sight, hooded ramp front sight. Select walnut stock with Monte Carlo comb and cheekpiece, checkered, pistol-grip cap, QD swivels and sling. Made from 1974 to 1979.
Standard calibers.................................. $250
Caliber 7mm Rem. Mag.............................. 260

Savage Model 112V Varmint Rifle.............. $230
Bolt action single shot. Calibers: 220 Swift, 222 Rem., 223 Rem., 22-250, 243 Win., 25-06. 26-inch heavy barrel with scope bases. Supplied without sights. Weight, 9¼ pounds. Select walnut stock in varmint style with checkered pistol grip, high comb, QD sling swivels. Made from 1975 to 1979.

Savage Model 170 Pump Action Center Fire Rifle.. $140
Calibers: 30-30, 35 Rem. 3-shot tubular magazine. 22-inch barrel. Weight, 6¾ pounds. Folding leaf rear sight, ramp front sight. Select walnut stock with checkered pistol grip, Monte Carlo comb, grooved slide handle. Made from 1970 to 1981.

Savage Model 110 B

Savage Model 110 BL

Savage Model 110 P

Savage Model 110 PE

Savage Model 110 C

Savage Model 110 CL

Savage Model 110 DL

Savage Model 111

Savage Model 112V

Savage Model 170 Rifle

Savage Model 170C Carbine

Savage/Anschutz Model 64

Savage/Anschutz Mark 10D

Savage/Anschutz Model 54 Sporter

Savage/Anschutz Model 164

Savage Model 170C Carbine..................... **$140**
Same as Model 170 Rifle, except has 18½-inch barrel, straight comb stock, weighs 6 pounds; caliber 30-30 only. Made from 1974 to 1981.

Savage/Anschutz Model 153 Bolt Action Sporting Rifle
.... **$370**
Caliber, 222 Rem. 3-shot clip magazine. 24-inch barrel. Folding leaf open rear sight, hooded ramp front sight. Weight, 6¾ pounds. French walnut stock with cheekpiece, skip checkering, rosewood fore-end tip and grip cap, swivels. Made from 1964 to 1967. (Manufactured for Savage by J. G. Anschutz GmbH, Ulm, West Germany.)

Savage/Anschutz Model 153S.................... **$400**
Same as Model 153, except has double-set trigger. Made from 1965 to 1967.

Savage/Anschutz Model 64 Bolt Action Target Rifle $250
Single shot. Caliber, 22 Long Rifle, 26-inch medium-heavy barrel. Weight, 7¾ pounds. Supplied without sights (add $40 for Anschutz match sight set). Target stock with thumb groove, checkered pistol grip, high comb and cheekpiece, adjustable butt plate, swivel rail. Model 64L has left-hand stock. Made from 1965 to 1981. (*Note:* Same as Anschutz Model 1403)

Savage/Anschutz Mark 10 Bolt Action Target Rifle.. **$240**
Single shot. Caliber 22 Long Rifle. 26-inch barrel. Weight, 8½ pounds. Anschutz micrometer rear sight, globe front sight. Target stock with full pistol grip and cheekpiece, adjustable hand stop and swivel. Made from 1967 to 1972.

Savage/Anschutz Mark 10D..................... **$240**
Same as Mark 10, except has redesigned stock with Monte Carlo comb, different rear sight; weight, 7¾ pounds. Made in 1972.

Savage/Anschutz Model 54 Custom Sporter..... **$300**
Bolt action. Caliber, 22 Long Rifle. 5-shot clip magazine. 24-inch barrel. Weight, 6¾ pounds. Folding leaf rear sight, hooded ramp front sight. Select walnut stock with Monte Carlo comb and rollover cheekpiece, checkered pistol grip and schnabel-type forearm, QD swivel studs. Made from 1969 to 1981. (*Note:* Same as Anschutz Model 1422D)

Savage/Anschutz Model 54M..................... **$470**
Same as Model 54, except chambered for 22 Win. Mag. R.F., 4-shot clip magazine. Made from 1972 to date: (*Note:* Same as Anschutz Model 1522D)

Savage/Anschutz Model 164 Custom Sporter.... $295
Bolt action. Caliber, 22 Long Rifle. 5-shot clip magazine. 23-inch barrel. Weight, 6 pounds. Folding leaf rear sight, hooded ramp front sight. Select walnut stock with Monte Carlo comb and cheekpiece, checkered pistol grip and schnabel-type forearm. Made from 1969 to 1981 (*Note*: Same as Anschutz Model 1416)

Savage/Anschutz Model 164M.................. $300
Same as Model 164, except chambered for 22 Win. Mag. R.F.; 4-shot clip magazine. Made from 1969 to date. (*Note*: Same as Anschutz Model 1516)

Savage/Anschutz Model 184 Sporter........... $225
Bolt action. Caliber, 22 Long Rifle. 5-shot clip magazine. 21½-inch barrel. Weight, 4½ pounds. Folding leaf rear sight, hooded ramp front sight. Monte Carlo stock with checkered pistol grip and schnabel-type forearm. Made from 1972 to 1975. (*Note*: Same as Anschutz Model 1441)

Note: In 1965, Savage began the importation of rifles manufactured by J. G. Anschutz GmbH, Ulm, West Germany. Models designated "Savage/Anschutz" are listed in this section; those marketed in the U.S. under the "Anschutz" name are included in that firm's listings. Anschutz rifles are now distributed in the U.S. by Talco Distributors.

Savage-Stevens Model 35....................... $ 60
Bolt action repeater. Caliber, 22 Long Rifle. 6-shot clip magazine. 22-inch barrel. Weight, about 5 pounds. Open rear sight, ramp front sight. Monte Carlo stock with checkered pistol grip and forearm. Made 1982 to date.

Savage-Stevens Model 35M..................... $ 70
Same as Model 35, except chambered for 22 Win. Mag. R.F. Made from 1982 to date.

Savage-Stevens Model 987-T Autoloading Rifle. $ 70
Caliber, 22 Long Rifle. 15-shot tubular magazine. 20-inch barrel. Weight, 6 pounds. Open rear sight, ramp front sight. Monte Carlo stock with checkered pistol grip and forearm. Made from 1981 to date.

Savage Model 71 "Stevens Favorite" Single Shot Lever Action Rifle....................................... $125
Replica of the original Stevens Favorite issued as a tribute to Joshua Stevens, "Father of 22 Hunting." Caliber, 22 Long Rifle. 22-inch full-octagon barrel. Brass-plated hammer and lever. Open rear sight, brass blade front sight. Weight, 4½ pounds. Plain straight-grip buttstock and schnabel fore-end; brass commemorative medallion inlaid in buttstock, brass crescent-shaped butt plate. 10,000 produced. Made in 1971 only. Value is for new, unfired specimen.

Savage-Stevens Model 72 "Crackshot" Single Shot Lever Action Rifle............................... $ 80
Falling block action. Casehardened frame. Caliber, 22 Short, Long, Long Rifle. 22-inch octagon barrel. Weight, 4½ pounds. Open rear sight, bead front sight. Plain straight-grip stock and forearm of walnut. Made from 1972 to date. (*Note*: Model 72 is a "Favorite" type single shot, unlike the smaller original "Crackshot" made by Stevens 1913-39.)

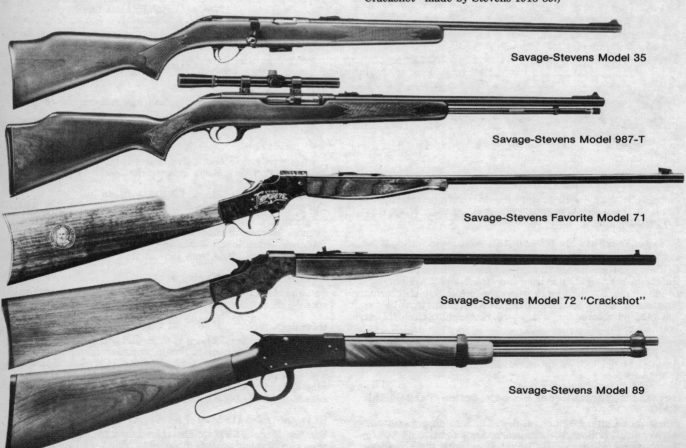

Savage-Stevens Model 35

Savage-Stevens Model 987-T

Savage-Stevens Favorite Model 71

Savage-Stevens Model 72 "Crackshot"

Savage-Stevens Model 89

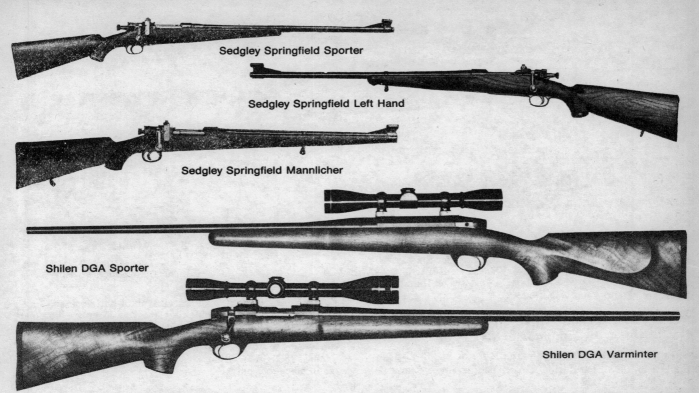

Sedgley Springfield Sporter

Sedgley Springfield Left Hand

Sedgley Springfield Mannlicher

Shilen DGA Sporter

Shilen DGA Varminter

Savage-Stevens Model 74 "Little Favorite"......$ 80
Same as Model 72 "Crackshot," except has black-finished frame, 22-inch round barrel, walnut-finished hardwood stock; weight, 4¾ pounds. Made from 1972 to 1974.

Savage-Stevens Model 89 Single Shot Lever Action Carbine...$ 50
Martini-type action. Caliber, 22 Short, Long, Long Rifle. 18½-inch barrel. Weight, 5 pounds. Open rear sight, bead front sight. Western-style carbine stock with straight grip, forearm with barrel band. Made from 1976 to date.

V. C. Schilling, Suhl, Germany

Schilling Mauser-Mannlicher Bolt Action Sporting Rifle...$350
Same general specifications as given for the Haenel Mauser-Mannlicher Sporter.

Schilling '88 Mauser Sporter.....................$350
Same general specifications as Haenel '88 Mauser Sporter.

Schultz & Larsen Gevaerfabrik, Otterup, Denmark

Schultz & Larsen Match Rifle No. 47............$560
Caliber, 22 Long Rifle. Bolt action single shot, set trigger. 28½-inch heavy barrel. Weight, about 14 pounds. Micrometer receiver sight, globe front sight. Free-rifle stock with cheekpiece, thumb hole, adjustable Schuetzen-type butt plate, swivels, palm-rest.

Schultz & Larsen Free Rifle Model 54..........$700
Calibers: 6.5x55mm or any standard American centerfire caliber. Schultz & Larsen M54 bolt action, single shot, set trigger. 27½-inch heavy barrel. Weight, about 15½ pounds. Micrometer receiver sight, globe front sight. Free-rifle stock with cheekpiece, thumb hole, adjustable Schuetzen-type butt plate, swivels, palm-rest.

Schultz & Larsen Model 54J Sporting Rifle......$600
Calibers: 270 Win., 30-06, 7x61 Sharpe & Hart. Schultz & Larsen bolt action. 3-shot magazine. 24-inch barrel in 270 and 30-06, 26-inch in 7x61 S&H. Checkered stock with Monte Carlo comb and cheekpiece. Value shown is for rifle less sights.

R. F. Sedgley, Inc., Philadelphia, Pennsylvania

Sedgley Springfield Sporter.....................$400
Springfield '03 bolt action. Calibers: 220 Swift, 218 Bee, 22-3000, R2, 22-4000, 22 Hornet, 25-35, 250-3000, 257 Roberts, 270 Win., 7mm, 30-06. 24-inch barrel. Weight, 7½ pounds. Lyman No. 48 receiver sight, bead front sight on matted ramp. Checkered walnut stock, grip cap, sling swivels. Discontinued 1941.

Sedgley Springfield Left-Hand Sporter..........$430
Bolt action reversed for left-handed shooter. Otherwise the same as the standard Sedgley Springfield Sporter.

Sedgley Springfield Mannlicher-Type Sporter...$460
Same as the standard Sedgley Springfield Sporter except, has 20-inch barrel, Mannlicher-type full stock with cheekpiece, weighs 7¾ pounds.

Shilen Rifles, Inc., Ennis, Texas

Shilen DGA Sporter..............................$530
DGA bolt action. Calibers: 17 Rem., 222 Rem., 223 Rem., 22-250, 220 Swift, 6mm Rem., 243 Win., 250 Sav., 257 Roberts, 284 Win., 308 Win., 358 Win. 3-shot blind magazine. 24-inch barrel. Average weight, 7½ pounds. No sights. Selected Claro walnut stock with cheekpiece, pistol grip, sling swivel studs. Currently manufactured.

Shilen DGA Varminter..........................$525
Same as Sporter, except has 25-inch medium-heavy barrel; average weight, 9 pounds.

Shilen DGA Benchrest Rifle.....................$595
DGA single-shot bolt action. Calibers as listed for Sporter. 26-inch medium-heavy or heavy barrel. Weight, from 10½ pounds. No sights. Fiberglass or walnut stock, classic or thumb-hole pattern. Currently manufactured.

Shiloh Arms Company
Farmingdale, N.Y.

Shiloh New Model 1863 Sharps Rifle........... $400
Replica of 1863 Sharps rifle. Breechloading single shot rifle.

Shilen DGA Benchrest Rifle

Calibers, 50 and 54. 30-inch barrel. Walnut buttstock and forearm. Color casehardened patchbox, receiver, lockplate, hammer and buttplate. Barrel finish is blue-black. Weight, 8¾ pounds.

Shiloh New Model 1863 Sharps Carbine........ $310
Same as 1863 Sharps Rifle, except has 22-inch barrel and available in 50 caliber only.

Shiloh 1863 Sharps Rifle

Shiloh 1863 Sharps Carbine

SIG Swiss Industrial Company,
Neuhausen-Rhine Falls, Switzerland

SIG AMT Sporting Rifle.........................$725
Semiautomatic version of SG510-4 automatic assault rifle based on Swiss Army StGW57. Roller-delayed blowback action. Caliber, 7.62x51mm NATO (308 Win.). 5-, 10-, and 20-round magazines. 19-inch barrel. Weight, about 10 pounds. Aperture rear sight, post front sight. Wood buttstock and forearm, folding bipod. Made from 1960 to 1974.

SIG AMT

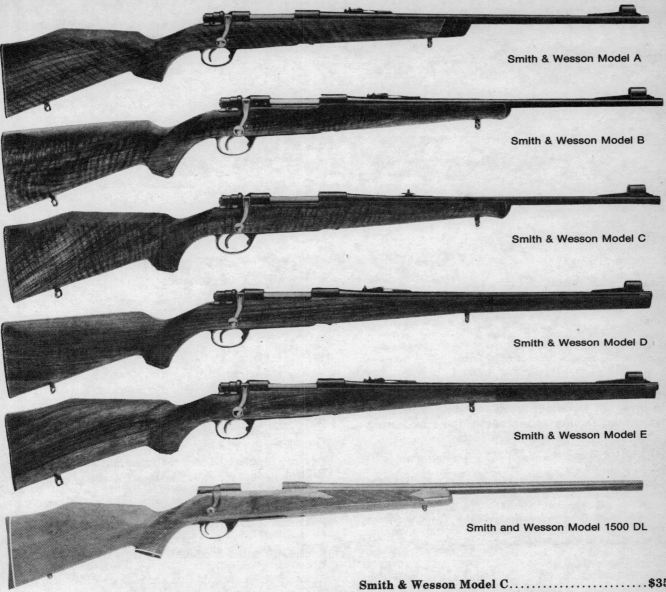

Smith & Wesson Model A

Smith & Wesson Model B

Smith & Wesson Model C

Smith & Wesson Model D

Smith & Wesson Model E

Smith and Wesson Model 1500 DL

Smith & Wesson Rifles manufactured for Smith & Wesson, Springfield, Massachusetts, by Husqvarna Vapenfabrik A.B., Huskvarna, Sweden

Smith & Wesson Model A Bolt-Action Sporting Rifle **$375**
Similar to Husqvarna Model 9000 Crown Grade. Mauser-type bolt action. Calibers: 22-250, 243 Win., 270 Win., 308 Win., 30-06, 7mm Rem. Mag., 300 Win. Mag. 5-shot magazine, except in latter two calibers for which magazine capacity is 3 rounds. 23¾-inch barrel. Weight, about 7 pounds. Folding leaf rear sight, hooded ramp front sight. Checkered walnut stock with Monte Carlo cheekpiece, rosewood fore-end tip and pistol-grip cap, swivels. Made from 1969 to 1972.

Smith & Wesson Model B **$350**
Same as Model A, except has 20¾-inch extra-light barrel, Monte Carlo cheekpiece with schnabel-style forearm, weighs about 6 lbs. 10 oz. Calibers: 243 Win., 30-06.

Smith & Wesson Model C **$350**
Same as Model B, except has cheekpiece stock with straight comb.

Smith & Wesson Model D **$400**
Same as Model C, except has full-length forearm (Mannlicher-style.)

Smith & Wesson Model E **$400**
Same as Model B, except has full-length forearm (Mannlicher-style.)

Smith & Wesson Model 1500 . . . . **$200**
Bolt action. Calibers: 243 Win., 270 Win., 30-06, 7mm Rem. Mag. 22-inch barrel (24-inch in 7mm Rem. Mag.) Weight, about 7½ pounds. American walnut stock with Monte Carlo comb and cheekpiece, cut checkering. Open rear sight, hooded ramp gold bead front. Introduced in 1979.

Smith & Wesson Model 1500 Deluxe **$225**
Same as standard Model, except without sights; has engine-turned bolt, decorative scroll on floorplate, French checkering.

Springfield Armory M1A

Squires Bingham Model 14D

Squires Bingham Model 15

Springfield Armory, Geneseo, Illinois; this is a private firm, not to be confused with the former U.S. Government facility of the same name in Springfield, Massachusetts

Springfield Armory Standard M1A Semiautomatic Rifle

Gas-operated. Similar to U.S. M14 service rifle, except has no provision for automatic firing. Caliber, 7.65mm NATO (308 Win.). 5-, 10-, or 20-round detachable box magazine. 25-1/16-inch barrel with flash suppressor. Weight, about 9 pounds. Adjustable aperture rear sight, blade front sight. Fiberglass, birch or walnut stock, fiberglass hand guard, sling swivels. Made from 1974 to date.
With fiberglass or birch stock........................ **$700**
With walnut stock................................. **800**

Springfield Armory Match M1A................. **$1000**
Same as Standard M1A, except has National Match grade barrel with modified flash suppressor, National Match sights, turned trigger pull, gas system assembly in one unit, modified mainspring guide, glass-bedded walnut stock.

Springfield Armory Super Match M1A......... **$1200**
Same as Match M1A, except has heavier barrel of premium grade, weighs about 10 pounds.

Squires Bingham Co., Inc., Makati, Rizal, Philippines

Squires Bingham Model 14D Deluxe Bolt Action Repeating Rifle....................................... **$ 60**
Caliber, 22 Long Rifle. 5-shot box magazine. 24-inch barrel. V-notch rear sight, hooded ramp front sight. Receiver grooved for scope mounting. Pulong Dalaga stock with contrasting fore-end tip and grip cap, checkered forearm and pistol grip. Weight, about 6 pounds. Currently manufactured.

Squires Bingham Model 15.......................**$ 70**
Same as Model 14D, except chambered for 22 Magnum R.F. Currently manufactured.

Squires Bingham Model M16 Semiautomatic Rifle... **$ 90**
Styled after U.S. M16 military rifle. Caliber, 22 Long Rifle. 15-shot box magazine. 19½-inch barrel with muzzle brake/flash hider. Rear sight in carrying handle, post front on high ramp. Black-painted mahogany buttstock and forearm. Weight, about 6½ pounds. Currently manufactured.

Squires Bingham Model M20D Deluxe Semiautomatic Rifle... **$ 90**
Caliber, 22 Long Rifle. 15-shot box magazine. 19½-inch barrel with muzzle brake/flash hider. V-notch rear sight, blade front sight. Receiver grooved for scope mounting. Pulong Dalaga stock with contrasting fore-end tip and grip cap, checkered forearm and pistol grip. Weight, about 6 pounds. Currently manufactured.

Standard Arms Company, Wilmington, Delaware

Standard Model G Automatic Rifle............... **$375**
Gas-operated. Autoloading. Hammerless. Takedown. Calibers: 25-35, 30-30, 25 Rem., 30 Rem., 35 Rem. Magazine capacity: 4 rounds in 35 Rem., 5 rounds in other calibers. 22⅜-inch barrel. Weight, about 7¾ pounds. Open sporting rear sight, ivory bead front sight. Shotgun-type stock. Made c. 1910. *Note:* This was the first gas-operated rifle manufactured in the U.S. While essentially an autoloader, the gas port can be closed and the rifle operated as a slide action repeater.

Standard Model M Hand-Operated Rifle........ **$240**
Slide action repeater with same general specifications as Model G, except lacks autoloading feature; weight, about 7 pounds.

Squires Bingham Model M16

Squires Bingham Model M20D

Standard Model G

Star Rolling Block

Star, Bonifacio Echeverria, S.A., Eibar, Spain

Star Rolling Block Carbine........................ **$160**
Single-shot action similar to Remington Rolling Block. Calibers: 30-30, 357 Mag., 44 Mag. 20-inch barrel. Weight, about 6 pounds. Folding leaf rear sight, ramp front sight. Walnut straight-grip stock with crescent butt plate, forearm with barrel band. Made from 1973 to 1975.

J. Stevens Arms Company, Chicopee Falls, Massachusetts; now a division of Savage Arms Corporation

Stevens "Ideal" No. 44 Single Shot Rifle........ **$370**
Rolling block. Lever Action. Takedown. Calibers: 22 Long Rifle, 25 R.F., 32 R.F., 25-20 S.S., 32-20, 32-40, 38-40, 38-55, 44-40. Barrel lengths: 24-inch, 26-inch (round, half-octagon, full-octagon). Weight, about 7 pounds with 26-inch round barrel. Open rear sight, Rocky Mountain front sight. Plain straight-grip stock and forearm. Made from 1894 to 1932.

Stevens "Ideal" No. 44½ Single Shot Rifle....... **$500**
Falling-block lever action. Aside from the new design action introduced in 1903, the specifications of this model are the same as those of Model 44. The Model 44½ was discontinued about 1916.

Stevens "Ideal" Single Shot Rifles No. 45 to 54

These are the higher grade models, differing from the standard No. 44 and No. 44½ chiefly in finish, engraving, set triggers, levers, barrels, stocks, etc. The Schuetzen types (including the "Stevens-Pope" models) are in this series. Model Nos. 45 to 54 were introduced about 1896 and originally had the No. 44-type rolling-block action which was superseded in 1903 by the No. 44½-type falling-block action. These models were all discontinued about 1916. Generally speaking the 45-54 series rifles, particularly the "Stevens-Pope" and higher grade Schuetzen models, are collector's items bringing very much higher prices than the ordinary No. 44 and 44½.

Stevens "Favorite" No. 17 Single Shot Rifle..... **$125**
Lever action. Takedown. Calibers: 22 Long Rifle, 25 R.F., 32 R.F. 24-inch round barrel, other lengths were available. Weight, about 4½ pounds. Open rear sight, Rocky Mountain front sight. Plain straight-grip stock, small tapered forearm. Made from 1894 to 1935.

Stevens "Favorite" No. 18......................... **$175**
Same as No. 17 except has Vernier peep rear sight, leaf middle sight, Beach combination front sight.

Stevens "Favorite" No. 19......................... **$180**
Same as No. 17 except has Lyman combination rear sight, leaf sight, Lyman front sight.

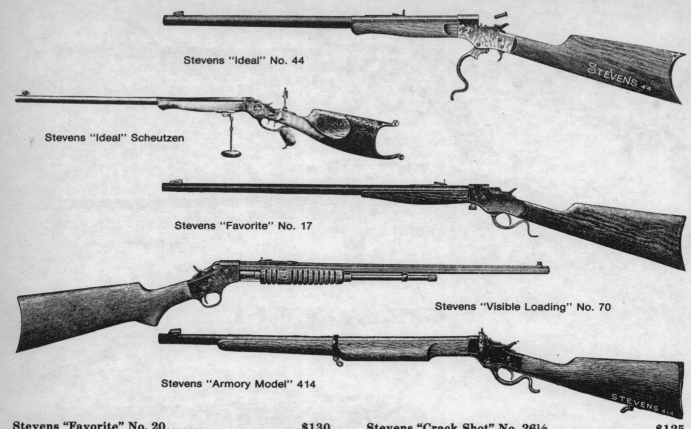

Stevens "Ideal" No. 44

Stevens "Ideal" Scheutzen

Stevens "Favorite" No. 17

Stevens "Visible Loading" No. 70

Stevens "Armory Model" 414

Stevens "Favorite" No. 20........................$130
Same as No. 17, except has smoothbore barrel for 22 R.F. and 32 R.F. shot cartridges.

Stevens "Favorite" No. 27........................$175
Same as No. 17, except has octagon barrel.

Stevens "Favorite" No. 28........................$205
Same as No. 18, except has octagon barrel.

Stevens "Favorite" No. 29........................$200
Same as No. 19, except has octagon barrel.

Stevens "Visible Loading" No. 70 Slide Action Repeating Rifle... $140
Exposed hammer. Caliber, 22 Long Rifle, Long, Short. Tubular magazine holds 11 Long Rifle, 13 Long, 15 Short. 22-inch barrel. Weight, about 4½ pounds. Open rear sight, bead front sight. Plain straight-grip stock, grooved slide handle. Made from 1907 to 1934. *Note:* Nos. 70½, 71, 71½, 72, 72½ are essentially the same as No. 70, differing chiefly in barrel length or sight equipment.

Stevens "Armory Model" No. 414 Single Shot Rifle... $325
No. 44-type lever action. Calibers: 22 Long Rifle only. 22 Short only. 26-inch barrel. Weight, about 8 pounds. Lyman receiver peep sight, blade front sight. Plain straight-grip stock, military-type forearm, swivels. Made from 1912 to 1932.

Stevens "Crack Shot" No. 26 Single Shot Rifle.. $135
Lever action. Takedown. Calibers: 22 Long Rifle, 32 R.F. 18-inch or 22-inch barrel. Weight, about 3¼ pounds. Open rear sight, blade front sight. Plain straight-grip stock, small tapered forearm. Made from 1913 to 1939.

Stevens "Crack Shot" No. 26½....................$125
Same as No. 26, except has smoothbore barrel for shot cartridges.

Stevens "Marksman" No. 12 Single Shot Rifle... $100
Lever action, tip-up. Takedown. Calibers: 22 Long Rifle, 25 R.F., 32 R.F. 22-inch barrel. Plain straight-grip stock, small tapered forearm.

Stevens "Little Scout" No. 14½ Single Shot Rifle... $ 85
Rolling block. Takedown. Caliber, 22 Long Rifle. 18- or 20-inch barrel. Weight, about 2¾ pounds. Open rear sight, blade front sight. Plain straight-grip stock, small tapered forearm.

Stevens No. 66 Bolt Action Repeating Rifle...... $ 45
Takedown. Caliber, 22 Short, Long, Long Rifle. Tubular magazine holds 13 Long Rifle, 15 Long, 19 Short. 24-inch barrel. Weight, about 5 pounds. Open rear sight, bead front sight. Plain pistol-grip stock with grooved forearm. Made from 1931 to 1935.

Stevens "Junior Target Model" No. 419 Bolt Action Single Shot Rifle................................$ 50
Takedown. Caliber, 22 Long Rifle. 26-inch barrel. Weight, about 5½ pounds. Lyman No. 55 rear peep sight, blade front sight. Plain junior target stock with pistol grip and grooved forearm, swivels, sling. Made from 1932 to 1936.

Stevens "Walnut Hill" No. 417-0 Single Shot Target Rifle... $500
Lever action. Calibers: 22 Long Rifle only, 22 Short only, 22 Hornet. 28-inch heavy barrel (extra heavy 29-inch barrel also available). Weight, about 10½ pounds. Lyman 52L extension rear sight, 17A front sight, scope bases. Target stock with full pistol grip, beavertail forearm, barrel band, swivels, sling. Made from 1932 to 1947.

Stevens "Crackshot" No. 26

Stevens "Marksman" No. 12

Stevens "Little Scout" No. 14½

Stevens No. 66

Stevens No. 419

Stevens "Walnut Hill" No. 417-1

Stevens "Walnut Hill" No. 417-2

Stevens "Walnut Hill" No. 417½

Stevens "Walnut Hill" No. 418

Stevens "Walnut Hill" No. 418½

Stevens "Walnut Hill" No. 417-1................ **$500**
Same as No. 417-0, except has Lyman 48L receiver sight.

Stevens "Walnut Hill" No. 417-2................ **$500**
Same as No. 417-0, except has Lyman No. 144 tang sight.

Stevens "Walnut Hill" No. 417-3................ **$475**
Same as No. 417-0, except without sights.

Stevens "Walnut Hill" No. 417½ Single Shot Rifle... **$500**
Lever action. Calibers: 22 Long Rifle, 22 W.R.F., 25 R.F., 22 Hornet. 28-inch barrel. Weight, about 8½ pounds. Lyman No. 144 tang peep sight, folding middle sight, bead front sight. Sporting stock with pistol grip, semi-beavertail forearm, swivels, sling. Made from 1932 to 1940.

Stevens "Walnut Hill" No. 418 Single Shot Rifle. $290
Lever action. Takedown. Calibers: 22 Long Rifle only, 22 Short only. 26-inch barrel. Weight, about 6½ pounds. Lyman No. 144 tang peep sight, blade front sight. Pistol-grip stock, semi-beavertail forearm, swivels, sling. Made from 1932 to 1940.

Stevens "Walnut Hill" No. 418½................ **$270**
Same as No. 418, except also available in calibers 22 W.R.F. and 25 Stevens R.F., has Lyman No. 2A tang peep sight, bead front sight.

Stevens "Buckhorn" Model 053 Bolt Action Single Shot Rifle.. **$ 40**
Takedown. Calibers: 22 Short, Long, Long Rifle, 22 W.R.F., 25 Stevens R.F. 24-inch barrel. Weight, about 5½ pounds. Receiver peep sight, open middle sight, hooded front sight. Sporting stock with pistol grip and black fore-end tip. Made from 1935 to 1948.

Stevens "Buckhorn" Model 53................... **$ 35**
Same as "Buckhorn" Model 053, except has open rear sight and plain bead front sight.

Stevens Model 053

Stevens Model 056

Stevens Model 066

Stevens-Springfield Model 82

Stevens-Springfield Model 83

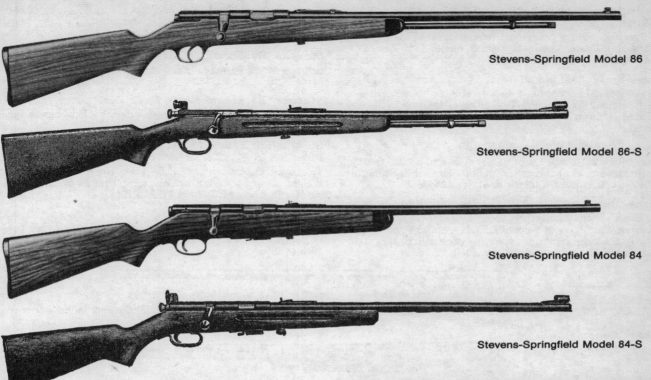

Stevens-Springfield Model 86

Stevens-Springfield Model 86-S

Stevens-Springfield Model 84

Stevens-Springfield Model 84-S

Stevens "Buckhorn" Model 056 Bolt Action Repeating Rifle .... **$ 45**
Takedown. Caliber, 22 Long Rifle, Long, Short. 5-shot detachable box magazine. 24-inch barrel. Weight, about 6 pounds. Receiver peep sight, open middle sight, hooded front sight. Sporting stock with pistol grip and black fore-end tip. Made from 1935 to 1948.

Stevens "Buckhorn" Model 56 .... **$ 40**
Same as "Buckhorn" Model 056, except has open rear sight and plain bead front sight.

Stevens "Buckhorn" Model 066 Bolt Action Repeating Rifle .... **$ 65**
Takedown. Caliber, 22 Long Rifle, Long, Short. Tubular magazine holds 21 Short, 17 Long, 15 Long Rifle. 24-inch barrel. Weight, about 6 pounds. Receiver peep sight, open middle sight, hooded front sight. Sporting stock with pistol grip and black fore-end tip. Made from 1935 to 1948.

Stevens "Buckhorn" Model 66 .... **$ 40**
Same as "Buckhorn" Model 066, except has open rear sight, plain bead front sight.

Stevens-Springfield Model 82 Bolt Action Single Shot Rifle .... **$ 30**
Takedown. Caliber, 22 Long Rifle, Long, Short. 22-inch barrel. Weight, about 4 pounds. Open rear sight, gold bead front sight. Plain pistol-grip stock with grooved forearm. Made from 1935 to 1939.

Stevens-Springfield Model 83 Bolt Action Single Shot Rifle .... **$ 30**
Takedown. Calibers: 22 Long Rifle, Long, Short; 22 W.R.F., 25 Stevens R.F. 24-inch barrel. Weight, about 4½ pounds. Peep rear sight, open middle sight, hooded front sight. Plain pistol-grip stock with grooved forearm. Made from 1935 to 1939.

Stevens-Springfield Model 86 Bolt Action Repeating Rifle .... **$ 45**
Takedown. Caliber, 22 Long Rifle, Long, Short. Tubular magazine holds 15 Long Rifle, 17 Long, 21 Short. 24-inch barrel. Weight, about 6 pounds. Open rear sight, gold bead front sight. Pistol-grip stock, black fore-end tip on current production. Made from 1935 to 1965. *Note:* This model originally bore the "Springfield" brand name which was discontinued in 1948.

Stevens-Springfield Model 86-S (086) .... **$ 45**
Same as Model 86, except has peep rear sight and hooded front sight. Pre-1948 rifles of this model were designated as Springfield Model 086, later known as Stevens Model 86-S. Discontinued.

Stevens-Springfield Model 84 .... **$ 45**
Same as Model 86, except has 5-shot detachable box magazine. Pre-1948 rifles of this model were designated as Springfield Model 84, later known as Stevens Model 84. Made from 1940 to 1965.

Stevens-Springfield Model 84-S (084) .... **$ 45**
Same as Model 84, except has peep rear sight and hooded front sight. Pre-1948 rifles of this model were designated as Springfield Model 084, later known as Stevens Model 84-S. Discontinued.

Stevens Model 416 Bolt Action Target Rifle **$150**
Caliber, 22 Long Rifle. 5-shot detachable box magazine. 26-inch heavy barrel. Weight, about 9½ pounds. Receiver peep sight, hooded front sight. Target stock, swivels, sling. Made from 1937 to 1949.

Stevens Model 87 Autoloading Rifle .... **$ 60**
Takedown. Caliber, 22 Long Rifle. 15-shot tubular magazine. 24-inch barrel (20-inch on current model). Weight, about 6 pounds. Open rear sight, bead front sight. Pistol-grip stock. Made from 1938 to date. *Note:* This model originally bore the "Springfield" brand name which was discontinued in 1948.

Stevens-Springfield Model 87-S (087).......... **$ 60**
Same as Model 87, except has peep rear sight and hooded front sight. Pre-1948 rifles of this model were designated as Springfield Model 087, later known as Stevens Model 87-S. Discontinued.

Stevens-Springfield Model 85.................... **$ 60**
Same as Model 87, except has 5-shot detachable box magazine. Made from 1939 to date. Pre-1948 rifles of this model were designated as Springfield Model 85, currently known as Stevens Model 85.

Stevens-Springfield Model 85-S (085).......... **$ 60**
Same as Model 85, except has peep rear sight and hooded front sight. Pre-1948 rifles of this model were designated as Springfield Model 085, currently known as Stevens Model 85-S.

Stevens "Buckhorn" No. 076 Autoloading Rifle.. **$ 55**
Takedown. Caliber, 22 Long Rifle. 15-shot tubular magazine. 24-inch barrel. Weight, about 6 pounds. Receiver peep sight, open middle sight, hooded front sight. Sporting stock with pistol grip, black fore-end tip. Made from 1938 to 1948.

Stevens "Buckhorn" No. 76.................... **$ 40**
Same as "Buckhorn" No. 076, except has open rear sight, plain bead front sight.

Stevens "Buckhorn" No. 57.................... **$ 40**
Same as Model 76, except has 5-shot detachable box magazine. Made from 1939 to 1948.

Stevens "Buckhorn" No. 057.................... **$ 40**
Same as Model 076, except has 5-shot detachable box magazine. Made from 1939 to 1948.

Stevens-Springfield Model 15 Single Shot Bolt Action Rifle.. **$ 30**
Takedown. Caliber, 22 Long Rifle, Long, Short. 22-inch barrel. Weight, about 4 pounds. Open rear sight, bead front sight. Plain pistol-grip stock. Made from 1937 to 1948.

Stevens Model 15................................ **$ 35**
Same as Stevens-Springfield Model 15, except has 24-inch barrel, weighs about 5 pounds, has redesigned stock. Made from 1948 to 1965.

Stevens Model 416
Stevens Model 87
Stevens-Springfield Model 85
Stevens No. 076
Stevens-Springfield Model 15

Stevens Youth's Model 15Y.................... **$ 40**
Same as Model 15, except has 21-inch barrel, short butt-stock, weighs about 4¾ pounds. Made from 1958 to 1965.

Stevens Model 322 Hi-Power Bolt Action Carbine.. **$125**
Caliber, 22 Hornet. 4-shot detachable box magazine. 21-inch barrel. Weight, about 6¾ pounds. Open rear sight, ramp front sight. Pistol-grip stock. Made from 1947 to 1950. (See Savage Models 340, 342).

Stevens Model 322-S............................ **$125**
Same as Model 325, except has peep rear sight. (See Savage Models 340S, 342S).

Stevens Model 325 Hi-Power Bolt Action Carbine.. **$110**
Caliber, 30-30. 3-shot detachable box magazine. 21-inch barrel. Weight, about 6¾ pounds. Open rear sight, bead front sight. Plain pistol-grip stock. Made from 1947 to 1950. (See Savage Model 340).

Stevens Model 325-S............................ **$120**
Same as Model 325, except has peep rear sight. (See Savage Model 340S).

Note: "Stevens" brand name is still used for some models by Savage Arms. See listings as "Savage-Stevens" in Savage section.

Stevens Youth's Model 15Y

Steyr Small Bore Carbine

Thompson Standard Model 27A-1

Thompson Deluxe Model 27A-1

Steyr-Daimler-Puch A.-G., Steyr, Austria (see listings under "Mannlicher")

Steyr Small Bore Carbine **$350**
Bolt action repeater. Caliber, 22 Long Rifle. 5-shot detachable box magazine. 19½-inch barrel. Leaf rear sight, hooded bead front sight. Mannlicher-type stock, checkered, swivels. Made from 1953 to 1967.

Stoeger Rifle made by Franz Jaeger & Co., Suhl, Germany, and distributed in the U.S. by A. F. Stoeger, Inc., New York City

Stoeger Hornet Rifle **$900**
Same as Herold Rifle. See listing of that rifle for specifications. Imported during the 1930's.

Thompson Carbines manufactured by Auto-Ordnance Corporation, West Hurley, New York

Thompson Standard Model 27A-1 Semiautomatic Carbine **$325**
Similar to Thompson submachine gun ("Tommy Gun"), except has no provision for automatic firing. Caliber, 45 Automatic. 20-shot detachable box magazine (5-, 15- and 30-shot box magazines, 39-shot drum also available). 16-inch plain barrel. Weight, about 14 pounds. Aperture rear sight, blade front sight. Walnut buttstock, pistol grip and grooved forearm, sling swivels. Made from 1976 to date.

Thompson Deluxe Model 27A-1 . . . . **$400**
Same as Standard Model 27A-1, except has finned barrel with compensator, adjustable rear sight, pistol-grip fore-stock, weighs about 15 pounds. Made from 1976 to date.

Thompson Model 22-27A-3 . . . . **$380**
Smallbore version of Deluxe Model 27A-1. Same general specifications, except caliber 22 Long Rifle, has lightweight alloy receiver, weighs about 6½ pounds; magazines include 5-, 20-, 30- and 50-shot box types, 80-shot drum. Introduced in 1977.

Tikka Rifles manufactured by Oy Tikkakoski AB, Tikkakoski, Finland

Tikka LSA55 Standard Bolt Action Repeating Rifle **$305**
Mauser type action. Calibers: 222 Rem., 22-250, 6mm Rem. Mag., 243 Win., 308 Win. 3-shot clip magazine. 22.8-inch barrel. Weight, 6.8 pounds. Folding leaf rear sight, hooded ramp front sight. Checkered walnut stock with Monte Carlo cheekpiece, swivels. Made from 1965 to date.

Tikka LSA55 Deluxe **$330**
Same as LSA55 Standard, except has roll-over cheekpiece, rosewood grip cap and fore-end tip, skip checkering, high-lustre blue. Made from 1965 to date.

Tikka LSA55 Sporter **$350**
Same as LSA55, except not available in 6mm Rem., has 22.8-inch heavy barrel, no sights, special stock with beavertail fore-arm, weighs about 9 pounds. Made from 1965 to date.

Tikka LSA55 Deluxe

Tikka LSA65 Deluxe

Tikka LSA65 Standard **$300**
Same as LSA55 Standard, except calibers: 25-06, 6.5x55, 270
Win., 30-06. 5-shot magazine, 22-inch barrel, weighs 7½ pounds.
Made from 1970 to date.

Tikka LSA65 Deluxe **$350**
Same as LSA65 Standard, except has special features of LSA55
Deluxe. Made from 1970 to date.

Note: Similar rifles manufactured by Oy Tikkakoski AB are
marketed in the U.S.A. as Ithaca-LSA.

Ultra-Hi Products Company, Hawthorne, New Jersey

Ultra-Hi Model 2200 Single Shot Bolt Action Rifle
.... **$ 35**
Caliber, 22 Long Rifle, Long, Short. 23-inch barrel. Weight,
about 5 pounds. Open rear sight, blade front sight. Monte Carlo
stock with pistol grip. Made in Japan. Introduced in 1977.

Unique Rifle manufactured by Manufacture d'Armes des Pyrénées Françaises, Hendaye, France

Unique T66 Match Rifle **$525**
Single-shot bolt action. Caliber, 22 Long Rifle. 25½-inch barrel.
Weight, about 10½ pounds. Micrometer aperture rear sight,
globe front sight. French walnut target stock with Monte Carlo
comb, bull pistol grip, wide and deep forearm, stippled grip
surfaces, adjustable swivel on accessory track, adjustable rubber
butt plate. Made from 1966 to date.

U.S. Military Rifles manufactured at Springfield Armory, Springfield, Massachusetts

U.S. Model 1898 Krag-Jorgensen Military Rifle. **$275**
Bolt action. Caliber, 30-40 Krag. 5-shot hinged box magazine.
30-inch barrel. Weight, about 9 pounds. Adjustable rear sight,
blade front sight. Military-type stock, straight grip. *Note:* The
foregoing specifications apply, in general, to Rifle Models 1892
and 1896 which differed from Model 1898 only in minor details.
Made from 1894 to 1904.

Ultra-Hi Model 2200

Unique T66 Match

U.S. Model 1898 Krag Rifle

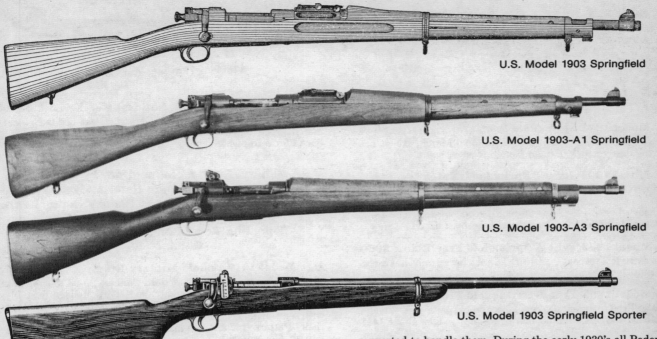

U.S. Model 1903 Springfield

U.S. Model 1903-A1 Springfield

U.S. Model 1903-A3 Springfield

U.S. Model 1903 Springfield Sporter

U.S. Model 1898 Krag-Jorgensen Carbine....... $295

Same general specifications as Model 1898 Rifle, except has 22-inch barrel, weighs about 8 pounds, carbine-type stock. *Note:* The foregoing specifications apply, in general, to Carbine Models 1896 and 1899 which differed from Model 1898 only in minor details.

U.S. Model 1903 Springfield Military Rifle

Modified Mauser-type bolt action. Caliber, 30-06. 5-shot box magazine. 23.79-inch barrel. Weight, about 8¾ pounds. Adjustable rear sight, blade front sight. Military-type stock, straight grip. *Note:* M/1903 rifles of Springfield manufacture with serial numbers under 800,000 (1903-1918) have casehardened receivers, those between 800,000 and 1,275,767 (1918-1927) were double-heat-treated, rifles numbered over 1,275,767 have nickel-steel bolts and receivers; Rock Island production from No. 1 to 285,507 have case-hardened receivers improved heat treatment was adopted in May 1918 with No. 285,207, about three months later with No. 319,921 the use of nickel steel was begun, but the production of some double-heat-treated carbon-steel receivers and bolts continued. Made from 1903 to 1930 at Springfield Armory; during World War I, M/1903 rifles were also made at Rock Island Arsenal, Rock Island, Ill.
With casehardened receiver........................... $150
With double-heat-treated receiver................... 175
With nickel steel reciever.......................... 200

U.S. Model 1903 Mark I Springfield............. $200

Same as Model 1903, except altered to permit use of the Pedersen Device. This device, officially designated as "U.S. Automatic Pistol Model 1918," converted the M/1903 to a semiautomatic weapon firing a 30 caliber cartridge similar to the 32 automatic pistol ammunition. The Mark I rifles have a slot milled in the left side of the receiver to serve as an ejection port when the Pedersen Device was in use, these rifles were also fitted with a special sear and cut-off. Some 65,000 of these devices were manufactured and presumably a like number of M/1903 rifles

converted to handle them. During the early 1930's all Pedersen Devices were ordered destroyed and the Mark I rifles were reconverted by replacement of the special sear and cut-off with standard components. Some 20-odd specimens are known to have escaped destruction and are in government museums and private collections. Probably more are extant. Rarely is a Pedersen Device offered for sale and so a current value cannot be assigned. However, many of the altered rifles were purchased by members of the National Rifle Association through the Director of Civilian Marksmanship. Value shown is for the Mark I rifle without the Pedersen Device.

U.S. Model 1903-A1 Springfield

Same general specifications as M-1903, except may have Type C pistol-grip stock adopted in 1930. The last Springfields produced at the Springfield Armory were of this type, final serial number was 1,532,878 made in 1939. *Note:* Late in 1941, the Remington Arms Company, Ilion, N.Y., began production under government contract of Springfield rifles of this type with a few minor modifications. These rifles are numbered from 3,000,001 to 3,348,085 and were manufactured prior to the adoption of Model 1903-A3.
Springfield manufacture.............................. $235
Remington manufacture............................. 200

U.S. Model 1903-A3 Springfield.................$180

Same general specifications as Model 1903-A1, except modified to permit increased production and lower cost, may have either straight-grip or pistol-grip stock, bolt is not interchangeable with earlier types, has receiver peep sight, many parts are stamped sheet steel including the trigger guard and magazine assembly. Quality of these rifles, lower than that of other M/1903 Springfields, reflects the emergency conditions under which they were produced. Manufactured during World War II by Remington Arms Co. and L. C. Smith Corona Typewriters, Inc.

U.S. Model 1903 National Match Springfield.....$600

Same general specifications as the standard Model 1903, except specially selected with star-gauged barrel, Type C pistol-grip stock, polished bolt assembly, early types have headless firing pin assembly and reversed safety lock. These rifles were produced especially for target shooting.

U.S. Rifle Cal. 30 M1 (Garand)

U.S. Model 1903 Springfield Sporter............. $650
Same general specifications as the National Match, except has sporting design stock, Lyman No. 48 receiver sight.

U.S. Model 1903 Style T Springfield Match Rifle.. $875
Same general specifications as the Springfield Sporter, except has heavy barrel (26-,28-or 30-inch), scope bases, globe front sight, weighs about 12½ pounds with 26-inch barrel.

U.S. Model 1903 Type A Springfield Free Rifle.. $950
Same as Style T, except made with 28-inch barrel only, has Swiss butt plate, weighs about 13¼ pounds.

U.S. Model 1903 Type B Springfield Free Rifle. $1185
Same as Type A, except has cheekpiece stock, palm-rest, Woodie double-set triggers, Garand fast firing pin, weighs about 14¾ pounds.

U.S. Model 1922-MI 22 Springfield Target Rifle. $375
Modified Model 1903. Caliber, 22 Long Rifle. 5-shot detachable box magazine. 24½-inch barrel. Weight, about 9 pounds. Lyman No. 48C receiver sight, blade front sight. Sporting-type stock similar to that of the Model 1903 Springfield Sporter. Issued 1927. *Note:* The earlier Model 1922, which is seldom encountered, differs from the foregoing chiefly in the bolt mechanism and magazine.

U.S. M2 22 Springfield Target Rifle............. $550
Same general specifications as Model 1922-MI, except has speedlock, improved bolt assembly adjustable for headspace. *Note:* These improvements were later incorporated in many rifles of the preceding models (M1922, M1922MI) and arms so converted were marked "M1922M2" or "M1922MII."

U.S. Rifle, Caliber 30, M1 (Garand) Military Rifle.. $740
Clip-fed, gas-operated, air-cooled, semiautomatic. Uses a clip containing eight rounds. 24-inch barrel. Weight (without bayonet), 9½ pounds. Adjustable peep rear sight, blade front sight with guards. Pistol-grip stock, handguards. Made from 1937 to 1957. *Note:* In addition to manufacture at Springfield Armory, Garand rifles have been produced by Winchester Repeating Arms Co., Harrington & Richardson Arms Co., and International Harvester Co.

U.S. Rifle, Caliber 30, M1, National Match...... $1100
Accurized target version of the Garand. Glass-bedded stock; match grade barrel, sights, gas cylinder. "NM" stamped on barrel forward of handguard.

U.S. Military Rifle manufactured by Remington Arms Company of Delaware (later Midvale Steel & Ordnance Co.), Eddystone, Pennsylvania; Remington Arms Company, Ilion, New York; Winchester Repeating Arms Company, New Haven, Connecticut

U.S. Model 1917 Enfield Military Rifle.......... $175
Modified Mauser-type bolt action. Caliber, 30-06. 5-shot box magazine. 26-inch barrel. Weight, about 9¼ pounds. Adjustable rear sight, blade front sight with guards. Military-type stock with semi-pistol grip. This design originated in Great Britain as their "Pattern '14" and was manufactured in caliber 303 for the British Government in three U.S. plants. In 1917, the U.S. Government contracted with these firms to produce the same rifle in caliber 30-06. Made only from 1917 to 1918, over two million of these Model 1917 Enfields were manufactured. While no more were produced after World War I, the U.S. supplied over a million of them to Great Britain during World War II.

U.S. Carbine manufactured by Inland Mfg. Div. of G.M.C., Dayton, Ohio; Winchester Repeating Arms Co., New Haven, Connecticut; other contractors. *

U.S. Carbine, Caliber 30, M1..................... $235
Gas-operated (short-stroke piston), semiautomatic. 15- or 30-round detachable box magazine. 18-inch barrel. Weight, about 5½ pounds. Adjustable rear sight, blade front sight with guards. Pistol-grip stock with handguard, side-mounted web sling. Made from 1942 to 1945. *Note:* In 1963, 150,000 surplus M1 Carbines were sold at $20 each to members of the National Rifle Assn. by the Dept. of the Army.

* International Business Machines Corp., Poughkeepsie, N.Y.; National Postal Meter Co., Rochester, N.Y.; Quality Hardware & Machine Co., Chicago, Ill.; Rock-Ola Co., Chicago, Ill.; Saginaw Steering Gear Div. of G.M.C., Saginaw, Mich.; Standard Products Co., Port Clinton, Ohio; Underwood-Elliott-Fisher Co., Hartford, Conn.

U.S. Model 1917 Enfield

U.S. Carbine Cal. 30 M1

Universal Standard 30 Carbine

Universal Deluxe 30 Carbine

Valmet M-62S

Vickers Jubilee Model

Vickers Empire Model

Universal Sporting Goods, Inc., Miami, Florida

Universal Standard M-1 Carbine............... **$140**
Same as U.S. Carbine, Cal. 30, M1, except may have either wood
or metal handguard, barrel band with or without bayonet lug; 5-
shot magazine standard. Made from 1964 to date.

Universal Deluxe Carbine.......................**$160**
Same as standard model, except also available in caliber 256, has
deluxe walnut Monte Carlo stock and handguard. Made from
1965 to date.

Valmet Oy, Punanotkonkatu, Finland

Valmet M-62S Semiautomatic Rifle............. **$600**
Semiautomatic version of Finnish M-62 automatic assault rifle
based on Russian AK-47. Gas-operated rotating-bolt action.
Caliber, 7.62mm x 39 Russian. 15- and 30-round magazines.
16⅝-inch barrel. Weight, about 8 pounds with metal stock.
Tangent aperture rear sight, hooded blade front sight with
luminous flip-up post for low-light use. Tubular steel or wood
stock. Made from 1962 to date.

Valmet M-71S....................................**$500**
Same specifications as M-62S, except caliber 5.56mm x 45 (223
Rem.), has open rear sight, reinforced resin or wood stock,
weighs 7¾ pounds with former. Made from 1971 to date.

Vickers Ltd., Crayford, Kent, England

Vickers Jubilee Model Single Shot Target Rifle. **$325**
Round-receiver Martini-type action. Caliber, 22 Long Rifle. 28-
inch heavy barrel. Weight, about 9½ pounds. Parker-Hale No.
2 front sight, Perfection rear peep sight. One-piece target stock
with full forearm and pistol grip. Made prior to World War II.

Vickers Empire Model........................... **$295**
Similar to Jubilee Model, except has 27- or 30-inch barrel,
straight-grip stock, weighs about 9¼ pounds with 30-inch barrel. Made prior to World War II.

Walther Rifles manufactured prior to World War II by Waffenfabrik Walther, Zella-Mehlis (Thür.), Germany

**Walther Olympic Bolt Action Single Shot
Match Rifle**.......................................**$700**
Caliber, 22 Long Rifle. 26-inch heavy barrel. Weight, about 13
pounds. Micrometer extension rear sight, interchangeable front
sights. Target stock with checkered pistol grip, thumb hole, full
beavertail forearm covered with corrugated rubber, palm-rest,
adjustable Swiss-type butt plate, swivels.

Walther Olympic

Walther Model 2

Walter Model V "Meisterbüchse"

Walther Model KKM

Walther Model KKJ

Walther Model SSV

Walther Model 2 Autoloading Rifle **$375**
Bolt action, may be used as autoloader, manually-operated repeater or single shot. Caliber, 22 Long Rifle. 5- or 9-shot detachable box magazine. 24½-inch barrel. Weight, about 7 pounds. Tangent curve rear sight, ramp front sight. Sporting stock with checkered pistol grip, grooved forearm, swivels.

Walther Model 1 Autoloading Rifle,
Light Model **$380**
Similar to Standard Model but with 20-inch barrel, lighter stock, weighs about 4½ pounds.

Walther Model V Bolt Action Single Shot
Sporting Rifle **$300**
Caliber, 22 Long Rifle. 26-inch barrel. Weight, about 7 pounds. Open rear sight, ramp front sight. Plain pistol-grip stock with grooved forearm.

Walther Model V "Meisterbüchse"
(Champion Rifle) **$375**
Same as standard Model V, except has micrometer open rear sight and checkered pistol grip.

Walther Rifles manufactured since World War II by Carl Walther Sportwaffenfabrik, Ulm/Donau, West Germany

Walther Model KKM International Match Rifle . **$740**
Bolt action, single shot. Caliber, 22 Long Rifle. 28-inch heavy barrel. Weight, 15½ pounds. Micrometer aperture rear sight, globe front sight. Thumb-hole stock with high comb, adjustable hook butt plate, accessory rail. Left-hand stock available.

Walther Model KKM-S **$750**
Same specifications as Model KKM, except has adjustable cheekpiece.

Walther Model KKJ Sporter **$525**
Bolt action. Caliber, 22 Long Rifle. 5-shot box magazine. 22½-inch barrel. Weight, 5½ pounds. Open rear sight, hooded ramp front sight. Stock with cheekpiece, checkered pistol grip and forearm, sling swivels.

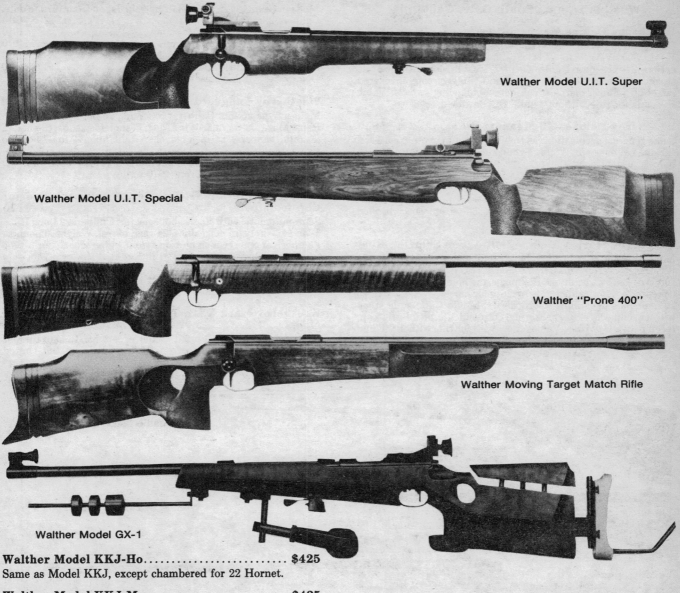

Walther Model U.I.T. Super

Walther Model U.I.T. Special

Walther "Prone 400"

Walther Moving Target Match Rifle

Walther Model GX-1

Walther Model KKJ-Ho.......................... **$425**
Same as Model KKJ, except chambered for 22 Hornet.

Walther Model KKJ-Ma.......................... **$425**
Same as Model KKJ, except chambered for 22 Win. Mag. R.F.

Walther Model SSV Varmint Rifle............... **$490**
Bolt action, single shot. Calibers: 22 Long Rifle, 22 Hornet. 25½-inch barrel. Weight, 6¾ pounds. Supplied without sights. Monte Carlo stock with high cheekpiece, full pistol grip and forearm.

Walther Model U.I.T. Super Match Rifle........ **$595**
Bolt action, single shot. Caliber, 22 Long Rifle. 25½-inch heavy barrel. Weight, 10.2 pounds. Micrometer aperture rear sight, globe front sight. Target stock with support for off-hand shooting, high comb, adjustable butt plate and swivel. Left-hand stock available.

Walther Model U.I.T. Special Match Rifle....... **$600**
Bolt action, single shot. Caliber, 22 Long Rifle. 25½-inch barrel. Weight, 10.2 pounds. Micrometer aperture rear sight, globe front sight. Target stock with high comb, adjustable butt plate, accessory rail. Left-hand stock available.

Walther "Prone 400" Target Rifle................ **$525**
Bolt action, single shot. Caliber, 22 Long Rifle. 25½-inch heavy barrel. Weight, 10¼ pounds. Supplied without sights. Prone stock with adjustable cheekpiece and butt plate, accessory rail. Left-hand stock available.

Walther Moving Target Match Rifle............. **$525**
Bolt action, single shot. Caliber, 22 Long Rifle. 23.6-inch barrel with weight. Weight, 8.6 pounds. Supplied without sights. Thumb-hole stock with adjustable cheekpiece and butt plate. Left-hand stock available.

Walther Model GX-1 Free Rifle.................. **$790**
Bolt action, single shot. Caliber, 22 Long Rifle. 25½-inch heavy barrel. Weight, 15.9 pounds. Micrometer aperture rear sight, globe front sight. Thumb-hole stock with adjustable cheekpiece and butt plate with removable hook, accessory rail. Left-hand stock available. Accessories furnished include hand stop and sling swivel, palm-rest, counter-weight assembly.

Weatherby, Inc., South Gate, California

Weatherby Deluxe Magnum Rifle................ **$510**
Calibers: 220 Rocket, 257 Weatherby Magnum, 270 W.M., 7mm W.M., 300 W.M., 375 W.M. Specially processed FN Mauser action. 24-inch barrel (26-inch in 375 cal.). Monte Carlo-style stock with cheekpiece, black fore-end tip, grip cap, checkered pistol grip and forearm, quick-detachable sling swivels. Value shown is for rifle without sights. Discontinued 1958.

Weatherby Deluxe 378 Magnum Rifle.......... **$650**
Same general specifications as Deluxe Magnum in other calibers, except: caliber, 378 W. M. Schultz & Larsen action; 26-inch barrel. Discontinued 1958.

Weatherby Deluxe Rifle......................... **$495**
Same general specifications as Deluxe Magnum, except chambered for standard calibers such as 270, 30-06, etc. Discontinued 1958.

Weatherby Mark V Deluxe Bolt Action Sporting Rifle
Mark V action, right or left hand. Calibers: 22/250, 30-06; 224 Weatherby Varmintmaster; 240, 257, 270, 7mm, 300, 340, 378, 460 Weatherby Magnums. Box magazine holds 2 to 5 cartridges depending upon caliber. 24- or 26-inch barrel. Weight, 6½ to 10½ pounds depending upon caliber. Monte Carlo-style stock with cheekpiece, skip checkering, fore-end tip, pistol-grip cap, recoil pad, QD swivels. Values shown are for rifle without sights.

Made in Germany from 1958 to 1969, in Japan from 1970 to date.
Calibers 22/250, 224.................................. **$ 600**
Caliber 378 Weatherby Magnum..................... **950**
Caliber 460 Weatherby Magnum..................... **1200**
Other calibers..................................... **700**
Add for left-hand action........................... **50**
Deduct 30% if Japanese-made

Weatherby Vanguard Bolt Action Sporting Rifle. **$310**
Mauser-type action. Calibers: 243 Win., 25-06, 270 Win., 7mm Rem. Mag., 30-06, 300 Win. Mag. 5-shot magazine (3-shot in magnum calibers). 24-inch barrel. Weight, about 7 lbs. 14 oz. No sights. Monte Carlo-type stock with cheekpiece, rosewood fore-end tip and pistol-grip cap, checkering, rubber butt pad, QD swivels. Made in Japan from 1970 to date.

Weatherby Mark XXII Deluxe 22 Automatic Sporter Clip-fed Model................................... **$175**
Semi-automatic with single shot selector. Caliber, 22 Long Rifle. 5- and 10-shot clip magazines. 24-inch barrel. Weight, 6 pounds. Folding leaf open rear sight, ramp front sight. Monte Carlo-type stock with cheekpiece, pistol grip, fore-end tip, grip cap, skip checkering, QD swivels. Made for 1964 to date. Made in Italy from 1964 to 1969, in Japan from 1970 to 1981, in the United States from 1982 to date.

Weatherby Mark XXII, Tubular Magazine Model.. **$175**
Same as Mark XXII, Clip-fed Model, except has 15-shot tubular magazine. Made in Japan from 1973 to 1981, in the United States from 1982 to date.

Weatherby Deluxe Magnum

Weatherby Deluxe 378 Magnum

Weatherby Mark V

Weatherby Vanguard

Weatherby Mark XXII Clip-fed

Westley Richards & Co., Ltd., London, England

Westley Richards Best Quality Double Rifle . . $13,000

Box Lock, hammerless, ejector. Hand detachable locks. Calibers: 30-06, 318 Accelerated Express, 375 Magnum, 425 Magnum Express, 465 Nitro Express, 470 Nitro Express, 25-inch barrels. Weights, 8½ to 11 pounds depending upon caliber. Leaf rear sight, Hooded front sight. French walnut stock with cheekpiece, checkered pistol grip and fore-end.

Westley Richards Best Quality Magazine Rifle $4,000

Mauser or Magnum Mauser Action. Calibers: 7mm High Velocity, 30-06, 318 Accelerated Express, 375 Magnum, 404 Nitro Express, 425 Magnum. Barrel lengths: 24-inch, except 7mm 22-inch and 425 caliber 25-inch. Weights, 7¼ to 9¼ pounds depending upon caliber. Leaf rear sight, hooded front sight. French walnut sporting stock with cheekpiece, checkered pistol grip and forearm, horn fore-end tip, swivels.

Whitworth Rifle manufactured for Interarms, Alexandria, Virginia, by Whitworth Rifle Company England

Whitworth Express Rifle, African Series $450

Mauser-type bolt action. Calibers, 375 H&H Mag., 458 Win. Mag. 3-shot magazine. 24-inch barrel. Weight, about 8 pounds.

3-leaf express open rear sight, ramp front sight with hood. English style stock of European walnut, with cheekpiece, black fore-end tip, checkered pistol grip and forearm, recoil pad, QD swivels. Made from 1974 to date.

Wickliffe Rifles manufactured by Triple-S Development Co., Inc., Wickliffe, Ohio

Wickliffe '76 Standard Model Single Shot Rifle . . $275

Falling block action. Calibers: 22 Hornet, 223 Rem., 22-250, 243 Win., 25-06, 308 Win., 30-06, 45-70. 22-inch lightweight barrel (243 and 308 only) or 26-inch heavy sporter barrel. Weight, 6¾ or 8½ pounds, depending upon barrel. No sights. Select American walnut Monte Carlo stock with right or left cheekpiece and pistol grip, semi-beavertail forearm. Made from 1976 to date.

Wickliffe '76 Deluxe Grade $350

Same as Standard Model, except 22-inch barrel in 30-06 only, has high-lustre blued finish, fancy grade figured American walnut stock with nickel silver grip cap.

Wickliffe '76 Commemorative Model $600

Limited edition of 100. Same as Deluxe Model, except has filled etching on receiver sidewalls, U.S. silver dollar inlaid in stock, 26-inch barrel only, comes in presentation case.

Westley Richards Best Quality Double Rifle

Westley Richards Best Quality Magazine Rifle

Whitworth Express

Wickliffe '76 Standard

Winchester-Western Div., Olin Corp. (formerly Winchester Repeating Arms Company), New Haven, Connecticut

Winchester Model 73 Lever Action Repeating Rifle $1500

Calibers: 32-20, 38-40, 44-40; a few were chambered for 22 rimfire. 15-shot magazine, also made with 6-shot half magazine. 24-inch barrel (round, half-octagon, octagon). Weight, about 8½ pounds. Open rear sight, bead or blade front sight. Plain straight-grip stock and forearm. Made from 1873 to 1924. 720,610 rifles of this model were manufactured.

Winchester Model 73 Special Sporting Rifle $2100

Same as Standard Model 73 Rifle, except this type has receiver casehardened in colors, pistol-grip stock of selected walnut, octagon barrel only.

Winchester Model 73 Lever Action Carbine $2800

Same as Standard Model 73 Rifle, except has 20-inch barrel, 12-shot magazine, weighs 7¼ pounds.

Winchester Model 73 Rifle

Winchester Model 73 One of One Thousand

Closeup of barrel engraving Winchester Model 73 One of One Thousand

Winchester Single Shot Sporting Rifle

Winchester Single Shot Schuetzen Rifle

Winchester Single Shot Musket

Winchester Model 73 Rifle — One of One Thousand $25,000

During the late 1870's Winchester offered Model 73 rifles of superior accuracy and extra finish, designated "One of One Thousand" grade, at a price of $100. These rifles are marked "1 of 1000" or "One of One Thousand." Only 136 of this model are known to have been manufactured. This is one of the rarest of shoulder arms and, because so very few have been sold in recent years, it is extremely difficult to assign a value; however, in the author's opinion, an "excellent" specimen would probably bring a price upward of $25,000

Winchester Single Shot Rifle

Design by John M. Browning, this falling-block lever action arm was manufactured from 1885 to 1920 in a variety of models and chambered for most of the popular cartridges of the period, rimfire and centerfire, from 22 to 50 caliber. There are two basic styles of frame, low-wall and high-wall. The former style was used only for low-powered calibers; the latter was supplied in all calibers and was made in three types: the standard model for #3 and heavier barrels is the type commonly encountered, the thin-walled version was supplied with #1 and #2 light barrels and the thick-walled action in the heavier calibers. Made in solid frame and take-down models. The latter are generally considered less desirable. Barrels were available in five weights ranging from the lightweight # 1 to the extra heavy #5 in round, half-octagon and full-octagon styles. Plain, single-set, double-set and double-Schuetzen triggers were offered. A complete listing of Winchester Single Shots is beyond the proper scope of this volume; included herein are the three standard types: Sporting Rifle, Musket and Schuetzen Rifle.

Winchester Single Shot Sporting Rifle $1000

Low-wall. Plain model. Solid frame. Plain trigger. Standard lever. No. 1 28-inch round or octagon barrel. Weight, 7 pounds. Open rear sight, blade front sight. Plain stock and forearm.

Winchester Single Shot Sporting Rifle $1650

High-wall. Plain model. Solid frame or takedown. Plain trigger. Standard lever. No. 3 30-inch barrel. Weight, 9½ pounds. Open rear sight, blade front sight. Plain stock and forearm.

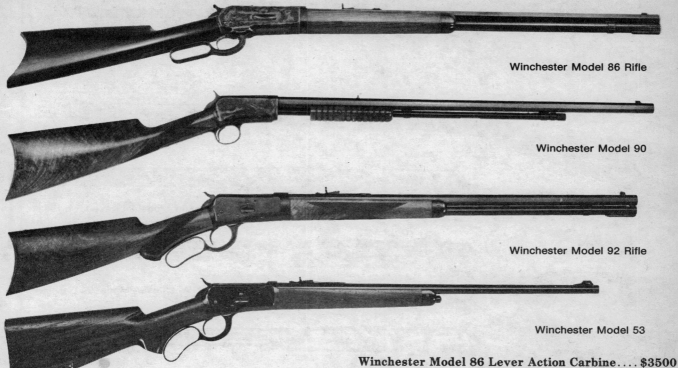

Winchester Model 86 Rifle

Winchester Model 90

Winchester Model 92 Rifle

Winchester Model 53

Winchester Single Shot Sporting Rifle......... $1850

Special Grade. Same as Plain Model High-wall, but with fancy walnut stock and forearm, checkered.

Winchester Single Shot Schuetzen Rifle....... $2300

Solid frame or takedown. High-wall action. Schuetzen double-set trigger. Spur finger level. No. 3 30-inch octagon barrel. Weight, 12 pounds. Vernier rear peep sight, wind-guage front sight. Fancy walnut Schuetzen stock with checkered pistol grip and forearm. Schuetzen butt plate. Adjustable palm-rest.

Winchester Single Shot "Winder" Musket....... $550

Solid frame or takedown. High-wall. Plain trigger. Standard finger lever. Calibers: 22 Short, 22 Long Rifle. 28-inch round barrel. Weight, 8½ pounds. Musket rear sight, blade front sight. Military-type stock and forearm.

Winchester Single Shot Musket................. $395

Solid frame. Low-wall. Plain trigger. Standard finger lever. Calibers: 22 Short, 22 Long Rifle. 28-inch round barrel. Weight, 8½ pounds. Lyman rear peep sight, blade front sight. Military-type stock and forearm. *Note:* The U.S. Government purchased a large quantity of these Single Shot Muskets during World War I for training purposes. Many of these rifles were later sold through the Director of Civilian Marksmanship, to National Rifle Association members. The price was $1.50.

Winchester Model 86 Lever Action Repeater.. $1250

Solid frame or takedown style. Calibers: 45/70, 38/56, 45/90/300, 40/82/260, 40/65/260, 38/56/255, 38/70/255, 40/70/330, 50/110/300, 50/100/450, 33 Win. All but the first cartridge listed are now obsolete. 33 Win. and 45/70 were the last calibers in which this model was supplied. 8-shot tubular magazine, also 4-shot half-magazine. 22- or 26-inch barrel (round, half-octagon, octagon). Weight, from 7½ pounds up. Open rear sight, bead or blade front sight. Plain straight-grip stock and forearm. Made from 1886 to 1935.

Winchester Model 86 Lever Action Carbine.... $3500

Same as standard Model 86 rifle, except with 22-inch barrel and weighs about 7¾ pounds.

Winchester Model 90 Slide Action Repeater.... $350

Visible hammer. Calibers: 22 Short, Long, Long Rifle; 22 W.R.F. (not interchangeable). Tubular magazine holds 15 Short, 12 Long, 11 Long Rifle; 12 W.R.F. 24-inch octagon barrel. Weight, 5¾ pounds. Open rear sight, bead front sight. Plain straight-grip stock, grooved slide handle. Originally solid frame, after No. 15,499 all rifles of this model were takedown type. Fancy checkered pistol-grip stock, stainless steel barrel supplied at extra cost. Made from 1890 to 1932.

Winchester Model 92 Lever Action Repeating Rifle.. $750

Solid frame or takedown. Calibers: 25/20, 32/20, 38/40, 44/40. 13-shot tubular magazine, also 7-shot half-magazine. 24-inch barrel (round, octagon, half-octagon). Weight, from 6¾ pounds up. Open rear sight, bead front sight. Plain straight-grip stock and forearm (stock illustrated was extra cost option). Made from 1892 to 1941.

Winchester Model 92 Lever Action Carbine.... $1600

Same as Model 92RR rifle, except has 20-inch barrel, 5-shot or 11-shot magazine, weighs about 5¾ pounds.

Winchester Model 53 Lever Action Repeating Rifle.. $750

Modification of Model 92. Solid frame or takedown. Calibers: 25/20, 32/20, 44/40. 6-shot tubular half-magazine in solid frame model. 7-shot in takedown. 22-inch nickel steel barrel. Weight, 5½ to 6½ pounds. Open rear sight, bead front sight. Redesigned straight-grip stock and forearm. Made from 1924 to 1932.

Winchester Model 65 Lever Action Repeating Rifle.. $875

Improved version of Model 53. Solid frame. Calibers: 25-20 and 32-20. Six-shot tubular half-magazine. 22-inch barrel. Weight, 6½ pounds. Open rear sight, bead front sight on ramp base. Plain pistol-grip stock and forearm. Made from 1933 to 1947.

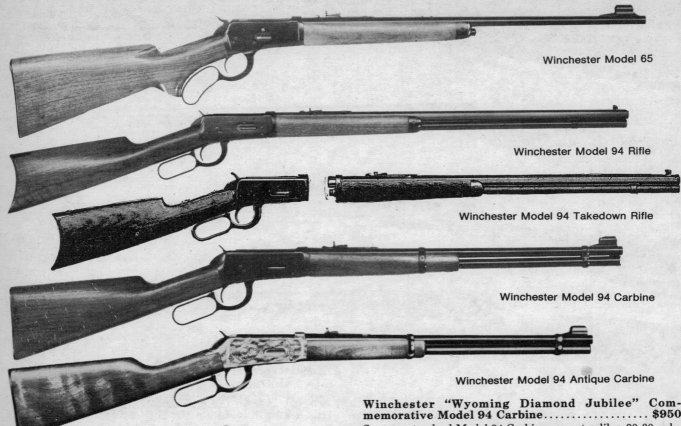

Winchester Model 65

Winchester Model 94 Rifle

Winchester Model 94 Takedown Rifle

Winchester Model 94 Carbine

Winchester Model 94 Antique Carbine

Winchester Model 65—218 Bee............... **$800**
Same as Standard Model 65, except has 24-inch barrel, peep rear sight. Made from 1938 to 1947.

Winchester Model 94 Lever Action Repeating Rifle
.... **$475**
Solid frame or takedown. Calibers: 25/35, 30/30, 32/40, 32 Special, 38/55. 7-shot tubular magazine or 4-shot half-magazine. 26-inch barrel (octagon, half-octagon, round). Weight, about 7¾ pounds. Open rear sight, bead front sight. Plain straight-grip stock and forearm. Made from 1894 to 1937.

Winchester Model 94 Carbine
Same as Model 94 Rifle, except 20-inch round barrel, 6-shot full-length magazine, weight, about 6½ pounds. Currently manufactured in calibers 30-30 and 32 Special, solid frame only.
Pre-World War II (under No. 1,300,000)............. **$475**
Postwar, pre-1964.. **295**
Current model... **110**

Winchester Model 94 Antique Carbine.......... **$150**
Same as standard Model 94 Carbine, except has receiver with decorative scrollwork and casehardened in colors, brass-plated loading gate, saddle ring; caliber 30-30 only. Made from 1964 to date.

Winchester Big Bore 94 XTR................... **$165**
Modified Model 94 action for added strength. Caliber: 375 Win. 20-inch barrel. Rubber butt pad. Checkered stock and forearm. Weight: 6½ pounds. Made from 1978 to date.

Winchester Model 94 Trapper................... **$145**
Same as Winchester Model 94 Carbine, except 16-inch barrel and weighs 6 pounds 2 ounces. Made from 1980 to date.

Winchester "Wyoming Diamond Jubilee" Commemorative Model 94 Carbine.................. **$950**
Same as standard Model 94 Carbine, except caliber 30-30 only, receiver engraved and casehardened in colors, brass saddle ring and loading gate, souvenir medallion embedded in buttstock, commemorative inscription on barrel. 1,500 made in 1964.

Winchester "Nebraska Centennial" Commemorative Model 94 Carbine............................... **$850**
Same as standard Model 94 Carbine, except caliber 30-30 only; gold-plated hammer, loading gate, barrel band, and butt plate; souvenir medallion embedded in stock, commemorative inscription on barrel. 2,500 made in 1966.

Winchester "Centennial '66" Commemorative Rifle
.... **$425**
Commemorates Winchester's 100th anniversary. Standard Model 94 action. Caliber, 30-30. Full-length magazine holds 8 rounds. 26-inch octagon barrel. Weight, 8 pounds. Gold-plated receiver and forearm cap. Open rear sight, post front sight. Saddle ring. Walnut buttstock and forearm with high-gloss finish, solid brass butt plate. Commemorative inscription on barrel and top tang of receiver. Made in 1966.

Winchester "Centennial '66" Carbine........... **$425**
Same as '66 Rifle, except has 20-inch barrel, magazine holds 6 rounds, weight is 7 pounds, forearm is shorter. Made in 1966.

Winchester "Centennial '66" Matched Set...... **$750**
Rifle and carbine were offered in sets with consecutive serial numbers. *Note:* 100,478 Centennial '66s were made.

Winchester "Canadian Centennial" Model 67 Commemorative Rifle............................... **$275**
Same as Centennial '66 Rifle, except receiver—engraved with maple leaves—and forearm cap are black-chromed, butt plate is blued, commemorative inscription in gold on barrel and top tang: "Canadian Centennial 1867-1967." Made in 1967.

Winchester "Canadian Centennial" Model 67 Carbine... $275

Same as Model 67 Rifle, except has 20-inch barrel, magazine holds 6 rounds, weight is 7 pounds, forearm is shorter. Made in 1967.

Winchester "Canadian Centennial" Model 67 Matched Set.. $730

Rifle and carbine were offered in sets with consecutive serial numbers. *Note:* 90,398 Model 67's were made.

Winchester Model 94 Classic Rifle............... $250

Same as Model 67 Rifle, except without commemorative details; has scroll-engraved receiver, gold-plated loading gate. Made from 1968 to 1970.

Winchester Model 94 Classic Carbine........... $250

Same as Model 67 Carbine, except without commemorative details; has scroll-engraved receiver, gold-plated loading gate. Made from 1968 to 1970.

Winchester "Alaskan Purchase Centennial," Commemorative Model 94 Carbine................. $1700

Same as "Wyoming" issue, except different medallion and inscription. 1,501 made in 1967.

Winchester "Buffalo Bill" Commemorative Model 94 Rifle.. $395

Same as Centennial '66 Rifle, except receiver is black chromed scroll-engraved and bears name "Buffalo Bill;" hammer, trigger, loading gate, saddle ring, forearm cap, and butt plate are nickel-plated; Buffalo Bill Memorial Assn. commemorative medallion embedded in buttstock; "Buffalo Bill Commemorative" inscribed on barrel, facsimile signature "W.F. Cody, Chief of Scouts" on tang. Made in 1968.

Winchester "Buffalo Bill" Model 94 Carbine..... $395

Same as Buffalo Bill Rifle, except has 20-inch barrel, magazine holds 6 rounds, weight is 7 pounds, forearm is shorter. Made in 1968.

Winchester "Buffalo Bill" Model 94 Matched Set...................................... $750

Rifle and carbine were offered in sets with consecutive serial numbers. *Note:* 120,751 Buffalo Bill 94's were made.

Winchester "Illinois Sesquicentennial" Commemorative Model 94 Carbine................... $395

Same as standard Model 94 Carbine, except caliber 30-30 only;

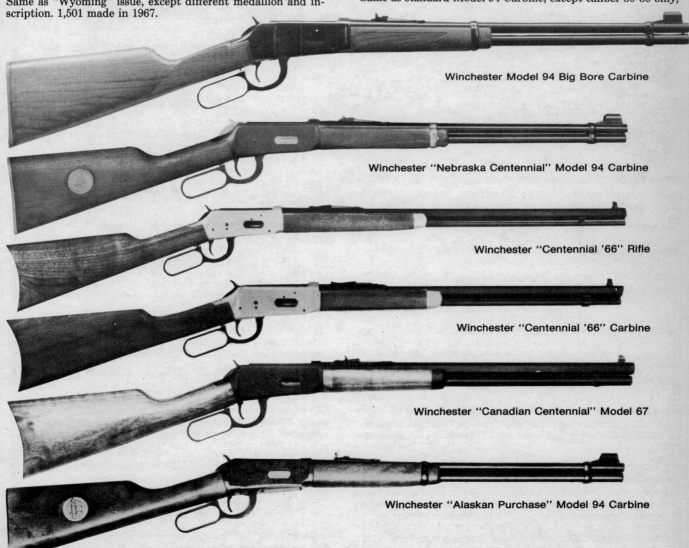

Winchester Model 94 Big Bore Carbine

Winchester "Nebraska Centennial" Model 94 Carbine

Winchester "Centennial '66" Rifle

Winchester "Centennial '66" Carbine

Winchester "Canadian Centennial" Model 67

Winchester "Alaskan Purchase" Model 94 Carbine

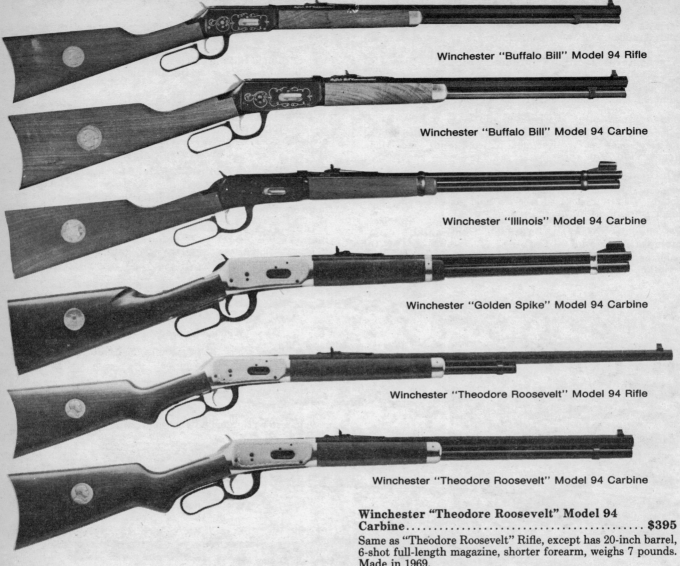

Winchester "Buffalo Bill" Model 94 Rifle

Winchester "Buffalo Bill" Model 94 Carbine

Winchester "Illinois" Model 94 Carbine

Winchester "Golden Spike" Model 94 Carbine

Winchester "Theodore Roosevelt" Model 94 Rifle

Winchester "Theodore Roosevelt" Model 94 Carbine

gold-plated butt plate, trigger, loading gate, and saddle ring; receiver engraved with profile of Lincoln, commemorative inscriptions on receiver, barrel; souvenir medallion embedded in stock. 31,124 made in 1968.

Winchester "Golden Spike" Commemorative Model 94 Carbine.. $395
Same as standard Model 94 Carbine, except caliber 30-30 only; gold-plated receiver, tangs and barrel bands; engraved receiver, commemorative medallion embedded in stock. 64,758 made in 1969.

Winchester "Theodore Roosevelt" Commemorative Model 94 Rifle.................................... $395
Standard Model 94 action. Caliber, 30-30. Half magazine holds 6 rounds. 26-inch octagon barrel. Weight, 7½ pounds. White gold-plated receiver, upper tang, and fore-end cap; receiver engraved with American Eagle, "26th President 1901-1909," and Roosevelt's signature. Commemorative medallion embedded in buttstock. Saddle ring. Half pistol grip, contoured lever. Made in 1969.

Winchester "Theodore Roosevelt" Model 94 Carbine.. $395
Same as "Theodore Roosevelt" Rifle, except has 20-inch barrel, 6-shot full-length magazine, shorter forearm, weighs 7 pounds. Made in 1969.

Winchester "Theodore Roosevelt" Matched Set. $800
Rifle and carbine were offered in sets with consecutive serial numbers. *Note:* 49,505 "T.R." 94's were made.

Winchester "Cowboy" Commemorative Model 94 Carbine.. $395
Same as standard Model 94 Carbine, except caliber 30-30 only; nickel-plated receiver, tangs, lever, barrel bands; engraved receiver, "Cowboy Commemorative" on barrel, commemorative medallion embedded in buttstock; curved butt plate. 20,915 made in 1970.

Winchester "Lone Star" Commemorative Model 94 Rifle.................................... $395
Same as "Theodore Roosevelt" Rifle, except yellow-gold plating; "Lone Star" engraving on receiver and barrel, commemorative medallion embedded in buttstock. Made in 1970.

Winchester "Lone Star" Matched Set........... $800
Rifle and carbine were offered in sets with consecutive serial numbers. *Note:* 30,669 Lone Star 94's were made.

Winchester "NRA Centennial" Model 94 Musket.. $450

Commemorates 100th anniversary of National Rifle Association of America. Standard Model 94 action. Caliber, 30-30. 7-shot magazine. 26-inch barrel. Military folding rear sight and blade front sight. Black chrome-finished receiver engraved "NRA 1871-1971" plus scrollwork. Barrel inscribed "NRA Centennial Musket." Musket-style buttstock and full-length forearm; commemorative medallion embedded in buttstock. Weight, 7⅛ pounds. Made in 1971.

Winchester "NRA Centennial" Model 94 Rifle... $395

Same as Model 64 Rifle, except has commemorative details as in "NRA Centennial" Musket (barrel inscribed "NRA Centennial Rifle"); caliber 30-30, 24-inch barrel, QD sling swivels. Made in 1971.

Winchester "NRA Centennial" Matched Set..... $800

Rifle and carbine were offered in sets with consecutive serial numbers. *Note:* Production figure not available. These rifles were again offered in Winchester's 1972 catalog.

Winchester "Texas Ranger" Commemorative Model 94 Carbine.. $750

Same as standard Model 94 Carbine, except caliber 30-30 only, stock and forearm of semi-fancy walnut, replica of Texas Ranger star embedded in buttstock, curved butt plate. 5,000 made in 1973.

Winchester Texas Ranger Association Model 94 Carbine.. $2000

Same as Texas Ranger Commemorative Model 94, except special edition of 150 carbines, numbered 1 through 150, with hand-checkered full-fancy walnut stock and forearm. Sold only through Texas Ranger Association. Made in 1973.

Winchester Bicentennial '76 Model 94 Carbine.. $695

Same as standard Model 94 Carbine, except caliber 30-30 only; antique silver-finished, engraved receiver; stock and forearm of fancy walnut, checkered, Bicentennial medallion embedded in buttstock, curved butt plate. 20,000 made in 1976.

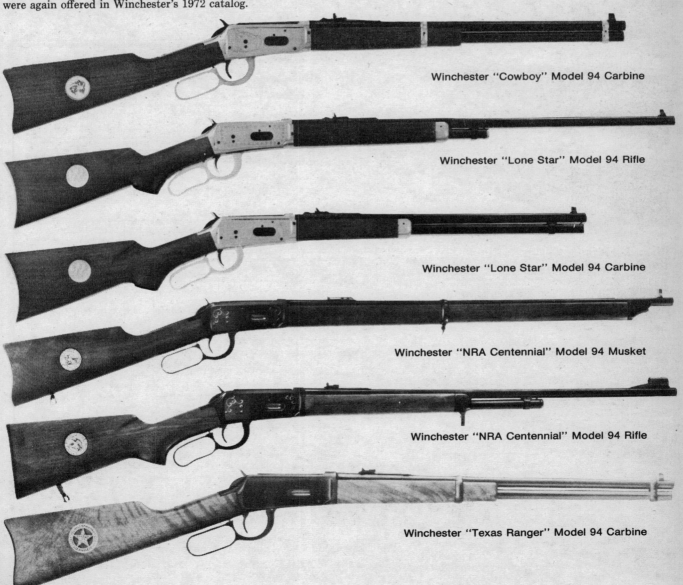

Winchester "Cowboy" Model 94 Carbine

Winchester "Lone Star" Model 94 Rifle

Winchester "Lone Star" Model 94 Carbine

Winchester "NRA Centennial" Model 94 Musket

Winchester "NRA Centennial" Model 94 Rifle

Winchester "Texas Ranger" Model 94 Carbine

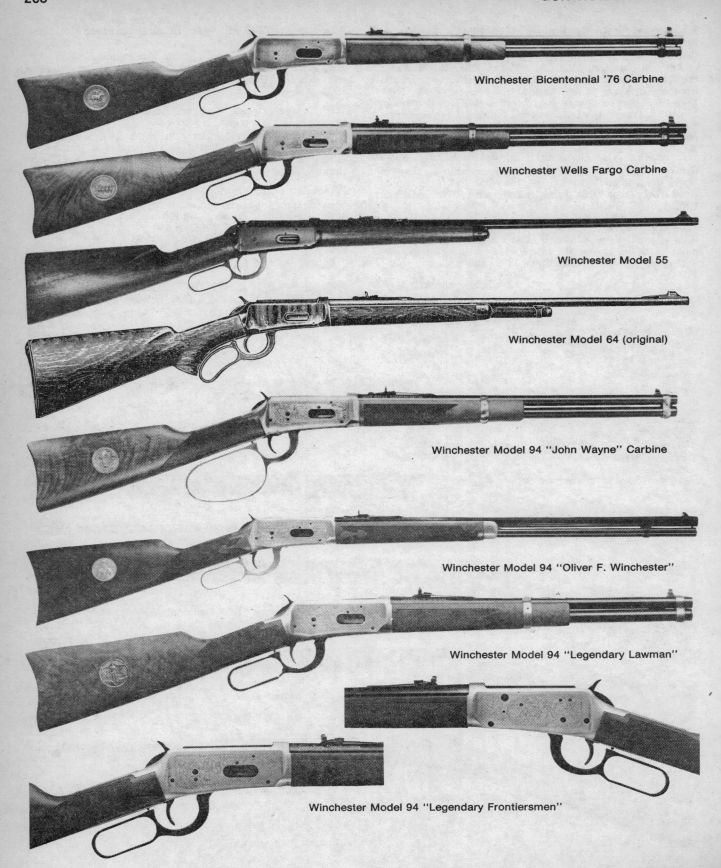

Winchester Bicentennial '76 Carbine

Winchester Wells Fargo Carbine

Winchester Model 55

Winchester Model 64 (original)

Winchester Model 94 "John Wayne" Carbine

Winchester Model 94 "Oliver F. Winchester"

Winchester Model 94 "Legendary Lawman"

Winchester Model 94 "Legendary Frontiersmen"

Winchester Wells Fargo & Co. Commemorative Model 94 Carbine **$525**
Same as standard Model 94 Carbine, except 30-30 only; antique silver-finished, engraved receiver; stock and forearm of fancy walnut, checkered, curved butt plate. Nickel-silver stagecoach medallion (inscribed "Wells Fargo & Co.–1852-1977–125 Years") embedded in buttstock. 20,000 made in 1977.

Winchester Cheyenne Commemorative Model 94 .... **$550**
Available in Canada only. Same as Standard Model 94 Carbine, except chambered for 44/40. 11,225 made in 1977.

Winchester Legendary Lawmen Commemorative Model 94 .... **$425**
Same as Standard Model 94 Carbine, except 30-30 only; Antique silver-plated receiver engraved with action law-enforcement scenes. 16-inch Trapper barrel, antique silver plated barrel bands. 19,999 made in 1978.

Winchester Antlered Game Commemorative Model 94 .... **$495**
Standard Model 94 action. Gold-colored medallion inlaid in stock. Antique gold plated receiver, lever tang and barrel bands. Medallion and receiver engraved with elk, moose, deer and caribou. 20½-inch barrel. Curved steel butt plate. In 30-30 caliber, 19,999 made in 1978.

Winchester Legendary Frontiersman Commemorative Model 94 .... **$450**
Standard Model 94 action. Caliber, 38-55. 24-inch round barrel. Nickel-silver medallion inlaid in stock. Antique silver-plated receiver engraved with scenes of the old frontier. Checkered walnut stock and forearm. 19,999 made in 1979.

Winchester Oliver F. Winchester Commemorative Model 94 .... **$550**
Standard Model 94 action. Caliber, 38-55. 24-inch octagonal barrel. Receiver is satin gold plated with distinctive engravings. Stock and forearm semi-fancy American walnut with high grade checkering. 19,999 made in 1980.

Winchester John Wayne Commemorative Model 94 .... **$895**
Standard Model 94 action. Caliber, 32-40. 18½-inch barrel. Receiver is pewter-plated with engraving of Indian attack and cattle drive scenes. Oversized bow on lever. Nickel-silver medallion in buttstock bears a bas-relief portrait of Wayne. Selected American walnut stock with deep-cut checkering.

Note on Commemorative Winchesters: Values indicated are for rifles in new condition. Data on these models supplied by Mr. Robert E. P. Cherry, Cherry's Sporting Goods, Geneseo, Illinois.

Winchester Model 55 Lever Action Repeating Rifle **$625**
Modification of Model 94. Solid frame or takedown. Calibers: 25/35, 30/30, 32 Win. Special. 3-shot tubular half magazine. 24-inch nickel steel barrel. Weight, about 7 pounds. Open rear sight, bead front sight. Plain straight-grip stock and forearm. Made from 1924 to 1932.

Winchester Model 64 Lever Action Repeating Rifle
Standard Grade. Improved version of Models 94 and 55. Solid frame. Calibers: 25/35, 30-30, 32 Win. Special. 5-shot tubular ⅔ magazine. 20- or 24-inch barrel. Weight, about 7 pounds. Open rear sight, bead front sight on ramp with sight cover. Plain pistol-grip stock and forearm. Made from 1933 to 1956. Production resumed in 1972–caliber 30-30, 24-inch barrel–discontinued 1974.
Original model **$500**
1972-74 model 225

Winchester Model 64—219 Zipper **$695**
Same as Standard Grade Model 64, except has 26-inch barrel, peep rear sight. Made from 1937 to 1947.

Winchester Model 64 Deer Rifle **$450**
Same as Standard Model 64, calibers 30-30 and 32 Win. Special, except has checkered pistol grip and semi-beavertail forearm, swivels and sling, weighs 7¾ pounds. Made from 1933 to 1956.

Winchester Model 64, 1972-74 type

Winchester Model 64 Deer Rifle

Winchester Model 95 Rifle

Winchester Model 95 Carbine

Winchester Lee Sporting Rifle

Winchester Model 1900

Winchester Model 02

Winchester Thumb Trigger Model

Winchester Model 95 Lever Action Repeating Rifle....................................$750
Calibers: 30-40 Krag, 30-30, 30-06, 303 British, 35 Win., 405 Win.; original model supplied in the now obsolete 38/72 and 40/72 calibers. 4-shot box magazine, except 30-40 and 303 which have 5-shot magazine. Barrel lengths: 24-, 26-, 28-inches (round, half-octagon, octagon). Weight, about 8½ pounds. Open rear sight, bead or blade front sight. Plain straight-grip stock and forearm (standard). Both solid frame and takedown models were available. Made from 1895 to 1931.

Winchester Model 95 Lever Action Carbine.....$950
Same as Model 95 Standard Rifle, except has 22-inch barrel, carbine style stock, weighs about 8 pounds, calibers 30-40, 30-30, 30-06 and 303, solid frame only.

Winchester Lee Straight-Pull Bolt Action Repeating Rifle—Musket Model............................$550
Commercial version of U.S. Navy Model 1895 Rifle, Caliber 6mm (1895-1897). Caliber, 236 U.S.N. 5-shot box magazine, clip-loaded. 28-inch barrel. Weight, 8½ pounds. Folding leaf rear sight, post front sight. Military type full stock with semi-pistol grip. Made from 1897 to 1902.

Winchester Lee Straight-Pull Sporting Rifle....$700
Same as Musket Model except has 24-inch barrel, sporter-style stock, open sporting rear sight, bead front sight, weighs about 7½ pounds. Made from 1897 to 1902.

Winchester Model 1900 Bolt Action Single Shot Rifle...$ 80
Takedown. Caliber, 22 Short and Long. 18-inch barrel. Weight, 2¾ pounds. Open rear sight, blade front sight. One-piece, straight-grip stock. Made from 1899 to 1902.

Winchester Model 02 Bolt Action Single Shot Rifle...$ 80
Takedown. Basically the same as Model 1900 with minor improvements. Calibers: 22 Short and Long, 22 Extra Long, 22 Long Rifle. Weight, 3 pounds. Made from 1902 to 1931.

Winchester Thumb Trigger Model Bolt Action Single Shot Rifle..$250
Takedown. Same as Model 02 except fired by pressing a button behind the cocking piece. Made from 1904 to 1923.

Winchester Model 04 Bolt Action Single Shot Rifle...$ 90
Similar to Model 02. Takedown. Caliber, 22 Short, Long, Extra Long, Long Rifle. 21-inch barrel. Weight, 4 pounds. Made from 1904 to 1931.

Winchester Model 03 Self-Loading Rifle........$300
Takedown. Caliber, 22 Win. Auto Rimfire. 10-shot tubular magazine in buttstock. 20-inch barrel. Weight, 5¾ pounds. Open rear sight, bead front sight. Plain straight-grip stock and forearm (stock illustrated was extra-cost option). Made from 1903 to 1936.

Winchester Model 05 Self-Loading Rifle........$350
Takedown. Calibers: 32 Win. S.L., 35 Win. S.L. 5- or 10-shot detachable box magazine. 22-inch barrel. Weight, 7½ pounds. Open rear sight, bead front sight. Plain pistol-grip stock and forearm. Made from 1905 to 1920.

Winchester Model 06 Slide Action Repeater.....$350
Takedown. Visible hammer. Caliber, 22 Short, Long, Long Rifle. Tubular magazine holds 20 Short, 16 Long or 14 Long Rifle. 20-inch barrel. Weight, 5 pounds. Open rear sight, bead front sight. Straight-grip stock and grooved forearm. Made from 1906 to 1932.

Winchester Model 07 Self-Loading Rifle........ $380
Takedown. Caliber, 351 Win. S.L. 5-shot or 10-shot detachable box magazine. 20-inch barrel. Weight, 7¾ pounds. Open rear sight, bead front sight. Plain pistol-grip stock and forearm. Made from 1907 to 1957.

Winchester Model 10 Self-Loading Rifle........ $350
Takedown. Caliber, 401 Win. S.L. 4-shot detachable box magazine. 20-inch barrel. Weight, 8½ pounds. Open rear sight, bead front sight. Plain pistol-grip stock and forearm. Made from 1910 to 1936.

Winchester Model 52 Bolt Action Target Rifle
Standard barrel. First type. Caliber, 22 Long Rifle. 5-shot box magazine. 28-inch barrel. Weight, 8¾ pounds. Folding leaf peep rear sight, blade front sight, standard sights, various other combinations available. Scope bases. Semi-military type target stock with pistol grip; original model has grasping grooves in forearm; higher comb and semi-beavertail forearm on later models. Numerous changes were made in this model, the most important being the adoption of the speed lock in 1929; Model 52 rifles produced prior to this change are generally referred to as "slow lock" models. Last arms of this type bore serial numbers followed by the letter "A." Made from 1919 to 1937.
Slow lock model.................................. $375
Speed lock model................................. 425

Winchester Model 52 Heavy Barrel............. $475
First type. Speed lock. Same general specifications as Standard Model 52 of this type, except has heavier barrel, Lyman 17G front sight, weighs 10 pounds.

Winchester Model 52 Sporting Rifle............ $895
First type. Same as Standard Model 52 of this type, except has lightweight 24-inch barrel, Lyman No. 48 receiver sight and gold bead front sight on hooded ramp, deluxe checkered sporting stock with cheekpiece, black fore-end tip, etc., weighs 7¾ pounds.

Winchester Model 52-B Bolt Action Target Rifle...................................... $425
Standard Barrel. Extensively redesigned action. Supplied with choice of "Target" stock, an improved version of the previous Model 52 stock, or "Marksman" stock with high comb, full pistol grip and beavertail forearm. Weight, 9 pounds. Offered with a wide choice of target sight combinations (Lyman, Marble-Goss, Redfield, Vaver, Winchester); value shown is for rifle less sight equipment. Other specifications as shown for first type. Made from 1935 to 1947.

Winchester Model 52-B Heavy Barrel.......... $475
Same general specifications as Standard Model 52-B, except has heavier barrel, weighs 11 pounds.

Winchester Model 52-B Bull Gun............... $500
Same general specifications as Standard Model 52-B, except has extra heavy barrel, Marksman stock only, weighs 12 pounds.

Winchester Model 52-B Sporting Rifle.......... $600
Model 52-B action, otherwise same as Model 52 Sporting Rifle.

Winchester Model 52-C Bolt Action Target Rifle...................................... $475
Heavy Barrel. Improved action with "Micro-Motion" trigger mechanism and new type "Marksman" stock. General specifications, same as shown for previous models. Made from 1947 to 1961. Value shown is for rifle less sights.

Winchester Model 52-C Standard Barrel....... $425
Same general specifications as Heavy Barrel Model, except has standard weight barrel, weighs 9¾ pounds. Made from 1947 to 1961.

Winchester Model 52-C Bull Gun............... $500
Same general specifications as Heavy Barrel Model, except has extra heavy "bull" barrel, weighs 12 pounds. Made from 1952 to 1961.

Winchester Model 04

Winchester Model 03

Winchester Model 05

Winchester Model 06

Winchester Model 07

Winchester Model 10

Winchester Model 52 Standard Barrel

Winchester Model 52B Standard Barrel

Winchester Model 52B Sporter

Winchester Model 52C Heavy Barrel

Winchester Model 52D Heavy Barrel

Winchester Model 52-D Bolt Action Target Rifle.................................. $400

Redesigned Model 52 action, single shot. Caliber, 22 Long Rifle. 28-inch standard or heavy barrel, free-floating, with blocks for standard target scopes. Weight: with standard barrel, 9¾ pounds; with heavy barrel, 11 pounds. Restyled Marksman stock with accessory channel and fore-end stop, rubber butt plate. Made from 1961 to 1978. Value shown is for rifle without sights.

Winchester Model 52 International Match Rifle

Similar to Model 52-D Heavy Barrel, except has special lead-lapped barrel, laminated "free rifle" style stock with high comb, thumb-hole, hook butt plate, accessory rail, handstop/swivel assembly, palm-rest; weight, 13½ pounds. Made from 1969 to 1978.

With standard trigger.............................. $540
With Kenyon or I.S.U. trigger....................... 670

Winchester Model 52 International Prone Target Rifle.................................. $550

Similar to Model 52-D Heavy Barrel, except has special lead-lapped barrel, prone stock with fuller pistol grip, roll-over cheekpiece removable for bore-cleaning; weight, 11½ pounds. Made from 1975 to date.

Winchester Model 54 Bolt Action High Power Sporting Rifle... $475

First type. Calibers: 270 Win., 7x57mm, 30-30, 30-06, 7.65x53mm, 9x57mm. 5-shot box magazine. 24-inch barrel. Weight, 7¾ pounds. Open rear sight, bead front sight. Checkered stock with pistol grip, tapered forearm with schnabel tip. This type has two-piece firing pin. Made from 1925 to 1930.

Winchester Model 52 International Match

Winchester Model 52 International Prone Target

Winchester Model 54 Standard Grade, Improved Type

Winchester Model 54 Super Grade

Winchester Model 54 Sniper's Rifle

Winchester Model 54 National Match

Winchester Model 54 Target

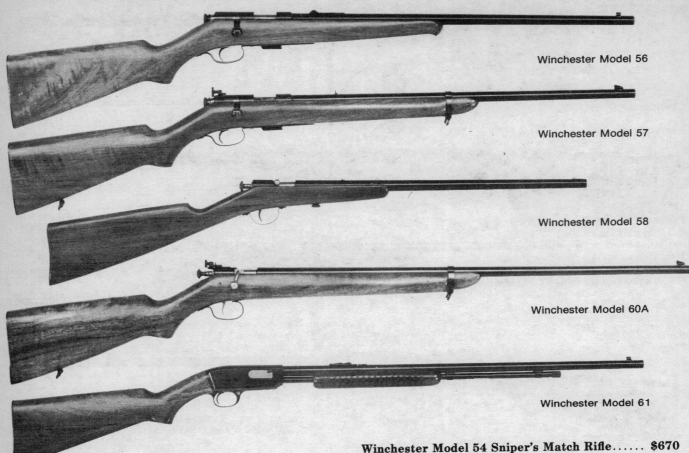

Winchester Model 56

Winchester Model 57

Winchester Model 58

Winchester Model 60A

Winchester Model 61

Winchester Model 54 Carbine................... **$450**
First type. Same as Model 54 rifle, except has 20-inch barrel, plain lightweight stock with grasping grooves in forearm. Weight, 7¼ pounds.

Winchester Model 54 Bolt Action High Power Sporting Rifle... **$450**
Standard grade. Improved type with speed lock and one-piece firing pin. Calibers: 22 Hornet, 220 Swift, 250/3000, 257 Roberts, 270 Win., 7x57mm, 30-06. 5-shot box magazine. 24-inch barrel, 26-inch in cal. 220 Swift. Weight, about 8 pounds. Open rear sight, bead front sight on ramp. NRA-type stock with checkered pistol grip and forearm. Made from 1930 to 1936.

Winchester Model 54 Carbine.................... **$550**
Improved type. Same as Model 54 Standard Grade Sporting Rifle of this type, except has 20-inch barrel. Weight, about 7½ pounds. This model may have either NRA-type stock or the lightweight stock found on the first type Model 54 Carbine.

Winchester Model 54 Super Grade.............. **$550**
Same as standard Model 54 Sporter, except has deluxe stock with cheekpiece, black fore-end tip, pistol-grip cap, quick detachable swivels, 1-inch sling strap.

Winchester Model 54 Sniper's Rifle............. **$575**
Same as standard Model 54, except has heavy 26-inch barrel, Lyman #48 rear peep sight and blade front sight, semi-military stock, weighs 11¾ pounds, caliber 30-06 only.

Winchester Model 54 Sniper's Match Rifle...... **$670**
Similar to the earlier Model 54 Sniper's Rifle, except has Marksman-type target stock, scope bases, weighs 12½ pounds. Available in same calibers as Model 54 Standard Grade.

Winchester Model 54 National Match Rifle...... **$685**
Same as standard Model 54, except has Lyman sights, scope bases, Marksman-type target stock, weighs 9½ pounds. Same calibers as standard model.

Winchester Model 54 Target Rifle.............. **$725**
Same as standard Model 54, except has 24-inch medium weight barrel (26-inch in cal. 220 Swift), Lyman sights, scope bases, Marksman-type target stock, weighs 10½ pounds, same calibers as standard model.

Winchester Model 56 Bolt Action Sporting Rifle. **$120**
Solid frame. Caliber, 22 Long Rifle, 22 Short. 5- or 10-shot detachable box magazine. 22-inch barrel. Weight, 4¾ pounds. Open rear sight, bead front sight. Plain pistol-grip stock with schnabel fore-end. Made from 1926 to 1929.

Winchester Model 57 Bolt Action Target Rifle.. **$195**
Solid frame. Same as Model 56, except available (until 1929) in 22 Short as well as Long Rifle, has semi-military style target stock, swivels and web sling, Lyman peep rear sight, blade front sight, weighs 5 pounds. Made from 1926 to 1936.

Winchester Model 58 Bolt Action Single Shot Rifle... **$ 90**
Similar to Model 02. Takedown. Caliber, 22 Short, Long, Long Rifle. 18-inch barrel. Weight, 3 pounds. Open rear sight, blade front sight. Plain, flat, straight-grip stock. Made from 1928 to 1931.

Winchester Model 59 Bolt Action Single Shot Rifle... **$125**
Improved version of Model 58, has 23-inch barrel, redesigned stock with pistol grip, weighs 4½ pounds. Made in 1930.

Winchester Model 60 Bolt Action Single Shot Rifle... **$ 90**
Redesign of Model 59. Caliber, 22 Short, Long, Long Rifle. 23-inch barrel (27-inch after 1933). Weight, 4¼ pounds. Open rear sight, blade front sight. Plain stock with pistol grip. Made from 1930 to 1934.

Winchester Model 60A Target Rifle............. **$145**
Essentially the same as Model 60, except has Lyman peep rear sight and square top front sight, semi-military target stock and web sling, weighs 5½ pounds. Made from 1932 to 1939.

Winchester Model 61 Hammerless Slide Action Repeater...**$395**
Takedown. Caliber, 22 Short, Long, Long Rifle. Tubular magazine holds 20 Short, 16 Long, 14 Long Rifle. 24-inch round barrel. Weight, 5½ pounds. Open rear sight, bead front sight. Plain pistol-grip stock, grooved semi-beavertail slide handle. Also available with 24-inch full-octagon barrel and chambered for 22 L.R. only, 22 Short only or 22 W.R.F. only. Made from 1932 to 1963.

Winchester Model 61 Magnum.................. **$425**
Same as standard Model 61, except chambered for 22 R.F. Magnum cartridge; magazine holds 12 rounds. Made from 1960 to 1963.

Winchester Model 62 Visible Hammer Slide Action Repeater.....................................**$395**
Modernized version of Model 1890. Caliber, 22 Short, Long, Long Rifle. 23-inch barrel. Weight, 5½ pounds. Plain straight-grip stock, grooved semi-beavertail slide handle. Also available in Gallery Model chambered for 22 Short only. Made from 1932 to 1959.

Winchester Model 63 Self-Loading Rifle........ **$395**
Takedown. Caliber, 22 Long Rifle High Speed only. 10-shot tubular magazine in buttstock. 23-inch barrel. Weight, 5½ pounds. Open rear sight, bead front sight. Plain pistol-grip stock and forearm. Originally available with 20-inch barrel as well as 23-inch. Made from 1933 to 1959.

Winchester Model 67 Bolt Action Single Shot Rifle... **$110**
Takedown. Calibers: 22 Short, Long, Long Rifle, 22 L.R. shot (smoothbore), 22 W.R.F. 27-inch barrel. Weight, 5 pounds. Open rear sight, bead front sight. Plain pistol-grip stock (original model had grasping grooves in forearm). Made from 1934 to 1963.

Winchester Model 67 Boy's Rifle................ **$110**
Same as Standard Model 67, except has shorter stock, 20-inch barrel, weighs 4¼ pounds.

Winchester Model 68 Bolt Action Single Shot Rifle... **$120**
Same as Model 67, except has rear peep sight. Made from 1934 to 1946.

Winchester Model 62

Winchester Model 63

Winchester Model 67

Winchester Model 68

Winchester Model 69

Winchester Model 69 Match

Winchester Model 70 Standard (pre-1964)

Winchester Model 70 Standard (1964)

**Winchester Model 69 Bolt Action
Repeating Rifle** **$125**
Takedown. Caliber, 22 Short, Long, Long Rifle. 5- or 10-shot box
magazine. 25-inch barrel. Weight, 5½ pounds. Peep or open rear
sight. Plain pistol-grip stock. Made from 1935 to 1963.

Winchester Model 69 Target Rifle **$135**
Same as Standard Model 69, except has Winchester Peep rear
sight, swivels and sling.

Winchester Model 69 Match Rifle **$145**
Same as Model 69 Target except has Lyman #57EW receiver
sight.

Winchester Model 70 Bolt Action Repeating Rifle
Introduced in 1937, this model was offered in a number of styles
and calibers; only minor design changes were made over a period
of 27 years. More than one-half million of these rifles weresold.
In 1964, the original Model 70 was superseded by a revised
version with redesigned action, improved bolt, swaged barrel,
restyled stock (barrel free-floating). This model again under-
went major changes in 1972–most visible: new stock with contrasting fore-end tip and grip cap, cut checkering (instead of
impressed as in predecessor), knurled bolt handle. Action (machined from a solid block of steel) and barrel are chrome
molybdenum steel.

Pre-1964 Type

Winchester Model 70 Standard Grade **$595**
Calibers: 22 Hornet, 220 Swift, 243 Win., 250-3000, 257 Roberts,
270 Win., 7x57mm, 30-06, 308 Win., 300 H&H Mag., 375 H&H
Mag. 5-shot box magazine (4-shot in Magnum calibers). 24-inch
barrel standard; 26-inch in 220 Swift and 300 Mag.; 25-inch in
375 Mag.; at one time, a 20-inch barrel was available. Open rear
sight, hooded ramp front sight. Checkered walnut stock; Monte
Carlo comb standard on later production. Weight, from 7¾
pounds, depending upon caliber and barrel length. Made from
1937 to 1963.

Winchester Model 70 Super Grade **$995**
Same as Standard Grade Model 70, except has deluxe stock with
cheekpiece, black fore-end tip, pistol-grip cap, quick detachable
swivels, sling. Discontinued 1960.

Winchester Model 70 Featherweight Sporter **$595**
Same as Standard Model 70, except has redesigned stock and 22-
inch barrel, aluminum trigger guard, floorplate and butt plate.
Calibers: 243 Win., 264 Win. Mag., 270 Win., 308 Win., 30-06,
358 Win. Weight, about 6½ pounds. Made from 1952 to 1963.

**Winchester Model 70 Super Grade
Featherweight** **$695**
Same as Standard Grade Featherweight except has deluxe stock
with cheekpiece, black fore-end tip, pistol-grip cap, quick detachable swivels, sling. Discontinued 1960.

Winchester Model 70 National Match Rifle **$650**
Same as Standard Model 70, except has scope bases, Marksman
type target stock, weighs 9½ pounds, caliber 30-06 only. Discontinued 1960.

Winchester Model 70 Target Rifle **$700**
Same as Standard Model 70, except has 24-inch medium-weight
barrel, scope bases, Marksman stock, weight about 10½ pounds.
Originally offered in all ofthe Model 70 calibers, this rifle later
was available in calibers 243 Win. and 30-06. Discontinued 1963.

Winchester Model 70 Bull Gun **$650**
Same as Standard Model 70, except has heavy 28-inch barrel,
scope bases, Marksman stock, weighs 13¼ pounds, caliber 300
H&H Magnum and 30-06 only. Discontinued 1963.

Winchester Model 70 Varmint Rifle **$550**
Same general specifications as Standard Model 70, except has
26-inch heavy barrel, scope bases, special varminter stock.
Calibers, 220 Swift, 243 Win. Made from 1956 to 1963.

Winchester Model 70 African Rifle **$1380**
Same general specifications as Super Grade Model 70, except
has 25-inch barrel, 3-shot magazine, Monte Carlo stock with
recoil pad. Weight, about 9½ pounds. Caliber, 458 Winchester
Magnum. Made from 1956 to 1963.

Winchester Model 70 Westerner **$895**
Same as Standard Model 70, except calibers 264 Win. Mag., 300
Win. Mag.; 3-shot magazine: 26-inch barrel in former caliber, 24-
inch in latter; weight, about 8¼ pounds. Made from 1960 to
1963.

Winchester Model 70 Magnum (1964)

Winchester Model 70 African (1964)

Winchester Model 70 Target (1964)

Winchester Model 70 Deluxe (1964)

Winchester Model 70 Mannlicher (1964)

Winchester Model 70 Alaskan................... **$795**
Same as Standard Model 70, except calibers 338 Win. Mag., 375 H&H Mag.; 3-shot magazine in 338, 4-shot in 375 caliber; 25-inch barrel; stock with recoil pad; weight, 8 pounds in 338, 8¾ pounds in 375 caliber. Made from 1960 to 1963.

1964 Type

Winchester Model 70 Standard................. **$280**
Calibers: 22-250, 222 Rem., 225, 243, 270, 308 Win., 30-06. 5-shot box magazine. 22-inch barrel. Weight, 7½ pounds. Open rear sight, hooded ramp front sight. Monte Carlo stock with cheekpiece, checkering, swivels. Made from 1964 to 1971.

Winchester Model 70 Magnum
Calibers: 7mm Rem. Mag.; 264, 300, 338 Win. Mag.; 375 H&H Mag. 3-shot magazine. 24-inch barrel. Weight, 7¾ to 8½ pounds. Open rear sight, hooded ramp front sight. Monte Carlo stock with cheekpiece, checkering, twin stock-reinforcing bolts, recoil pad, swivels. Made from 1964 to 1971.
Caliber 375 H&H Mag...............................$400
Other calibers....................................... 280

Winchester Model 70 African................... **$595**
Caliber, 458 Win. Mag. 3-shot magazine. 22-inch barrel. Weight, 8½ pounds. Special "African" sights. Monte Carlo stock with

ebony fore-end tip, hand-checkering, twin stock-reinforcing bolts, recoil pad, QD swivels. Made from 1964 to 1971.

Winchester Model 70 Varmint................... **$325**
Same as Model 70 Standard, except has 24-inch target weight barrel, blocks for target scope, no sights, available in calibers 22-250, 222 Rem., and 243 Win. only. Weight, 9¾ pounds. Made from 1964 to 1971.

Winchester Model 70 Target.................... **$450**
Calibers, 308 Win. (7.62 NATO) and 30-06. 5-shot box magazine. 24-inch heavy barrel. Blocks for target scope, no sights. Weight, 10¼ pounds. High comb Marksman-style stock, aluminum hand stop, swivels. Made from 1964 to 1971.

Winchester Model 70 Deluxe................... **$400**
Calibers: 243, 270 Win., 30-06, 300 Win. Mag. 5-shot box magazine (3-shot in Magnum). 22-inch barrel (24-inch in Magnum). Weight, 7½ pounds. Open rear sight, hooded ramp front sight. Monte Carlo stock with ebony fore-end tip, hand-checkering, QD swivels, recoil pad on Magnum. Made from 1964 to 1971.

Winchester Model 70 Mannlicher............... **$480**
Calibers: 243, 270, 308 Win., 30-06. 5-shot box magazine. 19-inch barrel. Open rear sight, hooded ramp front sight. Weight, 7½ pounds. Mannlicher-style stock with Monte Carlo comb and cheekpiece, checkering, steel fore-end cap, QD swivels. Made from 1969 to 1971.

Winchester Model 70A

Winchester Model 70 Standard

Winchester Model 70 Magnum (1972)

Winchester Model 70 International Army Match Rifle $550
Caliber, 308 Win. (7.62 NATO). 5-shot box magazine. 24-inch heavy barrel. Externally adjustable trigger. Weight, 11 pounds. ISU stock with military oil finish, forearm rail for standard accessories, vertically adjustable butt plate. Made in 1971. Value shown is for rifle without sights.

1972 Type

Winchester Model 70A $240
Calibers: 222 Rem., 22-250, 243 Win., 25-06, 270 Win., 30-06, 308 Win. 4-shot magazine. 22-inch barrel (except 24- or 26-inch in 25-06). Weight, about 7½ pounds. Open rear sight, hooded ramp front sight. Monte Carlo stock with checkered pistol grip and forearm, sling swivels. Made from 1972 to date.

Winchester Model 70A Magnum $250
Same as Model 70A, except has 3-shot magazine, 24-inch barrel, recoil pad; weight, about 7¾ pounds. Calibers: 264 Win. Mag., 7mm Rem. Mag., 300 Win. Mag. Made from 1972 to date.

Winchester Model 70 Standard $280
Same as Model 70A, except has 5-shot magazine, Monte Carlo stock with cheekpiece, black fore-end tip and pistol-grip cap with white spacers, checkered pistol grip and forearm, detachable sling swivels. Same calibers plus 225 Win. Made from 1972 to date.

Winchester Model 70 Magnum
Same as Model 70, except has 3-shot magazine, 24-inch barrel, reinforced stock with recoil pad; weight, about 7¾ pounds (except 8½ pounds in 375 H&H Mag.). Calibers: 264 Win. Mag., 7mm Rem. Mag., 300 Win. Mag., 338 Win. Mag., 375 H&H Mag. Made from 1972 to date.
375 H&H Magnum $395
Other magnum calibers 280

Winchester Model 70 African $455
Similar to Model 70 Magnum, except caliber 458 Win. Mag.; has 22-inch barrel, special African open rear sight, reinforced stock with ebony fore-end tip, detachable swivels and sling; weight, about 8½ pounds. Made from 1972 to date.

Winchester Model 70 African (1972)

Winchester Model 70 Varmint (1972)

Winchester Model 70 Target (1972)

Winchester Model 70 International Army Match

Winchester Model 70 XTR Featherweight

Winchester Model 670 Rifle

Winchester Model 670 Carbine

Winchester Model 670 Magnum

Winchester Model 770

Winchester Model 70 Varmint..................$475
Same as Model 70 Standard, except has medium-heavy 24-inch barrel, no sights, stock with less drop; weight, about 9¾ pounds. Calibers: 222 Rem., 22-250, 243 Win. Made from 1972 to date.

Winchester Model 70 Target...................$495
Calibers, 30-06 and 308 Win. (7.62mm NATO). 5-shot magazine. 26-inch heavy barrel. Weight, 10½ pounds. No sights. High-comb Marksman style target stock, aluminum hand stop, swivels. Made from 1972 to date.

Winchester Model 70 Ultra Match..............$500
Similar to Model 70 Target, but custom grade; has 26-inch heavy barrel with deep counterbore, glass bedding, externally adjustable trigger. Made from 1972 to date.

Winchester Model 70 International Army
Match..$500
Caliber, 308 Win. (7.62mm NATO). 5-shot magazine, clip slot in receiver bridge. 24-inch heavy barrel. Weight, 11 pounds. No sights. ISU target stock. Made from 1973 to date.

Winchester Model 70 Featherweight...........$280
Similar to standard Win. Model 70, except lightweight American walnut stock with classic schnabel forend, checkered. 22-inch barrel, hooded blade front sight, folding leaf rear sight. Stainless steel magazine follower. Weight, 6¾ pounds.

Winchester Model 670 Bolt Action
Sporting Rifle...................................$150
Calibers: 225 Win., 243 Win., 270 Win., 30-06, 308 Win. 4-shot magazine. 22-inch barrel. Weight, 7 pounds. Open rear sight, ramp front sight. Monte Carlo stock with checkered pistol grip and forearm. Made from 1967 to 1973.

Winchester Model 670 Carbine.................$140
Same as Model 670 Rifle, except has 19-inch barrel; weight, 6¾ pounds. Calibers: 243 Win., 270 Win., 30-06. Made from 1967 to 1970.

Winchester Model 670 Magnum.................$175
Same as Model 670 Rifle, except has 24-inch barrel, reinforced stock with recoil pad; weight, 7¼ pounds. Calibers: 264 Win. Mag., 7mm Rem. Mag., 300 Win. Mag. Made from 1967 to 1970.

Winchester Model 770 Bolt Action
Sporting Rifle...................................$250
Model 70 type action. Calibers: 22-250, 222 Rem., 243, 270 Win., 30-06. 4-shot box magazine. 22-inch barrel. Open rear sight, hooded ramp front sight. Weight, 7⅛ pounds. Monte Carlo stock, checkered, swivels. made from 1969 to 1971.

Winchester Model 770 Magnum.................$260
Same as standard Model 770, except 24-inch barrel, weight 7¼ pounds, recoil pad. Calibers: 7mm Rem. Mag., 264 and 300 Win. Mag. Made from 1969 to 1971.

Winchester Model 71 Special Lever Action Repeating Rifle... **$625**
Solid frame. Caliber, 348 Win. 4-shot tubular magazine, 20- or 24-inch barrel. Weight, 8 pounds. Open rear sight, bead front sight on ramp with hood. Walnut stock, checkered pistol grip and forearm, grip cap, quick-detachable swivels and sling. Made from 1935 to 1957.

Winchester Model 71 Standard Grade.......... **$475**
Plain Model. Same as Model 71 Special, except lacks checkering, grip car, sling and swivels.

Winchester Model 72 Bolt Action Repeating Rifle.................................. **$125**
Tubular magazine. takedown. Caliber, 22 Short, Long, Long Rifle. Magazine holds 20 Short, 16 Long or 15 Long Rifle. 25-inch barrel. Weight, 5¾ pounds. Peep or open rear sight, bead front sight. Plain pistol-grip stock. Made from 1938 to 1959.

Winchester Model 74 Self-Loading Rifle........ **$145**
Takedown. Calibers: 22 Short only, 22 Long Rifle only. Tubular magazine in buttstock holds 20 Short, 14 Long Rifle. 24-inch barrel. Weight, 6¼ pounds. Open rear sight, bead front sight. Plain pistol-grip stock, one-piece. Made from 1939 to 1955.

Winchester Model 75 Bolt Action Target Rifle.. **$250**
Caliber, 22 Long Rifle. 5- or 10-shot box magazine. 28-inch barrel. Weight, 8¾ pounds. Target sights (Lyman, Redfield or Winchester). Target stock with pistol grip and semi-beavertail forearm, swivels and sling. Made from 1938 to 1959.

Winchester Model 75 Sporting Rifle............. **$325**
Same as Model 75 Target, except has 24-inch barrel, checkered sporter stock, open rear sight and bead front sight on hooded ramp, weighs 5½ pounds.

Winchester Model 47 Bolt Action Single Shot Rifle... **$135**
Caliber, 22 Short, Long, Long Rifle. 25-inch barrel. Weight, 5½ pounds. Peep or open rear sight, bead front sight. Plain pistol-grip stock. Made from 1949 to 1954.

Winchester Model 43 Bolt Action Sporting Rifle. **$285**
Standard Grade. Calibers: 218 Bee, 22 Hornet, 25-20, 32-20 (latter two discontinued 1950). 3-shot detachable box magazine. 24-inch barrel. Weight, 6 pounds. Open rear sight, bead front sight on hooded ramp. Plain pistol-grip stock with swivels. Made from 1949 to 1957.

Winchester Model 43 Special Grade............. **$350**
Same as Standard Model 43, except has checkered pistol grip and forearm, grip cap.

Winchester Model 71 Special

Winchester Model 72

Winchester Model 74

Winchester Model 75 Target

Winchester Model 75 Sporter

Winchester Model 47

Winchester Model 43 Special Grade

Winchester Model 55

Winchester Model 88

Winchester Model 88 Carbine

Winchester Model 55 "Automatic" Single Shot Rifle **$130**
Caliber, 22 Short, Long, Long Rifle. 22-inch barrel. Open rear sight, bead front sight. One-piece walnut stock. Weight, about 5½ pounds. Made from 1958 to 1960.

Winchester Model 88 Lever Action Rifle **$275**
Hammerless. Calibers: 243 Win., 284 Win., 308 Win., 358 Win. 4-shot box magazine. 3-shot in pre-1963 models and in current 284. 22-inch barrel. Weight, about 7¼ pounds. One-piece walnut stock with pistol grip, swivels (1965 and later models have basket-weave ornamentation instead of checkering). Made from 1955 to 1973. *Note:* 243 and 358 introduced 1956, latter discontinued 1964; 284 introduced 1963.

Winchester Model 88 Carbine **$325**
Same as Model 88 Rifle, except has 19-inch barrel, plain carbine-style stock and forearm with barrel band; weight, 7 pounds. Made from 1968 to 1973.

Winchester Model 77 Semiautomatic Rifle, Clip Type **$150**
Solid frame. Caliber, 22 Long Rifle. 8-shot clip magazine. 22-inch barrel. Weight, about 5½ pounds. Open rear sight, bead front sight. Plain, one-piece stock with pistol grip. Made from 1955 to 1963.

Winchester Model 77, Tubular Magazine Type .. **$150**
Same as Model 77. Clip type, except has tubular magazine holding 15 rounds. Made from 1955 to 1963.

Winchester Model 100 Autoloading Rifle **$350**
Gas-operated semiautomatic. Calibers: 243, 284, 308 Win. 4-shot clip magazine (3-shot in 284). 22-inch barrel. Weight, 7¼ pounds. Open rear sight, hooded ramp front sight. One-piece stock with pistol grip, basket-weave checkering, grip cap, sling swivels. Made from 1961 to 1973.

Winchester Model 100 Carbine **$325**
Same as Model 100 Rifle, except has 19-inch barrel, plain carbine-style stock and forearm with barrel band; weight, 7 pounds. Made from 1967 to 1973.

Winchester Model 250 Standard Lever Action Rifle .... **$ 80**
Hammerless. Caliber, 22 Short, Long or Long Rifle. Tubular magazine holds 21 Short, 17 Long, 15 L.R. 20½-inch barrel. Open rear sight, ramp front sight. Weight, about 5 pounds. Plain stock and forearm on early production; later model has checkering. Made from 1963 to 1973.

Winchester Model 255 Standard Rifle .... **$ 90**
Same as Model 250 Standard Rifle, except chambered for 22 Win. mag. R.F. cartridge. Magazine holds 11 rounds. Made from 1964 to 1970.

Winchester Model 77 Clip Type

Winchester Model 77 Tubular Magazine

Winchester Model 100

Winchester Model 100 Carbine

Winchester Model 250 Standard

Winchester Model 150

Winchester Model 270 Standard

Winchester Model 250 Deluxe Rifle.............$100

Same as Model 250 Standard Rifle, except has fancy walnut Monte Carlo stock and forearm, sling swivels. Made from 1965 to 1971.

Winchester Model 255 Deluxe Rifle.............$120

Same as Model 250 Deluxe Rifle, except chambered for 22 Win. Mag. R.F. cartridge. Magazine holds 11 rounds. Made from 1965 to 1973.

Winchester Model 150 Lever Action Carbine.... $ 80

Same as Model 250, except has straight loop lever, plain carbine-style straight-grip stock and forearm with barrel band. Made from 1967 to 1973.

Winchester Model 270 Standard Slide Action Rifle... $ 80

Hammerless. Caliber, 22 Short, Long or Long Rifle. Tubular magazine holds 21 Short, 17 Long, 15 L.R. 20½-inch barrel. Open rear sight, ramp front sight. Weight, about 5 pounds. Early production had plain walnut stock and forearm (slide handle); latter also furnished in plastic (Cycolac); last model has checkering. Made from 1963 to 1973.

Winchester Model 275 Standard Rifle........... $ 90

Same as Model 270 Standard Rifle, except chambered for 22 Win. Mag. R.F. cartridge. Magazine holds 11 rounds. Made from 1964 to 1970.

Winchester Model 270 Deluxe Rifle.............$100

Same as Model 270 Standard Rifle, except has fancy walnut Monte Carlo stock and forearm. Made from 1965 to 1973.

Winchester Model 275 Deluxe Rifle.............$110

Same as Model 270 Deluxe Rifle, except chambered for 22 Win. Mag. R.F. cartridge. Magazine holds 11 rounds. Made from 1965 to 1970.

Winchester Model 290 Standard Semiautomatic Rifle

Caliber, 22 Long or Long Rifle. Tubular magazine holds 17 Long, 15 L.R. 20½-inch barrel. Open rear sight, ramp front sight. Weight, about 5 pounds. Plain stock and forearm on early production; current model has checkering. Made from 1963 to 1977.

With plain stock and forearm........................ $ 65
With checkered stock and forearm.................... 70

Winchester Model 290 Deluxe Rifle.............$ 95

Same as Model 290 Standard Rifle, except has fancy walnut Monte Carlo stock and forearm. Made from 1965 to 1973.

Winchester Model 190 Semiautomatic Rifle..... $ 70

Same as current Model 290, except has plain stock and forearm. Made from 1966 to 1978.

Winchester Model 190 Carbine.................. $ 75

Same as Model 190, except has carbine style forearm with barrel band. Made from 1967 to 1973.

Winchester Model 121 Standard Bolt Action Single Shot...$ 55

Caliber, 22 Short, Long, Long Rifle. 20¾-inch barrel. Weight, 5 pounds. Open rear sight, bead front sight. Monte Carlo style stock. Made from 1967 to 1973.

Winchester Model 121 Youth.................... $ 55

Same as Model 121 Standard, except has 1¼-inch shorter stock. Made from 1967 to 1973.

Winchester Model 121 Deluxe................... $ 60

Same as Model 121 Standard, except has ramp front sight, stock with fluted comb and sling swivels. Made from 1967 to 1973.

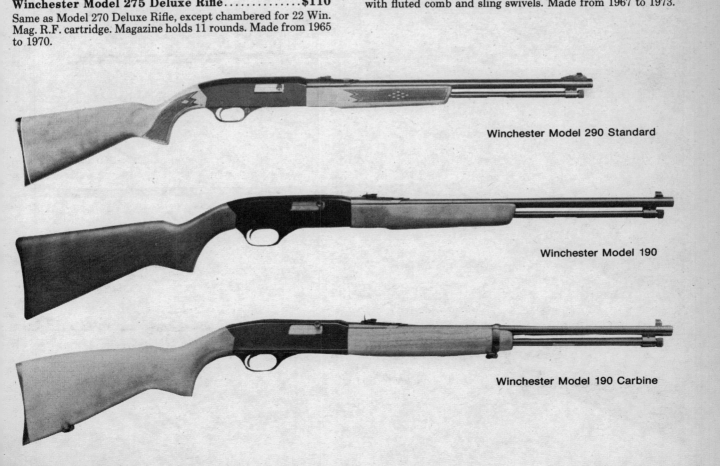

Winchester Model 290 Standard

Winchester Model 190

Winchester Model 190 Carbine

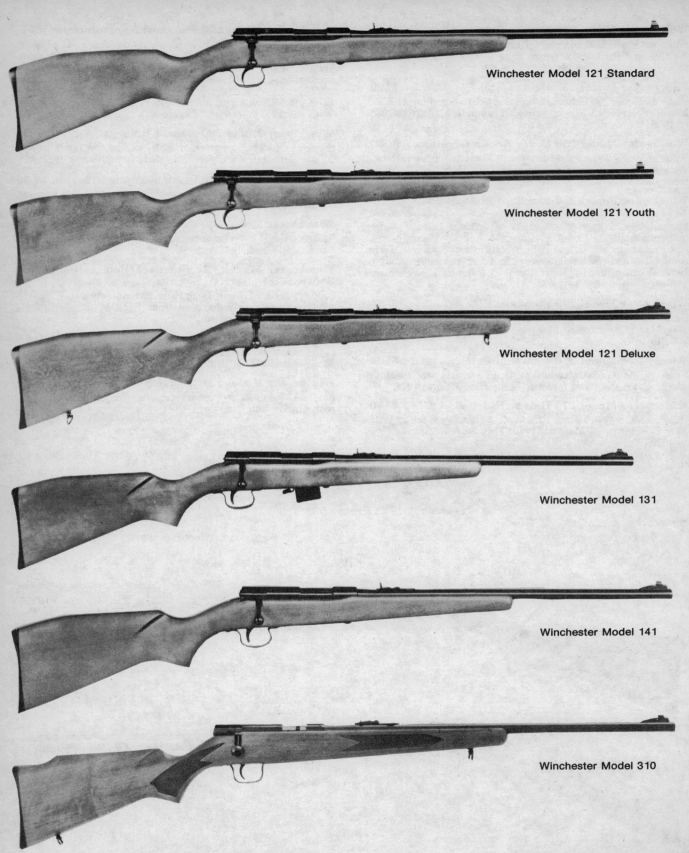

Winchester Model 121 Standard

Winchester Model 121 Youth

Winchester Model 121 Deluxe

Winchester Model 131

Winchester Model 141

Winchester Model 310

Winchester Model 131 Bolt Action Repeating Rifle.................................... $ 70
Caliber, 22 Short, Long or Long Rifle. 7-shot clip magazine. 20¾-inch barrel. Weight, 5 pounds. Open rear sight, ramp front sight. Plain Monte Carlo stock. Made from 1967 to 1973.

Winchester Model 135........................... $ 75
Same as Model 131, except chambered for 22 Win. Mag. R.F. cartridge. Magazine holds 5 rounds. Made in 1967.

Winchester Model 141 Bolt Action Tubular Repeater... $ 75
Same as Model 131, except has tubular magazine in buttstock; holds 19 Short, 15 Long, 13 Long Rifle. Made from 1967 to 1973.

Winchester Model 145........................... $ 75
Same as Model 141, except chambered for 22 Win. Mag. R.F.; magazine holds 9 rounds. Made in 1967.

Winchester Model 310 Bolt Action Single Shot .. $ 70
Caliber, 22 Short, Long, Long Rifle. 22-inch barrel. Weight, 5⅝ pounds. Open rear sight, ramp front sight. Monte Carlo stock with checkered pistol grip and forearm, sling swivels. Made from 1972 to 1975.

Winchester Model 320 Bolt Action Repeater.... $ 75
Same as Model 310, except has 5-shot clip magazine. Made from 1972 to 1974.

Winchester Model 9422 Lever Action Carbine.. $175
Styled after Model 94. Caliber, 22 Short, Long, Long Rifle. Tubular magazine holds 21 Short, 17 Long, 15 Long Rifle. 20½-inch barrel. Weight, 6¼ pounds. Open rear sight, hooded ramp front sight. Carbine style stock and forearm, barrel band. Made from 1972 to date.

Winchester Model 9422M........................ $190
Same as Model 9422, except chambered for 22 Win. Mag. R.F.; magazine holds 11 rounds. Made from 1972 to date.

Winchester Model 490 Semiautomatic Rifle..... $150
Caliber, 22 Long Rifle. 5-shot clip magazine. 22-inch barrel. Weight, 6 pounds. Folding leaf rear sight, hooded ramp front sight. One-piece walnut stock with checkered pistol grip and forearm. Made from 1975 to 1977.

Winchester Double Xpress Rifle................ $1750
Over/under double rifle. Caliber, 30-06. 23½-inch barrel. Weight, 8½ pounds. Made for Olin Corporation, Winchester Group, by Olin-Dodensha in Japan. Introduced in 1982.

Winchester Model 320

Winchester Model 9422

Winchester Model 490

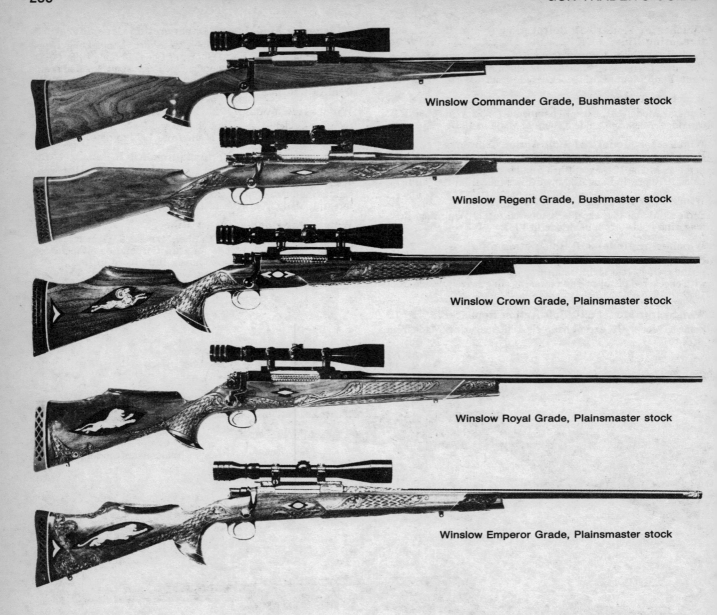

Winslow Commander Grade, Bushmaster stock

Winslow Regent Grade, Bushmaster stock

Winslow Crown Grade, Plainsmaster stock

Winslow Royal Grade, Plainsmaster stock

Winslow Emperor Grade, Plainsmaster stock

Winslow Arms Company, Camden, South Carolina

Winslow Bolt Action Sporting Rifle

Action: FN Supreme Mauser, Mark X Mauser, Remington 700 and 788, Sako, Winchester 70. Standard calibers: 17/222, 17/223, 222 Rem., 22-250, 243 Win., 6mm Rem., 25-06, 257 Roberts, 270 Win., 7x57, 280 Rem., 284 Win., 308 Win., 30-06, 358 Win.; magnum calibers: 17/222 mg, 257 Weatherby, 264 Win., 270 Weath., 7mm Rem., 7mm Weath., 300 H&H, 300 Weath., 300 Win., 308 Norma, 8mm Rem., 338 Win., 358 Norma, 375 H&H, 375 Weath., 458 Win. 3-shot magazine in standard calibers, 2-shot in magnum. 24-inch barrel in standard calibers, 26-inch in magnum. Weights: with 24-inch barrel, 7 to 7½ pounds; with 26-inch barrel, 8 to 9 pounds. No sights. Stocks: "Bushmaster" with slender pistol grip and beavertail forearm, "Plainsmaster" with full curl pistol grip and flat forearm; both styles have Monte Carlo cheekpiece; rosewood fore-end tip and pistol-grip cap, recoil pad, QD swivels; woods used include walnut, maple, myrtle. There are eight grades – Commander, Regal, Regent, Regimental, Royal, Imperial, Emperor – in ascending order of

quality of wood, carving, inlays, engraving. Values shown are for basic rifle in each grade; extras such as special fancy wood, more elaborate carving, inlays and engraving can increase these figures considerably. Made 1962 to date.

Commander Grade	$ 400
Regal Grade	485
Regent Grade	590
Regimental Grade	750
Crown Grade	1100
Royal Grade	1260
Imperial Grade	2770
Emperor Grade	5300

Z-B Rifle manufactured by Ceska Zbrojovka, Brno, Czechoslovakia

Z-B Mauser Varmint Rifle $650

Same as Brno Hornet Rifle. See listing of that rifle for specifications.

Section III
SHOTGUNS

AyA Matador II

Aguirre y Aranzabal (AyA), Eibar, Spain

**AyA Matador Hammerless Double Barrel
Shotgun** **$340**
Anson & Deeley box lock. Selective automatic ejectors. Selective single trigger. Gauges: 12, 16, 20, 20 magnum (3-inch). Barrels: 26-, 28-, 30-inch; any standard choke combination. Weights: from 6½ to 7½ pounds, depending upon gauge and barrel length. Checkered pistol-grip stock and beavertail fore-end. *Note:* This model, prior to 1956, was designated F. I. Model 400E by the U.S. importer, Firearms International Corp., Washington, D.C. Made from 1955 to 1963.

AyA Matador II **$375**
Improved version of Matador with same general specifications, except has ventilated-rib barrels. Made from 1964 to 1969.

AyA Bolero **$225**
Same general specifications as "Matador" except non-selective single trigger and extractors. Gauges: 12, 16, 20, 20 magnum (3-inch), 410 (3-inch). *Note:* This model, prior to 1956, was designated F. I. Model 400 by the importer. Made from 1955 to 1963.

**AyA Model 76 Hammerless Double Barrel
Shotgun** **$390**
Anson & Deeley box lock. Automatic ejectors. Selective single trigger. Gauges: 12, 20 (3-inch). Barrels: 26-, 28-, 30-inch (latter in 12 gauge only); any standard choke combination. Checkered pistol-grip stock and beavertail fore-end. Currently manufactured.

AyA Model 76 410 . . . . **$310**
Same general specifications as 12 and 20 gauge Model 76, except chambered for 3-inch shells in 410, has extractors, double triggers, 26-inch barrels only, English-style stock with straight grip and small fore-end. Currently manufactured.

**AyA Model 117 Hammerless Double Barrel
Shotgun** **$580**
Holland & Holland type side locks, hand-detachable. Engraved action. Automatic ejectors. Selective single trigger. Gauges: 12, 20 (3-inch). Barrels: 26-, 27-, 28-, 30-inch (27- and 30-inch in 12 gauge only); any standard choke combination. Checkered pistol-grip stock and beavertail fore-end of select walnut. Currently manufactured.

AyA Model 53E **$950**
Same general specifications as Model 117, except more elaborate engraving and select figured wood. Currently manufactured.

**AyA Model 37 Super Over-and-Under
Shotgun** **$1800**
Side lock. Automatic ejectors. Selective single trigger. Made in all gauges, barrel lengths and chokes. Ventilated-rib barrels. Elaborately engraved. Checkered stock (with straight or pistol grip) and fore-end. Currently manufactured.

AyA Model 76

AyA Model 117

AyA Model 53E

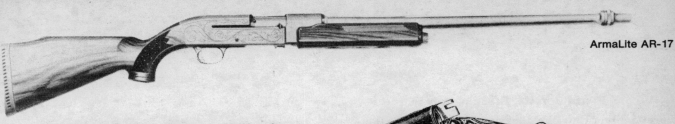

ArmaLite AR-17

ArmaLite, Inc., Costa Mesa, California

Armalite AR-17 Golden Gun.................... $440

Recoil-operated semiautomatic. High-test aluminum barrel and receiver housing. 12 gauge only. 2-shot. 24-inch barrel with interchangeable choke tubes: improved cylinder, modified, and full. Weight, 5.6 pounds. Polycarbonate stock and forearm, recoil pad. Gold anodized finish standard; also made with black finish. Made from 1964 to 1965. Less than 2,000 produced.

Baker Batavia Leader

Baker Shotguns made from 1903 to 1933 by Baker Gun Co., Batavia, N.Y.

Baker Batavia Leader Hammerless Double Barrel Shotgun

Side lock. Plain extractors or automatic ejectors. Double triggers. Gauges: 12, 16, 20. Barrels: 26- to 32-inch; any standard boring. Weight, about 7¾ pounds (12 gauge with 30-inch barrels). Checkered pistol-grip stock and forearm.
With plain extractors.................................. $325
With automatic ejectors.............................. 425

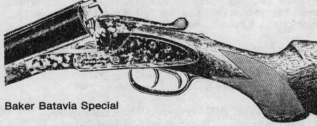

Baker Batavia Special

Baker Batavia Special........................... $270

Same general specifications as the Batavia Leader, except plainer finish, 12 and 16 gauge only; has plain extractors, Homotensile steel barrels.

Baker Black Beauty Special

Same general specifications as the Batavia Leader, except higher quality and finer finish throughout; has line engraving, special steel barrels, select walnut stock with straight, full- or half-pistol grip.
With plain extractors................................ $560
With automatic ejectors........................... 590

Baker Batavia Ejector......................... $675

Same general specifications as the Batavia Leader, except higher quality and finer finish throughout; has Damascus or Homotensile steel barrels, checkered pistol-grip stock and forearm of select walnut; automatic ejectors standard; 12 and 16 gauge only.

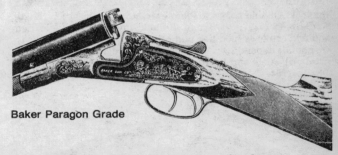

Baker Grade R

Baker Grade S

Same general specifications as the Batavia Leader, except higher quality and finer finish throughout; has Flui-tempered steel barrels, line and scroll engraving, checkered stock with half-pistol grip and forearm of semi-fancy imported walnut; 10, 12 and 16 gauges.
Nonejector... $675
With automatic ejectors.............................. 850

Baker Grade R

High grade gun with same general specifications as the Batavia Leader, except has fine Damascus or Krupp fluid steel barrels, engraving in line, scroll and game scene designs, checkered stock and forearm of fancy European walnut; 12 and 16 gauges only.
Nonejector... $ 875
With automatic ejectors........................... 1000

Baker Paragon Grade

Baker Paragon, Expert and Deluxe Grades

Made to order only, these are the higher grades of Baker hammerless side lock double barrel shotguns. After 1909, the Paragon Grade, as well as the Expert and Deluxe introduced that year, had a cross bolt in addition to the regular Baker system taper wedge fastening. There are early Paragon guns with Damascus barrels and some are non-ejector, but this grade was also produced with automatic ejectors and with the finest fluid steel barrels, in lengths to 34 inches, standard on Expert and Deluxe guns. Differences among the three models are in overall quality, finish, elaborateness of engraving and grade of fancy figured walnut in the stock and forearm; Expert and Deluxe wood may be carved as well as checkered. Choice of straight, half- or full-pistol grip was offered. A single trigger was available in the two higher grades. The Paragon was available in 10 gauge (Damascus barrels only); this and the other two models were regularly produced in 12, 16 and 20 gauges.
Paragon Grade, nonejector...........................$1200
Paragon Grade, automatic ejectors.................. 1300
Expert Grade.. 2400
Deluxe Grade.. 4500
Extra for single trigger............................ 150

Beretta Silver Hawk

Pietro Beretta, Brescia, Italy

Beretta Silver Hawk Featherweight Hammerless Double Barrel Shotgun
Box lock. Double triggers or non-selective single trigger. Plain extractor. Gauges: 12, 16, 20, 28, 12 mag. 26- to 32-inch barrels with high matted rib; all standard choke combinations. Weight, 12 ga. with 26-inch barrels, 7 pounds. Checkered walnut stock with beavertail forearm. Discontinued 1967.
With double triggers................................. $550
Extra for non-selective single trigger................. 50

Beretta Model 409 PB

Beretta Model 409PB Hammerless Double Barrel Shotgun..$625
Box lock. Double triggers. Plain extractors. Gauges: 12, 16, 20, 28. Barrels: 27½-, 28½- and 30-inch; improved cylinder and modified choke or modified and full choke. Weight, from 5½ to 7¾ pounds depending upon gauge and barrel length. Straight or pistol-grip stock and beavertail forearm, checkered. Made from 1934 to 1964.

Beretta Model 410 E

Beretta Model 410E.............................. $950
Same general specifications as Model 409PB, except has automatic ejectors and is of higher quality throughout. Made from 1934 to 1964.

Beretta Model 410, 10 Gauge Magnum......... $775
Same as Model 410E, except heavier construction. Plain extractors. Double triggers. 10 gauge magnum, 3½-inch chambers. 32-inch barrels, both full choke. Weight, about 10 pounds. Checkered pistol-grip stock and forearm, recoil pad. Made from 1934 to date.

Beretta Model 411E.............................. $975
Same general specifications as Model 409PB except has side plates, automatic ejectors and is of higher quality throughout. Made from 1934 to 1964.

Beretta Model 424 Hammerless Double Barrel Shotgun.. $600
Box lock. Light border engraving. Plain extractors. Gauges: 12, 20; chambers 2¾-inch in former, 3-inch in latter. Barrels: 28-inch modified and full choke, 26-inch improved cylinder and modified choke. Weight, 5 lbs.14 oz. to 6 lbs. 10 oz., depending upon gauge and barrel length. English style straight-grip stock and forearm, checkered. Introduced in 1977.

Beretta Model 426E............................. $800
Same as Model 424, except action body is finely engraved, silver pigeon inlaid in top lever; has selective automatic ejectors and selective single trigger, stock and forearm of select European walnut. Introduced in 1977.

Beretta Model GR-2 Hammerless Double Barrel Shotgun.. $500
Box lock. Plain extractors. Double triggers. Gauges: 12, 20; 2¾-inch chambers in former, 3-inch in latter. Barrels: ventilated rib; 30-inch modified and full choke (12 gauge only), 28-inch modified and full choke, 26-inch improved cylinder and modified choke. Weights, 6½ to 7¼ pounds, depending upon gauge and barrel length. Checkered pistol-grip stock and forearm. Made from 1968 to 1976.

Beretta Model GR-3............................. $600
Same as Model GR-2, except has selective single trigger; chambered for 12 gauge 3-inch as well as 2¾-inch shell. Magnum model has 30-inch modified and full choke barrel, recoil pad, weighs about 8 pounds. Made from 1968 to 1976.

Beretta Model GR-4............................. $700
Same as Model GR-2, except has automatic ejectors and selective single trigger, higher grade engraving and wood. 12 gauge, 2¾-inch chambers only. Made from 1968 to 1976.

Beretta Series "SO" Over-and-Under Shotguns
Side lock. Selective automatic ejectors. Selective single trigger or double triggers. 12 gauge only, 2¾- or 3-inch chambers. Barrels: ventilated rib (wide type on skeet and trap guns); 26-, 27-, 29-, 30-inch; any combination of standard chokes. Weights from about 7 to 7¾ pounds, depending upon barrel length, style of stock and density of wood. Stock and forearm of select walnut, finely checkered; straight or pistol grip; field, skeet and trap guns have appropriate styles of stock and forearm. The various models differ chiefly in quality of wood and grade of engraving. Models SO-3EL, SO-3EELL, SO-4 and SO-5 have hand-detachable locks. "SO-4" is used to designate current skeet and trap models derived from Model SO-3EL but with less elaborate engraving. Present Models SO-3EL and SO-3EELL are similar to the earlier SO-4 and SO-5 respectively. Made from 1948 to date.
Model SO-2... $2360
Model SO-3... 2800
Model SO-4 Skeet or Trap Gun (current)............ 3120
Model SO-4 (pre-1977) or SO-3EL.................. 3400
Model SO-5 or SO-3EELL......................... 4600

Beretta Models SO-6 and SO-7 Hammerless Double Barrel Shotguns

Side-by-side guns with same general specifications as Series "SO" over-and-unders. Higher grade Model SO-7 has more elaborate engraving, fancier wood. Made from 1948 to date.

Model SO-6. . . . . $5600
Model SO-7. 9250

Beretta Silver Snipe Over-and-Under Shotgun

Box lock. Non-selective or selective single trigger. Plain extractor. Gauges: 12, 20, 12 mag., 20 mag. Barrels: 26-, 28-, 30-inch; plain or ventilated rib; improved cylinder and modified choke, modified and full choke, skeet chokes #1 and #2, full and full. Weight, from about 6 pounds in 20 ga. to 8½ pounds in 12 ga. (trap gun). Checkered walnut pistol-grip stock and forearm. Made from 1955 to 1967.

With plain barrel, non-selective trigger. $420
With ventilated-rib barrel, non-selective single trigger. . 480
Extra for selective single trigger. 50

Beretta Golden Snipe Over-and-Under

Same as Silver Snipe, except has automatic ejectors, ventilated rib is standard feature. Made from 1959 to 1967.

With non-selective single trigger. $695
Extra for selective single trigger. 50

Beretta Model 57E Over-and-Under

Same general specifications as Golden Snipe, but higher quality throughout. Made from 1955 to 1967.

With non-selective single trigger. . . . . $ 750
With selective single trigger. 840

Beretta Model Asel Over-and-Under Shotgun. . $1000

Box lock. Single non-selective trigger. Selective automatic ejectors. Gauges: 12, 20. Barrels: 26-, 28-, 30-inch, improved cylinder and modified choke or modified and full choke. Weights: 20 gauge—about 5¾ pounds, 12 gauge—about 7 pounds. Checkered pistol-grip stock and forearm. Made from 1947 to 1964.

Beretta Model 57E

Beretta Model Asel

Beretta Model 424

Beretta Model 426E

Beretta Model GR-2

Beretta Model GR-3

Beretta Model GR-4

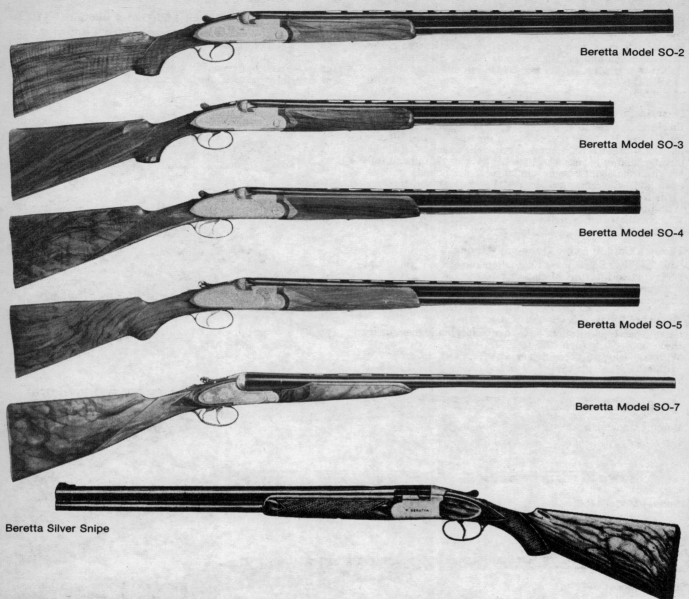

Beretta Model SO-2

Beretta Model SO-3

Beretta Model SO-4

Beretta Model SO-5

Beretta Model SO-7

Beretta Silver Snipe

Beretta Grade 100 Over-and-Under Shotgun.. $1710
Side lock. Double triggers. Automatic ejectors, 12 gauge only. Barrels: 26-, 28-, 30-inch; any standard boring. Weight, about 7½ pounds. Checkered stock and fore-end, straight grip or pistol grip. Discontinued.

Beretta Grade 200............................. **$2100**
Same general specifications as Grade 100 except higher quality, bores and action parts hard chrome-plated. Discontinued.

Beretta Model BL-1 Over-and-Under Shotgun.. $375
Box lock. Plain extractors. Double triggers. 12 gauge, 2¾-inch chambers only. Barrels: 30- and 28-inch modified and full choke, 26-inch improved cylinder and modified choke. Weight, 6¾ to 7 pounds, depending upon barrel length. Checkered pistol-grip stock and forearm. Made from 1968 to 1973.

Beretta Model BL-2............................. **$475**
Same as Model BL-1, except has more engraving, selective single trigger. Made from 1968 to 1973.

Beretta Model BL-2/S........................... **$500**
Similar to Model BL-1, except has selective "Speed-Trigger," ventilated-rib barrels, 2¾- or 3-inch chambers; weight, 7 to 7½ pounds. Made from 1974 to 1976.

Beretta Model BL-3............................. **$550**
Same as Model BL-1, except deluxe engraved receiver, selective single trigger, ventilated-rib barrels; 12 or 20 gauge, 2¾-inch or 3-inch chambers in former, 3-inch in latter; weights, 6 to 7½ pounds depending upon gauge and barrel length. Made from 1968 to 1976.

Beretta Models BL-4, BL-5 and BL-6
Higher grade versions of Model BL-3 with more elaborate engraving and fancier wood; Model BL-6 has side plates. Selective automatic ejectors standard. Made from 1968 to 1976 (Model BL-6 introduced in 1973).
Model BL-4.. $ 700
Model BL-5..   850
Model BL-6.. 1000

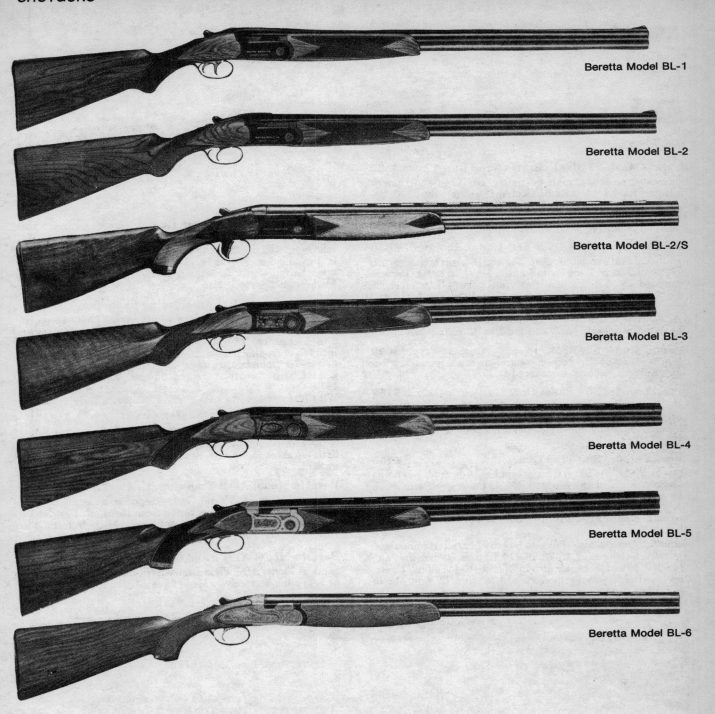

Beretta Model BL-1

Beretta Model BL-2

Beretta Model BL-2/S

Beretta Model BL-3

Beretta Model BL-4

Beretta Model BL-5

Beretta Model BL-6

Beretta Series "BL" Skeet Guns

Models BL-3, BL-4, BL-5 and BL-6 with standard features of their respective grades plus wider rib and skeet-style stock; 26-inch barrels skeet choked; weight, 6 to 7¼ pounds depending upon gauge.

Model BL-3 Skeet Gun..............................$ 550
Model BL-4 Skeet Gun.............................. 650
Model BL-5 Skeet Gun.............................. 900
Model BL-6 Skeet Gun..............................1100

Beretta Series "BL" Trap Guns

Models BL-3, BL-4, BL-5 and BL-6 with standard features of their respective grades plus wider rib and Monte Carlo stock with recoil pad; 30-inch barrels, improved modified and full or both full choke; weight, about 7½ pounds.

Model BL-3 Trap Gun.............................$ 575
Model BL-4 Trap Gun............................. 700
Model BL-5 Trap Gun............................. 900
Model BL-6 Trap Gun.............................1100

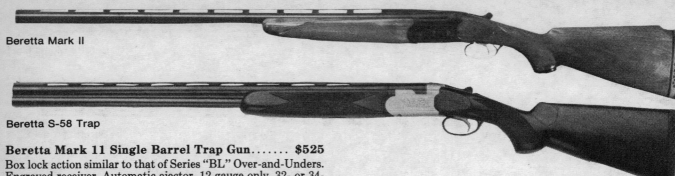

Beretta Mark II

Beretta S-58 Trap

Beretta Mark 11 Single Barrel Trap Gun....... $525

Box lock action similar to that of Series "BL" Over-and-Unders. Engraved receiver. Automatic ejector. 12 gauge only. 32- or 34-inch barrel with wide ventilated rib. Weight, about 8½ pounds. Monte Carlo stock with pistol grip and recoil pad, beavertail forearm. Made from 1972 to 1976.

Beretta Model S55B Over-and-Under Shotgun.. $550

Box lock. Plain extractors. Selective single trigger. Gauges: 12, 20; 2¾- or 3-inch chambers in former, 3-inch in latter. Barrels: ventilated rib; 30-inch modified and full choke or both full choke in 12 gauge 3-inch magnum only, 28-inch modified and full choke, 26-inch improved cylinder and modified choke. Weight, 6½ to 7½ pounds, depending upon gauge and barrel length. Checkered pistol-grip stock and forearm. Introduced in 1977.

Beretta Model S56E............................... $600

Same as Model S55B, except has scroll-engraved receiver, selective automatic ejectors. Introduced in 1977.

Beretta Model S58 Skeet Gun.................... $750

Same as Model S56E, except has 26-inch barrels of Boehler Antinit Anticorro steel, skeet choked, with wide ventilated rib; skeet-style stock and forearm; weight, 7½ pounds. Introduced in 1977.

Beretta Model S58 Trap Gun..................... $750

Same as Model S58 Skeet Gun, except has 30-inch barrels bored improved modified and full trap, Monte Carlo stock with recoil pad; weight, 7 lbs. 10 oz. Introduced in 1977.

Beretta Model FS-1 Folding Single Barrel Shotgun...$100

Formerly "Companion." Folds to length of barrel. Hammerless. Underlever. Gauges: 12, 16, 20, 28, 410. Barrels: 30-inch in 12 ga., 28-inch in 16 and 20 ga., 26-inch in 28 and 410 ga.; all full choke. Checkered semi-pistol-grip stock and forearm. Weight 4½ to 5½ pounds depending upon gauge. Discontinued 1971.

Beretta Model SL-2 Pump Gun.................. $240

Hammerless. Takedown. 12 gauge only. 3-shot magazine. Barrels: ventilated rib; 30-inch full choke, 28-inch modified, 26-inch improved cylinder. Weight, about 7 to 7¼ pounds, depending upon barrel length. Checkered pistol-grip stock and forearm. Made from 1968 to 1971.

Beretta Model AL-2 Autoloading Shotgun

Field Gun. Gas-operated. Engraved receiver (1968 version, 12 gauge only, had no engraving). Gauges: 12, 20. 2¾-inch chamber. 3-shot magazine. Barrels: ventilated rib; 30-inch full choke, 28-inch full or modified choke, 26-inch improved cylinder. Weights: 6½ to 7¼ pounds, depending upon gauge and barrel length. Checkered pistol-grip stock and forearm. Made from 1968 to 1975.

With plain receiver.................................... $275
With engraved receiver.............................. 325

Beretta Model AL-2 Skeet Gun.................. $390

Same as Model AL-2 Field Gun, except has wide rib, 26-inch barrel in skeet choke only, beavertail forearm. Made from 1969 to 1975.

Beretta Model AL-2 Trap Gun................... $410

Same as Model AL-2 Field Gun, except has wide rib, 30-inch barrel in full choke only, beavertail forearm. Monte Carlo stock with recoil pad; weight, about 7¾ pounds. Made from 1969 to 1975.

Beretta Model AL-1 Field Gun.................. $280

Same as Model AL-2 Field Gun, except has barrel without rib, no engraving on receiver. Made from 1971 to 1973.

Beretta FS-1

Beretta Model TR-1 Single Barrel Trap Gun.... $200

Hammerless. Underlever action. Engraved frame. 12 gauge only. 32-inch barrel with ventilated rib. Weight, about 8¼ pounds. Monte Carlo stock with pistol grip and recoil pad, beavertail forearm. Made from 1968 to 1971.

Beretta Model TR-2........................ $230

Same as Model TR-1, except has extended ventilated rib. Made from 1969 to 1973.

Beretta Model AL-2 Magnum.................... $390

Same as Model AL-2 Field Gun, except chambered for 12 gauge 3-inch magnum shells; 30-inch full, 28-inch modified choke barrels only; weight, about 8 pounds. Made from 1973 to 1975.

Beretta Model AL-3

Similar to corresponding AL-2 models in design and general specifications. Made from 1975 to 1976.

Field model...$360
Magnum model.................................... 390
Skeet model....................................... 390
Trap model.. 410

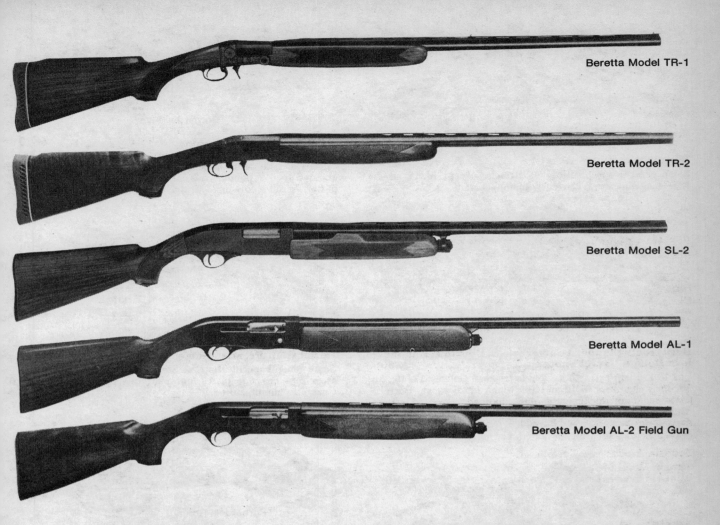

Beretta Model TR-1

Beretta Model TR-2

Beretta Model SL-2

Beretta Model AL-1

Beretta Model AL-2 Field Gun

Beretta Model AL-3 Deluxe Trap Gun........... **$700**
Same as standard Model AL-3 Trap Gun, except has fully
engraved receiver, gold-plated trigger and safety, stock and
forearm of premium grade European walnut, gold monogram
escutcheon inlaid in buttstock. Made from 1975 to 1976.

Beretta Model A-301 Autoloading Shotgun...... **$350**
Field Gun. Gas-operated. Scroll-decorated receiver. Gauges: 12,
20; 2¾-inch chamber in former, 3-inch in latter. 3-shot magazine. Barrels: ventilated rib; 28-inch full or modified choke, 26-
inch improved cylinder. Weights: 6 lbs. 5 oz. to 6 lbs. 14 oz.,
depending upon gauge and barrel length. Checkered pistol-grip
stock and forearm. Introduced in 1977.

Beretta Model A-301 Magnum.................. **$385**
Same as Model A-301 Field Gun, except chambered for 12 gauge
3-inch magnum shells; 30-inch full choke barrel only, stock with
recoil pad; weight, 7¼ pounds.

Beretta Model A-301 Skeet Gun................ **$350**
Same as Model A-301 Field Gun, except 26-inch barrel in skeet
choke only, has skeet style stock, gold-plated trigger.

Beretta Model A-301 Trap Gun................. **$350**
Same as Model A-301 Field Gun, except has 30-inch barrel in full
choke only, Monte Carlo stock with recoil pad, gold-plated
trigger; weight, 7 lbs. 10 oz.

Beretta Model A-301 Slug Gun................. **$350**
Same as Model A-301 Field Gun, except has plain 22-inch barrel,
slug choke, with rifle sights; weight, 6 lbs. 14 oz.

Bernardelli Brescia

Vincenzo Bernardelli, Gardone V.T. (Brescia), Italy

**Bernardelli Brescia Hammer Double Barrel
Shotgun**.. **$600**
Back-action side lock. Plain extractors. Double triggers. Gauges:
12, 20. Barrels: 27½ or 29½-inch modified and full choke in 12
gauge, 25½-inch improved cylinder and modified choke in 20
gauge. Weight, from 5¾ to 7 pounds, depending upon gauge and
barrel length. English-style stock and forearm, checkered. Currently manufactured.

Bernardelli Italia

Bernardelli Italia...................................$760

Same general specifications as Brescia, except higher grade engraving and wood. Currently manufactured.

Bernardelli Standard Gamecock

Bernardelli Standard Gamecock (S. Uberto 1) Hammerless Double Barrel Shotgun.....................$600

Box lock. Plain extractors. Double triggers. Gauges: 12, 16, 20; 2¾-inch chambers in 12 and 16, 3-inch in 20 gauge. Barrels: 25½-inch improved cylinder and modified choke, 27½-inch modified and full choke. Weight, from 5¾ to 6½ pounds, depending upon gauge and barrel length. English-style straight-grip stock and forearm, checkered. Currently manufactured.

Bernardelli S. Uberto 2

Bernardelli S. Uberto F.S.

Bernardelli S. Uberto 2 and S. Uberto F.S.

Same as Standard Gamecock (S. Uberto 1), except higher grade engraving and wood; S. Uberto F.S. has automatic ejectors. Currently manufactured.

S. Uberto 2...$780
S. Uberto F.S... 900

Bernardelli Elio

Bernardelli Elio....................................$870

Lightweight game gun, 12 gauge only, with same general specifications as Standard Gamecock (S. Uberto 1), except weighs about 6 to 6¼ pounds, has automatic ejectors, fine English pattern scroll engraving. Currently manufactured.

Bernardelli Premier Gamecock

Bernardelli Premier Gamecock (Roma 3).......$820

Same general specifications as Standard Gamecock (S. Uberto 1), except has side plates, automatic ejectors, single trigger. Currently manufactured.

Bernardelli Roma 6

Bernardelli Roma 4 and Roma 6

Same as Premier Gamecock (Roma 3), except higher grade engraving and wood, double triggers. Currently manufactured.

Roma 4...$ 960
Roma 6... 1080

Bernardelli V.B. Holland Deluxe

Bernardelli V.B. Holland Deluxe Hammerless Double Barrel Shotgun..................................$4560

Holland & Holland-type side lock action. Automatic ejectors. Double triggers. 12 gauge only. Any barrel length, chokes. Checkered stock (straight or pistol grip) and forearm. Currently manufactured.

Boss & Co., London, England

Boss Hammerless Double Barrel Shotgun
Side lock. Automatic ejectors. Double triggers, non-selective or selective single trigger. Made in all gauges, barrel lengths and chokes. Checkered stock and fore-end, straight or pistol grip.

With double triggers or non-selective
single trigger.................................... $15,000
With selective single trigger....................... 18,000

Boss Double Barrel

Boss Over-and-Under

Boss Hammerless Over-and-Under Shotgun ..$18,000
Side lock. Automatic ejectors. Selective single trigger. Made in all gauges, barrel lengths and chokes. Checkered stock and fore-end, straight or pistol grip. Discontinued.

Ernesto Breda, Milan, Italy

Breda Autoloading Shotgun
Recoil-operated. 12 gauge, 2¾-inch chamber. 4-shell tubular magazine. Barrels: 25½- and 27½-inch; plain, matted rib or ventilated rib; improved cylinder, modified or full choke; current model has 26-inch ventilated-rib barrel with interchangeable choke tubes. Weight, about 7¼ pounds. Checkered straight or pistol-grip stock and forearm. Currently manufactured.
With plain barrel................................... $250
With raised matted rib.............................. 260
With ventilated rib................................. 270
With ventilated rib, interchangeable choke tube....... 280

Breda Magnum
Same general specifications as standard model, except chambered for 12 gauge 3-inch magnum, 3-shot magazine; latest model has 29-inch ventilated-rib barrel. Currently manufactured.
With plain barrel................................... $350
With ventilated rib................................. 375

American Browning Shotguns distributed by Browning Arms Company, St. Louis, Mo.; manufactured by Remington Arms Company, Ilion, N.Y. These Browning models are almost identical to the Remington Model 11A and Sportsman.

American Browning Grade I Three or Five Shot Autoloading Shotgun................................. $260
Recoil-operated. Gauges: 12, 16, 20. 2- or 4-shell tubular magazine. Plain barrel, 26- to 32-inch, any standard boring. Weight, from about 6⅞ (20 gauge) to 8 pounds (12 gauge). Checkered pistol-grip stock and forearm. Made from 1940 to 1949.

American Browning Special
Same general specifications as Grade I, except supplied with raised matted rib or ventilated rib. Discontinued in 1949.
With raised matted rib.............................. $400
With ventilated rib................................. 425

American Browning Special Skeet Model........$430
Same general specifications as Grade I, except has 26-inch barrel with ventilated rib and Cutts Compensator. Discontinued in 1949.

American Browning Utility Field Gun........... $325
Same general specifications as Grade I, except has 28-inch plain barrel with Poly Choke. Discontinued in 1949.

Breda

Browning Automatic-5

Browning Automatic-5 Magnum

Browning Automatic-5
Buck Special

Browning Shotguns manufactured for Browning, Morgan, Utah, by Fabrique Nationale d'Armes de Guerre (now Fabrique Nationale Herstal), Herstal, Belgium, and by Miroku Firearms Mfg. Co., Tokyo, Japan. F.N. has also produced Browning design shotguns for sale under its own name

Browning Automatic-5, Standard (Grade I)
Recoil-operated. Gauges: 12 and 16 (16 gauge guns made prior to World War II were chambered for 2-9/16-inch shells; standard 16 discontinued 1964). 4-shell magazine in five-shot model, prewar guns were also available in three-shot model. Barrels: 26- to 32-inch; plain, raised matted rib, ventilated rib; choice of standard chokes. Weights: about 8 pounds in 12 gauge, 7¼ pounds in 16 gauge. Checkered pistol-grip stock and forearm. (*Note:* Browning Special, discontinued about 1940, is Grade I gun with either ventilated or raised matted rib.) Made from 1900 to 1973 by FN.
Grade I, plain barrel................................. $525
Grade I or Browning Special, raised matted rib....... 550
Grade I or Browning Special, ventilated rib........... 565

Browning Autoloading Shotguns, Grade III and IV
These higher grade models differ from the Standard or Grade I in general quality, grade of wood, checkering, engraving, etc., otherwise specifications are the same. Grade IV guns, sometimes called Midas Grade, are inlaid with yellow and green gold. Discontinued in 1940.
Grade III, plain barrel.............................. $ 950
Grade IV, plain barrel.............................. 1400
Extra for raised matted rib........................ 30
Extra for ventilated rib........................... 100

Browning Automatic-5, Trap Model.............. $540
12 gauge only. Same general specifications as Standard Model, except has trap-style stock, 30-inch ventilated-rib barrel, full choke; weighs 8½ pounds. Discontinued 1971.

Browning Automatic-5, Magnum 12 Gauge
Same general specifications as Standard Model. Chambered for 3-inch magnum 12 gauge shell. Barrels: 28-inch modified and full, 30- or 32-inch full and full; plain or ventilated rib. Buttstock has recoil pad. Weight, from 8½ to 9 pounds depending upon barrel. Made from 1958 to 1976 by FN, since then by Miroku.
FN manufacture, with plain barrel..................... $540
FN manufacture, with ventilated rib................. 560
Miroku manufacture, with ventilated rib............. 445

Browning Sweet 16 Automatic-5
16 gauge only. Same general specifications as Standard Model, except lightweight (about 6¾ pounds), has gold-plated trigger and guns without rib have striped matting on top of barrel. Made from 1937 to 1976 by FN.
With plain barrel.................................... $550
With raised matted rib.............................. 575
With ventilated rib................................. 600

Browning Light 12 Automatic-5
12 gauge only. Same general specifications as Standard Model, except lightweight (about 7¼ pounds), has gold-plated trigger and guns without rib have striped matting on top of barrel. Made from 1948 to 1976 by FN, since then by Miroku.
FN manufacture, with plain barrel..................... $525
FN manufacture, with raised matted rib.............. 550
FN manufacture, with ventilated rib................. 600
Miroku manufacture, with ventilated rib.............. 420

Browning Automatic-5, Buck Special Models
Same as Light 12, Magnum 12, Light 20, Magnum 20, in respective gauges, except 24-inch plain barrel specially bored for rifled slug and buckshot, fitted with rifle sights (open rear, ramp front). Weight, from 6⅛ pounds to 8¼ pounds, depending upon gauge. Made from 1964 to 1976 by FN, since then by Miroku.
FN manufacture...................................... $525
Miroku manufacture................................. 420

Browning Automatic-5, Magnum 20 Gauge
Same general specifications as Standard Model, except chambered for 3-inch magnum 20 gauge shell. Barrels: 26- or 28-inch, plain or ventilated rib. Weight, from 7 lbs. 5 oz. to 7 lbs. 7 oz., depending upon barrel. Made from 1967 to 1976 by FN, since then by Miroku.
FN manufacture, with plain barrel..................... $525
FN manufacture, with ventilated rib................. 625
Miroku manufacture, with ventilated rib............. 410

Browning Automatic-5, Skeet Model
12 gauge only. Same general specifications as Light 12; barrels: 26- or 28-inch, plain or ventilated rib, skeet choke; weighs from 7 lbs. 5 oz. to 7 lbs. 10 oz., depending upon barrel. Made by FN prior to 1976, since then by Miroku.
FN manufacture, with plain barrel..................... $525
FN manufacture, with ventilated-rib barrel........... 575
Miroku manufacture, with ventilated-rib barrel....... 400

Browning Light 20 Automatic-5
Same general specifications as Standard Model, except lightweight and 20 gauge. Barrels: 26- or 28-inch; plain or ventilated rib. Weight, from about 6¼ to 6½ pounds, depending upon barrel. Made from 1958 to 1976 by FN, since then by Miroku.
FN manufacture, with plain barrel..................... $525
FN manufacture, with ventilated-rib barrel........... 550
Miroku manufacture, with ventilated-rib barrel....... 420

Browning Superposed Shotguns, Hunting Models
Over-and-under. Box lock. Selective automatic ejectors. Selective single trigger; earlier models (worth 25% less) supplied with double triggers, twin selective triggers or non-selective single trigger. Gauges: 12, 20 (introduced 1949, 3-inch chambers in later production), 28, 410 (latter two gauges introduced 1960). Barrels: 26½-, 28-, 30-, 32-inch; raised matted rib or ventilated

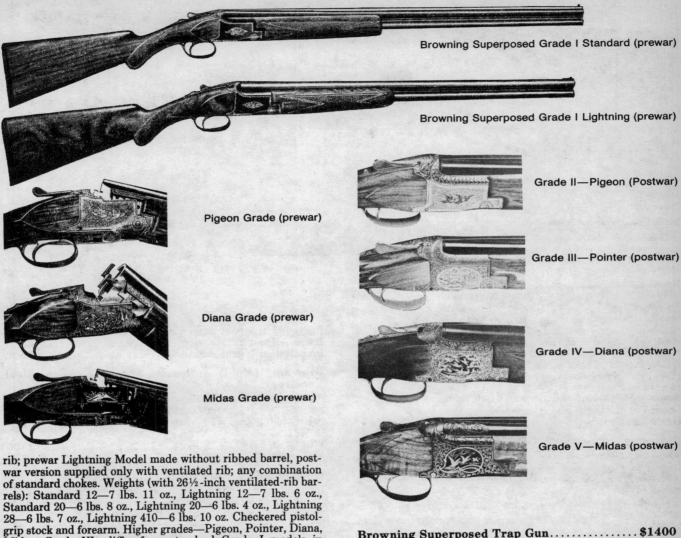

Browning Superposed Grade I Standard (prewar)

Browning Superposed Grade I Lightning (prewar)

Pigeon Grade (prewar)

Grade II—Pigeon (Postwar)

Diana Grade (prewar)

Grade III—Pointer (postwar)

Grade IV—Diana (postwar)

Midas Grade (prewar)

Grade V—Midas (postwar)

rib; prewar Lightning Model made without ribbed barrel, post-war version supplied only with ventilated rib; any combination of standard chokes. Weights (with 26½-inch ventilated-rib barrels): Standard 12—7 lbs. 11 oz., Lightning 12—7 lbs. 6 oz., Standard 20—6 lbs. 8 oz., Lightning 20—6 lbs. 4 oz., Lightning 28—6 lbs. 7 oz., Lightning 410—6 lbs. 10 oz. Checkered pistol-grip stock and forearm. Higher grades—Pigeon, Pointer, Diana, Midas, Grade VI—differ from standard Grade I models in overall quality, engraving, wood and checkering; otherwise, specifications are the same. Midas Grade and Grade VI guns are richly gold-inlaid. Made by FN from 1928 to 1976. Prewar models may be considered as discontinued in 1940 when Belgium was occupied by Germany. Grade VI offered 1955-1960. Pointer Grade discontinued 1966, Grade I Standard in 1973, Pigeon Grade in 1974. Lightning Grade I, Diana and Midas Grades were not offered after 1976.

Grade I Standard..................................	**$1300**
Grade I Lightning.................................	1400
Grade I Lightning, prewar, matted barrel, no rib......	1250
Grade II—Pigeon..................................	1750
Grade III—Pointer................................	2300
Grade IV—Diana..................................	3000
Grade V—Midas...................................	4000
Grade VI...	5000
Add for 28 or 410 gauge..........................	200
Values shown are for models with ventilated rib, if gun has raised matted rib, deduct....................	100

Browning Superposed—Magnum............... **$1595**
Same as Grade I, except chambered for 12 gauge 3-inch shells, 30-inch ventilated-rib barrels, stock with recoil pad, weighs about 8¼ pounds. Discontinued 1976.

Browning Superposed Trap Gun................ **$1400**
Same as Grade I, except has trap-style stock, beavertail forearm, 30-inch ventilated-rib barrels,12 gauge only. Discontinued 1976.

Browning Superposed BROADway 12 Trap Gun... **$1450**
Same as standard Trap Gun, except has 30- or 32-inch barrels with wider BROADway rib. Discontinued 1976.

Browning Superposed Skeet Guns, Grade I
Same as standard Lightning 12, 20, 28 and 410 Hunting Models, except has skeet-style stock and forearm, 26½- or 28-inch ventilated-rib barrels bored skeet choke. Available also in All Gauge Skeet Set: Lightning 12 with one removable forearm and three extra sets of barrels in 20, 28 and 410 gauge in fitted luggage case. Discontinued 1976.

12 or 20 gauge.....................................	**$1400**
28 or 410 gauge...................................	1600
All Gauge Skeet Set...............................	4250

Browning Superposed Super-Light Model...... **$1750**
Ultralight field gun version of Standard Lightning Model, has classic straight-grip stock and slimmer forearm. Available only in 12 and 20 gauges (2¾-inch chambers), with 26½-inch ventilated-rib barrels. Weights: 6½ pounds in 12 gauge, 6 pounds in 20 gauge. Made from 1967 to 1976.

Browning Superposed Trap

Browning Superposed Super-Light Model

Browning Superposed BROADway Tray

Browning Bicentennial Superposed (left side)

Browning Bicentennial Superposed (right side)

Browning Bicentennial Commemorative
Superposed **$9500**
Special limited edition issued to commemorate U.S. Bicentennial. 51 guns, one for each state in the Union plus one for Washington, D.C. Receiver with side plates has engraved and gold-inlaid hunter and wild turkey on right side, U.S. flag and bald eagle on left side, together with state markings inlaid in gold, on blued background. Checkered straight-grip stock and schnabel-style forearm of highly figured American walnut. Velvet-lined wooden presentation case. Made in 1976 by FN. Value shown is for gun in new, unfired condition.

Browning Superposed, Presentation Grades
Custom versions of Super-Light, Lightning Hunting, Trap and Skeet Models, with same general specifications as those of standard guns, but of higher overall quality. The four Presentation Grades differ in receiver finish (greyed or blued), engraving, gold inlays, wood and checkering; Presentation 4 has side plates. Made by FN, these models were introduced in 1977 and are the only Superposed guns currently marketed in the U.S.
Presentation 1 .... **$2100**
Presentation 1, gold-inlaid 3600
Presentation 2 3800
Presentation 2, gold-inlaid 5500

Presentation 3, gold-inlaid 5700
Presentation 4 6500
Presentation 4, gold-inlaid 7500

Browning Double Automatic, Standard Grade (Steel Receiver)
Short recoil system. Takedown. 12 gauge only. Two shots. Barrels: 26-, 28-, 30-inch; any standard choke. Checkered pistol-grip stock and forearm. Weight, about 7¾ pounds. Made from 1955 to 1961.
With plain barrel **$300**
With recessed-rib barrel 320

Browning Twelvette Double Automatic
Lightweight version of Double Automatic with same general specifications except aluminum receiver. Barrel with plain matted top or ventilated rib. Weight, from about 6¾ to 7 pounds, depending upon barrel. Receiver is finished in black with gold engraving; from 1956 to 1961, receivers were also anodized in grey, brown, and green with silver engraving. Made from 1955 to 1971.
With plain barrel **$295**
With ventilated-rib barrel 345

Browning Twentyweight Double Automatic
Same as Twelvette, but ¾ pound lighter. 26½-inch barrel only. Made from 1956 to 1971.
With plain barrel **$320**
With Ventilated-rib barrel 375

Browning BT-99 Grade I Single Barrel
Trap Gun **$550**
Box lock. Automatic ejector. 12 gauge only. 32- or 34-inch ventilated-rib barrel; modified, improved modified or full choke. Weight, about 8 pounds. Checkered pistol-grip stock and beavertail forearm, recoil pad. Made from 1971 to date by Miroku.

Browning BT-99 Grade I Competition **$550**
Same as BT-99, except has super-high wide rib and Monte Carlo stock. Made from 1976 to date.

Browning BSS Hammerless Double Barrel
Shotgun **$375**
Box lock. Automatic ejectors. Non-selective single trigger.

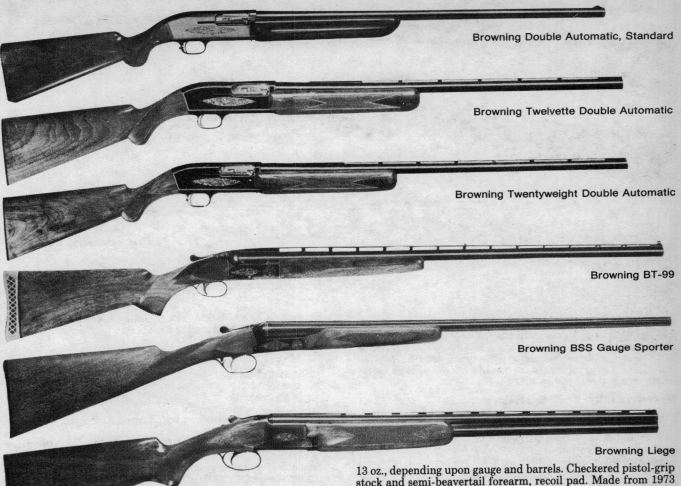

Browning Double Automatic, Standard

Browning Twelvette Double Automatic

Browning Twentyweight Double Automatic

Browning BT-99

Browning BSS Gauge Sporter

Browning Liege

Gauges: 12, 20; 3-inch chambers. Barrels: 26-, 28- or 30-inch (latter in 12 gauge only); improved cylinder and modified, modified and full, both barrels full choke; matted solid rib. Weights (with 28-inch barrels): 12 gauge—7 lbs. 5 oz., 20 gauge—7 pounds. Checkered pistol-grip stock and beavertail forearm. Made from 1972 to date by Miroku.

Browning BSS 20 Gauge Sporter................ **$375**
Same as standard BSS 20 gauge, except has selective single trigger, straight-grip stock. Introduced 1977.

Browning Liege Over-and-Under Shotgun....... **$600**
Box lock. Automatic ejectors. Non-selective single trigger. 12 gauge only. Barrels: 26½-, 28-, or 30-inch; 2¾-inch chambers in 26½- and 28-inch, 3-inch in 30-inch; improved cylinder and modified, modified and full, both barrels full choke; ventilated rib. Weight, from 7 lbs. 4 oz. to 7 lbs. 14 oz., depending upon barrels. Checkered pistol-grip stock and forearm. Made from 1973 to 1975 by FN.

Browning Citori Over-and-Under Shotgun, Hunting Model... **$500**
Box lock. Automatic ejectors. Selective single trigger. Gauges: 12, 20; 3-inch chambers. Barrels: 26-, 28-, 30- inch (latter in 12 gauge only); improved cylinder and modified, modified and full, full and full; ventilated rib. Weights: from 6 lbs. 13 oz. to 7 lbs.

13 oz., depending upon gauge and barrels. Checkered pistol-grip stock and semi-beavertail forearm, recoil pad. Made from 1973 to date by Miroku.

Browning Citori Trap Gun
Same as Hunting Model, except 12 gauge only, has Monte Carlo stock and beavertail forearm, trap style recoil pad; 30- or 32-inch barrels; modified and full, improved modified and full, or full and full. Available with either standard ventilated rib or special target-type, high-post, wide ventilated rib. Weight, about 8 pounds. Made from 1974 to date by Miroku.
With standard ventilated rib......................... **$500**
With target ventilated rib............................ 525

Browning Citori Skeet Gun
Same as Hunting Model, except has skeet-style stock and forearm, 26- or 28-inch barrels, both bored skeet choke. Available with either standard ventilated rib or special target-type, high-post, wide ventilated rib. Weights (with 26-inch barrels): 12 gauge—8 pounds, 20 gauge—7 pounds. Made from 1974 to date by Miroku.
With standard ventilated rib......................... **$485**
With target ventilated rib............................ 500

Browning 2000 Gas Automatic Shotgun, Field Model
Gas-operated. Gauges: 12, 20, 2¾-inch chamber. 4-shot magazine. Barrels: 26-, 28-, 30-inch; any standard choke; plain matted barrel (12 gauge only) or ventilated rib. Weights: from 6 lbs. 11 oz. to 7 lbs. 12 oz., depending upon gauge and barrel. Checkered pistol-grip stock and forearm. Made from 1974 to 1981 by FN.
With plain matted barrel............................. **$375**
With ventilated rib.................................. 400

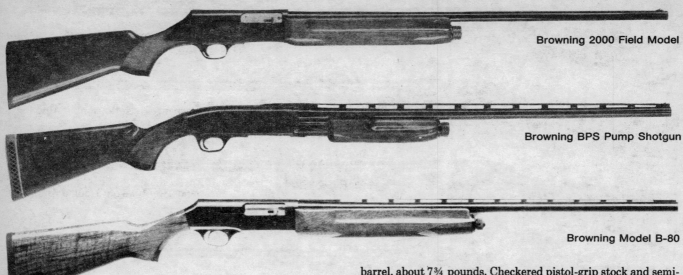

Browning 2000 Field Model

Browning BPS Pump Shotgun

Browning Model B-80

Browning 2000 Magnum Model................. **$375**
Same as Field Model, except chambered for 3-inch shells, 3-shot magazine. Barrels: 26-(20 gauge only), 28-, 30- or 32-inch (latter two 12 gauge only); any standard choke; ventilated rib. Weights, from 6 lbs. 11 oz to 7 lbs. 13 oz., depending upon gauge and barrel length. Made from 1974 to 1981 by FN.

Browning 2000 Buck Special.................... **$395**
Same as Field Model, except has 24-inch plain barrel specially bored for rifled slug and buck shot, fitted with rifle sights (open rear, ramp front). 12 gauge, 2¾-inch or 3-inch, 20 gauge, 2¾-inch chamber. Weights: 12 gauge—7 lbs. 8 oz, 20 gauge—6 lbs. 10 oz. Made from 1974 to 1981 by FN.

Browning 2000 Trap Model..................... **$400**
Same as Field Model, except has Monte Carlo stock with recoil pad, 30- or 32-inch barrel with high-post ventilated rib and receiver extension; modified, improved or full choke. 12 gauge, 2¾-inch chamber. Weight, about 8 lbs. 5 oz. Made from 1974 to 1981 by FN.

Browning 2000 Skeet Model.................... **$400**
Same as Field Model, except has skeet-style stock with recoil pad, 26-inch ventilated-rib barrel, skeet choke. 12 or 20 gauge, 2¾-inch chamber. Weights: 12 gauge—8 lbs. 1 oz., 20 gauge—6 lbs. 12 oz. Made from 1974 to 1981 by FN.

Browning Model B-80 Gas Operated Automatic Shotgun... **$375**
Gauges: 12, 20; 2¾-inch chamber. 4-shot magazine. Barrels: 26-, 28-, 30-inch; any standard choke; ventilated rib barrel. Weights: From 6 pounds 12 ounces to 8 pounds 1 ounce, depending upon gauge and barrel. Checkered pistol-grip stock and forearm. Made from 1981 to date.

Browning Model B-80 Superlight............... **$385**
Same as Standard Model, except weighs about 1 pound less.

Browning Model B-80 Magnum.................. **$395**
Same as Standard Model, except has 3-inch Magnum chambers.

Browning BPS Pump Shotgun................... **$250**
Takedown. 12 gauge. 3-inch chamber. Holds five 2¾-inch or four 3-inch shells. Barrels: 26-, 28-, 30-inch; improved cylinder, modified or full choke; ventilated rib. Weight, with 28-inch

barrel, about 7¾ pounds. Checkered pistol-grip stock and semi-beavertail forearm (slide handle), recoil pad. Introduced 1977. Made by Miroku.

Browning Choke Marks—The following markings are used to indicate chokes on Browning Shotguns:

    Full *
    Improved Modified *—
    Modified **
    Improved Cylinder **—
    Skeet **S
    Cylinder ***

E.J. Churchill, Ltd., London, England

Churchill Premiere Quality Hammerless Double Barrel Shotgun
Side lock. Automatic ejectors. Double triggers or selective single trigger. Gauges: 12, 16, 20, 28. Barrels: 25-, 28-, 30-, 32-inch; any degree of boring. Weight, from 5 to 8 pounds depending upon gauge and barrel length. Checkered stock and fore-end, straight or pistol grip.
With double triggers.............................. **$10,000**
Selective single trigger, extra.................... **400**

Churchill Premiere

Churchill Field Model Hammerless Double Barrel Shotgun
Side lock hammerless ejector gun with same general specifications as Premiere Model but of lower quality.
With double triggers............................... **$8000**
Selective single trigger, extra...................... **400**

Churchill Utility Model Hammerless Double Barrel Shotgun
Anson & Deeley box lock action. Double triggers or single trigger. Gauges: 12, 16, 20, 28, 410. Barrels: 25-, 28-, 30-, 32-inch; any degree of boring. Weight from 4½ to 8 pounds depending upon gauge and barrel length. Checkered stock and fore-end, straight or pistol grip.
With double triggers............................... **$3500**
Selective single trigger, extra...................... **400**

Churchill Premiere Quality Under-and-Over Shotgun

Side lock. Automatic ejectors. Double triggers or selective single trigger. Gauges: 12, 16, 20, 28. Barrels: 25-, 28-, 30-, 32-inch; any degree of boring. Weight, from 5 to 8 pounds depending upon gauge and barrel length. Checkered stock and fore-end, straight or pistol grip.

With double triggers	$11,000
Selective single trigger, extra	400
Raised ventilated rib, extra	400

Note: The preceding Churchill models have been discontinued. Current production consists of the following Series XXV guns.

Churchill XXV Premiere Hammerless Double Barrel Shotgun $10,000

Side lock. Assisted opening. Automatic ejectors. Double triggers. Gauges: 12, 20, 25-inch barrels with narrow, quick-sighting rib; any standard choke combination. English-style straight-grip stock and forearm, checkered.

Churchill XXV Imperial $9000
Similar to XXV Premiere, but without assisted opening feature.

Churchill XXV Hercules $6000
Box lock. Otherwise specifications same as for XXV Premiere.

Churchill XXV Regal $4200
Similar to XXV Hercules, but without assisted opening feature. Gauges: 12, 20, 28, 410.

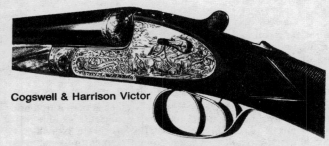

Cogswell & Harrison Victor

Cogswell & Harrison, Ltd., London, England

Cogswell & Harrison Best Quality Hammerless Side Lock Double Barrel Shotgun

Hand-detachable locks. Automatic ejectors. Double triggers or single trigger (selective or non-selective). Gauges: 12, 16, 20. Barrels: 25-, 26-, 28-, 30-inch; any choke combination. Checkered stock and fore-end, straight grip standard. Made in two models Victor (currently manufactured) and Primic (discontinued), the latter being of plainer finish, otherwise the same.

Victor Model	$6000
Primic Model	4000
Single trigger, non-selective, extra	225
Single trigger, selective, extra	300

Cogswell & Harrison Huntic Model Hammerless Double Barrel Shotgun

Side lock. Automatic ejectors. Double triggers or single trigger (selective or non-selective). Gauges: 12, 16, 20. Barrels: 25-, 27½-, 30-inch; any choke combination. Checkered stock and fore-end, straight grip standard. Discontinued.

With double triggers	$3500
Single trigger, non-selective, extra	225
Single trigger, selective extra	300

Cogswell & Harrison Avant Tout Series Hammerless Double Barrel Shotguns

Box lock. Side plates (except Avant Tout III Grade). Automatic ejectors. Double triggers or single trigger (selective or non-selective). Gauges: 12, 16, 20. Barrels: 25-, 27½-, 30-inch; any choke combination. Checkered stock and fore-end, straight grip standard. Made in three models—Avant Tout I or Konor, Avant Tout II or Sandhurst, Avant Tout III or Rex—which differ chiefly in overall quality, engraving, grade of wood, checkering, etc., general specifications are the same. Discontinued.

Avant Tout I	$2700
Avant Tout II	2500
Avant Tout III	1800
Single trigger, non-selective, extra	225
Single trigger, selective, extra	300

Cogswell & Harrison Markor Hammerless Double Barrel Shotgun

Box lock. Nonejector or ejector. Double triggers. Gauges: 12, 16, 20. Barrels: 27½- or 30-inch; any choke combination. Checkered stock and fore-end, straight grip standard. Discontinued.

Nonejector Model	$1800
Ejector Model	2000

Cogswell & Harrison Ambassador Hammerless Double Barrel Shotgun $3500

Box lock. Side plates with game scene or rose scroll engraving. Automatic ejectors. Double triggers. Gauges: 12, 16, 20. Barrels: 26-, 28-, 30-inch; any choke combination. Checkered straight-grip stock and forearm. Currently manufactured.

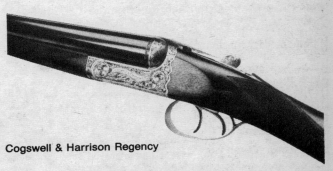

Cogswell & Harrison Regency

Cogswell & Harrison Regency Hammerless Double Barrel Shotgun $2800

Anson & Deeley box lock action. Automatic ejectors. Double triggers. Gauges: 12, 16, 20. Barrels: 26-, 28-, 30-inch; any choke combination. Checkered straight-grip stock and forearm. Introduced in 1970 to commemorate the firm's bicentenary, this model has deep scroll engraving and the name "Regency" inlaid in gold on the rib. Currently manufactured.

Colt's Firearms Division, Hartford, Connecticut

Colt Custom Double Barrel Hammerless Shotgun $320

Box lock. Double triggers. Automatic ejectors. Gauges: 12 Mag., 16. Barrels: 26-inch improved cylinder and modified, 28-inch modified and full, 30-inch full and full. Weight (12 ga.), about 7½ pounds. Checkered pistol-grip stock and beavertail forearm. Made in 1961.

Coltsman Standard Pump Shotgun $170

Takedown. Gauges: 12, 16, 20. Magazine holds 4 shells. Barrels: 26-inch improved cylinder, 28-inch modified or full choke, 30-inch full choke. Weight, about 6 pounds. Plain pistol-grip stock and forearm. Made from 1961 to 1965 by Manufrance.

Coltsman Custom Pump $225

Same as Standard Pump except has checkered stock, ventilated-rib barrel, weighs about 6½ pounds. Made from 1961 to 1963.

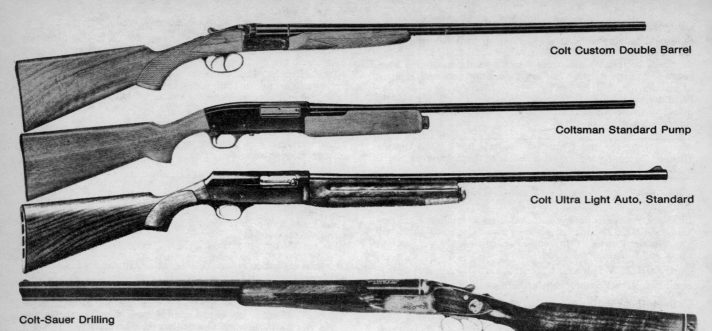

Colt Custom Double Barrel

Coltsman Standard Pump

Colt Ultra Light Auto, Standard

Colt-Sauer Drilling

Colt Ultra Light Auto Shotgun—Standard

Recoil-operated. Takedown. Alloy receiver. Gauges: 12, 20. Magazine holds 4 shells. Barrels: plain, solid rib, ventilated rib; chrome-lined; 26-inch improved cylinder or modified choke. 28-inch modified or full choke, 30-inch full choke, 32-inch full choke. Weight (12 ga.), about 6¼ pounds. Checkered pistol-grip stock and forearm. Made from 1964 to 1966.

With plain barrel................................... $195
With solid-rib barrel............................... 215
With ventilated-rib barrel.......................... 235

Colt Ultra Light Auto—Custom

Same as Standard Auto, except has engraved receiver, select walnut stock and forearm. Made from 1964 to 1966.

With solid-rib barrel................................ $265
With ventilated-rib barrel.......................... 290

Colt Magnum Auto Shotgun

Same as Standard Auto, except steel receiver, handles 3-inch magnum shells, 30- and 32-inch barrels in 12 gauge, 28-inch in 20 gauge; weight (12 ga.) about 8¼ pounds. Made from 1964 to 1966.

With plain barrel................................... $215
With solid-rib barrel............................... 235
With ventilated-rib barrel.......................... 255

Colt Magnum Auto—Custom

Same as Magnum, except has engraved receiver, select walnut stock and forearm. Made from 1964 to 1966.

With solid-rib barrel................................ $285
With ventilated-rib barrel.......................... 310

Note: Colt Auto Shotguns were made by Luigi Franchi S.p.A. and are similar to corresponding models of that manufacturer.

Colt-Sauer Drilling..............................$1850

Three-barrel combination gun. Box lock. Set rifle trigger. Tang barrel selector, automatic rear sight positioner. 12 gauge over 30-06 or 243 rifle barrel. 25-inch barrels, full and modified choke. Weight, about 8 pounds. Folding leaf rear sight, blade front sight with brass bead. Checkered pistol-grip stock and beavertail forearm, recoil pad. Made from 1974 to date by J.P. Sauer & Sohn, Eckernforde, West Germany.

Charles Daly, Inc., New York City

Charles Daly Hammerless Double Barrel Shotgun

Daly pattern Anson & Deeley system box lock action. Automatic ejectors—except "Superior Quality" is nonejector. Double triggers. Gauges: 10, 12, 16, 20, 28, 410. Barrels: 26- to 32-inch, any combination of chokes. Weight, from 4 pounds to 8½ pounds depending upon gauge and barrel length. Checkered pistol-grip stock and fore-end. The four grades—Regent Diamond, Diamond, Empire, Superior—differ in general quality, grade of wood, checkering, engraving, etc., otherwise specifications are the same. Discontinued about 1933.

Regent Diamond Quality........................... $5000
Diamond Quality................................... 3800
Empire Quality.................................... 2550
Superior Quality.................................. 1300

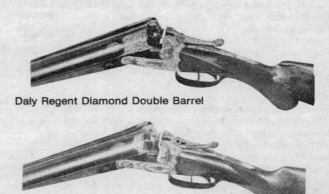

Daly Regent Diamond Double Barrel

Daly Diamond Double Barrel

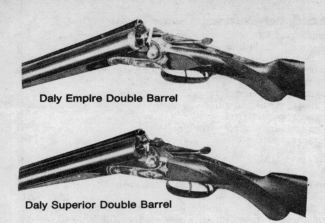

Daly Empire Double Barrel

Daly Superior Double Barrel

Charles Daly Over-and-Under Shotgun

Daly pattern Anson & Deeley system box lock action. Side plates. Automatic ejectors. Double triggers. Gauges: 12, 16, 20. Supplied in various barrel lengths and weights. Checkered pistol-grip stock and fore-end. The two grades—Diamond and Empire—differ in general quality, grade of wood, checkering, engraving, etc., otherwise specifications are the same. Discontinued about 1933.

Diamond Quality.................................... $5000
Empire Quality..................................... 4000

Daly Single Barrel Trap

Charles Daly Single Barrel Trap Gun.......... $4000

Daly pattern Anson & Deeley system box lock action. Automatic ejector. 12 gauge only. Barrels: 30-, 32-, 34-inch, ventilated rib. Weight, from 7½ to 8¼ pounds. Checkered pistol-grip stock and fore-end. This model was made in "Empire Quality" only. Discontinued about 1933.

Daly Sextuple Trap

Charles Daly Sextuple Model Single Barrel Trap Gun

Daly pattern Anson & Deeley system box lock action. Six locking bolts. Automatic ejector. 12 gauge only. Barrels: 30-, 32-, 34-inch, ventilated rib. Weight, from 7½ to 8¼ pounds. Checkered pistol-grip stock and fore-end. This model was made in two grades, "Empire" and "Regent Diamond;" the guns differ in general quality, grade of wood, checkering, engraving, etc., otherwise specifications are the same. Discontinued about 1933.

Regent Diamond Quality........................... $6000
Empire Quality..................................... 4500

Charles Daly Hammerless Drilling (Three Barrel Gun)

Daly pattern Anson & Deeley system box lock action. Plain extractors. Double triggers, front single set for rifle barrel. Gauges: 12, 16, 20, 25-20, 25-35, 30-30 rifle barrel. Supplied in various barrel lengths and weights. Checkered pistol-grip stock and fore-end. Automatic rear sight operated by rifle barrel selector. The three grades—Regent Diamond, Diamond, Superior—differ in general quality, grade of wood, checkering, engraving, etc., otherwise specifications are the same. Discontinued about 1933.

Regent Diamond Quality........................... $6000
Diamond Quality................................... 4800
Superior Quality................................... 3000

Note: The preceding prewar Charles Daly guns were manufactured by various firms in Suhl, Germany.

Charles Daly Commander Over-and-Under Shotgun

Daly pattern Anson & Deeley system box lock action. Automatic ejectors. Double triggers or Miller selective single trigger. Gauges: 12, 16, 20, 28, 410. Barrels: 26- to 30-inch, improved cylinder and modified or modified and full choke. Weight, from 5¼ to 7¼ pounds depending upon gauge and barrel length. Checkered stock and fore-end, straight or pistol grip. The two models, 100 and 200, differ in general quality, grade of wood, checkering, engraving, etc., otherwise specifications are the same. Made in Belgium cicra 1939.

Model 100... $475
Model 200... 600
Miller single trigger, extra......................... 75

Note: The following postwar Charles Daly over-and-under, double and single barrel shotguns were produced by Miroku Firearms Mfg. Co., Tokyo, Japan, while the Novomatic autoloader was made by Ernesto Breda, Milan, Italy.

Charles Daly Over-and-Under Shotguns

Box lock. Automatic ejectors or selective automatic/manual ejection. Selective single trigger. Gauges: 12, 12 magnum (3-inch chambers), 20 (3-inch chambers), 28, 410. Barrels: ventilated rib; 26-, 28-, 30-inch; standard choke combinations. Weight: from about 6 to 8 pounds, depending upon gauge and barrels. Select walnut stock with pistol grip, fluted forearm, checkered; Monte Carlo comb on trap guns; recoil pad on 12 gauge magnum and trap models. The various grades differ in quality of engraving and wood. Made from 1963 to 1976.

Venture Grade..................................... $520
Field Grade.. 530
Superior Grade..................................... 550
Diamond Grade.................................... 825

Daly Wildlife Commemorative

Charles Daly 1974 Wildlife Commemorative... $1200

Limited issue of 500 guns. Similar to Diamond Grade over-and-under. 12 gauge trap and skeet models only. Duck scene engraved on right side of receiver, fine scroll on left side. Made in 1974.

Charles Daly Superior Grade Single Barrel Trap Gun... $575

Box lock. Automatic ejector. 12 gauge only. 32- or 34-inch ventilated-rib barrel, full choke. Weight, about 8 pounds. Monte Carlo stock with pistol grip and recoil pad, beavertail forearm, checkered. Made from 1968 to 1976.

Charles Daly Empire Grade Hammerless Double Barrel Shotgun.. $375

Box lock. Plain extractors. Non-selective single trigger. Gauges: 12, 16, 20; 3-inch chambers in 12 and 20, 2¾-inch in 16 gauge. Barrels: ventilated rib; 26-, 28-, 30-inch (latter in 12 gauge only); improved cylinder and modified, modified and full, full and full. Weight, from 6 to 7¾ pounds, depending upon gauge and barrels. Checkered pistol-grip stock and beavertail forearm. Made from 1968 to 1971.

Charles Daly Novamatic 12 Gauge Magnum..... $250

Same as Novamatic Lightweight, except chambered for 12 gauge magnum 3-inch shell, has 3-shell magazine, 30-inch ventilated-rib barrel, full choke, and stock with recoil pad. Weight, 7¾ pounds. Made in 1968.

Charles Daly Novamatic Trap Gun............... $300

Same as Novamatic Lightweight, except has 30-inch ventilated-rib barrel, full choke, and Monte Carlo stock with recoil pad. Weight, 7¾ pounds. Made in 1968.

Charles Daly Novamatic Super Lightweight

Lighter version of Novamatic Lightweight. Gauges: 12, 20. Weights, with 26-inch ventilated-rib barrel: 12 gauge, 6 lbs. 10 oz.; 20 gauge, 6 pounds. Skeet choke available in 26-inch ventilated-rib barrel. 28-inch barrels in 12 gauge only. Quick-Choke in 20 gauge with plain barrel. Made in 1968.

12 gauge, plain barrel.................................	$275
12 gauge, ventilated rib..............................	290
20 gauge, plain barrel.................................	250
20 gauge, plain barrel with Quick-Choke..............	275
20 gauge, ventilated rib..............................	290

Charles Daly Novamatic Lightweight Autoloading Shotgun

Same as Breda. Recoil-operated. Takedown. 12 gauge, 2¾-inch chamber. 4-shell tubular magazine. Barrels: plain, ventilated rib; 26 inch improved cylinder or Quick-Choke with three interchangeable tubes, 28-inch modified or full choke. Weight, with 26-inch ventilated-rib barrel, 7 lbs. 6 oz. Checkered pistol-grip stock and forearm. Made in 1968.

With plain barrel.....................................	$250
With ventilated rib...................................	275
Extra for Quick-Choke.................................	10

Charles Daly Novamatic Super Lightweight 20 Gauge Magnum.. $275

Same as Novamatic Super Lightweight 20, except 3-inch chamber, has 3-shell magazine, 28-inch ventilated-rib barrel, full choke. Made in 1968.

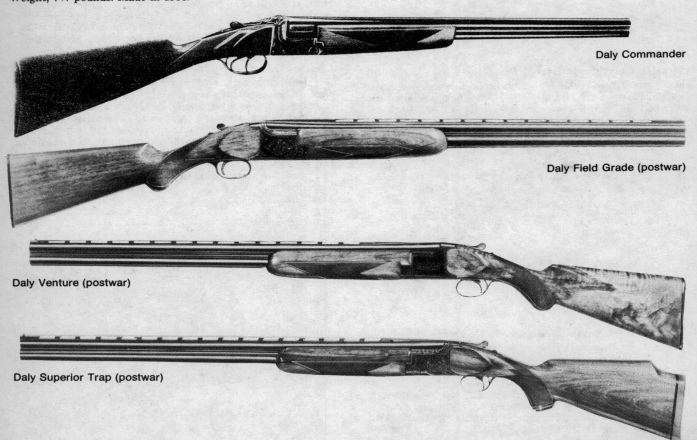

Daly Commander

Daly Field Grade (postwar)

Daly Venture (postwar)

Daly Superior Trap (postwar)

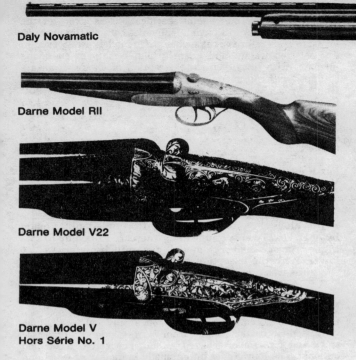

Daly Novamatic

Darne Model RII

Darne Model V22

Darne Model V
Hors Série No. 1

Darne S.A., Saint-Etienne, France

Darne Hammerless Double Barrel Shotguns

Sliding-breech action with fixed barrels. Automatic ejectors. Double triggers. Gauges: 12, 16, 20, 28; also 12 and 20 magnum with 3-inch chambers. Barrels: 27½-inch standard, other lengths from 25½- to 31½-inch available; any standard choke combination. Weights: from about 5½ to 7 pounds, depending upon gauge and barrel length. Checkered straight-grip or pistol grip stock and forearm. The various models differ in grade of engraving and wood. Currently manufactured.

Model R11 (Bird Hunter)	$ 800
Model R15 (Pheasant Hunter)	1225
Model R16 (Magnum)	1550
Model V19 (Quail Hunter)	1950
Model V22	3600
Model V Hors Série No. 1	4500

Davidson Guns, manufactured by Fabrica de Armas ILJA, Eibar, Spain; distributed by Davidson Firearms Co., Greensboro, North Carolina

Davidson Model 63B Double Barrel Shotgun.... $200

Anson & Deeley box lock action. Frame-engraved and nickel plated. Plain extractors. Automatic safety. Double triggers. Gauges: 12, 16, 20, 28, 410. Barrel lengths: 25 (410 only)-, 26-, 28-, 30-inch (latter 12 ga. only); chokes: improved cylinder and modified, modified and full, full and full. Weights, from 5 lb. 11 oz. (410) to 7 pounds (12 ga.). Pistol-grip stock and forearm of European walnut, checkered. Made from 1963 to date.

Davidson Model 63B Magnum

Similar to standard Model 63B, except chambered for 10 ga. 3½-inch, 12 and 20 ga. 3-inch magnum shells; 10 gauge has 32-inch barrels, choked full and full, weighs 10 lb. 10 oz. Made from 1963 to date.

12 and 20 gauge Magnum	$280
10 gauge Magnum	310

Davidson Model 69SL Double Barrel Shotgun... $340

Side lock action with detachable side plates, engraved and nickel-plated. Plain extractors. Automatic safety. Double triggers. 12 and 20 gauge. Barrels: 26-inch improved cylinder and modified, 28-inch modified and full. Weights: 12 ga., 7 pounds; 20 ga., 6½ pounds. Pistol-grip stock and forearm of European walnut, checkered. Made from 1963 to 1976.

Davidson Model 73 Stagecoach Hammer Double Barrel Shotgun.. $200

Side lock action with detachable side plates and exposed hammers. Plain extractors. Double triggers. Gauges: 12, 20; 3-inch chambers. 20-inch barrels, modified and full choke. Weights: 7 pounds in 12 gauge, 6½ pounds in 20 guage. Checkered pistol-grip stock and forearm. Made from 1976 to date.

Fox Shotguns made by A. H. Fox Gun Co., Philadelphia, Pennsylvania, from 1903 to 1930 and since then by Savage Arms, originally of Utica, New York, now of Westfield, Massachusetts.

Fox Sterlingworth Hammerless Double Barrel Shotgun

Box lock. double triggers (Fox-Kautzky selective single trigger extra). Plain extractors (automatic ejectors extra). Gauges: 12, 16, 20. Barrel lengths: 26-, 28-, 30-inch; chokes; full and full, modified and full, cylinder and modified (any combination of cylinder to full choke borings was available at no extra cost). Weights: 12 gauge—6⅛ to 8¼ pounds, 16 gauge—6 to 7 pounds, 20 gauge—5¾ to 6¾ pounds. Checkered pistol-grip stock and forearm.

With plain extractors	$550
With automatic ejectors	750
Selective single trigger, extra	150

Fox Sterlingworth

Davidson Model 63B

Fox Sterlingworth Deluxe

Same general specifications as Sterlingworth, except 32-inch barrel was also available, has recoil pad, ivory bead sights.

With plain extractors...............................**$600**
With automatic ejectors........................... 800

Fox Sterlingworth Skeet and Upland Game Gun

Same general specifications as the standard Sterlingworth, except has 26- or 28-inch barrels with skeet boring only, straight-grip stock; weighs 7 pounds in 12 gauge model.

With plain extractors...............................**$600**
With automatic ejectors........................... 800

Super Fox HE

Super Fox HE Grade...........................**$1100**

Long Range Gun made in 12 gauge only (chambered for 3-inch shells on order), 30- or 32-inch full choke barrels, weighs 8¾ to 9¾ pounds, automatic ejectors standard. General specifications same as standard sterlingworth.

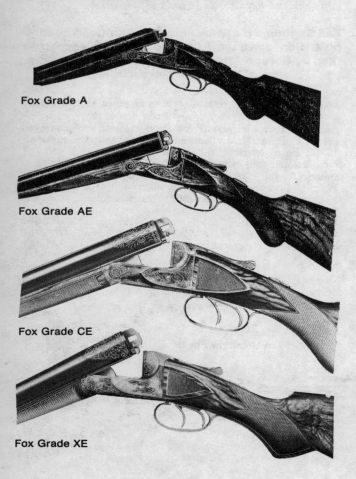

Fox Grade A

Fox Grade AE

Fox Grade CE

Fox Grade XE

Fox Hammerless Double Barrel Shotguns

In the higher grades have the same general specifications as given for the standard Sterlingworth model. Differences are chiefly in workmanship and materials; the higher grade models are stocked in fine selected walnut and quantity and quality of engraving increases with price. With the exception of Grade A, all are equipped with automatic ejectors.

Grade A...	$ 900
Grade AE..	1495
Grade BE..	1400
Grade CE..	1700
Grade XE..	3200
Grade DE..	5500
Grade FE..	9000
Fox-Kautzky selective single trigger, extra...........	150
Ventilated rib, extra................................	200
Beatvertail forearm, extra..........................	150

Note: Values shown are for 12 and 16 gauge doubles made by A. H. Fox. Twenty gauge guns often are valued up to 75% higher. Savage-made Fox models generally bring prices 25% lower. With the exception of Model B, production of Fox shotguns was discontinued about 1942.

Fox Single Barrel Trap Guns

Box lock. Automatic ejector. 12 gauge only. 30- or 32-inch ventilated-rib barrel. Weight, from 7½ to 8 pounds. Trapstyle stock and forearm of selected walnut, checkered, recoil pad optional. The four grades differ chiefly in quality of wood and engraving; Grade M guns, built to order, have finest Circassian walnut. Stock and receiver are elaborately engraved and inlaid with gold. Discontinued 1942. *Note:* In 1932 the Fox Trap Gun was redesigned and those manufactured after that date have a stock with full pistol grip and Monte Carlo comb; at the same time frame was changed to permit the rib line to extend across it to the rear.

Grade JE..	$1350
Grade KE..	2000
Grade LE..	2800
Grade ME..	5000

Fox Model B Hammerless Double Barrel Shotgun

....**$205**

Box lock. Double triggers. Plain extractor. Gauges: 12, 16, 20, 410. 24- to 30-inch barrels; ventilated rib on current production; chokes: modified and full, cylinder and modified, both full (410 only). Weight, about 7½ pounds in 12 gauge. Checkered pistol-grip stock and forearm. Made from about 1940 to date.

Fox Model B-ST...................................**$230**

Same as Model B except has non-selective single trigger. Made from 1955 to 1966.

Fox Model B-DL...................................**$300**

Same as Model B-ST except frame finished in satin chrome, select walnut buttstock with checkered pistol grip, side panels, beavertail forearm. Made from 1962 to 1966.

Fox Model B-DE...................................**$270**

Same as Model B-ST except frame finished in satin chrome, select walnut buttstock with checkered pistol grip and beavertail forearm. Made from 1965 to 1966.

Fox Model B-SE................................**$235**

Same as Model B except has selective ejectors and single trigger. Made from 1966 to date.

Fox Model B

Fox Model B-ST

Fox Model B-DL

Fox Model B-DE

Luigi Franchi S.p.A., Brescia, Italy

Franchi Airone Hammerless Double Barrel Shotgun.. **$1020**
Box lock. Anson & Deeley system action. Automatic ejectors. Double triggers. 12 gauge. Various barrel lengths, chokes, weights. Checkered straight-grip stock and forearm. Made from 1940 to 1950.

Franchi Airone

Franchi Astore Hammerless Double Barrel Shotgun... **$840**
Box lock. Anson & Deeley system action. Plain extractors. Double triggers. 12 gauge. Various barrel lengths, chokes, weights. Checkered straight-grip stock and forearm. Made from 1937 to 1960.

Franchi Astore

Franchi Astore 5................................... **$1820**
Same as Astore, except has higher grade wood, fine engraving. Automatic ejectors, single trigger, 28-inch barrel (modified and full or improved modified and full choke) are standard on current production.

Franchi Astore S

Franchi Astore II................................... **$975**
Similar to Astore S, but not as high grade. Furnished with either plain extractors or automatic ejectors, double triggers, pistol-grip stock; barrels: 27-inch improved cylinder and improved modified, 28-inch modified and full choke. Currently manufactured for Franchi in Spain.

Franchi Condor

Franchi Hammerless Side Lock Double Barrel Shotguns
Hand-detachable locks. Self-opening action. Automatic ejectors. Double triggers or single trigger. Gauges: 12, 16, 20. Barrel lengths, chokes, weights according to customer's specifications. Checkered stock and fore-end, straight or pistol grip. Made in six grades—Condor, Imperiale, Imperiale S, Imperiale Montecarlo No. 5, Imperiale Montecarlo No. 11, Imperiale Montecarlo Extra—which differ chiefly in overall quality, engraving, grade of wood, checkering, etc., general specifications are the same. Only the Imperiale Montecarlo Extra Grade is currently manufactured.

Condor Grade....................................	$ 6,000
Imperiale, Imperiale S Grades.....................	8,500
Imperiale Montecarlo Grades No. 5, 11.............	11,180
Imperiale Montecarlo Extra Grade...............	13,650

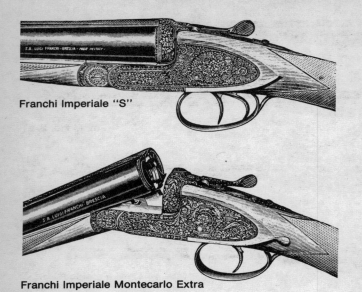

Franchi Imperiale "S"

Franchi Imperiale Montecarlo Extra

Franchi Standard Model Autoloader

Recoil operated. Light alloy receiver. Gauges: 12, 20. 4-shot magazine. Barrels: 26-, 28-, 30-inch; plain, solid rib, ventilated rib; improved cylinder, modified, full choke. Weights: 12 ga.— about 6¼ pounds, 20 ga.—5⅛ pounds. Checkered pistol-grip stock and forearm. Made from 1950 to date.
With plain barrel................................... **$275**
With solid rib.. 300
With ventilated rib................................. 320

Franchi Standard Model Magnum

Same general specifications as Standard Model, except has 3-inch chamber, 32-inch (12 gauge) or 28-inch (20 gauge) full choke barrel, recoil pad. Weights: 12 gauge, 8¼ pounds; 20 gauge, 6 pounds. Formerly designated "Superange Model." Made from 1954 to date.
With plain barrel................................... **$300**
With ventilated rib................................. 320

Franchi Hunter Model

Same general specifications as Standard Model except higher grade with engraved receiver; furnished with ribbed barrel only. Made from 1950 to date.
With solid rib.. **$290**
With ventilated rib................................. 310

Franchi Hunter Model Magnum.................. **$350**

Same as Standard Model Magnum, except higher grade with engraved receiver, ventilated-rib barrel only. Formerly designated "Wildfowler Model." Made from 1954 to 1973.

Franchi Turkey Gun............................. **$350**

Same as Standard Model Magnum, except higher grade with turkey scene engraved receiver, 12 gauge only, 36-inch matted-rib barrel, extra full choke. Made from 1963 to 1965.

Franchi Slug Gun............................... **$290**

Same as Standard Model, except has 22-inch plain barrel, cylinder bore; folding leaf open rear sight, gold bead front sight. Made from 1960 to date.

Franchi Skeet Gun.............................. **$325**

Same general specifications and appearance as Standard Model, except made only with 26-inch ventilated-rib barrel, skeet choke; stock and forearm of extra fancy walnut. Made from 1972 to 1974.

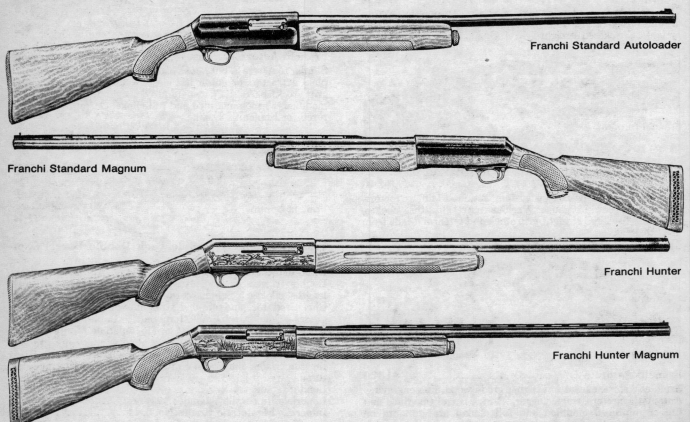

Franchi Standard Autoloader

Franchi Standard Magnum

Franchi Hunter

Franchi Hunter Magnum

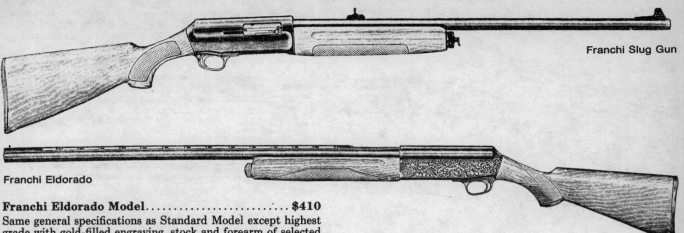

Franchi Slug Gun

Franchi Eldorado

Franchi Eldorado Model...........................$410
Same general specifications as Standard Model except highest grade with gold-filled engraving, stock and forearm of selected walnut; furnished with ventilated-rib barrel only. Made from 1954 to date.

Franchi Crown Grade

Franchi Diamond Grade

Franchi Crown, Diamond and Imperial Grade Autoloaders
Same general specifications as Standard Model, except these are custom guns of the highest quality. Crown Grade has hunting scene engraving; Diamond Grade has silver-inlaid scroll engraving; Imperial Grade has elaborately engraved hunting scenes with figures inlaid in gold. Stock and forearem of fancy walnut. Made from 1954 to 1975.

Crown Grade..................................	$1300
Diamond Grade................................	1625
Imperial Grade...............................	1950

Franchi Dynamic-12
Same general specifications and appearance as Standard Model, except 12 gauge only, has heavier steel receiver; weight, about 7¼ pounds. Made from 1965 to 1972.

With plain barrel............................	$290
With ventilated rib..........................	310

Franchi Dynamic-12 Slug Gun...................$300
Same as standard Slug Gun, except 12 gauge only, has heavier steel receiver. Made from 1965 to 1972.

Franchi Dynamic-12 Skeet Gun..................$325
Same general specifications and appearance as Standard Model, except has heavier steel receiver; made only in 12 gauge with 26-inch ventilated-rib barrel, skeet choke; stock and forearm of extra fancy walnut. Made from 1965 to 1972.

Franchi Aristocrat Field Model Over-and-Under Shotgun.. $425
Box lock. Selective automatic ejectors. Selective single trigger. 12 gauge. Barrels: 26-inch improved cylinder and modified, 28- and 30-inch modified and full choke; ventilated rib. Weight, with 26-inch barrels, 7 pounds. Checkered pistol-grip stock and forearm. Made from 1960 to 1969.

Franchi Aristocrat Magnum Model...............$425
Same as Field Model, except chambered for 3-inch shell, has 32-inch barrels, both full choke; weight, about 8 pounds; stock has recoil pad. Made from 1962 to 1965.

Franchi Model 3000/2 Combination Trap.......$2250
Box lock. Automatic ejectors. Selective single trigger. 12 gauge. Barrels: 32" over-and-under full and improved modified; 34" underbarrel modified choke; high ventilated rib. Weight with 32-inch barrels, 8 pounds 6 ounces. Choice of six different cast-off butt stocks. Made from 1979 to date.

Franchi Aristocrat Skeet Model..................$480
Same general specifications as Field Model, except made only with 26-inch ventilated-rib barrels bored skeet chokes #1 and #2; weight, about 7½ pounds; skeet-style stock and forearm. Later production had wider (10mm) rib. Made from 1960 to 1969.

Franchi Aristocrat Trap Model...................$525
Same general specifications as Field Model, except made only with 30-inch ventilated-rib barrels bored modified and full choke; trap style stock with recoil pad, beavertail forearm. Later production had Monte Carlo comb, wider (10mm) rib. Made from 1960 to 1969.

Franchie Aristocrat Silver King..................$525
Available in Field, Magnum, Skeet and Trap Models with the same general specifications as standard guns of these types. Silver King has stock and forearm of select walnut, more elaborately engraved silver finish receiver. Made from 1962 to 1969.

Franchi Aristocrat Deluxe and Supreme Grades
Available in Field, Skeet and Trap Models with the same general specifications as standard guns of these types. Deluxe and Supreme Grades are of higher quality with stock and forearm of select walnut, elaborate relief engraving of receiver, trigger guard, tang and top lever. Supreme Model has figures of game birds inlaid in gold. Made from 1960 to 1966.

Deluxe Grade......................................	$ 800
Supreme Grade....................................	1050

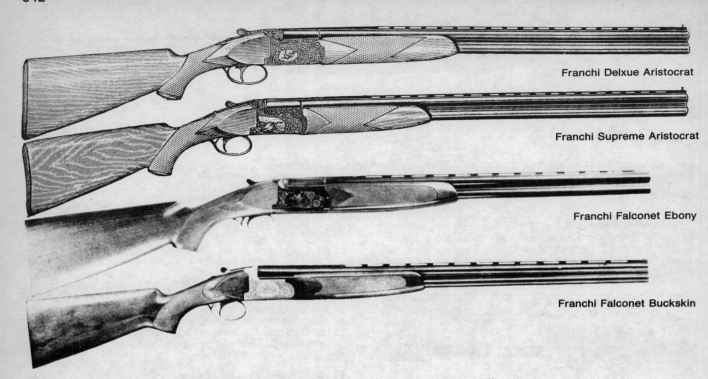

Franchi Delxue Aristocrat

Franchi Supreme Aristocrat

Franchi Falconet Ebony

Franchi Falconet Buckskin

Franchi Aristocrat Imperial and Monte Carlo Grades

Custom guns made in Field, Skeet and Trap Models with the same general specifications as standrd for these types. Imperial and Monte Carol Grades are of highest quality with stock and forearm of select walnut, fine engraving—elaborate on the latter grade. Made from 1967 to 1969.

Imperial Grade.................................... **$2000**
Monte Carlo Grade............................... **2600**

Franchi Falconet Over-and-Under Shotgun, Field Models

Box lock. Automatic ejectors. Selective single trigger. Gauges: 12, 16, 20, 28, 410. Barrels: 24-, 26-, 28-, 30-inch; ventilated rib. Chokes: cylinder and improved cylinder, improved cylinder and modified, modified and full. Weight, from about 6 pounds. Engraved lightweight alloy receiver; light-colored in Buckskin Model, blued in Ebony Model, pickled silver in Silver Model. Checkered walnut stock and forearm. Made from 1968 to 1975.

Buckskin or Ebony Model.......................... **$425**
Silver Model...................................... **500**

Franchi Falconet Standard Skeet Model........ **$850**

Same general specifications as Field Models, except made only with 26-inch barrels bored skeet chokes #1 and #2, wide ventilated rib, color-casehardened receiver, skeet-style stock and forearm; weight in 12 gauge, about 7¾ pounds. Made from 1970 to 1974.

Franchi Falconet International Skeet Model..... **$910**

Similar to Standard Skeet Model, but higher grade Made from 1970 to 1974.

Franchi Falconet Standard Trap Model......... **$845**

Same general specifications as Field Models, except made only in 12 gauge, with 30-inch barrels bored modified and full choke; wide ventilated rib, color-casehardened receiver, Monte Carlo trap-style stock and forearm, recoil pad; weight, about 8 pounds. Made from 1970 to 1974.

Franchi Falconet International Trap Model...... **$910**

Similar to Standard Trap Model, but higher grade; with either straight or Monte Carlo comb stock. Made from 1970 to 1974.

Franchi Peregrine Model 451 Over-and-Under Shotgun... **$490**

Box lock. Lightweight alloy receiver. Automatic ejectors. Selective single trigger. 12 gauge. Barrels: 26½-, 28-inch; cylinder and improved cylinder, improved cylinder and modified, modified and full choke; ventilated rib. Weight with 26½-inch barrels, 6 lbs. 1 oz. Checkered pistol-grip stock and forearm. Made from 1975 to 1978.

Franchi Peregrine Model 400.................... **$525**

Same general specifications as Model 451, except has steel receiver; weight, with 26½-inch barrel, 6 lbs. 15 oz. Made from 1975 to 1978.

Franchi Model 2003 Trap Over-and-Under Shotgun... **$1050**

Box lock. Automatic ejectors. Selective single trigger. 12 gauge. Barels: 30-, 32-inch; improved modified and full, full and full; high ventilated rib. Weight, with 30-inch barrel, 8¼ pounds. Checkered walnut beavertail forearm and stock with straight or Monte Carlo comb, recoil pad. Luggage-type carrying case. Made from 1976 to date.

Franchi Model 2004 Trap Single Barrel Shotgun... **$1050**

Same as Model 2003, except single barrel, 32- or 34-inch, full choke; weight, with 32-inch barrel, 8¼ pounds. Made from 1976 to date.

Franchi Model 2005 Combination Trap........ **$1620**

Model 2004/2005 type gun with two sets of barrels, single and over-and-under. Made from 1976 to date.

Franchi Model 2005/3 Combination Trap...... **$2100**

Model 2004/2005 type gun with three sets of barrels, any combination of single and over-and-under. Made from 1976 to date.

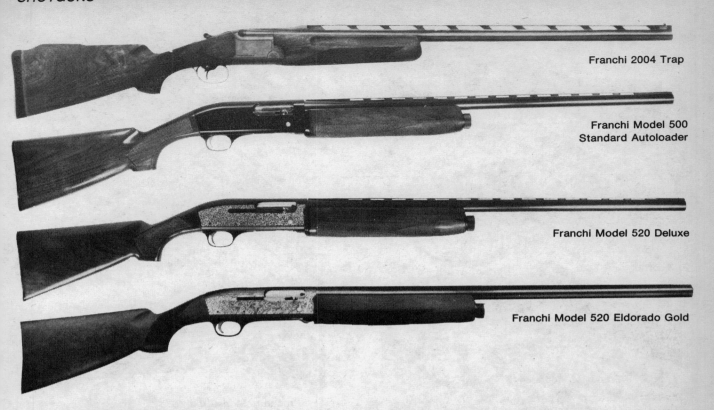

Franchi 2004 Trap

Franchi Model 500 Standard Autoloader

Franchi Model 520 Deluxe

Franchi Model 520 Eldorado Gold

Franchi Model 500 Standard Autoloader........**$260**
Gas operated. 12 gauge. 4-shot magazine. Barrels: 26-, 28- inch; ventilated rib; improved cylinder, modified, improved modified, full choke. Weight, about 7 pounds. Checkered pistol-grip stock and forearm. Made from 1976 to 1980.

Franchi Model 520 Deluxe.....................**$320**
Same as Model 500, except higher grade with engraved receiver. Made from 1975 to 1979.

Franchi Model 520 Eldorado Gold...............**$910**
Same as Model 520, except custom grade with engraved and gold-inlaid receiver, finer quality wood. Introduced 1977.

Auguste Francotte & Cie., S.A., Liege, Belgium

Francotte shotguns for many years were distributed in the United States by the Abercrombie & Fitch Company of New York City. This firm has used a series of model designations for Francotte guns which do not correspond to those of the manufacturer. Because so many Francotte owners refer to their guns by the A & F model names and numbers, the A & F series is included in a listing separate from that of the standard Francotte numbers.

Francotte Hammerless Double Barrel Shotguns

A & F Series. Box lock, Anson & Deeley type. Crossbolt. Side plate on all except Knockabout Model. Side clips. Automatic ejectors. Double triggers. Gauges: 12, 16, 20, 28, 410. Barrels: 26- to 32-inch in 12 gauge, 26- and 28-inch in other gauges; any boring. Weight, 4¾ to 8 pounds depending upon gauge and barrel length. Checkered stock and fore-end; straight-, half- or full-pistol grip. The seven grades—No. 45 Eagle Grade, No. 30, No. 25, No. 20, No. 14, Jubilee Model, Knockabout Model—differ chiefly in overall quality, engraving, grade of wood, checkering, etc., general specifications are the same. Discontinued.

No. 45 Eagle Grade.................................	**$6450**
No. 30...	5100
No. 25...	4800
No. 20...	4200
No. 14...	3800
Jubilee Model.....................................	3800
Knockabout Model.................................	2950

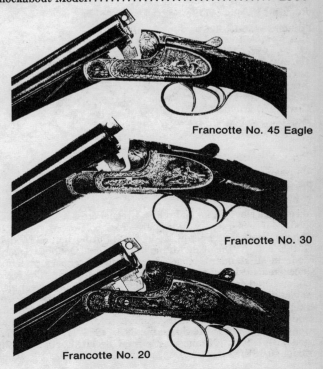

Francotte No. 45 Eagle

Francotte No. 30

Francotte No. 20

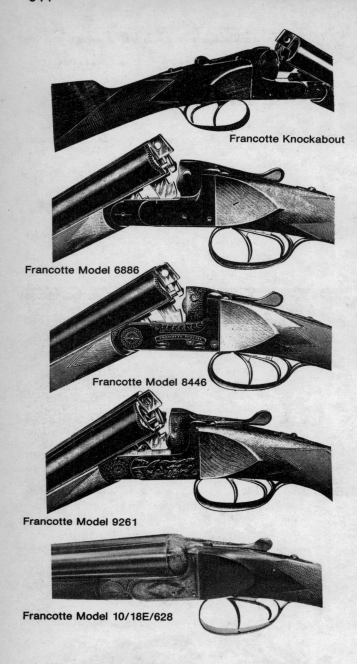

Francotte Knockabout

Francotte Model 6982

Francotte Model 6886

Francotte
Model SOB.E/11082

Francotte Model 8446

Francotte Model 9/40.SE

Francotte Model 9261

Francotte Model 10/18E/628

Francotte Box Lock Hammerless Double Barrel Shotguns

Anson & Deeley system. Side clips. Greener cross bolt on Models 6886, 8446, 4996 and 9261; square cross bolt on Model 6930; Greener-Scott cross bolt on Model 8457; Purdey bolt on Models 11/18E and 10/18E/628. Automatic ejectors. Double triggers. Made in all standard gauges, barrel lengths, chokes, weights. Checkered stock and fore-end, straight or pistol grip. The eight models listed vary chiefly in fastening as described above, finish and engraving, etc., general specifications are the same. All except Model 10/18E/628 have been discontinued.

Model 6886.................................... $2000
Model 8446 ("Francotte Special"), 6930, 4996....... 2475
Model 8457, 9261 ("Francotte Original"), 11/18E..... 2875
Model 10/18E/628................................. 4025

Francotte Box Lock Hammerless Double Barrel Shotguns With Sideplates

Anson & Deeley system. Reinforced frame with side clips. Purdley-type bolt except on Model 8455 which has Greener cross bolt. Automatic ejectors. Double triggers. Made in all standard gauges, barrel lengths, chokes, weights. Checkered stock and fore-end, straight or pristol grip. Models 10594, 8455 and 6982 are of equal quality, differ cheifly in style of engraving; Model 9/40E/38321 is a higher grade gun in all details and has fine English-style engraving. Currently manufactured.

Models 10594, 8455, 6982.......................... $3105
Model 9/40E/38321................................. 4025

Francotte Fine Side Lock Hammerless Double Barrel Shotgun... $8050

Model 120.HE/328 Automatic ejectors. Double triggers. Made in all standard gauges; barrel length, boring, weight to order. Checkered stock and fore-end, straight or pistol grip. Currently manufactured.

Francotte Half-Fine Over-and-Under Shotgun..$6325

Model SOB.E/11082. Box lock, Anson & Deeley system. Automatic ejectors. Double triggers. Made in all standard gauges; barrel length, boring to order. Checkered stock and fore-end, straight or pistol grip. Note: This model is quite similar to No. 9/40.SE except general quality is not as high and frame is not fully engraved or scalloped. Discontinued.

Francotte Fine Over-and-Under Shotgun....... $8625

Model 9/40.SE. Box lock, Anson & Deeley system. Automatic ejectors. Double triggers. Made in all standard gauges; barrel length, boring to order. Weight, about 6¾ pounds in 12 gauge. Checkered stock and fore-end, straight or pistol grip. Currently manufactured.

Galef Silver Hawk

Galef Zabala

Galef Silver Snipe

Carlo Monte Carlo

Galef Shotguns manufactured for J. L. Galef & Son, Inc., New York, New York, by M.A.V.I., Gardone V.T., Italy, by Zabala Hermanos, Elquetta, Spain, and by Antonio Zoli, Gardone V.T., Italy

Galef Silver Hawk Hammerless Double Barrel Shotgun... **$470**
Box lock. Plain extractors. Double triggers. Gauges: 12, 20; 3-inch chambers. Barrels: 26-, 28-, 30-inch (latter in 12 gauge only); improved cylinder and modified, modified and full choke. Weight, 12 gauge with 26-inch barrels, 6 lbs. 6 oz. Checkered walnut pistol-grip stock and beavertail forearm. Made by Antonio Zoli from 1968 to 1972.

Galef Zabala Hammerless Double Barrel Shotgun
Box lock. Plain extractors. Double triggers. Gauges: 10 mag., 12 mag., 16, 20 mag., 28, 410. Barrels: 22-, 26-, 28-, 30-, 32-inch; both improved cylinder, improved cylinder and modified, modified and full, both full choke. Weight, 12 gauge with 28-inch barrels, 7¾ pounds. Checkered walnut pistol-grip stock and beavertail forearm, recoil pad. Made by Zabala from 1972 to date.
10 gauge.. **$290**
Other gauges.. **250**

Galef Silver Snipe Over-and Under Shotgun.... **$435**
Box lock. Plain extractors. Single trigger. Gauges: 12, 20; 3-inch chambers. Barrels: 26-, 28-, 30-inch (latter in 12 gauge only); improved cylinder and modified, modified and full choke; ventilated rib. Weight, 12 gauge with 28-inch barrels, 6½ pounds. Checkered walnut pistol-grip stock and forearm. Made by Antonio Zoli from 1968 to date

Galef Golden Snipe................................ **$510**
Same as Silver Snipe, except has selective automatic ejectors. Made by Antonio Zoli from 1968 to date.

Galef Companion Folding Single Barrel Shotgun
Hammerless. Underlever. Gauges: 12 mag., 16, 20 mag., 28, 410. Barrels: 26-inch (410 only), 28-inch (12, 16, 20, 28), 30-inch (12 gauge only); full choke; plain or ventialted rib. Weights: from 4½ pounds for 410 to 5 lbs. 9 oz. for 12 gauge. Checkered pistol-grip stock and forearm. Made by M.A.V.I. from 1968 to date.
With plain barrel................................... **$75**
With ventilated rib................................... **80**

Galef Companion

Galef Monte Carlo Trap Single Barrel Shotgun..**$235**
Hammerless. Underlever. Plain extractor. 12 gauge. 32-inch barrel, full choke, ventilated rib. Weight, about 8¼ pounds. Checkered pistol-grip stock with Monte Carlo comb and recoil pad, beavertail forearm. Made by M.A.V.I. from 1968 to date.

Garcia Bronco 410

Garcia Bronco 22/410

Garcia Corporation
Teaneck, New Jersey

Garcia Bronco 410 Single Shot................... $60
Swing-out action. Takedown. 410 gauge. 18½-inch barrel. Weight, 3½ pounds. One-piece stock and receiver, crackle finish. Introduced in 1967. Discontinued.

Garcia Bronco 22/410 Over-and-Under Combination Gun $75
Swing-out action. Takedown. 18½-inch barrels; 22 Long Rifle over, 410 gauge under. Weight, 4½ pounds. One-piece stock and receiver, crackle finish. Introduced in 1976. Discontinued.

Golden Eagle Shotguns manufactured for Golden Eagle Firearms Inc., Houston Texas, by Nikko Firearms Ltd., Tochigi, Japan

Golden Eagle Model 5000 Grade I Field Over-and-Under Shotgun..................................... $675
Receiver engraved and inlaid with gold eagle head. Box lock. Automatic ejectors. Selective single trigger. Gauges: 12, 20; 2¾- or 3-inch chambers in 12 gauge, 3-inch in 20 gauge. Barrels: 26-, 28-, 30-inch (latter only in 12 gauge 3-inch magnum); improved cylinder and modified, modified and full choke; ventilated rib. Weight: 6¼ pounds in 20 gauge, 7¼ pounds in 12 gauge, 8 pounds in 12 gauge Magnum. Checkered pistol-grip stock and semi-beavertail forearm. Made from 1975 to date. *Note:* Guns marketed 1975-76 under the Nikko brand name have white recievers; those manufactured since 1976 have blued recievers.

Golden Eagle Model 5000 Grade I Skeet........ $750
Same as Field Model, except has 26- or 28-inch barrels with wide (11mm) ventilated rib, skeet choked. Made from 1975 to date.

Golden Eagle Model 5000 Grade I Trap......... $725
Same as Field Model, except has 30- or 32-inch barrels with wide (11mm) ventilated rib (modified and full, improved modified and full, both full choke), trap-style stock with recoil pad. Made from 1975 to date.

Golden Eagle Model 5000 Grade II Field........ $775
Same as Grade I Field Model, except higher grade with fancier wood, more elaborate engraving and "screaming eagle" inlaid in gold. Made from 1975 to date.

Golden Eagle Model 5000 Grade II Skeet....... $850
Same as Grade I Skeet Model, except higher grade with fancier wood, more elaborate engraving and "screaming eagle" inlaid in gold; inertia trigger, ventilated side ribs. Made from 1975 to date.

Golden Eagle Model 5000 Grade II Trap........ $875
Same as Grade I Trap Model, except higher grade with fancier wood, more elaborate engraving and "screaming eagle" inlaid in gold; inertia trigger, venilated side ribs. Made from 1975 to date.

Golden Eagle Model 5000 Grade III Grandee.. $2600
Best grade, available in Field, Skeet and Trap Models with same general specifications as lower grades. Has side plates with game scene engraving, scroll on frame and barrels, fancy wood (Monte Carlo comb, full pistol grip and recoil pad on Trap Model). Made from 1976 to date.

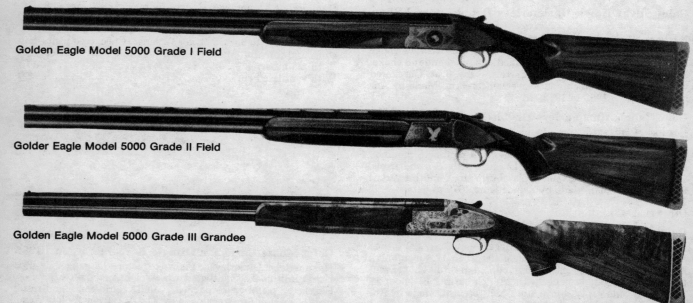

Golden Eagle Model 5000 Grade I Field

Golder Eagle Model 5000 Grade II Field

Golden Eagle Model 5000 Grade III Grandee

W.W. Greener, Ltd., Birmingham, England

Greener Hammerless Ejector Double Barrel Shotguns

Box lock. Automatic ejectors. Double triggers, non-selective or selective single trigger. Gauges: 12, 16, 20, 28, 410 (two latter gauges not supplied in Grades DH40 and DH35). Barrels: 26-, 28-, 30-inch; any choke combination. Weight, from 4¾ to 8 pounds depending upon gauge and barrel length. Checkered stock and fore-end, straight- or half-pistol grip. The Royal, Crown, Sovereign and Jubilee Models differ in quality, engraving, grade of wood, checkering, etc. General specifications are the same.

Royal Model Grade DH75	$3700
Crown Model Grade DH55	2775
Sovereign Model Grade DH40	2400
Jubilee Model Grade DH35	2000
Selective single trigger, extra	330
Non-selective single trigger, extra	250

Greener Royal

Greener Sovereign

Greener Jubilee

Greener Far-Killer Model Grade FH35 Hammerless Double Barrel Shotgun

Box lock. Non-ejector or with automatic ejectors. Double triggers. Gauges: 12 (2¾-inch or 3-inch), 10, 8. Barrels: 28,- 30- or 32-inch. Weight, from 7½ to 9 pounds in 12 gauge. Checkered stock and fore-end, straight- or half-pistol grip.

Nonejector, 12 gauge	$1950
Ejector, 12 gauge	2775
Nonejector, 10 or 8 gauge	2250
Ejector, 10 or 8 gauge	3000

Greener Far-Killer

Greener Empire Model Hammerless Double Barrel Shotgun

Box lock. Nonejector or with automatic ejectors. Double triggers. 12 gauge only (2¾-inch or 3-inch chamber). Barrels: 28- to 32-inch; any choke combination. Weight, from 7¼ to 7¾ pounds depending upon barrel length. Checkered stock and fore-end, straight- or half-pistol grip. Also furnished in "Empire Deluxe Grade;" this model has same general specifications but in deluxe finish.

Empire Model, nonejector	$1300
Empire Model, ejector	1500
Empire Deluxe Model, nonejector	1500
Empire Deluxe Model, ejector	1700

Greener Empire

Greener G. P. (General Purpose) Single Barrel Shotgun ... $275

Greener Improved Martini Lever Action. Takedown. Ejector. 12 gauge only. Barrel lengths: 26-, 30-, 32-inch. Modified or full choke. Weight, from 6¼ to 6¾ pounds, depending upon barrel length. Checkered straight-grip stock and forearm.

Greifelt & Co., Suhl, Germany

Greifelt Model 103 Hammerless Double Barrel Shotgun ... $1400

Anson & Deeley box lock. Plain extractors. Double triggers. Gauges: 12 and 16. Barrels: 28- or 30-inch, modified and full choke. Checkered stock and fore-end, pistol grip and cheekpiece standard, English-style stock also supplied. Manufactured since World War II.

Greifelt Model 103E Hammerless Double Barrel Shotgun ... $1665

Same as Model 103, except has automatic ejectors.

Greifelt Model 22 Hammerless Double Barrel Shotgun ... $1400

Anson & Deeley box lock. Plain extractors. Double triggers. Gauges: 12 and 16. Barrels: 28- or 30-inch, modified and full choke. Checkered stock and fore-end, pistol grip and cheekpiece standard, English-style stock also supplied. Manufactured since World War II.

Grefelt Model 22E Hammerless Double Barrel Shotgun ... $1900

Same as Model 22, except has automatic ejectors.

Greifelt No. 1

H&R No. 8

Harrington & Richardson Arms Co., Worcester, Massachusetts

Harrington & Richardson No. 8 Standard Single Barrel Hammer Shotgun.................................. **$ 75**
Takedown. Automatic ejector. Gauges: 12, 16, 20, 24, 28, 410.Barrels: plain, 26- to 32-inch, full choke. Weight, from 5½ to 6½ pounds depending upon gauge and barrel length. Plain pistol-grip stock and fore-end. Made from 1908 to 1942.

Greifelt Grade No. 1 Over-and-Under Shotgun
Anson & Deeley box lock, Kersten fastening. Automatic ejectors. Double triggers or single trigger. Elaborately engraved. Gauges: 12, 16, 20, 28, 410. Barrels: 26- to 32-inch, any combination of chokes, ventilated or solid matted rib. Weight, from 4¼ to 8¼ pounds depending upon gauge and barrel length. Straight-or pistol-grip stock, Purdey-type fore-end, both checkered. Manufactured prior to World War II.
With solid matted-rib barrel, in all gauges except 410. **$4500**
With solid matted-rib barrel, 410 gauge.............. 5550
Extra for ventilated rib............................ 280
Extra for single trigger............................ 335

Greifelt Grade No. 3 Over-and-Under Shotgun
Same general specifications as Grade No. 1 except not as fancy engraving. Manufactured prior to World War II.
With solid matted-rib barrel, in all gauges except 410. **$3200**
With solid matted-rib barrel, 410 gauge.............. 3885
Extra for ventilated rib............................ 280
Extra for single trigger............................ 335

H&R No. 6

Harrington & Richardson No. 6 Heavy Breech Single Barrel Hammer Shotgun......................... **$ 85**
Takedown. Automatic ejector. Gauges: 10, 12, 16, 20. Barrels: plain, 28- to 36-inch, full choke. Weight, about 7 to 7¼ pounds. Plain stock and fore-end. Discontinued 1942.

Greifelt Model 143E Over-and-Under Shotgun
General specifications same as prewar Grade No. 1 Over-and-Under except this model is not supplied in 28 and 410 gauge or with 32-inch barrels. Model 143 E is not as high quality as the Grade No. 1 gun. Manufactured since World War II.
With raised matted rib, double triggers.............. **$2000**
With ventilated rib, selective single trigger........... 5200

Greifelt Over-and-Under Combination Gun
Similar in design to this maker's over-and-under shotguns. Gauges: 12, 16, 20, 28, 410; rifle barrel in any caliber adapted to this type of gun. Barrels: 24- or 26-inch, solid matted rib. Weight, from 4¾ to 7¼ pounds. Folding rear sight. Manufactured prior to World War II. *Note:* Values shown are for gauges other than 410, with rifle barrel chambered for a cartridge readily obtainable; if in an odd foreign caliber, value will be considerably less. 410 gauge increses value by upwards of 50%.
With nonautomatic ejector...........................**$4800**
With automatic ejector............................. 5200

H&R No. 7

Harrington & Richardson Bay State No. 7 or 9 Single Barrel Hammer Shotgun......................... **$ 75**
Takedown. Automatic ejector. Gauges: 12, 16, 20, 410. Barrels: plain, 26- to 32-inch full choke. Weight, from 5½ to 6½ pounds depending upon gauge and barrel length. Plain pistol-grip stock and fore-end. Discontinued 1942.

Greifelt Hammerless Drilling (Three Barrel Combination Gun).. **$5700**
Box lock. Plain extractors. Double triggers, front single set for rifle barrel. Gauges: 12, 16, 20; rifle barrel in any caliber adapted to this type of gun. 26-inch barrels. Weight, about 7½ pounds. Automatic rear sight operated by rifle barrel selector. Checkered stock and forearm, pistol grip and cheekpiece standard. Manufactured prior to WW II. *Note:* Value shown is for guns chambered for cartridges readily obtainable; if rifle barrel is an odd foreign caliber, value will be considerably less.

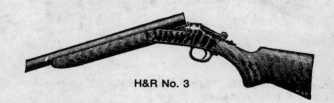

H&R No. 3

Harrington & Richardson No. 3 Hammerless Single Barrel Shotgun................................... **$ 75**
Takedown. Automatic ejector. Gauges: 12, 16, 20, 410. Barrels: plain, 26- to 32-inch, full choke. Weight, from 6½ to 7¼ pounds depending upon gauge and barrel length. Plain pistol-grip stock and fore-end. Discontinued 1942.

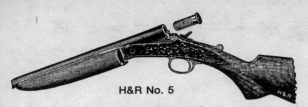

H&R No. 5

Harrington & Richardson Standard Light Weight No. 5 Hammer Single Barrel Shotgun................. $ 90

Takedown. Automatic ejector. Gauges: 24, 28, 410, 14mm. Barrels: 26- or 28-inch, full choke. Weight, about 4 to 4¾ pounds. Plain pistol-grip stock and fore-end. Discontinued 1942.

Harrington & Richardson Folding Gun.......... $120

Single barrel hammer shotgun hinged at the front of the frame, the barrel folds down against the stock. Light Frame Model: gauges—28, 14mm, 410; 22-inch barrel; weight, about 4½ pounds. Heavy Frame Model: gauges—12, 16, 20, 28, 410; 26-inch barrel; weight, from 5¾ to 6½ pounds. Plain pistol-grip stock and fore-end. Discontinued 1942.

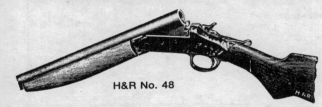

H&R No. 48

Harrington & Richardson No. 48 Topper Single Barrel Hammer Shotgun................................. $ 65

Similar to old Model 8 Standard. Takedown. Top lever. Automatic ejector. Gauges: 12, 16, 20, 410. Barrels: plain, 26- to 30-inch, modified or full choke. Weight, 5½ to 6½ pounds depending upon gauge and barrel length. Plain pistol-grip stock and fore-end. Made from 1946 to 1957.

Harrington & Richardson No. 488 Topper Deluxe.................................... $ 65

Same as standard No. 48 Topper, except chrome-plated frame, black lacquered stock and fore-end, recoil pad. Discontinued 1957.

Harrington & Richardson Topper Model 148 Single Barrel Hammer Shotgun....................... $ 65

Takedown. Side lever. Automatic ejection. Gauges: 12, 16, 20, 410. Barrels: 12 ga., 30-, 32- and 36-inch; 16 ga., 28- and 30-inch; 20 and 410 ga., 28-inch; full choke. Weight, 5 to 6½ pounds. Plain pistol-grip stock and fore-end, recoil pad. Made from 1958 to 1961.

Harrington & Richardson Topper Deluxe Model 188.. $ 60

Same as standard Topper Model 148, except has chromed frame, stock and fore-end in black, red, yellow, blue, green, pink, or purple colored finish. 410 gauge only. Made from 1958 to 1961.

Harrington & Richardson Topper Jr. Model 480. $ 65

Similar to No. 48 Topper, except has youth-size stock, 26-inch barrel, 410 gauge only. Made from 1958 to 1961.

Harrington & Richardson Topper Jr. Model 580. $ 60

Same as Model 480, except has colored stocks as on Model 188. Made from 1958 to 1961.

Harrington & Richardson Model 158 (058) Topper Single Barrel Hammer Shotgun..................... $ 65

Takedown. Side lever. Automatic ejection. Gauges: 12, 20, 410 (2¾-inch and 3-inch shells); 16 (2¾-inch). Barrel length and choke combinations: 12 ga.–36-inch/full, 32-inch/full, 30-inch/full, 28-inch/full or modified; 410–28-inch/full. Weight, about 5½ pounds. Plain pistol-grip stock and fore-end, recoil pad. Made from 1962 to 1981. *Note:* Designation changed to 058 in 1974.

Harrington & Richardson Model 198 (098) Topper Deluxe.. $ 65

Same as Model 158, except has chrome-plated frame, black finished stock and fore-end; 12, 20 and 410 gauges. Made from 1962 to 1981. *Note:* Designation changed to 098 in 1974.

Harrington & Richardson Model 099 Deluxe.... $ 60

Same as Model 158, except has matte nickel finish, semi-pistol grip walnut-finished American hardwood stock; semi-beavertail forearm; 12, 16, 20, and 410 gauges. Made from 1982 to date.

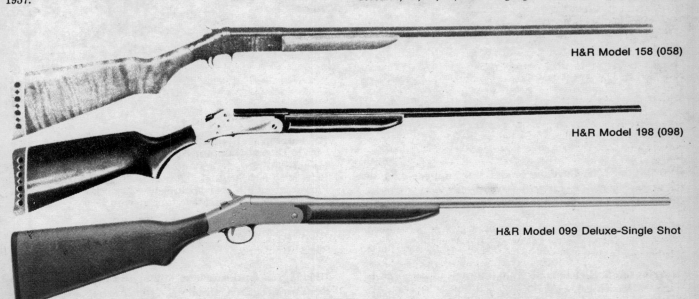

H&R Model 158 (058)

H&R Model 198 (098)

H&R Model 099 Deluxe-Single Shot

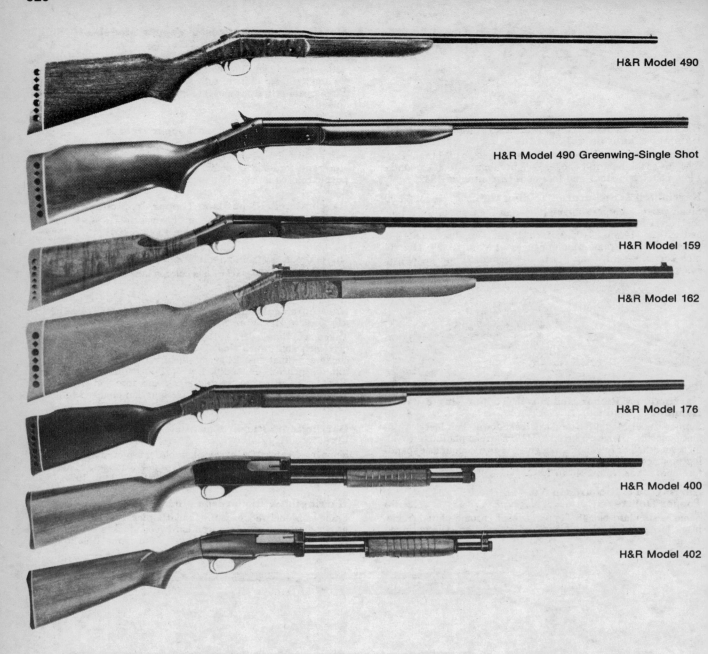

H&R Model 490

H&R Model 490 Greenwing-Single Shot

H&R Model 159

H&R Model 162

H&R Model 176

H&R Model 400

H&R Model 402

Harrington & Richardson Model 490 Topper.... $ 65
Same as Model 158, except has youth-size stock (3 inches shorter), 26-inch barrel; 20 and 28 gauge (modified choke), 410 (full). Made from 1962 to date.

Harrington & Richard Model 490 Greenwing.... $ 65
Same as the Model 490, except has a special high-polished finish. Made from 1981 to date.

Harrington & Richardson Model 590 Topper.... $ 65
Same as Model 490, except has chrome-plated frame, black finished stock and fore-end. Made from 1962 to 1963.

Harrington & Richardson Model 159 Golden Squire Single Barrel Hammer Shotgun.................... $80
Hammerless. Side lever. Automatic ejection. Gauges: 12, 20. Barrels: 30-inch in 12 ga., 28-inch in 20 ga., both full choke. Weight, about 6½ pounds. Straight-grip stock with recoil pad, forearm with schnabel. Made from 1964 to 1966.

Harrington & Richardson Model 459 Golden Squire Jr..................................... $80
Same as Model 159, except gauges 20 and 410, 26-inch barrel, youth-size stock. Made in 1964.

Harrington & Richardson Model 162 Slug Gun... $70
Same as Model 158, except has 24-inch barrel, cylinder bore, with rifle sights. Made from 1968 to date.

H&R Model 403

H&R Model 440

H&R Model 442

H&R Model 404C

Harrington & Richardson Model 176 10 Gauge Magnum... **$75**
Similar to Model 158, but has 36-inch heavy barrel chambered for 3½-inch 10 gauge magnum shells, weights 10 pounds; stock with Monte Carlo comb and recoil pad, longer and fuller forearm. Introduced 1977.

Harrington & Richardson Model 348 Gamester Bolt Action Shotgun.................................... **$65**
Takedown. 12 and 16 gauge. 2-shot tubular magazine, 28-inch barrel, full choke. Plain piston-grip stock. Weight, about 7½ pounds. Made from 1949 to 1954.

Harrington & Richardson Model 349 Gamester Deluxe.................................. **$80**
Same as Model 348, except has 26-inch barrel with adjustable choke device, recoil pad. Made from 1953 to 1955.

Harrington & Richardson Model 351 Huntsman Bolt Action Shotgun.................................... **$80**
Takedown. 12 and 16 gauge. 2-shot tubular magazine. Pushbutton safety. 26-inch barrel with H&R variable choke. Weight, about 6¾ pounds. Monte Carlo stock with recoil pad. Made from 1956 to 1958.

Harrington & Richardson Model 400 Pump Action Shotgun... **$175**
Hammerless. Gauges: 12, 16, 20. Tubular magazine holds 4 shells. 28-inch barrel, full choke. Weight, about 7¼ pounds. Plain pistol-grip stock (recoil pad in 12 and 16 ga.), grooved slide handle. Made from 1955 to 1967.

Harrington & Richardson Model 401............. **$190**
Same as Model 400, except has H&R variable choke. Made from 1956 to 1963.

Harrington & Richardson Model 402............. **$190**
Similar to Model 400, except 410 gauge, weighs about 5½ pounds. Made from 1959 to 1967

Harrington & Richardson Model 403 Autoloading Shotgun.. **$210**
Takedown. 410 gauge. Tubular magazine holds four shells. 26-inch barrel, full choke. Weight, about 5¾ pounds. Plain pistol-grip stock and forearm. Made in 1964.

Harrington & Richardson Model 440 Pump Action Shotgun.. **$150**
Hammerless. Gauges: 12, 16, 20. 2¾-inch chamber in 16 gauge, 3-inch in 12 and 20 gauges. 3-shot magazine. Barrels: 26-, 28-, 30-inch; improved cylinder, modified, full choke. Weight, 6¼ pounds. Plain pistol-grip stock and slide handle, recoil pad. Made from 1968 to 1973.

Harrington & Richardson Model 442............. **$190**
Same as Model 440, except has ventilated-rib barrel, checkered stock and forearm, weighs 6¾ pounds. Made from 1969 to 1973.

Harrington & Richardson Model 404 Double Barrel Shotgun.. **$195**
Box lock. Plain extractors. Double triggers. Gauges: 12, 20, 410. Barrels: 28-inch modified and full choke in 12 ga., 26-inch in 20 ga. (improved cylinder and modified) and 410 (full and full). Weight, 5½ to 7¼ pounds. Plain walnut-finished hardwood stock and fore-end. Made in Brazil by Amadeo Rossi from 1969 to 1972.

Harrington & Richardson Model 404C........... **$220**
Same as Model 404, except has checkered stock and fore-end. Made from 1969 to 1972.

H&R Harrich No. 1

H&R Model 1212 Field

H&R Model 1212 Waterfowl

Harrington & Richardson Harrich No. 1 Single Barrel Trap Gun **$2025**
Anson & Deeley-type locking system with Kersten top locks and double underlocking lugs. Side plates engraved with hunting scenes. 12 gauge. Barrels: 32-, 34-inch; full choke; high ventilated rib. Weight, 8½ pounds. Checkered Monte Carlo stock with pistol grip and recoil pad, beavertail forearm, of select walnut. Made in Ferlach, Austria, from 1971 to 1975.

Harrington & Richardson Model 1212 Over-and-Under Field Gun **$365**
Box lock. Plain extractors. Selective single trigger. 12 gauge, 2¾-inch chambers. 28-inch barrels, improved cylinder and improved modified, ventilated rib. Weight, 7 pounds. Checkered walnut pistol-grip stock and fluted forearm. Made from 1976 to 1980 by Lanber Arms S.A., Zaldibar (Vizcaya), Spain.

Harrington & Richardson Model 1212 Waterfowl Gun **$375**
Same as Field Gun, except chambered for 12 gauge 3-inch magnum shells, has 30-inch barrels, modified and full choke, stock and recoil pad, weighs 7½ pounds. Made from 1976 to 1980.

The High Standard Mfg. Corp., Hamden, Connecticut

High Standard Supermatic Field Autoloading Shotgun—12 Gauge **$165**
Gas-operated. Magazine holds four shells. Barrels: 26-inch improved cylinder, 28-inch modified or full choke, 30-inch full choke. Weight, about 7½ pounds. Plain pistol-grip stock and forearm. Made from 1960 to 1966.

High Standard Supermatic Special—12 Gauge . . . **$170**
Same as Supermatic Field 12, except has 27-inch barrel with adjustable choke. Made form 1960 to 1966.

High Standard Supermatic Deluxe Rib— 12 Gauge **$185**
Same as Supermatic Field 12, except ventilated-rib barrel (28-inch modified or full, 30-inch full), checkered stock and forearm. Made from 1961 to 1966.

High Standard Supermatic Trophy—12 Gauge . . **$195**
Same as Supermatic Deluxe Rib 12, except has 27-inch ventilated rib barrel with adjustable choke. Made from 1961 to 1966.

High Standard Supermatic Duck— 12 Gauge Magnum **$170**
Same as Supermatic Field 12, except chambered for 3-inch magnum shell, 30-inch full choke barrel, recoil pad. Made form 1961 to 1966.

High Standard Supermatic Duck Rib—12 Gauge Magnum **$195**
Same as Supermatic Duck 12 Magnum, except has ventilated-rib barrel, checkered stock and forearm. Made from 1961 to 1966.

High Standard Supermatic Deer Gun **$185**
Same as Supermatic Field 12, except has 22-inch barrel (cylinder bore) with rifle sights, checkered stock and forearm, recoil pad; weight, 7¾ pounds. Made in 1965.

High Standard Supermatic Skeet—12 Gauge **$195**
Same as Supermatic Deluxe Rib 12, except 26-inch ventilated-rib barrel bored skeet choke. Made from 1962 to 1966.

High Standard Superamtic Trip—12 Gauge **$205**
Same as Supermatic Deluxe rib 12, except 30-inch ventilated-rib barrel, full choke, special trap stock with recoil pad. Made from 1962 to 1966.

High Standard Supermatic Field Autoloading Shotgun—20 Gauge **$165**
Gas-operated Chambered for 3-inch magnum shells, also handles 2¾-inch. Magazine holds three shells. Barrels: 26-inch improved cylinder, 28-inch modified or full choke. Weight, about 7 pounds. Plain pistol-grip stock and forearm. Made from 1963 to 1966.

High Standard Supermatic Special— 20 Gauge **$175**
Same as Supermatic Field 20, except has 27-inch barrel with adjustable choke. Made from 1963 to 1966.

High Standard Supermatic Deluxe Rib— 20 Gauge **$190**
Same as Supermatic Field 20, except ventilated-rib barrel, (28-inch modified or full), checkered stock and forearm. Made from 1963 to 1966.

High Standard Supermatic Trophy—20 Gauge . . **$195**
Same as Supermatic Deluxe Rib 20, except has 27-inch ventilated-rib barrel with adjustable choke. Made from 1963 to 1966.

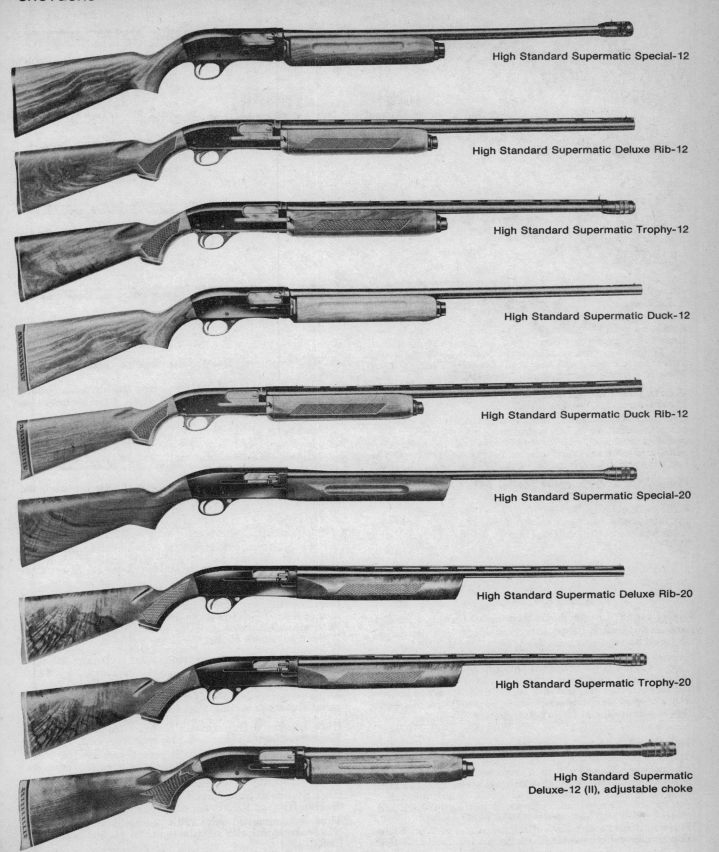

High Standard Supermatic Special-12

High Standard Supermatic Deluxe Rib-12

High Standard Supermatic Trophy-12

High Standard Supermatic Duck-12

High Standard Supermatic Duck Rib-12

High Standard Supermatic Special-20

High Standard Supermatic Deluxe Rib-20

High Standard Supermatic Trophy-20

High Standard Supermatic
Deluxe-12 (II), adjustable choke

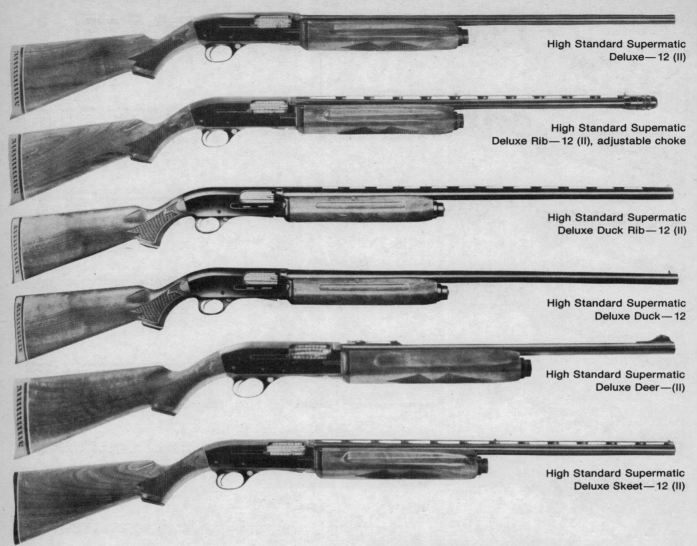

High Standard Supermatic
Deluxe—12 (II)

High Standard Supematic
Deluxe Rib—12 (II), adjustable choke

High Standard Supermatic
Deluxe Duck Rib—12 (II)

High Standard Supermatic
Deluxe Duck—12

High Standard Supermatic
Deluxe Deer—(II)

High Standard Supermatic
Deluxe Skeet—12 (II)

High Standard Supermatic Skeet—20 Gauge.... $200
Same as Supermatic Deluxe Rib 20, except 26-inch ventilated-rib barrel bored skeet choke. Made from 1964 to 1966.

Note: In 1966, High Standard introduced a new series of Supermatic autoloaders, readily identifiable by the damascened bolt and restyled checkering. To avoid confusion, these models are designated "Series II" in this text. This is *not* an official factory designation.

High Standard Supermatic Deluxe—12 Gauge (Series II)
Gas-operated autoloader. 4-shot magazine. Barrels: plain; 27-inch with adjustable choke (discontinued about 1970); 26-inch improved cylinder, 28-inch modified or full, 30-inch full choke. Weight, about 7½ pounds. Checkered pistol-grip stock and forearm, recoil pad. Made from 1966 to 1975.
With adjustable choke................................ **$190**
Without adjustable choke........................... **185**

High Standard Supermatic Deluxe Rib—12 Gauge (Series II)
Same as Supermatic Deluxe 12 (II), except has ventilated-rib barrel; available in 27-inch with adjustable choke, 28-inch modified or full, 30-inch full choke. Made from 1966 to 1975.
With adjustable choke............................... **$215**
Without adjustable choke............................ **195**

High Standard Supermatic Deluxe Duck Rib—12 Gauge Magnum (Series II)...................... **$210**
Same as Supermatic Deluxe Rib 12 (II), except chambered for 3-inch magnum shell, 3-shot magazine; 30-inch ventilated-rib barrel, full choke; weight, 8 pounds. Made from 1966 to 1975.

High Standard Supermatic Deluxe Duck—12 Gauge Magnum (Series II).............................**$175**
Same as Supermatic Deluxe 12 (II), except chambered for 3-inch magnum shell, 3-shot magazine; 30-inch plain barrel, full choke, weight 8 pounds. Made from 1966 to 1974.

High Standard Supermatic Deluxe Deer Gun (Series II)..**$190**
Same as Supermatic Deluxe 12 (II), except has 22-inch barrel, cylinder bore, with rifle sights; weight, 7¾ pounds. Made from 1966 to 1974.

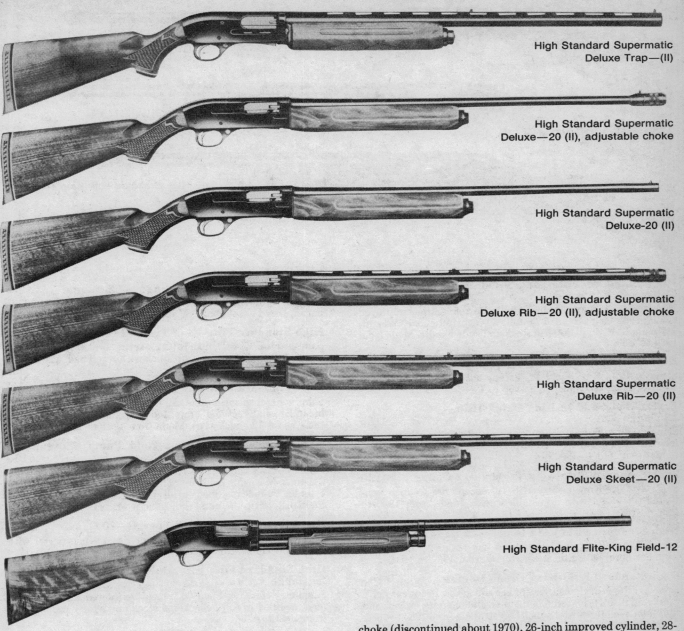

High Standard Supermatic
Deluxe Trap—(II)

High Standard Supermatic
Deluxe—20 (II), adjustable choke

High Standard Supermatic
Deluxe-20 (II)

High Standard Supermatic
Deluxe Rib—20 (II), adjustable choke

High Standard Supermatic
Deluxe Rib—20 (II)

High Standard Supermatic
Deluxe Skeet—20 (II)

High Standard Flite-King Field-12

High Standard Supermatic Deluxe Skeet Gun—12 Gauge (Series II).................... $200
Same as Supermatic Deluxe Rib 12 (II), except available only with 26-inch ventilated-rib barrel, skeet choke. Made from 1966 to 1975.

High Standard Supermatic Deluxe Trap Gun (Series II).....................$210
Same as Supermatic Deluxe Rib 12 (II), except available only with 30-inch ventilated-rib barrel, full choke; trap-style stock. Made from 1966 to 1975.

High Standard Supermatic Deluxe—20 Gauge (Series II)
Same as Supermatic Deluxe 12 (II), except chambered for 20 gauge 3-inch shell; barrels available in 27-inch with adjustable

choke (discontinued about 1970), 26-inch improved cylinder, 28-inch modified or full choke; weight, about 7 pounds. Made from 1966 to 1975.
With adjustable choke................................. $190
Without adjustable choke........................... 175

High Standard Supermatic Deluxe Rib—20 Gauge (Series II)
Same as Supermatic Deluxe 20 (II), except has ventilated-rib barrel. Made from 1966 to 1975.
With adjustable choke................................. $210
Without adjustable choke........................... 190

High Standard Supermatic Deluxe Skeet Gun—20 Gauge (Series II)................................ $195
Same as Supermatic Deluxe Rib 20 (II), except available only with 26-inch ventilated-rib barrel, skeet choke. Made from 1966 to 1975.

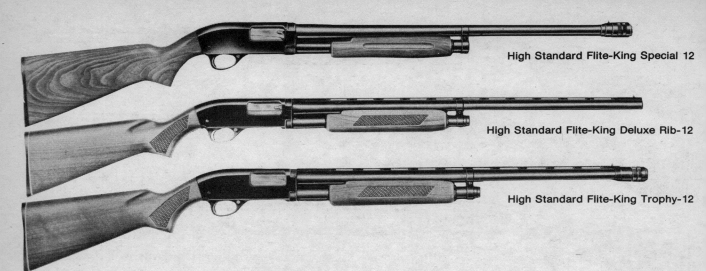

High Standard Flite-King Special 12

High Standard Flite-King Deluxe Rib-12

High Standard Flite-King Trophy-12

High Standard Flite-King Field Pump Shotgun—12 Gauge **$130**
Hammerless. Magazine holds 5 shells. Barrels: 26-inch improved cylinder, 28-inch modified or full, 30-inch full choke. Weight, 7¼ pounds. Plain pistol-grip stock and slide handle. Made from 1960 to 1966.

High Standard Flite-King Special—12 Gauge **$140**
Same as Flite-King Field 12, except has 27-inch barrel with adjustable choke. Made from 1960 to 1966.

**High Standard Flite-King Deluxe Rib—
12 Gauge** **$155**
Same as Flite-King Field 12, except ventilated-rib barrel (28-inch modified or full 30-inch full), checkered stock and forearm. Made from 1961 to 1966.

High Standard Flite-King Trophy—12 Gauge **$160**
Same as Flite-King Deluxe Rib 12, except has 27-inch ventilated-rib barrel with adjustable choke. Made from 1960 to 1966.

High Standard Flite King Brush—12 Gauge **$150**
Same as Flite-King Field 12, except has 18- or 20-inch barrel (cylinder bore) with rifle sights. Made from 1962 to 1964.

High Standard Flite-King Brush Deluxe **$165**
Same as Flite-King Brush, except has adjustable peep rear sight, checkered pistol grip, recoil pad, fluted slide handle, swivels and sling. Not available with 18-inch barrel. Made from 1964 to 1966.

High Standard Flite-King Skeet—12 Gauge **$170**
Same as Flite-King Deluxe Rib, except 26-inch ventilated-rib barrel, bored skeet choke. Made from 1962 to 1966.

High Standard Flite-King Trap-12 Gauge **$180**
Same as Flite-King Deluxe Rib 12, except 30-inch ventilated-rib barrel, full choke; special trap stock with recoil pad. Made from 1962 to 1966.

High Standard Flite-King Pump Shotguns—16 Gauge
Same general specifications as Flite-King 12, except not available in Brush, Skeet and Trap Models, or 30-inch barrel. Values same as for 12 gauge guns. Made from 1961 to 1965.

High Standard Flite-King Field Pump Shotgun—20 Gauge **$130**
Hammerless. Chambered for 3-inch magnum shells, also handles 2¾-inch. Magazine holds four shells. Barrels: 26-inch improved cylinder, 28-inch modified or full choke. Weight, about 6 pounds. Plain pistol-grip stock and slide handle. Made from 1961 to 1966.

High Standard Flite-King Special—20 Gauge **$140**
Same as Flite-King Field 20, except has 27-inch barrel with adjustable choke. Made from 1961 to 1966.

**High Standard Flite King Deluxe Rib—
20 Gauge** **$155**
Same as Flite-King Field 20, except ventilated-rib barrel (28-inch modified or full), checkered stock and slide handle. Made from 1962 to 1966.

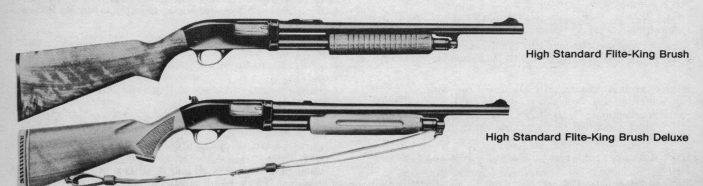

High Standard Flite-King Brush

High Standard Flite-King Brush Deluxe

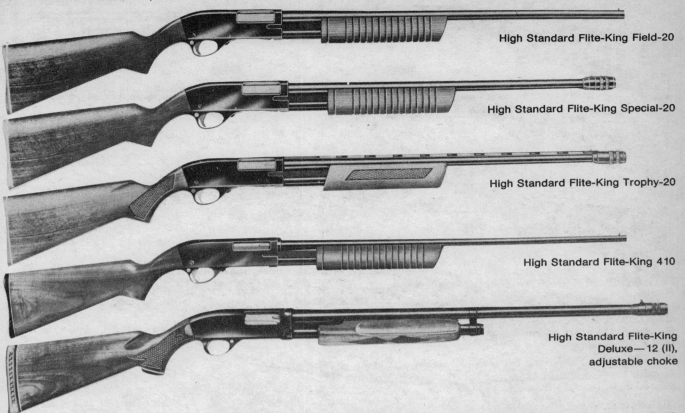

High Standard Flite-King Field-20

High Standard Flite-King Special-20

High Standard Flite-King Trophy-20

High Standard Flite-King 410

High Standard Flite-King
Deluxe—12 (II),
adjustable choke

High Standard Flite-King Trophy—20 Gauge.... $160
Same as Flite-King Deluxe Rib 20, except has 27-inch ventilated-rib barrel with adjustable choke. Made from 1962 to 1966.

High Standard Flite-King Pump Shotguns—410 Gauge
Same general specifications as Flite-King 20, except not available in Special and Trophy Models, or with other than 26-inch full choke barrel. Values same as for 20-gauge guns. Made from 1962 to 1966.

Note: In 1966, High Standard introduced a new series of Flite-King pumps, readily indentifiable by the damascened bolt and restyled checkering. To avoid confusion, these models are designated "Series II" in this text. This is *not* an official factory designation.

High Standard Flite-King Deluxe—12 Gauge (Series II)
Hammerless. 5-shot magazine. Barrels: plain; 27-inch with adjustable choke. 26-inch improved cylinder, 28-inch modified or full, 30-inch full choke. Weight, about 7¼ pounds. Checkered pistol-grip stock and forearm, recoil pad. Made from 1966 to 1975.
With adjustable choke.................................. $140
Without adjustable choke............................. 125

High Standard Flite-King Deluxe Rib—12 Gauge (Series II)
Same as Flite-King Deluxe 12 (II), except has ventilated-rib barrel; available in 27-inch with adjustable choke, 28-inch modified or full, 30-inch full choke. Made from 1966 to 1975.
With adjustable choke.................................. $175
Without adjustable choke............................. 160

High Standard Flite-King Brush (Series II)......$150
Same as Flite-King Deluxe 12 (II), except has 20-inch barrel, cylinder bore, with rifle sights; weight, 7 pounds. Made from 1966 to 1975.

High Standard Flite-King Brush Deluxe (Series II)..$165
Same as Flite-King Brush (II), except has adjustable peep rear sight, swivels and sling. Made from 1966 to 1975.

High Standard Flite-King Deluxe Skeet Gun—12 Gauge (Series II)................................. $165
Same as Flite-King Deluxe Rib 12 (II), except available only with 26-inch ventilated-rib barrel, skeet choke; recoil pad optional. Made from 1966 to 1975.

High Standard Flite-King Deluxe Trap Gun (Series II)..$175
Same as Flite-King Deluxe Rib 12 (II), except available only with 30-inch ventilated-rib barrel, full choke; trap-style stock. Made from 1966 to 1975.

High Standard Flite-King Deluxe—20, 28, 410 Gauge (Series II)..$125
Same as Flite-King Deluxe 12 (II), except chambered for 20 and 410 gauge 3-inch shell, 28 gauge 2¾-inch shell; plain barrel in improved cylinder (20), modified (20, 28), full choke (20, 28, 410); weight, about 6 pounds. Made from 1966 to 1975.

High Standard Flite-King Deluxe Rib—20, 28, 410 Gauge (Series II)
Same as Flite-King Deluxe 20, 28, 410 (II), except 20 gauge available with 27-inch adjustable choke, 28-inch modified or full choke; weight, about 6¼ pounds. Made from 1966 to 1975.
With adjustable choke.................................. $175
Without adjustable choke............................. 160

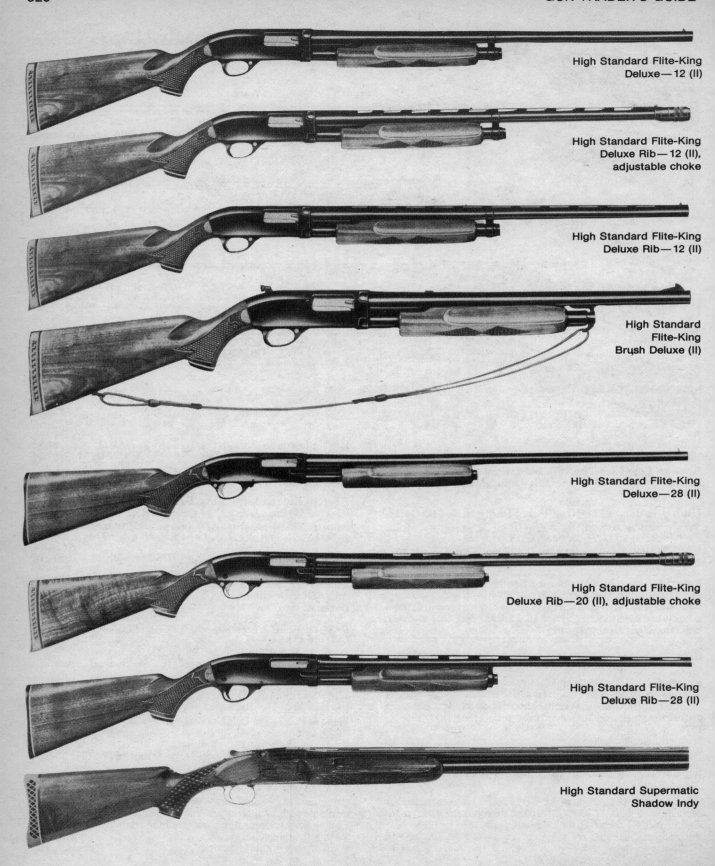

High Standard Flite-King
Deluxe—12 (II)

High Standard Flite-King
Deluxe Rib—12 (II),
adjustable choke

High Standard Flite-King
Deluxe Rib—12 (II)

High Standard
Flite-King
Brush Deluxe (II)

High Standard Flite-King
Deluxe—28 (II)

High Standard Flite-King
Deluxe Rib—20 (II), adjustable choke

High Standard Flite-King
Deluxe Rib—28 (II)

High Standard Supermatic
Shadow Indy

High Standard Supermatic
Shadow Seven

High Standard Supermatic
Shadow Automatic

High Standard Flite-King Deluxe Skeet Gun—20, 28, 410 Gauge (Series II)............................ **$175**

Same as Flite-King Deluxe Rib 20, 28, 410 (II), except available only with 26-inch ventilated-rib barrel, skeet choke. Made from 1966 to 1975.

High Standard Supermatic Shadow Indy Over-and-Under Shotgun....................................... **$615**

Box lock. Fully engraved receiver. Selective automatic ejectors. Selective single trigger. 12 gauge. 2¾-inch chambers. Barrels: full-size airflow rib; 27½-inch both skeet choke, 29¾-inch improved modified and full or both full choke. Weight, with 29¾-inch barrels, 8 lbs. 2 oz. Pistol-grip stock with recoil pad, ventilated forearm, skip checkering. Made from 1974 to 1975 by Caspoll International, Inc., Tokyo, Japan.

High Standard Supermatic Shadow Seven....... **$525**

Same general specifications as Shadow Indy, except has conventional ventilated rib, less elaborate engraving, standard checkering; forearm is not vented, no recoil pad. 27½-inch barrels also available in improved cylinder and modified, modified and full choke. Made from 1974 to 1975.

High Standard Supermatic Shadow Automatic Shotgun... **$260**

Gas-operated. Gauges: 12, 20. 2¾- or 3-inch chamber in 12 gauge, 3-inch in 20 gauge. Magazine holds four 2¾-inch shells, three 3-inch. Barrels: full-size airflow rib; 26-inch (improved cylinder or skeet choke), 28-inch (modified, improved modified or full); 30-inch (trap or full choke); 12-gauge 3-inch magnum available only in 30-inch full choke; 20 gauge not available in 30-inch. Weight in 12 gauge, 7 pounds. Checkered walnut stock and forearm. Made from 1974 to 1975 by Caspoll International, Inc., Tokyo, Japan.

Holland & Holland, Ltd., London, England

Holland & Holland Royal Model Under-and-Over Gun

Side locks, hand-detachable. Automatic ejectors. Double triggers or single trigger. 12 gauge. Built to customer's specifications as to barrel length, chokes, etc. Made as a Game Gun or Pigeon and Wildfowl Gun. Checkered stock and fore-end, straight grip standard. *Note:* In 1951 Holland & Holland introduced their New Model Under-and-Over Gun with an improved, narrower action body. Discontinued 1960.

New Model with double triggers..................**$14,000**
New Model with single trigger.................... 15,000
Old Model with double triggers................... 11,000
Old Model with single trigger.................... 12,000

Holland & Holland Royal Model Hammerless Double Barrel Shotgun

Self-opening. Side locks, hand detachable. Automatic ejectors. Double triggers or single trigger. Gauges: 12, 16, 20, 28, 410. Built to customer's specifications as to barrel length, chokes, etc. Made as a Game Gun or Pigeon and Wildfowl Gun, the latter having treble-grip action and side clips. Checkered stock and fore-end, straight grip standard. Made from 1885 to date.

With double triggers............................**$10,000**
With single trigger............................... 10,700

Holland & Holland Model Deluxe Hammerless Double Barrel Shotgun

Same as Royal Model, except has special engraving and exhibition grade stock and forearm. Currently manufactured.

With double triggers............................**$11,000**
With single trigger............................... 11,700

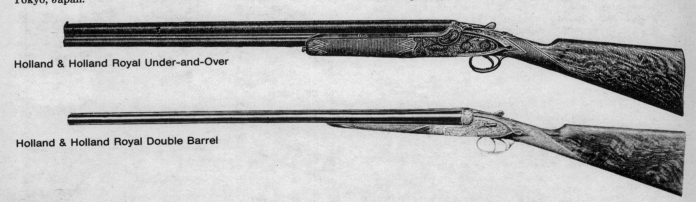

Holland & Holland Royal Under-and-Over

Holland & Holland Royal Double Barrel

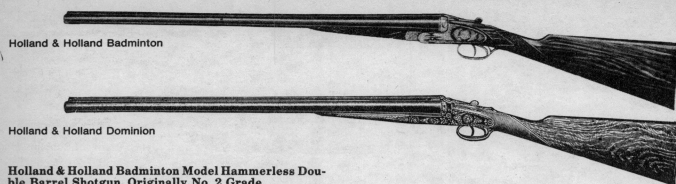

Holland & Holland Badminton

Holland & Holland Dominion

Holland & Holland Badminton Model Hammerless Double Barrel Shotgun. Originally No. 2 Grade

General specifications same as Royal Model except without self-opening action. Made as a Game Gun or Pigeon and Wildfowl Gun. Made from 1902 to date.

With double triggers	$7000
With single trigger	7700

Holland & Holland Riviera Model Pigeon Gun . . $8500

Same as Badminton Model but supplied with two sets of barrels, double triggers. Discontinued 1967.

Holland & Holland Dominion Model Hammerless Double Barrel Shotgun $3500

Game Gun. Side lock. Automatic ejectors; Double triggers. Gauges: 12, 16, 20. Barrels: 25- to 30-inch, any standard boring. Checkered stock and fore-end, straight grip standard. Discontinued 1967.

Holland & Holland Centenary Model Hammerless Double Barrel Shotgun

Lightweight (5½-pound). 12 gauge game gun designed for 2-inch shell. Made in four grades—Modele Deluxe, Royal, Badminton, Dominion—values same as shown for standard guns in those grades. Discontinued 1962.

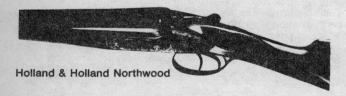

Holland & Holland Northwood

Holland & Holland Northwood Model Hammerless Double Barrel Shotgun $1900

Anson & Deeley system box lock. Automatic ejectors. Double triggers. Gauges: 12, 16, 20, 28 in Game Model; 28 gauge not offered in Pigeon Model; Wildfowl Model in 12 gauge only (3-inch chambers available). Barrels: 28-inch standard in Game and Pigeon Models, 30-inch in Wildfowl Model; other lengths, any standard choke combination available. Weights: from 5 pounds to 7¾ pounds, depending upon gauge and barrels. Checkered straight-grip or pistol-grip stock and forearm, checkered. Discontinued.

Holland & Holland Single Barrel Super Trap Gun

Anson & Deeley system box lock. Automatic ejector. No safety. 12 gauge. Barrels: wide ventilated rib, 30- or 32-inch, bored extra full choke. Weight, about 8¾ pounds. Monte Carlo stock with pistol grip and recoil pad, full beavertail forearm. The three models differ in grade of engraving and wood. Discontinued.

Standard Grade	$ 8000
Deluxe Grade	9000
Exhibition Grade	10,000

Holland & Holland Super Trap, Standard Grade

Holland & Holland Super Trap, Deluxe Grade

Hunter Arms Company, Fulton, New York

Hunter Fulton Hammerless Double Barrel Shotgun

Box lock. Plain extractors. Double triggers or non-selective single trigger. Gauges: 12, 16, 20. Barrels: 26- to 32-inch, various choke combinations. Weight, about 7 pounds. Checkered pistol-grip stock and forearm. Discontinued 1948.

With double triggers	$300
With single trigger	350

Hunter Special Hammerless Double Barrel Shotgun

Box lock. Plain extractors. Double triggers or non-selective single trigger. Gauges: 12, 16, 20: Barrels: 26- to 30-inch, various choke combinations. Weight, 6½ to 7¼ pounds depending upon barrel length and gauge. Checkered full pistol-grip stock and forearm. Discontinued 1948.

With double triggers	$375
With single trigger	400

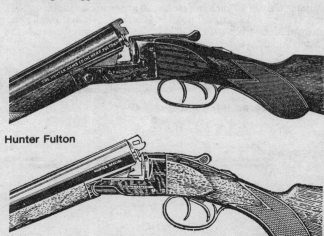

Hunter Fulton

Hunter Special

Ithaca Single Barrel Super Trap

Ithaca Gun Company, Ithaca, New York

Ithaca Hammerless Double Barrel Shotguns

Box lock. Plain extractors, automatic ejectors standard on the
"E" grades. Double triggers, non-selective or selective single
trigger extra. Gauges: Magnum 10, Magnum 12, 12, 16, 20, 28,
410. Barrels: 26- to 32-inch, any standard boring. Weight, 5¾
(410) to 10½ pounds (Magnum 10). Checkered pistol-grip stock
and forearm standard. The higher grades differ from the Field
Grade chiefly in quality of workmanship, grade of wood, checkering, engraving, etc.; general specifications are the same. Ithaca
doubles made before 1925 had underbolts and a bolt through the
rib extension. In 1925 (serial number 425,000) the rotary bolt
and a stronger frame were adopted. Values shown are for this
latter type; earlier models bring prices about 50 percent under
those of the more recent types. Smaller gauge guns often bring
prices up to 75 percent higher. Ithaca double guns were discontinued in 1948.

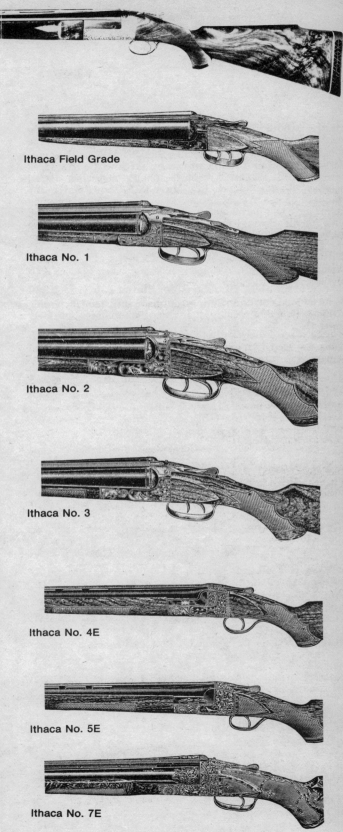

Ithaca Field Grade

Ithaca No. 1

Ithaca No. 2

Ithaca No. 3

Field Grade	$500
No. 1 Grade	600
No. 2 Grade	$ 900
No. 3 Grade	1000
No. 4-E Grade (ejector)	1900
No. 5-E Grade (ejector)	3250
No. 7-E Grade (ejector)	7250
$2000 (prewar $1000) Grade (ejector and selective single trigger standard)	11,000

Extras:

Magnum 10 or 12 gauge (in other than the four highest grades), add	200
Automatic ejectors (Grades No. 1, 2, 3, with ejectors are designated No. 1E, 2E, 3E) add	200
Selective single trigger, add	150
Non-selective single trigger, add	100
Beavertail fore-end (Field No. 1 or 2), add	150
Beavertail fore-end (No. 3 or 4), add	175
Beavertail fore-end (No. 5, 7 or $2000 Grade), add	250
Ventilated rib (No. 4, 5, 7 or $2000 Grade), add	250
Ventilated rib (lower grades), add	175

Ithaca Single Barrel Trap Victory Grade

Ithaca Single Barrel Trap Guns, Flues and Knick Models

Box lock. Hammerless. Ejector. 12 gauge only. Barrel lengths:
30-, 32-, 34-inch (32-inch only in Victory Grade). Ventilated rib.
Weight, about 8 pounds. Checkered pistol-grip stock and fore-
end. The five grades differ only in quality of workmanship, grade
of engraving, checkering, wood, etc. Flues Model, serial number
under 400,000, made from 1908 to 1921. Triple-bolted Knick
Model, serial number above 400,000 made since 1921. Victory
Model discontinued in 1938, No. 7-E in 1964, No. 4-E in 1976.
No. 5-E and $5000 Grade currently manufactured. Values shown
are for Knick Model; Flues Model guns bring prices about 50
percent lower.

Ithaca No. 4E

Ithaca No. 5E

Ithaca No. 7E

Victory Grade	$1200
No. 4-E	2700
No. 5-E	3500
No. 7-E	5200
$5000 Grade (prewar $1000 Grade)	7000

Ithaca No. 5E Single Barrel Trap

Ithaca Model 37 Featherlight Standard Grade Slide Action Repeating Shotgun

Adaptation of the earlier Remington Model 17, a Browning design patented in 1915. Hammerless. Takedown. Gauges: 12, 16 (discontinued 1973), 20. 4-shell tubular magazine. Barrel lengths: 26-, 28-, 30-inch (the latter in 12 gauge only); any standard choke. Weight, from 5¾ to 7½ pounds depending upon gauge and barrel length. Checkered pistol-grip stock and slide handle. Some guns made in the 1950's and 1960's have grooved slide handle; pistol grip on these may be plain or checkered. Made from 1937 to date.
With checkered pistol grip..........................**$190**
With plain stock...................................**175**

Ithaca Model 37V Standard Ventilated Rib...... $220

Same as Model 37 Standard, except has ventilated rib, adding about ¼-pound of weight. Made from 1962 to date.

Ithaca Model 37D Deluxe....................... $225

Same as Model 37 Standard except checkered stock and beavertail forearm, recoil pad. Made from 1954 to 1977.

Ithaca Model 37DV Deluxe Ventilated Rib...... $235

Same as Model 37D Deluxe, except has ventilated rib. Made from 1962 to date.

Ithaca Model 37R Solid Rib Grade

Same general specifications as the Model 37 Featherlight, except has a raised solid rib, adding about ¼-pound of weight. Made from 1937 to 1967.
With checkered grip and slide handle.................**$215**
With plain stock...................................**180**

Ithaca Model 37R Deluxe Solid Rib............. $255

Same general specifications as Model 37R, except has fancy walnut stock and slide handle, checkered. Made from 1955 to 1961.

Ithaca Model 37S Skeet Grade................... $330

Same general specifications as the Model 37 Featherlight, except has ventilated rib and large extension-type fore-end, weighs about ½-pound more than the Featherlight. Made from 1937 to 1955.

Ithaca Model 37T Trap Grade................... $350

Same general specifications as Model 37S, except has straighter trap-style stock of selected walnut, recoil pad, weighs about ½-pound more than Model 37S. Made from 1937 to 1955.

Ithaca Model 37T Target Grade................. $370

Same general specifications as Model 37 Featherlight, except has ventilated-rib barrel, checkered stock and slide handle of fancy walnut (choice of skeet- or trap-style stock). *Note:* This model replaced Model 37S Skeet and Model 37T Trap. Made from 1955 to 1961.

Ithaca Model 37 Supreme Grade................. $350

Available in Skeet or Trap Gun, similar to Model 37T. Made from 1967 to date.

Ithaca Model 37 Standard Deerslayer........... $210

Same as Model 37 Standard, except has 20- or 26-inch barrel bored for rifled slugs, rifle-type open rear sight and ramp front sight, weighs 5¾ to 6½ pounds, depending upon gauge and barrel length. Made from 1959 to date.

Ithaca Model 37 Super Deluxe Deerslayer...... $250

Formerly "Deluxe Deerslayer." Same as Model 37 Standard Deerslayer, except has stock and slide handle of fancy walnut. Made from 1962 to date.

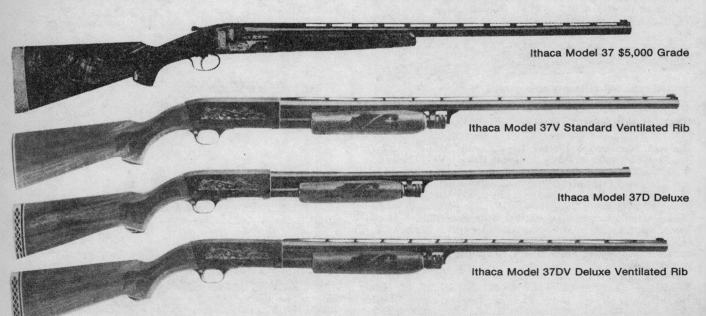

Ithaca Model 37 $5,000 Grade

Ithaca Model 37V Standard Ventilated Rib

Ithaca Model 37D Deluxe

Ithaca Model 37DV Deluxe Ventilated Rib

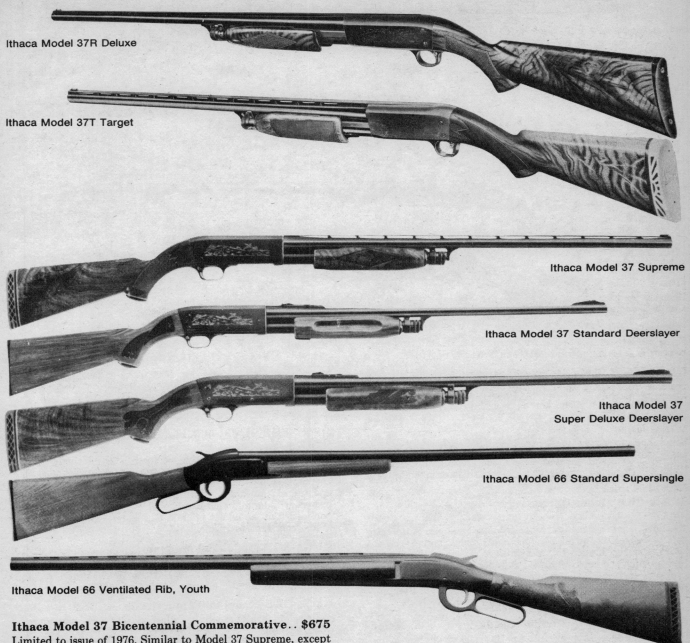

Ithaca Model 37R Deluxe

Ithaca Model 37T Target

Ithaca Model 37 Supreme

Ithaca Model 37 Standard Deerslayer

Ithaca Model 37
Super Deluxe Deerslayer

Ithaca Model 66 Standard Supersingle

Ithaca Model 66 Ventilated Rib, Youth

Ithaca Model 37 Bicentennial Commemorative.. $675

Limited to issue of 1976. Similar to Model 37 Supreme, except has special Bicentennial design etched on receiver, full-fancy walnut stock and slide handle. Serial numbers U.S.A. 0001 to U.S.A. 1976. Comes in presentation case with cast pewter belt buckle. Made in 1976. Value is for gun in new, unfired condition.

Ithaca Model 37 $5000 Grade................... $5400

Custom built, elaborately engraved and inlaid with gold, hand-finished working parts, stock and fore-end of selected figured walnut. General specifications same as standard Model 37. *Note:* the same gun was designated the $1000 Grade prior to World War II. Made from 1937 to 1967.

Ithaca Model 66 Standard Supersingle Lever Action
Shotgun.. $ 75

Single shot. Hand-cocked hammer. Gauges: 12 (discontinued 1974), 20, 410; 3-inch chambers. Barrels: 12 ga.—30-inch/full choke, 28-inch/full or modified; 20 ga.—28-inch/full or modified; 410—26-inch/full. Weight, about 7 pounds. Plain or checkered straight-grip stock, plain fore-end. Made from 1963 to 1978.

Ithaca Model 66 Youth........................... $ 75

Same as Model 66 Standard, except 26-inch barrel, shorter stock and recoil pad; 20 and 410 gauges only. Made from 1965 to 1978.

Ithaca Model 66 Ventilated Rib................. $ 95

Same as Model 66 Standard and Youth Model, except has ventilated-rib barrel, made in 20 gauge only, checkered stock and recoil pad standard. Made from 1969 to 1974.

Ithaca Model 66 Long Tom

Ithaca Model 66RS Buckbuster

Ithaca-SKB Model 100

Ithaca-SKB Model 200E Field

Ithaca Model 66 Long Tom.......................$ 80
Same as Model 66 Standard, except has 36-inch full choke
barrel, 12 gauge only, checkered stock and recoil pad standard.
Made from 1969 to 1974.

Ithaca Model 66RS Buckbuster.................$ 80
Same as Model 66 Standard, except has 22-inch barrel, cylinder
bore with rifle sights; later version has recoil pad. Originally
offered in 12 and 20 gauges; the former was discontinued in 1970.
Made from 1967 to 1978.

**Ithaca-SKB Model 100 Side-by-Side
Double Gun**.......................................$300
Box lock. Plain extractors. Selective single trigger. Automatic
safety. Gauges: 12 and 20; 2¾-inch and 3-inch chambers respectively. Barrels: 30-inch/full and full (12 ga. only), 28-inch/full
and modified, 26-inch/improved cylinder and modified (12 ga.
only), 25-inch/improved cylinder and modified choke (20 ga.
only). Weights: 12 ga., about 7 pounds; 20 ga. about 6 pounds.
Checkered stock and fore-end. Made from 1966 to 1976.

Ithaca-SKB Model 150 Field Grade.............$555
Same as Model 100, except has fancier scroll engraving,
beavertail forearm. Made from 1972 to 1974.

**Ithaca-SKB Model 200E Field Grade
Side-by-Side**......................................$505
Same as Model 100, except automatic selective ejectors, engraved and silver-plated frame, gold-plated nameplate and trigger, beavertail forearm. Made from 1966 to 1976.

Ithaca-SKB Model 200E Skeet Gun.............$600
Same as Model 200E Field Grade, except 26-inch (12 ga.) and 25-
inch (20 ga./2¾-inch chambers) barrels bored skeet choke; has
nonautomatic safety and recoil pad. Made from 1966 to 1976.

Ithaca-SKB Model 280 English.................$535
Same as Model 200E, except has scrolled game scene engraving
on frame, English-style straight-grip stock; 30-inch barrels not

available; special quail gun in 20 gauge has 25-inch barrels, both
bored improved cylinder. Made from 1971 to 1976.

**Ithaca-SKB Model 500 Field Grade Over-and-Under
Gun**...$540
Box lock. Automatic selective ejectors. Selective single trigger.
Nonautomatic safety. Gauges: 12 and 20; 2¾-inch and 3-inch
chambers respectively. Ventilated-rib barrels: 30-inch/modified
and full (12 ga. only), 28-inch/modified and full, 26-inch/im-
proved cylinder and modified choke. Weights: 12 ga., about 7½
pounds; 20 ga., about 6½ pounds. Checkered stock and forearm.
Made from 1966 to 1976.

Ithaca-SKB Model 500 Magnum.................$550
Same as Model 500 Field Grade, except chambered for 3-inch 12
gauge shells, has 30-inch barrels, improved modified and full
choke, weighs about 8 pounds. Made from 1973 to 1976.

Ithaca-SKB Model 600 Field Grade.............$650
Same as Model 500, except has silver-plated frame, higher grade
wood. Made from 1969 to 1976.

Ithaca-SKB Model 600 Magnum.................$675
Same as Model 600 Field Grade, except chambered for 3-inch 12
gauge shells, has 30-inch barrels, improved modified and full
choke, weighs 8½ pounds. Made from 1969 to 1972.

**Ithaca-SKB Model 600 Trap Grade Over-and-Under
Gun**...$700
Same as Model 500, except 12 gauge only, has silver-plated
frame, 30- or 32-inch barrels bored full and full or full and
improved modified choke, choice of Monte Carlo or straight
stock of higher grade wood, recoil pad, weight about 8 pounds.
Made from 1966 to 1976.

Ithaca-SKB Model 600 Doubles Gun............$700
Same as Model 600 Trap Grade, except specially choked for 21-
yard first target, 30-yard second target. Made from 1973 to 1975.

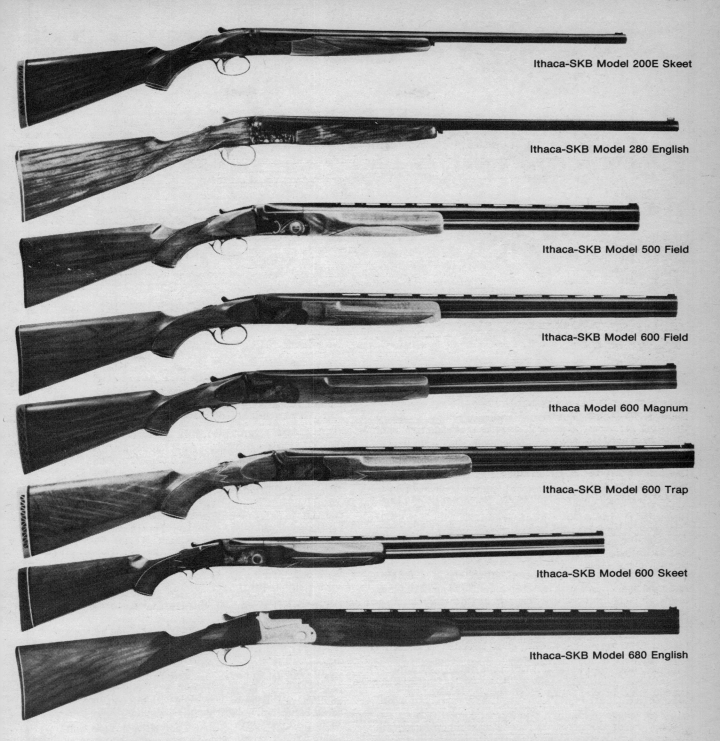

Ithaca-SKB Model 200E Skeet

Ithaca-SKB Model 280 English

Ithaca-SKB Model 500 Field

Ithaca-SKB Model 600 Field

Ithaca Model 600 Magnum

Ithaca-SKB Model 600 Trap

Ithaca-SKB Model 600 Skeet

Ithaca-SKB Model 680 English

Ithaca-SKB Model 600 Skeet Grade

Same as Model 500, except also available in 28 and 410 gauge, has silver-plated frame, higher grade wood, recoil pad, 26- or 28-inch barrels (28-inch only in 28 and 410) bored skeet choke; weight, 7 to 7¾ pounds depending upon gauge and barrel length. Made from 1966 to 1976.

12 or 20 gauge.. **$675**
28 or 410 gauge..................................... **700**

Ithaca-SKB Model 600 Skeet Combo Set....... $2100
Model 600 Skeet Grade with matched set of 20, 28 and 410 gauge barrels, 28-inch, in fitted case. Made from 1970 to 1976.

Ithaca-SKB Model 680 English.................. $625
Same as Model 600 Field Grade, except has intricate scroll engraving, English-style straight-grip stock and forearm of extra-fine walnut; 30-inch barrels not available. Made from 1973 to 1976.

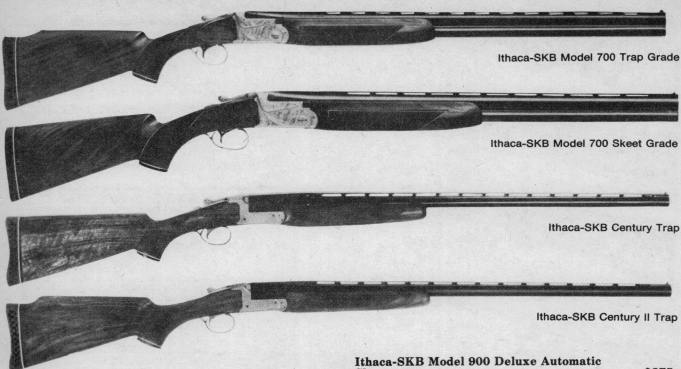

Ithaca-SKB Model 700 Trap Grade

Ithaca-SKB Model 700 Skeet Grade

Ithaca-SKB Century Trap

Ithaca-SKB Century II Trap

Ithaca-SKB Model 700 Trap Grade.............. **$700**
Same as Model 600 Trap Grade, except has more elaborate scroll engraving, extra-wide rib, higher grade wood. Made from 1969 to 1975.

Ithaca-SKB Model 700 Doubles Gun............. **$750**
Same as Model 700 Trap Grade, except specially choked for 21-yard first target, 30-yard second target. Made from 1973 to 1975.

Ithaca-SKB Model 700 Skeet Grade............. **$750**
Same as Model 600 Skeet Grade, except not available in 28 and 410 gauge, has more elaborate scroll engraving, extra-wide rib, higher grade wood. Made from 1969 to 1975.

Ithaca-SKB Model 700 Skeet Combo Set....... **$2100**
Model 700 Skeet Grade with matched set of 20, 28 and 410 gauge barrels, 28-inch, in fitted case. Made from 1970 to 1971.

Ithaca-SKB Century Single Barrel Trap Gun.... **$540**
Box lock. Automatic ejector. 12 gauge. Barrels: 32- or 34-inch, ventilated rib, full choke. Weight, about 8 pounds. Checkered walnut stock with pistol grip, straight or Monte Carlo comb, recoil pad, beavertail forearm. Made from 1973 to 1974. *Note:* Current SKB "Century" is same as Ithaca-SKB Century II.

Ithaca-SKB Century II......................... **$500**
Improved version of Century. Same general specifications, except has higher stock, reverse-taper beavertail forearm with redesigned locking iron. Made from 1975 to 1976.

Ithaca-SKB Model 300 Standard Automatic Shotgun
Recoil-operated. Gauges: 12, 20 (3-inch). 5-shot. Barrels: plain or ventilated rib; 30-inch full choke (12 gauge only), 28-inch full or modified, 26-inch improved cylinder. Weight, about 7 pounds. Checkered pistol-grip stock and forearm. Made from 1968 to 1972.
With plain barrel................................... **$230**
With ventilated rib................................. 250

Ithaca-SKB Model 900 Deluxe Automatic Shotgun.. **$275**
Same as Model 300, except has game scene etched and gold-filled on receiver, ventilated rib standard. Made from 1968 to 1972.

Ithaca-SKB Model 900 Slug Gun................. **$255**
Same as Model 900 Deluxe, except has 24-inch plain barrel with slug boring, rifle sights; weight, about 6½ pounds. Made from 1970 to 1972.

Ithaca-SKB Model XL300 Standard Automatic Shotgun
Gas-operated. Gauges: 12, 20 (3-inch). 5-shot. Barrels: plain or ventilated rib; 30-inch full choke (12 gauge only), 28-inch full or modified, 26-inch improved cylinder. Weight, 6 to 7½ pounds depending upon gauge and barrel. Checkered pistol-grip stock and forearm. Made from 1972 to 1976.
With plain barrel................................... **$235**
With ventilated rib................................. 255

Ithaca-SKB Model XL900 Deluxe Automatic Shotgun.. **$275**
Same as Model XL300, except has game scene finished in silver on receiver, ventilated rib standard. Made from 1972 to 1976.

Ithaca-SKB Model XL900 Trap Grade........... **$300**
Same as Model XL900 Deluxe, except 12 gauge only, has scrolled receiver finished in black chrome, 30-inch barrel only, improved modified or full choke, trap style with straight or Monte Carlo comb, recoil pad; weight, about 7¾ pounds. Made from 1972 to 1976.

Ithaca-SKB Model XL900 Skeet Grade.......... **$285**
Same as Model XL900 Deluxe, except has scrolled receiver finished in black chrome, 26-inch barrel only, skeet choke, skeet-style stock; weight, 7 or 7½ pounds depending upon gauge. Made from 1972 to 1976.

Ithaca-SKB Model XL900 Slug Gun............. **$265**
Same as Model XL900 Deluxe, except has 24-inch plain barrel with slug boring, rifle sights; weight, 6½ or 7 pounds, depending upon gauge. Made from 1972 to 1976.

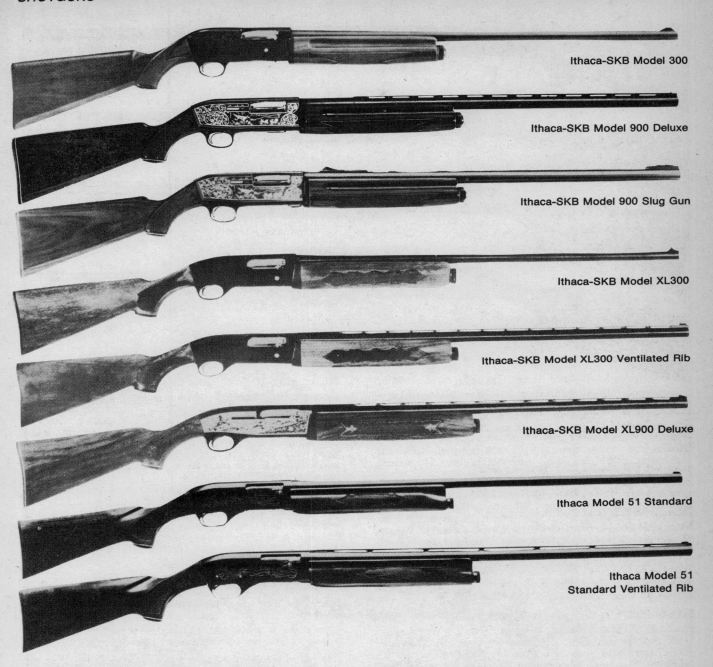

Ithaca-SKB Model 300

Ithaca-SKB Model 900 Deluxe

Ithaca-SKB Model 900 Slug Gun

Ithaca-SKB Model XL300

Ithaca-SKB Model XL300 Ventilated Rib

Ithaca-SKB Model XL900 Deluxe

Ithaca Model 51 Standard

Ithaca Model 51 Standard Ventilated Rib

Note: Ithaca-SKB shotguns, manufactured by SKB Arms Company, Tokyo, Japan, were distributed in the United States by Ithaca Gun Company from 1966 to 1976. See also listing under SKB.

Ithaca Model 51 Standard Automatic Shotgun

Gas-operated. Gauges: 12, 20. 3-shot. Barrels: plain or ventilated rib; 30-inch full choke (12 gauge only), 28-inch full or modified, 26-inch improved cylinder. Weight, 7¼ to 7¾ pounds depending upon gauge and barrel. Checkered pistol-grip stock and forearm. Made from 1970 to 1979.
With plain barrel $250
With ventilated rib 270

Ithaca Model 51 Standard Magnum

Same as Model 51 Standard, except has 3-inch chamber, handles magnum shells only; 30-inch barrel in 12 gauge, 28-inch in 20 gauge, full or modified choke, stock with recoil pad; weight, 7¾ or 8 pounds depending upon gauge. Made from 1972 to date.
With plain barrel (discontinued 1976) $250
With ventilated rib 290

Ithaca Model 51 Deluxe Trap Grade

Same as Model 51 Standard, except 12 gauge only, 30-inch barrel with broad floating rib, full choke, trap-style stock with straight or Monte Carlo comb, semi-fancy wood, recoil pad; weight, about 8 pounds. Made from 1970 to date.
With straight stock $255
With Monte Carlo stock 265

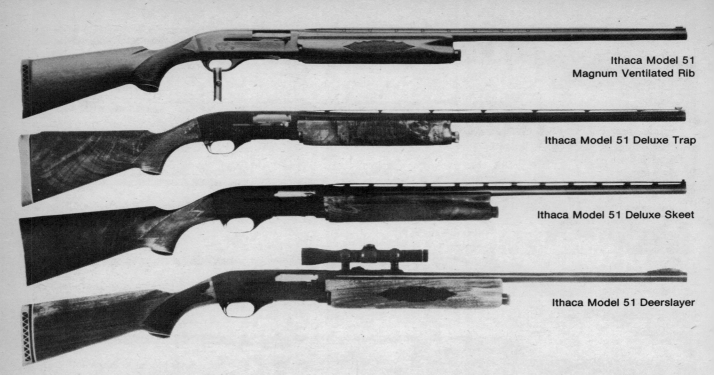

Ithaca Model 51
Magnum Ventilated Rib

Ithaca Model 51 Deluxe Trap

Ithaca Model 51 Deluxe Skeet

Ithaca Model 51 Deerslayer

Ithaca Model 51 Deluxe Skeet Grade **$255**
Same as Model 51 Standard, except 26-inch ventilated-rib barrel
only, skeet choke, skeet-style stock, semi-fancy wood; weight,
about 8 pounds. Made from 1970 to date.

Ithaca Model 51 Deerslayer **$260**
Same as Model 51 Standard, except has 24-inch plain barrel with
slug boring, rifle sights, recoil pad; weight, about 7¼ pounds.
Made from 1972 to date.

Ithaca LSA-55 Turkey Gun **$475**
Over-and-under shotgun/rifle combination. Box lock. Exposed
hammer. Plain extractor. Single trigger. 12 gauge/222 Rem.
24½-inch ribbed barrels (rifle barrel has muzzle brake). Weight,
about 7 pounds. Folding leaf rear sight, bead front sight. Checkered Monte Carlo stock and forearm. Made from 1970 to date by
Oy Tikkakoski AB, Tikkakoski, Finland.

Ithaca Mag-10 Automatic Shotgun
Gas-operated. 10 gauge 3½-inch magnum. 3-shot. 32-inch plain
(Standard Grade only) or ventilated-rib barrel, full choke.
Weight: 11 pounds with plain barrel, 11½ pounds with ven-
tilated rib. Standard Grade has plain stock and forearm. Deluxe
and Supreme Grades have checkering, semi-fancy and fancy
wood respectively, and stud swivel. All have recoil pad. Deluxe
and Supreme Grades made from 1974 to date. Standard Grade
introduced in 1977.
Standard Grade, plain barrel **$450**
Standard Grade, ventilated rib **425**
Deluxe Grade **520**
Supreme Grade **615**

Ithaca LSA-55 Turkey Gun

Ithaca Mag-10 Standard

Ithaca Mag-10 Standard Ventilated Rib

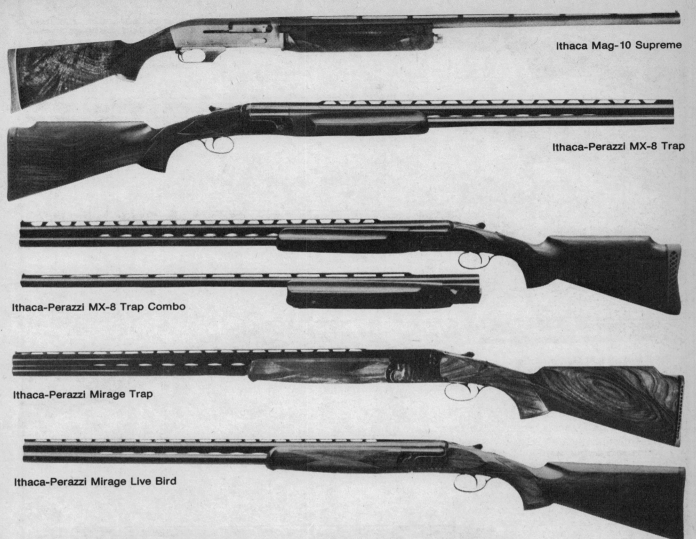

Ithaca Mag-10 Supreme

Ithaca-Perazzi MX-8 Trap

Ithaca-Perazzi MX-8 Trap Combo

Ithaca-Perazzi Mirage Trap

Ithaca-Perazzi Mirage Live Bird

Ithaca-Perazzi MX-8 Trap Over-and-Under Shotgun... **$2160**

Box lock. Automatic selective ejectors. Non-selective single trigger. 12 gauge. Barrels: vented, with high ventilated rib; 30- or 32-inch, improved modified and full choke. Weight, 8¼ or 8½ pounds. Checkered Monte Carlo stock and forearm, recoil pad. Made from 1969 to 1978.

Ithaca-Perazzi MX-8 Trap Combo.............. **$3310**

MX-8 with extra single barrel, ventilated rib, 32- or 34-inch, full choke, forearm; two trigger groups included. Made from 1973 to 1978.

Ithaca-Perazzi Mirage Trap.................... **$2160**

Same general specifications as MX-8 Trap, except has tapered rib. Made from 1973 to 1978.

Ithaca-Perazzi Mirage Live Bird.............. **$2160**

Same as Mirage Trap, except has 28-inch barrels, modified and extra full choke, special stock and forearm for live bird shooting; weight, about 8 pounds. Made from 1973 to 1978.

Ithaca-Perazzi Mirage Skeet................... **$2160**

Same as Mirage Trap, except has 28-inch barrels with integral muzzle brakes, skeet choke, skeet-style stock and forearm; weight, about 8 pounds. Made from 1973 to 1978.

Ithaca-Perazzi Competition I Trap Over-and-Under Shotgun.. **$1485**

Box lock. Automatic ejectors. Single trigger. 12 gauge. 30- or 32-inch ventilated-rib barrels, improved modified and full choke. Weight, about 8½ pounds. Checkered pistol-grip stock and forearm, recoil pad. Made from 1969 to 1974.

Ithaca-Perazzi Competition I Skeet........... **$1485**

Same as Competition I Trap, except has 26¾-inch barrels with integral muzzle brakes, skeet choke, skeet-style stock and forearm; weight, 7¾ pounds. Made from 1969 to 1974.

Ithaca-Perazzi Single Barrel Trap Gun........ **$1485**

Box lock. Automatic ejection. 12 gauge. 34-inch ventilated-rib barrel, full choke. Weight, about 8½ pounds. Checkered pistol-grip stock and forearm, recoil pad. Made from 1971 to 1972.

Ithaca-Perazzi Light Game Model Over-and-Under Field Gun.. **$1485**

Box lock. Automatic ejectors. Single trigger. 12 gauge. 27½-inch ventilated-rib barrels, modified and full or improved cylinder and modified choke. Weight, 6¾ pounds. Checkered field-style stock and forearm. Made from 1972 to 1974.

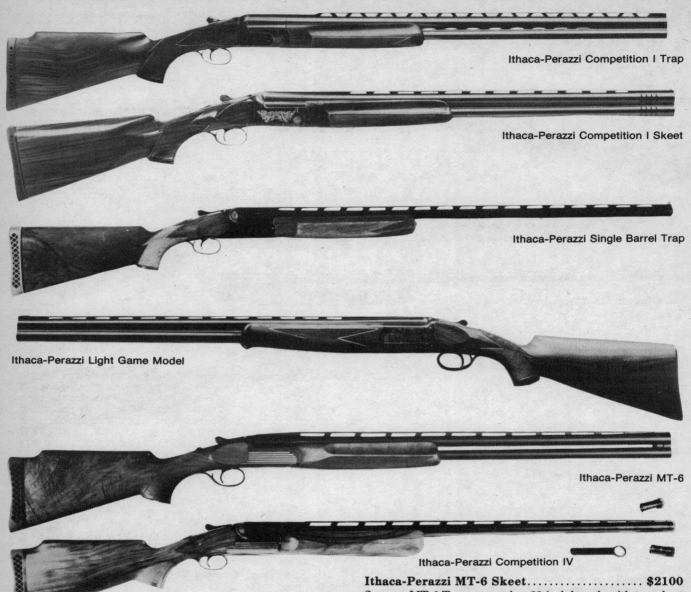

Ithaca-Perazzi Competition I Trap

Ithaca-Perazzi Competition I Skeet

Ithaca-Perazzi Single Barrel Trap

Ithaca-Perazzi Light Game Model

Ithaca-Perazzi MT-6

Ithaca-Perazzi Competition IV

Ithaca-Perazzi Competition I Single Barrel Trap Gun... **$1690**
Box lock. Automatic ejection. 12 gauge. 32- or 34-inch barrel, ventilated rib, full choke. Weight, 8½ pounds. Checkered Monte Carlo stock and beavertail forearm, recoil pad. Made from 1973 to 1978.

Ithaca-Perazzi MT-6 Trap Over-and-Under Shotgun.. **$1900**
Box lock. Automatic selective ejectors. Non-selective single trigger. 12 gauge. Barrels: separated, wide ventilated rib, 30- or 32-inch, five interchangeable choke tubes (extra full, full, improved modified, modified, improved cylinder). Weight, about 8½ pounds. Checkered pistol-grip stock and forearm, recoil pad. Fitted case. Made from 1976 to date.

Ithaca-Perazzi MT-6 Skeet.................... **$2100**
Same as MT-6 Trap, except has 28-inch barrels with two skeet choke tubes instead of extra full and full, skeet-style stock and forearm; weight, about 8 pounds. Made from 1976 to 1978.

Ithaca-Perazzi MT-6 Trap Combo............. **$4185**
MT-6 with extra single under barrel with high-rise aluminum ventilated rib, 32- or 34-inch; seven interchangeable choke tubes (improved cylinder through extra full). Fitted case. Introduced in 1977.

Ithaca-Perazzi Competition IV Single Barrel Trap Gun.. **$2025**
Box lock. Automatic ejection. 12 gauge. 32- or 34-inch barrel with high, wide ventilated rib, four interchangeable choke tubes (extra full, full, improved modified, modified). Weight, about 8¾ pounds. Checkered Monte Carlo stock and beavertail forearm, recoil pad. Fitted case. Introduced in 1977.

Note: Manufacturer of Ithaca-Perazzi shotguns is Manifatura Armi Perazzi, Brescia, Italy.

Iver Johnson Champion

Iver Johnson Trap

Iver Johnson Hercules

Iver Johnson Silver Shadow

Iver Johnson's Arms & Cycle Works, Fitchburg, Massachusetts

Iver Johnson Champion Grade Single Barrel Hammer Shotgun.. $ 65
Automatic ejector. Gauges: 12, 16, 20, 410. Barrels: 26- to 32-inch, full choke. Weight, from 5¾ to 6½ pounds depending upon gauge and barrel length. Plain pistol-grip stock and fore-end. Made from 1909 to date.

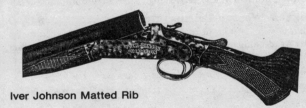

Iver Johnson Matted Rib

Iver Johnson Matted Rib Grade Single Barrel Hammer Shotgun.. $ 80
Same general specifications as Champion Grade except has solid matted top rib, checkered stock and fore-end, weighs about ¼-pound more. Discontinued 1948.

Iver Johnson Special Trap Single Barrel Hammer Shotgun.. $115
Automatic ejector. 12 gauge only. 32-inch barrel with ventilated rib, full choke. Weight, about 7½ pounds. Checkered pistol-grip stock and fore-end. Discontinued 1942.

Iver Johnson Hercules Grade Hammerless Double Barrel Shotgun
Box lock. Plain extractors or automatic ejectors. Double triggers or Miller single trigger (selective or non-selective). Gauges: 12, 16, 20, 410. Barrel lengths: 26- to 32-inch, chokes both full or modified and full. Weight, from 5¾ to 7¾ pounds, depending upon gauge and barrel length. Checkered straight- or pistol-grip stock and fore-end. Discontinued 1948.
With double triggers, plain extractors.................. $375
With double triggers, automatic ejectors.............. 435
Extra for non-selective single trigger.................. 100
Extra for selective single trigger...................... 135

Iver Johnson Skeeter Model Hammerless Double Barrel Shotgun
Box lock. Plain extractors or automatic ejectors. Double triggers or Miller single trigger (selective or non-selective). Gauges: 12, 16, 20, 28, 410. 26- or 28-inch barrels, skeet boring standard. Weight, about 7½ pounds. Straight- or pistol-grip stock, beavertail fore-end, both checkered. Discontinued 1942.
With double triggers, plain extractors.................. $475
With double triggers, automatic ejectors.............. 575
Extra for non-selective single trigger.................. 100
Extra for selective single trigger...................... 135

Iver Johnson Super Trap

Iver Johnson Super Trap Hammerless Double Barrel Shotgun
Box lock. Plain extractors. Double triggers or Miller single trigger (selective or non-selective), 12 gauge only, 32-inch full choke barrels, ventilated rib. Weight, about 8½ pounds. Checkered pistol-grip stock and beavertail fore-end, recoil pad. Discontinued 1942.
With double triggers.................................. $650
Extra for non-selective single trigger.................. 100
Extra for selective single trigger...................... 135

Iver Johnson Silver Shadow Over-and-Under Shotgun
Box lock. Plain extractors. Double triggers or non-selective single trigger. 12 gauge. 3-inch chambers. Barrels: 26-inch improved cylinder and modified, 28-inch modified and full, 30-inch both full choke; ventilated rib. Weight, with 28-inch barrels, 7½ pounds. Checkered pistol-grip stock and forearm. Made by F. Marocchi, Brescia, Italy, from 1973 to date.
Model 412, with double triggers....................... $310
Model 422, with single trigger........................ 400

Kessler Arms Corp., Silver Creek, New York

Kessler Three Shot Bolt Action Repeating Shotgun..$ 50
Takedown. Gauges: 12, 16, 20. 2-shell detachable box magazine. Barrels: 28-inch in 12 and 16 gauge, 26-inch in 20 gauge, full choke. Weight, from 6¼ to 7¼ pounds, depending upon gauge and barrel length. Plain one-piece pistol-grip stock, recoil pad. Made from 1951 to 1953.

Kessler Lever-Matic Repeating Shotgun........ $ 75
Lever action. Takedown. Gauges: 12, 16, 20, 3-shot magazine. Barrels: 26-, 28-, 30-inch; full choke. Plain pistol-grip stock, recoil pad. Weight, 7 to 7¾ pounds. Discontinued in 1953.

H. Krieghoff Jagd-und Sportwaffenfabrik, Ulm (Donau), West Germany

Krieghoff "Teck" Over-and-Under Shotgun.... $1950
Box lock. Kersten double crossbolt system. Automatic ejector. Double triggers or single trigger. Gauges: 12, 16, 20; latter with either 2¾- or 3-inch chambers. 28-inch ventilated-rib barrel, modified and full choke. Weight, about 7 pounds. Checkered walnut pistol-grip stock and forearm. Made from 1967 to date.

Krieghoff "Ulm" Over-and-Under Shotgun..... $3100
Same general specifications as "Teck" model, except has side locks with leaf arabesque engraving. Made from 1958 to date.

Krieghoff "Ulm-Primus" Over-and-Under Shotgun..$3770
Deluxe version of "Ulm" model; has detachable side locks, higher grade engraving and fancier wood. Made from 1958 to date.

Krieghoff "Ulm" Over-and-Under Rifle-Shotgun Combination....................................$2860
Same general specifications as "Teck" model, except has side locks with leaf arabesque engraving. Made from 1963 to date. *Note:* This combination gun is similar in appearance to the same model shotgun.

Krieghoff "Teck" Over-and-Under Rifle-Shotgun Combination....................................$2000
Box lock. Kersten double crossbolt system. Steel or dural receiver. Split extractor or ejector for shotgun barrel. Double triggers or single trigger. Gauges: 12, 16, 20; latter with either 2¾- or 3-inch chamber. Calibers: 22 Hornet, 222 Rem., 222 Rem. Mag., 7x57R, 7x64, 7x65R, 30-30, 300 Win. Mag., 30-06, 308, 9.3x74R. 25-inch barrels with solid rib, folding leaf rear sight, post or bead front sight; over barrel is shotgun, under barrel rifle (later fixed or interchangeable; extra rifle barrel, $175). Weights: 7.9 to 9.5 pounds depending upon type of receiver and caliber. Checkered pistol-grip stock with cheekpiece and semi-beavertail forearm of figured walnut, sling swivels. Made from 1967 to date. *Note:* This combination gun is similar in appearance to the same model shotgun.

Krieghoff "Ulm-Primus" Over-and-Under Rifle-Shotgun Combination............................$3500
Deluxe version of "Ulm" model; has detachable side locks, higher grade engraving and fancier wood. Made from 1963 to date. *Note:* This combination gun is similar in appearance to the same model shotgun.

Krieghoff "Trumpf" Drilling.................... $2700
Box lock. Steel or dural receiver. Split extractor or ejector for shotgun barrels. Double triggers. Gauges: 12, 16, 20; latter with either 2¾- or 3-inch chambers. Calibers: 243, 6.5x57R, 7x57R, 7x65R, 30-06; other calibers available. 25-inch barrels with solid rib, folding leaf rear sight, post or bead front sight; rifle barrel may be soldered or free floating. Weights: 6.6 to 7.5 pounds depending upon type of receiver, gauge and caliber. Checkered pistol-grip stock with cheekpiece and forearm of figured walnut, sling swivels. Made from 1953 to date.

Krieghoff "Neptun" Drilling.................... $3800
Same general specifications as "Trumpf" model, except has side locks with hunting scene engraving. Currently manufactured.

Krieghoff "Neptun-Primus" Drilling............ $4300
Deluxe version of "Neptun" model; has detachable side locks, higher grade engraving and fancier wood. Currently manufactured.

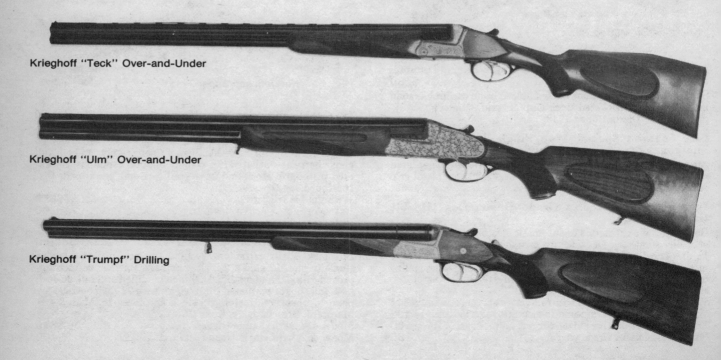

Krieghoff "Teck" Over-and-Under

Krieghoff "Ulm" Over-and-Under

Krieghoff "Trumpf" Drilling

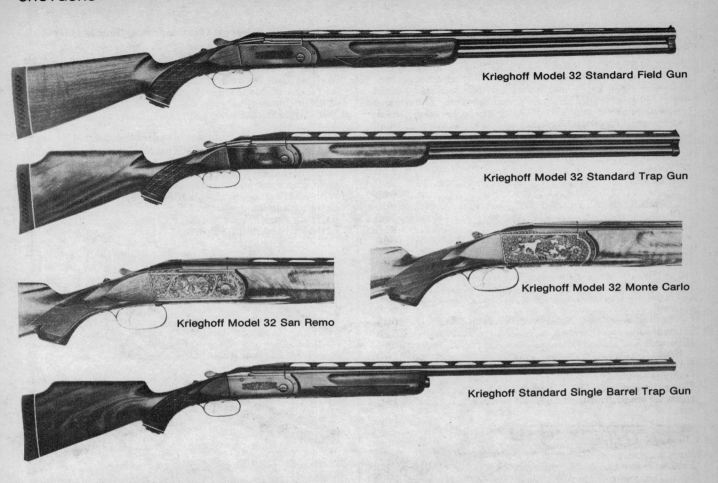

Krieghoff Model 32 Standard Field Gun

Krieghoff Model 32 Standard Trap Gun

Krieghoff Model 32 San Remo

Krieghoff Model 32 Monte Carlo

Krieghoff Standard Single Barrel Trap Gun

Krieghoff Model 32 Standard Grade Over-and-Under Shotgun

Similar to prewar Remington Model 23. Box lock. Automatic ejector. Single trigger. Gauges: 12, 20, 28, 410. Barrels: ventilated rib, 26½- to 32-inch, any chokes. Weight, 12 gauge field gun with 28-inch barrels, about 7½ pounds. Checkered pistol-grip stock and forearm of select walnut; available in field, skeet and trap styles. Made from 1958 to date.

With one set of barrels............................. $2621
Low-rib Two-barrel Trap Combo.................... 3300
Vandalia (high-rib) Two-barrel Trap Combo........ 4160

Krieghoff Model 32 Four-barrel Skeet Set

Over-and-Under gun with four sets of matched barrels in 12, 20, 28 and 410 gauge, in fitted case. Available in six grades which differ in quality of engraving and wood. Currently manufactured.

Standard Grade.................................. $ 4940
München Grade.................................. 6370
San Remo Grade................................ 7280
Monte Carlo Grade............................. 13,650
Crown Grade................................... 14,560
Super Crown Grade............................. 16,500
Exhibition Grade.............................. 27,300

Krieghoff Model 32 Standard Grade Single Barrel Trap Gun $1690

Same action as over-and-under. 12 gauge. 32- or 34-inch barrel with high ventilated rib; modified, improved modified, or full choke. Monte Carlo stock with recoil pad, beavertail forearm. Currently manufactured.

Lefever Arms Company, Syracuse and Ithaca, New York

Lefever side lock hammerless double barrel shotguns were made by Lefever Arms Company in Syracuse, New York, from about 1885 to 1915 (serial numbers 1 to 70,000) when the firm was sold to Ithaca Gun Company of Ithaca, New York. Production of these models was continued at the Ithaca plant until 1919 (serial numbers 70,001 to 72,000). Grades listed are those which appear in the last catalog of the Lefever Gun Company, Syracuse, New York. In 1921, Ithaca introduced the box lock Lefever Nitro Special double, followed in 1934 by the Lefever Grade A; there also were two single barrel Lefevers made from 1927 to 1942. Manufacture of Lefever brand shotguns was discontinued in 1948. *Note:* "New Lefever" box lock shotguns made circa 1904-1906 by D. M. Lefever Company, Bowling Green, Ohio, are included in a separate listing.

Lefever DS Grade

Lefever Side Lock Hammerless Double Barrel Shotguns

Plain extractors or automatic ejectors. Double triggers or selective single trigger. Gauges: 10, 12, 16, 20. Barrels: 26- to 32-inch, standard choke combinations. Weights: 5¾ to 10½ pounds, depending upon gauge and barrel length. Checkered walnut straight-grip or pistol-grip stock and forearm. The various grades differ chiefly in quality of workmanship, engraving, wood, checkering, etc.; general specifications are the same. DS and DSE Grade guns lack the cocking indicators found on all other models. Suffix "E" means model has automatic ejector; also standard on A, AA, Optimus, and Thousand Dollar Grade guns.

DS Grade	$ 550
DSE Grade	700
H Grade	650
HE Grade	800
G Grade	780
GE Grade	950
F Grade	1000
FE Grade	1200
E Grade	1270
EE Grade	1460
D Grade	1590
DE Grade	1780
C Grade	1900
CE Grade	2095
B Grade	2520
BE Grade	2690
A Grade	3100
AA Grade	3690
Optimus Grade	4000
Thousand Dollar Grade	8000
Extra for single trigger	150

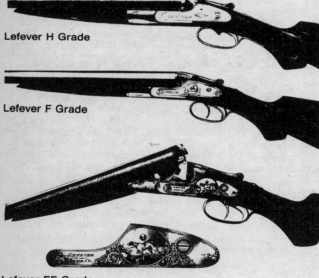

Lefever H Grade

Lefever F Grade

Lefever EE Grade

Lefever DE Grade

Lefever Nitro Special Hammerless Double Barrel Shotgun

Box lock. Plain extractors. Double triggers or single trigger. Gauges: 12, 16, 20, 410. Barrels: 26- to 32-inch, standard chokes. Weight, about 7 pounds in 12 gauge. Checkered pistol-grip stock and fore-end. Made from 1921 to 1948.

With double triggers	$500
With single trigger	550

Lefever Grade A Hammerless Double Barrel Shotgun

Box lock. Plain extractors or automatic ejector. Double triggers or single trigger. Gauges: 12, 16, 20, 410. Barrels: 26- to 32-inch, standard chokes. Weight, about 7 pounds in 12 gauge. Checkered pistol-grip stock and forearm. Made from 1934 to 1942.

With plain extractors, double triggers	$650
Extra for automatic ejector	75
Extra for single trigger	75
Extra for beavertail forearm	50

Lefever CE Grade

Lefever BE Grade

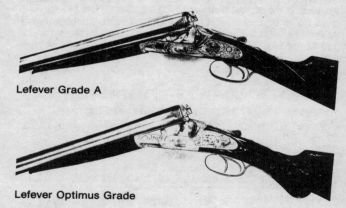

Lefever Grade A

Lefever Optimus Grade

Lefever Nitro Special

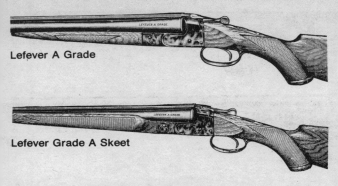

Lefever A Grade

Lefever Grade A Skeet

Lefever Grade A Skeet Model................... $900

Same as Grade A, except standard features include automatic ejector, single trigger, beavertail forearm; 26-inch barrels, skeet boring. Discontinued 1942.

Lefever Single Barrel Trap

Lefever Hammerless Single Barrel Trap Gun... $375

Box lock. Ejector. 12 gauge only. Barrel lengths: 30- or 32-inch. Ventilated rib. Weight, about 8 pounds. Checkered pistol-grip stock and fore-end, recoil pad. Made from 1927 to 1942.

Lefever Long Range

Lefever Long Range Hammerless Single Barrel Field Gun.. $225

Box lock. Plain extractor. Gauges: 12, 16, 20, 410. Barrel lengths: 26- to 32-inch. Weight, 5½ to 7 pounds depending upon gauge and barrel length. Checkered pistol-grip stock and fore-end. Made from 1927 to 1942.

D. M. Lefever Company, Bowling Green, Ohio

In 1901, D. M. "Uncle Dan" Lefever, founder of the Lefever Arms Company, withdrew from that firm to organize D. M. Lefever, Sons & Company (later D. M. Lefever Company) to manufacture the "New Lefever" box lock double and single barrel shotguns. These were produced at Bowling Green, Ohio, from about 1904 to 1906 when Dan Lefever died and the factory closed permanently. Grades listed are those which appear in the last catalog of D. M. Lefever Company.

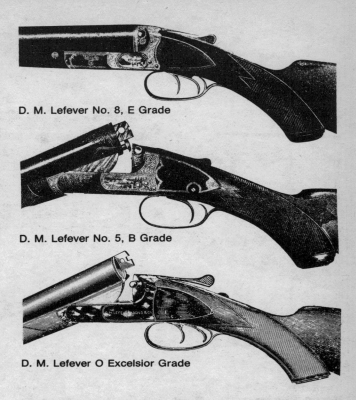

D. M. Lefever No. 8, E Grade

D. M. Lefever No. 5, B Grade

D. M. Lefever O Excelsior Grade

D. M. Lefever Hammerless Double Barrel Shotguns

"New Lefever." Box lock. Automatic ejector standard on all grades except O Excelsior which was regularly supplied with plain extractors (automatic ejector offered as an extra). Double triggers or selective single trigger (latter standard on Uncle Dan Grade, extra on all others). Gauges: 12, 16, 20. Barrels: any length and choke combination. Weights: 5½ to 8 pounds, depending upon gauge and barrel length. Checkered walnut straight-grip or pistol-grip stock and forearm. The various grades differ chiefly in quality of workmanship, engraving, wood, checkering, etc.; general specifications are the same.

O Excelsior Grade with plain extractors	$ 750
O Excelsior Grade with automatic ejector	980
No. 9, F Grade	1260
No. 8, E Grade	1520
No. 6, C Grade	2040
No. 5, B Grade	2640
No. 4, AA Grade	3900
Uncle Dan Grade	6400
Extra for single trigger	150

D. M. Lefever Single Barrel Trap Gun.......... $750

Box lock. Automatic ejector. 12 gauge only. Barrels: 26- to 32-inches, full choke. Weights: from 6½ to 8 pounds, depending upon barrel length. Checkered walnut pistol-grip stock and forearm.

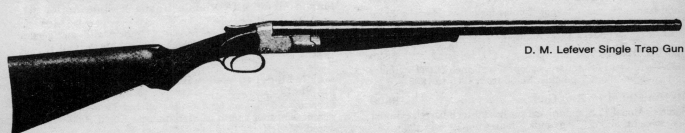

D. M. Lefever Single Trap Gun

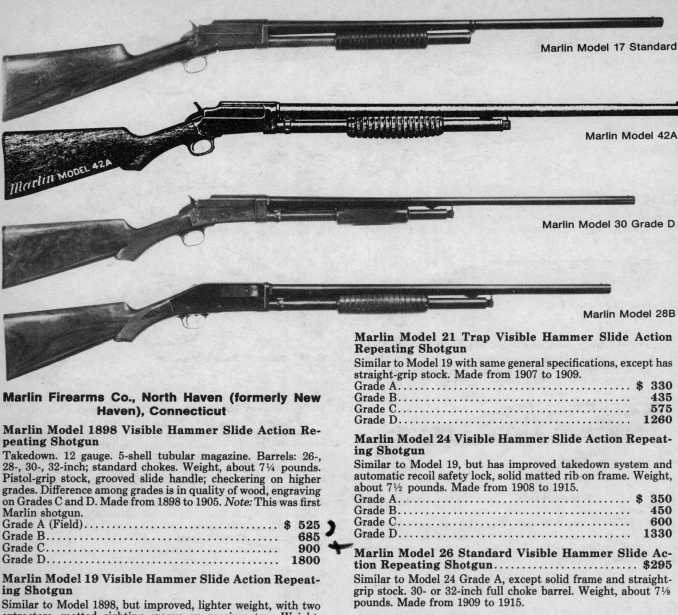

Marlin Model 17 Standard

Marlin Model 42A

Marlin Model 30 Grade D

Marlin Model 28B

Marlin Firearms Co., North Haven (formerly New Haven), Connecticut

Marlin Model 1898 Visible Hammer Slide Action Repeating Shotgun

Takedown. 12 gauge. 5-shell tubular magazine. Barrels: 26-, 28-, 30-, 32-inch; standard chokes. Weight, about 7¼ pounds. Pistol-grip stock, grooved slide handle; checkering on higher grades. Difference among grades is in quality of wood, engraving on Grades C and D. Made from 1898 to 1905. *Note:* This was first Marlin shotgun.

Grade A (Field)	$ 525
Grade B	685
Grade C	900
Grade D	1800

Marlin Model 19 Visible Hammer Slide Action Repeating Shotgun

Similar to Model 1898, but improved, lighter weight, with two extractors, matted sighting groove on receiver top. Weight, about 7 pounds. Made from 1906 to 1907.

Grade A	$ 330
Grade B	435
Grade C	575
Grade D	1125

Marlin Model 17 Standard Visible Hammer Slide Action Repeating Shotgun $325

Solid frame. 12 gauge. 5-shot tubular magazine. Barrels: 30- or 32-inch, full choke. Weight, about 7½ pounds. Straight-grip stock, grooved slide handle. Made from 1906 to 1908.

Marlin Model 17 Brush Gun $325

Same as Model 17 Standard, except has 26-inch barrel, cylinder bore; weight, about 7 pounds. Made from 1906 to 1908.

Marlin Model 17 Riot Gun $300

Same as Model 17 Standard, except has 20-inch barrel, cylinder bore; weight, about 6⅞ pounds. Made from 1906 to 1908.

Marlin Model 21 Trap Visible Hammer Slide Action Repeating Shotgun

Similar to Model 19 with same general specifications, except has straight-grip stock. Made from 1907 to 1909.

Grade A	$ 330
Grade B	435
Grade C	575
Grade D	1260

Marlin Model 24 Visible Hammer Slide Action Repeating Shotgun

Similar to Model 19, but has improved takedown system and automatic recoil safety lock, solid matted rib on frame. Weight, about 7½ pounds. Made from 1908 to 1915.

Grade A	$ 350
Grade B	450
Grade C	600
Grade D	1330

Marlin Model 26 Standard Visible Hammer Slide Action Repeating Shotgun $295

Similar to Model 24 Grade A, except solid frame and straight-grip stock. 30- or 32-inch full choke barrel. Weight, about 7⅛ pounds. Made from 1909 to 1915.

Marlin Model 26 Brush Gun $315

Same as Model 26 Standard, except has 26-inch barrel, cylinder bore; weight, about 7 pounds. Made from 1909 to 1915.

Marlin Model 26 Riot Gun $350

Same as Model 26 Standard, except has 20-inch barrel, cylinder bore; weight, about 6⅞ pounds. Made from 1909 to 1915.

Marlin Model 42A Visible Hammer Slide Action Repeating Shotgun $225

Similar to pre-World War I Model 24 Grade A with same general specifications, but not of as high quality. Made from 1922 to 1934.

Marlin Model 49 Visible Hammer Slide Action Repeating Shotgun $325

Economy version of Model 42A, offered as a bonus on the purchase of four shares of Marlin stock. About 3000 were produced. Made from 1925 to 1928.

Marlin Model 43A

Marlin Model 43T

Marlin Model 53

Marlin Model 60

Marlin Model 16 Visible Hammer Slide Action Repeating Shotgun

Takedown. 16 gauge. 5-shell tubular magazine. Barrels: 26- or 28-inch, standard chokes. Weight, about 6¼ pounds. Pistol-grip stock, grooved slide handle; checkering on higher grades. Difference among grades is in quality of wood, engraving on Grades C and D. Made from 1904 to 1910.

Grade A	$ 315
Grade B	380
Grade C	570
Grade D	1150

Marlin Model 30 Visible Hammer Slide Action Repeating Shotgun

Similar to Model 16, but with Model 24 improvements. Made from 1910 to 1914.

Grade A	$ 300
Grade B	350
Grade C	525
Grade D	1175

Marlin Model 30 Field Gun $375

Same as Model 30 Grade B, except has 25-inch barrel, modified choke, straight-grip stock. Made from 1913 to 1914.

Marlin Models 30A, 30B, 30C, 30D

Same as Model 30; designations were changed in 1915. Also available in 20 gauge with 25- or 28-inch barrel; matted-top barrel on all grades. Suffixes "A," "B," "C" and "D" correspond to former grades. Made in 1915.

Model 30A	$ 300
Model 30B	390
Model 30C	580
Model 30D	1050

Marlin Model 28 Hammerless Slide Action Repeating Shotgun

Takedown. 12 gauge. 5-shot tubular magazine. Barrels: 26-, 28-, 30-, 32-inch, standard chokes; matted-top barrel except on Model 28D which has solid matted rib. Weight, about 8 pounds. Pistol-grip stock, grooved slide handle; checkering on higher grades. Difference among grades is in quality of wood, engraving on Models 28C and 28D. Made from 1913 to 1922; all but Model 28A discontinued in 1915.

Model 28A	$ 300
Model 28B	425
Model 28C	650
Model 28D	1200

Marlin Model 28T Trap Gun $545

Same as Model 28, except has 30-inch matted-rib barrel, full choke, straight-grip stock with high fluted comb of fancy walnut, checkered. Made in 1915.

Marlin Model 28TS Trap Gun $330

Same as Model 28T, except has matted-top barrel, plainer stock. Made in 1915.

Marlin Model 43 Hammerless Slide Action Repeating Shotgun

Similar to pre-World War I Models 28A, 28T and 28TS, with same general specifications, but not of as high quality. Made from 1923 to 1930.

Model 43A	$200
Model 43T	475
Model 43TS	400

Marlin Model 53 Hammerless Slide Action Repeating Shotgun $225

Similar to Model 43A, with same general specifications. Made from 1929 to 1930.

Marlin Model 410

Marlin Model 90

Marlin Model 55 Hunter

Marlin Model 55 Goose Gun

Marlin Swamp Gun Model 55

Marlin Model 55S Slug Gun

Marlin Model 5510 Super Goose 10

Marlin Model 59

Marlin Model 63 Hammerless Slide Action Repeating Shotgun

Similar to Models 43A and 43T with same general specifications. Model 63TS Trap Special is same as Model 63T Trap Gun except stock style and dimensions to order. Made from 1931 to 1935.

Model 63A.. **$230**
Model 63T or 63TS................................... **370**

Marlin Model 31 Hammerless Slide Action Repeating Shotgun

Similar to Model 28, except scaled down for smaller gauges, 16 and 20. Barrels: 25-inch (20 gauge only), 26-inch (16 gauge only), 28-inch; all with matted top; standard chokes. Weights: 16 gauge, about 6¾ pounds; 20 gauge, about 6 pounds. Pistol-grip stock, grooved slide handle; checkering on higher grades; straight-grip stock optional on Model 31D. Made from 1915 to 1922; all but Model 31A discontinued in 1917.

Model 31A.. **$ 300**
Model 31B.. **420**
Model 31C.. **600**
Model 31D.. **1150**

Marlin Model 31F Field Gun..................... **$400**

Same as Model 31B, except has 25-inch barrel, modified choke, straight- or pistol-grip stock. Made from 1915 to 1917.

Marlin Model 44 Hammerless Slide Action Repeating Shotgun

Similar to pre-World War I Model 31A, with same general specifications, but not of as high quality. 20 gauge only. Model 44A is a standard grade field gun. Model 44S Special Grade has checkered stock and slide handle of fancy walnut. Made from 1923 to 1935.

Model 44A.. **$240**
Model 44S.. **360**

Marlin Model 60 Single Barrel Shotgun........ **$160**

Visible hammer. Takedown. Box lock. Automatic ejector. 12 gauge. 30- or 32-inch barrel, full choke. Weight, about 6½ pounds. Pistol-grip stock, beavertail forearm. Made in 1923. *Note:* Only about 600 were produced.

Marlin Model 410 Lever Action Repeating Shotgun.. **$495**

Action similar to that of Marlin Model 93 rifle. Visible hammer. Solid frame. 410 gauge (2½-inch shell). 5-shot tubular magazine. 22- or 26-inch barrel, full choke. Weight, about 6 pounds. Plain pistol-grip stock and grooved beavertail forearm. Made from 1929 to 1932.

Marlin Model 90 Standard Over-and-Under Shotgun

Hammerless. Box lock. Double triggers; non-selective single trigger was available as an extra on prewar guns except 410. Gauges: 12, 16, 20, 410. Barrels: plain; 26-, 28- or 30-inch; chokes improved cylinder and modified or modified and full; barrel design changed in 1949, eliminating full-length rib between barrels. Weights: 12 gauge about 7½ pounds, 16 and 20 gauge about 6¼ pounds. Checkered pistol-grip stock and forearm, recoil pad standard on prewar guns. Postwar production: Model 90-DT (double trigger), Model 90-ST (single trigger). Made from 1937 to 1958.

With double triggers................................ **$350**
With single trigger.................................. **450**

Marlin Model 55 Hunter Bolt Action Repeating Shotgun

Takedown. Gauges: 12, 16, 20. 2-shot clip magazine. 28-inch barrel (26-inch in 20 ga.), full choke or with adjustable choke. Plain pistol-grip stock; 12 ga. has recoil pad. Weight, about 7¼ pounds (20 ga., 6½ pounds). Made from 1950 to 1965.

With plain barrel................................... **$ 65**
With adjustable choke............................... **75**

Marlin Model 55 Goose Gun..................... **$ 85**

Same as Model 55 Hunter, except chambered for 12 gauge 3-inch magnum shell, has 36-inch barrel, full choke, swivels and sling; weight, about 8 pounds. Made from 1962 to date.

Marlin Model 55 Swamp Gun.................... **$ 90**

Same as Model 55 Hunter except chambered for 12 gauge 3-inch magnum shell, has 20½-inch barrel with adjustable choke, sling swivels, weighs about 6½ pounds. Made from 1963 to 1965.

Marlin Model 55S Slug Gun..................... **$100**

Same as Model 55 Goose Gun, except has 24-inch barrel, cylinder bore, rifle sights; weight, about 7½ pounds. Made from 1974 to date.

Marlin Model 5510 Super Goose 10.............. **$160**

Similar to Model 55 Goose Gun, except chambered for 10 gauge 3½-inch magnum shell, has 34-inch heavy barrel, full choke; weight, about 10½ pounds. Made from 1976 to date.

Marlin Model 59 Auto-Safe Bolt Action Single Shotgun.................................... **$ 60**

Takedown. Automatic thumb safety. 410 gauge. 24-inch barrel, full choke. Weight, about 5 pounds. Plain pistol-grip stock. Made from 1959 to 1961.

Marlin-Glenfield Model 50 Bolt Action Repeating Shotgun.................................. **$ 60**

Similar to Model 55 Hunter, except chambered for 12 or 20 gauge 3-inch magnum shell; has 28-inch barrel in 12 gauge, 26-inch in 20 gauge, full choke. Made from 1966 to 1974.

Marlin-Glenfield 778 Slide Action Repeating Shotgun

Hammerless. 12 gauge 2¾-inch or 3-inch. 4-shot tubular magazine. Barrels: 26-inch improved cylinder, 28-inch modified, 30-inch full, 38-inch MXR, 20-inch slug barrel. Weight, 7¾ pounds. Checkering on pistol grip. Made from 1979 to date.

With plain barrel................................... **$140**
With ventilated-rib barrel........................... **175**

Marlin-Glenfield Model 50

Marlin Premier Mark I

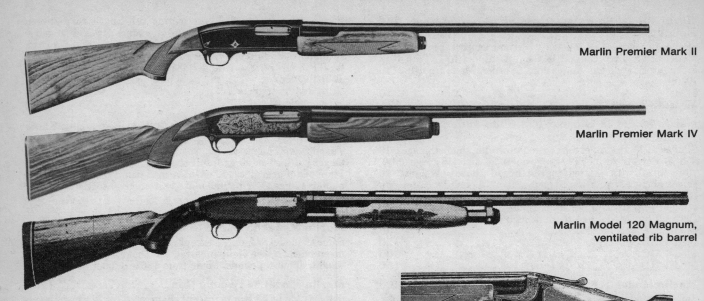

Marlin Premier Mark II

Marlin Premier Mark IV

Marlin Model 120 Magnum,
ventilated rib barrel

Marlin Premier Mark I Slide Action Repeating Shotgun.. **$140**
Hammerless. Takedown. 12 gauge. Magazine holds 3 shells. Barrels: 30-inch full choke, 28-inch modified, 26-inch improved cylinder or skeet choke. Weight, about 6 pounds. Plain pistol-grip stock and forearm. Made in France from 1960 to 1963.

Marlin Premier Mark II..........................**$190**
Same as Premier Mark I, except engraved receiver, checkered stock and forearm. Made from 1960 to 1963.

Marlin premier Mark IV
Same as Premier Mark II, except more elaborate engraving, fancier wood. Made from 1960 to 1963.
With plain barrel.................................... **$260**
With ventilated-rib barrel........................... 360

Marlin Model 120 Magnum Slide Action Repeating Shotgun... **$185**
Hammerless. Takedown. 12 gauge (3-inch). 4-shot tubular magazine. Barrels: 26-inch ventilated rib, improved cylinder; 28-inch ventilated rib, modified choke; 30-inch ventilated rib, full choke; 38-inch plain, full choke; 40-inch plain, full choke; 26-inch slug barrel with rifle sights, improved cylinder. Weight, about 7¾ pounds. Checkered pistol-grip stock and forearm, recoil pad. Made from 1971 to date.

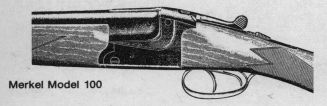

Merkel Model 100

Gebrüder Merkel, Suhl, Germany

Merkel Model 100 Over-and-Under Shotgun
Hammerless. Box lock. Greener crossbolt. Plain extractor. Double triggers. Gauges: 12, 16, 20. Made with plain or ribbed barrels in various lengths and chokes. Plain finish, no engraving. Checkered fore-end and stock with pistol grip and cheekpiece or English style. Made prior to World War II.
With plain barrel.................................... **$700**
With ribbed barrel................................... 735

Merkel Model 101

Merkel Models 101 and 101E Over-and-Under Shotguns
Same as Model 100, except ribbed barrel standard, has separate extractors (ejectors on Model 101E), English engraving. Made prior to World War II.
Model 101... **$900**
Model 101E.. 980

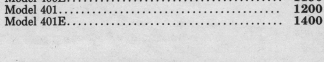

Merkel Model 400

Merkel Models 400, 400E, 401 and 401E Over-and-Under Shotguns
Similar to Model 101 except have Kersten double crossbolt, arabesque engraving on Models 400 and 400E, hunting engraving on Models 401 and 401E, finer general quality. "E" models have Merkel ejectors, others have separate extractors. Made prior to World War II.
Model 400... **$1015**
Model 400E.. 1190
Model 401... 1200
Model 401E.. 1400

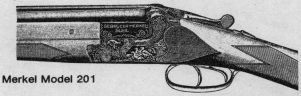

Merkel Model 201

Merkel Models 200, 200E, 201, 201E, 202 and 202E Over-and-Under Shotguns

Hammerless. Box lock. Kersten double crossbolt. Scalloped frame. Sideplates on Models 202 and 202E. Arabesque engraving, hunting engraving, also supplied on all except Models 200 and 200E. "E" models have ejectors, others have separate extractors. Signal pins. Double triggers. Gauges: 12, 16, 20, 24, 28, 32 (last three gauges are not available in postwar guns). Ribbed barrels in various lengths and chokes. Weight, from 5¾ to 7½ pounds depending upon barrel length and gauge. Checkered fore-end and stock with pistol-grip and cheekpiece or English style. The three grades—200, 201, 202—differ in overall quality, engraving, wood, checkering, etc., aside from the dummy sideplates on Models 202 and 202E, general specifications are the same. Models 200, 201, 202, and 202E, which were made before World War II, are discontinued.

Model 200...	$ 900
Model 200E..	1100
Model 201...	1100
Model 201E..	2000
Model 202...	2240
Model 202E..	2520

Merkel Model 203E

Merkel Model 203E Over-and-Under Shotgun. $3800

Hammerless. Hand detachable side locks. Kersten fastening. Automatic ejectors. Double triggers. Arabesque engraving standard, hunting engraving also supplied. Gauges: 12, 16, 20. Ribbed barrels in various lengths and chokes. Checkered fore-end and stock with pistol grip and cheekpiece or English style. Currently manufactured.

Merkel Model 204E Over-and-Under Shotgun. $4420

Similar to Model 203E. Has Merkel sidelocks, fine English engraving. Made prior to World War II.

Merkel Model 303E Over-and-Under Shotgun. $4500

Similar to Model 203E. Has Kersten crossbolt, double underlugs, Holland & Holland-type hand-detachable side locks, automatic ejectors. This is a finer gun than Model 203E. Currently manufactured.

Merkel Model 300E

Merkel Model 304E

Merkel Model 304E Over-and-Under Shotgun. $7200

Special model of the Model 303E-type, but higher quality throughout. This is the top grade Merkel Over-and-Under. Currently manufactured.

Merkel Model 302

Merkel Model 210 O/U Combination

Merkel Models 300, 300E, 301, 301E and 302 Over-and-Under Shotguns

Merkel-Anson system box lock. Kersten double cross bolt. Two underlugs. Scalloped frame. Sideplates on Model 302. Arabesque or hunting engraving. "E" models and Model 302 have automatic ejectors, others have separate extractors. Signal pins. Double triggers. Gauges: 12, 16, 20, 24, 28, 32. Ribbed barrels in various lengths and chokes. Checkered fore-end and stock with pistol-grip and cheekpiece or English style. The three grades—300, 301, 302—differ in overall quality, engraving, wood, checkering, etc., aside from the dummy sideplates on Model 302, general specifications are the same. Manufactured prior to World War II.

Model 300...	$1700
Model 300E..	2100
Model 301...	2100
Model 301E..	4500
Model 302...	4800

Merkel Over-and-Under Combination Guns ("Bock-Büchsflinten")

Shotgun barrel over, rifle barrel under. Gauges: 12, 16, 20; calibers: 5.6x35 Vierling, 7x57R, 8x57JR, 8x60R Magnum, 9.3x53R, 9.3x72R, 9.3x74R and others. Various barrel lengths, chokes and weights. Other specifications and values correspond to those of Merkel Over-and-Under Shotguns listed below. Currently manufactured.

Models 410, 410E, 411E........**see shotgun Models 400, 400E, 401, 401E respectively**

Models 210, 210E, 211, 211E, 212, 212E........**see shotgun Models 200, 200E, 201, 201E, 202, 202E respectively**

Models 310, 310E, 311, 311E, 312............ **see shotgun Models 300, 300E, 301, 301E, 302 respectively**
Model 213E..................**see shotgun Model 203E**
Model 214E..................**see shotgun Model 204E**
Model 313..................**see shotgun Model 303E**
Model 314..................**see shotgun Model 304E**

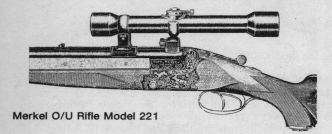

Merkel O/U Rifle Model 221

Merkel Over-and-Under Rifles ("Bock-Doppelbüch-sen")

Calibers: 5.6x35 Vierling, 6.5x58R, 7x57R, 8x57JR, 8x60R Magnum, 9.3x53R, 9.3x72R, 9.3x74R, 10.3x60R as well as most of the British calibers for African and Indian big game. Various barrel lengths, weights. In general, specifications correspond to those of Merkel Over-and-Under Shotguns listed below. Values of these over-and-under rifles (in calibers for which ammunition is obtainable) are about the same as those of comparable shotgun models. Currently manufactured.
Models 220, 220E, 221, 221E......... **see shotgun Models 200, 200E, 201, 201E respectively**
Models 320, 320E, 321, 321E, 322............ **see shotgun Models 300, 300E, 301, 301E, 302 respectively**
Model 323..................**see shotgun Model 303E**
Model 324..................**see shotgun Model 304E**

Merkel Interchangeable Barrels

This manufacturer's over-and-under guns were often supplied with accessory barrels, interchangeable to convert the gun into an arm of another type; for example, a set might consist of one pair each of shotgun, rifle and combination gun barrels. Each pair of interchangeable barrels has a value of approximately one-third that of the gun with which they are supplied.

Merkel Model 130

Merkel Model 130 Hammerless Box Lock Double Barrel Shotgun.....................................$5080

Anson & Deeley system. Side plates. Automatic ejectors. Double triggers. Elaborate hunting scene engravings or arabesque engraving. Made in all standard gauges, various barrel lengths and chokes. Checkered fore-end and stock with pistol grip and cheekpiece of English style. Manufactured prior to World War II.

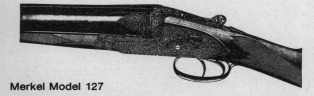

Merkel Model 127

Merkel Model 127 Hammerless Side Lock Double Barrel Shotgun.....................................$12,000

Holland & Holland system, hand detachable locks. Automatic ejectors. Double triggers. Made in all standard gauges, barrel lengths and chokes. Checkered fore-end and stock with pistol grip and cheekpiece or English style. This is a highest quality deluxe gun, elaborately engraved in arabesque or hunting scene pattern. Manufactured prior to World War II.

Merkel Model 147E Hammerless Box Lock Double Barrel Shotgun.....................................$900

Anson & Deeley system. Automatic ejectors. Double triggers. Gauges: 12, 16, 20 (3-inch chambers available in 12 and 20 gauge). Barrels: 26-inch standard, other lengths available; any standard choke combination. Weight, about 6½ pounds. Checkered straight-grip stock and forearm, checkered. Currently manufactured.

Merkel Models 147S and 47S Hammerless Double Barrel Shotguns

Side-lock action. Otherwise same general specifications as Model 147E. Model 147S has hunting scene engraving, Model 47S has less elaborate arabesque engraving. Currently manufactured.
Model 147S..**$2700**
Model 47S...1600

Merkel Model 144 Drilling

Merkel Anson Drillings

Three-barrel combination guns; usually made with double shotgun barrels, over rifle barrel, although "Doppel-büchsdrillingen" were made with two rifle barrels over and shotgun barrel under. Hammerless. Box lock. Anson & Deeley system. Side clips. Plain extractors. Double triggers. Gauges: 12, 16, 20; rifle calibers: 7x57R, 8x57JR and 9.3x74R are most common, but these guns were produced in other calibers from 5.6mm to 10.75mm. Barrels: standard drilling, 25.6 inches; short drilling, 21.6 inches. Checkered pistol-grip stock and fore-end. The three models listed differ chiefly in overall quality, grade of wood, etc., general specifications are the same. Manufactured prior to World War II.
Model 144.. **$6000**
Model 142.. 5400
Model 145.. 4800

Miida Shotguns manufactured for Marubeni America Corp., New York, New York, by Olin-Kodensha Co., Tochigi, Japan

Miida Model 612 Field Grade Over-and-Under Shotgun...$600

Box lock. Automatic ejectors. Selective single trigger. 12 gauge. Barrels: ventilated rib; 26-inch, improved cylinder and modified; 28-inch, modified and full choke. Weight with 26-inch barrel, 6 lbs. 11 oz. Checkered pistol-grip stock and forearm. Made from 1972 to 1974.

Miida Model 2100 Skeet Gun.................... $700

Similar to Model 612, except has more elaborate engraving on

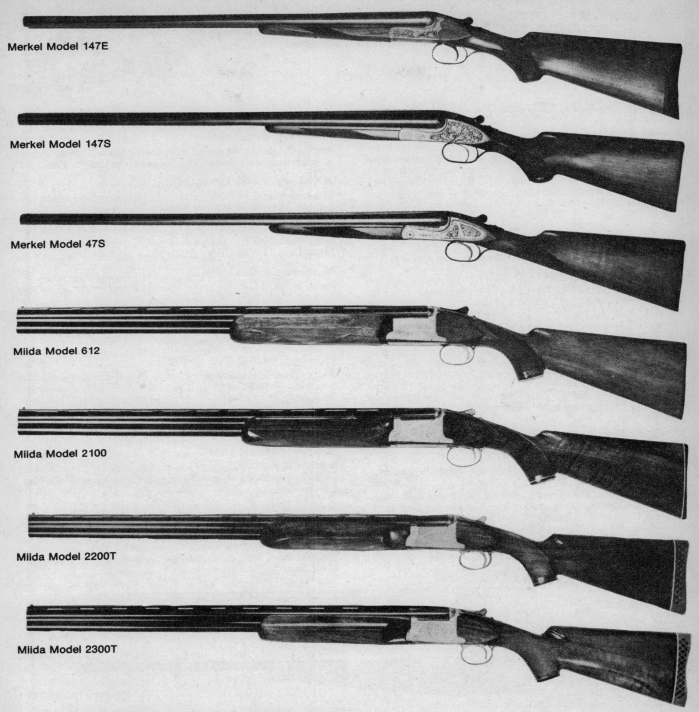

Merkel Model 147E

Merkel Model 147S

Merkel Model 47S

Miida Model 612

Miida Model 2100

Miida Model 2200T

Miida Model 2300T

frame (50 percent coverage), skeet-style stock and forearm of select grade wood; 27-inch ventilated-rib barrels, skeet choke; weight, 7 lbs. 11 oz. Made from 1972 to 1974.

Miida Model 2200T Trap Gun, Model 2200S Skeet Gun.. **$800**
Similar to Model 612, except more elaborate engraving on frame (60 percent coverage), trap- or skeet-style stock and semi-beavertail forearm of fancy walnut, recoil pad on trap stock. Barrels: wide ventilated rib; 29¾-inch, improved modified and

full choke, on Trap Gun; 27-inch, skeet choke, on Skeet Gun. Weight: Trap Gun, 7 lbs. 14 oz.; Skeet Gun, 7 lbs. 11 oz. Made from 1972 to 1974.

Miida Model 2300T Trap Gun, Model 2300S Skeet Gun.. **$950**
Same as Models 2200T and 2200S, except more elaborate engraving on frame (70 percent coverage). Made from 1972 to 1974.

Miida Grandee Model GRT

Miida Grandee Model GRT Trap Gun, Model GRS Skeet Gun... $1650

Box lock with side plates. Frame, breech ends of barrels, trigger guard and locking lever fully engraved and gold inlaid. Automatic ejectors. Selective single trigger. 12 gauge. Barrels: wide ventilated rib; 29-inch, full choke, on Trap Gun; 27-inch, skeet choke, on Skeet Gun. Weight: Trap Gun, 7 lbs. 14 oz.; Skeet Gun, 7 lbs. 11 oz. Trap- or skeet-style stock and semi-beavertail forearm of extra fancy wood, recoil pad on trap stock. Made from 1972 to 1974.

Morrone Shotgun manufactured by Rhode Island Arms Company, Hope Valley, Rhode Island

Morrone Standard Model 46 Over-and-Under Shotgun.. $640

Box lock. Plain extractors. Non-selective single trigger. Gauges: 12, 20. Barrels: plain, ventilated rib; 26-inch, improved cylinder and modified, 28-inch, modified and full choke. Weight: about 7 pounds in 12 gauge, 6 pounds in 20 gauge. Checkered straight or pistol-grip stock and forearm. Made from 1949 to 1953. *Note:* Less than 500 of these guns were produced, about 50 in 20 gauge; a few had ventilated-rib barrels. Value shown is for 12 gauge with plain barrels; the very rare 20 gauge and ventilated-rib types should bring considerably more.

O. F. Mossberg & Sons, Inc., North Haven (formerly in New Haven), Connecticut

Mossberg Model 85D or 185D Bolt Action Repeating Shotgun... $65

Takedown. 3-shot. 20 gauge only. 2-shell detachable box magazine. 25-inch barrel, three interchangeable choke tubes (full, modified, improved cylinder). Later production had 26-inch barrel with full and improved cylinder choke tubes. Weight, about 6¼ pounds. Plain, one-piece, pistol-grip stock. Originally designated Model 85D, changed in 1947 to Model 185D. Made from 1940 to 1971.

Mossberg Model 185K............................. $ 70

Same as Model 185D, except has variable C-Lect-Choke instead of interchangeable choke tubes. Made from 1950 to 1963.

Mossberg Model 195K............................. $ 75

Same as Model 185K, except in 12 gauge, weighs about 7½ pounds. Made from 1956 to 1963.

Mossberg Model 190D............................. $ 60

Same as Model 185D, except in 16 gauge, weighs about 6 pounds. Made from 1955 to 1971.

Mossberg Model 190K............................. $ 65

Same as Model 185K, except in 16 gauge, weighs about 6¾ pounds. Made from 1956 to 1963.

Mossberg Model 195D............................. $ 65

Same as Model 185D, except in 12 gauge, weighs about 6¾ pounds. Made from 1955 to 1971.

Mossberg Model 83D or 183D..................... $ 60

3-shot. Takedown. 410-gauge only. 2-shell fixed, top-loading magazine. 23-inch barrel with two interchangeable choke tubes (modified, full). Later production had 24-inch barrel. Plain, one-piece, pistol-grip stock. Weight, about 5½ pounds. Originally designated Model 83D, changed in 1947 to Model 183D. Made from 1940 to 1971.

Mossberg Model 183K............................. $ 60

Same as Model 183D, except has 25-inch barrel with variable C-Lect-Choke instead of interchangeable choke tubes. Made from 1953 to date.

Mossberg Model 395K Bolt Action Repeating Shotgun... $ 70

Takedown. 3-shot (detachable clip magazine holds two shells). 12 gauge (3-inch chamber). 28-inch barrel with C-Lect-Choke. Weight, about 7½ pounds. Monte Carlo stock with recoil pad. Made from 1963 to date.

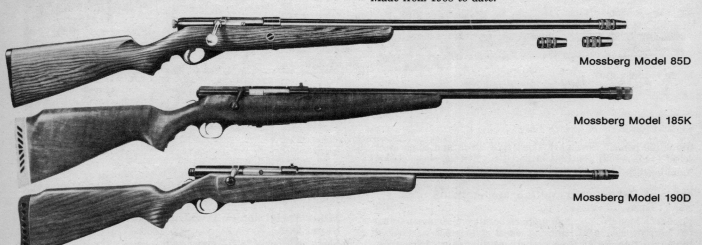

Mossberg Model 85D

Mossberg Model 185K

Mossberg Model 190D

Mossberg Model 195D

Mossberg Model 83D

Mossberg Model 183K

Mossberg Model 395K

Mossberg Model 395S

Mossberg Model 200K

Mossberg Model 390K............................ **$ 60**
Same as Model 395K, except 16 gauge (2¾-inch). Made from 1963 to 1974.

Mossberg Model 385K............................ **$ 70**
Same as Model 395K, except 20 gauge (3-inch), 26-inch barrel with C-Lect-Choke; weight, about 6¼ pounds. Made from 1963 to date.

Mossberg Model 395S Slugster................... **$ 75**
Same as Model 395K, except has 24-inch barrel, cylinder bore, rifle sights, swivels and web sling; weight, about 7 pounds. Made from 1968 to 1981.

Mossberg Model 200K Slide Action Repeater... **$ 90**
12 gauge. 3-shot detachable box magazine. 28-inch barrel. C-Lect-Choke. Plain pistol-grip stock. Black nylon slide handle. Weight, about 7½ pounds. Made from 1955 to 1959.

Mossberg Model 200D............................ **$ 90**
Same as Model 200K, except with two interchangeable choke tubes instead of C-Lect-Choke. Made from 1955 to 1959.

Mossberg Model 500 Field Grade Hammerless Slide Action Repeater

Pre-1977 type. Takedown. Gauges: 12, 16, 20, 410. 3-inch chamber (2¾-inch in 16 gauge). Tubular magazine holds five 2¾-inch shells or four three-inch. Barrels: plain; 30-inch regular or heavy magnum, full choke (12 gauge only); 28-inch, modified or full; 26-inch, improved cylinder or adjustable C-Lect-Choke; 24-inch Slugster, cylinder bore, with rifle sights. Weight: from 5¾ to 8 pounds, depending upon gauge and barrel. Plain pistol-grip stock with recoil pad, grooved slide handle. After 1973, these guns have checkered stock and slide handle, Models 500AM and 500AS have receivers etched with game scenes. The latter has swivels and sling. Made from 1962 to 1976.

Model 500A, 12 gauge.................................. **$150**
Model 500AM, 12 gauge, heavy magnum barrel........ **150**
Model 500AK, 12 gauge, C-Lect-Choke................ **185**
Model 500AS, 12 gauge, Slugster..................... **165**
Model 500B, 16 gauge................................. **150**
Model 500BK, 16 gauge, C-Lect-Choke................ **185**
Model 500BS, 16 gauge, Slugster..................... **150**
Model 500C, 20 gauge................................. **150**
Model 500CK, 20 gauge, C-Lect-Choke................ **185**
Model 500CS, 20 gauge, Slugster..................... **150**
Model 500E, 410 gauge................................ **150**
Model 500EK, 410 gauge, C-Lect-Choke............... **185**

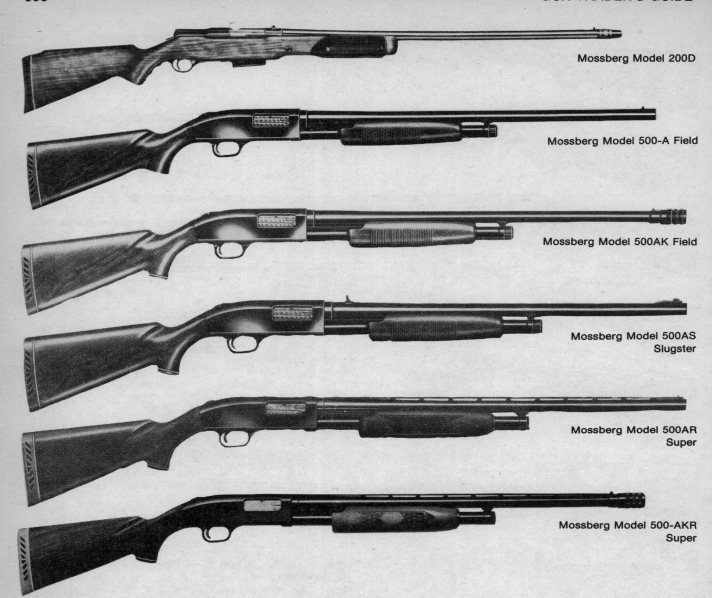

Mossberg Model 200D

Mossberg Model 500-A Field

Mossberg Model 500AK Field

Mossberg Model 500AS Slugster

Mossberg Model 500AR Super

Mossberg Model 500-AKR Super

Mossberg Model 500 Super Grade
Same as pre-1977 Model 500 Field Grade, except not made in 16 gauge, has ventilated-rib barrel, checkered pistol grip and slide handle. Made from 1965 to 1976.

Model 500AR, 12 gauge..............................**$210**
Model 500AMR, 12 gauge, heavy magnum barrel........ **235**
Model 500AKR, 12 gauge, C-Lect-Choke.............. **235**
Model 500CR, 20 gauge............................. **210**
Model 500CKR, 20 gauge, C-Lect-Choke.............. **235**
Model 500ER, 410 gauge............................ **210**
Model 500EKR, 410 gauge, C-Lect-Choke............. **235**

Mossberg Model 500ATR Super Grade
Trap Gun.. **$225**
Same as pre-1977 Model 500 Field Grade, except 12 gauge only, has ventilated-rib barrel—30-inch full choke; Monte Carlo stock with recoil pad, beavertail forearm (slide handle)—both checkered. Made from 1968 to 1971.

Mossberg Model 500 Pigeon Grade
Same as Model 500 Super Grade, except higher quality with fancy wood, floating ventilated rib; field gun hunting dog etching, trap and skeet guns have scroll etching. Barrels: 30-inch, full choke (12 gauge only); 28-inch, modified choke; 26-inch, skeet choke or C-Lect-Choke. Made from 1971 to 1975.

Model 500 APR, 12 gauge, Field, Trap or Skeet Gun... **$275**
Model 500 APKR, 12 gauge, Field Gun, C-Lect-Choke.. **300**
Model 500 CPR, 20 gauge, Field or Skeet Gun........ **275**
Model 500 EPR, 410 gauge, Field or Skeet Gun....... **300**

Mossberg Model 500APTR Pigeon Grade
Trap Gun.. **$300**
Same as Model 500APR Trap Gun, except has Monte Carlo style trap stock. Made from 1971 to 1975.

Mossberg Model 500DSPR Duck Stamp Commemorative $500

Limited edition of 1000 to commemorate the Migratory Bird Hunting Stamp Program. Same as Model 500DSPR Pigeon Grade 12 Gauge Magnum Heavy Duck Gun with heavy 30-inch ventilated-rib barrel, full choke; receiver has special Wood Duck etching. Gun accompanied by a special wall plaque. Made in 1975. *Note:* Value is for gun in new, unfired condition.

Mossberg Model 500 "L" Series

"L" in model designation. Same as pre-1977 Model 500 Field Grade, except not available in 16 gauge, has receiver etched with different game scenes; Accu-choke with three interchangeable tubes (improved cylinder, modified, full choke) is standard, restyled stock and slide handle. Barrels: plain or ventilated rib; 30-, 32-inch, heavy, full choke (12 gauge magnum and ventilated rib only), 28-inch, Accu-choke (12 and 20 gauge); 26-inch, full choke (410 gauge only), 18½-inch (12 gauge only), 24-inch (12 and 20 gauge) Slugster with rifle sights, cylinder bore. Weight: from 6 to 8½ pounds, depending upon gauge and barrel. Introduced in 1977.

Model 500ALD, 12 gauge, plain barrel (Disc. 1980).... **$190**
Model 500ALDR, 12 gauge, ventilated rib............. **200**

Model 500ALMR, 12 gauge, Heavy Duck Gun (Disc. 1980).. **$225**
Model 500ALS, 12 gauge, Slugster (Disc. 1981)....... **190**
Model 500CLD, 20 gauge, plain barrel (Disc. 1980)..... **190**
Model 500CLDR, 20 gauge, ventilated rib............. **200**
Model 500CLS, 20 gauge, Slugster (Disc. 1980)........ **190**
Model 500EL, 410 gauge, plain barrel (Disc. 1980)..... **190**
Model 500ELR, 410 gauge, ventilated rib............. **195**

Mossberg Model 500 "Persuader" Law Enforcement Shotgun

Similar to pre-1977 Model 500 Field Grade, except 12 gauge only, 6- or 8-shot, has 18½- or 20-inch plain barrel, cylinder bore, either shotgun or rifle sights, plain pistol-grip stock and grooved slide handle, sling swivels. Special Model 500ATP8-SP has bayonet lug, Parkerized finish. Currently manufactured.

Model 500ATP6, 6-shot, 18½-inch barrel, shotgun sights.. **$150**
Model 500ATP6S, 6-shot, 18½-barrel, rifle sights...... **190**
Model 500ATP8, 8-shot, 20-inch barrel, shotgun sights. **200**
Model 500ATP8S, 8-shot, 20-inch barrel, rifle sights.... **200**
Model 500ATP8-SP Special Enforcement Shotgun..... **225**

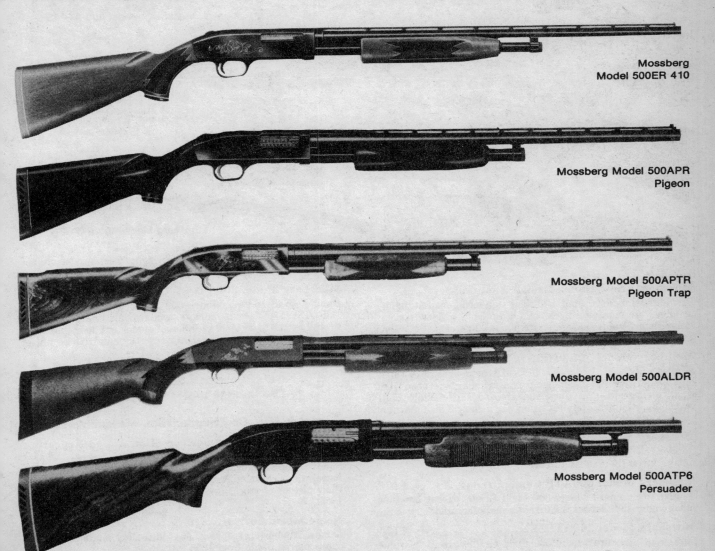

Mossberg Model 500ER 410

Mossberg Model 500APR Pigeon

Mossberg Model 500APTR Pigeon Trap

Mossberg Model 500ALDR

Mossberg Model 500ATP6 Persuader

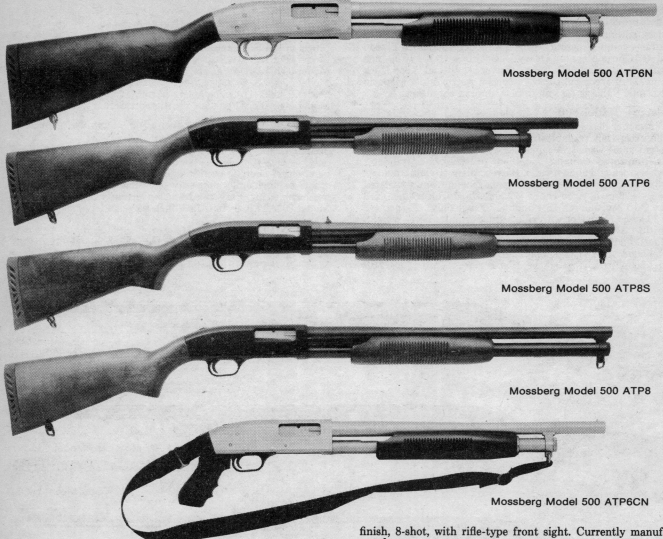

Mossberg Model 500 ATP6N

Mossberg Model 500 ATP6

Mossberg Model 500 ATP8S

Mossberg Model 500 ATP8

Mossberg Model 500 ATP6CN

Mossberg "New Haven Brand" Shotguns
Promotional models, similar to their standard guns but plainer in finish, are marketed by Mossberg under the "New Haven" brand name. Values generally are about 20 percent lower than for corresponding standard models.

Mossberg Model 500ATP6N................... **$190**
Similar to Standard Model 500 Field Grade, except 12 gauge only, 6-shot, has 18½-inch plain barrel, cylinder bore, bead front sight, plain-pistol grip stock and grooved slide handle, sling swivel, nickel finish. Handles either 2¾ inch or 3 inch magnum shells. Currently manufactured.

Mossberg Model 500ATP6.................... **$180**
Similar to Standard Model 500 Field Grade, except has blue finish. Currently manufactured.

Mossberg Model 500ATP8.................... **$170**
Similar to Standard Model 500 Field Grade, except has blue finish and 8-shot capacity. Currently manufactured.

Mossberg Model 500ATP8S.................... **$175**
Similar to Standard Model 500 Field Grade, except has blue finish, 8-shot, with rifle-type front sight. Currently manufactured.

Mossberg Model 500ATP6CN.................... **$190**
Similar to Standard Model 500 Field Grade, except new "CRUISER" pistol grip replaces standard butt stock, shortening overall length to 28 inches for 6-shot model and 30 inches on 8-shot version, and reducing weight by ¾ of a pound. Nickel finish. Currently manufactured.

Nikko Firearms Ltd., Togichi, Japan
See listings under Golden Eagle.

Noble Mfg. Co., Haydenville, Massachusetts

Noble Model 40 Hammerless Slide Action Repeating Shotgun... **$110**
Solid frame. 12 gauge only. 5-shell tubular magazine. 28-inch barrel with ventilated Multi-Choke. Weight, about 7½ pounds. Plain pistol-grip stock, grooved slide handle. Made from 1950 to 1955.

Noble Model 50.................................. **$105**
Same as Model 40, except without Multi-Choke. Modified or full choke barrel. Made from 1953 to 1955.

Noble Model 60 Hammerless Slide Action Repeating Shotgun..................................**$120**
Solid frame. 12 and 16 gauge. 5-shot tubular magazine. 28-inch barrel with adjustable choke. Plain pistol-grip stock with recoil pad, grooved slide handle. Weight, about 7½ pounds. Made from 1955 to 1966.

Noble Model 65..................................**$110**
Same as Model 60, except without adjustable choke and recoil pad. Modified or full choke barrel. Made from 1955 to 1966.

Noble Model 70CLP Hammerless Slide Action Repeating Shotgun..................................**$135**
Solid frame. 410 gauge. Magazine holds 5 shells. 26-inch barrel with adjustable choke. Weight, about 6 pounds. Checkered buttstock and forearm, recoil pad. Made from 1958 to 1970.

Noble Model 70XL..................................**$115**
Same as Model 70CLP, except without adjustable choke and checkering on buttstock. Made from 1958 to 1970.

Noble Model 70RCLP..................................**$155**
Same as Model 70CLP, except has ventilated rib. Made from 1967 to 1970.

Noble Model 70RLP..................................**$140**
Same as Model 70CLP, except has ventilated rib and no adjustable choke. Made from 1967 to 1970.

Noble Model 602RCLP Hammerless Slide Action Repeating Shotgun..................................**$150**
Solid frame. Key lock fire control mechanism. 20 gauge. 3-inch chamber. 5-shot tubular magazine. 28-inch barrel, ventilated rib, adjustable choke. Weight, about 6½ pounds. Checkered pistol-grip stock and slide handle, recoil pad. Made from 1967 to 1970.

Noble Model 602RLP..................................**$140**
Same as Model 602RCLP, except without adjustable choke, bored full or modified choke. Made from 1967 to 1970.

Noble Model 602CLP..................................**$130**
Same as Model 602RCLP, except has plain barrel. Made from 1958 to 1970.

Noble Model 662..................................**$160**
Same as Model 602CLP, except has aluminum receiver and barrel; weight, about 4½ pounds. Made from 1966 to 1970.

Noble Model 602XL..................................**$110**
Same as Model 602RCLP, except has plain barrel, full or modified choke, slide handle only checkered, no recoil pad. Made from 1958 to 1970.

Note: Series 602 and 70 are similar in appearance to the corresponding Model 66 guns.

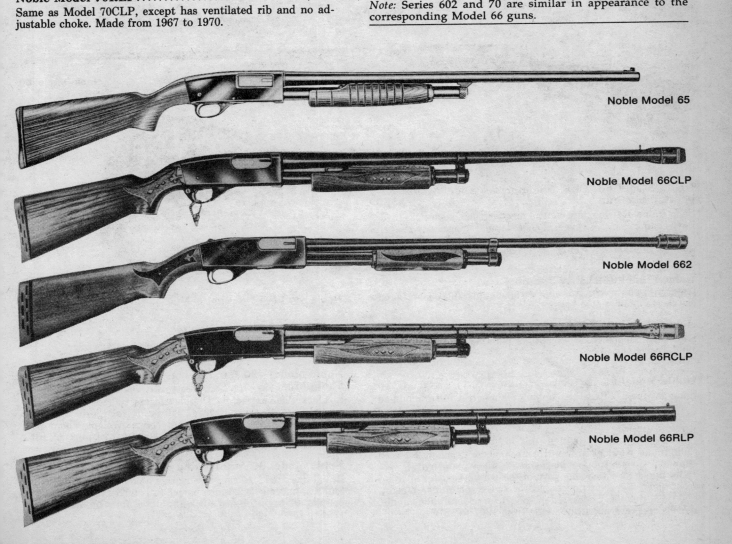

Noble Model 65

Noble Model 66CLP

Noble Model 662

Noble Model 66RCLP

Noble Model 66RLP

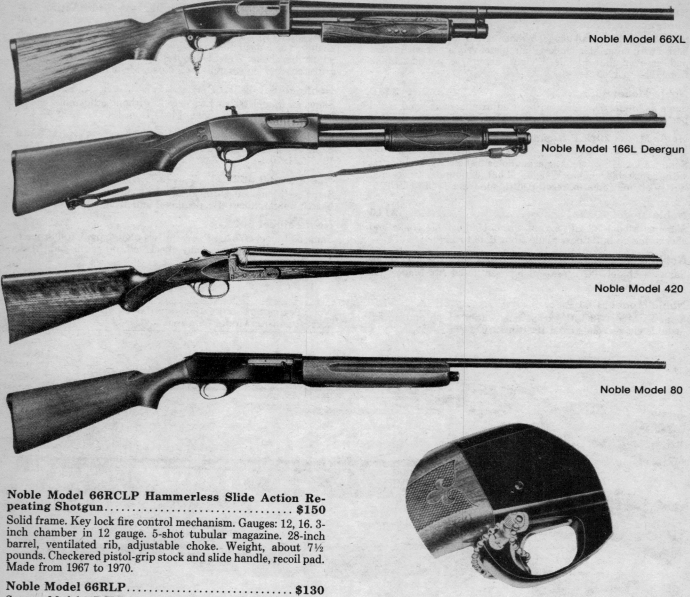

Noble Model 66XL

Noble Model 166L Deergun

Noble Model 420

Noble Model 80

Noble Key Lock Fire Control Mechanism

Noble Model 66RCLP Hammerless Slide Action Repeating Shotgun.................................. **$150**
Solid frame. Key lock fire control mechanism. Gauges: 12, 16. 3-inch chamber in 12 gauge. 5-shot tubular magazine. 28-inch barrel, ventilated rib, adjustable choke. Weight, about 7½ pounds. Checkered pistol-grip stock and slide handle, recoil pad. Made from 1967 to 1970.

Noble Model 66RLP.............................. **$130**
Same as Model 66RCLP, except without adjustable choke, bored full or modified choke. Made from 1967 to 1970.

Noble Model 66CLP.............................. **$135**
Same as Model 66RCLP, except has plain barrel. Introduced in 1967. Discontinued.

Noble Model 66XL.............................. **$115**
Same as Model 66RCLP, except has plain barrel, full or modified choke, slide handle only checkered, no recoil pad. Made from 1967 to 1970.

Noble Model 166L Deergun...................... **$140**
Solid frame. Key lock fire control mechanism. 12 gauge. 2¾-inch chamber. 5-shot tubular magazine. 24-inch plain barrel, specially bored for rifled slug. Lyman peep rear sight, post ramp front sight. Receiver dovetailed for scope mounting. Weight, about 7¼ pounds. Checkered pistol-grip stock and slide handle, swivels and carrying strap. Made from 1967 to 1970.

Noble Model 420 Hammerless Double Barrel Shotgun.. **$200**
Box lock. Plain extractors. Double triggers. Gauges: 12 ga. 3-inch mag., 16 ga., 20 ga. 3-inch mag., 410 ga. Barrels: 28-inch, except 410 in 26-inch, modified and full choke. Weight, about 6¾ pounds. Engraved frame. Checkered walnut stock and forearm. Made from 1958 to 1970.

Noble Model 80 Autoloading Shotgun............ **$175**
Recoil-operated. 410 gauge. Magazine holds three 3-inch shells, four 2½-inch shells. 26-inch barrel, full choke. Weight, about 6 pounds. Plain pistol-grip stock and fluted forearm. Made from 1964 to 1966.

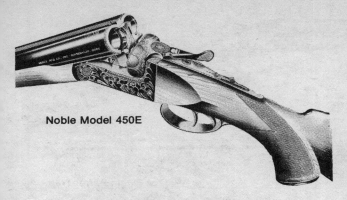

Noble Model 450E

Noble Model 450E Hammerless Double Barrel Shotgun $225

Box lock. Engraved frame. Selective automatic ejectors. Double triggers. Gauges: 12, 16, 20. 3-inch chambers in 12 and 20 gauge. 28-inch barrels, modified and full choke. Weight, about 6 lbs. 14 oz. in 12 gauge. Checkered pistol-grip stock and beavertail forearm, recoil pad. Made from 1967 to 1970.

Parker Brothers, Meriden, Connecticut. This firm was taken over by Remington Arms Company in 1934 and its production facilities removed to Remington's Ilion, New York plant

Parker Trojan Hammerless Double Barrel Shotgun

Box lock. Plain extractors. Double trigger or single trigger. Gauges: 12, 16, 20. Barrels: 30-inch both full choke (12 gauge only), 26- or 28-inch modified and full choke. Weight, 6¼ to 7¾ pounds depending upon gauge and barrel length. Checkered pistol-grip stock and forearm. Discontinued in 1939.

12 or 16 gauge......................................	$ 800
20 gauge..	1265

Parker Hammerless Double Barrel Shotguns

Grades V.H.E. through A-1 Special. Box lock. Automatic ejectors. Double triggers or selective single trigger. Gauges: 10, 12, 16, 20, 28, 410. Barrels: 26- to 32-inch, any standard boring. Weight, 6⅞ to 8½ pounds in 12 gauge. Stock and forearm of select walnut, checkered; straight, half- or full- pistol-grip. The various grades differ only in quality of workmanship, grade of wood, engraving, checkering, etc.; general specifications are the same for all. Discontinued about 1940.

V.H.E. Grade, 12 or 16 gauge........................	$ 2175
V.H.E. Grade, 20 gauge.............................	3000
V.H.E. Grade, 28 gauge.............................	5750
V.H.E. Grade, 410 gauge............................	7000
G.H.E. Grade, 12 or 16 gauge........................	2500
G.H.E. Grade, 20 gauge.............................	4500
G.H.E. Grade, 28 gauge.............................	6000
G.H.E. Grade, 410 gauge............................	9000
D.H.E. Grade, 12 or 16 gauge........................	3500
D.H.E. Grade, 20 gauge.............................	5400
D.H.E. Grade, 28 gauge.............................	6500
D.H.E. Grade, 410 gauge............................	15,000
C.H.E. Grade, 12 or 16 gauge........................	7000
C.H.E. Grade, 20 gauge.............................	10,500
C.H.E. Grade, 28 gauge.............................	18,200
C.H.E. Grade, 410 gauge............................	28,000
B.H.E. Grade, 12 or 16 gauge........................	6500
B.H.E. Grade, 20 gauge.............................	8000
B.H.E. Grade, 28 gauge.............................	10,000
B.H.E. Grade, 410 gauge............................	30,000
A.H.E. Grade, 12 or 16 gauge........................	6000
A.H.E. Grade, 20 gauge.............................	8000
A.H.E. Grade, 28 gauge.............................	15,000
A.A.H.E. Grade, 12 or 16 gauge......................	8000
A.A.H.E. Grade, 20 gauge...........................	12,000
A.A.H.E. Grade, 28 gauge...........................	25,000
A-1 Special Grade, 12 or 16 gauge....................	15,000
A-1 Special Grade, 20 gauge.........................	20,000
A-1 Special Grade, 28 gauge.........................	95,000

Nonejector guns, deduct 30 percent from values shown. Ventilated-rib barrels, add 20 percent to values shown.

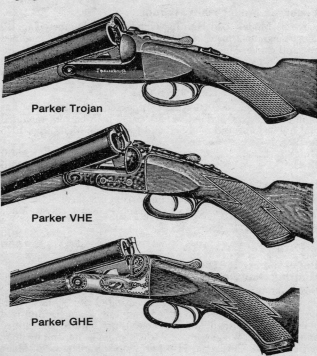

Parker Trojan

Parker VHE

Parker GHE

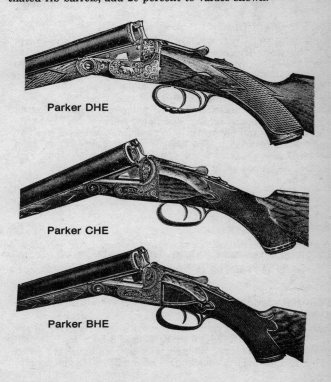

Parker DHE

Parker CHE

Parker BHE

Parker Skeet Gun

Parker Single Barrel Trap

Parker AHE

Parker AAHE

Parker A-1 Special

Parker Skeet Gun

Same as other Parker doubles from Grade V.H.E. up, except selective single trigger and beavertail forearm are standard on this model, as are 26-inch barrels, skeet choke. Discontinued about 1940. Values are 20 percent higher.

Parker Single Barrel Trap Guns

Hammerless. Box lock. Ejector. 12 gauge only. Barrel lengths: 30-, 32-, 34-inch; any boring. Ventilated rib. Weight, 7½ to 8½ pounds. Stock and forearm of select walnut, checkered; straight, half- or full-pistol grip. The five grades differ only in quality of workmanship, grade of wood, checkering, engraving, etc., general specifications same for all. Discontinued about 1940.

S.C. Grade.. $ 2000
S.B. Grade..   3000
S.A. Grade..   4200
S.A.A. Grade......................................   6200
S.A.1 Special..................................... 10,000

Pedersen Custom Guns, division of O. F. Mossberg & Sons, Inc., North Haven, Connecticut

Pedersen Model 1000 Over-and-Under Hunting Shotgun

Box lock. Automatic ejectors. Selective single trigger. Gauges: 12, 20, 2¾-inch chambers in 12 gauge, 3-inch in 20 gauge. Barrels: ventilated rib; 30-inch, modified and full (12 gauge only); 28-inch, improved cylinder and modified (12 gauge only),

modified and full; 26-inch, improved cylinder and modified choke. Checkered pistol-grip stock and forearm. Grade I is the higher quality gun with custom stock dimensions, fancier wood, more elaborate engraving, silver inlays. Made from 1973 to 1975.

Grade I.. $1780
Grade II... 1500

Pedersen Model 1000 Magnum

Same as Model 1000 Hunting Gun, except chambered for 12 gauge magnum 3-inch shells, 30-inch barrels, improved modified and full choke. Made from 1973 to 1975.

Grade I.. $1780
Grade II... 1525

Pedersen Model 1000 Trap Gun

Same as Model 1000 Hunting Gun, except 12 gauge only, has Monte Carlo trap-style stock, 30- or 32-inch barrels, modified and full or improved modified and full choke. Made from 1973 to 1975.

Grade I.. $1850
Grade II... 1525

Pedersen Model 1000 Skeet Gun

Same as Model 1000 Hunting Gun, except has skeet-style stock; barrels, 26-inch, 28-inch (12 gauge only), skeet choke. Made from 1973 to 1975.

Grade I.. $1900
Grade II... 1550

Pedersen Model 1500 Over-and-Under

Hunting Shotgun................................. $500

Box lock. Automatic ejectors. Selective single trigger. 12 gauge. 2¾- or 3-inch chambers. Barrels: ventilated rib; 30-inch, modified and full; 28-inch, modified and full; 26-inch, improved cylinder and modified; Magnum has 30-inch, improved modified and full choke. Weight, about 7 to 7½ pounds, depending upon barrel length. Checkered pistol-grip stock and forearm. Made from 1973 to 1975.

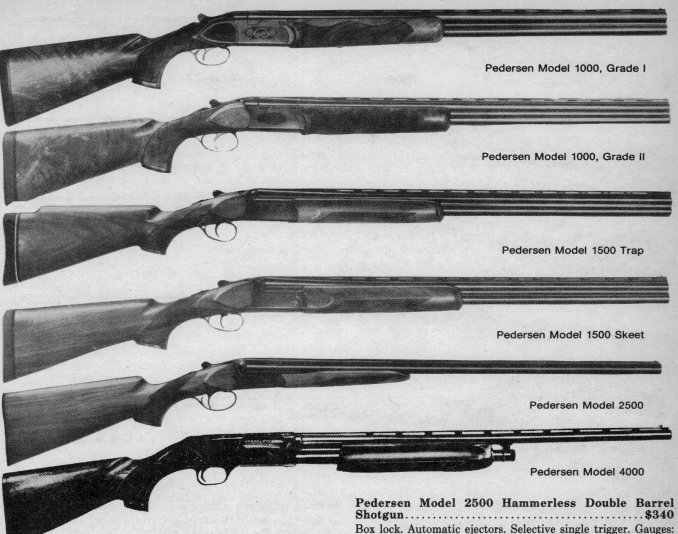

Pedersen Model 1000, Grade I

Pedersen Model 1000, Grade II

Pedersen Model 1500 Trap

Pedersen Model 1500 Skeet

Pedersen Model 2500

Pedersen Model 4000

Pedersen Model 1500 Trap Gun............... **$525**
Same as Model 1500 Hunting Gun, except has Monte Carlo trap-style stock, 30- or 32-inch barrels, modified and full or improved modified and full choke. Made from 1973 to 1975.

Pedersen Model 1500 Skeet Gun............... **$500**
Same as Model 1500 Hunting Gun, except has skeet-style stock, 27-inch barrels, skeet choke. Made from 1973 to 1975.

Pedersen Model 2000 Hammerless Double Barrel Shotgun
Box lock. Automatic ejectors. Selective single trigger. Gauges: 12, 20. 2¾-inch chambers in 12 gauge, 3-inch in 20 gauge. Barrels: ventilated rib; 30-inch, modified and full (12 gauge only); 28-inch, modified and full; 26-inch, improved cylinder and modified choke. Checkered pistol-grip stock and forearm. Grade I is the higher quality gun with custom dimensions, fancier wood, more elaborate engraving, silver inlays. Made from 1973 to 1974.
Grade I... **$1950**
Grade II.. **1500**

Pedersen Model 2500 Hammerless Double Barrel Shotgun... **$340**
Box lock. Automatic ejectors. Selective single trigger. Gauges: 12, 20. 2¾-inch chambers in 12 gauge, 3-inch in 20 gauge. Barrels: ventilated rib; 28-inch, modified and full; 26-inch, improved cylinder and modified choke. Checkered pistol-grip stock and forearm. Made from 1973 to 1974.

Pedersen Model 4000 Hammerless Slide Action Repeating Shotgun.................................. **$325**
Custom version of Mossberg Model 500. Full-coverage floral engraving on receiver. Gauges: 12, 20, 410. 3-inch chamber. Barrels: ventilated rib; 26-inch, improved cylinder or skeet choke; 28-inch, full or modified; 30-inch, full. Weight: from about 6 to 8 pounds, depending upon gauge and barrel. Checkered stock and slide handle of select wood. Made in 1975.

Pedersen Model 4000 Trap Gun............... **$325**
Same as standard Model 4000, except 12 gauge only, has 30-inch full choke barrel, Monte Carlo trap-style stock with recoil pad. Made in 1975.

Pedersen Model 4500........................... **$310**
Same as Model 4000, except has simpler scroll engraving. Made in 1975.

Pedersen Model 4500 Trap Gun............... **$340**
Same as Model 4000 Trap Gun, except has simpler scroll engraving. Made in 1975.

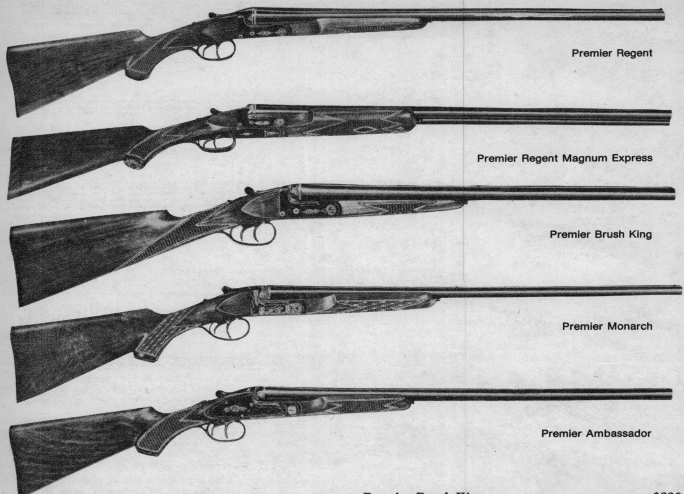

Premier Regent

Premier Regent Magnum Express

Premier Brush King

Premier Monarch

Premier Ambassador

Manifattura Armi Perazzi, Brescia, Italy
See listings under Ithaca.

Premier Shotguns, Brooklyn, New York

Premier Regent Model Field Grade Hammerless Double Barrel Shotgun **$225**
Box lock. Plain extractors. Double triggers. Gauges: 12, 16, 20, 28, 410. 3-inch chambers in 20 and 410 gauge, 2¾-inch in other gauges. Barrels: 26-inch, improved cylinder and modified, modified and full (28 and 410 gauge only); 28-inch, modified and full; 30-inch, modified and full (12 gauge only). Weight: 6 lbs. 2 oz. to 7 lbs. 4 oz., depending upon gauge and barrel. Checkered pistol-grip stock and beavertail forearm. Made from 1955 to date.

Premier Regent 12 Gauge Magnum Express **$250**
Same as standard Regent Model, except chambered for 12 gauge magnum 3-inch shells, has 30-inch barrels choked full and full, stock with recoil pad; weight, 7¼ pounds. Made from 1957 to date.

Premier Regent 10 Gauge Magnum Express **$275**
Same as standard Regent Model, except chambered for 10 gauge magnum 3½-inch shells, has heavier construction, 32-inch barrels choked full and full, stock with recoil pad; weight, 11¼ pounds. Made from 1957 to date.

Premier Brush King **$230**
Same as standard Regent Model, except chambered for 12 (2¾-inch) and 20 gauge (3-inch) only; has 22-inch barrels, improved cylinder and modified choke, straight-grip stock; weight, about 6 lbs. 3 oz. in 12 gauge, 5 lbs. 12 oz. in 20 gauge. Made from 1959 to date.

Premier Monarch Supreme Grade Hammerless Double Barrel Shotgun **$365**
Box lock. Automatic ejectors. Double triggers. Gauges: 12, 20. 2¾-inch chambers in 12 gauge, 3-inch in 20 gauge. Barrels: 28-inch, modified and full; 26-inch, improved cylinder and modified choke. Weight: from 6 lbs. 6 oz. to 7 lbs. 2 oz., depending upon gauge and barrel. Checkered pistol-grip stock and beavertail forearm of fancy walnut. Made from 1959 to date.

Premier Presentation Custom Grade **$850**
Similar to Monarch model, but made to order; of higher quality with hunting scene engraving gold- and silver-inlaid, fancier wood. Made from 1959 to date.

Premier Ambassador Model Field Grade Hammerless Double Barrel Shotgun **$310**
Side lock. Plain extractors. Double triggers. Gauges: 12, 16, 20, 410. 3-inch chambers in 20 and 410 gauge, 2¾-inch in 12 and 16 gauge. Barrels: 26-inch in 410 gauge, 28-inch in other gauges; choked modified and full. Weight: from about 6 lbs. 3 oz. to 7 lbs. 3 oz. depending upon gauge. Checkered pistol-grip stock and beavertail forearm. Made from 1957 to date.

Premier Continental

Purdey Over-and-Under

Purdey Single Barrel Trap

Premier Continental Model Field Grade Hammer Double Barrel Shotgun............................. $300

Side lock. Exposed hammers. Plain extractors. Double triggers. Gauges: 12, 16, 20, 410. 3-inch chambers in 20 and 410 gauge, 2¾-inch in 12 and 16 gauge. Barrels: 26-inch in 410 gauge; 28-inch in other gauges; choked modified and full. Weight: from about 6 lbs. 3 oz. to 7 lbs. 3 oz., depending upon gauge. Checkered pistol-grip stock and English-style forearm. Made from 1957 to date.

Note: Premier shotguns have been produced by various gunmakers in Italy and Spain.

Purdey Double Barrel

James Purdey & Sons, Ltd., London, England

Purdey Hammerless Double Barrel Shotgun

Side lock. Automatic ejectors. Double triggers or single trigger. Gauges: 12, 16, 20. Barrels: 26-, 27-, 28-, 30-inch (latter in 12 gauge only); any boring, any shape or style of rib. Weight, from 5¼ to 6½ pounds depending upon model, gauge and barrel length. Checkered stock and forearm, straight grip standard, pistol-grip also available. Purdey guns of this type have been made from about 1880 to date. Models include: Game Gun, Featherweight Game Gun, Two-Inch Gun (chambered for 12 gauge 2-inch shells), Pigeon Gun (with 3rd fastening and side clips); values of all models are the same.

With double triggers............................. $14,000
With single trigger.............................. 19,000

Purdey Over-and-Under Gun

Side lock. Automatic ejectors. Double triggers and single trigger. Gauges: 12, 16, 20. Barrels: 26-, 27-, 28, 30-inch (latter in 12 gauge only); any boring, any style rib. Weight, from 6 to 7½ pounds depending upon gauge and barrel length. Checkered stock and fore-end, straight or pistol grip. Prior to World War II, the Purdey Over-and-Under Gun was made with a Purdey action; since the war James Purdey & Sons have acquired the business of James Woodward & Sons and all Purdey Over-and-Under Guns are now built on the Woodward principle. General specifications of both types are the same.

With Purdey action, double triggers.............. $15,000
With Woodward action, double triggers........... 18,000
Single trigger, extra............................ 1000

Purdey Single Barrel Trap Gun.............. $15,000

Side lock. Mechanical features similar to those of the Over-and-Under model with Purdey action. 12 gauge only. Built to customer's specifications. Made prior to World War II.

Remington Arms Co., Ilion, New York

Remington New Model 1882 Hammer Double Barrel Shotgun... $385

Gauges: 10, 12, 16. Plain or Damascus barrels, 28- to 32-inch. Weight, 6¾ to 10¼ pounds, depending upon gauge and barrel length. Checkered pistol-grip stock and forearm. Made from 1882 to 1910. *Note:* Value shown is for standard grade; this model was made in six higher grades, varying in quality of workmanship, engraving, grade of wood, etc.

Remington Model 1889 Hammer Double Barrel Shotgun.. $575

Gauges: 10, 12, 16. Steel or Damascus barrels, 28- to 32-inch. Weight, 7 to 10 pounds, depending upon gauge and barrel length. Checkered pistol-grip stock and forearm. Made from 1889 to 1908.

Remington Rider No. 3 Single Barrel Shotgun.. $160

Semi-hammerless. Gauges: 10, 12, 16, 20, 24, 28. Plain barrel, 30- to 32-inch. Weight, about 6 pounds. Plain pistol-grip stock and forearm. Made from 1893 to 1903.

Remington Rider No. 9 Single Barrel Shotgun.. $150

Improved version of No. 3 Single; same general specifications, except has automatic ejector. Made from 1902 to 1910.

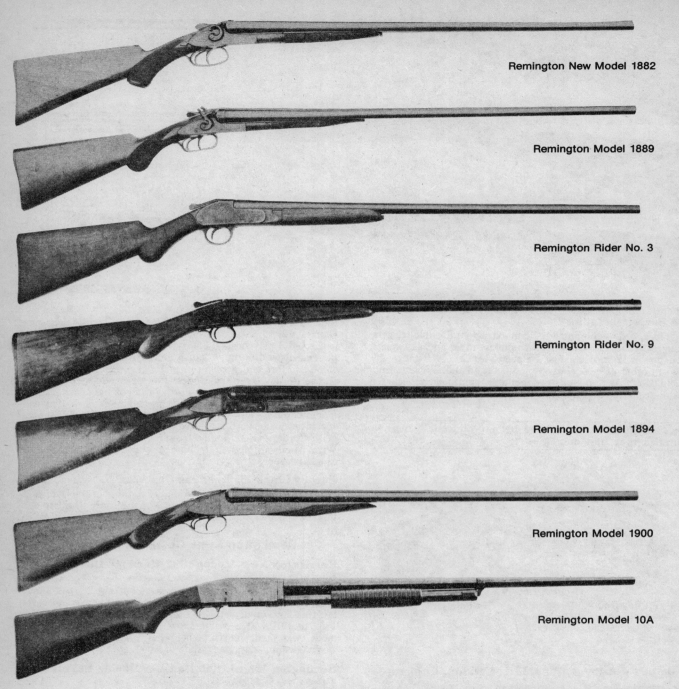

Remington New Model 1882

Remington Model 1889

Remington Rider No. 3

Remington Rider No. 9

Remington Model 1894

Remington Model 1900

Remington Model 10A

Remington Model 1894 Hammerless Double Barrel Shotgun **$800**
Box lock. Automatic ejector. Double triggers. Gauges: 10, 12, 16. Ordnance steel barrels, 28- to 32-inch. Weight, 7 to 10 pounds, depending upon gauge and barrel length. Checkered stock and forearm. Made from 1894 to 1910. *Note:* This model was made in seven higher grades, including a trap gun; these, of course, have a higher value than the standard grade for which valuation is given. Guns with Damascus barrels have about 50 percent lower value.

Remington Model 1900 Hammerless Double Barrel Shotgun **$690**
Improved version of Model 1894. Same general specifications as that model. Made from 1900 to 1910. Value shown is for standard grade with ordnance steel barrels; see note under Model 1894.

Remington Model 10A Standard Grade Slide Action Repeating Shotgun **$290**
Hammerless. Takedown. 6-shot. 12 gauge only. 5-shell tubular magazine. Barrels: plain, 26- to 32-inch; chokes: full, modified or cylinder bore. Weight, about 7½ pounds. Plain pistol-grip stock, grooved slide handle. Made from 1907 to 1929.

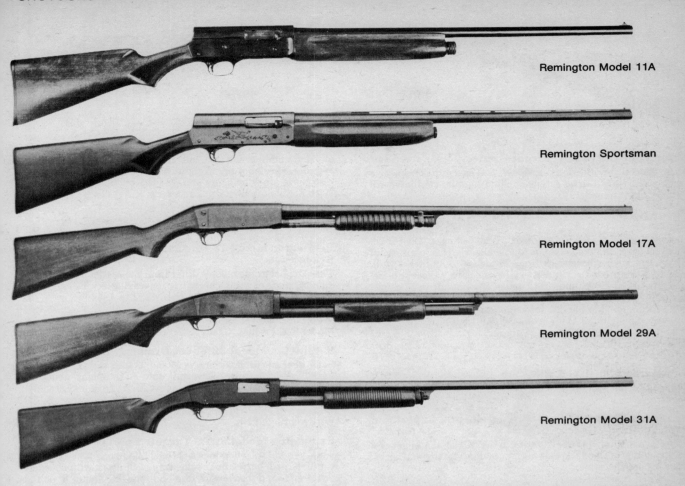

Remington Model 11A

Remington Sportsman

Remington Model 17A

Remington Model 29A

Remington Model 31A

Remington Model 11A Standard Grade 5-Shot Auto-loader

Hammerless. Browning type. Takedown. Gauges: 12, 16, 20. Tubular magazine holds four shells. Barrels: plain, solid rib or ventilated rib; lengths from 26 inches to 32 inches; full, modified, improved cylinder, cylinder bore, skeet choke. Weights: about 8 pounds in 12 gauge, about 7½ pounds in 16 gauge, about 7¼ pounds in 20 gauge. Checkered pistol grip and fore-end. Made from 1905 to 1949.

With plain barrel.................................. **$160**
With solid-rib barrel.............................. **190**
With ventilated-rib barrel........................ **220**

Remington Model 11R Riot Gun................. **$175**

Same as Model 11A Standard Grade, except has 20-inch plain barrel, 12 gauge only.

Remington Model 11 Special, Tournament, Expert and Premier Grade Guns

These higher grade models differ from the Model 11A in general quality, grade of wood, checkering, engraving, etc. General specifications are the same.

Model 11B Special Grade...........................**$ 250**
Model 11D Tournament Grade....................... **600**
Model 11E Expert Grade............................ **870**
Model 11F Premier Grade........................... **1200**

Remington Sportsman A Standard Grade 3-Shot Auto-loader

Same general specifications as Model 11A, except magazine holds two shells. Also available in "B" Special Grade, "D" Tournament Grade, "E" Expert Grade, "F" Premier Grade. Made from 1931 to 1948. Values same as shown for Model 11A, etc.

Remington Sportsman Skeet Gun

Same general specifications as the Sportsman A, except has 26-inch barrel (plain, solid rib or ventilated rib), skeet boring, beavertail fore-end. Discontinued 1949.

With plain barrel................................... **$310**
With solid-rib barrel.............................. **340**
With ventilated-rib barrel......................... **375**

Remington Model 17A Standard Grade Slide Action Repeating Shotgun................................ **$225**

Hammerless. Takedown. 5-shot. 20 gauge only. 4-shell tubular magazine. Barrels: plain, 26- to 32-inch; chokes: full, modified or cylinder bore. Weight, about 5¾ pounds. Plain pistol-grip stock, grooved slide handle. Made from 1921 to 1933. *Note:* The present Ithaca Model 37 is an adaptation of this Browning design.

Remington Model 29A Standard Grade Slide Action Repeating Shotgun................................ **$300**

Hammerless. Takedown. 6-shot. 12 gauge only. 5-shell tubular magazine. Barrels: plain, 26- to 32-inch; chokes: full, modified or cylinder bore. Weight, about 7½ pounds. Checkered pistol-grip stock and slide handle. Made from 1929 to 1933.

Remington Model 32A

Remington Model 29T Target Grade.............$340
Same general specifications as Model 29A, except has trap-style stock with straight grip, extension slide handle, ventilated-rib barrel. Discontinued 1933.

Remington Model 31A Standard Grade Slide Action Repeater
Hammerless. Takedown. 3-shot or 5-shot. Gauges: 12, 16, 20. Tubular magazine holds two or four shells. Barrels: plain, solid rib or ventilated rib; lengths from 26 inches to 32 inches; full, modified, improved cylinder, cylinder bore, skeet choke. Weights: about 7½ pounds in 12 gauge, 6¾ pounds in 16 gauge, 6½ pounds in 20 gauge. Earlier models have checkered pistol-grip stock and slide handle: later models have plain stock and grooved slide handle. Made from 1931 to 1949.
With plain barrel....................................... $260
With solid-rib barrel.................................. 350
With ventilated-rib barrel............................ 375

Remington Model 31R Riot Gun.................$210
Same as Model 31A, except has 20-inch plain barrel, 12 gauge only.

Remington Model 31 Special, Tournament, Expert and Premier Grade Guns
These higher grade models differ from the Model 31A in general quality, grade of wood, checkering, engraving, etc. General specifications are the same.
Model 31B Special Grade............................$ 390
Model 31D Tournament Grade...................... 790
Model 31E Expert Grade............................ 1140
Model 31F Premier Grade.......................... 1700

Remington Model 31TC Trap Grade.............$640
Same general specifications as Model 31A, except 12 gauge only, has 30- or 32-inch ventilated-rib barrel, full choke, trap stock with full pistol grip and recoil pad, extension beavertail fore-end, both checkered, weighs about 8 pounds.

Remington Model 31S Trap Special.............$420
Same general specifications as Model 31TC, except has solid-rib barrel, half-pistol-grip stock and fore-end of standard walnut.

Remington Model 31H Hunters' Special........ $390
Same as Model 31S, except has sporting-style stock (shorter and with more drop).

Remington Model 31 Skeet Grade
Same general specifications as Model 31A, except has 26-inch barrel with raised solid rib or ventilated rib, skeet boring, checkered pistol-grip stock and beavertail fore-end, weighs about 8 pounds in 12 gauge.
With raised solid rib.................................. $480
With ventilated rib.................................... 800

Remington Model 32A Standard Grade Over-and-Under Gun
Hammerless. Takedown. Automatic ejectors. Early model had double triggers, later built with selective single trigger only. 12 gauge only. Barrels: plain, raised matted solid rib, ventilated rib; 26-, 28-, 30-, 32-inch; full and modified choke standard, option of any combination of full, modified, improved cylinder, cylinder, skeet boring. Weight, about 7¾ pounds. Checkered pistol-grip stock and fore-end. Made from 1932 to 1942.
With double triggers................................. $660
With selective single trigger......................... 900
Extra for raised solid rib............................. 75
Extra for ventilated rib.............................. 125

Remington Model 32 Tournament, Expert and Premier Grade Guns
These higher grade models differ from the Model 32A in general quality, grade of wood, checkering, engraving, etc. General specifications are the same. Made from 1932 to 1942.
Model 32D Tournament Grade.....................$1800
Model 32E Expert Grade............................ 2500
Model 32F Premier Grade.......................... 2800

Remington Model 32 Skeet Grade
Same general specifications as Model 32A, except 26- or 28-inch barrel, skeet boring, beavertail fore-end, weighs about 7½ pounds, selective single trigger only. Made from 1932 to 1942.
With plain barrels....................................$1100
With raised solid rib................................. 1200
With ventilated rib.................................. 1350

Remington Model 32TC Target (Trap) Grade
Same general specifications as Model 32A, except 30- or 32-inch ventilated-rib barrel, full choke, trap-style stock with checkered pistol-grip and beavertail fore-end, weighs about 8 pounds. Made from 1932 to 1942.
With double triggers.................................$1150
With selective single trigger......................... 1350

Remington Sportsman-48A Standard Grade 3-Shot Autoloader
Streamlined receiver. Hammerless. Takedown. Gauges: 12, 16, 20. Tubular magazine holds two shells. Barrels: plain, matted top surface or ventilated rib; 26-inch improved cylinder, 28-inch modified or full choke, 30-inch full choke (12 gauge only). Weights: about 7½ pounds in 12 gauge, about 6¾ pounds in 16 gauge, about 6½ pounds in 20 gauge. Pistol-grip stock, grooved fore-end, both checkered. Made from 1949 to 1959.
With plain barrel..................................... $210
With matted top-surface barrel...................... 225
With ventilated-rib barrel............................ 275

Remington Sportsman 48D

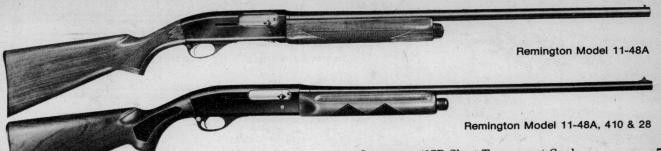

Remington Model 11-48A

Remington Model 11-48A, 410 & 28

Remington Sportsman-48 Special, Tournament and Premier Grade Guns

These higher grade models differ from the Sportsman-48A in general quality, grade of wood, checkering, engraving, etc. General specifications are the same. Made from 1949 to 1959.

Sportsman-48B Special Grade...................... $ 325
Sportsman-48D Tournament Grade.................. 685
Sportsman-48F Premier Grade...................... 1500

Remington Model 11-48A Standard Grade 5-Shot Autoloader

Same general specifications as Sportsman-48A, except magazine holds four shells, fore-end not grooved. Also available in Special Grade (11-48B), Tournament Grade (11-48D) and Premier Grade (11-48F). Made from 1949 to 1969. Prices same as shown for Sportsman-48A.

Remington Model 11-48A Standard Grade 4-Shot Autoloader, 410 & 28 Gauge

Same general specifications as Sportsman-48A, except gauge, 3-shell magazine, 25-inch barrel, weighs about 6¼ pounds. 28 gauge introduced 1952, 410 in 1954. Discontinued in 1969. Prices same as shown for Sportsman-48A.

Remingon Model 11-48A Riot Gun.............. $210

Same as Model 11-48A, except 20-inch plain barrel and 12 gauge only. Discontinued in 1969.

Remington Sportsman-48SA Skeet Gun

Same general specifications as Sportsman-48A, except has 26-inch barrel with matted top surface or ventilated rib, skeet choke, ivory bead front sight, metal bead rear sight. Made from 1949 to 1960.

With matted top-surface barrel..................... $ 245
With ventilated-rib barrel.......................... 290
Sportsman-48SC Skeet Target Grade................ 385

Sportsman-48SD Skeet Tournament Grade.......... 785
Sportsman-48SF Skeet Premier Grade.............. 1400

Remington Model 11-48SA 28 Gauge
Skeet Gun...................................... $395

Same general specifications as Model 11-48A 28 Gauge, except has 25-inch ventilated-rib barrel, skeet choke. 28 gauge introduced 1952, 410 in 1954.

Remington Wingmaster Model 870AP Standard Grade 5-Shot Slide Action Repeater

Hammerless. Takedown. Gauges: 12, 16, 20. Tubular magazine holds four shells. Barrels: plain, matted top surface or ventilated rib; 26-inch improved cylinder, 28-inch modified or full choke, 30-inch full choke (12 gauge only). Weights: about 7 pounds in 12 gauge, about 6¾ pounds in 16 gauge, about 6½ pounds in 20 gauge. Plain pistol-grip stock, grooved fore-end. Made from 1950 to 1963.

With plain barrel................................. $ 165
With matted top-surface barrel..................... 180
With ventilated-rib barrel......................... 185
Left-hand model.................................. 185

Remington Model 870 Wingmaster Field Gun

Same general specifications as Model 870AP, except checkered stock and fore-end. Made from 1964 to date.

With plain barrel................................. $190
With ventilated-rib barrel   220

Remington Wingmaster Model 870 Magnum Standard Grade................................ $190

Same as Model 870AP, except chambered for 12 gauge 3-inch magnum, 30-inch full choke barrel, recoil pad, weighs about 8¼ pounds. Made from 1955 to 1963.

Remington Wingmaster Model 870 Magnum Deluxe Grade................................... $205

Same as Model 870 Magnum Standard Grade, except has checkered stock and extension beavertail forearm, barrel with matted top surface. Discontinued in 1963.

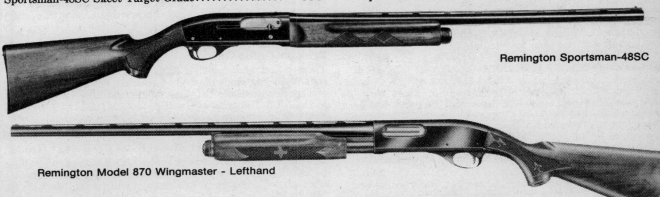

Remington Sportsman-48SC

Remington Model 870 Wingmaster - Lefthand

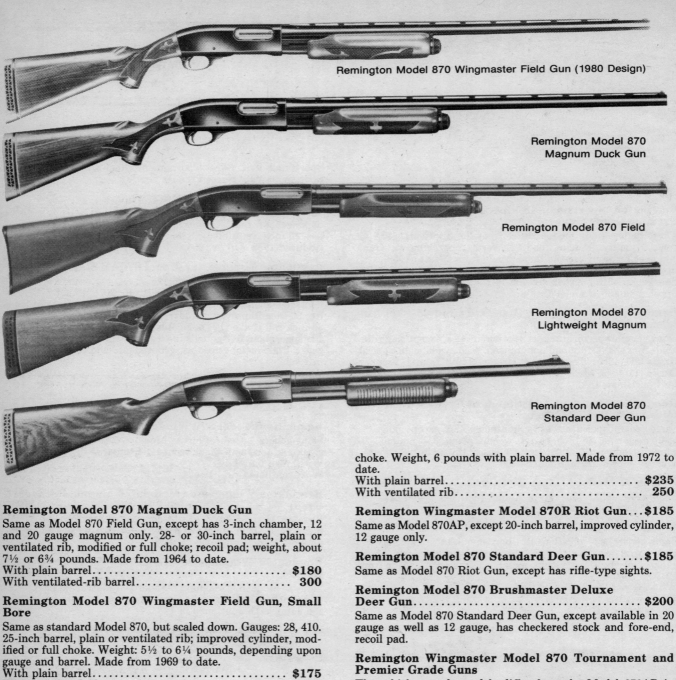

Remington Model 870 Wingmaster Field Gun (1980 Design)

Remington Model 870 Magnum Duck Gun

Remington Model 870 Field

Remington Model 870 Lightweight Magnum

Remington Model 870 Standard Deer Gun

Remington Model 870 Magnum Duck Gun

Same as Model 870 Field Gun, except has 3-inch chamber, 12 and 20 gauge magnum only. 28- or 30-inch barrel, plain or ventilated rib, modified or full choke; recoil pad; weight, about 7½ or 6¾ pounds. Made from 1964 to date.

With plain barrel..................................... **$180**
With ventilated-rib barrel............................ **300**

Remington Model 870 Wingmaster Field Gun, Small Bore

Same as standard Model 870, but scaled down. Gauges: 28, 410. 25-inch barrel, plain or ventilated rib; improved cylinder, modified or full choke. Weight: 5½ to 6¼ pounds, depending upon gauge and barrel. Made from 1969 to date.

With plain barrel..................................... **$175**
With ventilated rib................................... **190**

Remington Model 870 Lightweight

Same as standard Model 870, but with scaled-down receiver and lightweight mahogany stock; 20 gauge only. 2¾-inch chamber. Barrels: plain or ventilated rib; 26-inch, improved cylinder; 28-inch, modified or full choke. Weight: 5¾ pounds with 26-inch plain barrel. Made from 1972 to date.

With plain barrel..................................... **$200**
With ventilated rib................................... **225**

Remington Model 870 Lightweight Magnum

Same as Model 870 Lightweight, but chambered for 20 gauge magnum 3-inch shell; 28-inch barrel, plain or ventilated rib, full

choke. Weight, 6 pounds with plain barrel. Made from 1972 to date.

With plain barrel..................................... **$235**
With ventilated rib................................... **250**

Remington Wingmaster Model 870R Riot Gun...$185

Same as Model 870AP, except 20-inch barrel, improved cylinder, 12 gauge only.

Remington Model 870 Standard Deer Gun.......$185

Same as Model 870 Riot Gun, except has rifle-type sights.

Remington Model 870 Brushmaster Deluxe Deer Gun.. $200

Same as Model 870 Standard Deer Gun, except available in 20 gauge as well as 12 gauge, has checkered stock and fore-end, recoil pad.

Remington Wingmaster Model 870 Tournament and Premier Grade Guns

These higher grade models differ from the Model 870AP in general quality, grade of wood, checkering, engraving, etc. General specifications are the same. Made from 1950 to date.

Model 870D Tournament Grade.....................$1080
Model 870F Premier Grade......................... 2160
Model 870F Premier Grade with gold inlay........... 3175

Remington Wingmaster Model 870ADL Deluxe Grade

Same general specifications as Model 870AP, except has pistol-grip stock and extension beavertail fore-end, both finely checkered; matted top surface or ventilated-rib barrel. Made from 1950 to 1963.

With matted top-surface barrel.......................$185
With ventilated-rib barrel............................ 205

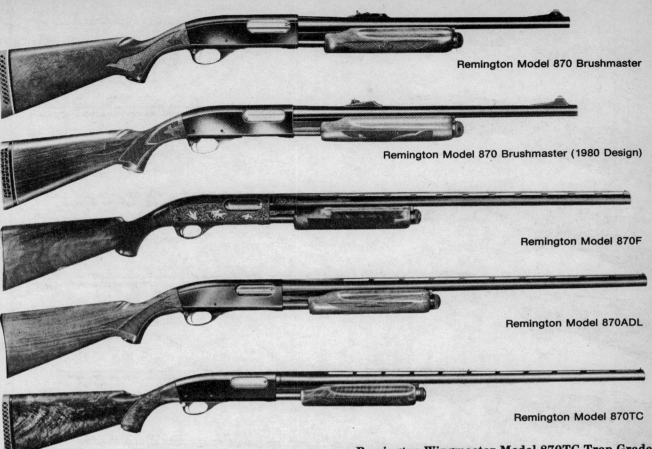

Remington Model 870 Brushmaster

Remington Model 870 Brushmaster (1980 Design)

Remington Model 870F

Remington Model 870ADL

Remington Model 870TC

Remington Wingmaster Model 870BDL Deluxe Special Grade

Same as Model 870ADL, except selected American walnut stock and fore-end. Made from 1950 to 1963.
With matted top-surface barrel........................$200
With ventilated-rib barrel............................ 225

Remington Wingmaster Model 870SA Skeet Gun

Same general specifications as Model 870AP, except has 26-inch ventilated-rib barrel, skeet boring, ivory bead front sight, metal bead rear sight, pistol-grip stock and extension beavertail fore-end, both finely checkered, weighs 6¾ to 7½ pounds depending upon gauge. Made from 1950 to date.
Model 870SA Skeet Grade (Disc. 1982)............. $ 210
Model 870SC Skeet Target Grade (Disc. 1980)........ 355
Model 870SD Skeet Tournament Grade.............. 1080
Model 870SF Skeet Premier Grade................. 2000

Remington Model 870SA Skeet Gun, Small Bore.......................................$225

Similar to Model 870SA, except chambered for 28 and 410 gauge (2½-inch chamber for latter); 25-inch ventilated-rib barrel, skeet choke. Weight: 6 pounds in 28 gauge, 6½ pounds in 410. Made from 1969 to date.

Remington Wingmaster Model 870TB Trap Special.......................................$250

Same general specifications as Model 870AP, except has 28-or 30-inch ventilated-rib barrel, full choke, metal bead front sight, no rear sight, "Special" grade trap-style stock and fore-end, both checkered, recoil pad, weighs about 8 pounds. Made from 1950 to 1981.

Remington Wingmaster Model 870TC Trap Grade

Same as Model 870TB, except higher grade walnut in stock and fore-end, has both front and rear sights. Made from 1950 to 1979.
Model 870TC Trap Grade........................... $ 390
Model 870TD Trap Tournament Grade.............. 1080
Model 870TF Trap Premier Grade.................. 2040

Remington Model 870 Competition Trap.........$390

Based on standard Model 870 receiver, except is a single-shot with a gas-assisted recoil-reducing system, new choke design, a high step-up ventilated rib and redesigned stock and fore-end with cut checkering and a satin finish. Weight: 8½ pounds. Made from 1981 to date.

Remington Model 870 "All American"

Remington Model 870 "All American" Trap Gun...$560

Same as Model 870TB, except custom grade with engraved receiver, trigger guard and barrel; Monte Carlo or straight-comb stock and fore-end of fancy walnut; available only with 30-inch full choke barrel. Made from 1972 to 1977.

Note: Remington changed the stock styling for all Model 870 shotguns in 1980.

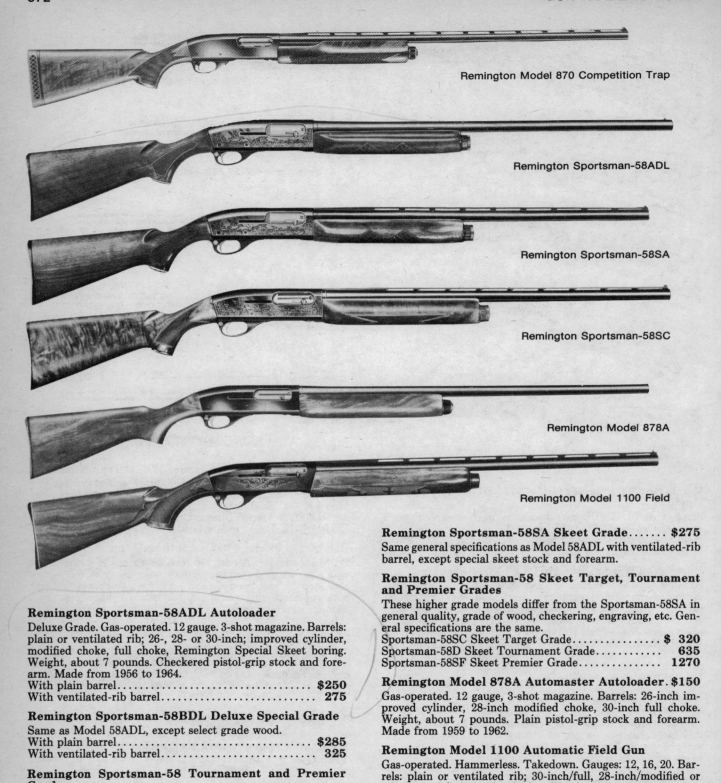

Remington Model 870 Competition Trap

Remington Sportsman-58ADL

Remington Sportsman-58SA

Remington Sportsman-58SC

Remington Model 878A

Remington Model 1100 Field

Remington Sportsman-58ADL Autoloader

Deluxe Grade. Gas-operated. 12 gauge. 3-shot magazine. Barrels: plain or ventilated rib; 26-, 28- or 30-inch; improved cylinder, modified choke, full choke, Remington Special Skeet boring. Weight, about 7 pounds. Checkered pistol-grip stock and forearm. Made from 1956 to 1964.

With plain barrel.................................... $250
With ventilated-rib barrel........................... 275

Remington Sportsman-58BDL Deluxe Special Grade

Same as Model 58ADL, except select grade wood.

With plain barrel.................................... $285
With ventilated-rib barrel........................... 325

Remington Sportsman-58 Tournament and Premier Grades

These higher grade models differ from the Sportsman-58ADL with ventilated-rib barrel in general quality, grade of wood, checkering, engraving, etc. General specifications are the same.

Sportsman-58D Tournament Grade................... $ 690
Sportsman-58F Premier Grade...................... 1300

Remington Sportsman-58SA Skeet Grade....... $275

Same general specifications as Model 58ADL with ventilated-rib barrel, except special skeet stock and forearm.

Remington Sportsman-58 Skeet Target, Tournament and Premier Grades

These higher grade models differ from the Sportsman-58SA in general quality, grade of wood, checkering, engraving, etc. General specifications are the same.

Sportsman-58SC Skeet Target Grade................ $ 320
Sportsman-58D Skeet Tournament Grade............ 635
Sportsman-58SF Skeet Premier Grade.............. 1270

Remington Model 878A Automaster Autoloader. $150

Gas-operated. 12 gauge, 3-shot magazine. Barrels: 26-inch improved cylinder, 28-inch modified choke, 30-inch full choke. Weight, about 7 pounds. Plain pistol-grip stock and forearm. Made from 1959 to 1962.

Remington Model 1100 Automatic Field Gun

Gas-operated. Hammerless. Takedown. Gauges: 12, 16, 20. Barrels: plain or ventilated rib; 30-inch/full, 28-inch/modified or full, 26-inch/improved cylinder. Weights, average 7¼ to 7½ pounds, depending upon gauge and barrel length. Checkered pistol-grip stock and forearm. Made from 1963 to date.

With plain barrel.................................... $265
With ventilated-rib barrel........................... 270
Left-hand action.................................... 285

Remington Model 1100 Lightweight

Remington Model 1100 Lightweight (1979 Model)

Remington Model 1100 - Lefthand Action

Remington Model 1100

Magnum Duck Gun

Remington Model 1100 Deer Gun

Remington Model 1100 Deer Gun (1979 Model)

Remington Model 1100 Field Grade, Small Bore
Same as standard Model 1100, but scaled down. Gauges: 28, 410. 25-inch barrel, plain or ventilated rib; improved cylinder, modified or full choke. Weight: 6¼ to 7 pounds, depending upon gauge and barrel. Made from 1969 to date.

With plain barrel.................................... **$275**
With ventilated rib................................... 290

Remington Model 1100 Lightweight
Same as standard Model 1100, but scaled-down receiver and lightweight mahogany stock; 20 gauge only, 2¾-inch chamber. Barrels: plain or ventilated rib; 26-inch, improved cylinder; 28-inch, modified and full choke. Weight, about 6¼ pounds. Made from 1971 to date.

With plain barrel.................................... **$270**
With ventilated rib................................... 295

Remingon Model 1100 Lightweight Magnum
Same as Model 1100 Lightweight, but chambered for 20 gauge magnum 3-inch shell; 28-inch barrel, plain or ventilated rib, full choke. Weight, about 6½ pounds. Made from 1971 to date.

With plain barrel..................................... **$285**
With ventilated rib................................... 300

Note: New stock checkering patterns and receiver scroll markings were incorporated on all standard Model 1100 field, magnum, skeet and trap models in 1979.

Remington Model 1100 Magnum Duck Gun
Same as Model 1100 Field Gun, except has 3-inch chamber, 12 and 20 gauge magnum only. 30-inch plain or ventilated-rib barrel in 12 gauge, 28-inch in 20 gauge; modified or full choke. Recoil pad. Weight, about 7¾ pounds. Made from 1963 to date.

With plain barrel..................................... **$330**
With ventilated-rib barrel............................ 345

Remington Model 1100 Deer Gun................$325
Same as Model 1100 Field Gun, except has 22-inch barrel, improved cylinder, with rifle-type sights; 12 and 20 gauge only; recoil pad; weighs about 7¼ pounds. Made from 1963 to date.

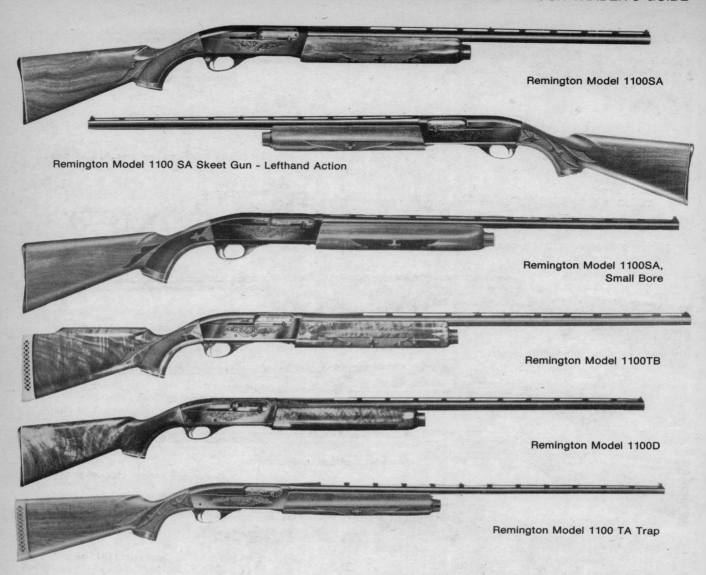

Remington Model 1100SA

Remington Model 1100 SA Skeet Gun - Lefthand Action

Remington Model 1100SA, Small Bore

Remington Model 1100TB

Remington Model 1100D

Remington Model 1100 TA Trap

Remington Model 1100SA Skeet Gun

Same as Model 1100 Field Gun, 12 and 20 gauge, except has 26-inch ventilated-rib barrel, skeet choke or with Cutts Compensator; weight, 7¼ to 7½ pounds. Made from 1963 to date.

With skeet-choked barrel............................ $325
With Cutts Comp.................................... 380
Left-hand action................................... 390

Remington Model 1100SB Skeet Gun........... $350

Same as Model 1100SA, except has selected wood. Made from 1963 to date.

Remington Model 1100SA Skeet Gun, Small Bore...$325

Similar to standard Model 1100SA, except chambered for 28 and 410 gauge (2½-inch chamber for latter); 25-inch ventilated-rib barrel, skeet choke. Weight: 6¾ pounds in 28 gauge, 7¼ pounds in 410. Made from 1969 to date.

Remington Model 1100SA Lightweight Skeet Gun.. $325

Same as Model 1100 Lightweight, except has skeet-style stock and forearm, 26-inch ventilated-rib barrel, skeet choke. Made from 1971 to date.

Remington Model 1100SB Lightweight Skeet Gun.. $350

Same as Model 1100SA Lightweight, except has selected wood. Introduced in 1977.

Remington Model 1100TB Trap Gun

Same as Model 1100 Field Gun, except has special trap stock, straight or Monte Carlo comb, recoil pad; 30-inch ventilated-rib barrel, full or modified trap choke; 12 gauge only; weight, 8¼ pounds. Made from 1963 to 1979.

With straight stock................................$300
With Monte Carlo stock............................ 305

Remington Model 1100TA Trap Gun............ $275

Similar to Model 1100TB Trap Gun, except with regular-grade stocks. Available in both left and right-hand versions. Made from 1979 to date.

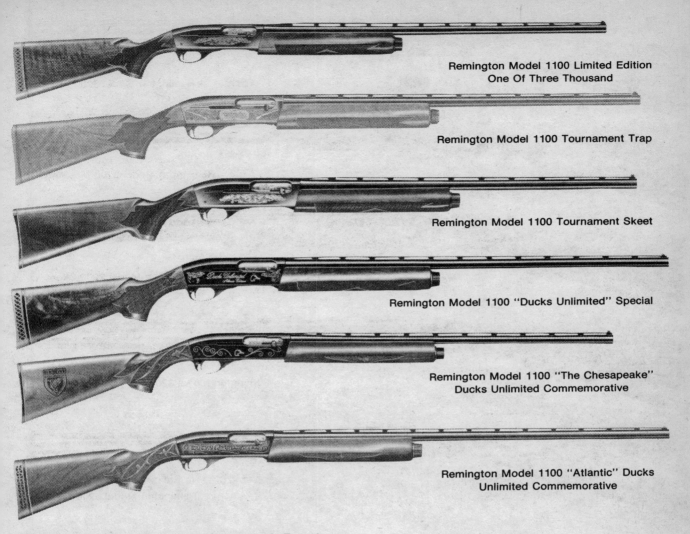

Remington Model 1100 Limited Edition
One Of Three Thousand

Remington Model 1100 Tournament Trap

Remington Model 1100 Tournament Skeet

Remington Model 1100 "Ducks Unlimited" Special

Remington Model 1100 "The Chesapeake"
Ducks Unlimited Commemorative

Remington Model 1100 "Atlantic" Ducks
Unlimited Commemorative

Remington Model 1100 Tournament and Premier Grades

These higher grade guns differ from standard models in overall quality, grade of wood, checkering, engraving, gold inlays, etc. General specifications are the same. Made from 1963 to date.

Model 1100D Tournament........................... **$1080**
Model 1100F Premier............................. 2160
Model 1100F Premier with gold inlay............... 3175

Remington Model 1100 Tournament Trap...... $400

Similar to Model 1100 Field Gun, except with 30-inch full or modified trap barrels. 12-gauge. Features select walnut stocks with cut-checkering patterns. Made from 1979 to date.

D Grade............................. **$1295**
F Grade............................. 2590
F Grade w/Gold Inlay............................ 3885

Remington Model 1100 "One of 3000" Field..... $790

Limited edition, numbered 1 to 3000. Similar to Model 100 Field, except with fancy wood and gold-trimmed etched hunting scenes on receiver. 12 gauge with 28" Modified, vent rib barrel. Made in 1980.

Remington Model 1100 Magnum................. $325

Limited production. Similar to the Model 1100 Field, except with 26-inch full choke, vent rib barrel and 3-inch chamber. Made in 1981.

Remington Model 1100 Tournament Skeet...... $400

Similar to Model 1100 Field, except with 26-inch barrel, skeet bore. Gauges, 12, LT-20, 28, and 410. Features select walnut stocks and new cut-checkering patterns. Made from 1979 to date.

Remington Model 1100 Ducks Unlimited "The Chesapeake" Commemorative........................... $385

Limited edition 1 to 2400. Same general specifications as Model 1100 Field, except sequentially serial numbered with markings "The Chesapeake". 12-gauge Magnum with 30-inch full choke, vent rib barrel. Made in 1981.

Remington Model 1100 LT-20 Ducks Unlimited "Special" Commemorative............................$385

Limited edition 1 to 2400. Same general specifications as Model 1100 Field, except sequentially serial numbered with markings "The Chesapeake". 20-gauge only. 26-inch Improved Cylinder, vent rib barrel. Made in 1981.

Remington Model 1100 Ducks Unlimited "Atlantic" Commemorative.................................... $385

Limited production for one year. Similar specifications to Model 1100 Field, except with 32-inch full choke, vent rib barrel. 12-gauge magnum only. Made in 1982.

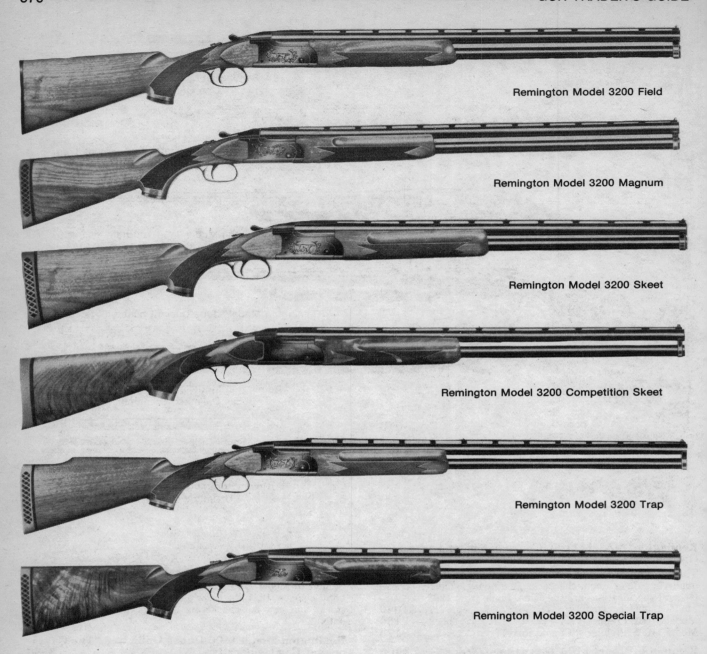

Remington Model 3200 Field

Remington Model 3200 Magnum

Remington Model 3200 Skeet

Remington Model 3200 Competition Skeet

Remington Model 3200 Trap

Remington Model 3200 Special Trap

Remington Model 3200 Field Grade Over-and-Under Shotgun...**$800**
Box lock. Automatic ejectors. Selective single trigger. 12 gauge. 2¾-inch chambers. Barrels: ventilated rib; 26-inch, modified and full, 30-inch improved cylinder and modified; 28-inch, modified and full choke. Weight, about 7¾ pounds with 26-inch barrels. Checkered pistol-grip stock and forearm. Made from 1973 to 1978.

Remington Model 3200 Field Grade Magnum....**$825**
Same as Model 3200 Field Grade, except chambered for 12 gauge magnum 3-inch shell; 30-inch barrels, modified and full or both full choke. Made from 1975 to date.

Remington Model 3200 Skeet Gun..............**$950**
Same as Model 3200 Field Grade, except skeet-style stock and full beavertail forearm; 26- or 28-inch barrels, skeet choke. Made from 1973 to 1980.

Remington Model 3200 Competition Skeet Gun.......................................**$1125**
Same as Model 3200 Skeet Gun, except has gilded scrollwork on frame, engraved fore-end latch plate and trigger guard, select fancy wood. Made from 1973 to date.

Remington Model 3200 Trap Gun...............**$840**
Same as Model 3200 Field Grade, except trap-style stock with Monte Carlo or straight comb, beavertail forearm; 30- or 32-inch barrels, improved modified and full or both full choke. Made from 1973 to 1977.

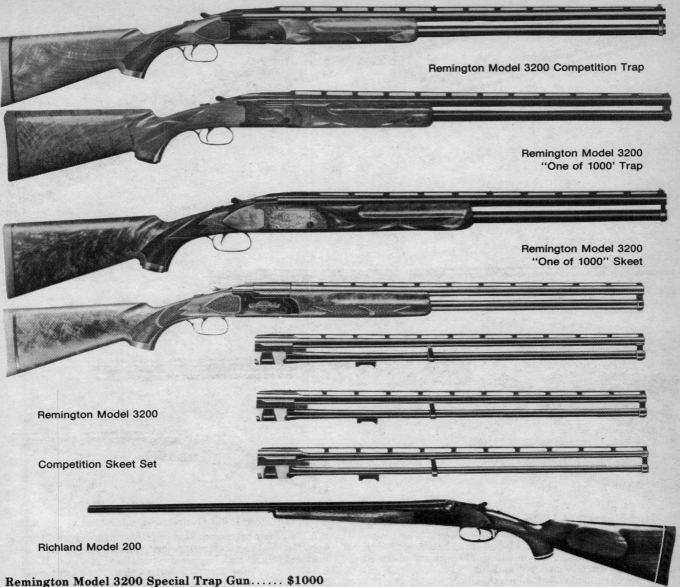

Remington Model 3200 Competition Trap

Remington Model 3200 "One of 1000' Trap

Remington Model 3200 "One of 1000'' Skeet

Remington Model 3200

Competition Skeet Set

Richland Model 200

Remington Model 3200 Special Trap Gun...... **$1000**
Same as Model 3200 Trap Gun, except has select wood. Made from 1973 to date.

Remington Model 3200 Competition Trap Gun. **$1175**
Same as Model 3200 Trap Gun, except has gilded scrollwork on frame, engraved fore-end latch plate and trigger guard, select fancy wood. Made from 1973 to date.

Remington Model 3200 "One of 1000"
Trap Gun.. **$2700**
Limited edition numbered 1 to 1000. Same general specifications as Model 3200 Trap Gun, but has frame, trigger guard and fore-end latch elaborately engraved (designation "One of 1,000" on frame side), stock and forearm of high grade walnut. Supplied in carrying case. Made in 1973.

Remington Model 3200 "One of 1000"
Skeet Gun... **$2700**
Same as Model 3200 "One of 1000" Trap Gun, except has 26- or 28-inch barrels bored skeet choke, skeet-style stock and forearm. Made in 1974.

Remington Model 3200 Competition Skeet Set. **$4000**
Similar specifications to Model 3200 Field. 12-gauge over-and-under with additional, interchangeable barrels in 20, 28, and 410 gauges. Cased. Made from 1980 to date.

Richland Shotguns manufactured in Italy and Spain for Richland Arms Company, Blissfield, Michigan

Richland Model 200 Field Grade Double Barrel
Shotgun.. **$195**
Hammerless, box lock, Anson & Deeley type. Plain extractors. Double triggers. Gauges: 12, 16, 20, 28, 410 (3-inch chambers in 20 and 410; others have 2¾-inch). Barrels: 28-inch modified and full choke, 26-inch improved cylinder and modified; 410 with 26-inch modified and full only; 22-inch improved cylinder and modified in 20 gauge only. Weights: 6 lbs. 2 oz. to 7 lbs. 4 oz. Checkered walnut stock with cheekpiece, pistol grip, recoil pad; beavertail fore-end; both checkered. Made in Spain 1963 to date.

Richland Model 202

Richland Model 711

Richland Model 707

Richland Model 808

Rigby Regal

Richland Model 202 All-Purpose Field Gun...... $265
Same as Model 200, except has two sets of barrels same gauge. 12 gauge: 30-inch barrels full and full, 3-inch chambers; 26-inch barrels improved cylinder and modified, 2¾-inch chambers. 20 gauge: 28-inch barrels modified and full; 22-inch barrels improved cylinder and modified; 3-inch chambers. Made from 1963 to date.

Richland Model 711 Long Range Waterfowl Magnum Double Barrel Shotgun
Hammerless, box lock, Anson & Deeley type, Purdey triple lock. Plain extractors. Double triggers. Automatic safety. Gauges: 10 gauge (3½-inch chambers), 12 gauge (3-inch chambers). Barrels: 10 gauge, 32-inch; 12 gauge, 30-inch; full and full. Weights: 10 gauge, 11 pounds; 12 gauge, 7¾ pounds. Checkered walnut stock and beavertail fore-end; recoil pad. Made in Spain 1963 to date.
10 Gauge Magnum.................................. **$235**
12 Gauge Magnum.................................. **220**

Richland Model 707 Deluxe Field Gun.......... $300
Hammerless, box lock, triple bolting system. Plain extractors. Double triggers. Gauges: 12 (2¾-inch chambers), 20 (3-inch chambers). Barrels: 12 gauge—28-inch modified and full, 26-inch improved cylinder and modified; 20 gauge—30-inch full and full, 28-inch modified and full, 26-inch improved cylinder and modified. Weights: 6 lbs. 4 oz. to 6 lbs. 15 oz. Checkered walnut stock and fore-end, recoil pad. Made from 1963 to 1972.

Richland Model 808 Over-and-Under Gun...... $360
Box lock. Plain extractors. Non-selective single trigger. 12 gauge only. Barrels (Vickers steel): 30-inch full and full, 28-inch modified and full, 26-inch improved cylinder and modified. Weight, 6 lbs. 12 oz. to 7 lbs. 3 oz. Checkered walnut stock and fore-end. Made in Italy from 1963 to 1968.

John Rigby & Co., London, England
Rigby Hammerless Side Lock Double Barrel Shotgun
Automatic ejectors. Double triggers. Made in all gauges, barrel lengths and chokes. Checkered stock and fore-end, straight grip standard. Made in two grades: Regal (best quality) and Sandringham; these guns differ in general quality, engraving, etc.; specifications are the same.
Regal Grade..................................... **$17,000**
Sandringham Grade............................... **12,000**

Rigby Hammerless Box Lock Double Barrel Shotgun
Automatic ejectors. Double triggers. Made in all gauges, barrel lengths and chokes. Checkered stock and fore-end, straight grip standard. Made in two grades: Sackville and Chatsworth; these guns differ in general quality, engraving, etc., specifications are the same.
Sackville Grade.................................. **$5000**
Chatsworth Grade................................ **3800**

Rossi Overland

Rossi Hammerless Double

Ruger Red Label

Ruger Red Label - 12 GAUGE

Sarasqueta Model 3

Sarasqueta Model 4

Sarasqueta Model 203

Amadeo Rossi, S.A.
Sao Leopoldo, Brazil

Rossi Overland Hammer Double Barrel Shotgun
.... **$200**

Side lock. Plain extractors. Double triggers. Gauges: 12, 410; 3-inch chambers. Barrels: 20-inch, improved cylinder and modified in 12 gauge; 26-inch, both full choke in 410. Weight: 7 pounds in 12 gauge, 6 pounds in 410. Pistol-grip stock and beavertail forearm, uncheckered. *Note:* Because of its resemblance to the short-barrelled doubles carried by guards riding shotgun on 19th century stage-coaches, the 12 gauge version originally was called the "Coach Gun." Made from 1968 to date.

Rossi Hammerless Double Barrel Shotgun...... **$225**

Box lock. Plain extractors. Double triggers. 12 gauge. 3-inch chambers. Barrels: 26-inch improved cylinder and modified, 28-inch modified and full choke. Weight: 7 or 7½ pounds. Pistol-grip stock and beavertail forearm, uncheckered. Made from 1974 to date. *Note:* H&R Model 404 (1969-72) is same gun.

Ruger Shotgun manufactured by
Sturm, Ruger & Company, Southport, Connecticut

Ruger Plain Grade Red Label Over-and-Under Shotgun...**$560**

Box lock. Automatic ejectors. Selective single trigger. 20 gauge. 3-inch chambers. 26-inch ventilated-rib barrel, improved cylinder and modified or skeet choke. Weight, about 7 pounds. Checkered pistol-grip stock and forearm. Introduced in 1977. 12 gauge version introduced in 1982. Chambers: 2¾-inch and 3-inch. Barrels: 26-inch, 28-inch, and 30-inch. Weight: about 7½ pounds.

Victor Sarasqueta, S. A., Eibar, Spain

Sarasqueta Model 3 Hammerless Box Lock Double Barrel Shotgun

Plain extractors or automatic ejectors. Double triggers. Gauges: 12, 16, 20. Made in various barrel lengths, chokes and weights. Checkered stock and fore-end, straight grip standard. Currently manufactured.
Model 3, plain extractors............................ **$400**
Model 3E, automatic ejectors........................ **460**

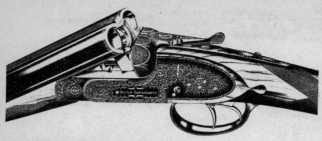

Sarasqueta Model 6E

Sarasqueta Model 10E

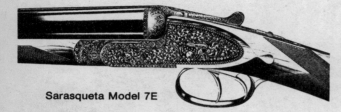

Sarasqueta Model 7E

Sarasqueta Model 11E

Sarasqueta Hammerless Side Lock Double Barrel Shotguns

Automatic ejectors (except on Models 4 and 203 which have plain extractors). Double triggers. Gauges: 12, 16, 20. Barrel lengths, chokes and weights made to order. Checkered stock and fore-end, straight grip standard. The various models differ chiefly in overall quality, engraving, grade of wood, checkering, etc. General specifications are the same. Currently manufactured.

Model 4	$ 500
Model 4E	540
Model 203	510
Model 203E	560
Model 6E	625
Model 7E	690
Model 10E	1440
Model 11E	1530
Model 12E	1600

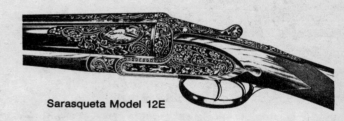

Sarasqueta Model 12E

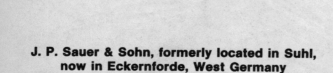

Sauer Royal

J. P. Sauer & Sohn, formerly located in Suhl, now in Eckernforde, West Germany

Sauer "Royal" Double Barrel Shotgun..........$1200

Anson & Deeley action (box lock) with Greener crossbolt, double underlugs, signal pins, selective single trigger, selective automatic ejectors, automatic safety. Scalloped frame with arabesque engraving. Krupp-Special steel barrels. Gauges: 12 (2¾-inch chambers), 20 (3-inch chambers). Barrels: 30-inch (12 ga. only) and 28-inch, modified and full; 26-inch (20 ga. only), improved cylinder and modified. Weights: 12 ga. about 6½ pounds; 20 ga., about 6 pounds. Checkered walnut pistol-grip stock and beavertail fore-end; recoil pad. Made from 1955 to 1977.

Sauer "Artemis" Double Barrel Shotgun

Holland & Holland-type side lock with Greener crossbolt, double underlugs, double sear safeties, selective single trigger, selective automatic ejectors. Grade I with fine line engraving; Grade II with full English arabesque engraving. 12 gauge (2¾-inch chambers). Krupp-Special steel barrels, 28-inch, modified and full choke. Weight, about 6½ pounds. Checkered walnut pistol-grip stock and beavertail fore-end; recoil pad. Made from 1966 to 1977.

Grade I	$4000
Grade II	4880

Sauer Model 66 Over-and-Under Field Gun

Purdey system action with Holland & Holland-type side locks. Selective single trigger. Selective automatic ejectors. Automatic safety. Available in three grades of engraving. 12 gauge only. Krupp-Special steel barrels with ventilated rib, 28-inch, modified and full choke. Weight, about 7¼ pounds. Checkered walnut stock and fore-end; recoil pad. Made from 1966 to 1975.

Grade I	$1500
Grade II	2100
Grade III	2900

Sauer Artemis Grade II

Sauer Model 66 Field Grade I

Sauer Model 66 Over-and-Under Skeet Gun

Same as Model 66 Field Gun, except 26-inch barrels with wide ventilated rib, skeet choked; skeet-style stock and ventilated beavertail forearm; nonautomatic safety. Made from 1966 to 1975.

Grade I... $1400
Grade II.. 2000
Grade III... 2800

Sauer Model 66 Over-and-Under Trap Gun

Same as Model 66 Skeet Gun, except has 30-inch barrels bored full and full or modified and full; trap-style stock. Values same as for Skeet Model. Made from 1966 to 1975.

Sauer Model 3000E Drilling

Combination rifle and double barrel shotgun. Blitz action with Greener crossbolt, double underlugs, separate rifle cartridge extractor, front set trigger, firing pin indicators, Greener side safety, sear slide selector locks right shotgun barrel for firing rifle barrel. Gauge/calibers: 12 gauge (2¾-inch chambers); 222, 243, 30-06, 7x65R. 25-inch Krupp-Special steel barrels; modified and full choke, automatic folding leaf rear rifle sight. Weight, 6½ to 7¼ pounds depending on rifle caliber. Checkered walnut stock and fore-end; pistol grip, modified Monte Carlo comb and cheekpiece, sling swivels. Standard Model with arabesque engraving; Deluxe Model with hunting scenes engraved on action. Currently manufactured. *Note:* Also see listing under Colt.

Standard Model.................................... $1650
Deluxe Model...................................... 3200

Sauer BBF Over-and-Under Combination Rifle/Shotgun

Blitz action with Kersten lock, front set trigger fires rifle barrel, slide-operated sear safety. Gauge/calibers: 16 gauge; 30-30, 30-06, 7x65R. 25-inch Krupp-Special steel barrels; shotgun barrel full choke, folding leaf rear sight. Weight, about 6 pounds. Checkered walnut stock and fore-end; pistol grip, modified Monte Carlo comb and cheekpiece, sling swivels. Standard Model with arabesque engraving; Deluxe Model with hunting scenes engraved on action. Currently manufactured.

Standard Model.................................... $1700
Deluxe Model...................................... 2715

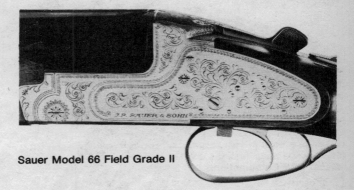

Sauer Model 66 Field Grade II

Sauer Model 66 Field Grade III

Sauer Model 66 Trap Grade II

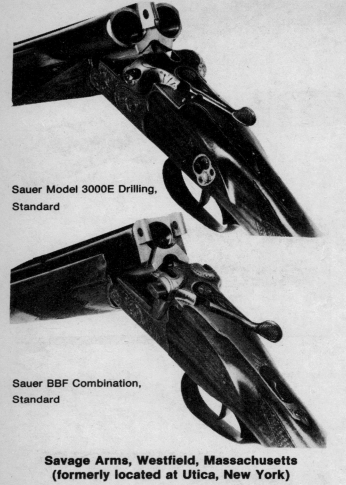

Sauer Model 3000E Drilling,
Standard

Sauer BBF Combination,
Standard

Savage Arms, Westfield, Massachusetts (formerly located at Utica, New York)

Savage Model 28A Standard Grade Slide Action Repeating Shotgun **$200**
Hammerless. Takedown. 12 gauge. 5-shell tubular magazine. Plain barrel; lengths: 26-, 28-, 30-, 32-inches; chokes: cylinder, modified, full. Weight, about 7½ pounds with 30-inch barrel. Plain pistol-grip stock, grooved slide handle. Made from 1928 to 1931.

Savage Model 28B **$215**
Raised matted rib; otherwise the same as Model 28A.

Savage Model 28D Trap Grade **$285**
Same general specifications as Model 28A, except has 30-inch full choke barrel with matted rib, trap-style stock with checkered pistol grip, checkered slide handle of selected walnut.

Savage Model 420 Over-and-Under Shotgun
Box lock. Hammerless. Takedown. Automatic safety. Double triggers or non-selective single trigger. Gauges: 12, 16, 20 gauge. Plain barrels; lengths: 26- to 30-inch (the latter in 12 gauge only); chokes: modified and full, cylinder and improved cylinder. Weights with 28-inch barrels: 12 gauge 7¾ pounds, 16 gauge 7½ pounds, 20 gauge 6¾ pounds. Plain pistol-grip stock and forearm. Made from 1938 to 1942.
With double triggers **$320**
With single trigger 415

Savage Model 430
Same as Model 420, except has matted top barrel, checkered

stock of selected walnut with recoil pad, checkered forearm. Made from 1938 to 1942.
With double triggers **$370**
With single trigger 440

Savage Model 220 Single Barrel Shotgun .... **$ 80**
Hammerless. Takedown. Automatic ejector. Gauges: 12, 16, 20, 410. Single shot. Barrel lengths: 12 gauge—28- to 36-inch, 16 gauge—28- to 32-inch, 20 gauge—26- to 32-inch, 410 bore—26- and 28-inch. Full choke. Weight, about 6 pounds. Plain pistol-grip stock and wide forearm. Made from 1938 to 1965.

Savage Model 220P .... **$ 85**
Same as Model 220, except has Poly Choke built integrally with barrel; made in 12 gauge with 30-inch barrel, 16 gauge and 20 gauge with 28-inch barrel, not made in 410 bore; has recoil pad.

Savage Model 220AC .... **$ 65**
Same as Model 220, except has Savage adjustable choke.

Savage Model 220L .... **$ 60**
Same general specifications as Model 220, except has side lever opening instead of top lever. Made from 1965 to 1972.

Savage Utility Gun
See listing under "Rifles."

Savage Model 720 Standard Grade 5-Shot Autoloading Shotgun **$190**
Browning type. Takedown. 12 and 16 gauge. 4-shell tubular magazine. Plain barrel; lengths: 26- to 32-inch (the latter in 12 gauge only); chokes: cylinder, modified, full. Weight, about 8¼ pounds in 12 gauge with 30-inch barrel; 16 gauge about ½ pound lighter. Checkered pistol-grip stock and forearm. Made from 1930 to 1949.

Savage Model 726 Upland Sporter Grade 3-Shot Autoloading Shotgun **$190**
Same as Model 720, except has 2-shell magazine capacity. Made from 1931 to 1949.

Savage Model 740C Skeet Gun **$210**
Same as Model 726, except has special skeet stock and full-beavertail forearm, equipped with Cutts Compensator, barrel length overall with spreader tube is about 24½-inches. Made from 1936 to 1949.

Savage Model 745 Lightweight Autoloading Shotgun **$200**
Three-shot or five-shot model. Same general specifications as Model 720, except has lightweight alloy receiver, 12 gauge only, 28-inch plain barrel, weighs about 6¾ pounds. Made from 1940 to 1949.

Savage Model 755 Standard Grade Autoloading Shotgun **$200**
Streamlined receiver. Takedown. 12 and 16 gauge. 4-shell tubular magazine (a three-shot model with magazine capacity of two shells was also produced until 1951). Plain barrel; 30-inch full choke (12 gauge only), 28-inch full or modified, 26-inch improved cylinder. Weight, about 8¼ pounds in 12 gauge. Checkered pistol-grip stock and forearm. Manufactured from 1949 to 1958.

Savage Model 755-SC **$210**
Same as Model 755, except has 26-inch barrel with recoil-reducing, adjustable Savage Super Choke.

Savage Model 775 Lightweight **$215**
Same general specifications as Model 755, except has lightweight alloy receiver and weighs about 6¾ pounds. Made from 1950 to 1965.

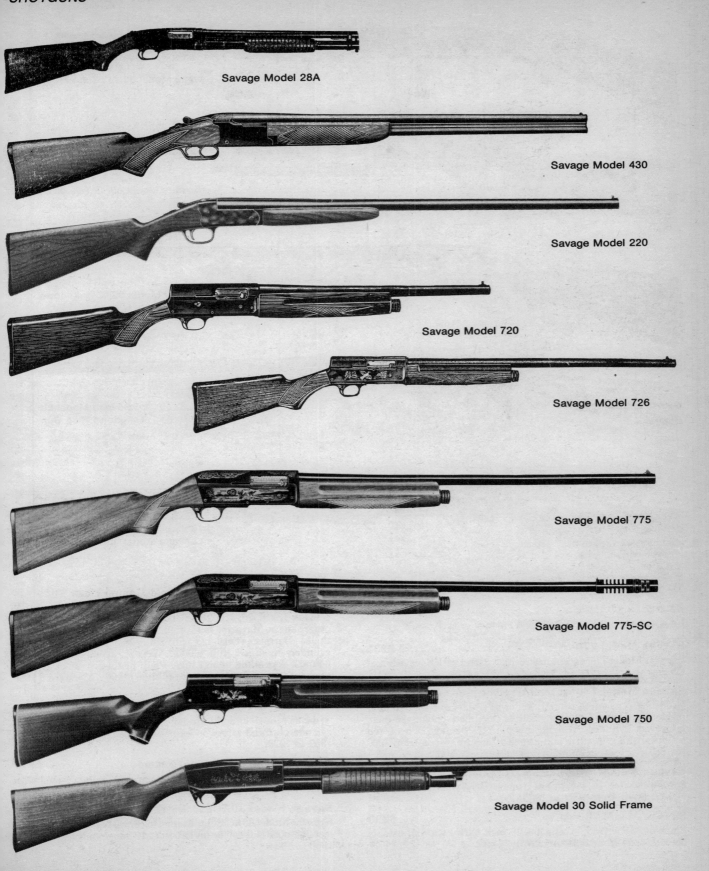

Savage Model 28A

Savage Model 430

Savage Model 220

Savage Model 720

Savage Model 726

Savage Model 775

Savage Model 775-SC

Savage Model 750

Savage Model 30 Solid Frame

Savage Model 30 AC Solid Frame

Savage Model 30FG Takedown

Savage Model 30AC Takedown

Savage Model 30
Takedown Slug Gun

Savage Model 30D Takedown

Savage Model 775-SC **$235**
Same as Model 775, except has 26-inch barrel with Savage Super Choke.

Savage Model 750 Automatic Shotgun **$190**
Browning-type autoloader. Takedown. 12 gauge. 4-shot tubular magazine. Barrels: 28-inch, full or modified choke; 26-inch, improved cylinder. Weight, about 7¼ pounds. Checkered walnut pistol-grip stock and grooved forearm. Made from 1960 to 1967.

Savage Model 750-SC **$200**
Same as Model 750, except has 26-inch barrel with Savage Super Choke. Made from 1962 to 1963.

Savage Model 750-AC **$200**
Same as Model 750, except has 26-inch barrel with adjustable choke. Made from 1964 to 1967.

Savage Model 30 Solid Frame Hammerless Slide Action Shotgun **$160**
Gauges: 12, 16, 20, 410. 2¾-inch chamber in 16 gauge, 3-inch in other gauges. Magazine holds four 2¾-inch shells or three 3-inch shells. Barrels: ventilated rib; 26-, 28-, 30-inch; improved cylinder, modified, full choke. Weight: average 6¼ to 6¾ pounds, depending upon gauge. Plain pistol-grip stock (checkered on later production), grooved slide handle. Made from 1958 to 1970.

Savage Model 30L Solid Frame **$160**
Same as Model 30 Solid Frame, except left-handed model with ejection port and safety on left side; 12 gauge only. Made from 1959 to 1970.

Savage Model 30AC Solid Frame **$170**
Same as Model 30 Solid Frame, except has 26-inch barrel with adjustable choke; 12 gauge only. Made from 1959 to 1970.

Savage Model 30ACL Solid Frame **$180**
Same as Model 30AC Solid Frame, except left-hand model with ejection port and safety on left side; 12 gauge only. Made from 1960 to 1964.

Savage Model 30T Solid Frame Trap and Duck Gun..**$170**
Same as Model 30 Solid Frame, except only in 12 gauge with 30-inch full choke barrel; has Monte Carlo stock with recoil pad; weight, about 8 pounds. Made from 1963 to 1970.

Savage Model 30FG Takedown Hammerless Slide Action Shotgun.......................................**$140**
Field Grade. Gauges: 12, 20, 410. 3-inch chamber. Magazine holds four 2¾-inch shells or three 3-inch shells. Barrels: plain; 26-inch, full choke (410 gauge only); 28-inch, modified, full choke; 30-inch, full choke (12 gauge only). Weight: average 7 to 7¾ pounds, depending upon gauge. Checkered pistol-grip stock, fluted slide handle. Made from 1970 to 1979.

Savage Model 30T Takedown Trap Gun.........**$160**
Same as Model 30D, except only in 12 gauge with 30-inch full choke barrel; has Monte Carlo stock with recoil pad. Made from 1970 to 1973.

Savage Model 30AC Takedown...................**$170**
Same as Model 30FG, except has 26-inch barrel with adjustable choke; 12 and 20 gauge only. Made from 1971 to 1972.

Savage Model 30 Takedown Slug Gun...........**$165**
Same as Model 30FG, except 21-inch cylinder bore barrel with rifle sights. Made from 1971 to 1979.

Savage Model 30D Takedown....................**$170**
Deluxe Grade. Same as Model 30FG, except has receiver engraved with game scene, ventilated-rib barrel, recoil pad. Made from 1971 to date.

Savage Model 24 22- 410 Over-and-Under Combination Gun..**$110**
Same as Stevens No. 22- 410, has walnut stock and forearm. Made from 1950 to 1965.

Savage Model 24S Over-and-Under Combination Gun..**$120**
Box lock. Visible hammer. Side lever opening. Plain extractors. Single trigger. 20 or 410 gauge shotgun barrel under 22 long rifle barrel; 24-inch; open rear sight and ramp front sight, dovetail for scope mounting. Weight, about 6¾ pounds. Plain pistol-grip stock and forearm. Made from 1965 to 1971.

Savage Model 24MS.............................**$125**
Same as Model 24S, except rifle barrel chambered for 22 Win. magnum rimfire. Made from 1965 to 1971.

Savage Model 24DL.............................**$110**
Same general specifications as Model 24S, except top lever opening; has satin-chrome-finished frame decorated with game scenes, checkered Monte Carlo stock and forearm. Made from 1965 to 1969.

Savage Model 24MDL...........................**$130**
Same as Model 24DL, except rifle barrel chambered for 22 Win. magnum rimfire. Made from 1965 to 1969.

Savage Model 24D..............................**$140**
Same as Models 24DL and 24MDL, except frame has black or casehardened finish. Game scene decoration of frame eliminated in 1974; forearm uncheckered after 1976. Made from 1970 to date.

Savage Model 24V..............................**$160**
Similar to Model 24D, except 20 gauge under 222 Rem, 22 Rem., 357 Mag., 22 Hornet or 30-30 rifle barrel. Made from 1971 to date.

Savage Model 24FG Field Grade.................**$100**
Same general specifications as Model 24S, except top lever opening. Made from 1972 to date.

Savage Model 24S

Savage Model 24D

Savage Model 24V

Savage Model 24FG

Savage Model 24C

Savage Model 242

Savage Model 24C Camper's Companion........$120
Same as Model 24FG, except made in 22 magnum/20 gauge only; has 20-inch barrels, shotgun tube cylinder bore; weight, 5¾ pounds; trap in butt provides ammunition storage; comes with carrying case. Made from 1972 to date.

Savage Model 242 Over-and-Under Shotgun.... $140
Similar to Model 24D, except both barrels 410 gauge, full choke; weight, about 7 pounds. Made from 1977 to 1980.

Savage Model 440 Over-and-Under Shotgun.... $450
Box lock. Plain extractors. Selective single trigger. Gauges: 12, 20. 2¾-inch chambers in 12 gauge, 3-inch in 20 gauge. Barrels: ventilated rib; 26-inch, skeet choke, improved cylinder and modified; 28-inch, modified and full; 30-inch, modified and full choke (12 gauge only). Weight: average 6 to 6½ pounds, depending upon gauge. Made from 1968 to 1972.

Savage Model 440T Trap Gun................... $575
Similar to Model 440, except only in 12 gauge with 30-inch barrels, extra-wide ventilated rib, improved modified and full choke; has trap-style Monte Carlo stock and semi-beavertail forearm of select walnut, recoil pad; weight, 7½ pounds. Made from 1969 to 1972.

Savage Model 444 Deluxe Over-and-Under Shotguns...$575
Similar to Model 440, except has automatic ejectors, select walnut stock and semi-beavertail forearm. Made from 1969 to 1972.

Savage Model 550 Hammerless Double Barrel Shotgun..$240
Box lock. Automatic ejectors. Non-selective single trigger. Gauges: 12, 20. 2¾-inch chamber in 12 gauge, 3-inch in 20 gauge. Barrels: ventilated rib; 26-inch, improved cylinder and modified; 28-inch, modified and full; 30-inch, modified and full choke (12 gauge only). Weight, average 7 to 8 pounds. Checkered pistol-grip stock and semi-beavertail forearm. Made from 1971 to 1973.

Savage Model 330 Over-and-Under Shotgun.... $405
Box lock. Plain extractors. Selective single trigger. Gauges: 12, 20. 2¾-inch chambers in 12 gauge, 3-inch in 20 gauge. Barrels: 26-inch, improved cylinder and modified; 28-inch, modified and full; 30-inch, modified and full choke (12 gauge only). Weight, average 6¼ to 7¼ pounds, depending upon gauge. Checkered pistol-grip stock and forearm. Made from 1969 to 1978.

Savage Model 333T Trap Gun................... $500
Similar to Model 330, except only in 12 gauge with 30-inch ventilated-rib barrels, improved modified and full choke; has Monte Carlo stock with recoil pad; weight, 7¾ pounds. Made from 1972 to 1979.

Savage Model 333 Over-and-Under Shotgun.... $525
Box lock. Automatic ejectors. Selective single trigger. Gauges: 12, 20. 2¾-inch chambers in 12 gauge, 3-inch in 20 gauge. Barrels: ventilated rib; 26-inch, skeet choke, improved cylinder and modified; 28-inch, modified and full; 30-inch, modified and full choke (12 gauge only). Weight: average 6¼ to 7¼ pounds, depending upon gauge. Checkered pistol-grip stock and forearm. Made from 1973 to 1979.

Savage Model 2400 Over-and-Under Combination Gun...$530
Box lock action similar to that of Model 330. Plain extractors. Selective single trigger. 12 gauge (2¾-inch chamber) shotgun barrel, full choke, over 308 Win. or 222 Rem. rifle barrel; 23½-inch; solid matted rib with blade front sight and folding leaf rear sight, dovetail for scope mounting. Weight, about 7½ pounds. Monte Carlo stock with pistol grip and recoil pad, semi-beavertail forearm, checkered. Made from 1975 to 1979.

Savage Model 69-RXL Slide Action Shotgun.... $130
Hammerless, side ejection, top tang safe for left or right hand use. 12 gauge, chambered for 2-¾" and 3" magnum shells. 18¼-inch barrel. Tubular magazine holds 6 rounds (one less for 3" mag.) Walnut finish hardwood stock with recoil pad, grooved operating handle. Weight: about 6½ pounds. Made from 1982 to date.

Note: Savage Models 330, 333T, 333, and 2400 were manufactured by Valmet Oy, Helsinki, Finland.

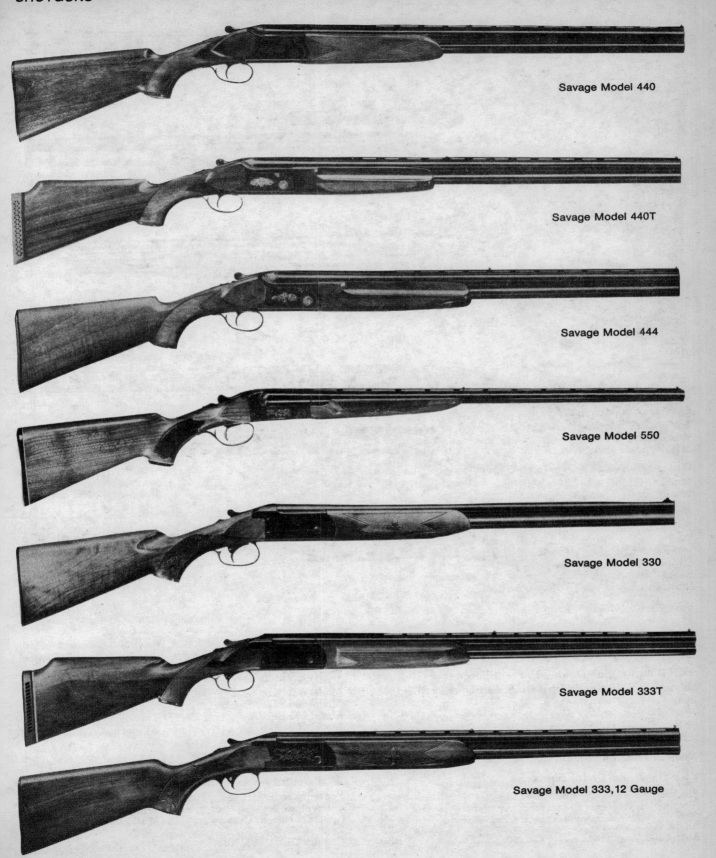

Savage Model 440

Savage Model 440T

Savage Model 444

Savage Model 550

Savage Model 330

Savage Model 333T

Savage Model 333, 12 Gauge

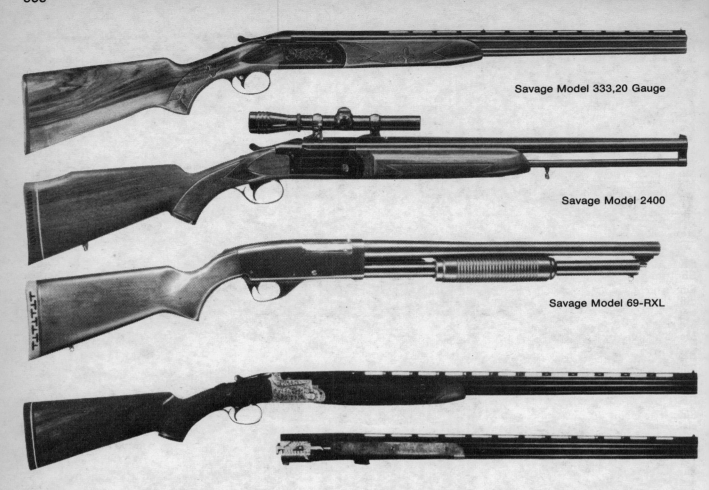

Savage Model 333, 20 Gauge

Savage Model 2400

Savage Model 69-RXL

SKB Model 600 Field

SKB Model 880

SKB Arms Company, Tokyo, Japan

SKB Side-by-Side Double Barrel Shotguns
For data see listings under Ithaca, U.S. distributor for SKB 1966 to 1976.

Model 100..	$365
Model 150..	380
Model 200E..	525
Model 200E Skeet...................................	525
Model 280 English..................................	535

SKB Over-and-Under Shotguns
For data see listings under Ithaca.

Model 500...	$ 515
Model 500 Magnum.................................	520
Model 600...	625
Model 600 Magnum.................................	630
Model 600 Trap.....................................	635
Model 600 Doubles..................................	635
Model 600 Skeet — 12 or 20 gauge..............	600
Model 600 Skeet — 28 or 410.....................	625
Model 600 Skeet Combo............................	1875
Model 680 English..................................	635
Model 700 Trap.....................................	790
Model 700 Doubles..................................	790
Model 700 Skeet....................................	790
Model 700 Skeet Combo............................	2000

SKB Century Single Barrel Trap Gun
For data see listings under Ithaca. *Note:* SKB catalog does not differentiate between Century and Century II; however, specifications of current Century are those of Ithaca-SKB Century II.

Century...	$580
Century II...	600

SKB Recoil-operated Automatic Shotguns
For data see listings under Ithaca.
Model 300—with plain barrel	$220
Model 300—with ventilated rib	240
Model 900	300
Model 900 Slug	260

SKB Gas-operated Automatic Shotguns
For data see listings under Ithaca.
Model XL300—with plain barrel	$270
Model XL300—with ventilated rib	310
Model XL900	330
Model XL900 Trap	350
Model XL900 Skeet	335
Model XL900 Slug	270

Note: The following currently manufactured SKB shotguns were not imported by Ithaca Gun Company.

SKB Models 300 and 400 Side-by-Side Double Barrel Shotguns
Similar to Model 200E, except higher grade. Models 300 and 400 differ in that the latter has more elaborate engraving and fancier wood.
Model 300	$650
Model 400	870

SKB Model 400 Skeet $870
Similar to Model 200E Skeet, except higher grade with more elaborate engraving and full fancy wood.

SKB Model 480 English $870
Similar to Model 280 English, except higher grade with more elaborate engraving and full fancy wood.

SKB Model 500 Small Gauge Over-and-Under Shotgun
.... $525
Similar to Model 500, except gauges 28 and 410; has 28-inch ventilated-rib barrels, modified and full choke; weight, about 6½ pounds.

SKB Model 600 Small Gauge $600
Same as Model 500 Small Gauge, except higher grade with more elaborate engraving and fancier wood.

SKB Model 800 Skeet Over-and-Under
Shotgun $925
Similar to Model 700 Skeet, except higher grade with more elaborate engraving and fancier wood.

SKB Model 800 Trap $950
Similar to Model 700 Trap, except higher grade with more elaborate engraving and fancier wood.

SKB Model 880 Skeet $1500
Similar to Model 800 Skeet, except has side plates.

SKB Model 880 Trap $1500
Similar to Model 800 Trap, except has side plates.

L. C. Smith Shotguns made from 1890 to 1945 by Hunter Arms Company, Fulton, New York; from 1946 to 1951 and from 1968 to 1973 by Marlin Firearms Company, New Haven, Connecticut

L. C. Smith Hammerless Double Barrel Shotguns
Side lock. Automatic ejectors standard on higher grades, extra on Field and Ideal Grades. Double triggers or Hunter single trigger (non-selective or selective). Gauges: 12, 16, 20, 410. Barrels: 26-to 32-inch, any standard boring. Weight, 6½ to 8¼ pounds in 12 gauge. Checkered stock and fore-end; choice of straight, half-or full-pistol grip, beavertail or standard-type fore-end. Grades differ only in quality of workmanship, wood, checkering, engraving, etc. Same general specifications apply to all. Manufacture of these L. C. Smith guns was discontinued in 1951. Production of Field Grade 12 gauge was resumed 1968-1973.

Note: L. C. Smith Shotguns manufactured by the Hunter Arms Co. from 1890 to 1913 were designated by numerals to indicate grade, with the exception of Pigeon and Monogram.

L. C. Smith, Hammerless double barrel, 00 Grade	$875
L. C. Smith, Hammerless double barrel, 0 Grade	1000
L. C. Smith, Hammerless double barrel, 1 Grade	1200
L. C. Smith, Hammerless double barrel, 2 Grade	1300
L. C. Smith, Hammerless double barrel, 3 Grade	1200
L. C. Smith, Hammerless double barrel, Pigeon	2800
L. C. Smith, Hammerless double barrel, 4 Grade	3800
L. C. Smith, Hammerless double barrel, 5 Grade	4000
L. C. Smith, Hammerless double barrel, Monogram	7000
L. C. Smith, Hammerless double barrel, A1	4800
L. C. Smith, Hammerless double barrel, A2	7000
L. C. Smith, Hammerless double barrel, A3	15,000+

L. C. Smith Field

Field Grade, double triggers, plain extractors	$650
Field Grade, double triggers, automatic ejectors	750
Field Grade, non-selective single trigger, plain extractors	690
Field Grade, selective single trigger, automatic ejectors	875

L. C. Smith Ideal

Ideal Grade, double triggers, plain extractors	900
Ideal Grade, double triggers, automatic ejectors	1250
Ideal Grade, selective single trigger, automatic ejectors	1050

L. C. Smith Olympic

Olympic Grade, selective single trigger, automatic ejectors	$1275

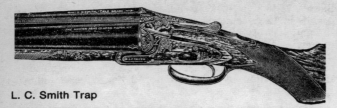

L. C. Smith Trap

Trap Grade, selective single trigger, automatic
  ejectors.. **$1200**

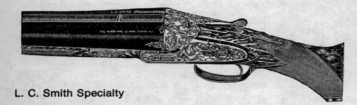

L. C. Smith Specialty

Specialty Grade, double triggers, automatic ejectors... **$1500**
Specialty Grade, selective single trigger, automatic
  ejectors.. 1600

L. C. Smith Skeet

Skeet Special, non-selective single trigger, automatic
  ejectors.. **$1200**
Skeet Special, selective single trigger, automatic
  ejectors.. 1300

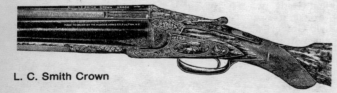

L. C. Smith Crown

Crown Grade, double triggers, automatic ejectors..... **$3800**
Crown Grade, selective single trigger, automatic
  ejectors.. 4100

L. C. Smith Monogram

Monogram Grade, selective single trigger, automatic
  ejectors.. **$6800**

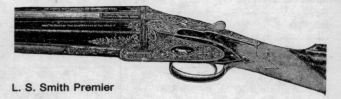

L. S. Smith Premier

Premier Grade, selective single trigger, automatic
  ejectors.. **$9000**
Deluxe Grade, selective single trigger, automatic
  ejectors.. 14,000

Note: Values shown are for L. C. Smith doubles made by Hunter. Those of 1946-1951 Marlin manufacture generally bring prices about ⅓ lower. Smaller gauge guns, especially in the higher grades, command premium prices: up to 50 percent more for 20 gauge, up to 200 percent for 410 gauge.

L. C. Smith Field Grade Hammerless Double Barrel Shotgun, 1968 Model............................ **$365**
"Re-creation" of the original L. C. Smith double. Side lock. Plain extractors. Double triggers. 12 gauge. 28-inch ventilated-rib barrels, modified and full choke. Weight, about 6¾ pounds. Checkered pistol-grip stock and forearm. Made from 1968 to 1973.

L. C. Smith Deluxe Model........................ **$425**
Same as 1968 Field Grade, except has Simmons floating ventilated rib, beavertail forearm. Made from 1971 to 1973.

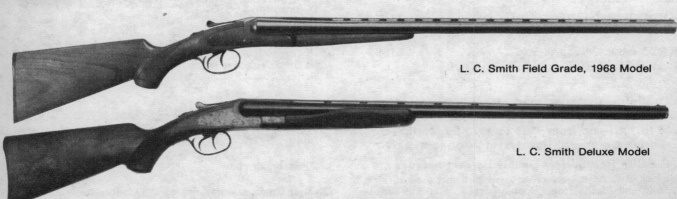

L. C. Smith Field Grade, 1968 Model

L. C. Smith Deluxe Model

L. C. Smith Barrel Trap, Olympic

L. C. Smith Single Barrel Trap Guns

Box lock. Hammerless. Automatic ejector. 12 gauge only. Barrel lengths: 32- or 34-inch. Ventilated rib. Weight, 8 to 8¼ pounds. Checkered pistol-grip stock and fore-end, recoil pad. The three grades vary in quality of workmanship, wood, engraving, etc.; general specifications are the same. Discontinued in 1951.

Olympic Grade	$1000
Specialty Grade	1200
Crown Grade	3200
Monogram Grade	4000
Premier Grade	6400
Deluxe Grade	9000

Note: Values shown are for L. C. Smith single barrel trap guns made by Hunter. Those of Marlin manufacture generally bring prices about one-third lower.

Smith & Wesson Shotguns manufactured for Smith & Wesson, Springfield, Massachusetts, by Howa Machinery, Ltd., Nagoya, Japan

Smith & Wesson Model 916 Slide Action Repeating Shotgun

Hammerless. Solid frame. Gauges: 12, 16, 20. 3-inch chamber in 12 and 20 gauge. 5-shot tubular magazine. Barrels: plain or ventilated rib; 20-inch, cylinder bore (12 gauge, plain only); 26-inch, improved cylinder; 28-inch, modified or full; 30-inch, full choke (12 gauge only). Weight, with 28-inch plain barrel, 7¼ pounds. Plain pistol-grip stock, fluted slide handle. Made from 1972 to 1981.

With plain barrel	$135
With ventilated rib	160

Smith & Wesson Model 916T

Same as Model 916, except takedown, 12 gauge only. Not available with 20-inch barrel. Made from 1976 to 1981.

With plain barrel	$150
With ventilated rib	175

Smith & Wesson Model 1000 Autoloading Shotgun $285

Gas-operated. Takedown. Gauges: 12, 20. 2¾-inch chamber in 12 gauge, 3-inch in 20 gauge. 4-shot magazine. Barrels: ventilated rib; 26-inch, skeet choke, improved cylinder; 28-inch, modified or full; 30-inch, full choke (12 gauge only). Weight, with 28-inch barrel, 6½ pounds in 20 gauge, 7½ pounds in 12 gauge. Checkered pistol-grip stock and forearm. Made from 1972 to date.

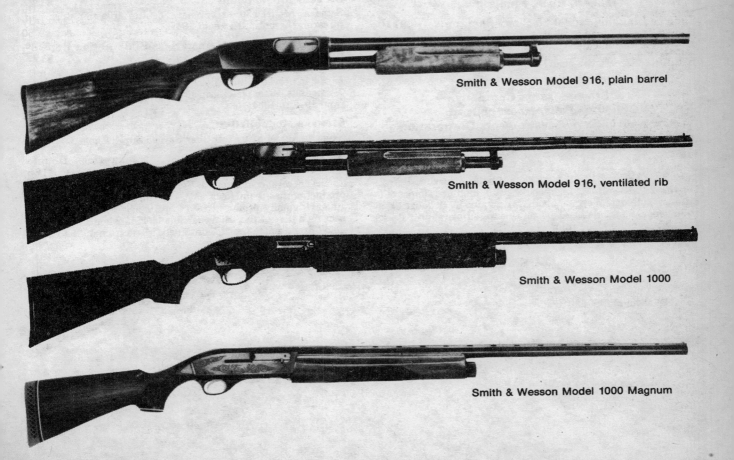

Smith & Wesson Model 916, plain barrel

Smith & Wesson Model 916, ventilated rib

Smith & Wesson Model 1000

Smith & Wesson Model 1000 Magnum

Smith And Wesson Model 3000

Squires Bingham Model 30

Smith & Wesson Model 1000 Magnum.......... $325
Same as standard Model 1000, except chambered for 12 gauge magnum 3-inch shell; 30-inch barrel only, modified or full choke; stock with recoil pad; weight, about 8 pounds. Introduced in 1977.

Smith & Wesson Model 3000 Slide Action...... $285
Hammerless. 20-gauge. Barrels: 26-inch improved cylinder, 28-inch modified and 28-inch full. Chambered for 3-inch Magnum and 2¾-inch loads. American walnut stock and forearm. Checkered pistol grip and forearm. Introduced in 1982.

Squires Bingham Co., Inc.
Makati, Rizal, Philippines

Squires Bingham Model 30 Pump Shotgun...... $110
Hammerless. 12 gauge. 5-shot magazine. Barrels: 20-inch cylinder, 28-inch modified, 30-inch full choke. Weight, about 7 pounds. Pulong Dalaga stock and slide handle. Currently manufactured.

J. Stevens Arms Company,
Chicopee Falls, Massachusetts;
now a division of Savage Arms Corporation

Stevens Model 620 Hammerless Slide Action Repeating Shotgun...$150
Takedown. Gauges: 12, 16, 20. 5-shell tubular magazine. Barrel lengths: 26-, 28-, 30-, 32-inch; chokes: full, modified, improved cylinder, cylinder. Weights: about 7¾ pounds in 12 gauge, 7¼ in 16 gauge, 6 pounds in 20 gauge. Checkered pistol-grip stock and slide handle. Made from 1927 to 1953.

Stevens Model 621............................... $180
Same as Model 620, except has raised solid matted-rib barrel. Discontinued.

Stevens Model 530 Hammerless Double Barrel Shotgun...$160
Box lock. Double triggers. Gauges: 12, 16, 20, 410. Barrel lengths: 26- to 32-inch; chokes: modified and full, cylinder and modified, full and full. Weight, from 6 to 7½ pounds depending upon gauge and barrel length. Checkered pistol-grip stock and forearm, some early models were fitted with recoil pad. Made from 1936 to 1954.

Stevens Model 530ST Double Gun............... $175
Same as Model 530, except has non-selective single trigger. Discontinued.

Stevens Model 530M............................. $120
Same as Model 530, except has "Tenite" (plastic) stock and forearm. Discontinued about 1947.

Stevens Model 820 Hammerless Slide Action Repeating Shotgun.......................................$125
Solid frame. 12 gauge only. 5-shell tubular magazine. 28-inch barrel; improved cylinder, modified or full choke. Weight, about 7½ pounds. Plain pistol-grip stock, grooved slide handle. Made from 1949 to 1954.

Stevens Model 820-SC........................... $145
Same as Model 820, except has Savage Super Choke.

Stevens-Springfield Model 311 Hammerless Double Barrel Shotgun................................. $185
Same general specifications as Stevens Model 530, except earlier production has plain stock and forearm; checkered on current guns. Originally produced as a "Springfield" gun, this model became a part of the "Stevens" line in 1948 when the "Springfield" brand name was discontinued. Made from 1931 to date.

Stevens Model 620

Stevens Model 530ST

Stevens Model 311

Stevens Model 311-R

Stevens Model 258

Stevens Model 58-410

Stevens Model 58

Stevens Model 59

Stevens Model 311-R Hammerless Double Barrel Shotgun..$165
Same general specifications as Stevens Model 311 except compact design for law enforcement use. Barrels: 18¼-inch 12 gauge with solid rib, chambered for 2¾" and 3" mag. shells. Double triggers and automatic top tang safety. Walnu finished hardwood stock with recoil pad and semi-beavertail forend. Weight About 6¾ pounds. Made from 1982 to date.

Stevens No. 22-410 Over-and-Under Combination Gun
22 caliber rifle barrel over 410 bore shotgun barrel. Visible hammer. Takedown. Single trigger. 24-inch barrels, shotgun barrel full choke. Weight, about 6 pounds. Open rear sight and ramp front sight of sporting rifle type. Plain pistol-grip stock and forearm; originally supplied with walnut stock and forearm, "Tenite" (plastic) was used in later production. Made from 1938 to 1950. *Note:* This gun is now manfactured as the Savage Model 24.
With wood stock and forearm.........................$115
With Tenite stock and forearm........................ 105

Stevens Model 240 Over-and-Under Shotgun... $225
Visible hammer. Takedown. Double triggers. 410 gauge. 26-inch barrels, full choke. Weight, about 6 pounds. "Tenite" (plastic) pistol-grip stock and forearm. Made from 1940 to 1949.

Stevens Model 258 Bolt Action Repeating Shotgun..$ 70
Takedown. 20-gauge. 2-shell detachable box magazine. 26-inch barrel, full choke. Weight, about 6¼ pounds. Plain one-piece pistol-grip stock. Made from 1937 to 1965.

Stevens Model 58 Bolt Action Repeating Shotgun..$70
Takedown. Gauges: 12, 16, 20. 2-shell detachable box magazine. 26-inch barrel, full choke. Weight, about 7¼ pounds. Plain one-piece pistol-grip stock. Made from 1933 to 1981. *Note:* Later production models have 3-inch chamber in 20 gauge, checkered stock with recoil pad.

Stevens Model 58- 410 Bolt Action Repeating Shotgun..$ 70
Takedown. 410 gauge. 3-shell detachable box magazine. 24-inch barrel, full choke. Weight, about 5½ pounds. Plain one-piece pistol-grip stock, checkered on later production. Made from 1937 to 1981.

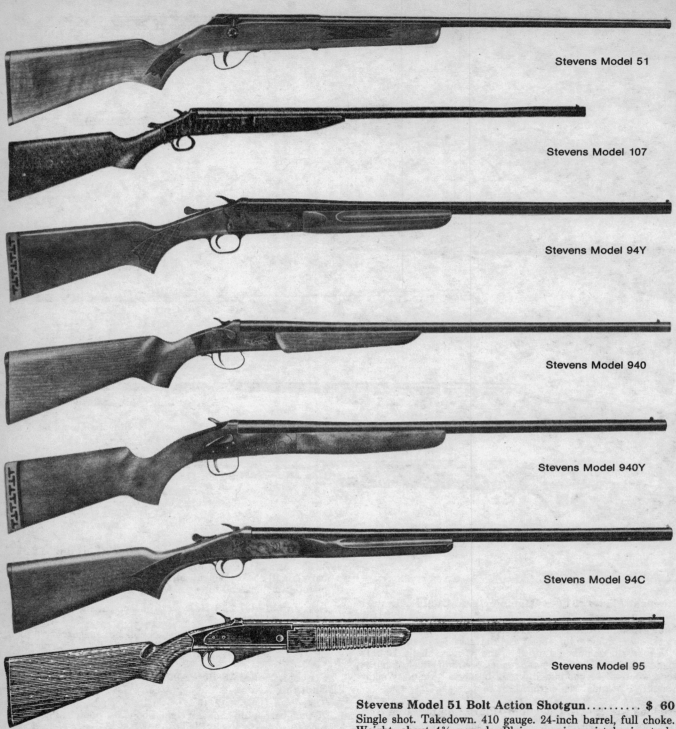

Stevens Model 51

Stevens Model 107

Stevens Model 94Y

Stevens Model 940

Stevens Model 940Y

Stevens Model 94C

Stevens Model 95

Stevens Model 51 Bolt Action Shotgun.........$ 60
Single shot. Takedown. 410 gauge. 24-inch barrel, full choke.
Weight, about 4¾ pounds. Plain one-piece pistol-grip stock,
checkered on later production. Made from 1962 to 1971.

**Stevens Model 107 Single Barrel Hammer
Shotgun...$ 55**
Takedown. Automatic ejector. Gauges: 12, 16, 20, 410. Barrel
lengths: 28- and 30-inch (12 and 16 gauge), 28-inch (20 gauge),
26-inch (410 gauge); full choke only. Weight, about 6 pounds (12
gauge). Plain pistol-grip stock and forearm. Made from about
1937 to 1953.

**Stevens Model 59 Bolt Action Repeating
Shotgun...$ 70**
Takedown. 410 gauge. 5-shell tubular magazine. 24-inch barrel,
full choke. Weight, about 6 pounds. Plain, one-piece pistol-grip
stock, checkered on later production. Made from 1934 to 1973.

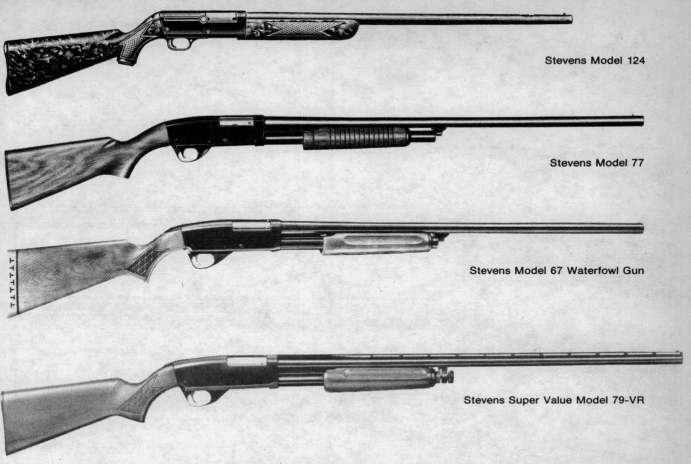

Stevens Model 124

Stevens Model 77

Stevens Model 67 Waterfowl Gun

Stevens Super Value Model 79-VR

Stevens Model 94 Single Barrel Shotgun....... **$ 55**
Takedown. Visible hammer. Automatic ejector. Gauges: 12, 16, 20, 28, 410. Barrels: 26-, 28-, 30-, 32-, 36-inch; full choke. Weight, average 6 pounds, depending upon gauge and barrel. Plain pistol-grip stock and forearm. Made from 1939 to 1961.

Stevens Model 94Y Youth's Gun................. **$ 55**
Same as Model 94, except made in 20 and 410 gauge only; has 26-inch full choke barrel, 12½-inch buttstock with recoil pad; checkered pistol grip and fluted forearm on late production. Made from 1959 to date.

Stevens Model 940 Single Barrel Shotgun....... **$ 55**
Same general specifications as Model 94, except has side lever opening instead of top lever. Made from 1961 to 1970.

Stevens Model 940Y Youth's Gun................ **$ 55**
Same general specifications as Model 94Y, except has side lever opening instead of top lever. Made from 1961 to 1970.

Stevens Model 94C.............................. **$ 55**
Same as Model 94, except has checkered stock, fluted forearm on late production. Made from 1965 to date.

Stevens Model 95 Single Barrel Shotgun....... **$ 55**
Solid frame. Visible hammer. Plain extractor. 12 gauge. 3-inch chamber. Barrels: 28-inch, modified; 30-inch, full choke. Weight, about 7¼ pounds. Plain pistol-grip stock, grooved forearm. Made from 1965 to 1969.

Stevens Model 124 Cross Bolt Repeater........ **$ 85**
Hammerless. Solid frame. 12 gauge only. 2-shot tubular magazine. 28-inch barrel; improved cylinder, modified or full choke. Weight, about 7 pounds. Tenite stock and forearm. Made from 1947 to 1952.

**Stevens Model 77 Slide Action Repeating
Shotgun**..**$140** ✓
Solid frame. Gauges: 12, 16, 20. 5-shot tubular magazine. Barrels: 26-inch, improved cylinder; 28-inch, modified or full choke. Weight, about 7½ pounds. Plain pistol-grip stock with recoil pad, grooved slide handle. Made from 1954 to 1971.

Stevens Model 77-AC............................ **$135**
Same as Model 77, except has Savage Super Choke.

Stevens Model 67 Waterfowl Shotgun.......... **$115**
Hammerless. Gauge: 12. 3-shot tubular magazine. Walnut finished hardwood stock. Weight: about 7½ pounds. Made from 1972 to date.

Stevens Model 67 Shotgun....................... **$115**
Same general specifications as Model 67 Waterfowl, except chambered for 12, 16, 20 and 410 gauges with various barrel lengths and chokes from 26-inch to 30-inch. Weight: 6¼ - 7½ pounds.

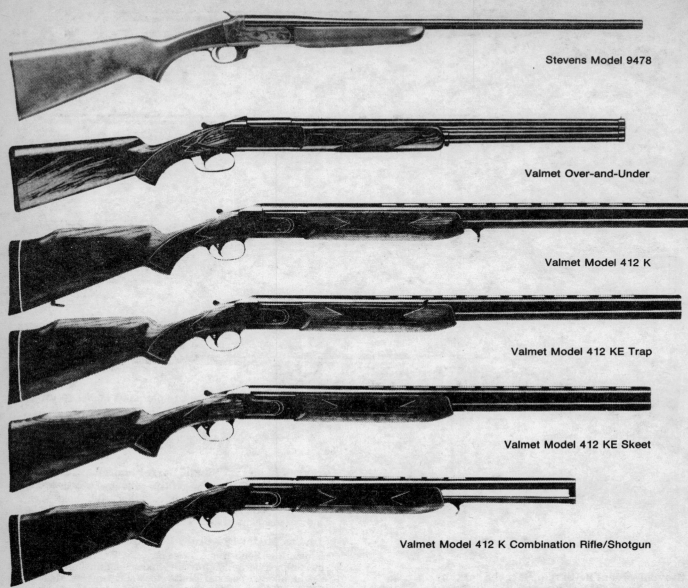

Stevens Model 9478

Valmet Over-and-Under

Valmet Model 412 K

Valmet Model 412 KE Trap

Valmet Model 412 KE Skeet

Valmet Model 412 K Combination Rifle/Shotgun

Stevens Super Value Model 79-VR.............. $140
Hammerless, side ejection. Barrel: chambered for 2¾-inch and 3-inch mag. shells. 12, 20, and 410 gauge. Ventilated rib. Walnut finished hardwood stock with checkering on grip. Weight: 6¾-7 pounds. Made from 1979 to date.

Stevens Model 9478............................. $ 50
Takedown. Visible hammer. Automatic ejector. Gauges: 12, 20, 410. Barrels: 26-, 28-, 30-, 36-inch; full choke. Weight, average 6 pounds, depending upon gauge and barrel. Plain pistol-grip stock and forearm. Made from 1978 to date.

Valmet Oy, Helsinki, Finland

Valmet Lion Over-and-Under Shotgun.......... $425
Box lock. Selective single trigger. Plain extractors. 12 gauge only. Barrels: 26-inch, improved cylinder and modified; 28-inch, modified and full; 30-inch, modified and full, full and full. Weight, about 7 pounds. Checkered pistol-grip stock and forearm. Made from 1947 to 1968. See also listings under Savage, whose Models 330, 333T, 333, and 2400 are Valmet guns.

Valmet Model 412K Over-and-Under Field Shotgun... $490
Hammerless. 12-gauge, 3-inch chamber. 36-inch barrel, full/full chokes. American walnut Monte Carlo stock. Made from 1982 to date.

Valmet Model 412 KE Over-and-Under Field Shotgun... $490
12-gauge chambered for 2¾-inch shells; 26-inch barrel, IC/M chokes; 28-inch barrel, M/F chokes; 12-gauge chambered for 3-inch shells, 30-inch barrel, M/F chokes. 20-guage chambered for 3-inch shells; 26-inch barrel IC/M chokes; 28-inch barrel, M/F chokes. American walnut Monte Carlo stock.

Valmet Model 412 KE Trap..................... $500
Similar to Model 412 K Field, except trap stock, recoil pad. 30-inch barrels (IM/F chokes).

Valmet Model 412 KE Skeet.................... $500
Similar to Model 412 K, except Skeet stock and chokes. 12 and 20 gauges.

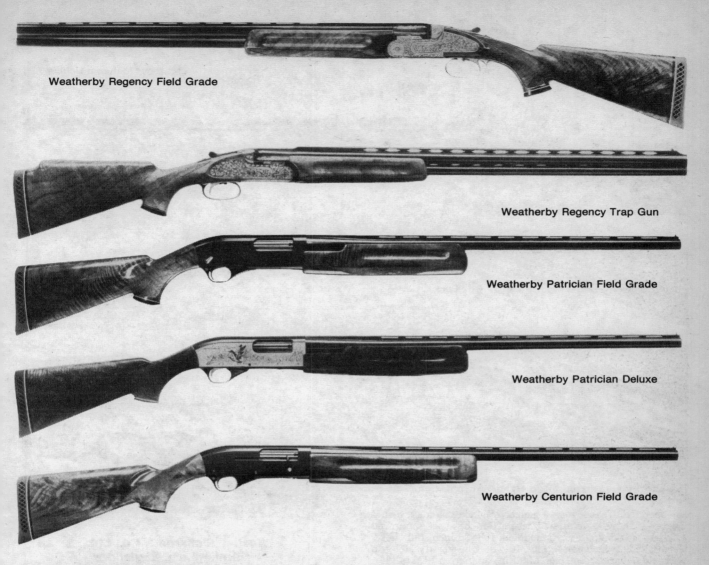

Weatherby Regency Field Grade

Weatherby Regency Trap Gun

Weatherby Patrician Field Grade

Weatherby Patrician Deluxe

Weatherby Centurion Field Grade

Valmet Model 412 K Combination Shotgun/Rifle **$550**
Similar to Model 412 K, except bottom barrel chambered for either .222 Rem., 223 Rem., 243 Win., 308 Win. or 30-06. 12-gauge shotgun barrel IMP/MOD. Monte Carlo American walnut stock, recoil pad.

Weatherby, Inc., South Gate, California

Weatherby Regency Field Grade Over-and-Under Shotgun **$800**
Box lock with side plates, elaborately engraved. Automatic ejectors. Selective single trigger. Gauges: 12, 20. 2¾-inch chamber in 12 gauge, 3-inch in 20 gauge. Barrels: ventilated rib; 26-inch, skeet, improved cylinder and modified, modified and full (20 gauge only); 28-inch, skeet; improved cylinder and modified, modified and full; 30-inch, modified and full (12 gauge only). Weight, with 28-inch barrels, 7 lbs. 6 oz. in 12 gauge, 6 lbs. 14 oz. in 20 gauge. Checkered pistol-grip stock and forearm of fancy walnut. Made in Italy from 1965 to 1982.

Weatherby Regency Trap Gun **$950**
Similar to Regency Field Grade, except has trap-style stock with straight or Monte Carlo comb; barrels have ventilated side ribs and high, wide ventilated top rib: 30- or 32-inch, modified and full, improved modified and full, both full choke; weight, with 32-inch barrels, 8 pounds. Made in Italy from 1965 to 1982.

Weatherby Patrician Field Grade Slide Action Shotgun **$285**
Hammerless. Takedown. 12 gauge. 2¾-inch chamber. 4-shot tubular magazine. Barrels: ventilated rib; 26-inch, skeet, improved cylinder, modified; 28-inch, modified, full; 30-inch, full choke. Weight, with 28-inch barrel, 7 lbs. 7 oz. Checkered pistol-grip stock and slide handle, recoil pad. Made in Japan from 1972 to 1982.

Weatherby Patrician Trap Gun **$325**
Same as Patrician Field Grade, except has 30-inch full choke barrel only, trap-style stock; weight, 7 lbs. 9 oz. Made in Japan from 1972 to 1982.

Weatherby Patrician Deluxe **$375**
Same as Patrician Field Grade, except has etched receiver, fancy grade wood. Made in Japan from 1972 to 1982.

Weatherby Centurion Deluxe

Westley Richards Best Quality Side Lock

Westley Richards Modele Deluxe Box Lock

Westley Richards Model E

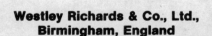

Western Long Range

Weatherby Centurion Field Grade Automatic Shotgun..$285
Gas-operated. Takedown. 12 gauge. 2¾-inch chamber. 3-shot magazine. Barrels; ventilated ribs; 26-inch, skeet, improved cylinder, modified; 28-inch, modified, full; 30-inch, full choke. Weight, with 28-inch barrel, 7 lbs. 10½ oz. Checkered pistol-grip stock and forearm, recoil pad. Made in Japan from 1972 to 1981.

Weatherby Centurion Trap Gun....................$305
Same as Centurion Field Grade, except has 30-inch full choke barrel only, trap-style stock; weight, 7 lbs. 11¾ oz. Made in Japan from 1972 to 1981.

Weatherby Centurion Deluxe......................$335
Same as Centurion Field Grade, except has etched receiver, fancy grade wood. Made in Japan from 1972 to date.

Weatherby Ducks Unlimited Shotgun............$700

Western Arms Corp., a division of Ithaca Gun Co., Ithaca, New York

Western Long Range Hammerless Double Barrel Shotgun
Box lock. Plain extractors. Double triggers or single trigger. Gauges: 12, 16, 20, 410. Barrels: 26- to 32-inch, modified and full choke standard. Weight, about 7½ pounds in 12 gauge. Plain pistol-grip stock and fore-end. Made from 1929 to 1946.
With double triggers...................................$175
With single trigger.................................... 200

Westley Richards & Co., Ltd., Birmingham, England

Westley Richards Best Quality Side Lock Hammerless Double Barrel Shotgun
Hand-detachable side locks. Selective ejectors. Double triggers or selective single trigger. Gauges: 12, 16, 20, 28, 410. Barrel lengths and boring to order. Weight, from 4¾ to 6¾ pounds depending upon gauge and barrel length. Checkered stock and fore-end, straight- or half-pistol grip. Also supplied in Pigeon and Wildfowl Model for which values are the same. Currently manufactured.
With double triggers..............................$12,000
With selective single trigger..................... 13,000

Westley Richards Modele Deluxe Side Lock

Winchester Model 1887

Winchester Model 1901

Winchester Model 97

Westley Richards Modele Deluxe Side Lock

Same as Best Quality Side Lock, except higher grade engraving and wood. Currently manufactured.

With double triggers............................ $16,000
With single trigger............................... 17,000

Westley Richards Best Quality Box Lock Hammerless Double Barrel Shotgun

Box lock. Hand-detachable locks and hinged cover plate. Selective ejectors. Double triggers or selective single trigger. Gauges: 12, 16, 20. Barrel lengths and boring to order. Weight, from 5½ to 6¼ pounds depending upon gauge and barrel length. Checkered stock and fore-end, straight or half-pistol grip. Also supplied in Pigeon and Wildfowl Model for which values are the same. Currently manufactured, guns of this type have been produced by Westley Richards & Co. since 1899.

With double triggers............................... $7000
With selective single trigger........................ 7500

Westley Richards Modele Deluxe Box Lock Hammerless Double Barrel Shotgun

Same general specifications as standard Best Quality gun, except higher quality throughout, has Westley Richards top-projection and treble-bite lever-work, hand-detachable locks. Also supplied in Pigeon and Wildfowl Model; values are the same. Currently manufactured.

With double triggers............................... $7500
With selective single trigger........................ 8200

Westley Richards Model E Hammerless Double Barrel Shotgun

Anson & Deeley-type box lock action. Selective ejector or nonejector. Double triggers. Gauges: 12, 16, 20. Barrel lengths and boring to order. Weight, from 5½ to 7¼ pounds depending upon type, gauge and barrel length. Checkered stock and fore-end, straight- or half-pistol grip. Also supplied in Pigeon and Wildfowl Model; values are the same. Currently manufactured.

Ejector model...................................... $3000
Nonejector model................................... 2500

Note: Pigeon and Wildfowl Gun, available in all of the foregoing Westley Richards models, has the same general specifications as the corresponding standard field gun, except has magnum action of extra strength and treble bolting, is chambered for 12 gauge only (2¾- or 3-inch); 30-inch full choke barrels are standard; weight is about 8 pounds. The manufacturer warns that 12 gauge magnum shells should not be used in their standard weight double barrel shotguns.

Westley Richards Ovundo (Over-and-Under) Shotgun.. $14,000

Hammerless. Box lock. Hand-detachable locks. Dummy side plates. Selective ejectors. Selective single trigger. 12 gauge. Barrel lengths and boring to order. Checkered stock and fore-end, straight- or half-pistol grip. Manufactured prior to World War II.

Winchester-Western Div., Olin Corp. (formerly Winchester Repeating Arms Co.), New Haven, Connecticut

Winchester Model 1887 Lever Action Repeater. $475

Solid frame. Gauges: 10 and 12, 4-shot tubular magazine. Plain barrel; 30- and 32-inch, full choke. Plain pistol-grip stock and fore-end. Weights: 9 pounds in 10 ga., 8 pounds in 12 ga. (*Note:* This model was also offered in Deluxe Grade with Damascus barrel, checkered stock and fore-end.) Made from 1887 to 1901.

Winchester Model 1901 Lever Action Repeater. $800

Same general specifications as Model 1887 of which this is a redesigned version. 10 gauge only. Made from 1901 to 1920.

Winchester Model 97 Visible Hammer Slide Action Repeating Shotgun................................ $340

Standard Grade. Takedown or solid frame. Gauges: 12 and 16. 5-shell tubular magazine. Plain barrel; lengths: 26- to 32-inches (the latter made in 12 gauge only); chokes: full to cylinder. Weight, about 7¾ pounds (12 gauge with 28-inch barrel). Plain pistol-grip stock, grooved slide handle. Made from 1897 to 1957.

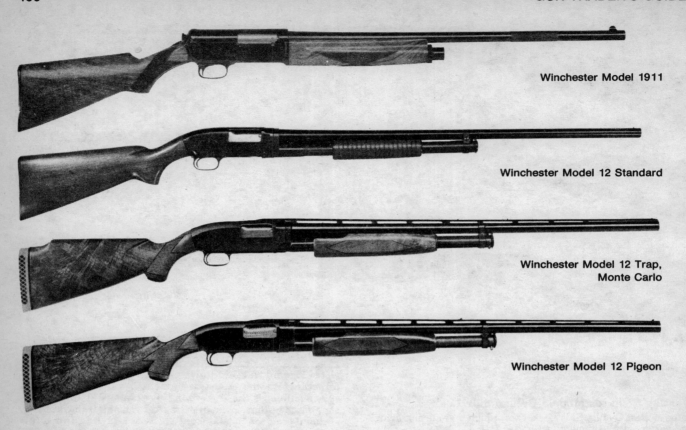

Winchester Model 1911

Winchester Model 12 Standard

Winchester Model 12 Trap, Monte Carlo

Winchester Model 12 Pigeon

Winchester Model 97 Riot Gun **$400**
Takedown or solid frame. Same general specifications as standard Model 97, except 12 gauge only, 20-inch cylinder bore barrel. Made from 1897 to 1957.

Winchester Model 97 Trench Gun **$450**
Solid frame. Same as Model 97 Riot Gun, except has handguard and is equipped with a bayonet. World War I government issue, 1917-1918.

Winchester Model 97 Trap, Tournament and Pigeon Grade Guns
These higher grade models, no longer produced, differ from the standard grade in type and forearm and higher general quality. Discontinued in 1939.
Trap Gun **$600**
Tournament Grade **700**
Pigeon Grade **900**

Winchester Model 1911 Autoloading Shotgun . . . **$250**
Hammerless. Takedown. 12 gauge only. 4-shell tubular magazine. Barrels: plain, 26- to 32-inch, standard borings. Weight, about 8½ pounds. Plain or checkered pistol-grip stock and forearm. Made from 1911 to 1925.

Winchester Model 12 Standard Slide Action Repeating Shotgun **$525**
Hammerless. Takedown. Gauges: 12, 16, 20, 28. 6-shell tubular magazine. Plain barrel. Lengths: 26- to 32-inches; chokes: full to cylinder. Weights: about 7½ pounds in 12 gauge 30-inch, about 6½ pounds in other gauges with 28-inch barrel. Plain pistol-grip stock, grooved slide handle. Made from 1912 to 1964.

Winchester Model 12 Featherweight **$495**
Same as Plain Barrel Model 12 Standard, except has alloy guard, modified takedown. 12 gauge only. Barrels: 26-inch, improved cylinder; 28-inch, modified or full; 30-inch, full choke. Weight, about 6¾ pounds. Made from 1959 to 1962.

Winchester Model 12 Standard Grade, Matted Rib **$550**
Same general specifications as Plain Barrel Model 12 Standard, except has solid raised matted rib. Discontinued after World War II.

Winchester Model 12 Standard Grade, Ventilated Rib **$675**
Same general specifications as Plain Barrel Model 12 Standard, except has ventilated rib. 26¾- or 30-inch barrel, 12 gauge only. Discontinued after World War II.

Winchester Model 12 Riot Gun **$350**
Same general specifications as Plain Barrel Model 12 Standard, except has 20-inch cylinder bore barrel, 12 gauge only. Made from 1918 to 1963.

Winchester Model 12 Heavy Duck Gun **$745**
12 gauge only, chambered for 3-inch shells. Same general specifications as Standard Grade, except 30- or 32-inch plain full choke barrel only, 3-shot magazine, recoil pad, weighs about 8¾ pounds. Discontinued in 1964.

Winchester Model 12 Heavy Duck Gun, Matted Rib Barrel **$795**
Same as Plain Barrel Model 12 Heavy Duck Gun, except has solid raised matted rib. Discontinued in 1959.

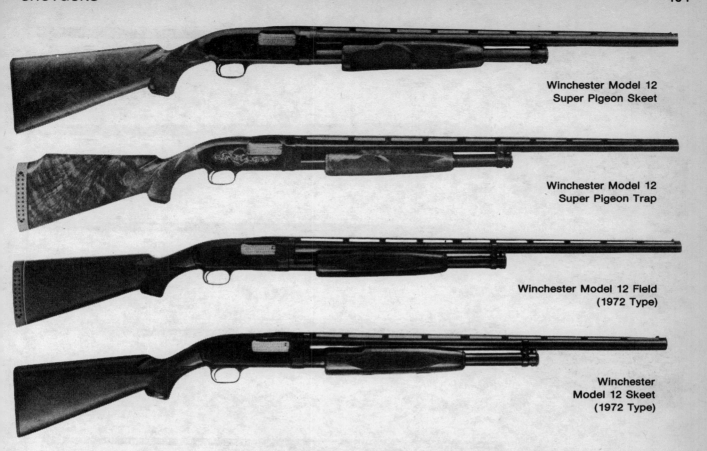

Winchester Model 12
Super Pigeon Skeet

Winchester Model 12
Super Pigeon Trap

Winchester Model 12 Field
(1972 Type)

Winchester
Model 12 Skeet
(1972 Type)

Winchester Model 12 Skeet Gun................ **$600**
Gauges: 12, 16, 20, 28. 5-shot tubular magazine. 26-inch matted rib barrel, skeet choke. Weights: about 7¾ pounds in 12 gauge, about 6¾ pounds in other gauges. Bradley red or ivory bead front sight. Winchester 94B middle sight. Checkered pistol-grip stock and extension slide handle. Discontinued after World War II.

**Winchester Model 12 Skeet Gun,
Ventilated Rib**..................................... **$700**
Same general specifications as standard Model 12 Skeet Gun, except has 26-inch barrel with ventilated rib, 12 and 20 gauge. Discontinued in 1965.

Winchester Model 12 Skeet Gun, Plain Barrel...**$550**
Same general specifications as standard Model 12 Skeet Gun, except has plain barrel. Made from 1937 to 1947.

**Winchester Model 12 Skeet Gun,
Cutts Compensator**............................... **$525**
Same general specifications as standard Model 12 Skeet Gun, except has plain barrel fitted with Cutts Compensator, 26 inches overall. Discontinued in 1954.

Winchester Model 12 Trap Gun................. **$700**
Same general specifications as standard Model 12, except has straighter stock, checkered pistol grip and extension slide handle, recoil pad, 30-inch matted-rib barrel, full choke, 12 gauge only. Discontinued after World War II.

**Winchester Model 12 Trap Gun, Ventilated Rib
Barrel**.. **$800**
Same as standard Model 12 Trap Gun, except has ventilated rib. Discontinued in 1965.

**Winchester Model 12 Trap Gun, Monte Carlo
Stock**.. **$750**
Same as Model 12 Ventilated Rib Trap Gun, except has Monte Carlo stock. Discontinued in 1965.

Winchester Model 12 Pigeon Grade
Deluxe versions of the regular Model 12 Standard or Field Gun, Duck Gun, Skeet Gun and Trap Gun made on special order. This grade has finer finish throughout, hand-smoothed action, engine-turned breech bolt and carrier, stock and extension slide handle of high grade walnut, fancy checkering, stock dimensions to individual specifications. Engraving and carving available at extra cost ranging from about $35 to over $200. Discontinued in 1965.

Field Gun, plain barrel........................	**$ 800**
Field Gun, ventilated rib......................	950
Skeet Gun, matted rib.........................	860
Skeet Gun, ventilated rib.....................	1035
Skeet Gun, Cutts Compensator..............	860
Trap Gun, matted rib..........................	1025
Trap Gun, ventilated rib......................	1200

Winchester Model 12 Super Pigeon Grade..... **$1800**
Custom version of Model 12 with same general specifications as standard models. 12 gauge only. 26-, 28-, or 30-inch ventilated-rib barrel, any standard choke. Engraved receiver. Hand-smoothed and fitted action. Full fancy walnut stock and forearm made to individual order. Made from 1965 to 1972.

Winchester Model 12 Field Gun, 1972 Type..... **$600**
Same general specifications as Standard Model 12. 12 gauge only. 26-, 28-, or 30-inch ventilated-rib barrel, standard chokes. Engine-turned bolt and carrier. Hand-checkered stock and slide handle of semi-fancy walnut. Made from 1972 to 1975.

Winchester Model 12 Trap
(1972 Type)

Winchester Single Shot

Winchester Model 20

Winchester Model 36

Winchester Model 41

Winchester Model 12 Skeet Gun, 1972 Type.... $700
Same general specifications as Standard Model 12. 12 gauge
only. 26-inch ventilated-rib barrel, skeet choke. Engine-turned
bolt and carrier. Hand-checkered skeet-style stock and slide
handle of choice walnut, recoil pad. Made from 1972 to 1975.

Winchester Model 12 Trap Gun, 1972 Type..... $800
Same general specifications as Standard Model 12. 12 gauge
only. 30-inch ventilated-rib barrel, full choke. Engine-turned
bolt and carrier. Hand-checkered trap-style stock (straight or
Monte Carlo comb) and slide handle of select walnut, recoil pad.
Made from 1972 to date.

Winchester Single Shot Lever Action Shotgun.. $675
Falling-block action, same as in Single Shot Rifle. High-wall
receiver. Solid frame or takedown. 20 gauge. 3-inch chamber. 26-
inch barrel; plain, matted, or matted rib; cylinder bore, modified,
or full choke. Weight, about 5½ pounds. Straight-grip stock and
forearm. Made from 1914 to 1916.

Winchester Model 20 Single Shot Hammer Gun. $225
Takedown. 410—2½-inch. 26-inch barrel, full choke. Checkered
pistol-grip stock and forearm. Weight, about 6 pounds. Made
from 1919 to 1924.

**Winchester Model 36 Single Shot Bolt Action
Shotgun...$175**
Takedown. Uses 9mm Short or Long shot or ball cartridges
interchangeably. 18-inch barrel. Plain stock. Weight, about 3
pounds. Made from 1920 to 1927.

**Winchester Model 41 Single Shot Bolt Action
Shotgun...$175**
Takedown. 410—2½-inch (chambered for 3-inch shells after
1932). 24-inch barrel, full choke. Plain straight stock standard.
Made from 1920 to 1934.

Winchester Model 21 Double Barrel Field Gun
Hammerless. Box lock. Automatic safety. Double triggers or
selective single trigger, selective or non-selective ejection (all
postwar Model 21 shotguns have selective single trigger and
selective ejection). Gauges: 12, 16, 20. Barrels: raised matted rib
or ventilated rib; 26-, 28-, 30-, 32-inch, the latter in 12 gauge
only; full choke, improved modified, modified, improved
cylinder, skeet chokes. Weights: 12 gauge with 30-inch barrel,
about 7½ pounds; 16 or 20 gauge with 28-inch barrel, about 6½
pounds. Pistol-grip or straight-grip stock, regular or beavertail
fore-end, both checkered. Made from 1930 to 1958.
With double trigger, non-selective ejection........... **$1600**
With double trigger, selective ejection.............. 1800
With selective single trigger, non-selective ejection.... 1850
With selective single trigger, selective ejection........ 1950
Extra for ventilated rib............................ 175

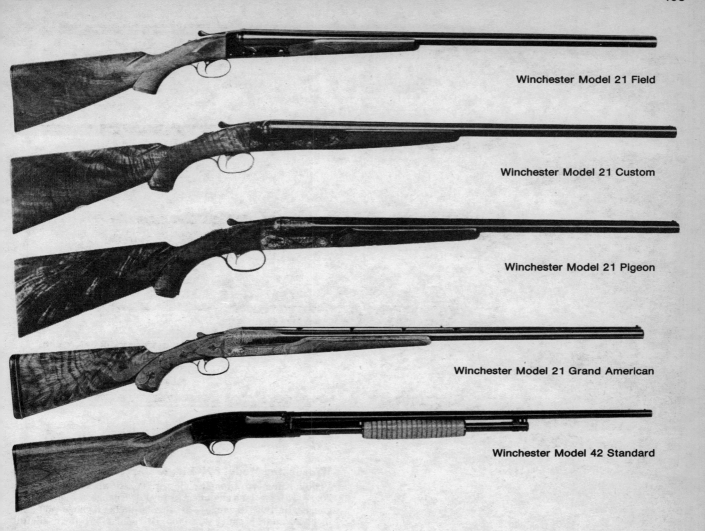

Winchester Model 21 Field

Winchester Model 21 Custom

Winchester Model 21 Pigeon

Winchester Model 21 Grand American

Winchester Model 42 Standard

Winchester Model 21 Duck Gun
Same general specifications as Model 21 Field Gun, except chambered for 12 gauge 3-inch shells, 30- or 32-inch barrels only, full choke, selective single trigger, selective ejection, pistol-grip stock with recoil pad, beavertail forearm, both checkered. Discontinued 1958.
With matted-rib barrels.............................$1950
With ventilated-rib barrels......................... 2200

Winchester Model 21 Skeet Gun
Same general specifications as Model 21 Standard, except has 26- or 28-inch barrels only, skeet chokes No. 1 and 2, Bradley red bead front sight, selective single trigger, selective ejection, nonautomatic safety, checkered pistol-grip or straight-grip stock without butt plate or pad (wood butt checkered), checkered beavertail forearm. Discontinued in 1958.
With matted-rib barrels............................ $2300
With ventilated-rib barrels......................... 3000

Winchester Model 21 Trap Gun
Same general specifications as Model 21 Standard, except has 30- or 32-inch barrels only, full choke, selective single trigger, selective ejection, nonautomatic safety, checkered pistol-grip or straight-grip stock with recoil pad, checkered beavertail forearm. Discontinued in 1958.
With matted-rib barrels............................ $2300
With ventilated-rib barrels......................... 3000

Winchester Model 21 Custom, Pigeon, Grand American
Since 1959, the Model 21 has been offered only in deluxe models: Custom, Pigeon, Grand American—on special order. General specifications same as for Model 21 standard models, except these custom guns have full fancy American walnut stock and forearm with fancy checkering, finely polished and hand-smoothed working parts, etc.; engraving inlays, carved stocks and other extras are available at additional cost. Made from 1960 to date.
Custom Grade.. $4500
Pigeon Grade.. 6300
Grand American..................................... 9950

Winchester Model 42 Standard Slide Action Repeating Shotgun...$545
Hammerless. Takedown. 410 Bore (3- or 2½-inch shell). Tubular magazine holds five 3-inch or six 2½-inch shells. 26- or 28-inch plain barrel; cylinder bore, modified or full choke. Weight, about 6 pounds. Plain pistol-grip stock; grooved slide handle. Made from 1933 to 1963.

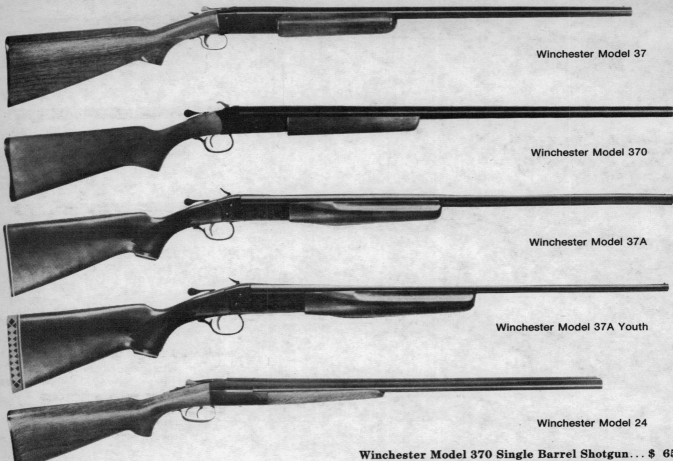

Winchester Model 37

Winchester Model 370

Winchester Model 37A

Winchester Model 37A Youth

Winchester Model 24

**Winchester Model 42 Standard Grade,
Matted Rib Barrel**............................... **$675**
Same general specifications as Plain Barrel Model 42, except has
solid raised matted rib. Discontinued in 1963.

Winchester Model 42 Skeet Gun................. **$975**
Same general specifications as Model 42 Standard, except has
checkered straight-grip or pistol-grip stock and extension slide
handle, 26- or 28-inch matted-rib barrel, skeet choke. *Note:*
Some Model 42 Skeet Guns are chambered for 2½-inch shells
only. Discontinued in 1963.

Winchester Model 42 Deluxe................... **$825**
Same general specifications as the Model 42 Standard, except
has ventilated rib, finer finish throughout, hand-smoothed action, engine turned breech bolt and carrier, stock and extension
slide handle of high grade walnut, fancy checkering, stock
dimensions to invididual specifications. Engraving and carving
were offered at extra cost. Made from 1933 to 1963.

Winchester Model 37 Single Barrel Shotgun.... **$135**
Semi-hammerless. Automatic ejection. Takedown. Gauges: 12,
16, 20, 28, 410. Barrel lengths: 28-, 30-, 32-inch in all gauges
except 410, 26- or 28-inch in 410; all barrels plain and full choke.
Weight, about 6½ pounds in 12 gauge. Made from 1937 to 1963.

Winchester Model 370 Single Barrel Shotgun... **$ 65**
Visible hammer. Automatic ejector. Takedown. Gauges: 12, 16,
20, 28, 410. 2¾-inch chambers in 16 and 28 gauge, 3-inch in other
gauges. Barrels: 12 gauge—30-, 32-, 36-inch; 16 gauge—30-, 32-
inch; 20 and 28 gauge—28-inch; 410 gauge—26-inch; all full
choke. Weight, 5½ to 6¼ pounds, depending upon gauge and
barrel. Plain pistol-grip stock and forearm. Made from 1968 to
1973.

Winchester Model 370 Youth.................... **$ 75**
Same as standard Model 370, except has 26-inch barrel and
12½-inch stock with recoil pad; 20 gauge with improved modified choke, 410 gauge with full choke. Made from 1968 to 1973.

Winchester Model 37A Single Barrel Shotgun... **$ 75**
Similar to Model 370, except has engraved receiver and gold
trigger, checkered pistol-grip stock, fluted forearm; 16 gauge
available with 30-inch barrel only. Made from 1973 to date.

Winchester Model 37A Youth.................... **$ 75**
Similar to Model 370 Youth, except has engraved receiver and
gold trigger, checkered pistol-grip stock, fluted forearm. Made
from 1973 to date.

**Winchester Model 24 Hammerless Double Barrel
Shotgun**... **$300**
Box lock. Double triggers. Plain extractors. Automatic safety.
Gauges: 12, 16, 20. Barrels: 26-inch improved cylinder and
modified, 28-inch modified and full (also improved cylinder and
modified in 12 gauge only), 30-inch modified and full in 12 gauge
only. Weight, about 7½ pounds in 12 gauge. Metal bead front
sight. Plain pistol-grip stock, semi-beavertail forearm. Made
from 1939 to 1957.

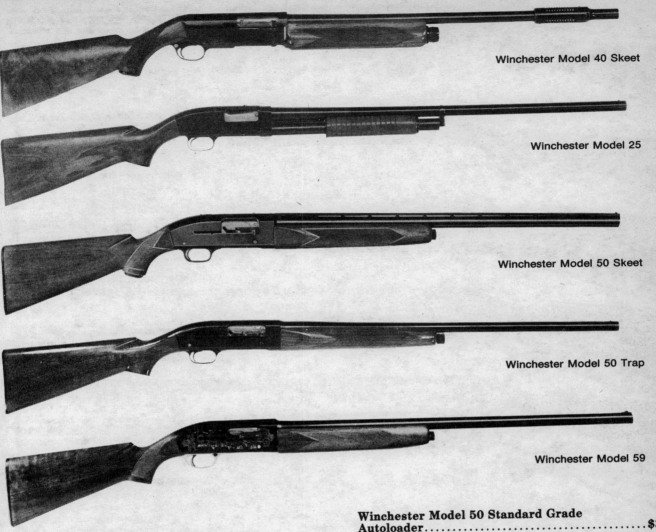

Winchester Model 40 Skeet

Winchester Model 25

Winchester Model 50 Skeet

Winchester Model 50 Trap

Winchester Model 59

Winchester Model 40 Standard Autoloading Shotgun..**$400**
Streamlined receiver. Hammerless. Takedown. 12 gauge only. 4-shell tubular magazine. 28- or 30-inch barrel; modified or full choke. Weight, about 8 pounds. Bead sight on ramp. Plain pistol-grip stock, semi-beavertail forearm. Made from 1940 to 1941.

Winchester Model 40 Skeet Gun................**$475**
Same general specifications as Model 40 Standard, except has 24-inch plain barrel with Cutts Compensator, checkered forearm and pistol grip, grip cap. Made from 1940 to 1941.

Winchester Model 25 Slide Action Repeating Shotgun...**$275**
Hammerless. Solid frame. 12 gauge only. 4-shell tubular magazine. 28-inch plain barrel; improved cylinder, modified or full choke. Weight, about 7½ pounds. Metal bead front sight. Plain pistol-grip stock, grooved slide handle. Made from 1949 to 1955.

Winchester Model 25 Riot Gun...................**$250**
Same as Model 25 Standard, except has 20-inch cylinder bore barrel, 12 gauge only. Made from 1949 to 1955.

Winchester Model 50 Standard Grade Autoloader...**$375**
Non recoiling barrel and independent chamber. Gauges: 12 and 20. 2-shot tubular magazine. Barrels: 12 ga.—26-, 28-, 30-inch; 20 ga.—26-, 28-inch; improved cylinder, skeet choke, modified, full choke. Checkered pistol-grip stock and forearm. Weight, about 7¾ pounds. Made from 1954 to 1961.

Winchester Model 50 Field Gun, Ventilated Rib. $425
Same as Model 50 Standard, except has ventilated rib.

Winchester Model 50 Skeet Gun................**$475**
Same as Model 50 Standard, except has 26-inch ventilated-rib barrel with skeet choke, skeet-style stock of selected walnut.

Winchester Model 50 Trap Gun..................**$525**
Same as Model 50 Standard, except 12 gauge only, has 30-inch ventilated-rib barrel with full choke, Monte Carlo stock of selected walnut.

Winchester Model 59 Autoloading Shotgun......**$400**
12 gauge. Magazine holds two shells. Alloy receiver. Win-Lite steel and fiberglass barrel: 26-inch improved cylinder, 28-inch modified or full choke, 30-inch full choke; also furnished with 26-inch barrel with Versalite choke (interchangeable full, modified, improved cylinder tubes; one supplied with gun). Weight, about 6-12 pounds. Checkered pistol-grip stock and forearm. Made from 1959 to 1965.

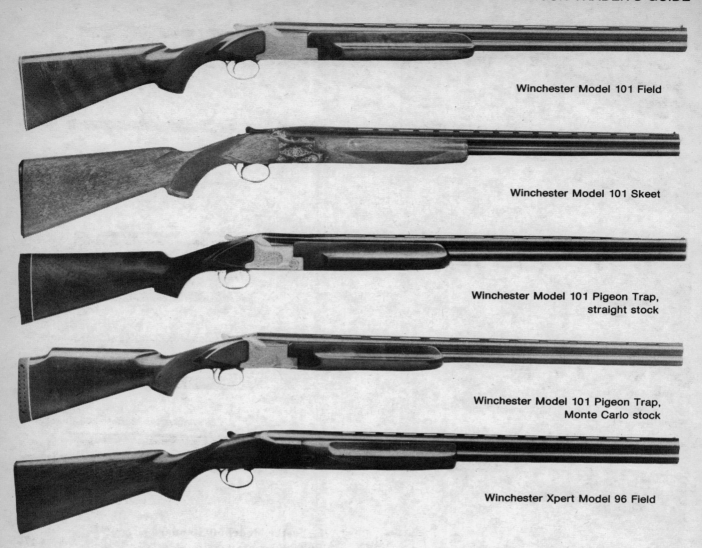

Winchester Model 101 Field

Winchester Model 101 Skeet

Winchester Model 101 Pigeon Trap,
straight stock

Winchester Model 101 Pigeon Trap,
Monte Carlo stock

Winchester Xpert Model 96 Field

Winchester Model 101 Over-and-Under Field Gun

Box lock. Engraved receiver. Automatic ejectors. Single selective trigger. Combination barrel selector and safety. Gauges: 12 and 28—2¾-inch chambers, 20 and 410—3-inch chambers. Ventilated-rib barrels: 30- (12 ga. only) and 26½-inch, improved cylinder and modified. Weight, 6¼ to 7¾ pounds depending upon gauge and barrel length. Hand-checkered French walnut stock and forearm. Made from 1963 to date. (gauges other than 12 introduced in 1966).

12 and 20 gauge...$700
28 and 410 gauge................................... 820

Winchester Model 101 Magnum Field Gun.......$750

Same as Model 101 Field Gun, except chamber for 12 or 20 ga. 3-inch magnum shells only, 30-inch barrels (full and full or modified and full), recoil pad. Made from 1966 to date.

Winchester Model 101 Skeet Gun

Same as Model 101 Field Gun, except skeet-style stock and forearm; barrels: 12 ga., 26-inch; 20 ga. 26½-inch; 28 and 410 ga., 28-inch; all skeet choked. Made from 1966 to date.

12 and 20 gauge.....................................$750
28 and 410 gauge.................................... 800

Winchester Model 101 Pigeon Grade

Same general specifications as standard Model 101 Field, Skeet, and Trap Guns, except higher grade with more elaborately engraved satin gray steel receiver, fancier wood and finer checkering. 12 and 20 gauge only. Made from 1974 to date.

Field Gun..$850
Skeet Gun... 950
Trap Gun with straight stock........................ 950
Trap Gun with Monte Carlo stock.................... 975

Winchester Xpert Model 96 Over-and-Under
Field Gun..$550

Box lock action similar to Model 101. Plain receiver. Automatic ejectors. Selective single trigger. Gauges: 12, 20. 3-inch chambers. Barrels: ventilated rib; 26-inch, improved cylinder and modified; 28-inch modified and full; 30-inch, both full choke (12 gauge only). Weight, 6¼ to 8¼ pounds, depending upon gauge and barrels. Checkered pistol-grip stock and forearm. Made from 1976 to date.

Winchester Xpert Model 96 Skeet Gun.........$600

Same as Xpert Field Gun, except has 2¾-inch chambers, 27-inch barrels, skeet choke, skeet-style stock and forearm. Made from 1976 to date.

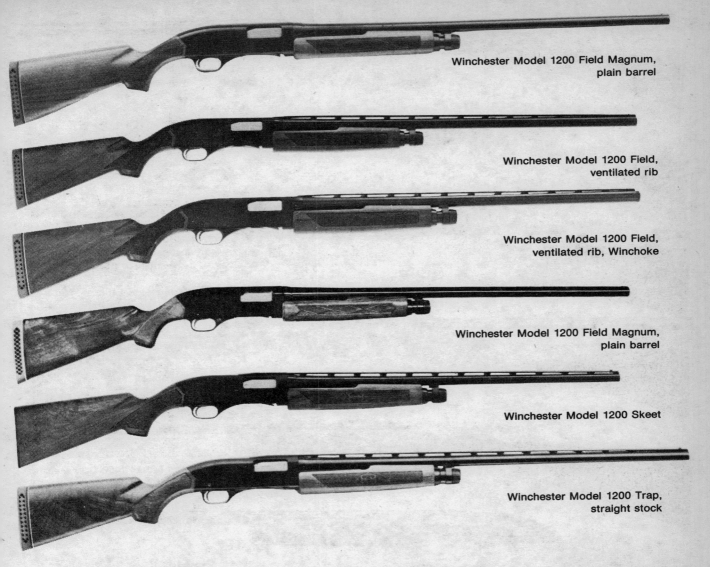

Winchester Model 1200 Field Magnum, plain barrel

Winchester Model 1200 Field, ventilated rib

Winchester Model 1200 Field, ventilated rib, Winchoke

Winchester Model 1200 Field Magnum, plain barrel

Winchester Model 1200 Skeet

Winchester Model 1200 Trap, straight stock

Winchester Xpert Model 96 Trap Gun

Same as Xpert Field Gun, except 12 gauge only, 2¾-inch chambers, has 30-inch barrels, improved modified and full or both full choke, trap-style stock (straight or Monte Carlo comb) with recoil pad. Made from 1976 to date.
With straight stock.....................................$650
With Monte Carlo stock.............................. 675

Note: Models 101 and Xpert Model 96 shotguns are manufactured by Olin-Kodensha Company, Tochigi, Japan.

Winchester Model 1200 Slide Action Field Gun

Front-locking rotary bolt. Takedown. 4-shot magazine. Gauges: 12, 16, 20 (2¾-inch chamber). Barrel: plain or ventilated rib; 26-, 28-, 20-inch; improved cylinder, modified, full choke, or with Winchoke (interchangeable tubes IC-M-F). Weights: 6½ to 7¼ pounds. Checkered pistol-grip stock and forearm (slide handle), recoil pad; also available 1966-70 with Winchester Recoil Reduction System (Cycolac stock). Made from 1964 to date.
With plain barrel.....................................$160
With ventilated-rib barrel............................ 170

Add for Winchoke.................................... 5
Add for Winchester Recoil Reduction System.......... 50

Winchester Model 1200 Field Gun—Magnum

Same as standard Model 1200, except chambered for 3-inch 12 and 20 gauge magnum shells; plain or ventilated-rib barrel, 28- or 30-inch, full choke; weight, 7⅜ to 7⅞ pounds. Made from 1964 to date.
With plain barrel.....................................$165
With ventilated-rib barrel............................ 175
Add for Winchester Recoil Reduction System.......... 50

Winchester Model 1200 Deer Gun...............$165

Same as standard Model 1200, except has special 22-inch barrel, with rifle-type sights, for rifled slug or buckshot; 12 gauge only; weight, 6½ pounds. Made from 1965 to 1974.

Winchester Model 1200 Skeet Gun.............$200

Same as standard Model 1200, except 12 and 20 gauge only; has 2-shot magazine, specially tuned trigger, 26-inch ventilated-rib barrel—skeet choke, semi-fancy walnut stock and forearm; also available 1966-70 with Winchester Recoil Reduction System (add $50 to value); weight, 7¼ to 7½ pounds. Made from 1965 to 1973.

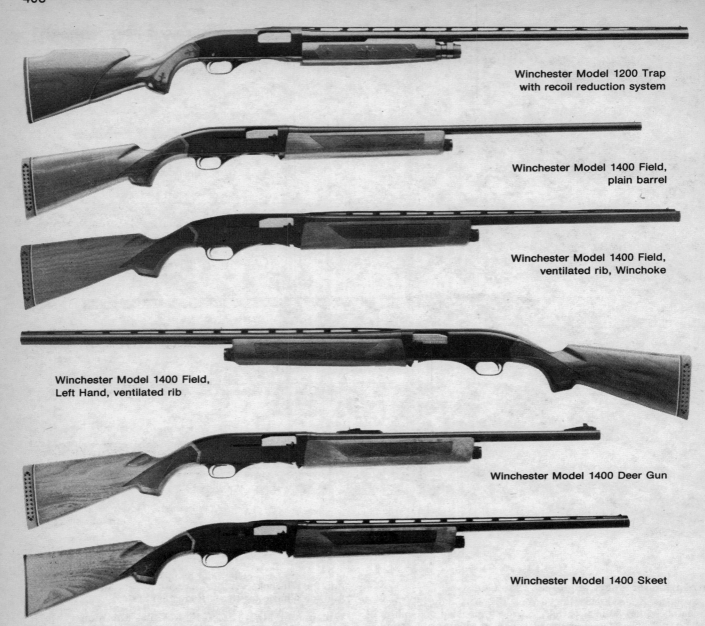

Winchester Model 1200 Trap
with recoil reduction system

Winchester Model 1400 Field,
plain barrel

Winchester Model 1400 Field,
ventilated rib, Winchoke

Winchester Model 1400 Field,
Left Hand, ventilated rib

Winchester Model 1400 Deer Gun

Winchester Model 1400 Skeet

Winchester Model 1200 Trap Gun

Same as standard Model 1200, except 12 gauge only; has 2-shot magazine, 30-inch ventilated-rib barrel—full choke or 28-inch with Winchoke; semi-fancy walnut stock, straight or Monte Carlo trap style; also available 1966-70 with Winchester Recoil Reduction System; weight, about 8¼ pounds. Made from 1965 to 1973.

With straight-trap stock.............................. **$265**
With Monte Carlo stock.............................. 275
Add for Winchester Recoil Reduction System.......... 50
Add for Winchoke.................................... 5

Winchester Model 1400 Automatic Field Gun

Gas-operated. Front-locking rotary bolt. Takedown. 2-shot magazine. Gauges: 12, 16, 20 (2¾-inch chamber). Barrel: plain or ventilated rib; 26-, 28-, 30-inch; improved cylinder, modified, full choke, or with Winchoke (interchangeable tubes IC-M-F). Weights: 6½ to 7¼ pounds. Checkered pistol-grip stock and forearm, recoil pad; also available with Winchester Reduction System (Cycolac stock). Made from 1964 to 1968.

With plain barrel.................................... **$205**
With ventilated-rib barrel............................ 225
Add for Winchoke.................................... 5
Add for Winchester Recoil Reduction System.......... 50

Winchester Model 1400 Deer Gun............... **$210**

Same as standard Model 1400, except has special 22-inch barrel, with rifle-type sights, for rifle slug or buckshot; 12 gauge only; weight, 6½ pounds. made from 1965 to 1968.

Winchester Model 1400 Skeet Gun.............. **$275**

Same as standard Model 1400, except 12 and 20 gauge only; 26-inch ventilated-rib barrel—skeet choke, semi-fancy walnut stock and forearm; also available with Winchester Recoil Reduction System (add $50 to value); weight, 7¼ to 7½ pounds. Made from 1965 to 1968.

SHOTGUNS ─────────────────────────────────── 409

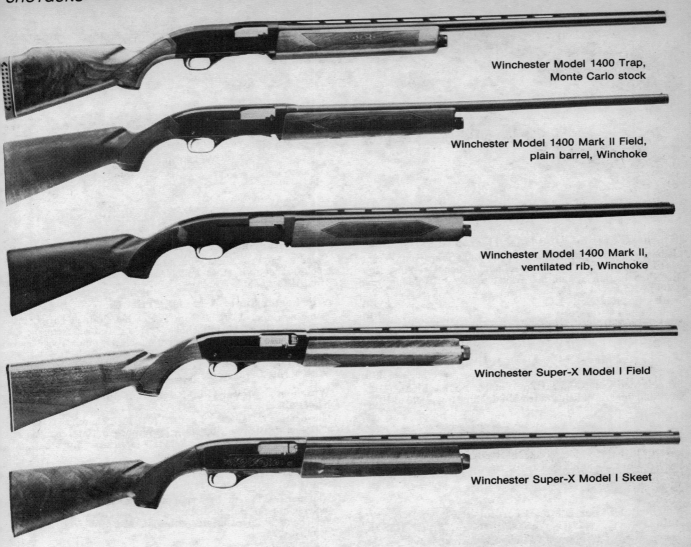

Winchester Model 1400 Trap,
Monte Carlo stock

Winchester Model 1400 Mark II Field,
plain barrel, Winchoke

Winchester Model 1400 Mark II,
ventilated rib, Winchoke

Winchester Super-X Model I Field

Winchester Super-X Model I Skeet

Winchester Model 1400 Trap Gun

Same as standard Model 1400, except 12 gauge only, 30-inch ventilated-rib barrel—full choke; semi-fancy walnut stock, straight or Monte Carlo trap style; also available with Winchester Recoil Reduction System; weight, about 8¼ pounds. Made from 1965 to 1968.

With straight stock.....................................$275
With Monte Carlo stock........................... 310
Add for Winchester Recoil Reduction System.......... 50

Note: Model 1400 shotguns were available in left-hand versions (ejection port and safety on left side). Values are the same as for right-hand models.

In 1968, Model 1400 was replaced by Model 1400 Mark II, which is the same gun with an improved action release and restyled checkering on stock and forearm. Winchester dropped the "Mark II" designation in 1972; however, to distinguish between the two types, it has been retained in the following listings.

Winchester Model 1400 Mark II Field Gun

Same general specifications as Model 1400 Field Gun, except not chambered for 16 gauge; Winchester Recoil Reduction System

not available after 1970; only 28-inch barrels with Winchoke furnished after 1973. Made from 1968 to date.

With plain barrel.....................................**$205**
With plain barrel and Winchoke...................... 225
With ventilated-rib barrel........................... 230
With ventilated-rib barrel and Winchoke.............. 240
Add for Winchester Recoil Reduction System.......... 50

Winchester Model 1400 Mark II Deer Gun...... $225

Same general specifications as Model 1400 Deer Gun. Made from 1968 to 1973.

Winchester Model 1400 Mark II Skeet Gun..... $280

Same general specifications as Model 1400 Skeet Gun. Made from 1968 to 1973.

Winchester Model 1400 Mark II Utility
Skeet Gun... **$240**

Same general specifications as Model 1400 Mark II Skeet Gun, except has stock and forearm of field grade walnut. Made from 1970 to 1973.

Winchester Super-X Model I Trap,
straight stock

Winchester Super-X Model I Trap,
Monte Carlo stock

Winchester Model 1400 Mark II Trap Gun

Same general specifications as Model 1400 Trap Gun, except also furnished with 28-inch barrel and Winchoke; Winchester Recoil Reduction System not available after 1970. Made from 1968 to 1973.
With straight stock....................................$280
With Monte Carlo stock............................ 300
Add for Winchoke.................................... 5
Add for Winchester Recoil Reduction System.......... 50

Winchester Model 1400 Mark II Utility Trap Gun..$260

Same as Model 1400 Mark II Trap Gun, except has Monte Carlo stock and forearm of field grade walnut. Made from 1970 to 1973.

Note: Until 1973, Model 1400 Mark II shotguns were available in left-hand versions (ejection port and safety on left side). Values are the same as for right-hand models.

Winchester Super-X Model I Automatic Field Gun..$375

Gas-operated. Takedown. 12 gauge. 2¾-inch chamber. 4-shot magazine. Barrels: ventilated rib; 26-inch, improved cylinder; 28-inch, modified or full; 30-inch, full choke. Weight, about 7 pounds. Checkered pistol-grip stock and forearm. Made from 1974 to date.

Winchester Super-X Model I Skeet Gun........ $430

Same as Super-X Field Gun, except has 26-inch barrel, skeet choke, skeet-style stock and forearm of select walnut. Made from 1974 to date.

Winchester Super-X Model I Trap Gun

Same as Super-X Field Gun, except has 30-inch barrel, improved modified or full choke, trap-style stock (straight or Monte Carlo Comb) and forearm of select walnut, recoil pad. Made from 1974 to date.
With straight stock....................................$430
With Monte Carlo stock............................ 440

Winchester Model 1500 XTR Semi-automatic Shotgun..$320

Gas-operated. Gauges: 12 and 20 (2¾-inch chambers). Barrel: plain or ventilated rib; 28-inch; Winchoke (interchangeable tubes IC-M-F). Weight: 7¼ pounds. American walnut stock and forend; checkered grip and forend.

Winchester Model 1300 XTR Slide Action Shotgun..$245

Hammerless. Takedown. 4-shot magazine. Gauges: 12 and 20 (3-inch chambers). Barrel: plain or ventilated rib; 28-inch barrels; Winchoke (interchangeable tubes IC-M-F). Weight: about 7 pounds.

Winchester Model 1300 Deer Gun.............. $250

Same as standard Model 1300, except has special 24⅛-inch barrel with rifle-type sights, for rifled slug or buckshot; 12 gauge only; weight, 6½ pounds.

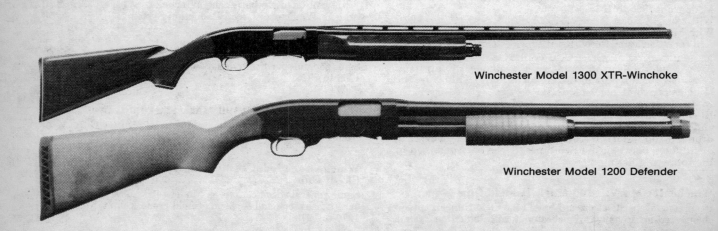

Winchester Model 1300 XTR-Winchoke

Winchester Model 1200 Defender

Winchester RANGER Model - Winchoke

Winchester Model 1200 Defender.............. **$175**
Hammerless slide action. 12 gauge only. 18-inch barrels. 7-shot magazine. Cylinder bore. Weight, 7 pounds.

Winchester Model 1200 Police................. **$200**
Same general specifications as 1200 Defender, except has rifle-type front and rear sights. Stainless-steel barrel and satin chrome finish on all external metal parts.

Winchester Model 1200 Stainless.............. **$225**
Same as standard Model 1200 Defender, except has stainless-steel barrel and special bright chrome finish on external metal parts.

Winchester Ranger Slide Action Shotgun....... **$175**
Hammerless. 12-gauge, 3-inch chambers; 20-gauge, 3-inch chambers. Walnut finished hardwood stock, ribbed forearm. 28-inch ventilated-rib barrel; Winchoke system. Weight: 7¼ pounds. Made from 1982 to date.

Note: The follwing Winchester shotguns are made for Olin Corporation, Winchester Group, at its Olin-Kodensha Japanese facility.

Winchester Model 23 Side By Side Shotgun..... **$875**
Box lock. Single trigger. Automatic safety. Gauges: 12, 20 3-inch chambers. 25½ to 28-inch barrels. Combination of IC&M, IC&IM or M&F chokes. Weight: average 6¾ pounds. Engraved receiver, hand checkered walnut stock and forend. Made from 1979 to date.

Winchester Model Shotgun/Rifle Combination.. **$1550**
12-gauge Winchoke barrel on top and rifle barrel chambered for 30-06 on bottom (over/under). 25-inch barrels. Engraved receiver. Hand checkered walnut stock and forend. Weight: 8½ pounds.

James Woodward & Sons, London, England. The business of this firm was acquired by James Purdey & Sons after World War II

Woodward Best Quality Hammerless Double Barrel Shotun
Side lock. Automatic ejectors. Double triggers or single trigger. Built to order in all standard gauges, barrel lengths, boring and other specifications; made as a field gun, pigeon and wildfowl gun, skeet gun or trap gun. Manufactured prior to World War II.
With double triggers............................. **$17,000**
With single trigger............................. **18,000**

Woodward Best Quality Under/Over

Woodward Best Quality Under-and-Over Shotgun
Side lock. Automatic ejectors. Double triggers or single trigger. Built to order in all standard gauges, barrel lengths, boring and other specifications, including Special Trap Grade with ventilated rib. Woodward introduced this type of gun in 1908. Made until World War II. See listing of Purdey Over-and-Under Gun.
With double triggers............................. **$20,000**
Single trigger, extra............................. **1000**

Woodward Best Quality Single Barrel Trap Gun..................................... **$18,000**
Side lock. Mechanical features of the Under & Over Gun. Ventilated-rib barrel. 12 gauge only. Built to customers' specifications. Made prior to World War II.

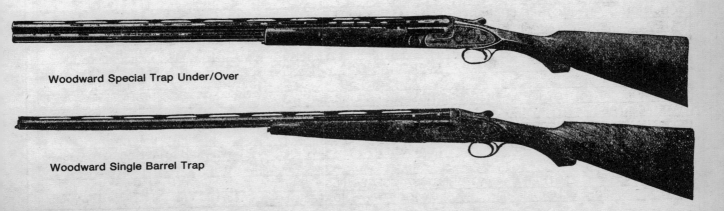

Woodward Special Trap Under/Over

Woodward Single Barrel Trap

HANDGUNS

MAKE:		MODEL NAME/NUMBER:		SERIAL NUMBER:	
CALIBER:		CAPACITY:	GRIPS:	BARREL LENGTH:	
FINISH:			SIGHTS:		ACTION:
CONDITION:	OTHER CHARACTERISTICS/ACCESSORIES:				
DATE ACQUIRED:	FROM:	COST:	DATE SOLD:	TO:	PRICE:

MAKE:		MODEL NAME/NUMBER:		SERIAL NUMBER:	
CALIBER:		CAPACITY:	GRIPS:	BARREL LENGTH:	
FINISH:			SIGHTS:		ACTION:
CONDITION:	OTHER CHARACTERISTICS/ACCESSORIES:				
DATE ACQUIRED:	FROM:	COST:	DATE SOLD:	TO:	PRICE:

MAKE:		MODEL NAME/NUMBER:		SERIAL NUMBER:	
CALIBER:		CAPACITY:	GRIPS:	BARREL LENGTH:	
FINISH:			SIGHTS:		ACTION:
CONDITION:	OTHER CHARACTERISTICS/ACCESSORIES:				
DATE ACQUIRED:	FROM:	COST:	DATE SOLD:	TO:	PRICE:

MAKE:		MODEL NAME/NUMBER:		SERIAL NUMBER:	
CALIBER:		CAPACITY:	GRIPS:	BARREL LENGTH:	
FINISH:			SIGHTS:		ACTION:
CONDITION:	OTHER CHARACTERISTICS/ACCESSORIES:				
DATE ACQUIRED:	FROM:	COST:	DATE SOLD:	TO:	PRICE:

MAKE:		MODEL NAME/NUMBER:		SERIAL NUMBER:	
CALIBER:		CAPACITY:	GRIPS:	BARREL LENGTH:	
FINISH:			SIGHTS:		ACTION:
CONDITION:	OTHER CHARACTERISTICS/ACCESSORIES:				
DATE ACQUIRED:	FROM:	COST:	DATE SOLD:	TO:	PRICE:

MAKE:		MODEL NAME/NUMBER:		SERIAL NUMBER:	
CALIBER:		CAPACITY:	GRIPS:	BARREL LENGTH:	
FINISH:			SIGHTS:		ACTION:
CONDITION:	OTHER CHARACTERISTICS/ACCESSORIES:				
DATE ACQUIRED:	FROM:	COST:	DATE SOLD:	TO:	PRICE:

MAKE:		MODEL NAME/NUMBER:		SERIAL NUMBER:	
CALIBER:		CAPACITY:	GRIPS:	BARREL LENGTH:	
FINISH:			SIGHTS:		ACTION:
CONDITION:	OTHER CHARACTERISTICS/ACCESSORIES:				
DATE ACQUIRED:	FROM:	COST:	DATE SOLD:	TO:	PRICE:

MAKE:		MODEL NAME/NUMBER:		SERIAL NUMBER:	
CALIBER:		CAPACITY:	GRIPS:	BARREL LENGTH:	
FINISH:			SIGHTS:		ACTION:
CONDITION:	OTHER CHARACTERISTICS/ACCESSORIES:				
DATE ACQUIRED:	FROM:	COST:	DATE SOLD:	TO:	PRICE:

MAKE:		MODEL NAME/NUMBER:		SERIAL NUMBER:	
CALIBER:		CAPACITY:	GRIPS:	BARREL LENGTH:	
FINISH:			SIGHTS:		ACTION:
CONDITION:	OTHER CHARACTERISTICS/ACCESSORIES:				
DATE ACQUIRED:	FROM:	COST:	DATE SOLD:	TO:	PRICE:

RIFLES

MAKE: | MODEL NAME/NUMBER: | SERIAL NUMBER:
CALIBER: | CAPACITY: | BARREL LENGTH:
FINISH: | STOCK/FORE-END: | SIGHTS: | ACTION:
CONDITION: | OTHER CHARACTERISTICS/ACCESSORIES:
DATE ACQUIRED: | FROM: | COST: | DATE SOLD: | TO: | PRICE:

MAKE: | MODEL NAME/NUMBER: | SERIAL NUMBER:
CALIBER: | CAPACITY: | BARREL LENGTH:
FINISH: | STOCK/FORE-END: | SIGHTS: | ACTION:
CONDITION: | OTHER CHARACTERISTICS/ACCESSORIES:
DATE ACQUIRED: | FROM: | COST: | DATE SOLD: | TO: | PRICE:

MAKE: | MODEL NAME/NUMBER: | SERIAL NUMBER:
CALIBER: | CAPACITY: | BARREL LENGTH:
FINISH: | STOCK/FORE-END: | SIGHTS: | ACTION:
CONDITION: | OTHER CHARACTERISTICS/ACCESSORIES:
DATE ACQUIRED: | FROM: | COST: | DATE SOLD: | TO: | PRICE:

MAKE: | MODEL NAME/NUMBER: | SERIAL NUMBER:
CALIBER: | CAPACITY: | BARREL LENGTH:
FINISH: | STOCK/FORE-END: | SIGHTS: | ACTION:
CONDITION: | OTHER CHARACTERISTICS/ACCESSORIES:
DATE ACQUIRED: | FROM: | COST: | DATE SOLD: | TO: | PRICE:

MAKE: | MODEL NAME/NUMBER: | SERIAL NUMBER:
CALIBER: | CAPACITY: | BARREL LENGTH:
FINISH: | STOCK/FORE-END: | SIGHTS: | ACTION:
CONDITION: | OTHER CHARACTERISTICS/ACCESSORIES:
DATE ACQUIRED: | FROM: | COST: | DATE SOLD: | TO: | PRICE:

MAKE: | MODEL NAME/NUMBER: | SERIAL NUMBER:
CALIBER: | CAPACITY: | BARREL LENGTH:
FINISH: | STOCK/FORE-END: | SIGHTS: | ACTION:
CONDITION: | OTHER CHARACTERISTICS/ACCESSORIES:
DATE ACQUIRED: | FROM: | COST: | DATE SOLD: | TO: | PRICE:

MAKE: | MODEL NAME/NUMBER: | SERIAL NUMBER:
CALIBER: | CAPACITY: | BARREL LENGTH:
FINISH: | STOCK/FORE-END: | SIGHTS: | ACTION:
CONDITION: | OTHER CHARACTERISTICS/ACCESSORIES:
DATE ACQUIRED: | FROM: | COST: | DATE SOLD: | TO: | PRICE:

MAKE: | MODEL NAME/NUMBER: | SERIAL NUMBER:
CALIBER: | CAPACITY: | BARREL LENGTH:
FINISH: | STOCK/FORE-END: | SIGHTS: | ACTION:
CONDITION: | OTHER CHARACTERISTICS/ACCESSORIES:
DATE ACQUIRED: | FROM: | COST: | DATE SOLD: | TO: | PRICE:

MAKE: | MODEL NAME/NUMBER: | SERIAL NUMBER:
CALIBER: | CAPACITY: | BARREL LENGTH:
FINISH: | STOCK/FORE-END: | SIGHTS: | ACTION:
CONDITION: | OTHER CHARACTERISTICS/ACCESSORIES:
DATE ACQUIRED: | FROM: | COST: | DATE SOLD: | TO: | PRICE:

SHOTGUNS

MAKE:	MODEL NAME/NUMBER:	SERIAL NUMBER:
GAUGE:	TYPE:	CAPACITY:	CHOKE(S):	BARREL LENGTH:
FINISH:	STOCK/FORE-END:	SIGHTS:	ACTION:
CONDITION:	OTHER CHARACTERISTICS/ACCESSORIES:
DATE ACQUIRED:	FROM:	COST:	DATE SOLD:	TO:	PRICE:

MAKE:	MODEL NAME/NUMBER:	SERIAL NUMBER:
GAUGE:	TYPE:	CAPACITY:	CHOKE(S):	BARREL LENGTH:
FINISH:	STOCK/FORE-END:	SIGHTS:	ACTION:
CONDITION:	OTHER CHARACTERISTICS/ACCESSORIES:
DATE ACQUIRED:	FROM:	COST:	DATE SOLD:	TO:	PRICE:

MAKE:	MODEL NAME/NUMBER:	SERIAL NUMBER:
GAUGE:	TYPE:	CAPACITY:	CHOKE(S):	BARREL LENGTH:
FINISH:	STOCK/FORE-END:	SIGHTS:	ACTION:
CONDITION:	OTHER CHARACTERISTICS/ACCESSORIES:
DATE ACQUIRED:	FROM:	COST:	DATE SOLD:	TO:	PRICE:

MAKE:	MODEL NAME/NUMBER:	SERIAL NUMBER:
GAUGE:	TYPE:	CAPACITY:	CHOKE(S):	BARREL LENGTH:
FINISH:	STOCK/FORE-END:	SIGHTS:	ACTION:
CONDITION:	OTHER CHARACTERISTICS/ACCESSORIES:
DATE ACQUIRED:	FROM:	COST:	DATE SOLD:	TO:	PRICE:

MAKE:	MODEL NAME/NUMBER:	SERIAL NUMBER:
GAUGE:	TYPE:	CAPACITY:	CHOKE(S):	BARREL LENGTH:
FINISH:	STOCK/FORE-END:	SIGHTS:	ACTION:
CONDITION:	OTHER CHARACTERISTICS/ACCESSORIES:
DATE ACQUIRED:	FROM:	COST:	DATE SOLD:	TO:	PRICE:

MAKE:	MODEL NAME/NUMBER:	SERIAL NUMBER:
GAUGE:	TYPE:	CAPACITY:	CHOKE(S):	BARREL LENGTH:
FINISH:	STOCK/FORE-END:	SIGHTS:	ACTION:
CONDITION:	OTHER CHARACTERISTICS/ACCESSORIES:
DATE ACQUIRED:	FROM:	COST:	DATE SOLD:	TO:	PRICE:

MAKE:	MODEL NAME/NUMBER:	SERIAL NUMBER:
GAUGE:	TYPE:	CAPACITY:	CHOKE(S):	BARREL LENGTH:
FINISH:	STOCK/FORE-END:	SIGHTS:	ACTION:
CONDITION:	OTHER CHARACTERISTICS/ACCESSORIES:
DATE ACQUIRED:	FROM:	COST:	DATE SOLD:	TO:	PRICE:

MAKE:	MODEL NAME/NUMBER:	SERIAL NUMBER:
GAUGE:	TYPE:	CAPACITY:	CHOKE(S):	BARREL LENGTH:
FINISH:	STOCK/FORE-END:	SIGHTS:	ACTION:
CONDITION:	OTHER CHARACTERISTICS/ACCESSORIES:
DATE ACQUIRED:	FROM:	COST:	DATE SOLD:	TO:	PRICE:

MAKE:	MODEL NAME/NUMBER:	SERIAL NUMBER:
GAUGE:	TYPE:	CAPACITY:	CHOKE(S):	BARREL LENGTH:
FINISH:	STOCK/FORE-END:	SIGHTS:	ACTION:
CONDITION:	OTHER CHARACTERISTICS/ACCESSORIES:
DATE ACQUIRED:	FROM:	COST:	DATE SOLD:	TO:	PRICE:

BIBLIOGRAPHY

Allen, W.G.B. *Pistols, Rifles and Machine Guns.* London: English Universities Press, 1953.

Bady, Donald B. *Colt Automatic Pistols, 1896-1955.* Beverly Hills: FADCO Publishing Co., 1956.

Baer, Larry L. *The Parker Gun.* 2 vols. North Hollywood: Beinfeld Publishing Inc., 1974, 1976.

Bearse, Ray. *Sporting Arms of the World.* New York: Outdoor Life/Harper & Row, 1976.

Brassey's Infantry Weapons of the World. J. I. H. Owen, editor. London: Brassey's Naval and Shipping Annual Ltd., 1975.

Brassey's Warsaw Pact Infantry and its Weapons. J. I. H. Owen, editor. London: Brassey's Publishers Ltd., 1976.

British War Office. *Textbook of Small Arms 1929.* London: H. M. Stationery Office, 1929.

Brophy, William S. *L. C. Smith Shotguns.* North Hollywood: Beinfeld Publishing Inc., 1977.

—*Plans and Specifications of the L. C. Smith Shotgun.* Montezuma, Iowa: F. Brownell & Son Publishers.

Browning, John, and Gentry, Curt. *John M. Browning, American Gunmaker.* Garden City: Doubleday & Co., 1964.

Buxton's Guide, Foreign Firearms. Greenwich, CT: John S. Herold Inc., 1963.

Colt's 100th Anniversary Fire Arms Manual: A Century of Achievement. Hartford: Colt's Patent Fire Arms Mfg. Co., 1937.

Crossman, Edward C., and Dunlap, Roy F. *The Book of the Springfield.* Georgetown, SC: Small-Arms Technical Publishing Co., 1951.

Datig, Fred A. *The Luger Pistol.* Beverly Hills: FADCO Publishing Co., 1955.

Ezell, Edward Clinton. *Small Arms of the World.* 11th rev. ed. Harrisburg: Stackpole Books, 1977.

Fuller, Claude E. *The Breech-Loader in the Service, 1816-1917.* 1933. Reprint. New Milford, CT: N. Flayderman & Co., 1965.

Gardner, Robert E. *Small Arms Makers: A Directory of Fabricators of Firearms, Edged Weapons, Crossbows and Polearms.* New York: Crown Publishers, 1963.

Grant, James J. *Single-Shot Rifles.* New York: William Morrow & Co., 1947.

Hatch, Alden. *Remington Arms in American History.* New York: Rinehart & Co., 1956.

Hatcher, Julian S. *Book of the Garand.* Washington: Infantry Journal Press, 1948.

Haven, Charles T., and Belden, Frank A. *A History of the Colt Revolver.* New York: William Morrow & Co., 1940.

Hicks, James E. *French Military Weapons, 1717-1938.* 1938. Reprint. New Milford, CT: N. Flayderman & Co. 1964.

—*German Weapons, Uniforms, Insignia, 1841-1918.* Rev. ed. La Canada, CA: James E. Hicks & Son.

—*Notes on United States Ordnance. Vol. I. Small Arms, 1776 to 1946.* Mt. Vernon, NY: James E. Hicks, 1946.

Hogg, Ian V. *German Pistols and Revolvers, 1871-1945.* Harrisburg: Stackpole Books, 1971.

Hogg, Ian V., and Weeks, John. *Military Small Arms of the 20th Century.* New York: Hippocrene Books, 1977.

Jane's Infantry Weapons. Edited by F. Hobart, Denis H. R. Archer. Published annually. New York: Franklin Watts Inc., 1975, 1976, 1977.

Jinks, Roy G. *History of Smith & Wesson.* North Hollywood: Beinfeld Publishing Inc., 1977.

Johnson, George B., and Lockhaven, Hans Bert. *International Armament.* 2 vols. Cologne: International Small Arms Publishers, 1965.

Johnson, Peter H. *Parker, America's Finest Shotgun.* 2nd ed. Harrisburg: Stackpole Co., 1963.

Karr, Charles Lee, Jr., and Karr, Caroll Robbins. *Remington Handguns.* Harrisburg: Military Service Publishing Co., 1947.

Keith, Elmer. *Shotguns by Keith.* Harrisburg: Stackpole & Heck Inc., 1950.

Lugs, Jaroslav. *Firearms Past and Present.* 2 vols. English edition. London: Grenville Publishing Co., 1975.

Madis, George. *The Winchester Book.* Dallas: George Madis, 1961.

Mahrholdt, Richard. *Waffen-Lexikon.* Munich: F. C. Mayer Verlag, 1952.

Mathews, J. Howard. *Firearms Identification.* 3 vols. Madison: University of Wisconsin Press, 1962 (Vols. I and II). Springfield, IL: Charles C. Thomas, Publisher, 1973. (Vol. III).

McHenry, Roy C., and Roper, Walter F. *Smith & Wesson Handguns.* Huntington, WV: Standard Publications Inc., 1945.

Moyer, Frank A. *Special Forces Foreign Weapons Handbook.* Boulder, CO: Panther Publications, 1970.

Neal, Robert J., and Jinks, Roy G. *Smith & Wesson, 1857-1945.* South Brunswick, NJ: A. S. Barnes & Co., 1966.

Olson, Ludwig. *Mauser Bolt Rifles.* 3rd ed. Montezuma, IA: F. Brownell & Son Publishers, 1976.

Parsons, John E. *The Peacemaker and Its Rivals.* New York: William Morrow & Co., 1950.

Reese, Michael, II. *Luger Tips.* Union City, TN: Pioneer Press, 1976.

Reynolds, E. G. B. *The Lee-Enfield Rifle.* New York: Arco Publishing Co., 1962.

Satterlee, L. D., and Gluckman, Arcadi. *American Gun Makers.* Buffalo: Otto Ulbrich Co., 1945.

Sell, DeWitt E. *Collector's Guide to American Cartridge Handguns.* Harrisburg: Stackpole Co., 1963.

Serven, James E. *Colt Firearms, 1836-1960.* Santa Ana, CA: Serven Books, 1960.

Sharpe, Philip B. *The Rifle in America.* 2nd ed. New York: Funk & Wagnalls Co., 1947.

Smith, W. H. B. *Mauser, Walther and Mannlicher Firearms.* Harrisburg: Stackpole Books, 1971.

Smith, W. H. B., and Bellah, Kent. *The Book of Pistols and Revolvers.* 6th ed. Harrisburg: Stackpole Books, 1965.

Smith, W. H. B., and Smith, Joseph E. *The Book of Rifles.* 4th ed. Harrisburg: Stackpole Books, 1972.

Sutherland, Robert Q., and Wilson, R. L. *The Book of Colt Firearms.* Kansas City, MO: Robert Q. Sutherland, 1971.

Wahl, Paul. *Carbine Handbook.* New York: Arco Publishing Co., 1964.

Watrous, George R. *The History of Winchester Firearms, 1866-1975.* 4th ed. New York: Winchester Press, 1975.

West, Bill. *Marlin and Ballard Firearms and History.* Azusa, CA: Bill West, 1968.

—*Remington Arms and History.* Azusa, CA: Bill West, 1970.

—*Savage and Stevens Arms and History.* Azusa, CA: Bill West, 1971.

—*Winchester For Over a Century.* Azusa, CA: Bill West, 1966.

Williamson, Harold F. *Winchester, The Gun That Won the West.* Washington: Combat Forces Press, 1952.

Wilson, R. K. *Textbook of Automatic Pistols.* Plantersville, SC: Small-Arms Technical Publishing Co., 1943.

Wilson, R. L. *Colt Commemorative Firearms.* 2nd rev. ed. Geneseo, IL: Robert E. P. Cherry, 1973.

Note: Many of the books listed are out of print.